HATHAWAY SHIRTS:
Their History, Design, and Advertising

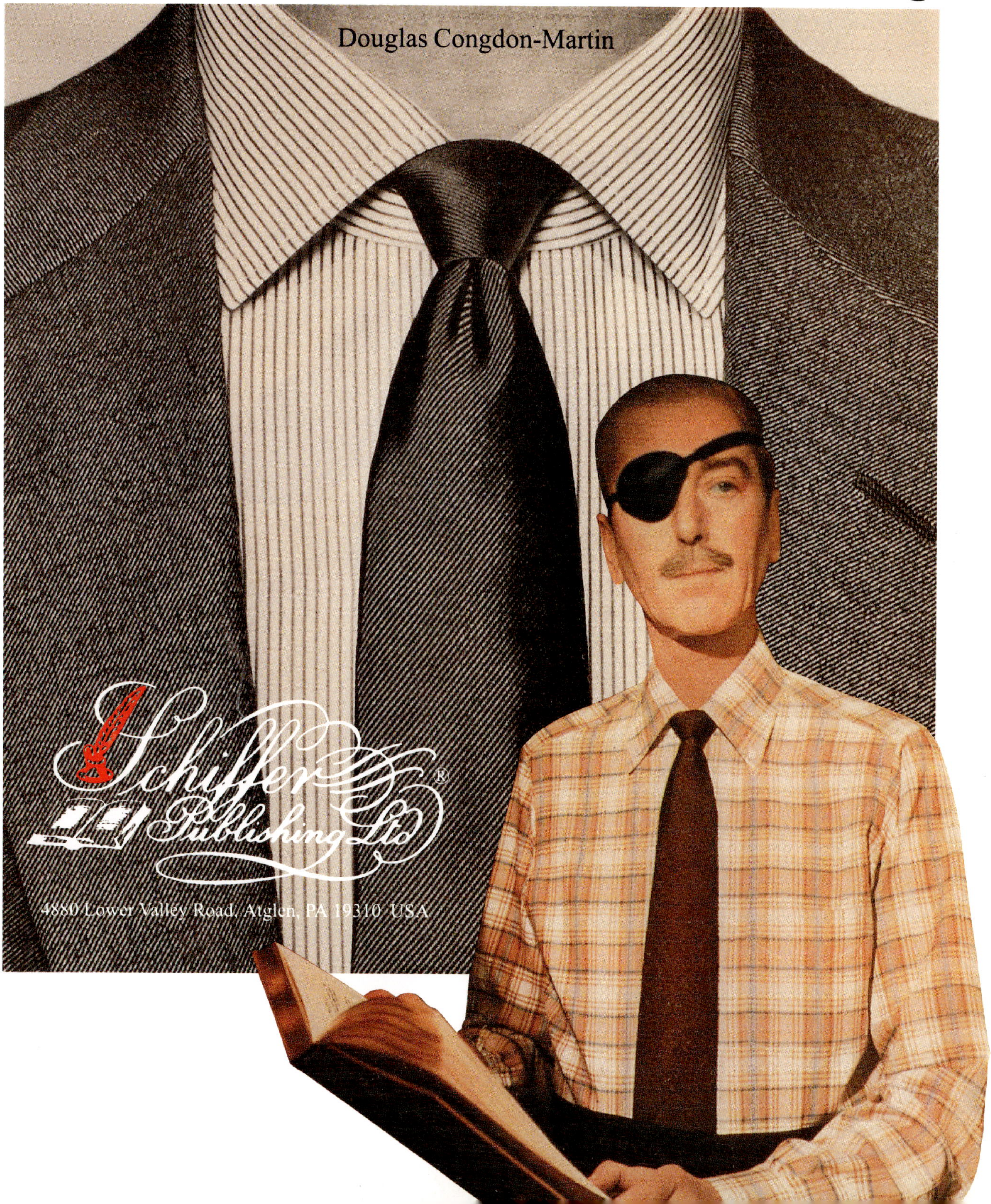

Douglas Congdon-Martin

Schiffer Publishing Ltd
4880 Lower Valley Road, Atglen, PA 19310 USA

Acknowledgments

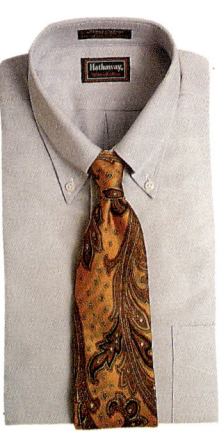

I would like to thank the fine people at Hathaway for their assistance in making this book a reality, especially Don Sappington, who welcomed us into the archives and gave us the time and space we needed. Elaine Scott, also of Hathaway has been most helpful in providing latest information about Hathaway's renaissance.

Donna S. Baker helped organize the photo shoot and recorded the information as I photographed.

My wife, Beth, saw her way through multiple crises at home during this project.

To all of them I express my sincere thanks.

Copyright © 1998 by Schiffer Publishing Ltd.
Library of Congress Catalog Card Number: 98-86372

All rights reserved. No part of this work may be reproduced or used in any form or by any means—graphic, electronic, or mechanical, including photocopying or information storage and retrieval systems—without written permission from the copyright holder.

"Schiffer," "Schiffer Publishing Ltd. & Design," and the "Design of pen and ink well" are registered trademarks of Schiffer Publishing, Ltd.

Design by Blair Loughrey
Typeset in University Extended/Times New Roman

ISBN: 0-7643-0628-6
Printed in China
1 2 3 4

Published by Schiffer Publishing Ltd.
4880 Lower Valley Road
Atglen, PA 19310
Phone: (610) 593-1777; Fax: (610) 593-2002
E-mail: Schifferbk@aol.com
Please write for a free catalog.
This book may be purchased from the publisher.
Please include $3.95 for shipping.

In Europe, Schiffer books are distributed by
Bushwood Books
6 Marksbury Avenue
Kew Gardens
Surrey TW9 4JF England
Phone: 44 (0) 392-8585; Fax: 44 (0) 181 392-9876
E-mail: Bushwd@aol.com

Please try your bookstore first.

We are interested in hearing from authors
with book ideas on related subjects

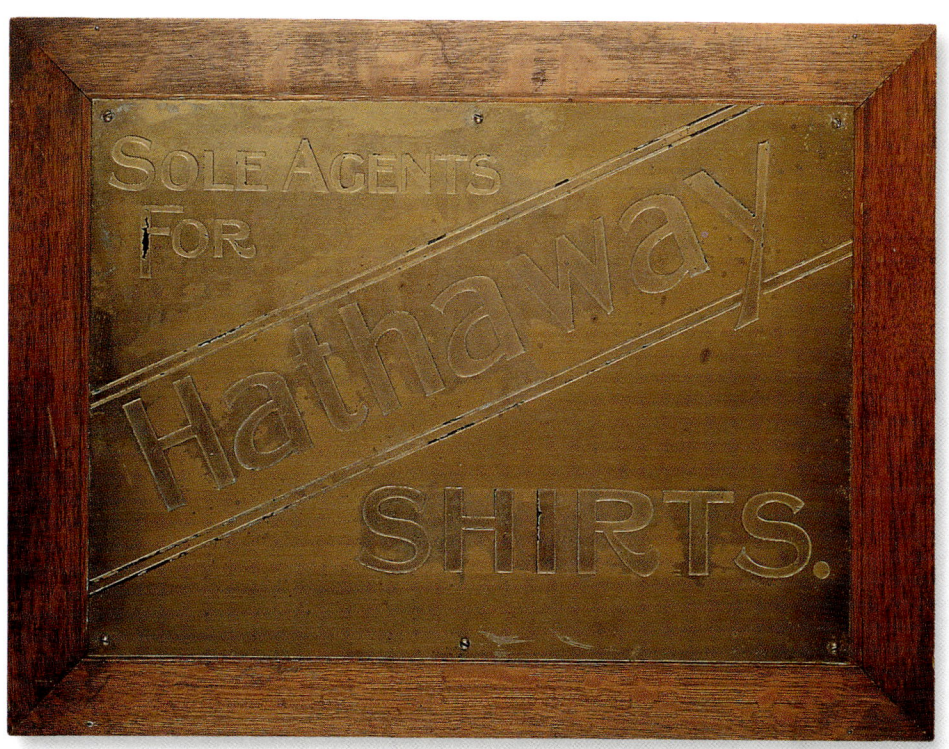

Contents

Introduction   5

East of the Hudson: The First Hundred Years   6
     C.F. Hathaway and His "Laundry"   6
     Colonel Leighton   12

The National Company   16
     Ellerton M. Jette   16

The Man in the Hathaway Shirt   19

The Warner/Warnaco Years   49
     Entering the Eighties   129

Saving a Great Shirt Company   156

Bibliography   160

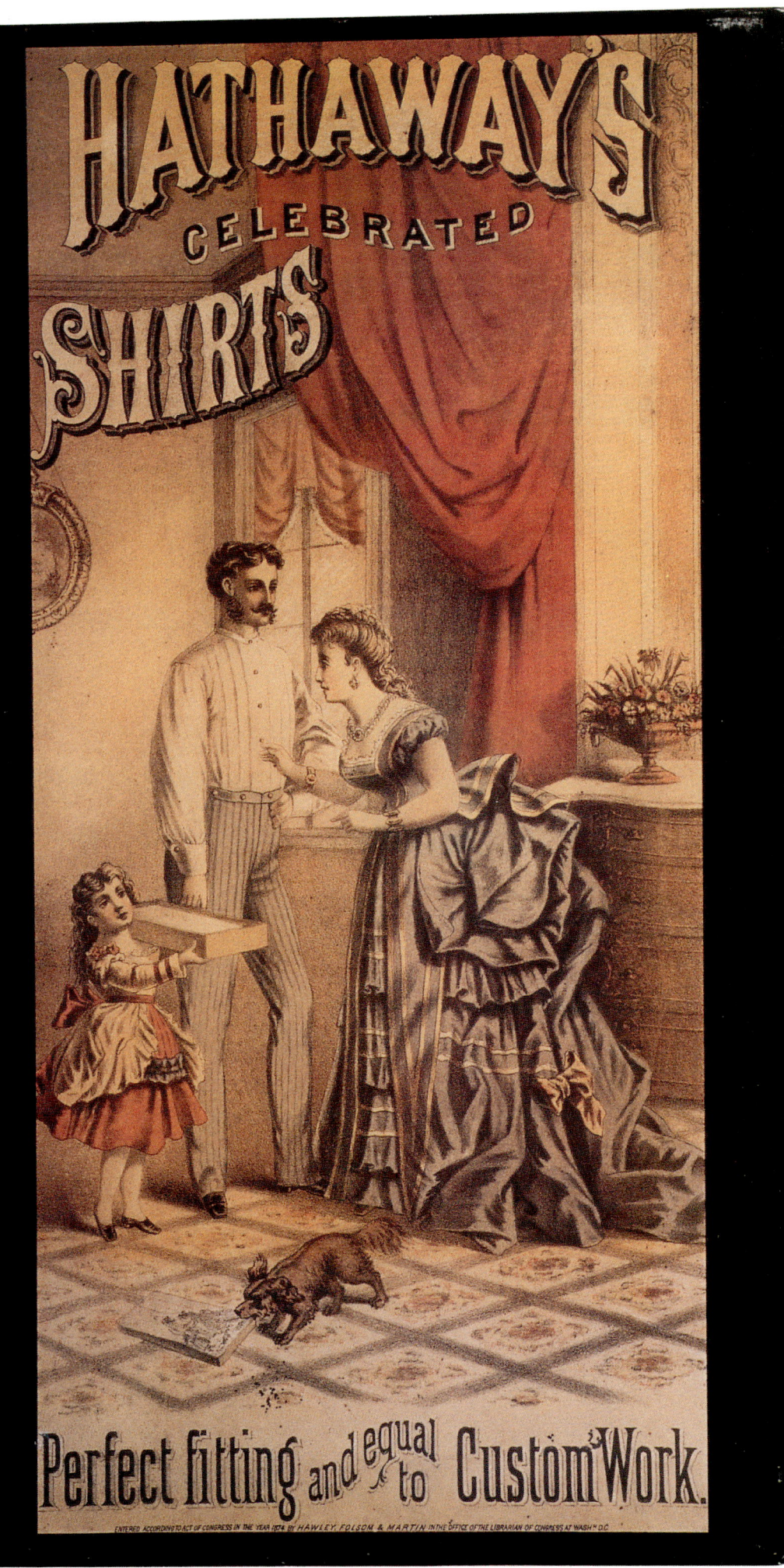

Early Hathaway shirt box, c. 1880.

Introduction

The record of American enterprise is built upon people who took a germ of an idea and nurtured it into a vital, successful reality. When their stories are compared, some common traits emerge, which, though not universal, are encountered consistently enough to give us pause.

In nearly every story of success, we encounter incidents of failure. Products fail to find their market, inventions fail to do what they are meant to do, plants close down, entrepreneurs go into bankruptcy. Sometimes these failings can be attributed to ineptitude or incompetence, and for many businesses that is the answer. When viewed from the vantage point of a successful endeavor, it might be more accurately ascribed to the entrepreneur's willingness to take risks in pursuit of his or her goals. When they fall short, they learn from their experiences, moving ahead with new wisdom, and often with renewed energy and dedication.

This willingness to risk points is the second common trait among successful enterprises: a full-out commitment. To create a business out of little more than an idea takes an enormous investment of thought, energy, and talent. A look at those who succeed shows people who have given their lives over to the enterprise. It is not a job they go to and then return home to a quiet retreat. It is a way of life, occupying every waking and many sleeping moments. It is not unusual to see health fail or families sacrificed in the pursuit of the dream. Nor is it unusual to find that all the members of a family share in the goal and the commitments it demands.

But risk and the commitment to face it head on are not enough to make success. The final key is clarity of vision. All the commitment and sacrifice in the world will not make a bad idea tenable. If the vision is not based in reality, if it does not fill a real need or is not rooted in a real possibility, no level of effort, however heroic, will be able to save it from defeat. Successful entrepreneurs are those who are students of the world around them. They are based in the real needs and desires of people, and from that vantage point can see clearly the products or services they need and want. More, they are also aware of the opportunities that the world brings in terms of technologies and materials, and how they may be used and manipulated to fulfill the dream. It is in the marriage of need and possibility that the entrepreneurial genius lies.

Among the American success stories is that of Charles F. Hathaway and his shirts. From its origins in 1837 to its present resurgence the company and its people have pursued the dream of excellence, and have committed the energies and made the sacrifices that an American success story requires.

This book tells that story. More than that it celebrates the designs and advertising that have made Hathaway synonymous with quality and style in men's and women's shirts.

A Word About Prices...

For the vintage clothing collector most of the shirts illustrated have an estimated value at the end of the caption. These values reflect the price you may expect to pay for the illustrated clothing if found in excellent to mint condition from a dealer specializing in vintage apparel. Prices, of course, vary from place to place, store to store, and even from day to day. These values are meant only as a guide.

East of the Hudson:
The First Hundred Years

C.F. Hathaway and His "Laundry"

The early years of C.F. Hathaway are somewhat confused by legend and the early histories of the company. Fortunately an extensive study of the company and the man was written as a master's thesis by Louis Leonard LaPierre in 1978, entitled: "C.F. Hathaway Company: The First One Hundred and Twenty-Five Years." It is the source of much of the information that follows.

C.F. Hathaway was born in Plymouth, Massachusetts, in 1816 of an old New England family. In the Yankee tradition, he was ambitious, going to work for a nail manufacturer at age 11 and for a printer, E. Marriam & Company, in West Brookfield, Massachusetts, at age 15 (LaPierre, p. 4). He spent seven years in the printing business.

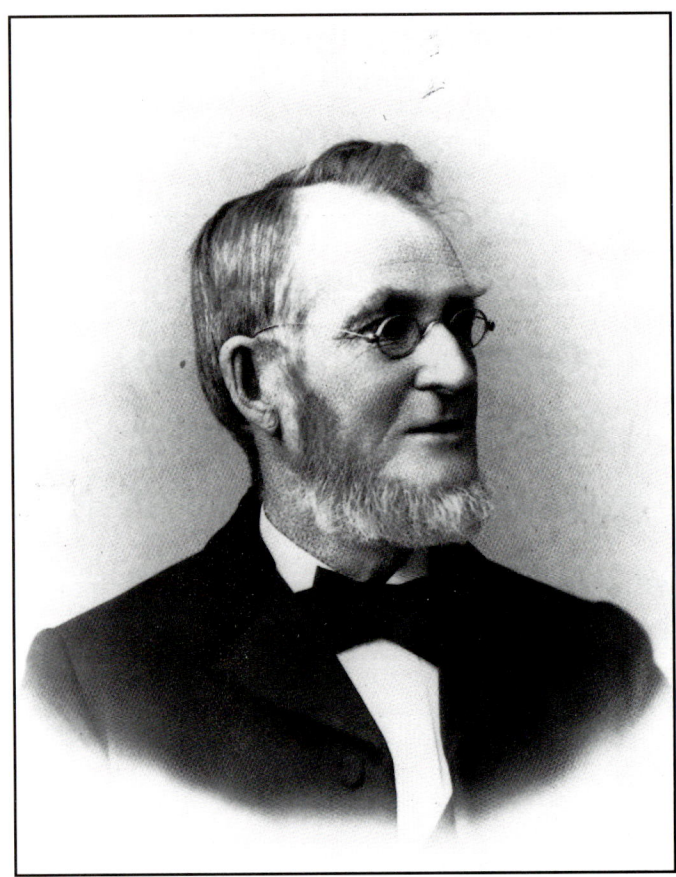

Charles F. Hathaway.

In 1837 he first entered the shirt business started by his uncle, Benjamin, in Plymouth. A letter from that period indicates that he held some stock in the ownership of the company. This date is cited as the birth of the Hathaway Shirt Company, and when liberally interpreted, it probably was. But the company that we know today, came into being by fits and starts.

Something during that year took Hathaway to Waterville, Maine. The city was in the midst of a growing economy. Textiles had moved north from Massachusetts, and Saco, 90 miles southeast of Waterville, had the largest cotton factory in the world. It is not known whether Hathaway's journey there was for business or pleasure, but it was fortuitous trip. While there he met Temperance Blackwell. Three years later, in 1840, they would marry in Waterville, and return back to Massachusetts to continue in the shirt business. He sold the business in 1843 and moved to Waterville, where he once again turned his hand to printing. In 1847 he bought an existing printing business and by April had published the first issue of the *Waterville Union*. A religious person, Hathaway put out a paper that was heavily theological in content, consisting of sermons, moral stories and the like. There was some national and international news, but, according to LaPierre, the first edition had not a word of local news. (LaPierre, p. 7.) The paper folded in less than four months.

Hathaway stayed in Waterville until 1850, though it is unclear how he was employed during that period. In April, 1850 he entered a partnership with Josiah Tillson, a former employee from Plymouth, to begin a shirt factory in Watertown, Massachusetts. In addition they bought and ran a retail store in Boston.

In March 31, 1853, Hathaway sold his "property in the firm" to Tillson for $9000. Exactly what that meant is unclear. He mailed out a letter bearing the name "Late Hathaway & Tillson" in August, 1853. He apparently had partial ownership of the retail store until 1864. While his motivations are not totally clear, he did record in his diary the desire "to get away from sweat shop conditions." The next day he agreed to go into the shirt business with his brother George, though LaPierre notes that George was virtually a silent partner, putting up one-fourth of the capital and receiving one third of the profits (p. 13).

The company opened back in Waterville, the work being done in the Hathaway's home and in the homes of those who worked for him. The early output, before the introduction of the sewing machine, was two dozen shirts per week. Hathaway himself served as the first salesman, taking the finished product to Boston when the numbers were great enough.

But he moved into the future with all due haste and determination. By late May and early June, 1853 he had hired two other salesmen, signing them to three-year contracts, with base salaries increasing each year plus a one percent sales commission and travel expenses. By the middle of May he had purchased a 100 acre site on Appleton Street, and by June 1 they had broken ground. The new factory opened in October, and would be the home for the company for the next century.

The factory was known as "The Laundry" by the locals. Perhaps this is because much of the hand sewing was done outside of the building. The shirts, with their separate collars and stiff full bosoms, needed to heavily starched and ironed to complete the manufacturing process. This operation was located at the factory, and the work was compensated based on production. Learners received $3 per week, provided they stayed for one year. Those who ironed 16 shirts per day received $5.50 per week. Even though the days were long, starting at 7 a.m. and finishing at 6 p.m., the wage was thought to be "liberal" as attested to by employees in 1865.

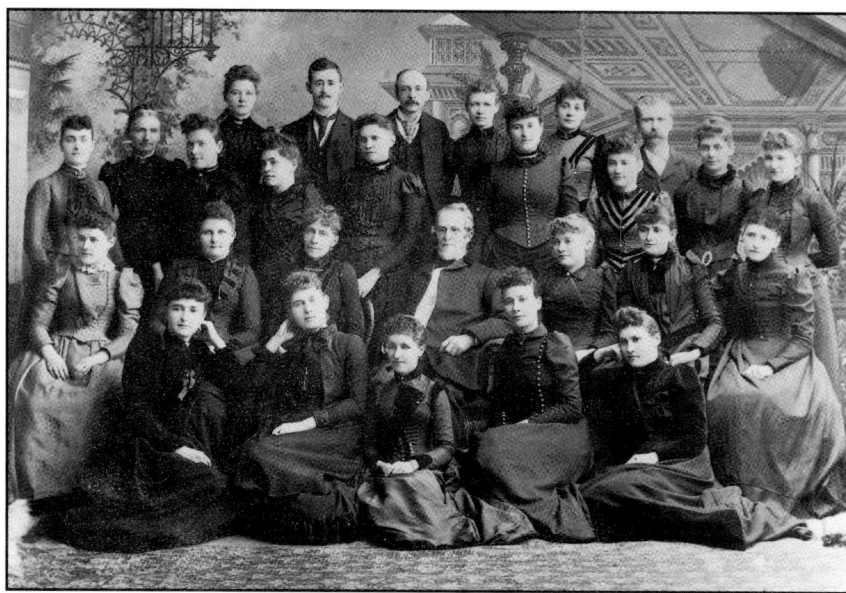

C.F. Hathaway seated in the midst of his employees. c. 1870.

The significance of Hathaway's new shirt company was that this was the first in the country to produce ready-to-wear merchandise. The quality of the work was well respected and orders always exceeded the capacity to fulfill them.

In 1860 the first sewing machine arrived at the Hathaway factory. The new technology put Hathaway in the position of being able to supply the Union Army during the Civil War. The growth continued after the war, until by 1872 the equipment account was up to $17,000. (LaPierre, p. 32.) The plant converted to steam in that year and gas lighting was installed. By 1874 Hathaway employed 100 workers and was producing lady's fine muslin underwear. (LaPierre, p. 32.)

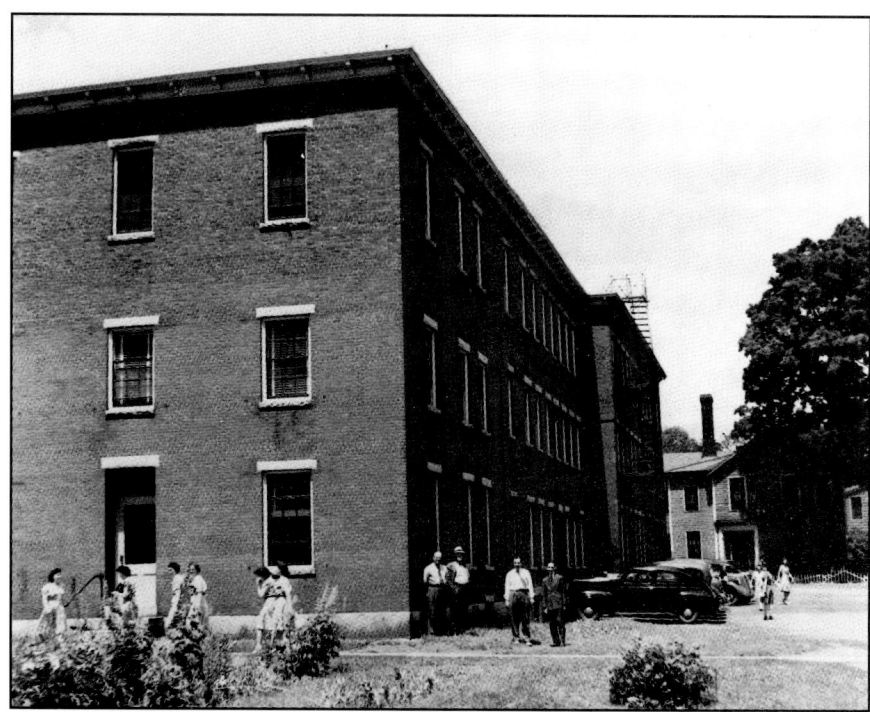

The Appleton Street Factory.

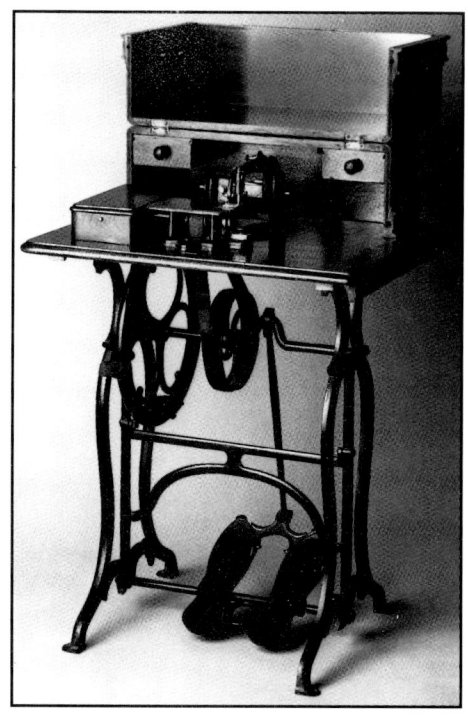

Early treadle sewing machine of the kind used from 1860 until 1874, when steam machines were installed.

The shirts were marketed primarily in New England and major east coast cities. The sales force in these locations got Hathaway into the finest department specialty stores. As the business grew C.F. Hathaway brought in a new salesman, with a unique contract. Colonel Clarence Leighton was hired at a commission of ten percent, a considerably higher rate than other salesmen at the time. With the higher commission came larger responsibilities. Leighton was required to cover all sales expenses, including boxes, wrapping, or any other presentations. More, Leighton acted as bill collector as well as salesman, being responsible for receiving payment for all the shirts he sold and passing them on to Hathaway. For a less talented person this may have been a disastrous arrangement, but Leighton was a talented businessman. He sold all the Hathaway shirts that the company could produce, as well as new ventures in lady's pantaloons and petticoats, and American flags. (LaPierre, p. 32-33.) As Ellerton M. Jette described him some 80 years later, Leighton was "a super-salesman of his day." ("History of Hathaway," a speech given in 1953.)

Leighton's task was made easier by the quality of the Hathaway shirts. Though they were not the least expensive of the ready-to-wear shirts, they were arguably the finest, and much sought after by the leading men's wear outlets. There was, of course, competition, even in Waterville. In the July 18, 1879, issue of *The Waterville Mail* are two advertisements in the same column. The top piece, headlined "Waterville Shirts," offers "A New Departure." The Hathaway Shirt Company was introducing an affordable product that they called "Waterville Shirts." In "finished" condition they cost $1.00, though the customer could save even more by leaving off the buttons (cost: $.75) or taking the shirt in an

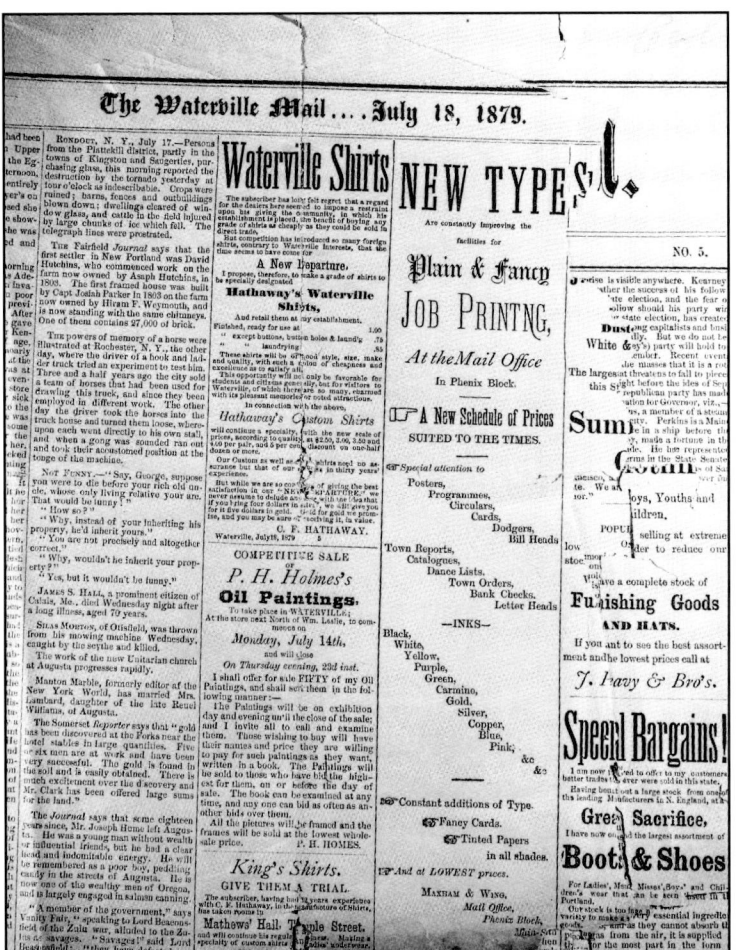

The Waterville Mail from July 18, 1879, with advertisements for both Hathaway and it competitor, King Shirts.

unlaundered condition (cost: $.85). This compared with Hathaway's custom shirts, also offered at reduced prices of "$2.50, 3.00, 3.50 and 4.00 per pair."

Why this generous offer? It may have had something to do with the advertisement a bit farther down in the same column. "King's Shirts" are being sold at Mathews' Hall on Temple Street by someone who claims to have worked for Hathaway for twelve years. The price for a half dozen of his best shirts is $9.00. As LaPierre explains, Hathaway had little tolerance for competition, usually including a contractual clause that forbade a worker from going into competition if they should leave his employ. This juxtaposition of advertisements may show the seriousness with which Hathaway regarded his competitors and the steps he would take to undermine their success.

The business continued to grow until Hathaway's death on December 5, 1893 at the age of 73. In keeping with his deep faith, he left the company to the Baptist Missionary Society. Having little or no knowledge about manufacturing shirts, the Baptists immediately sold the company to Leighton. At the time of the transfer its total assets were $100,900, with net assets of $44,000. Of the total assets, $38,000 were owed to Leighton and his wife. (LaPierre, pg. 37) His hard work and "super" salesmanship had insured that the company was in excellent condition to enter the new century. His leadership would take it there.

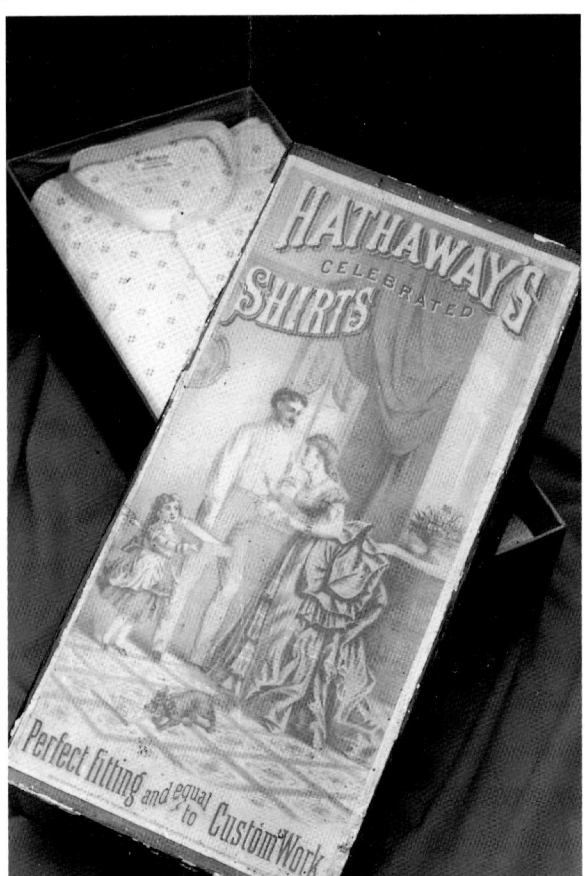

Early Hathaway box. c. 1885.

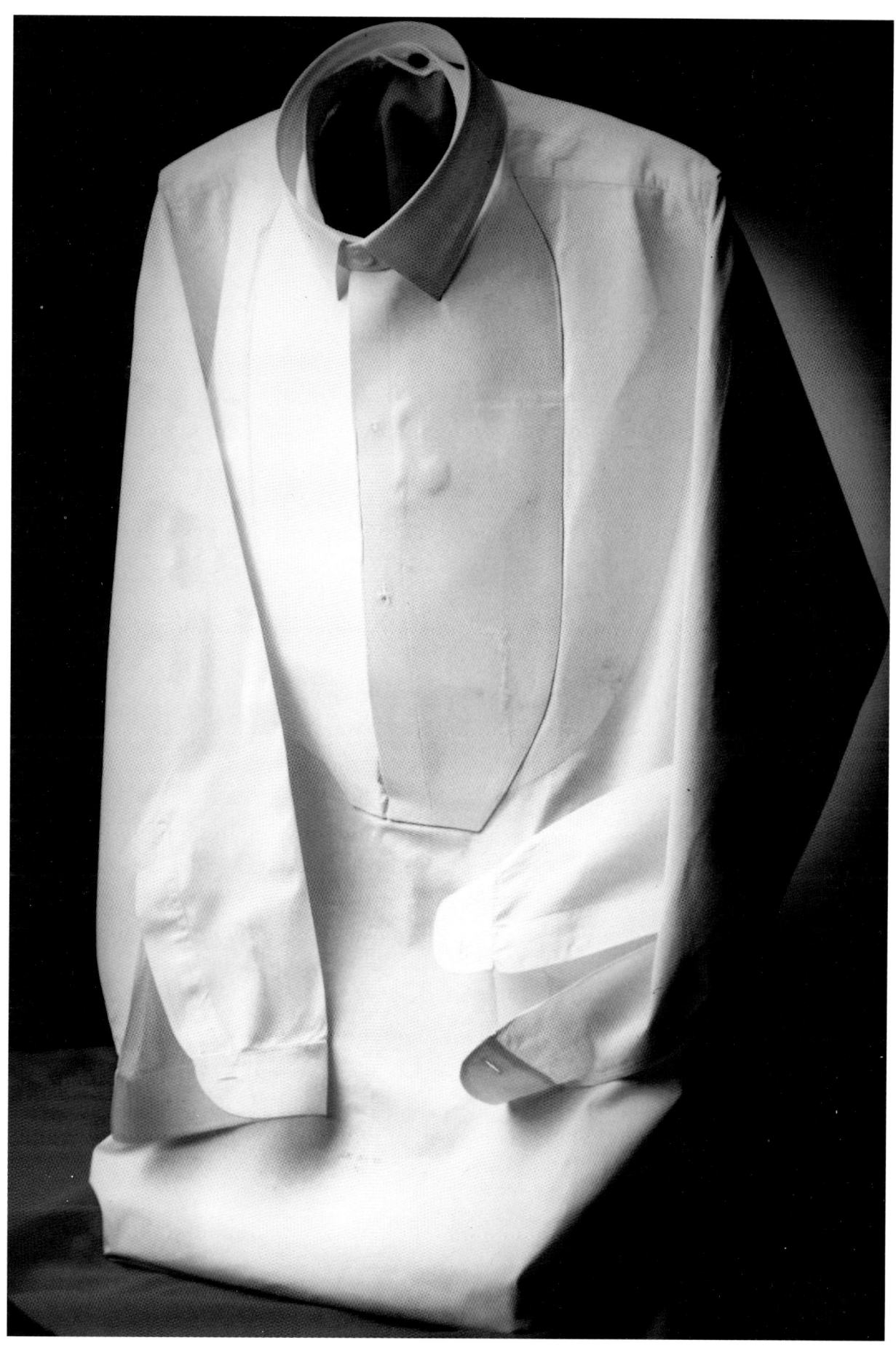

The oldest known Hathaway shirt, a full-bosomed model with attached collar.

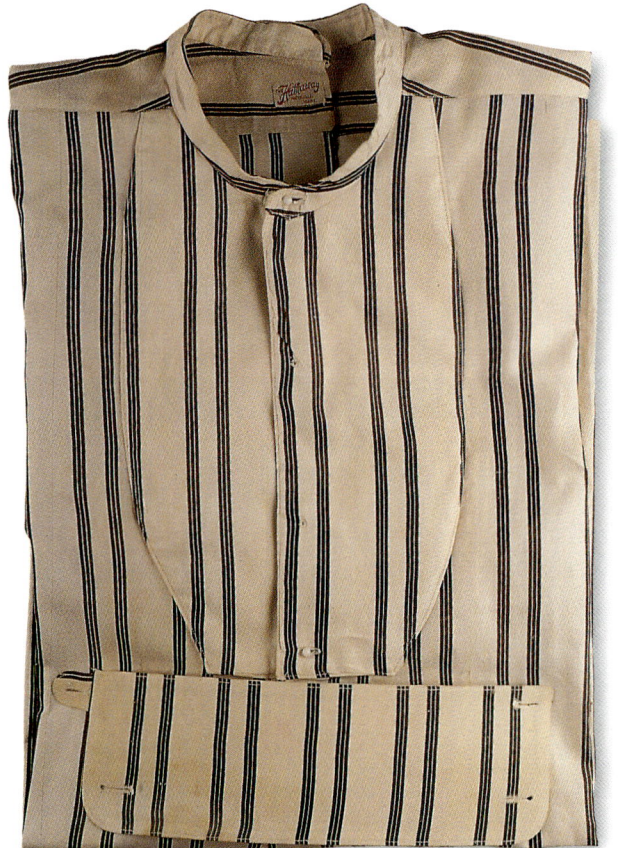

c. 1870s.

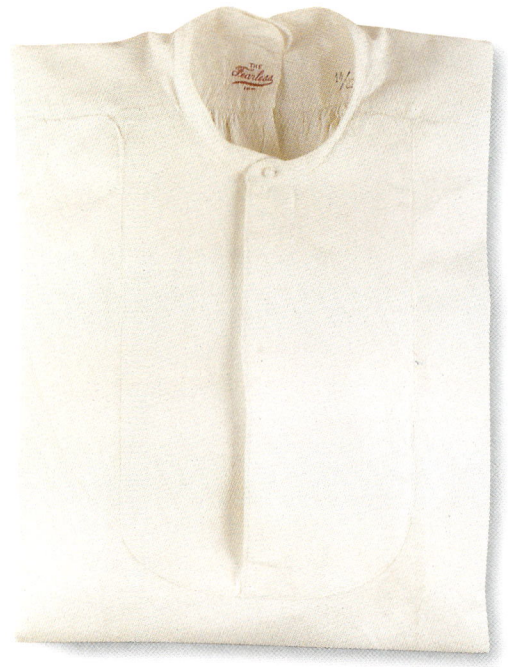

c. 1870s.

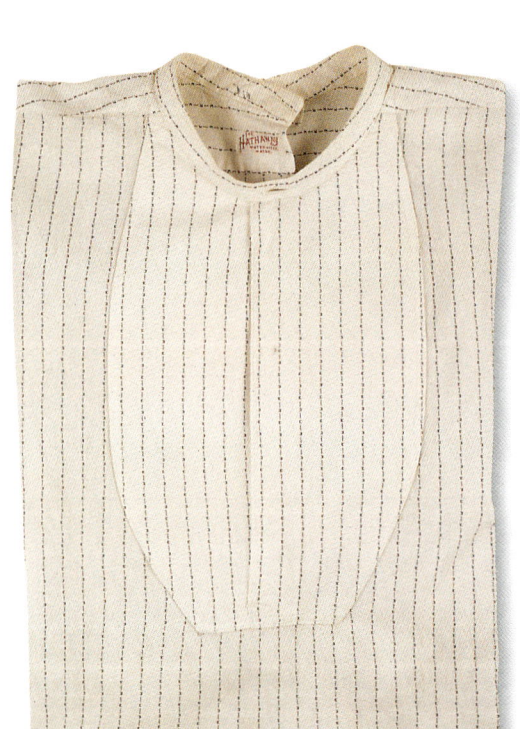

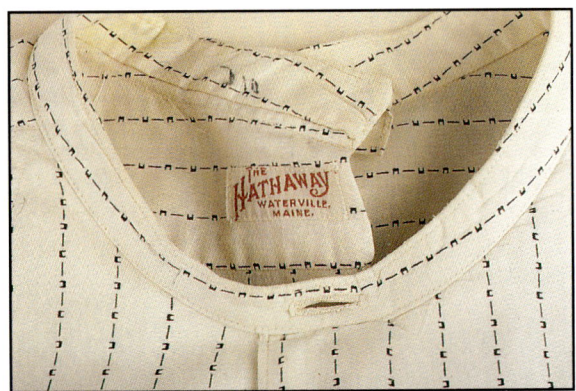

Above & right: c. 1870s.
White shirt with blue stripes.

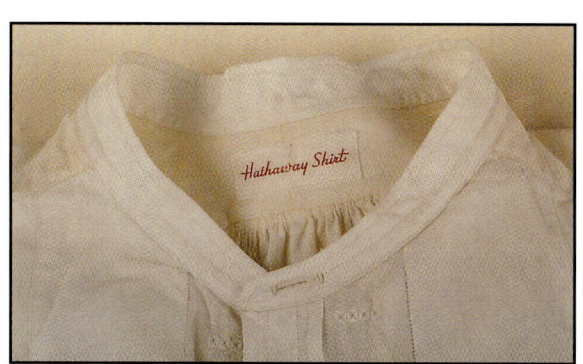

c. 1870s.

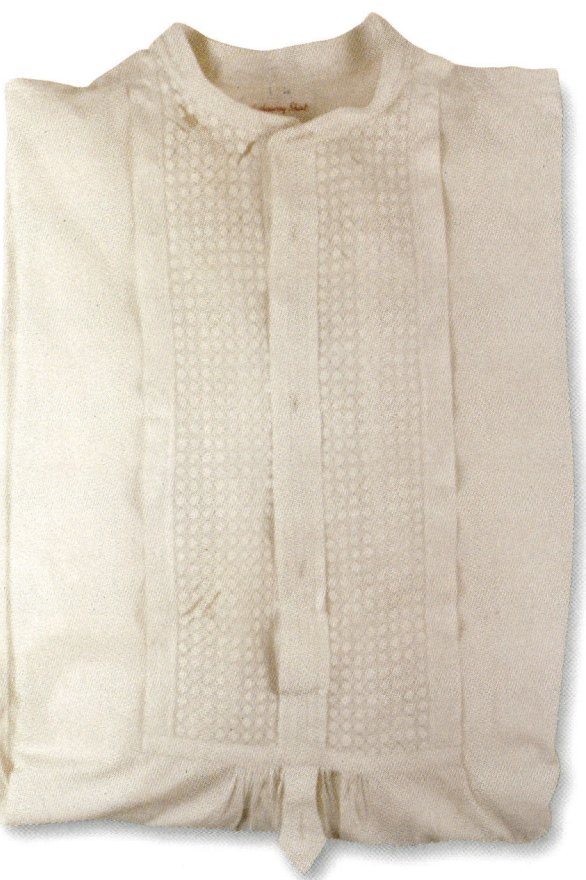

c. 1880s.

c. 1890s. White shirt with diamond patterned front.

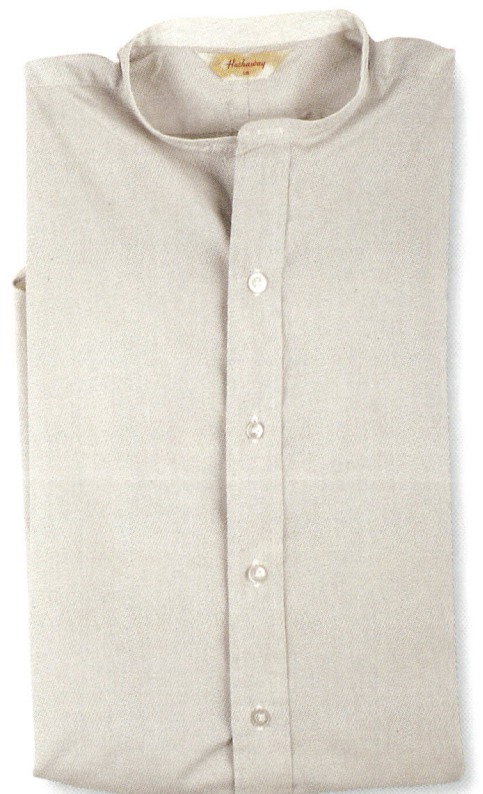

c. 1900s. Light blue shirt.

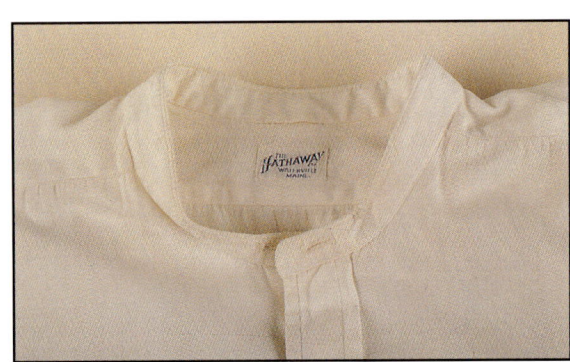

Above & left: c. 1900s.

Colonel Leighton

Clarence Leighton was an astute businessman, and his rise to the presidency of Hathaway ushered in an era of growth and innovation. The continued mechanization of the factory meant that by the turn of the century all the equipment was driven by steam. His successful promotion of the product kept the machinery running twenty-four hours a day to keep up with the demand.

This success was built upon the reputation of quality that C.F. Hathaway had established from the beginning, but, in truth, Leighton was a much better businessman than Hathaway.

Men's fashions during this period underwent some significant changes. In shirts, the use of ruffles disappeared, and was replaced by heavily starched plain bosoms and cuffs. As Ellerton Jette, a future president of Hathaway, would observe in a company history presented in 1953, "Colonel Leighton saw the beginning of a trend in shirts that was to completely revolutionize the type of garment worn.…This was not the stiff bosomed shirt

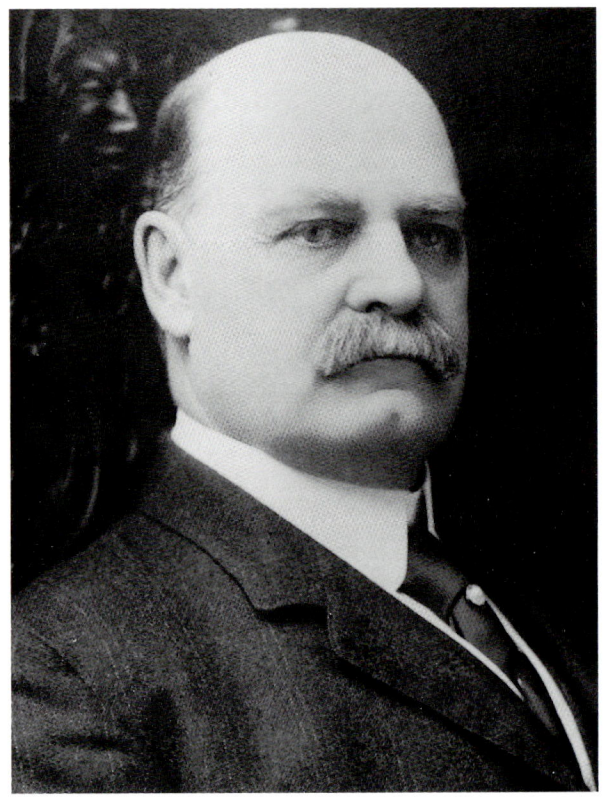

Colonel Clarence Leighton. c. 1900. Leighton took over Hathaway's leadership after the founder's death in 1893.

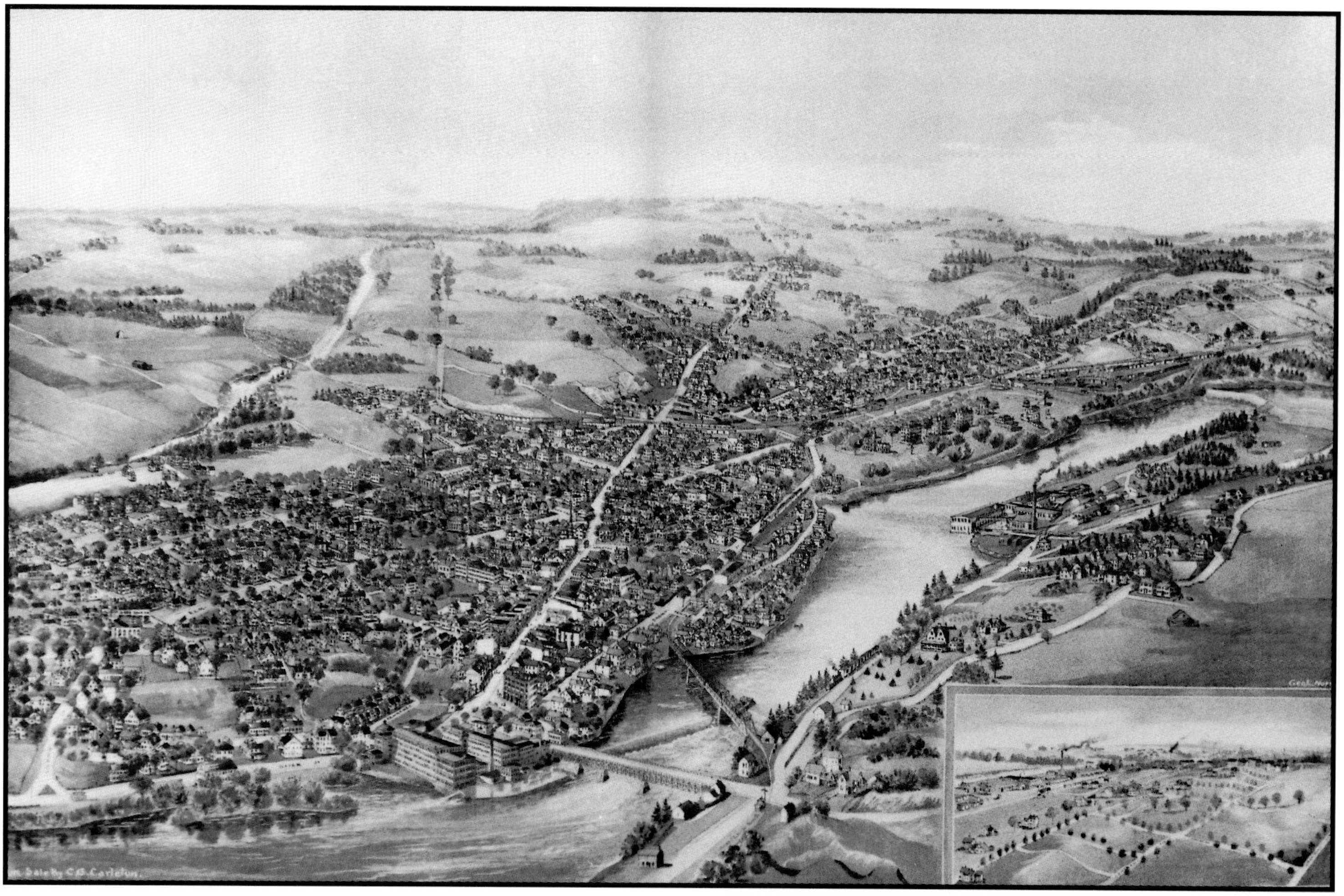

Above: Drawing of Waterville, Maine in 1895.

Right: Reverse painted store sign advertising Hathaway Shirts, with C.A. Leighton's name on it. C. 1900.

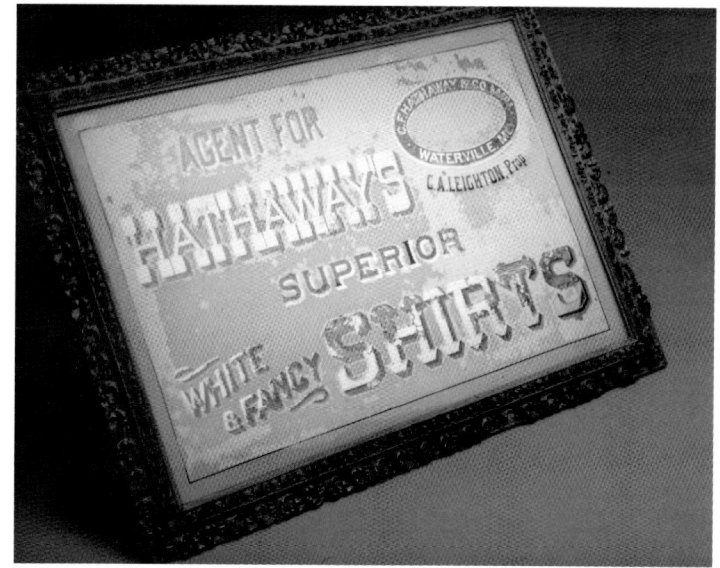

as we knew it in the 20's, but a garment with the entire front a large long stiff bosom. We can only guess the complication of manufacturing such a radically different garment by our own experience of only slight changes we have gone through." In Jette's estimation, Colonel Leighton "left his mark of ability, character, and soundness" on the company.

As with the Civil War, the Hathaway company responded to the Spanish American War (1898) by producing shirts for officers and enlisted soldiers, as well as American flags. Being a smaller and shorter conflict, the war production did not occupy all of the manufacturing capacity, so Hathaway continued to make shirts for civilians, and the company continued to grow. According to LaPierre, Hathaway had between 150 and 175 employees in 1902, with a payroll of $60,000 annually. One hundred steam and electrically powered sewing machines ran around the clock in a newly enlarged and modernized plant. (LaPierre, pg. 39.)

C.F. Hathaway and Company was incorporated on June 28, 1909. Its 500 shares, valued at $100 each, were divided between Clarence Leighton, his son and future president, Edward K. Leighton, and Frank W. Smith, who had come to the company as a young boy under C.F. Hathaway, and became production manager under Leighton. These three held all the shares of the company (O.M. Leighton, Clarence's widow, took over ownership of 200 shares in 1915 after his death) until 1922 when the company was recapitalized. (LaPierre, pp. 38-39)

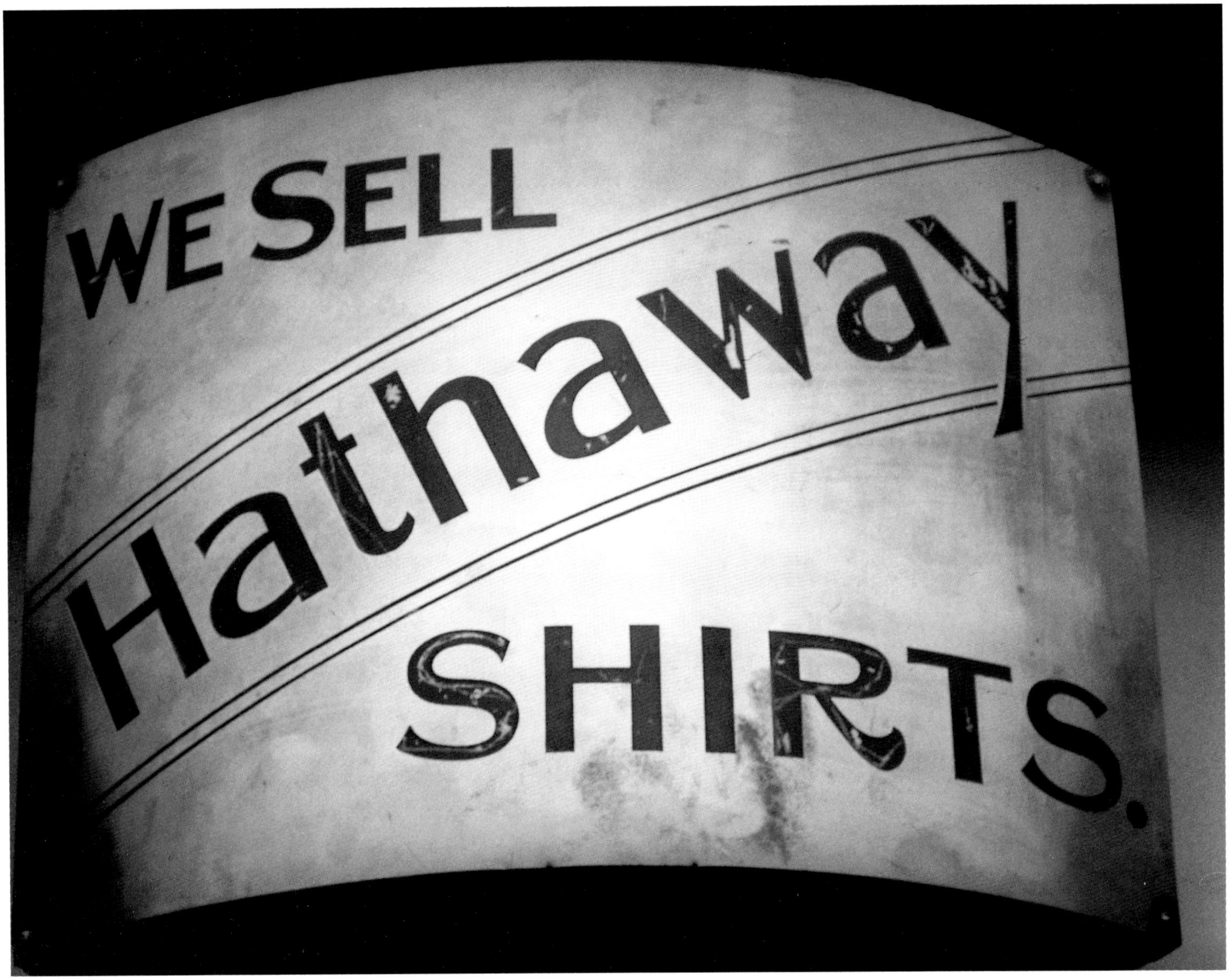

Hathaway store sign, c. 1910

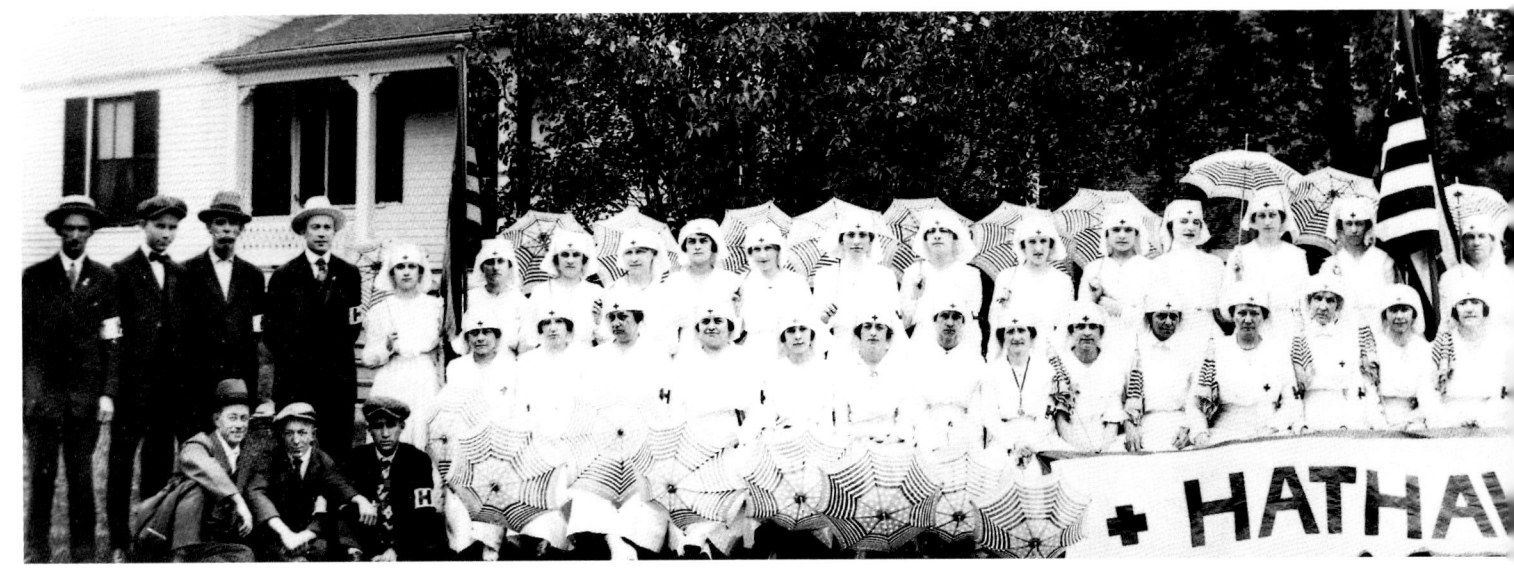

The Hathaway employees show their patriotism during World War I. The periods of war were mutually beneficial. Hathaway provided much needed uniforms, and the wars allowed Hathaway to increase their markets.

With the death of Colonel Leighton in 1915, controlling ownership moved to Edward, known as Ned. Frank Smith became the general manager, and the company began to move into the fast changing future.

Jette looked back on these times as difficult:

> The old long, wide, stiff bosom continually got shorter and narrower and over a period of about twenty years from 1915, completely disappeared…A radically new shirt made its appearance, the first completely soft shirt except the neckband, which was starched so as to accommodate the white and colored stiff collar to match the shirt. Also, in this Leighton-Smith regime, there were many other problems to haunt them, but Hathaway emerged successfully through the ability of these men.
>
> Prior to 1915, about all shirts were white. From 1915 on, there was a violent switch-over to colored shirts, so much so that the white shirt pretty much disappeared from the picture during the early 1920's. Then in addition to all this, the soft collar attached shirt started to creep into view.

Jette concludes that, all in all, "this was a fast moving period when many manufacturers were eliminated because they didn't move fast enough to keep up with rapid changes." (Jette, pg. 7 ff.)

The attached collar that Jette mentioned had its origins in the uniforms of World War I. Beginning in 1914, Hathaway was contracted to make khaki shirts for U.S. soldiers that had the collars attached and had no broad bosom. According to LaPierre the uniforms were not uniform. Some had fully starched attached collars, some had semi-starched attached collars, some used button-down collars and some used a cheaper fused collar. (LaPierre, pg. 43) Upon their return to civilian life, veterans wanted the same comfort and convenience in their shirts that they had had in their uniforms.

The problem posed by collar attached shirts was finding a way to keep the points of the collar from curling up. Hathaway introduced the use of celluloid collar stays, a not wholly satisfactory solution. As LaPierre points out, the collar pin became a stylish solution to the problem, neatly holding the ends of the collar together.

In his 1964 history of the company, *The Future Out of the Past,* Arthur W. Pearce summarizes the era of the late teens and early twenties as "a fast moving period when many names in the industry vanished because the management couldn't move fast enough to keep up." Under Ned Leighton and Frank Smith, Hathaway maintained its quality while staying current with the ever-changing fashion demands.

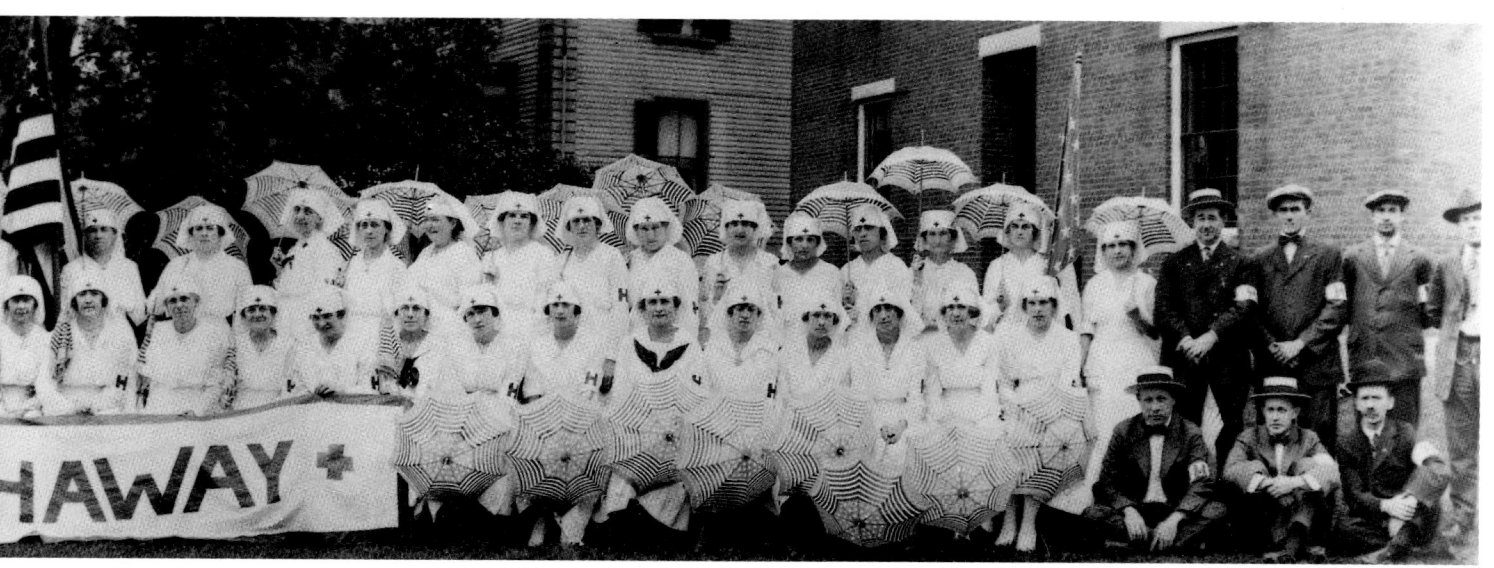

The National Company

Ellerton M. Jette

Despite their efforts Hathaway did not escape the ravages of the Great Depression. Sales reached $800,000, an all time high, in 1929. By 1932 sales had dropped to $150,000. (LaPierre, pg. 45) In 1932 Hathaway entered into an agreement with Ellerton M. Jette to become President of the company, in the hope of bringing it out of its decline. Born in 1900, Jette worked for the Brown-Durrell Company of Boston, in the men's furnishings division, from 1917 until he moved to the Buffalo Shirt Company in 1924. He was the New England sales representative, before moving to New York in 1929 to open an office there. Working with him at Buffalo Shirt was Charles McCarthy, who had previously worked for Simons, Hatch & Whitfield in Boston. When Jette took the presidency of Hathaway in 1932, McCarthy moved with him.

Writing in 1953, Jette looks back on the move:

> In 1932, Charles McCarthy and I joined Hathaway. What Charles's reasons were for deciding to make the move, I don't really know (we both had good secure jobs), but I do know why I came. Because as a competitor of Hathaway's from 1919 to 1932, I was just as inquisitive then as now and bought a shirt of any make that gave me a problem in selling my line...Among all I bought, Hathaway shirts were in my judgment, the best shirt made in the U.S.A. Then, as now, they were fundamentally the same garment they are today. Same general body, patterns built for a generous comfortable fit and, believe it or not at that time the shirts had the expensive French construction which we use today. Also with us in 1932 were Ned Leighton and Frank Smith and many of you here today. It is my opinion that the real reason these two gentlemen sold to us in 1932 was because they realized that they were approaching an age whereby younger men were needed and their foremost desire was to see the continuation of this business which they had worked so hard to preserve for the future. (Jette History, pg. 9.)

If those were the intentions of Leighton and Frank, Jette and McCarthy did not disappoint. Brought in with the agree-

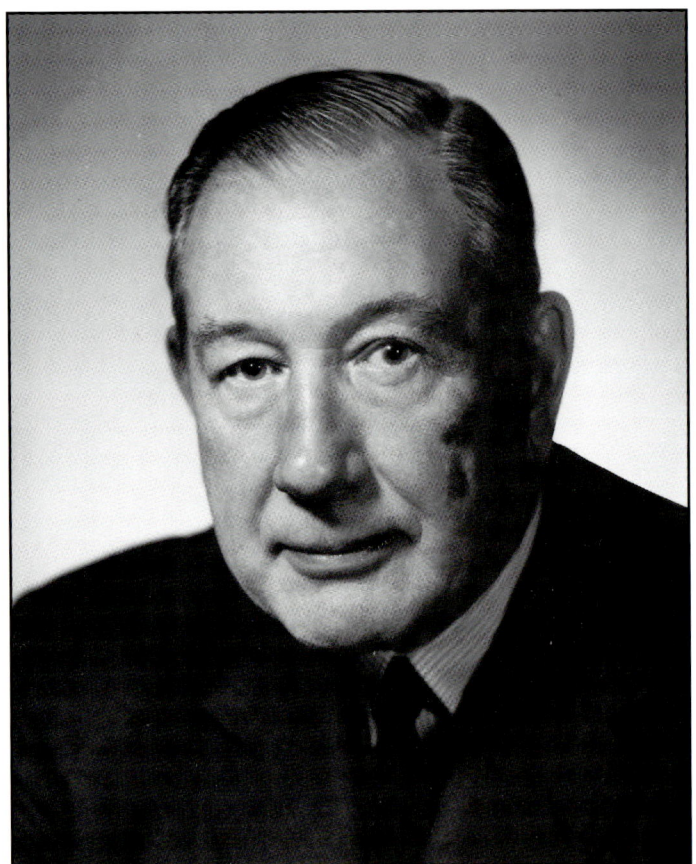

Ellerton M. Jette.

ment that he could buy all the capital stock for $60,000 if he made the company profitable in a year, Jette succeeded and became the controlling stock owner at the age of 33.

Change was in the air. Although colored shirts had become a strong part of the market in the 1920s, Jette made them the gospel of the company with his famous commandment: "Never wear a white shirt before sundown." At the same time the collar-attached shirt became the industry standard and the front of a man's shirt took on a smooth, flat appearance which improved the general fit. (LaPierre, pg. 50.) Other innovations included a redesigned collar shape. Ashley Logan, who had joined the company in 1927, made the "discovery" that men's necks were not round but oval, and that the neck was angled forward from the shoulder. Why it took so long to see this is unclear, but the result was a new collar design that matched the shape of the neck, making it more comfortable and more attractive. The new design required fifteen extra steps in manufacturing, but the result was a superior collar design that is still being used today. (Pearce, pg. 97)

In 1938 Hathaway introduced single-needle stitching throughout its shirts. The construction costs involved in this were immense, doubling the sewing time and, therefore, the seamstresses, and increasing the costs by sixty percent. But the quality it produced was comparable only to the most expensive custom made shirts.

In his 1953 history Jette highlights some of the other Hathaway firsts during the first twenty years of his Presidency: the "low slope collar, bi-angle stay collar...king size ocean pearl buttons, webbing collar linings, one piece sleeves, not to mention collar shapes and designs which have led the fashion parade of shirts all over the country for twenty years." (Jette History, pg. 10)

Jette was always on the lookout for new ideas. On a trip to England he encountered a shop in London that used three-hole buttons. The shirtmaker told him that the three holes made the strongest arrangement because the thread did not weaken the fabric. Hathaway adopted the button in 1938 and has used it since, except during World War II when they were unavailable. It is one of two traditional Hathaway marks. The other is a red H on the gusset of the shirt. Introduced in 1939 it was originally a simple way of strengthening the joint. It has since become something of a symbol. A more recent advertising piece called it the "Hathaway Hallmark of Quality." It continues "The girls that sew on the H know that they carry a great responsibility …. theirs is the last stitching operation (the 77th) and no shirt qualifies for this stamp of approval until it passes all the tests.

Other trips turned up an interesting variety of fabrics: Indian Madras; Batiste Madras; Batiste Broadcloth and Oxford; silk from India; gingham from Scotland; French prints; broadcloth from Japan; and Viyella from England.

Under Jette's leadership, Hathaway sought to expand its market. In 1936, for the first time, Hathaway marketed shirts west of the Hudson River. In 1937 it opened Hathaway House in New York City, a handsome brick home that served as a sales center for Hathaway and a residence for Jette.

In the late 1930s Hathaway introduced a fitted shirt with a shaped waist. Called the "Trim Shirt" it was developed for one of the larger accounts and became quite famous. (LaPierre, pg. 55.)

In 1937 Hathaway introduced two "staple shirts," stock shirts produced in numbers great enough to have ready inventory for their customers. The first two were Style 6, a low slope attached collar, with button cuffs and a pocket, and Style 7, similar to Style 6, but with a button down collar. Both were of regular weight fine yarn Oxford cloth. They were available with the collar standing or flat folded. (LaPierre, pg. 55.)

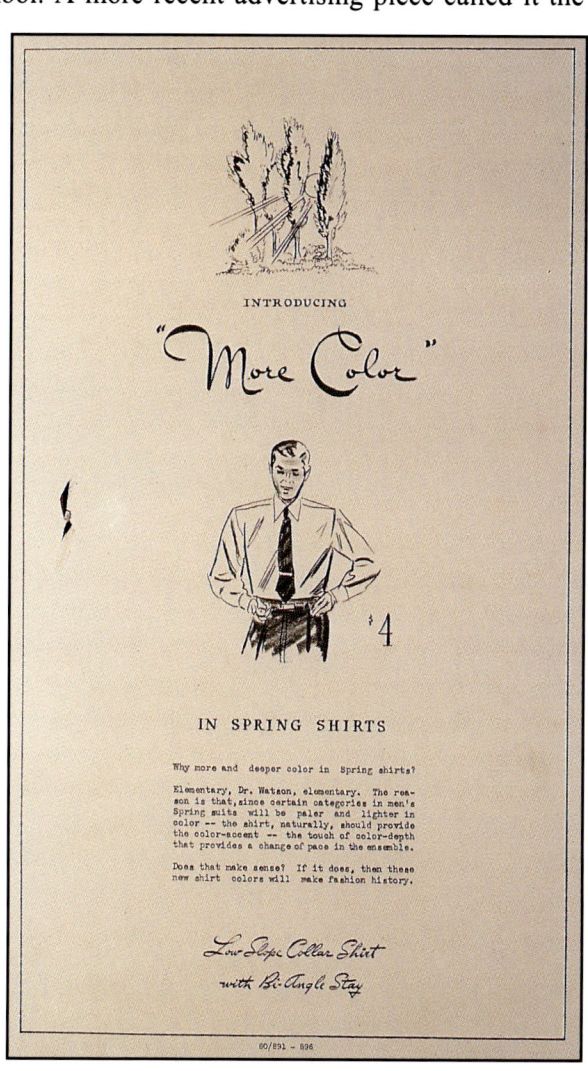

Trade advertisements from the 1940s.

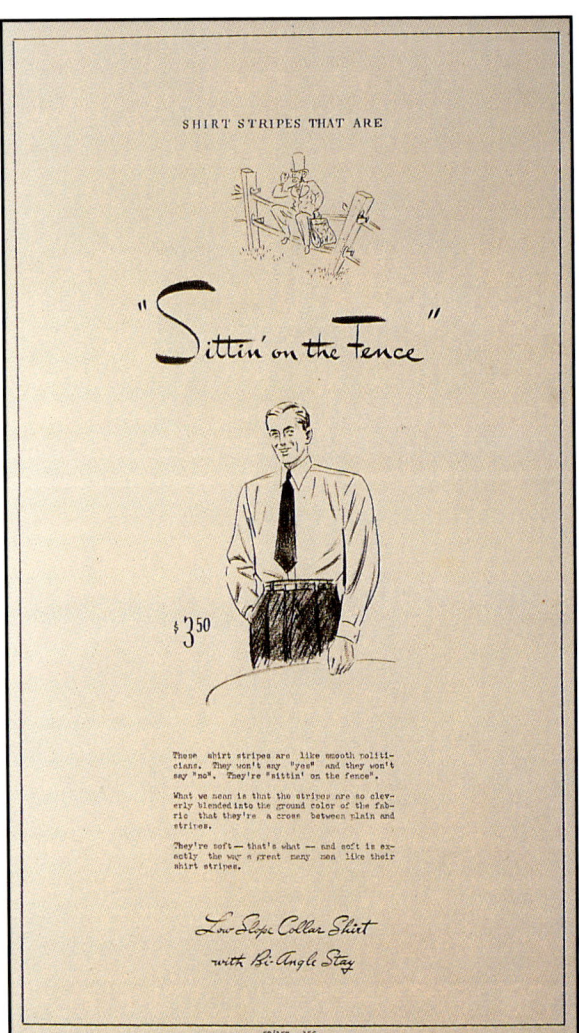
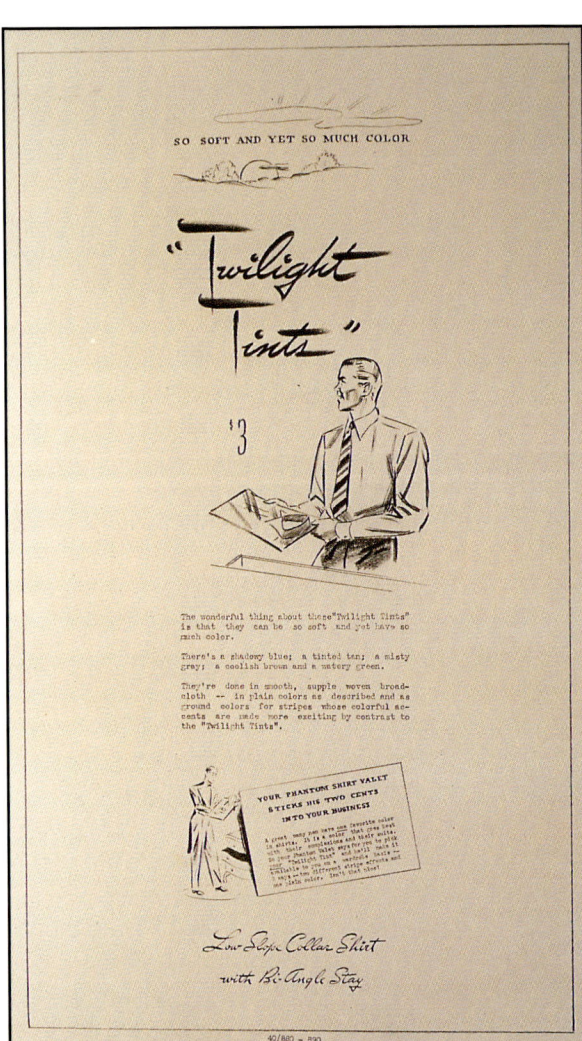

Trade advertisements from the 1940s.

Summarizing the Jette years from 1932 to 1941, Pearce writes:

> When World War II broke out, Hathaway was established as a national and international company selling goods in every state of the union and buying the finest fabrics, not only in the United States, but also from many of the finest shirting mills of Britain and Europe. Most of the fabrics purchased were of specially created designs, colors, and construction made to Mr. Jette's specifications.
>
> In the same pre-World War II period, Hathaway became famous not only for its high quality but also as a fashion leader of the industry. Its designs and colorings, and its fabrics and collar styles were copied freely in the market places. (Pearce, pg. 97)

From 1941 to 1945, almost all of Hathaway's resources were devoted to war production. As they had in the past, the company made shirts for military uniforms, both for officers and enlisted men. One new wrinkle in the patriotic fabric was the production of shirts for the WAC's and the Waves. This would have repercussions after the war, when Hathaway introduced the Lady Hathaway line. During the war, due to a limited supply of fabric, civilian production was at a bare minimum, with shirts allocated to regular customers.

Following the war consumers sought to put hardships behind them and to begin to experience some of the pleasures and niceties the war had forestalled. Demand for shirts was greater than ever and customers were seeking higher quality, both of which, of course, were good omens for Hathaway. Moreover there was a new interest in sports shirts and other casual wear, a market for which Hathaway was well-positioned. In 1945 they opened a new factory in Waterville, and by 1950 they opened a 100,000 square foot facility in Lowell, Massachusetts. The new capacity was 3500 dozen shirts per week. (Pearce, pg. 98.)

Riding this crest of economic boom times, Hathaway began a new marketing effort that was to significantly alter their future. Up until this time, Hathaway's customers had been the retail stores that carried their shirts. The wonderful reputation the company had built for quality, design innovation, and style were known only to a limited number of shop keepers, buyers for major department stores, and a few of the most knowledgeable consumers, because the Hathaway name was not to be found on the shirt. The label in the neck would have the retailer's name, and if the buyer couldn't identify the three-holed buttons or the little red H on the gusset, they would assume that the shirt they were buying was just a store brand. This began to change in 1947, when a concentrated effort began to get the stores to accept the Hathaway name on the label in addition to their own. It was a difficult idea to sell and took well into the 1950s before it was successful.

The Man in the Hathaway Shirt

No one could blame the retailers for balking at the idea of adding Hathaway's name to the label. What purpose would it serve? Outside of the Waterville newspaper, in its first 113 years the only advertising that Hathaway did was aimed not at the men who wore their shirts, but at the stores that sold them. In 1932 the total advertising budget for the company was $371. The name Hathaway had no meaning in the larger population. That would all change in September, 1951.

David Ogilvy was a principal in the firm of Ogilvy, Benson, and Mather, which was only three years old and struggling when Jette approached them about creating a national campaign in 1951. As Ogilvy recalled the meeting some years later, Jette approached him apologetically, "Our account is very small. But I will make you two promises. First, I will never fire you. Second, I will never change a word of your copy." The creative outcome of that meeting set the future for both companies.

On September 22, 1951, a distinguished, handsome gentleman appeared in a full color advertisement in *New Yorker* magazine. Dressed in a white shirt and tie, he was at the tailor's being fitted for a suit. And he was sporting a black eye patch over his right eye. This exotic touch caught the public's attention and from then until now the eye patch recalls "The man in the Hathaway shirt." Hathaway and Ogilvy had scored a direct hit on the consumer's consciousness. With this advertisement and the barrage that followed, Hathaway was established as a quality product for men of sophisticated tastes.

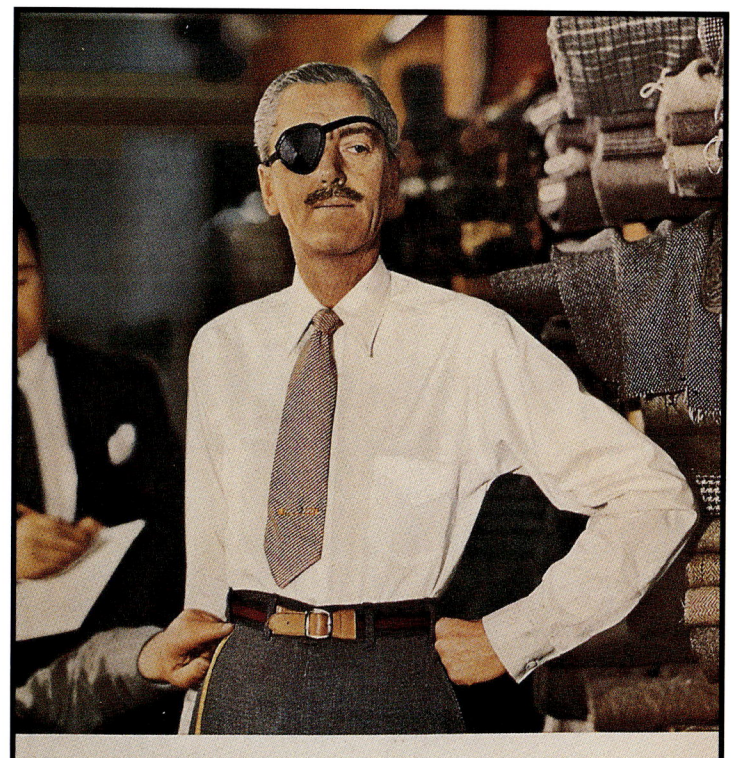

The original advertisement featuring the man in the Hathaway, Baron George Wrangell. It first ran in the *New Yorker* magazine on September 22, 1951. $18-20.

The first Hathaway man was Baron George Wrangell, the son of a Russian Navy Captain, Peter Baron Wrangell. The family emigrated west during the Bolshevik revolution, settling first in Europe and later in New York City. George Wrangell was born in 1903 and studied for the hotel business as a youth in Europe, before turning to journalism. In New York, he opened his own outdoor advertising business.

The advertisements placed Wrangell in a number of glamorous settings, taking him around the world and engaging him in a number of glamorous endeavors. He was the renaissance man personified, who could paint, lead symphony orchestras, fence, play pool, or cook gourmet meals. In every situation he was nattily dressed in a Hathaway shirt. The copy talked about the good life and how the style, comfort, and quality of the shirt was perfect for its pursuit.

Wrangell served as the Hathaway man until 1962, when he resigned. He was followed by Colin Leslie Fox, an adventurer who first made a name for himself by sailing solo across the Atlantic. In fact, his first appearance in a Hathaway advertisement was under his own name and without the patch! That was in 1958 when Fox was featured for having sailed his 24-foot cutter across the Atlantic singlehanded, alternating between two Viyella shirts for eighty-nine days. He became the Hathaway man in 1963.

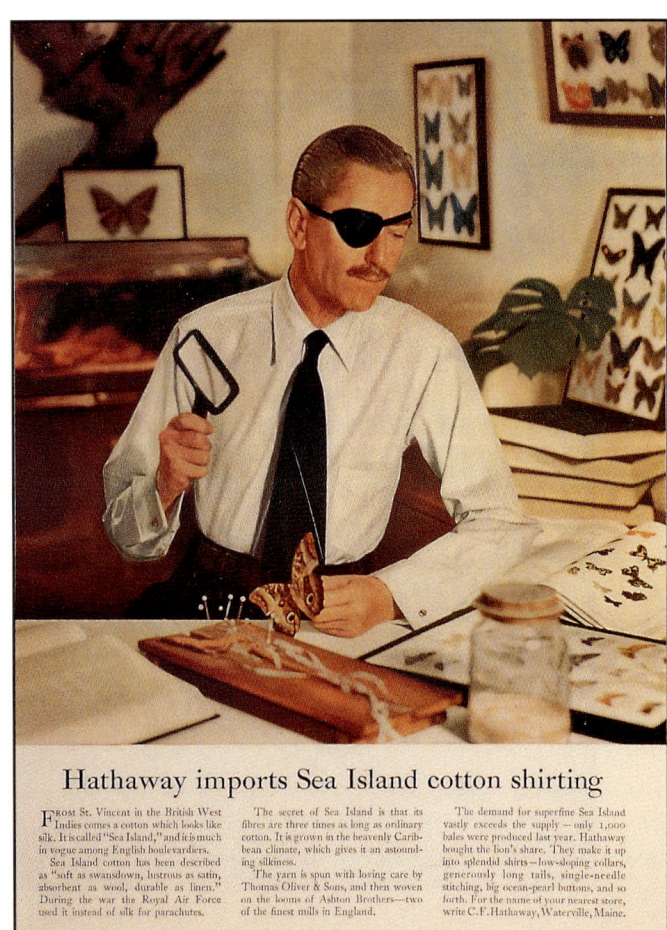

1951. Sea Island cotton shirt. $20-24.

In the early 1950s Hathaway introduced the Lady Hathaway line. Hathaway drew upon its considerable experience with uniforms for women in the war, and brought that knowledge to creating a "man-tailored" shirt for women. It was the first time this had been done, and as LaPierre points out, it marked a trend toward casual clothing for women. (LaPierre, pg. 65) The concept was welcomed by retailers, and soon the line expanded to include a Bermuda collar, and other varieties.

With increased advertising, a broadened line, and an expanding economy the 1950s were a time of significant growth for Hathaway. Their shirts were in demand across the nation, leading to a shift in their marketing strategy. Until then their outlets had been upscale specialty stores, making their shirts hard to find. It was decided to make the Hathaway shirt available to all the best stores in the nation, but to do so without sacrificing either quality or price. In Waterville the growing market meant expansion and growth in the factory and work force. It also meant a severe financial burden for the company. In 1957 the company experienced a net loss of $800,716 on sales of $11,062,921. Changes in management and an austerity program which included the cancellation of the annual Christmas party in 1958, meant improved performance for the next year with a net profit of $105,341 on sales of $9,895,968. In 1959 sales had returned to $10,391,339 with a net profit of $540,431. In the decade of the fifties, Hathaway sales had grown nearly 300 percent.

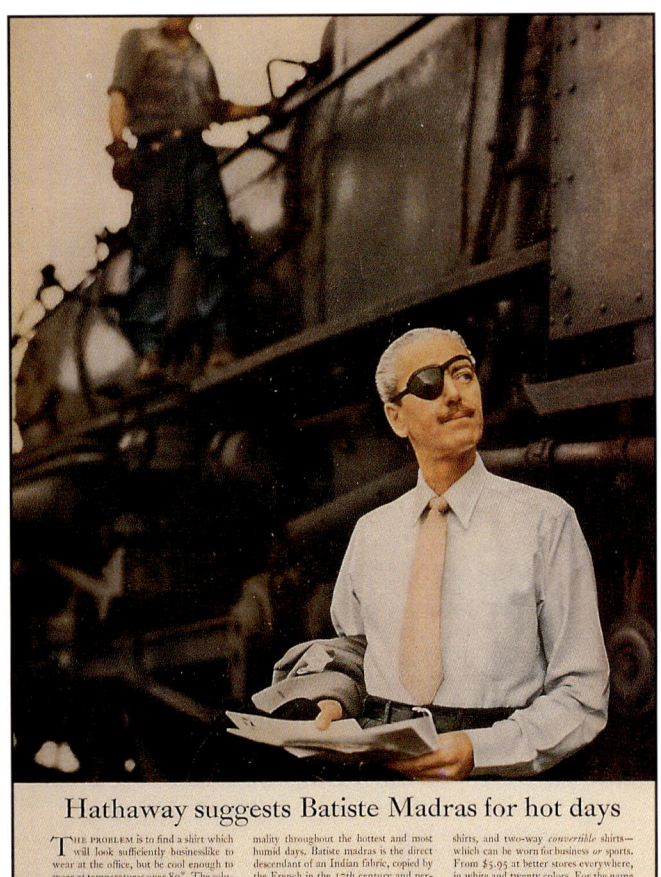

1951. Dress shirt in Batiste Batik. $20-24.

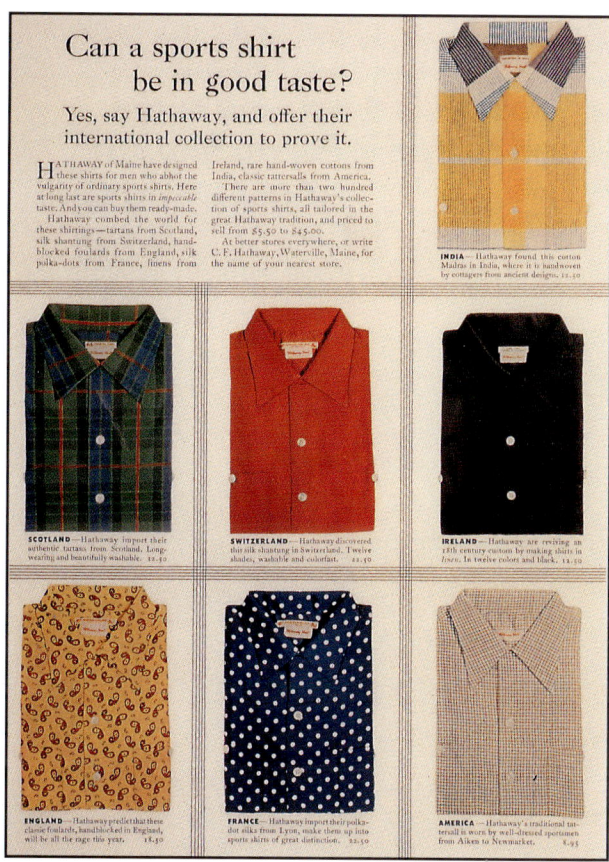

1952. While dress shirts were still considered proper dress, Hathaway recognized the growth of leisure time in post-War America, and produced a wide range of sports shirts, "in good taste," of course. The ad boasts of over 200 styles. $24-28.

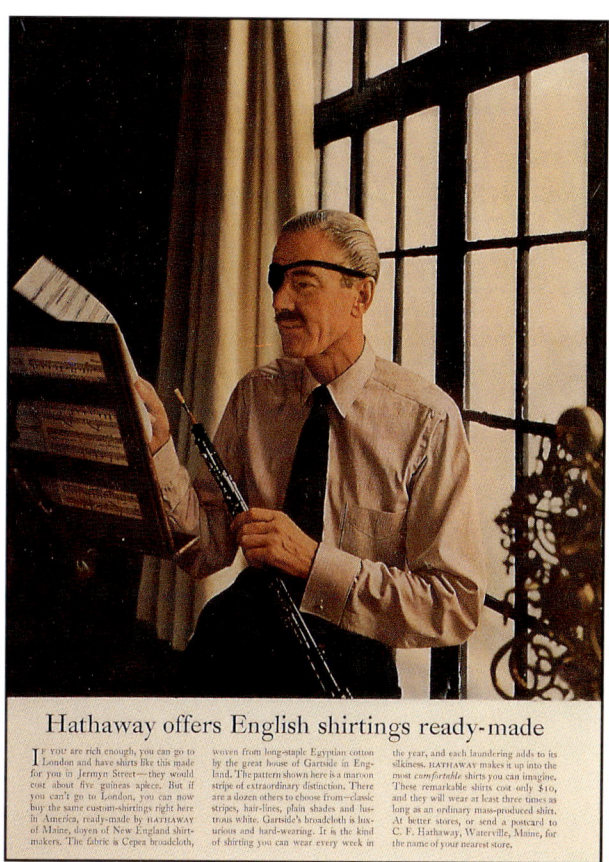

1952. $20-24.

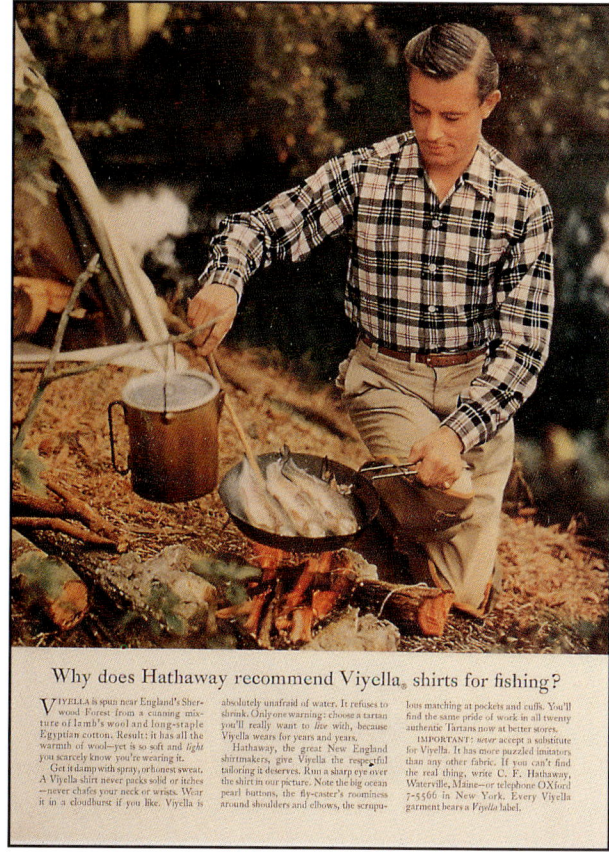

1952. Hathaway began using Viyella in the 1930s and continued until it was replaced by Lochlana in the 1960s. It is a blend of wool and cotton, perfect for sports shirts. $24–28.

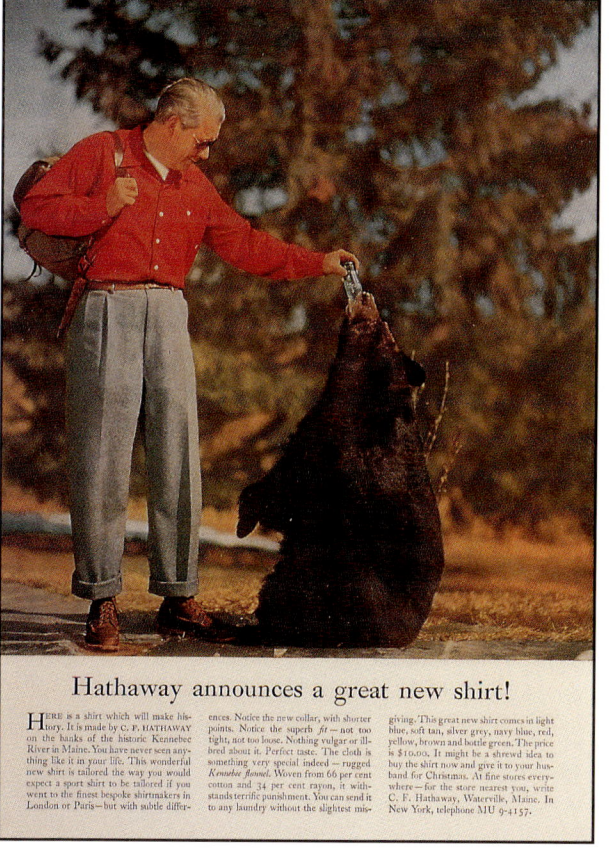

1952. Another sport shirt using "Kennebec flannel," a woven blend of 66% wool and 34% rayon. $24-28.

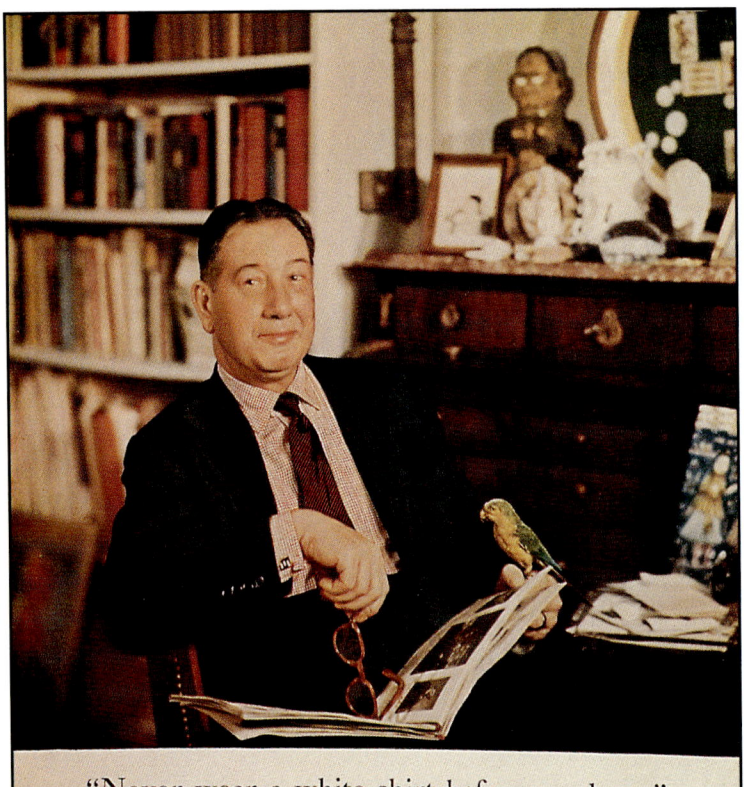

Left: 1952. "Never wear a white shirt before sundown" was a slogan originated by Ellerton Jette in the 1930s, which became an accepted fashion rule. Here he is in his own Hathaway advertisement. $18-20.

Lower left: 1952. Hathaway began using Indian madras in the 1930s. $28-30.

Lower right: 1952. $28-30.

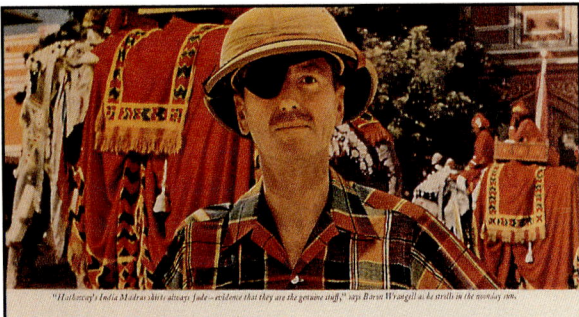

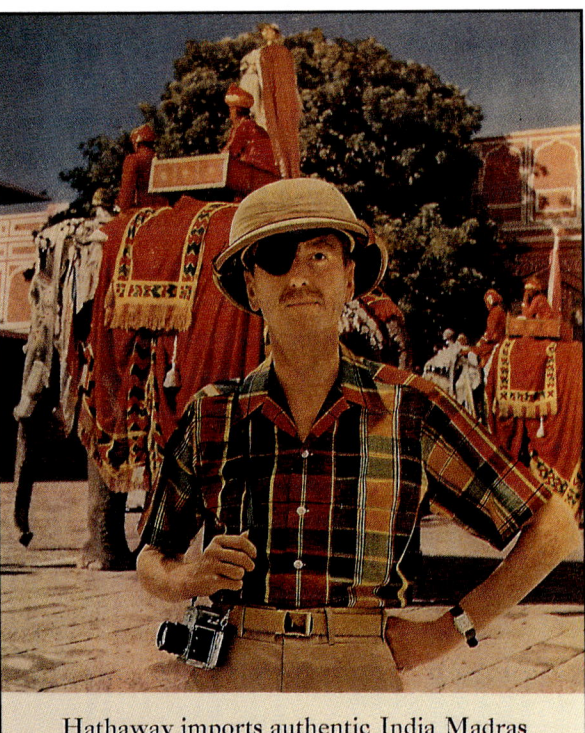

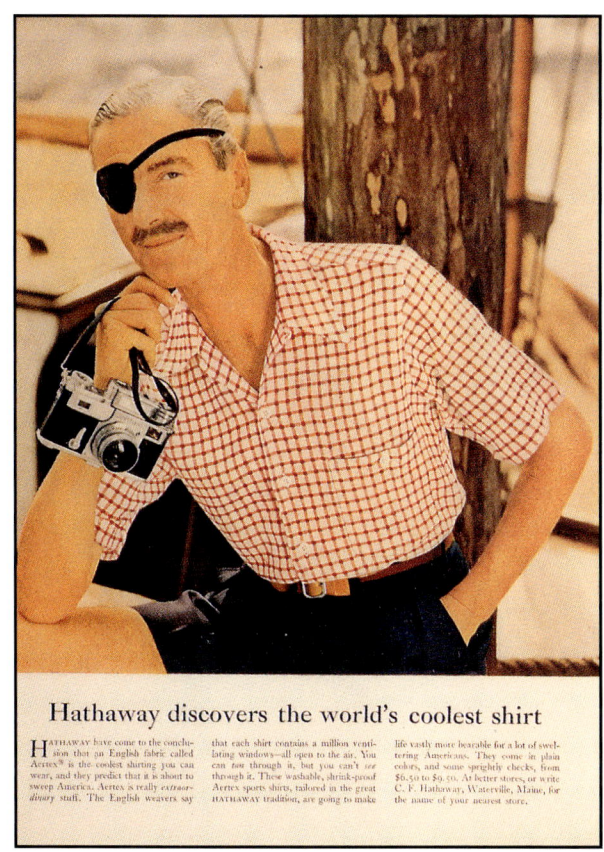

Hathaway discovers the world's coolest shirt

HATHAWAY have come to the conclusion that an English fabric called Aertex® is the coolest shirting you can wear, and they predict that it is about to sweep America. Aertex is really *extraordinary* stuff. The English weavers say that each shirt contains a million ventilating windows—all open to the air. You can see through it, but you can't *see* through it. These washable, shrink-proof Aertex sports shirts, tailored in the great HATHAWAY tradition, are going to make life vastly more bearable for a lot of sweltering Americans. They come in plain colors, and some sprightly checks, from $6.50 to $9.50. At better stores, or write C. F. Hathaway, Waterville, Maine, for the name of your nearest store.

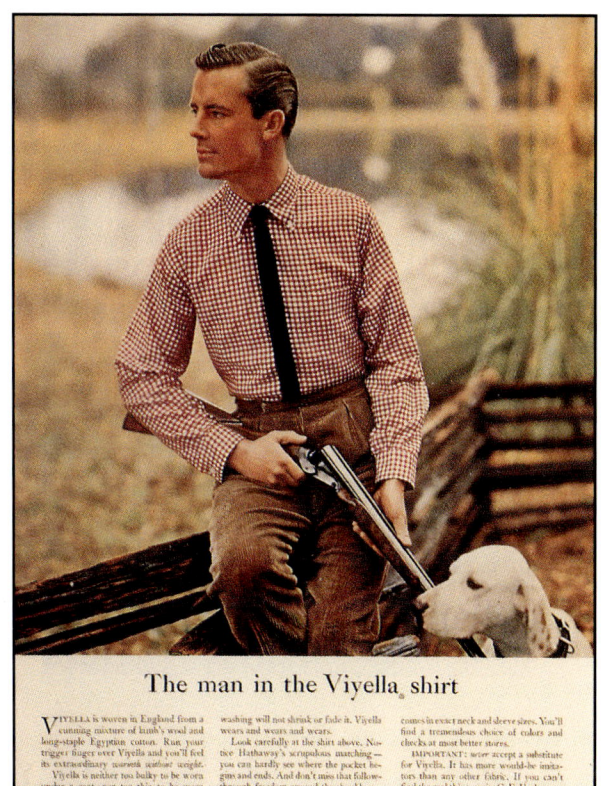

The man in the Viyella shirt

VIYELLA is woven in England from a cunning mixture of lamb's wool and long-staple Egyptian cotton. Run your trigger finger over Viyella and you'll feel its extraordinary smooth *without weight*. Viyella is neither too bulky to be worn under a coat—nor too thin to be worn alone. Take it on the toughest field trial—and it will never chafe at the neck or wrist. Send Viyella to the laundry. Decades of washing will not shrink or fade it. Viyella wears and wears and wears.

Look carefully at the shirt above. Notice Hathaway's scrupulous matching—you can hardly see where the pocket begins and ends. And don't miss that follow-through freedom around the shoulders.

We call this particular Hathaway style the "Suburban Shirt." Unlike most outdoor shirts, it takes a tie perfectly, and it comes in exact neck and sleeve sizes. You'll find a tremendous choice of colors and checks at most better stores.

IMPORTANT: never accept a substitute for Viyella. It has more would-be imitators than any other fabric. If you can't find the real thing, write C. F. Hathaway, Waterville, Maine—or telephone OXford 7-5566 in New York. Every Viyella garment bears a *Viyella* label.

Above left: 1952. $20–24.

Above right: 1952. Not all the early advertising featured the Hathaway man. $20–24.

Right: 1952. "The Girl in Hathaway shirt." Hathaway introduced man-tailored shirts for women in the early 1950s. This cigar smoking woman is just a little daring for its time. $20–22.

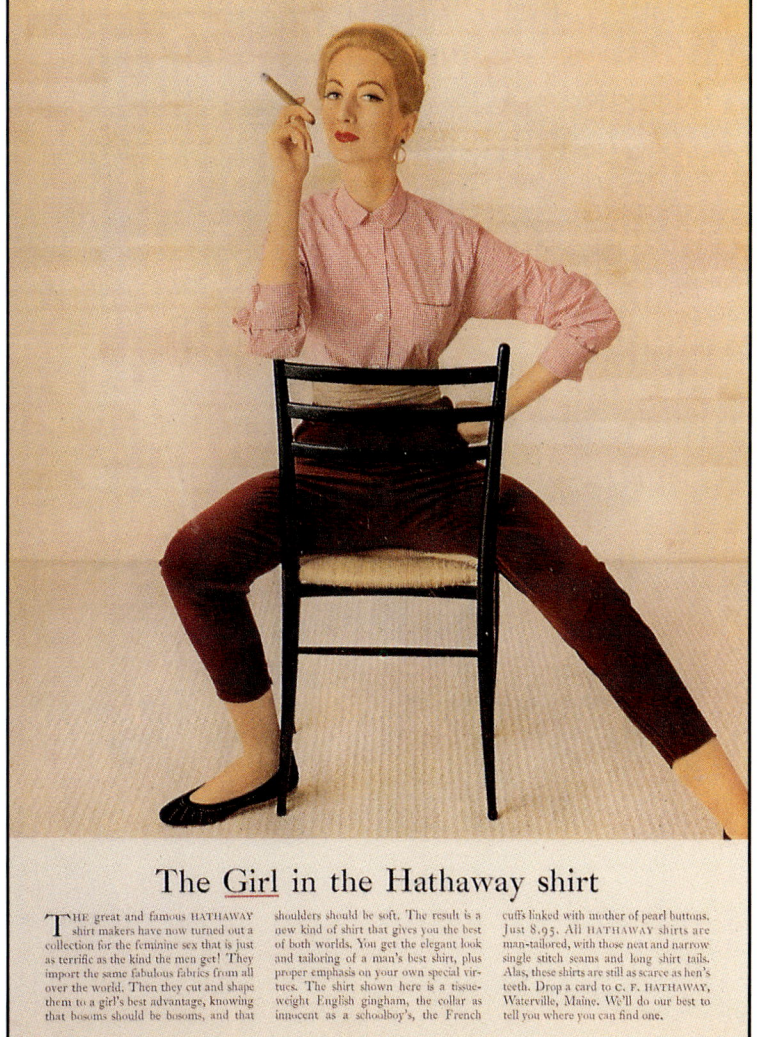

The Girl in the Hathaway shirt

THE great and famous HATHAWAY shirt makers have now turned out a collection for the feminine sex that is just as terrific as the kind the men get! They import the same fabulous fabrics from all over the world. Then they cut and shape them to a girl's best advantage, knowing that bosoms should be bosoms, and that shoulders should be soft. The result is a new kind of shirt that gives you the best of both worlds. You get the elegant look and tailoring of a man's best shirt, plus proper emphasis on your own special virtues. The shirt shown here is a tissue-weight English gingham, the collar as innocent as a schoolboy's, the French cuffs linked with mother of pearl buttons. Just 8.95. All HATHAWAY shirts are man-tailored, with those neat and narrow single stitch seams and long shirt tails. Alas, these shirts are still as scarce as hen's teeth. Drop a card to C. F. HATHAWAY, Waterville, Maine. We'll do our best to tell you where you can find one.

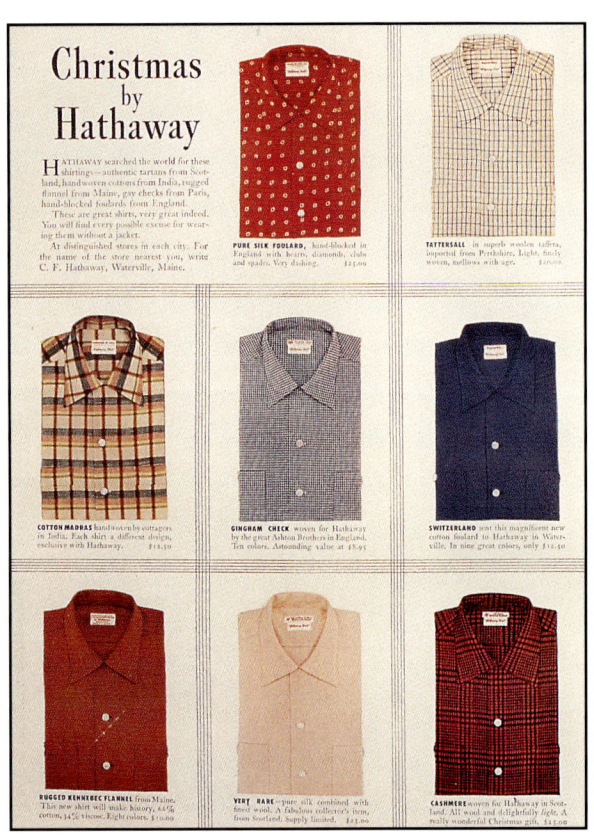

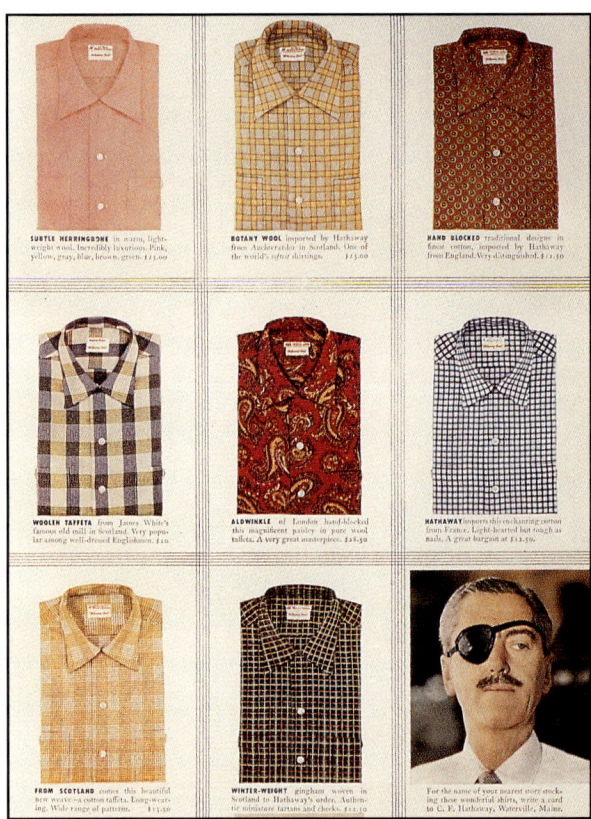

1952. Sports shirts for Christmas. $24–28.

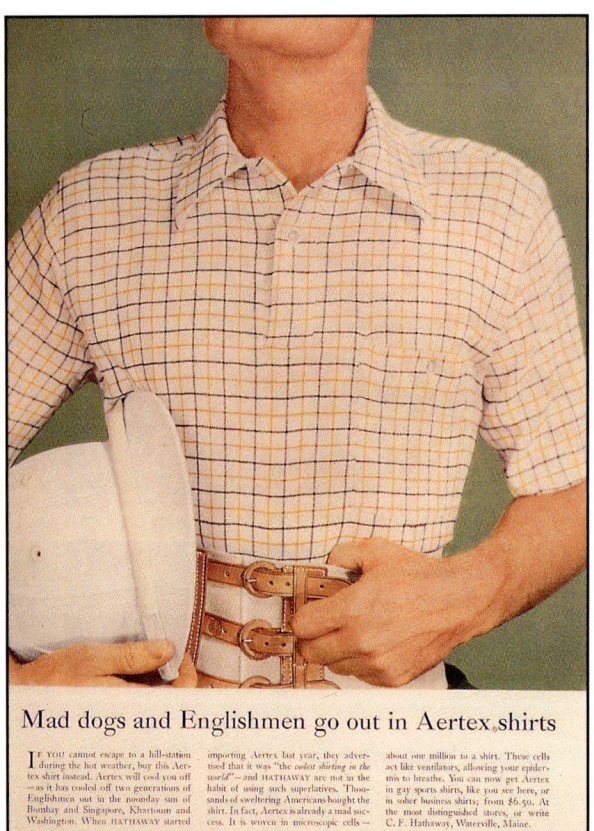

1953. A 1953 advertising campaign featured nearly headless torsos. While this gave the shirt more prominence, the romance of the Hathaway man was lost. He returned in 1954.

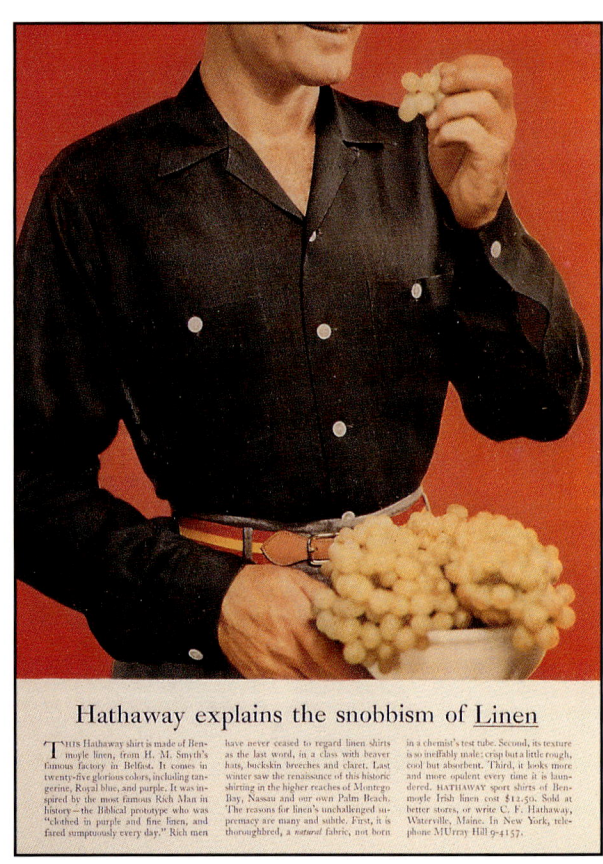

1953. $24–28.

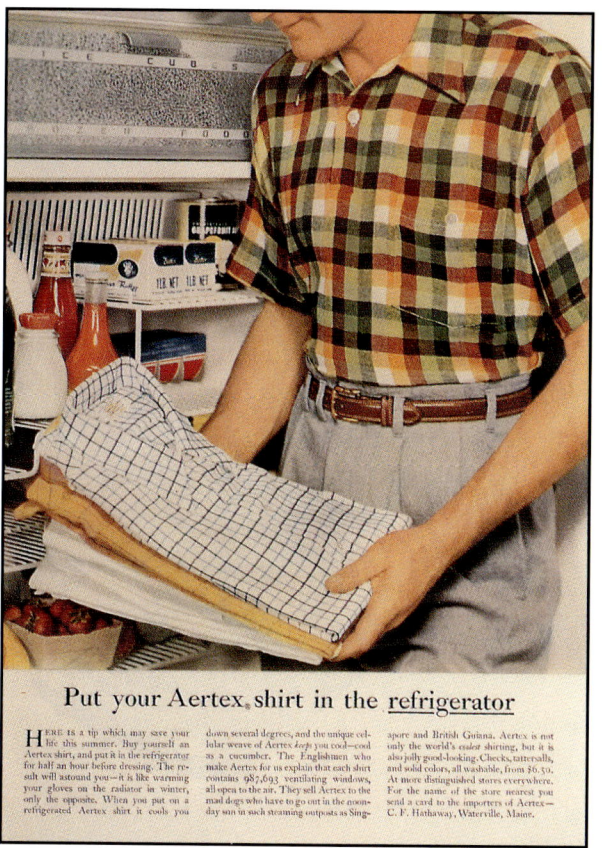

1953. $28–30

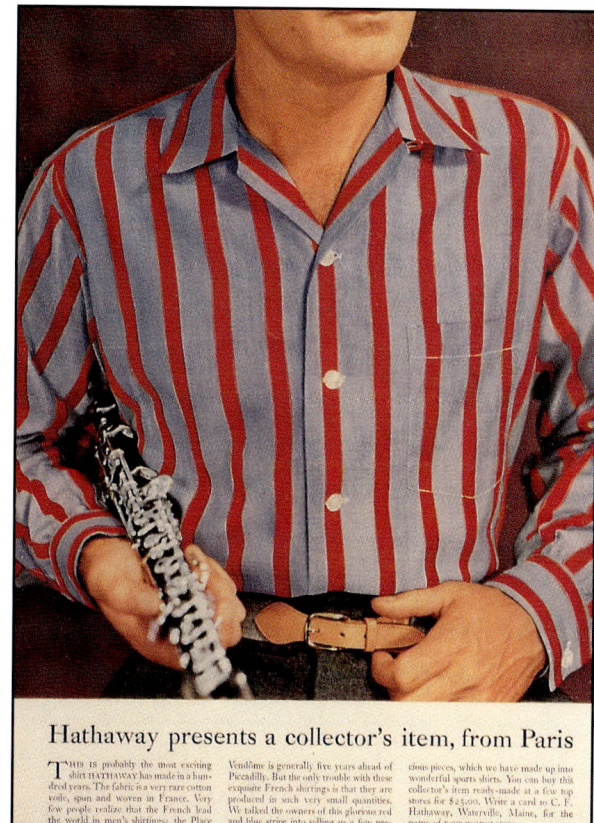

1953. $24–28

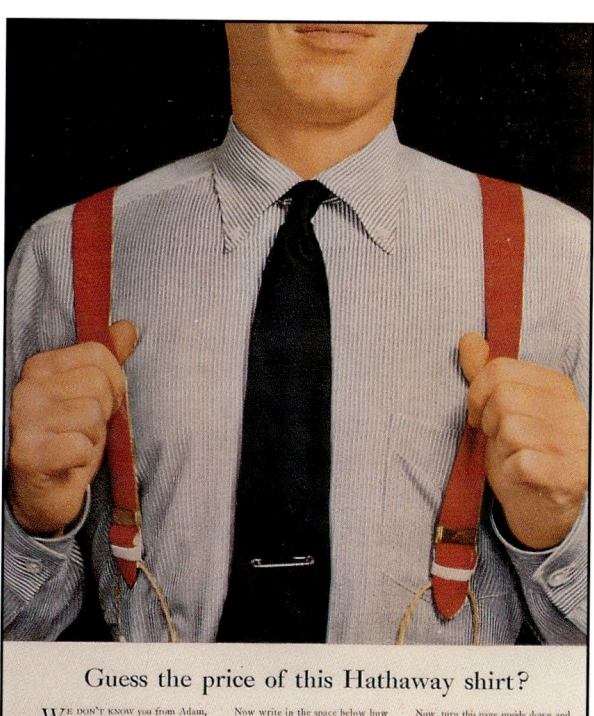

1953. The price was $6.50 as shown and $5.95 in white. $20–22.

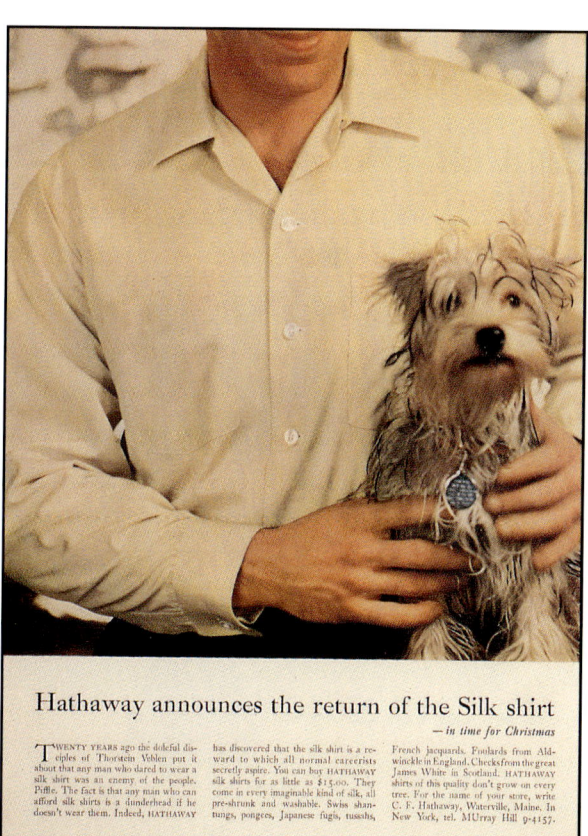

1953. $40–45

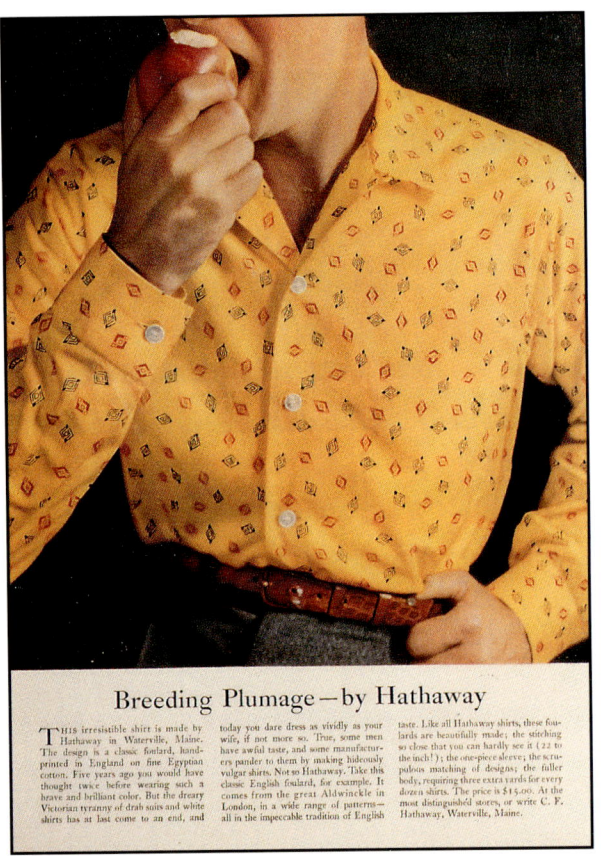

1953. The ad says "The dreary Victorian tyranny of drab suits and white shirts has come to an end." This brilliant English foulard print certainly confirms it. $22–24.

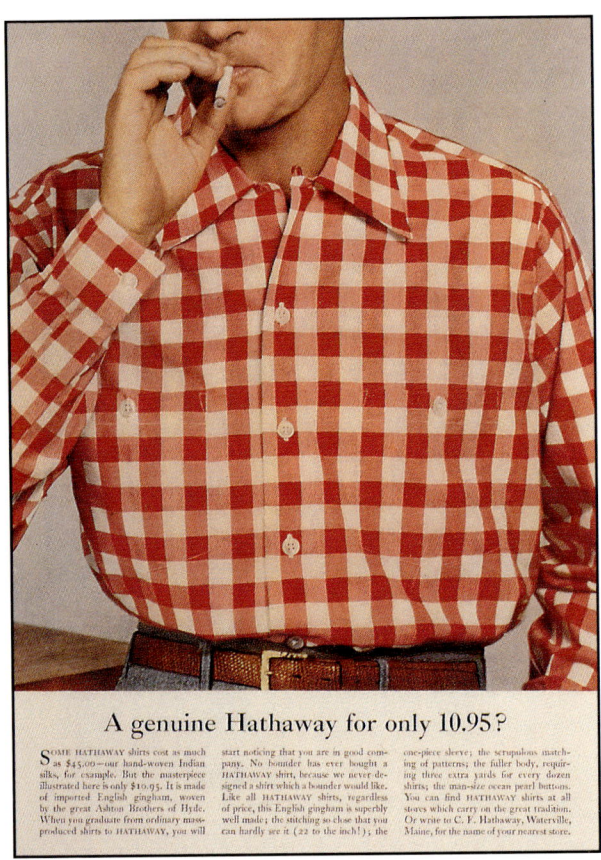

1953. $24–28.

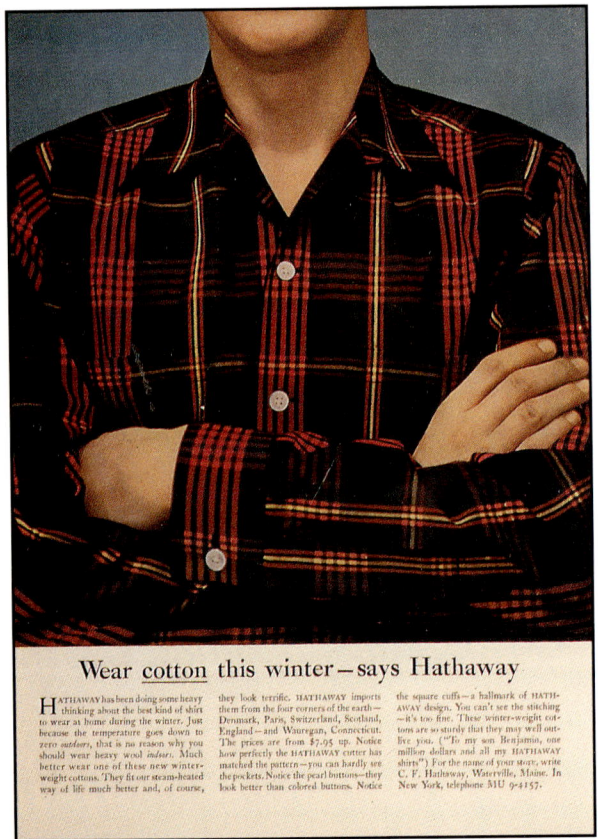

1953. $24–28.

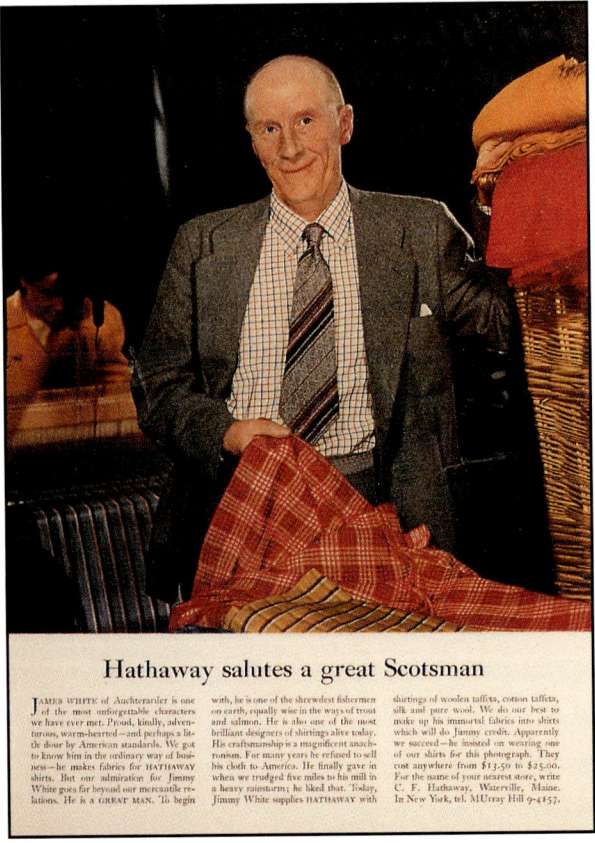

1953. This ad recognizes James White, of Auchterarder, a manufacturer of shirtings for Hathaway in woolen taffeta, cotton taffeta, silk, and pure wool.

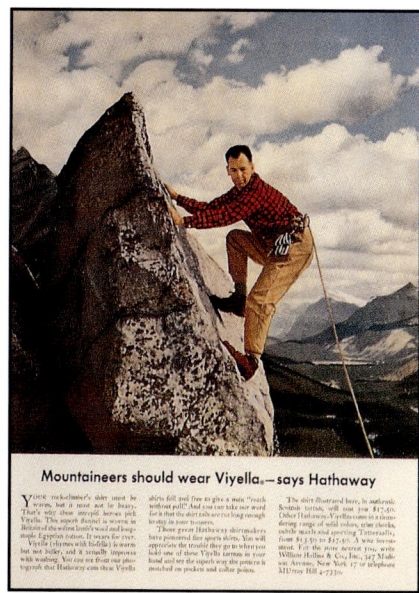

1953. This unidentified mountaineer is being kept warm and comfortable in a Viyella shirt. $28–30.

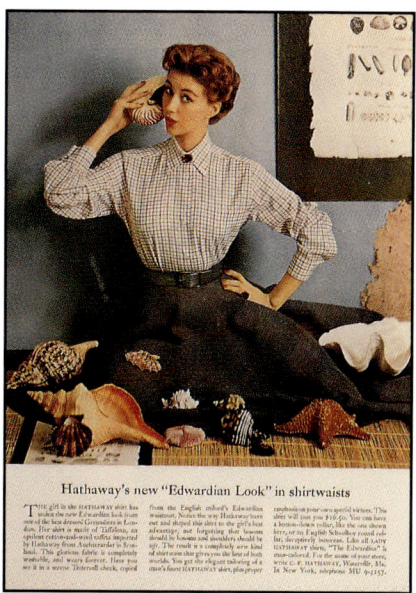

1953. Lady Hathaway's new "Edwardian Look" in Taffalean, a blend of wool and cotton from the Auchterarder mills. $24–28.

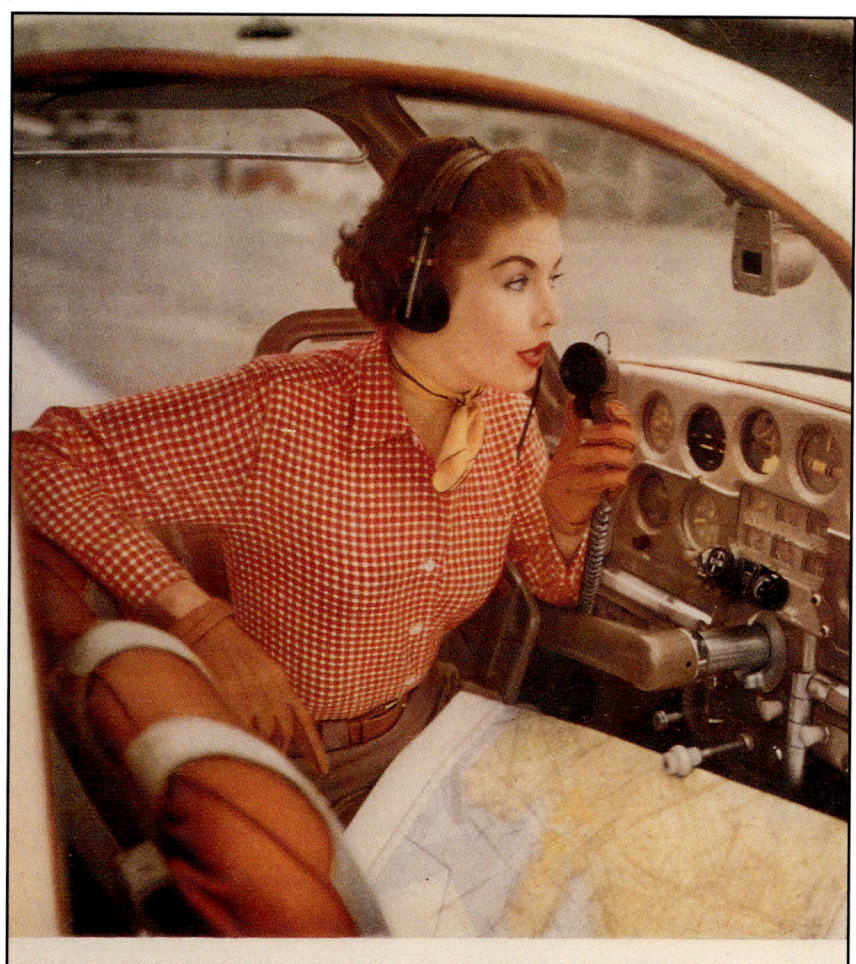

1953. The copy for this Lady Hathaway reveals the changes in "politically correct" advertising. In part it says, "...for the fair sex they cut and shape them for a girl's best advantage, knowing full well that bosoms should be bosoms and that shoulder should be soft." $24–28.

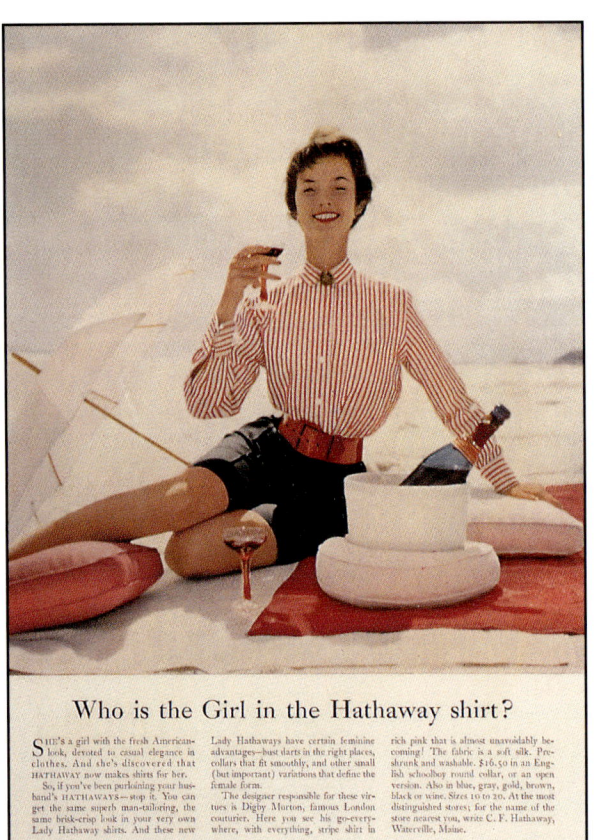

1954. This Lady Hathaway ad credits Digby Morton, a London couturier, with the feminine design of the man-tailored shirt. $20–22.

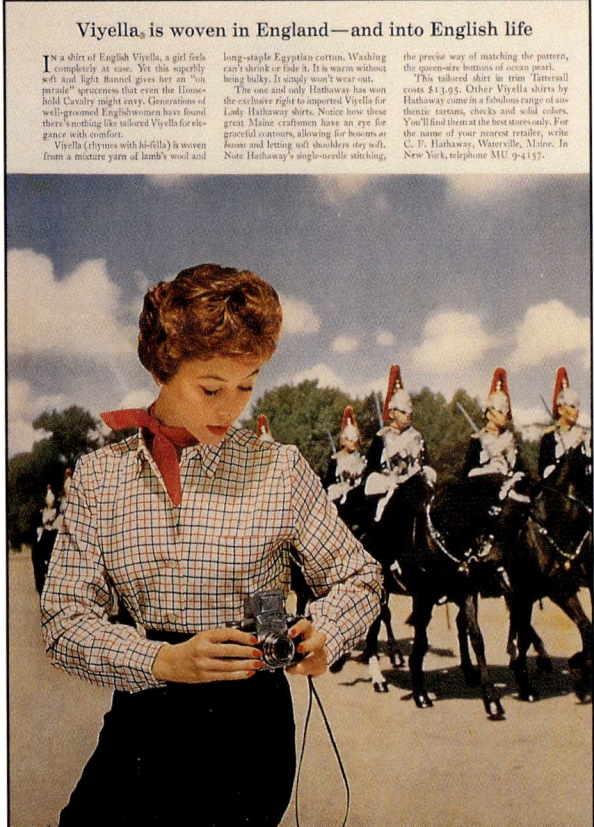

1954. $22–24

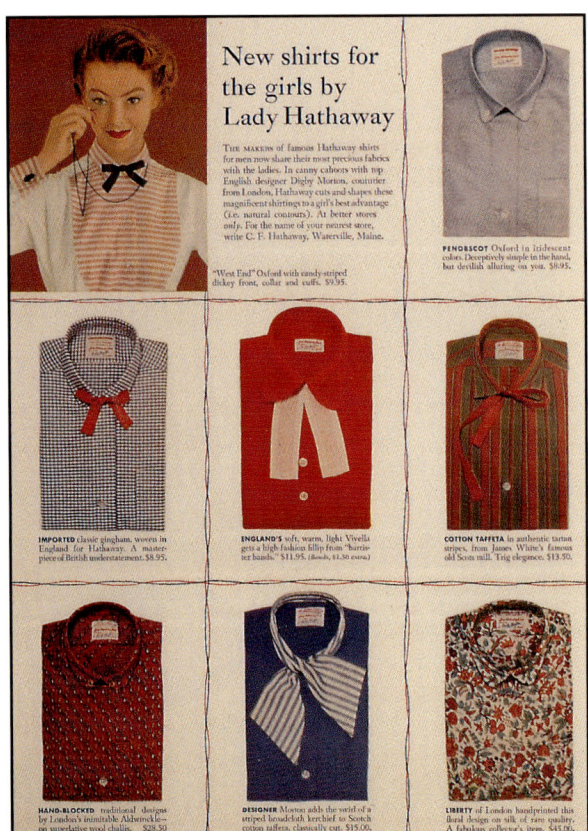

1954. $24–28.

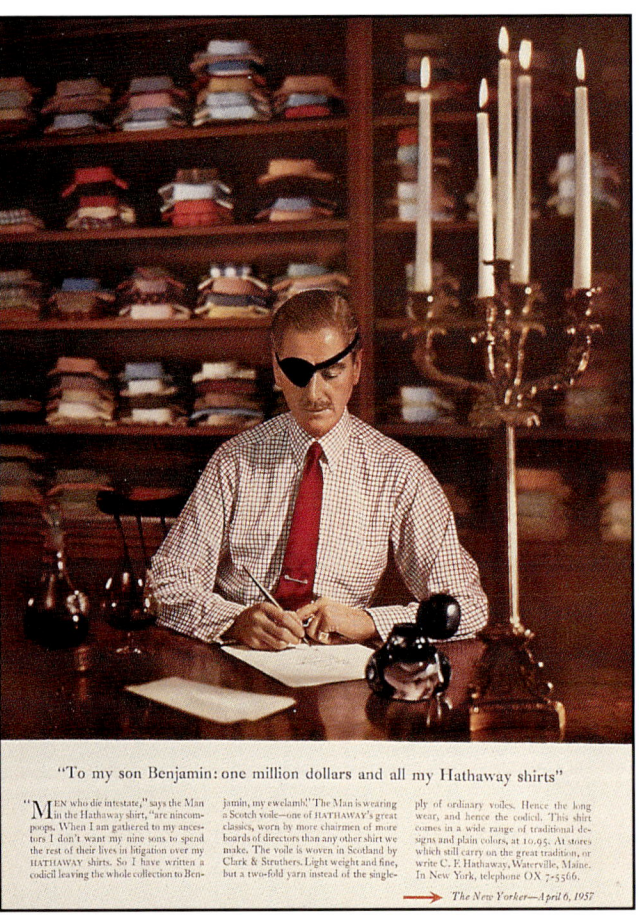

1954. Baron Wrangell returns. This ad ran at least until 1957. $20–24.

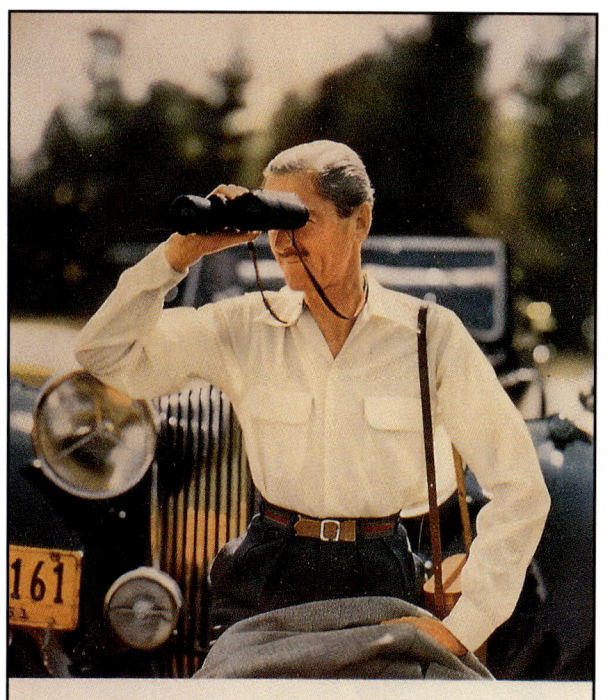

1954. $20–24.

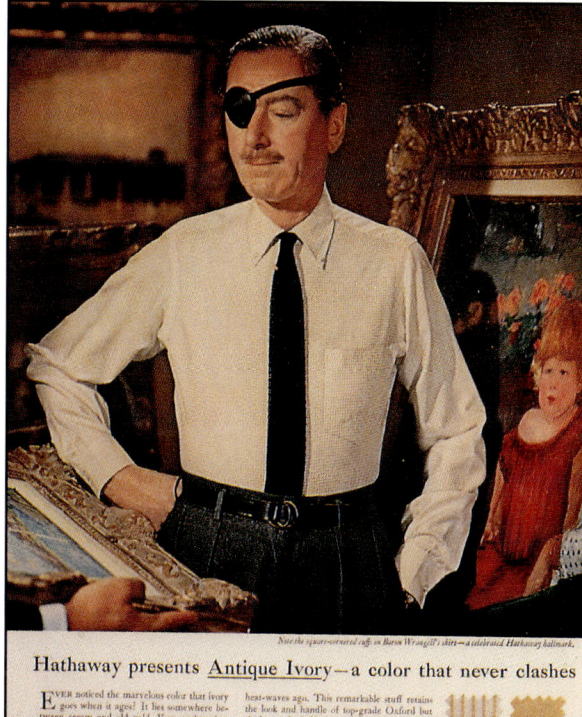

1954. $20–24.

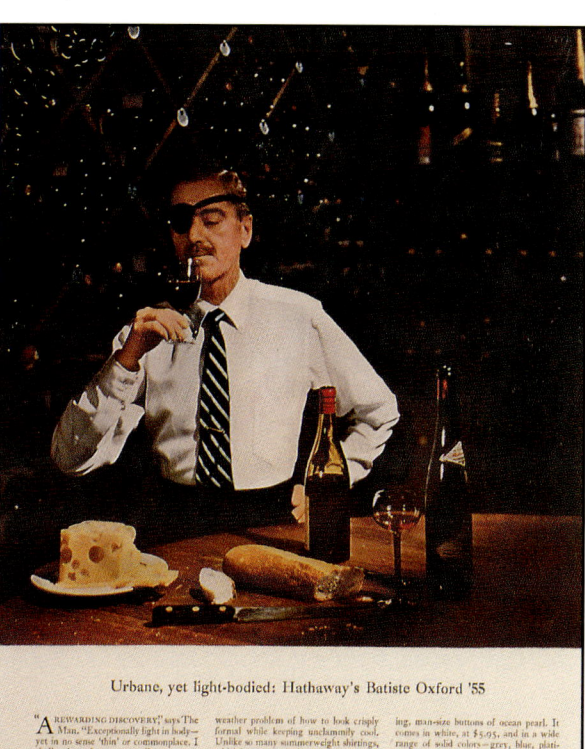

1954. $20–24.

1954. $20–24.

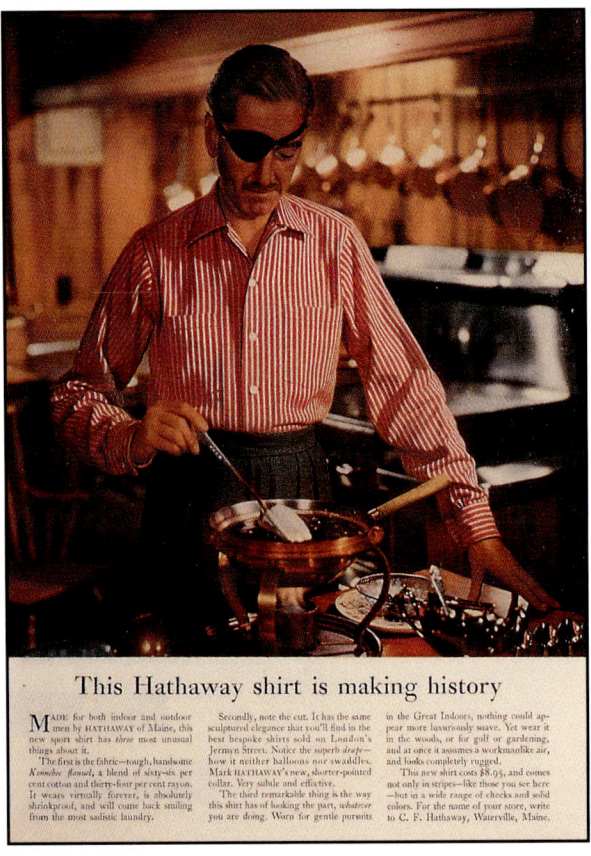

1954. $24–28

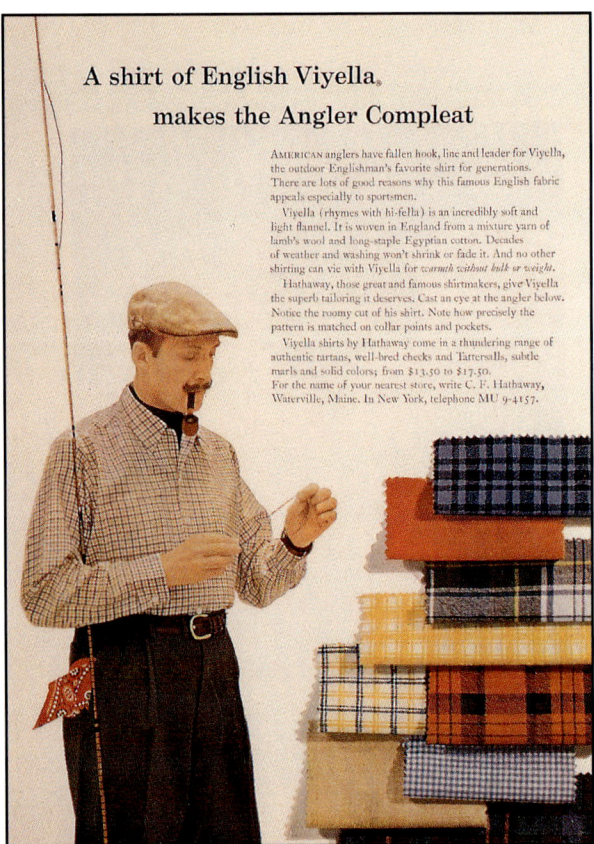

1954. $24–28

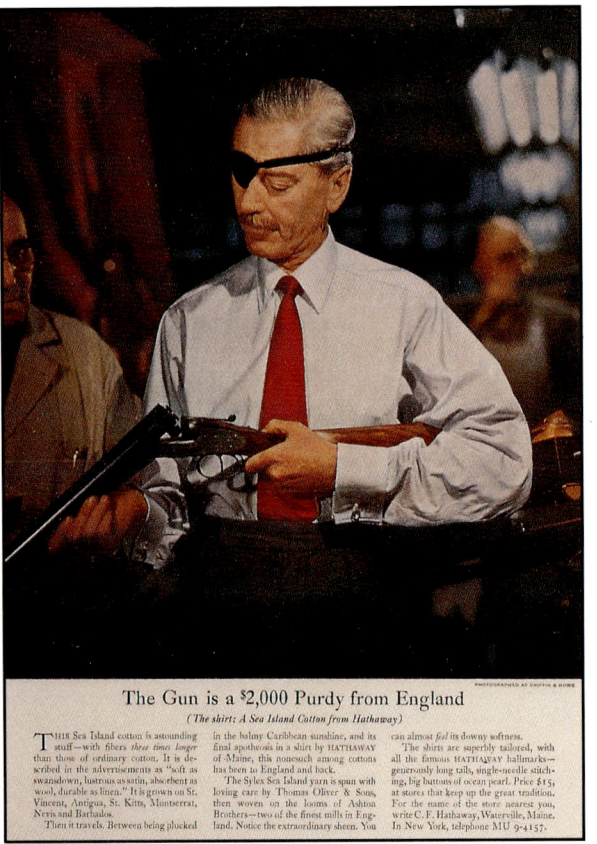

1955. $22–24.

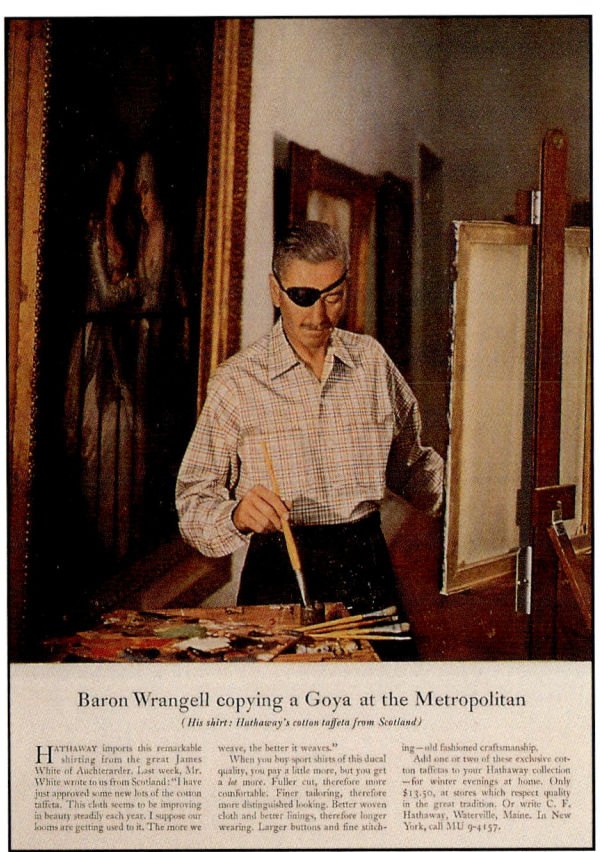

1955. The Hathaway man is nothing if not Renaissance. $28–30.

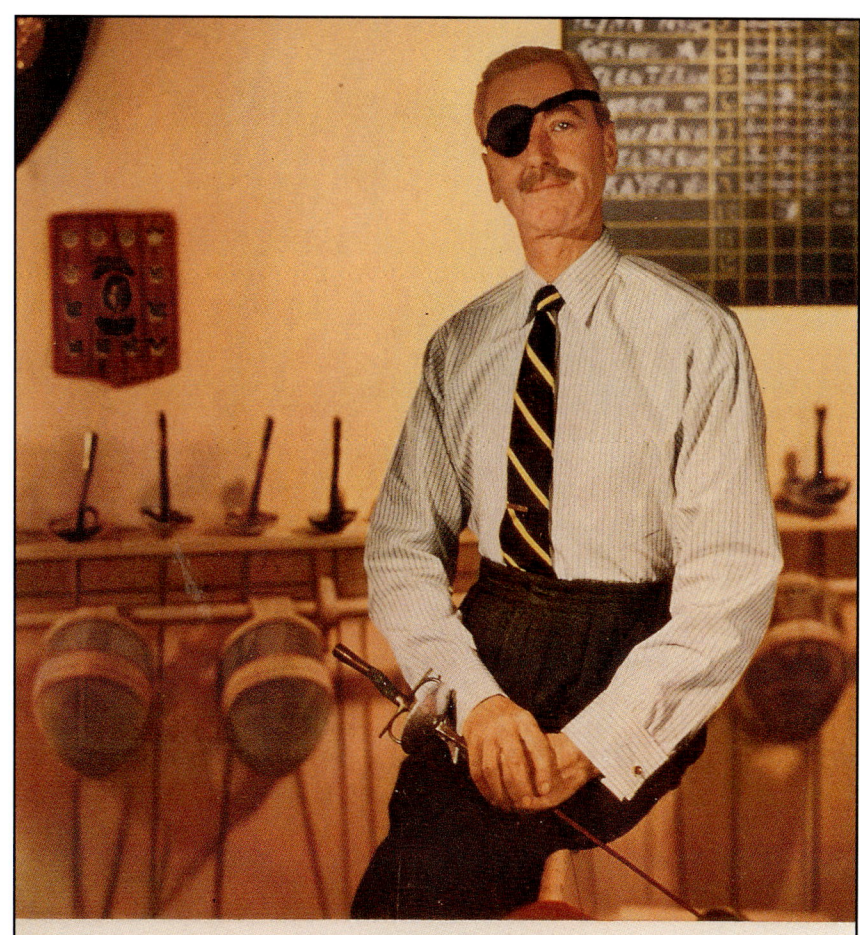

1955. A restatement of Hathaway's haberdashery rule. An ad with the same image appeared in 1955 sharing the 5 ways to identify a Hathaway shirt: 1. Ample room; 2. large buttons and small stitches; 3. square cornered cuffs; 4. the red H; and 5. all men who wear Hathaway "are individualists, so they seldom wear white shirts." $22–24.

"Never wear a white shirt before sundown"
— *says Hathaway*

HATHAWAY takes the view that no well-dressed man should wear a white shirt before sundown. A white shirt with a business suit is really the loudest thing you can wear. It looks clean in the morning, but by afternoon it gets soiled at the collar and cuffs. This looks awful. Wearing a white shirt at the office is like wearing a uniform—a pitiful abdication of individuality. Gentle reader, you may be wearing a white shirt at this very moment. HATHAWAY has no desire to insult you— heaven knows, we have been making white shirts for 120 years, and expect to go on making them. But we also make patterned shirts, and we would never dream of wearing anything else—before sundown.

Classic stripes, checks, plain colors are so much more interesting. So much more practical. So much better looking. Next time you are in the market for shirts, ask the store to show you some of HATHAWAY's patterned shirts. They are in superb taste, and they are a whole lot better made than ordinary mass-produced shirts. The prices start at $6.95. It isn't every store that stocks HATHAWAY shirts—only the most distinguished in each city.

Write C. F. Hathaway, Waterville, Maine, for the name of your nearest store.

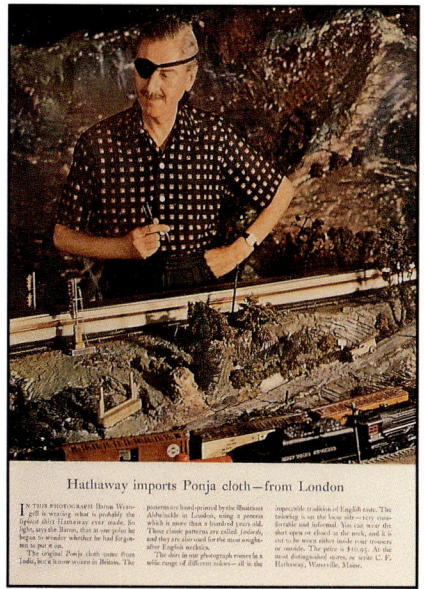

1955. $24–28.

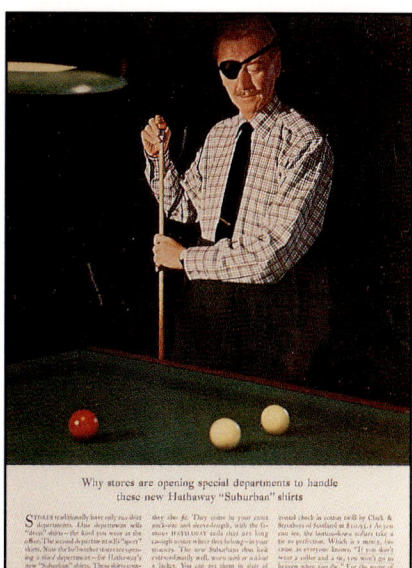

1955. $24–28.

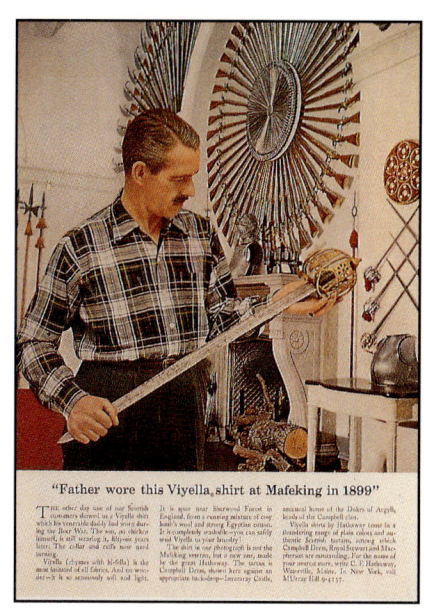

1955/1956. $24–28

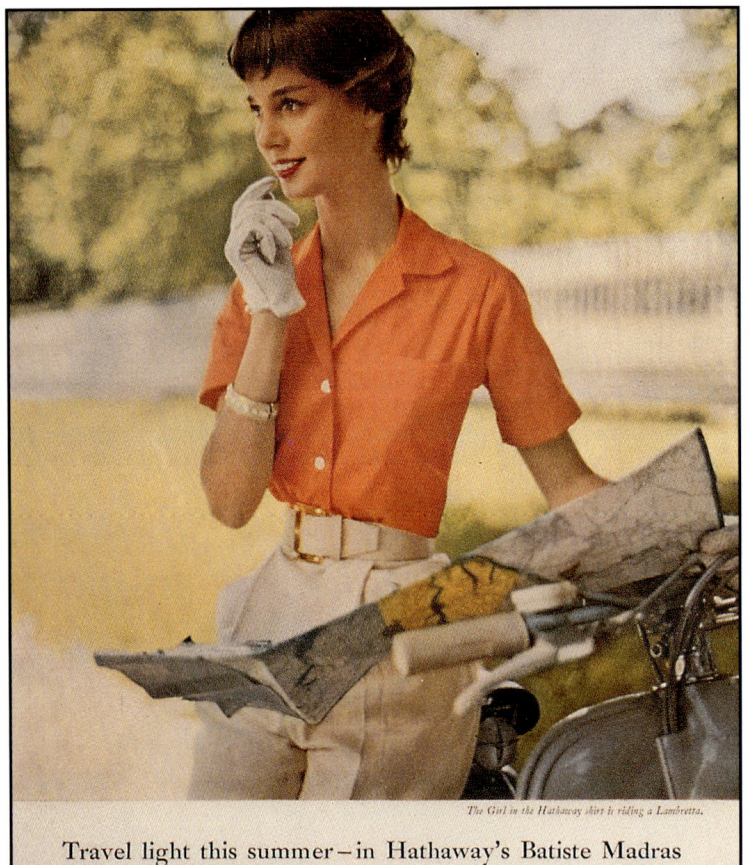

Left: 1955. A batiste Madras shirt. The ad points out that the "Lady in the Hathaway shirt is riding a Lambretta."

Lower left: 1955. Another Digby Morton design. The woman is in a 1906 Buick. $22–24.

Lower right: 1955. $18–22.

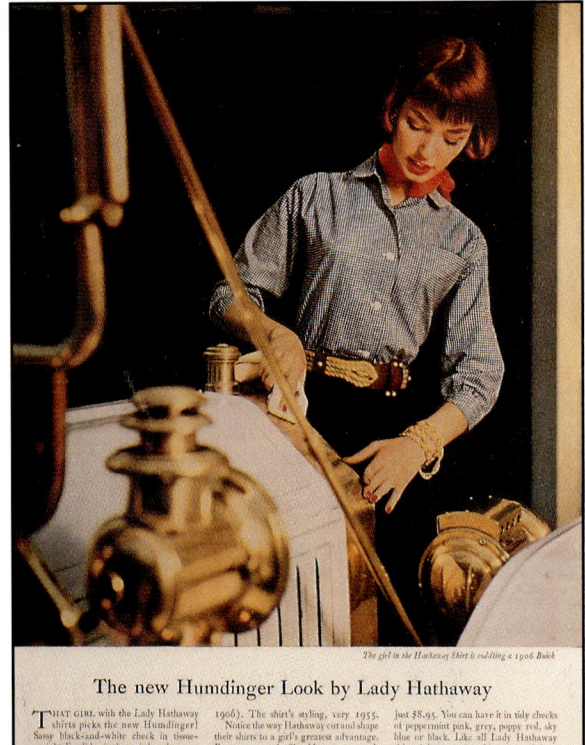

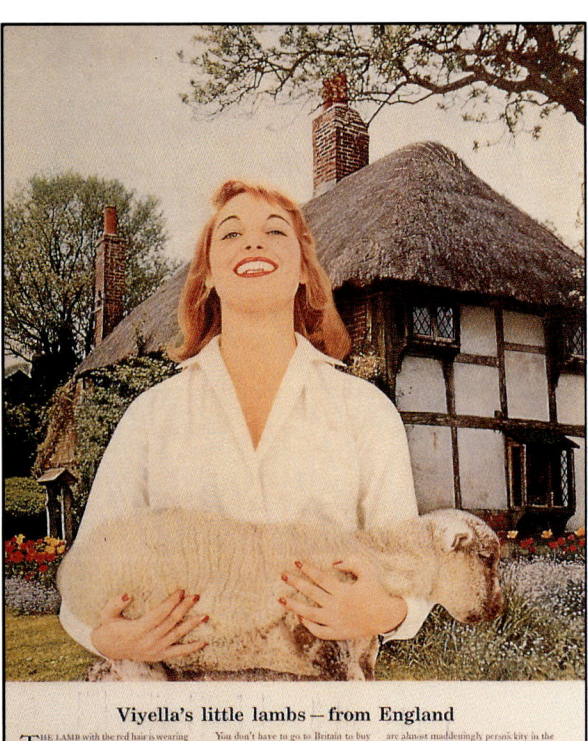

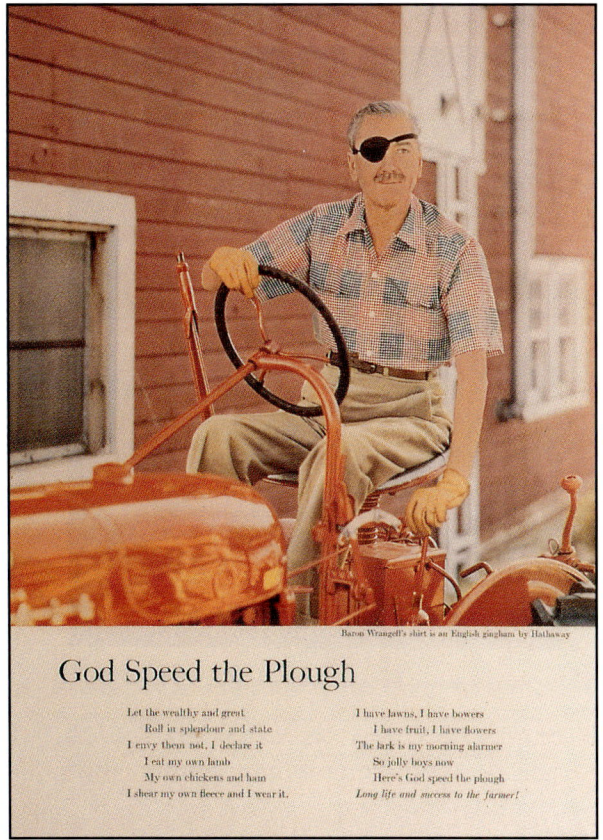

1956. English gingham shirt. $28–30.

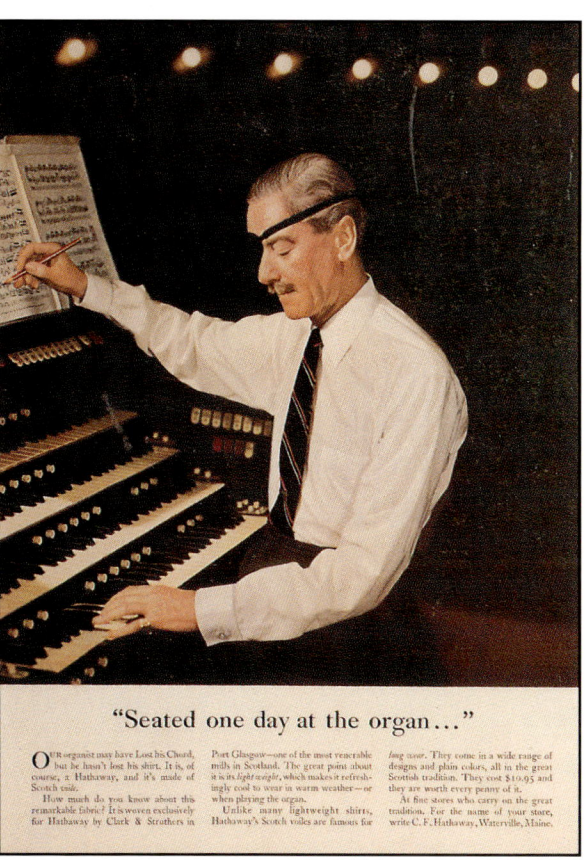

1956. A voile dress shirt, with fabric from Clark & Struthers, Port Glasgow, Scotland. $24–28.

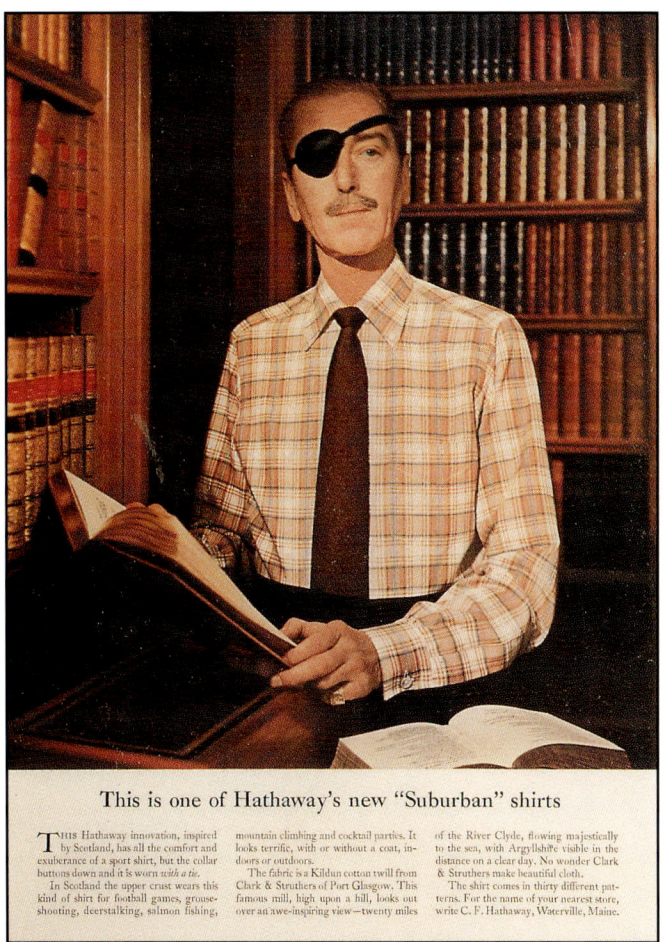

1956. Kildun cotton from Clark & Struthers. $24–28.

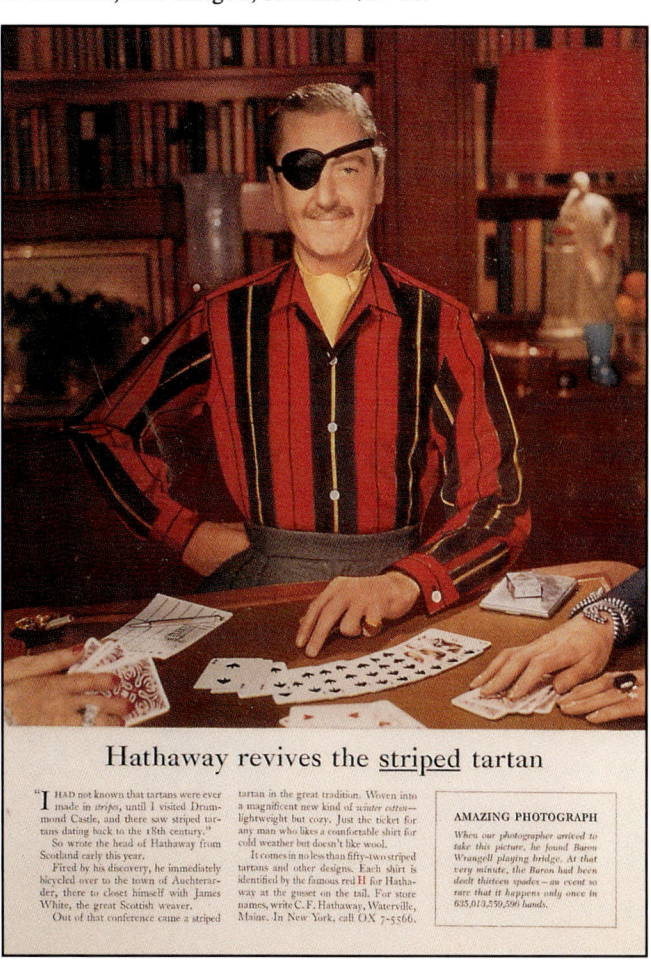

1956. Tartan stripes, woven by James White, Auchterarder, Scotland. $28–30.

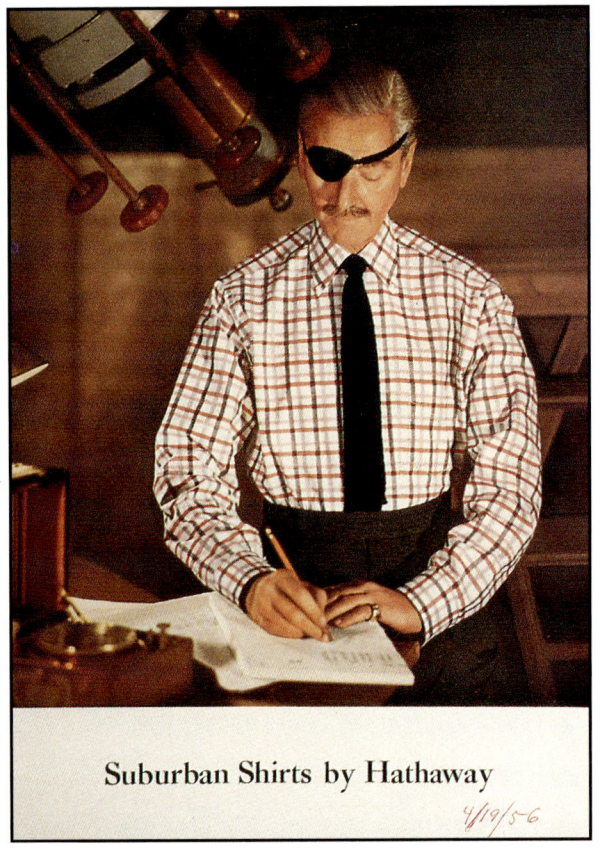

1956. $24–28.

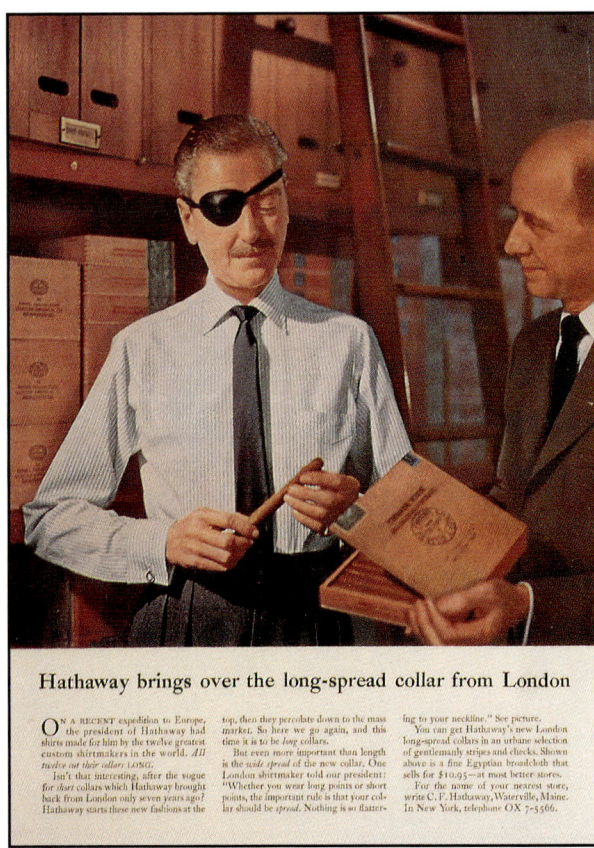

1956. Introducing the English long spread collar. $22–24.

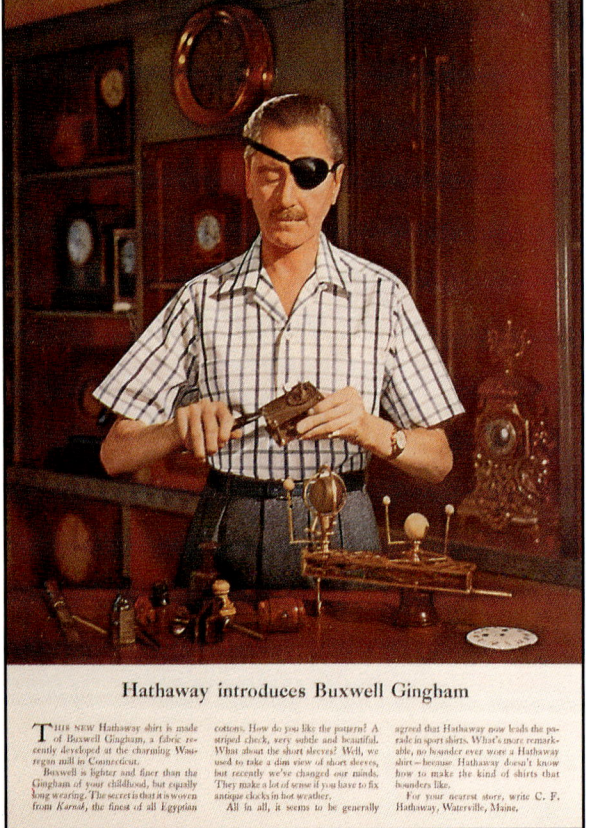

1956. Buxwell gingham from the Wauregan mill, Connecticut. $28–30.

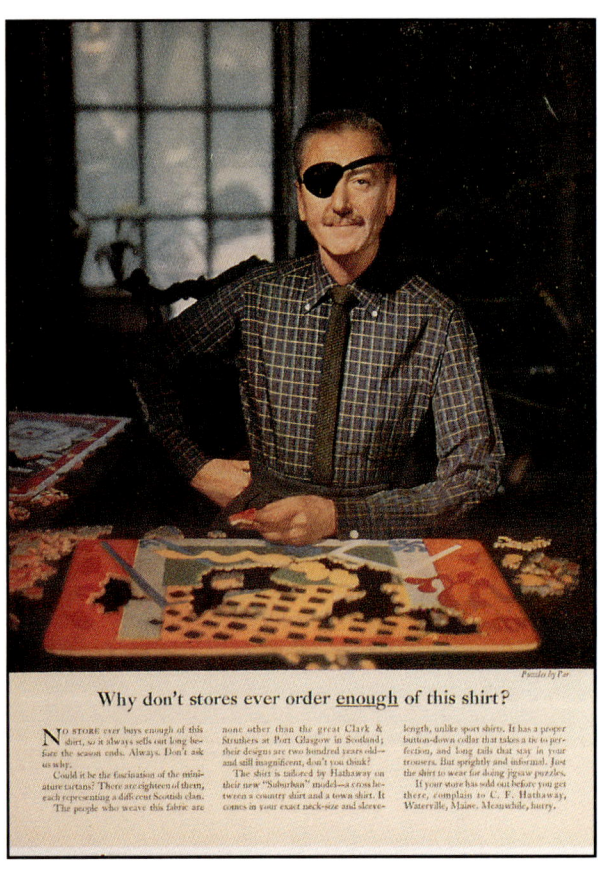

1956. The miniature tartan fabric in this button down shirt is from Clark & Struthers. $28–30.

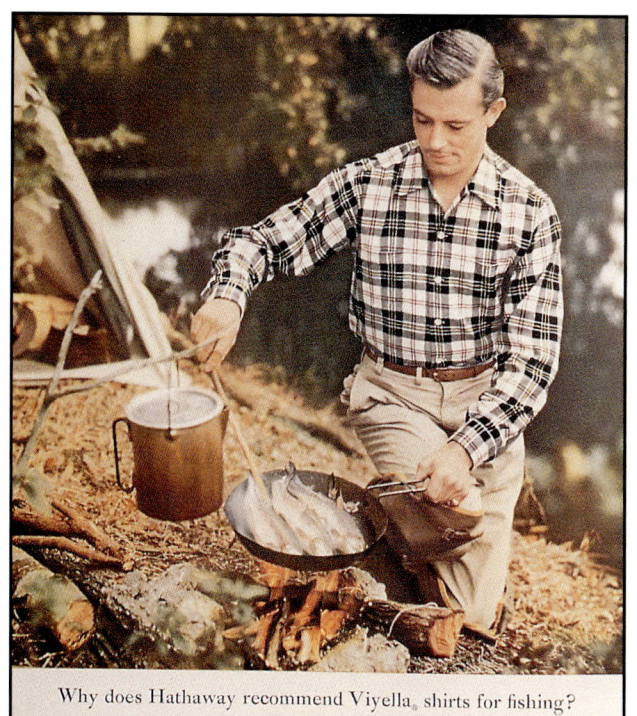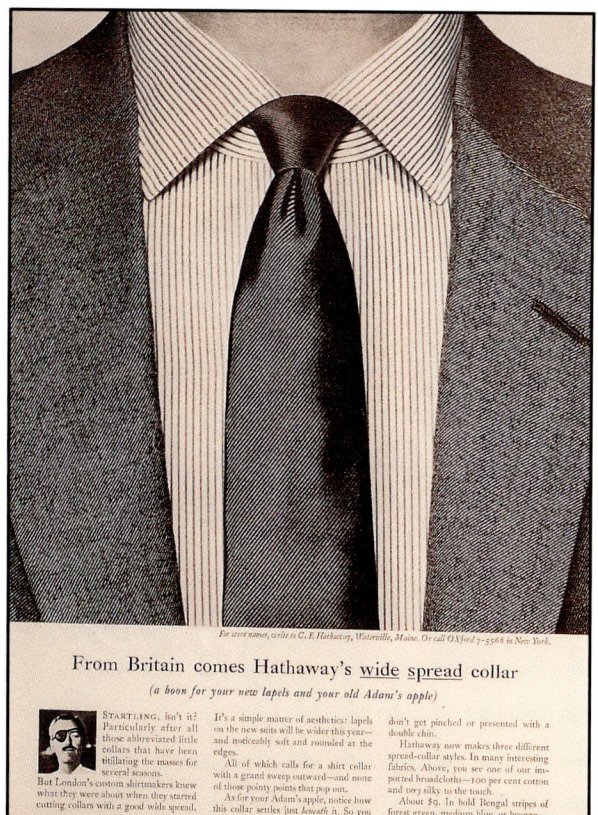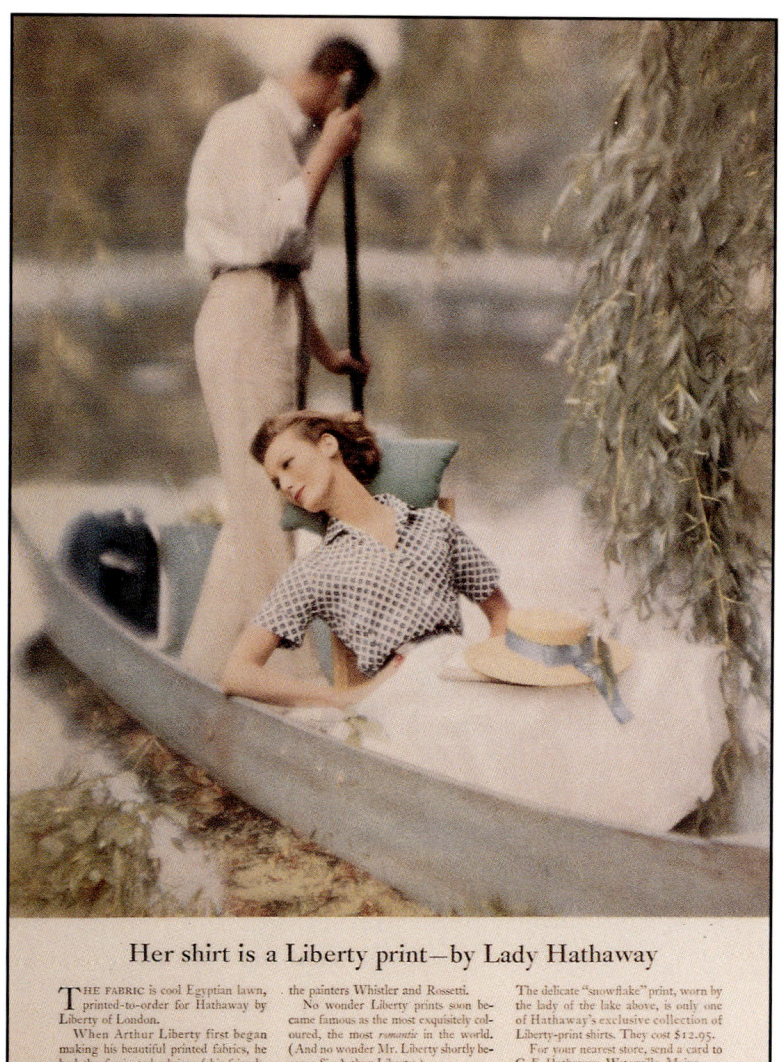

Above left: 1956. $22–24.

Above right: 1956. The introduction of the wide spread collar. $15–18.

Right: 1956. Lady Hathaway shirt with fabric by Liberty of London. $22–24.

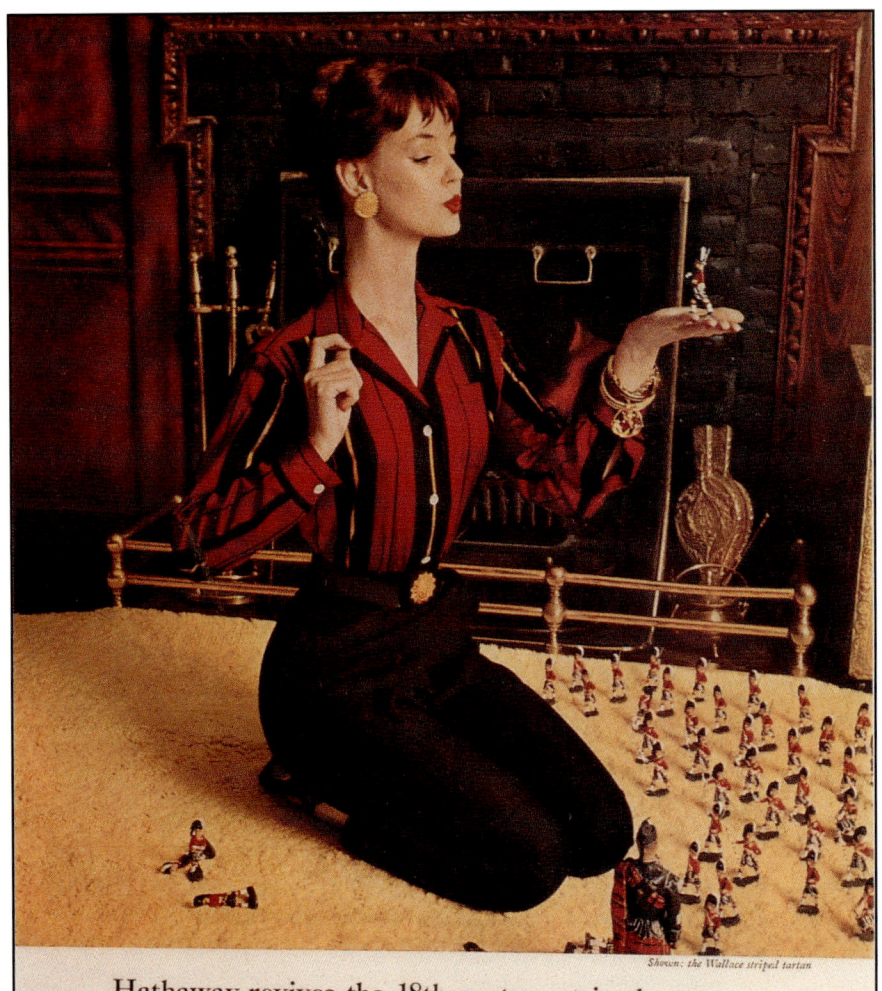

Shown: the Wallace striped tartan

Hathaway revives the 18th century striped tartan

"I HAD NOT KNOWN that tartans were ever made in *stripes*, until I visited Drummond Castle, and there saw with my own eyes *striped* tartans dating back to the 18th century."

So wrote the head of Hathaway from Scotland early this year.

Fired by his discovery, he immediately bicycled from the castle to the town of Auchterarder, there to closet himself with James White, the great Scottish weaver.

Out of that conference came a striped tartan in the old tradition. Woven into a magnificent *new* kind of *winter cotton* — lightweight but cozy, warm as wool but with the sheen of taffeta.

Now enters our third hero — Digby Morton of London. This famous couturier was commissioned to cut and shape the new Lady Hathaway striped tartan shirt. You can see his creation in our photograph. Impeccably man-tailored, but triumphantly *feminine*. A shirt guaranteed to put a regiment of men at your feet—and at least one in the palm of your hand. Or double your money back.

Price? $13.95, in a choice of authentic striped tartans. For the store nearest you write C. F. Hathaway, Waterville, Maine. In New York, call OX 7-5566.

Left: 1956. The same tartan fabric used in men's shirts. $22–24.

Lower left: 1956. $22–24.

Lower right: 1956. $22–24.

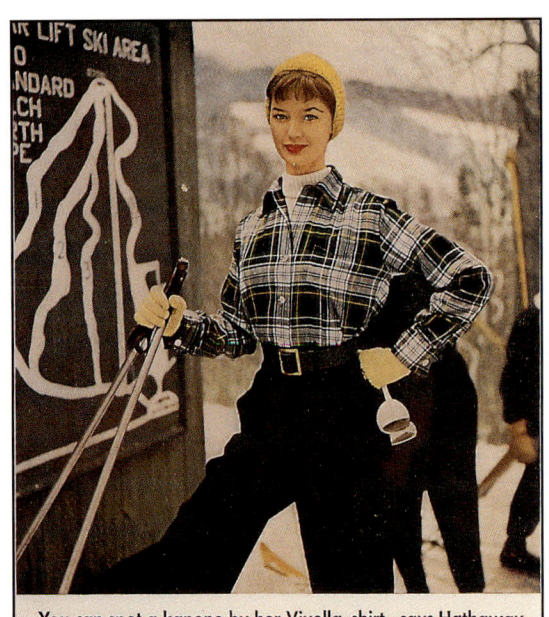

You can spot a kanone by her Viyella® shirt—says Hathaway

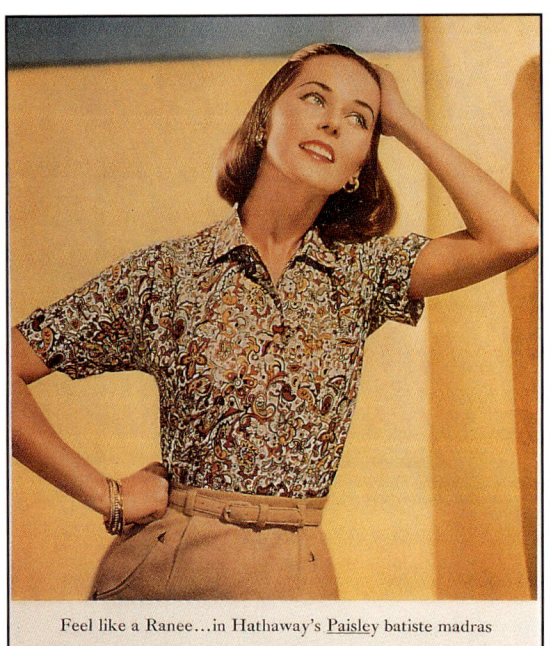

Feel like a Ranee...in Hathaway's Paisley batiste madras

36

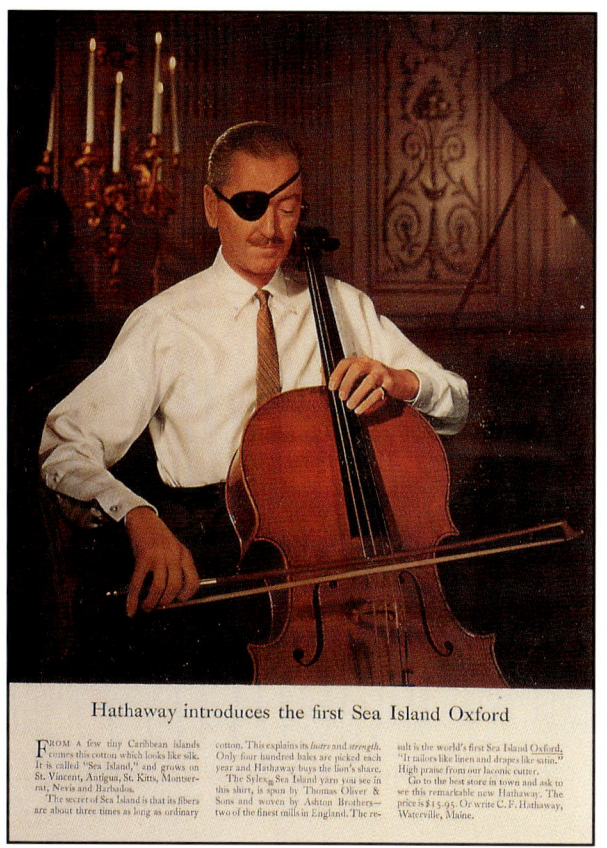

A dress shirt of Sylex Sea Isle yarn spun by Thomas Oliver & Sons and woven by Aston Mills, both of England. $18–20.

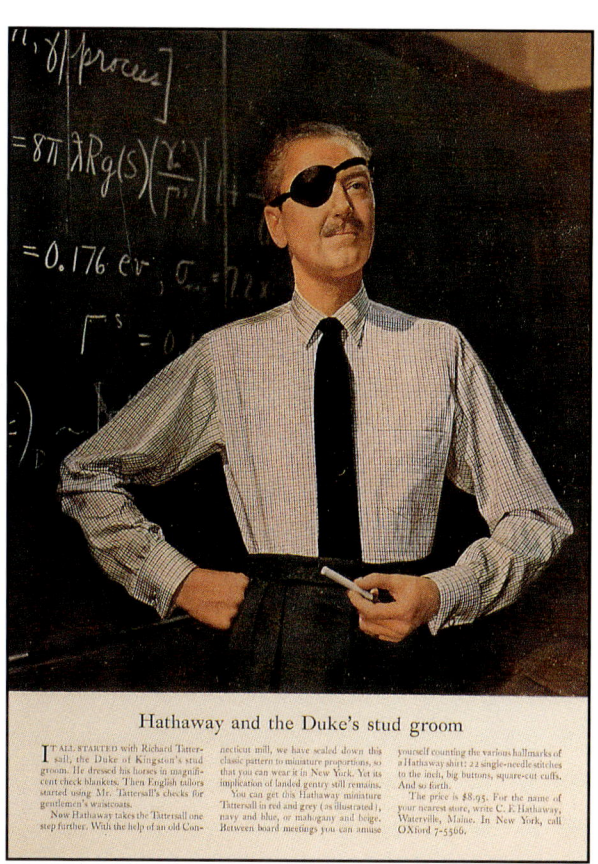

1957. Tattersall checks from a Connecticut mill. $18–20.

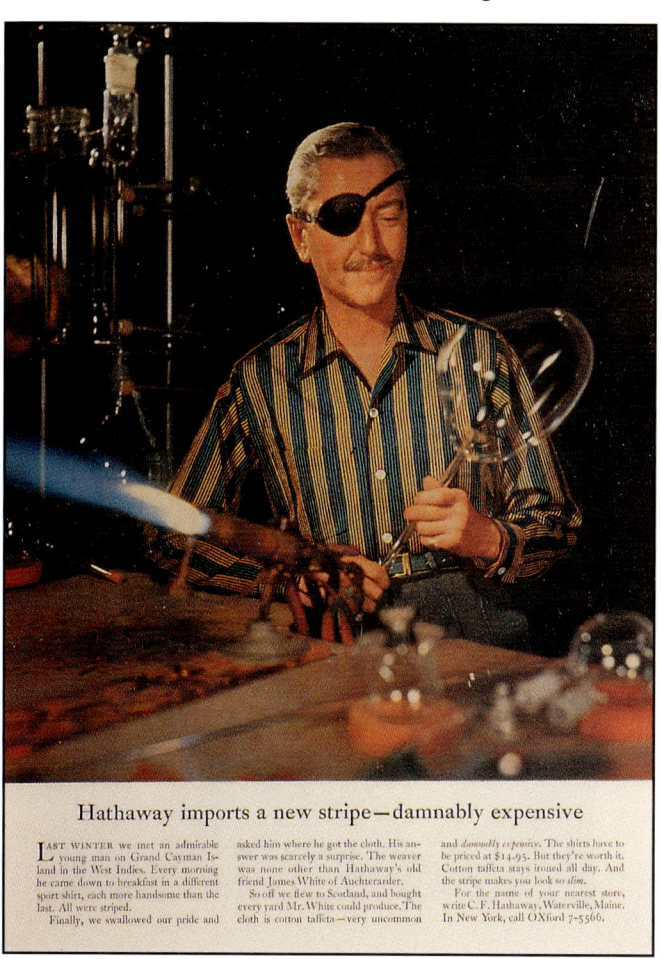

1957. Cotton taffeta strips from the James White mills. $24–28.

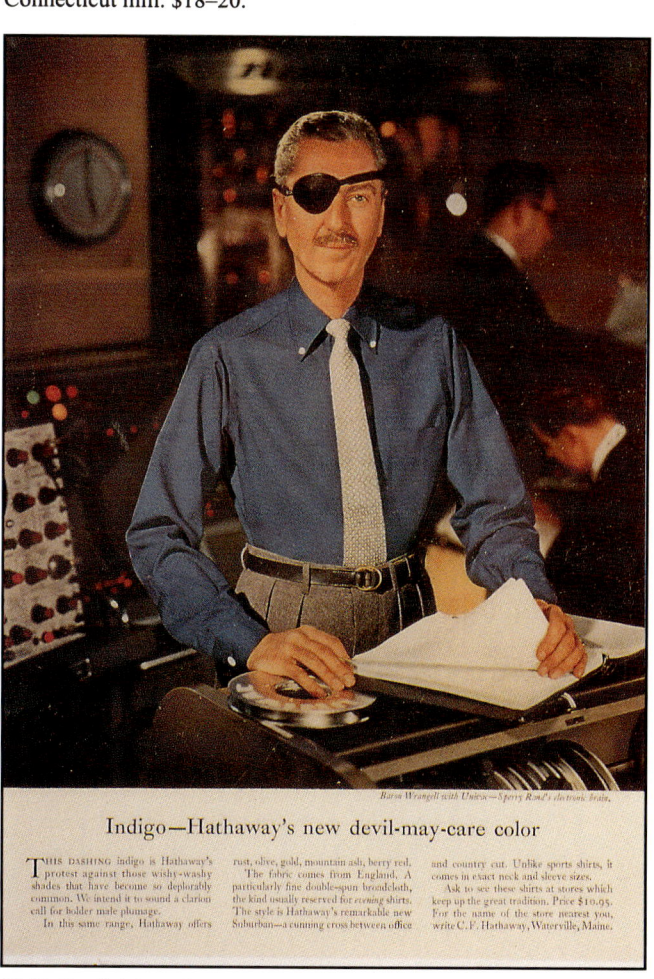

1957. English broadcloth with spread button down collar. $22–24.

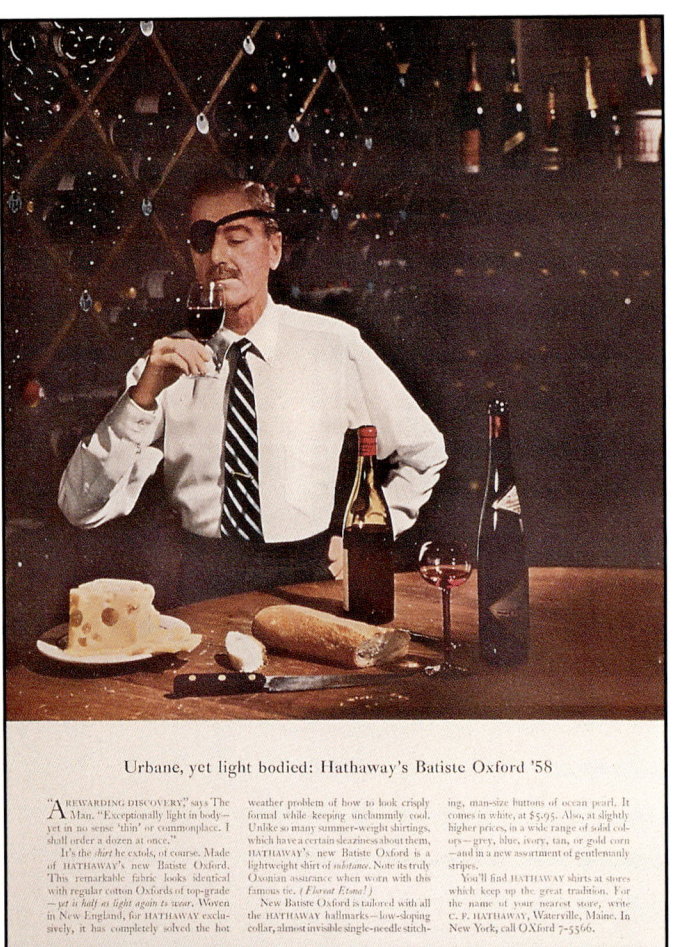

1957. $18–20.

1957. Viyella sports shirts. $24–28.

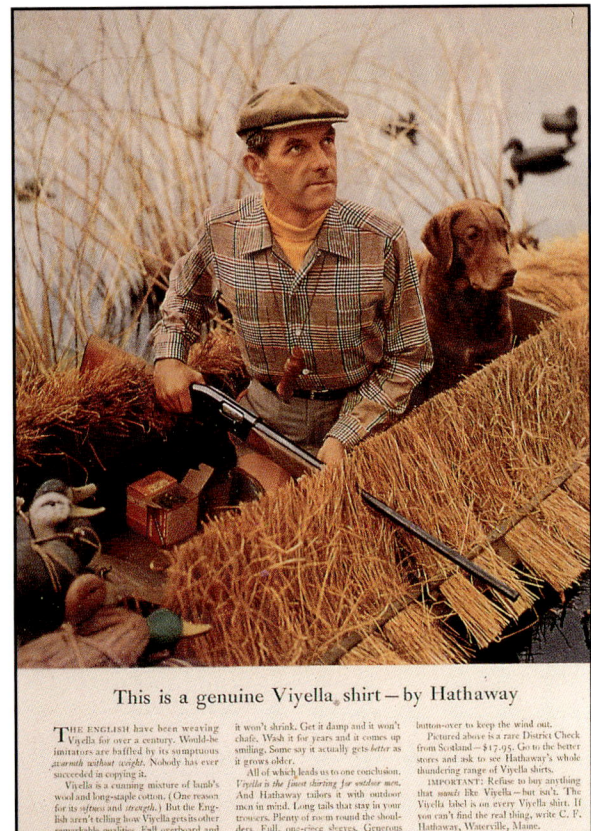

1957. $24–28.

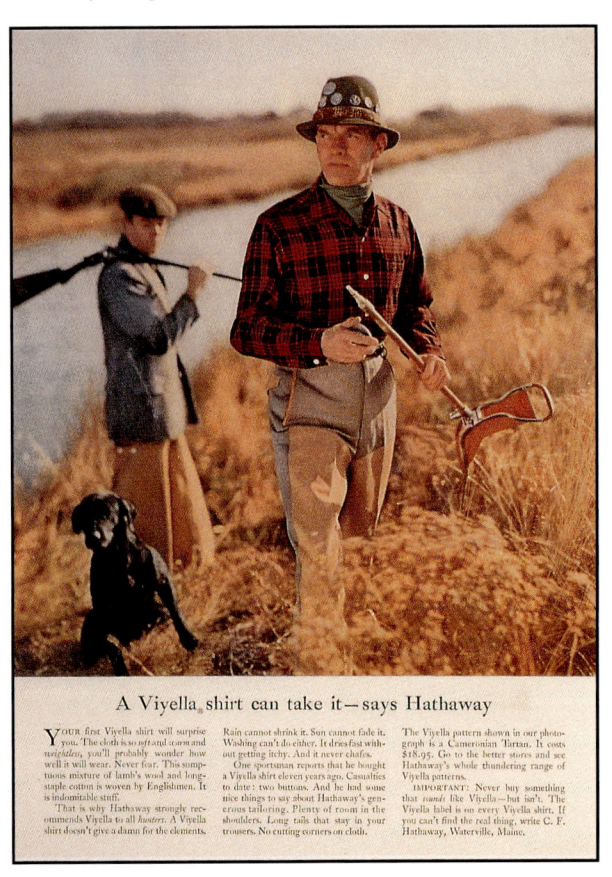

1957. $24–28.

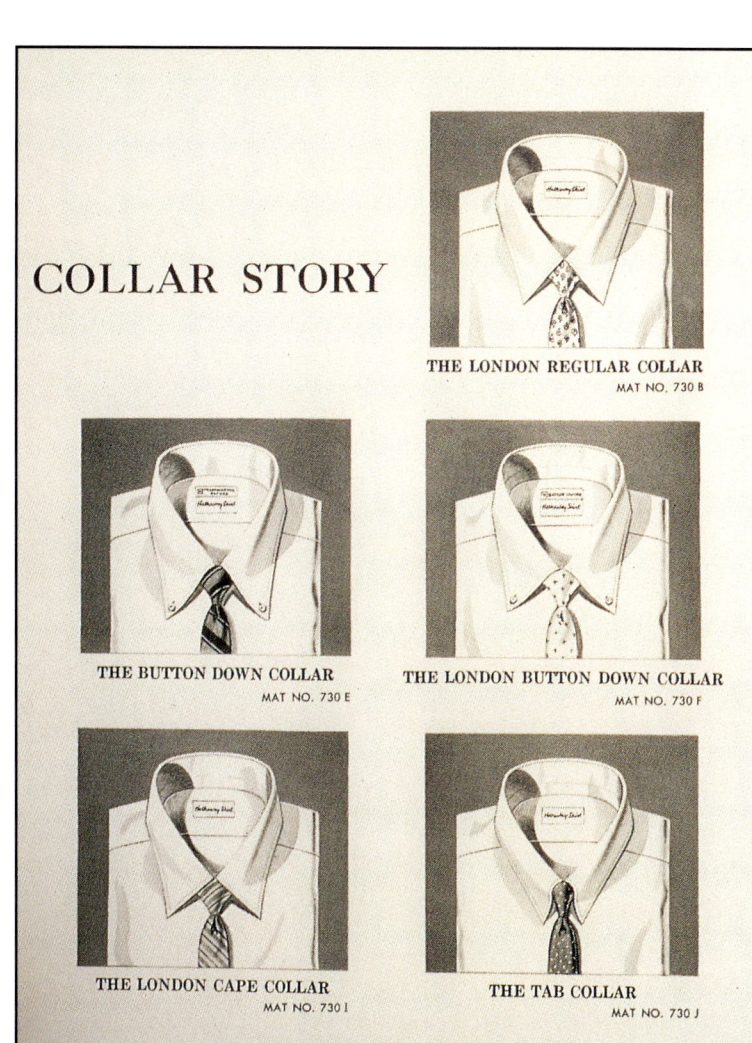

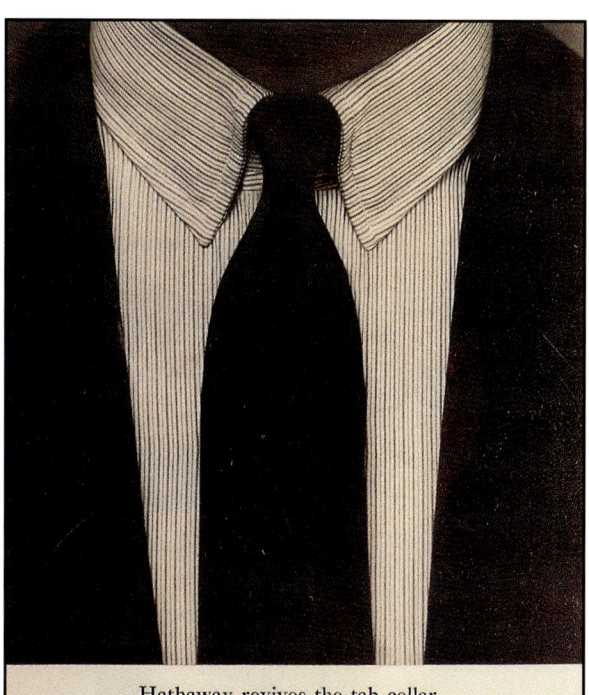

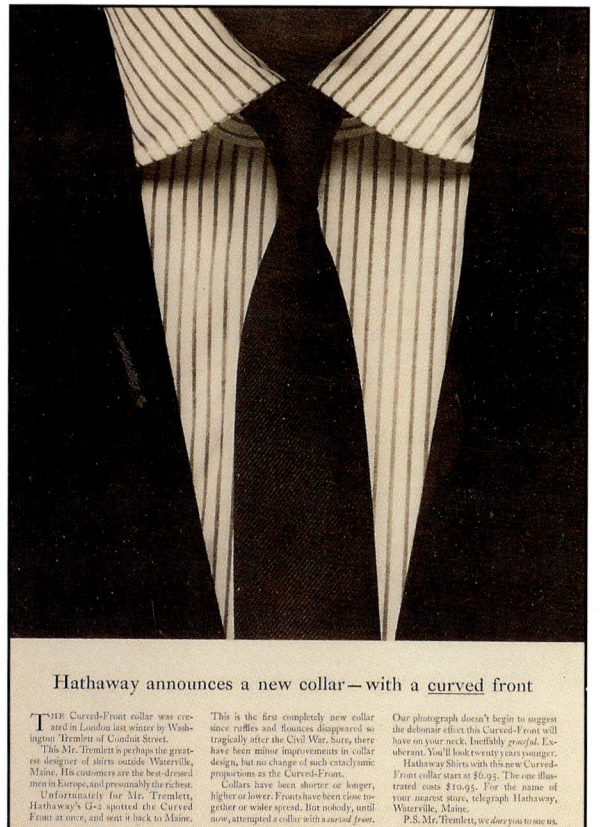

Left: 1957. Collar styles available.

Lower left: 1957. The tab collar. $18–20.

Lower right: 1957. Introducing the Curved-Front collar, created in London by Washington Tremlett of Conduit Street. $18–20.

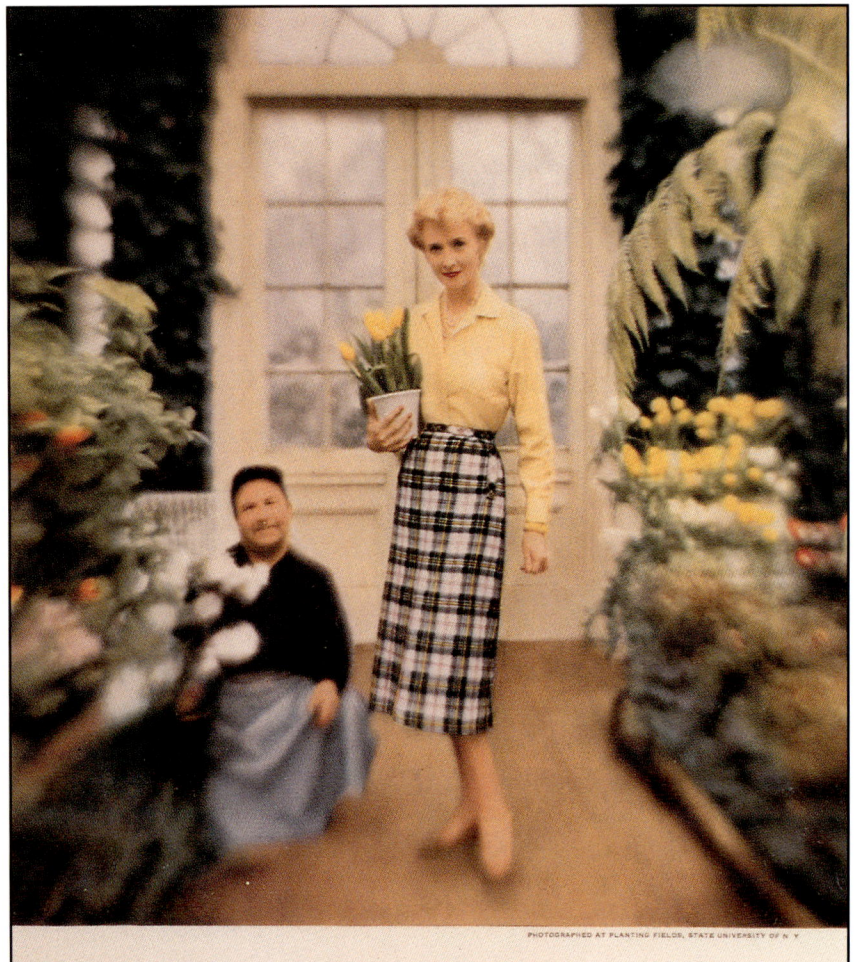

Left: 1957. Viyella shirt and skirt designed by Digby Morton. $18–20.

Lower left: 1957. Digby Morton designed this Japanese silk striped shirt. $30–34.

Lower center: 1957. A classically designed shirt with French cuffs. $28–30.

Lower right: c. 1957. Viyella shirt in paisley. $22–24.

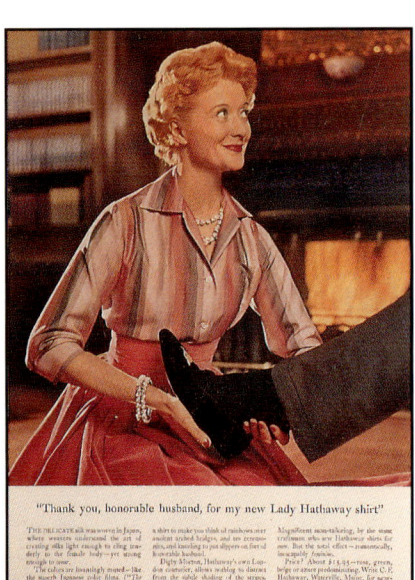

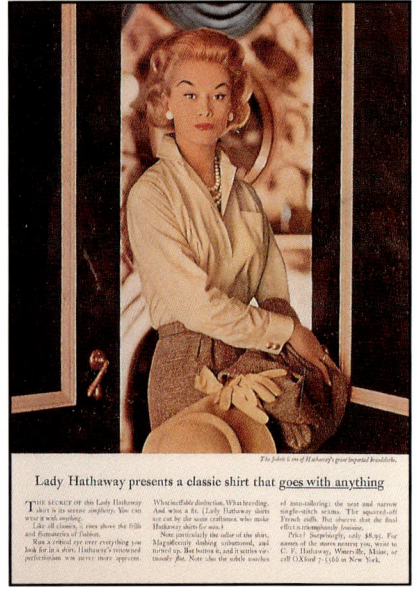

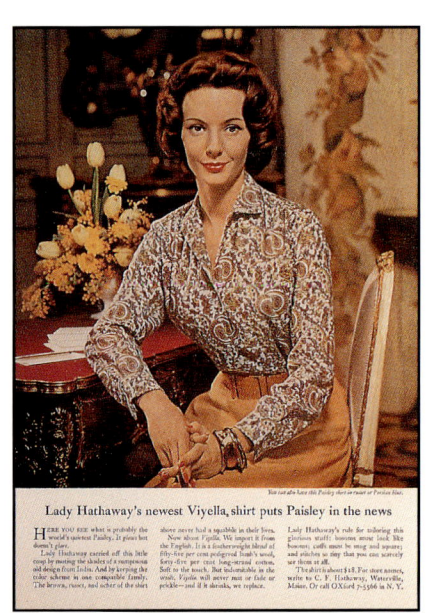

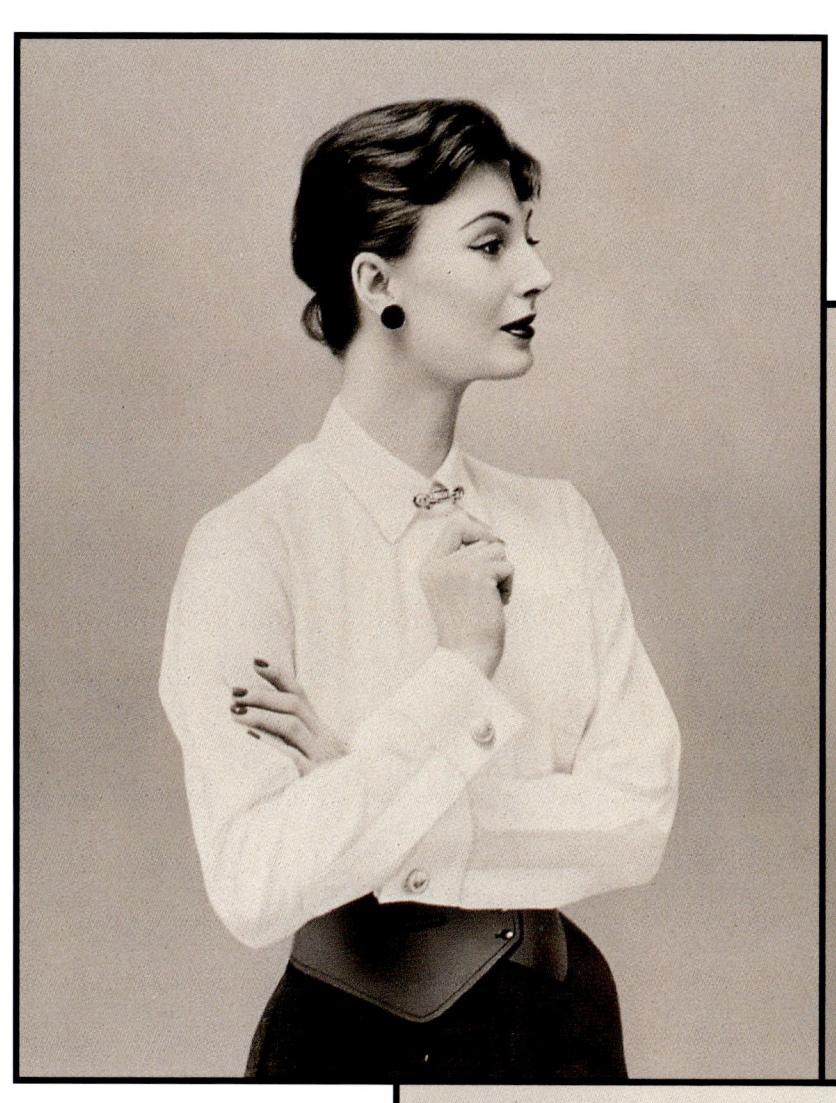
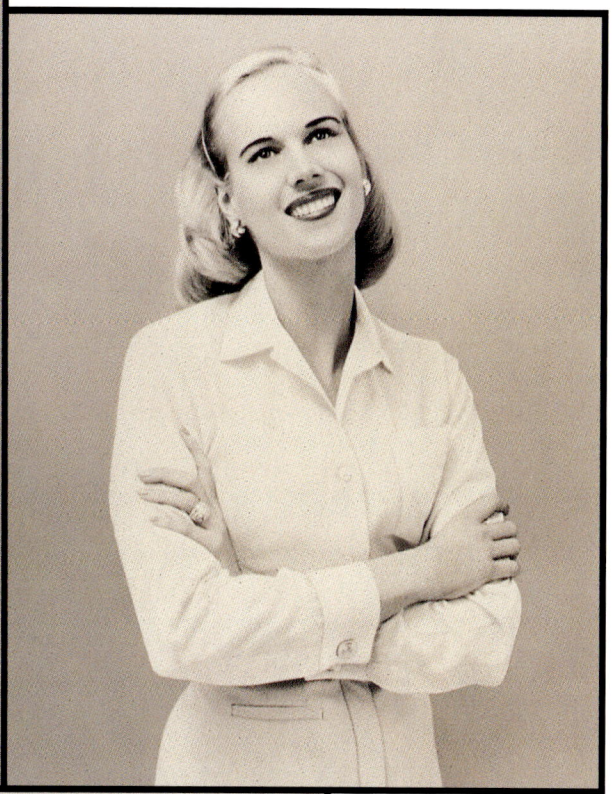

Above left: 1957.

Above right: 1957. $20–22.

Right: 1957. $22–24.

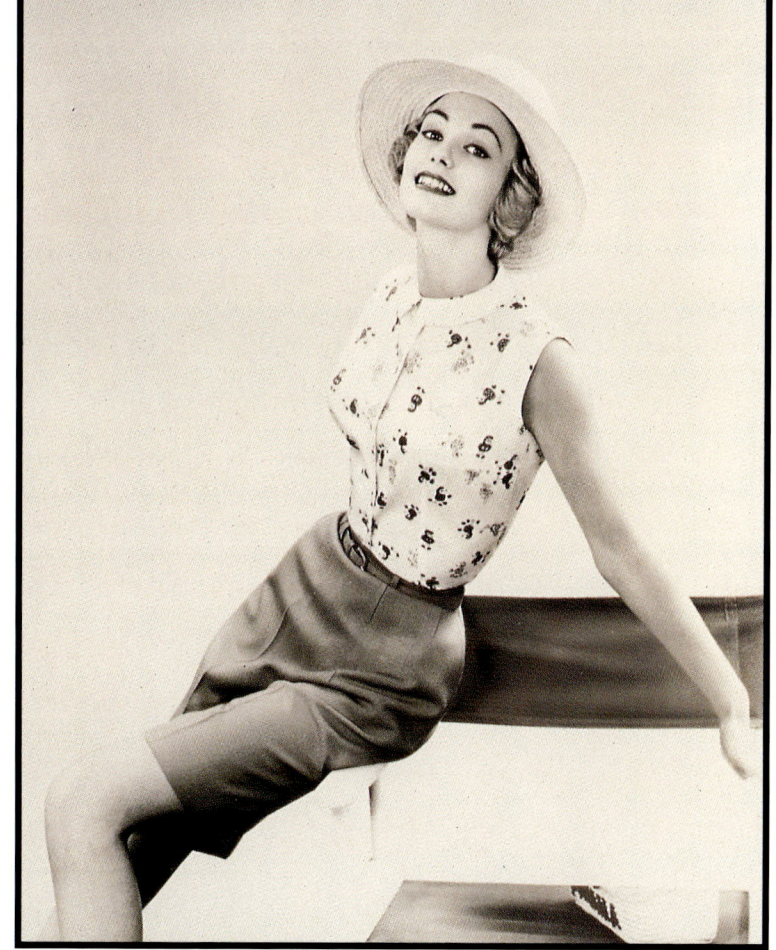

41

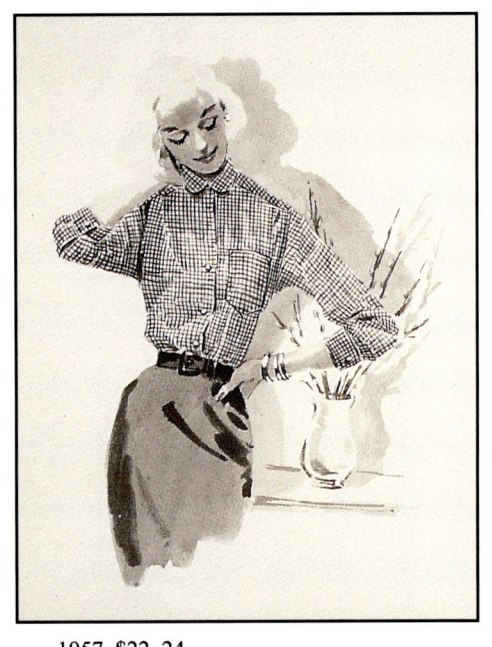

1957. $22–24.

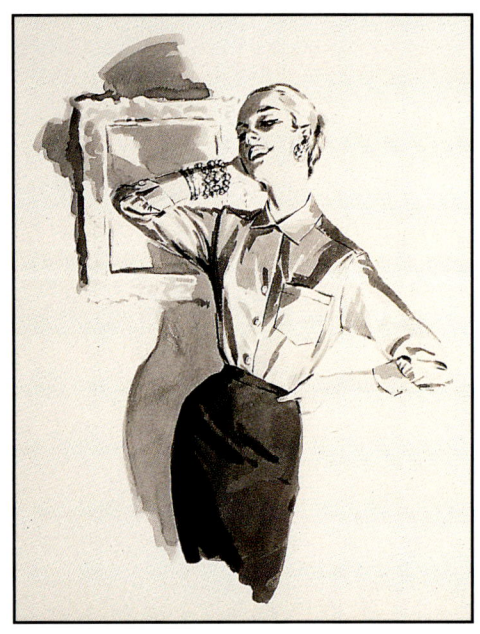

1957. $20–22.

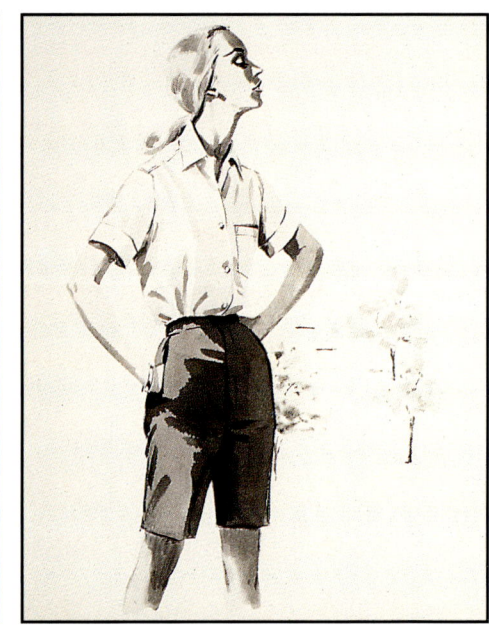

1957. $18–20.

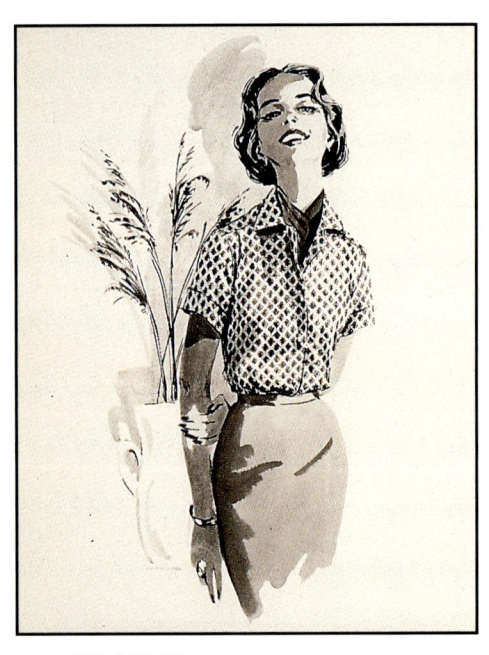

1957. $22–24.

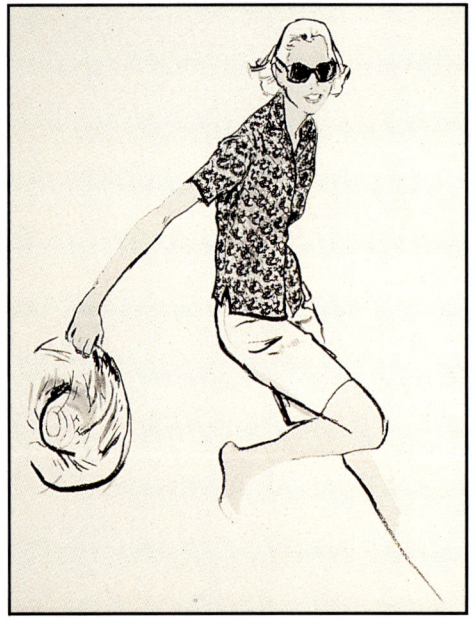

1957. $22–24.

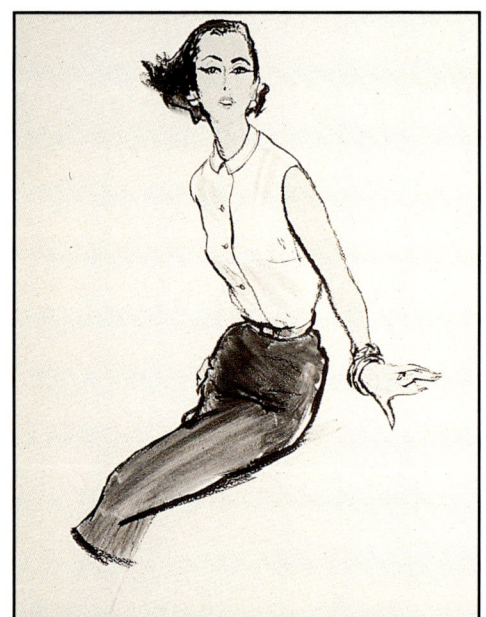

1957. $18–20.

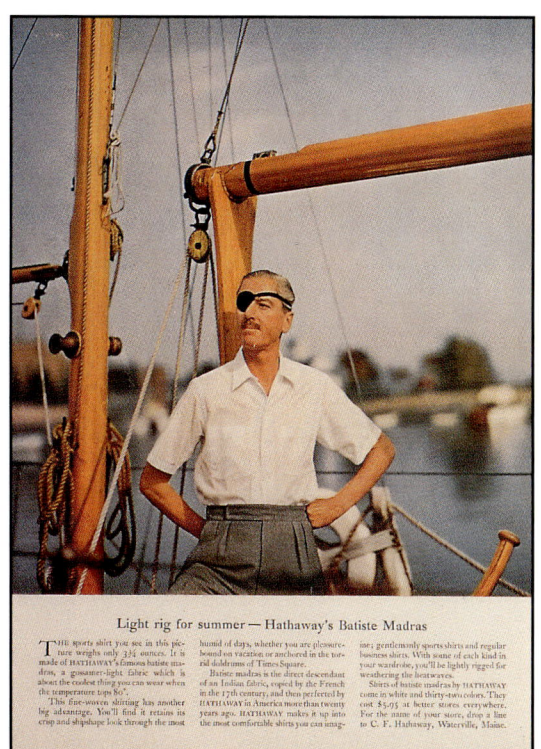

Light rig for summer — Hathaway's Batiste Madras

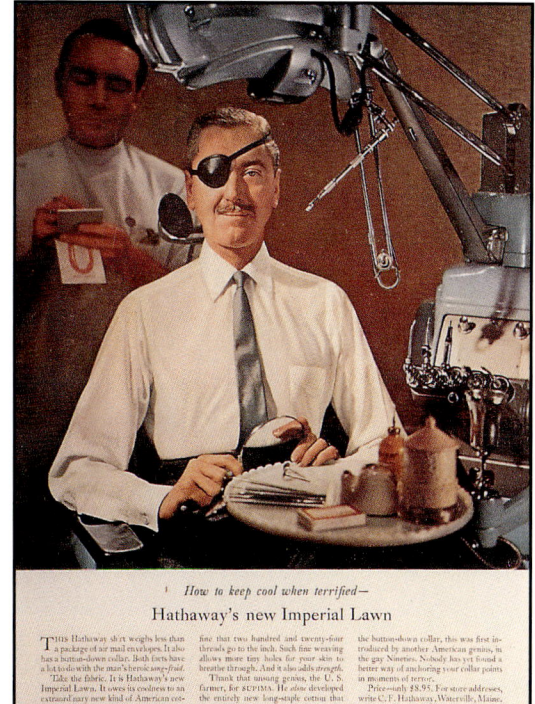

How to keep cool when terrified —
Hathaway's new Imperial Lawn

Above left: 1958. Batiste madras short sleeve shirt. $28–32.

Above right: 1958. Supima cotton dress shirt. $20–24.

Right: 1958. His and her foulards. $24–28.

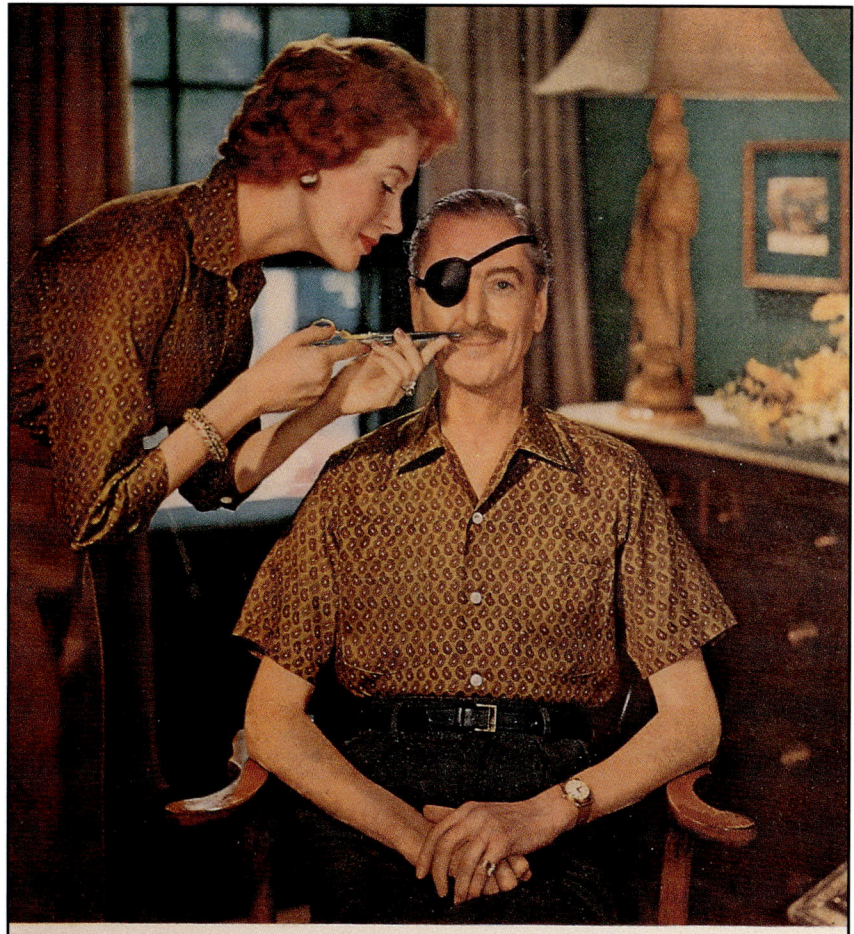

Matching Foulards by Hathaway
(and vive la différence!)

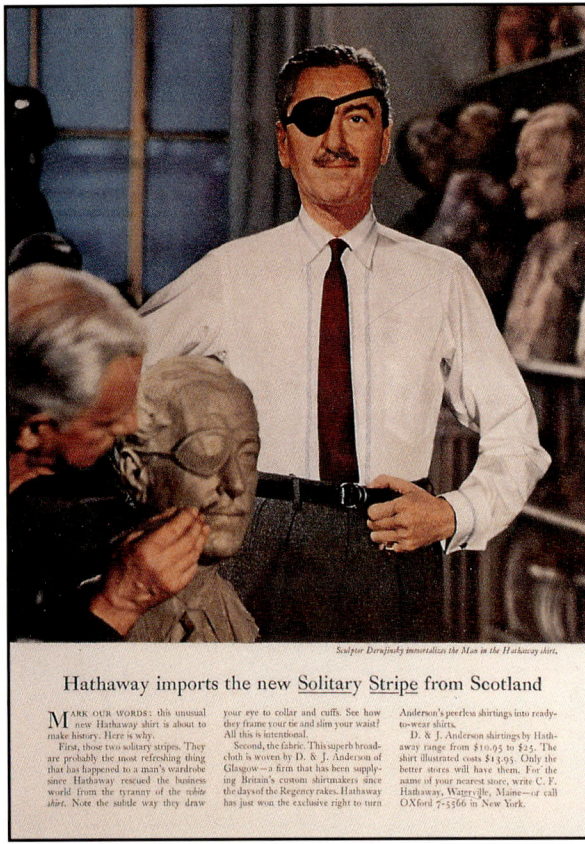

1958. Solitary strips border the tie and trim the cuffs of this shirt. The fabric is by D&J Anderson mills of Glasgow. $28–30.

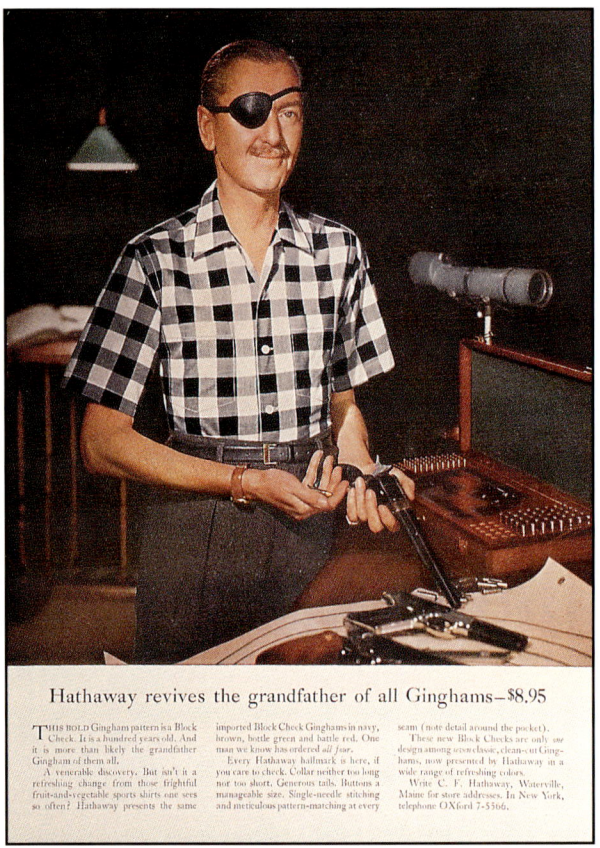

c. 1958. This black check gingham also came in navy, brown, green, and red. $24–28.

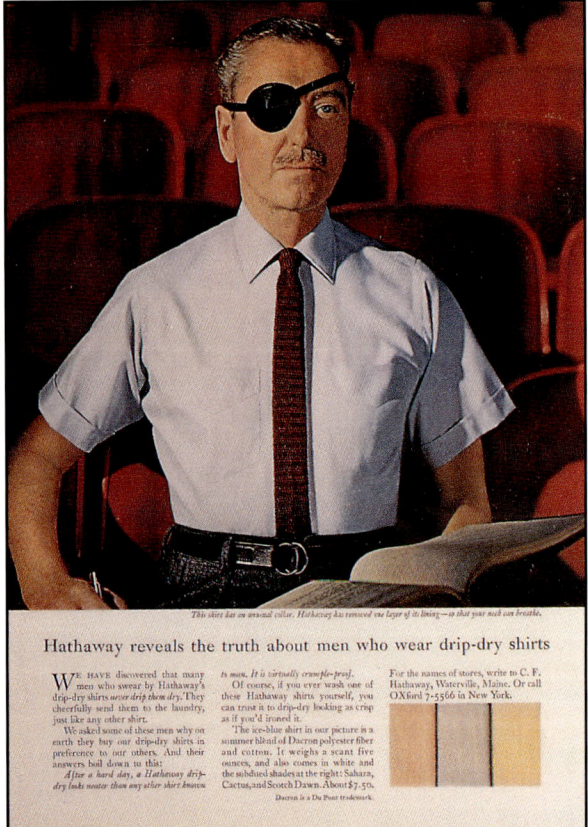

c. 1958. One of the first advertisements for a drip dry shirt, a blend of Dacron polyester and cotton. $20–22.

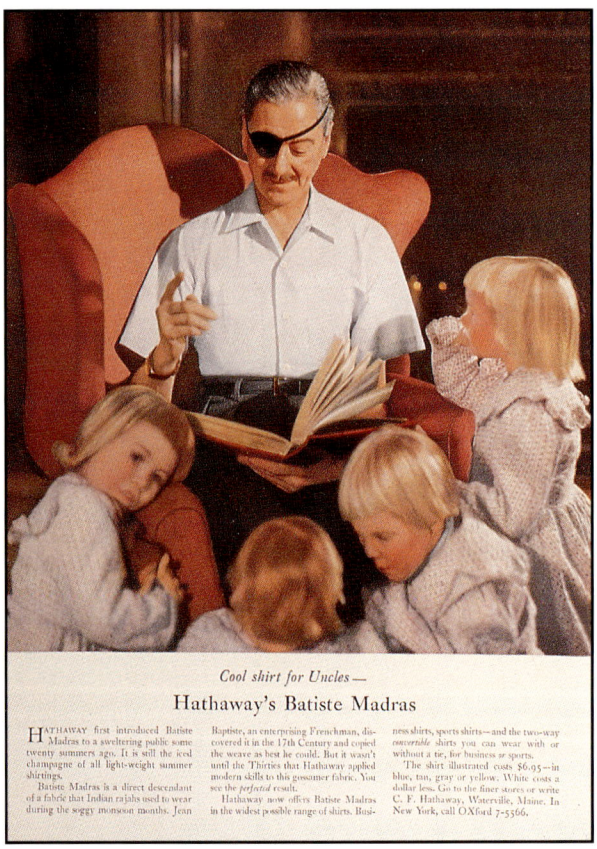

c. 1958. Batiste Madras shirt for dress or casual wear.

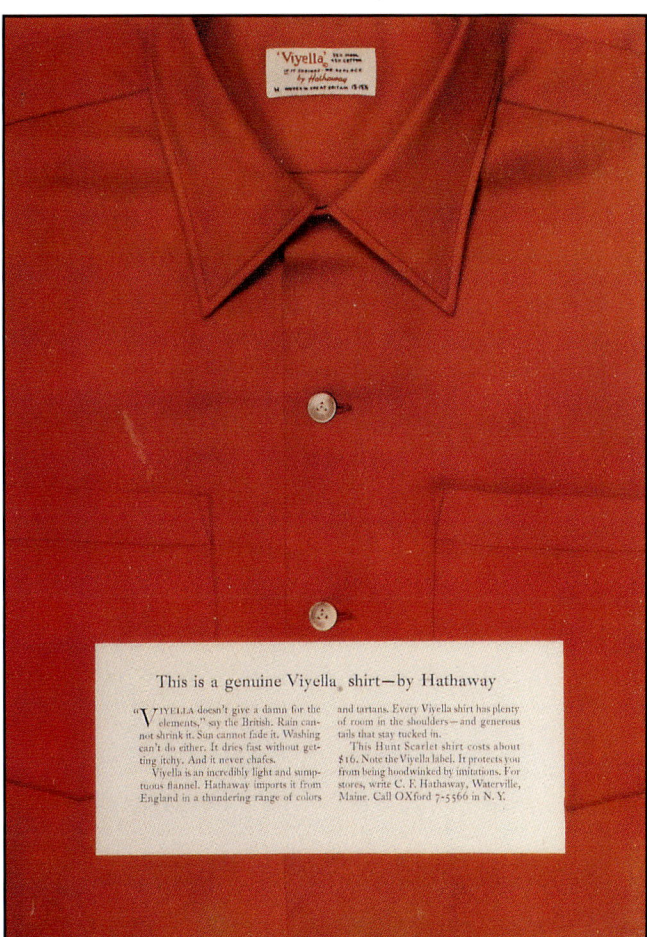

1958. Attention was brought to the labels of Viyella shirts at this time. Apparently other companies were introducing similarly named products to take advantage of Hathaway's marketing of this exclusive fabric. $24–28.

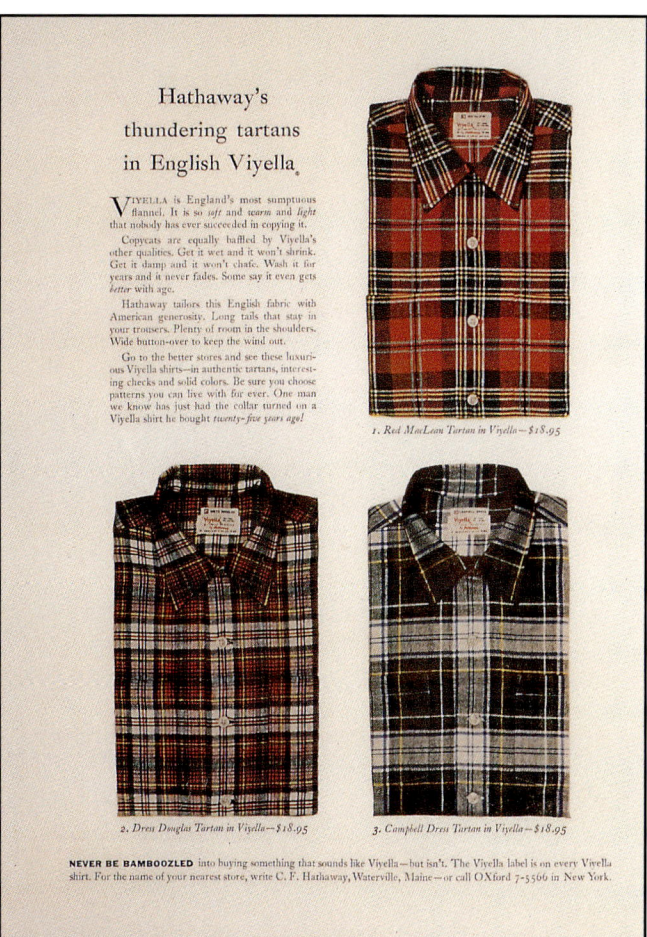

1958. Viyella in authentic clan tartans. $24–28

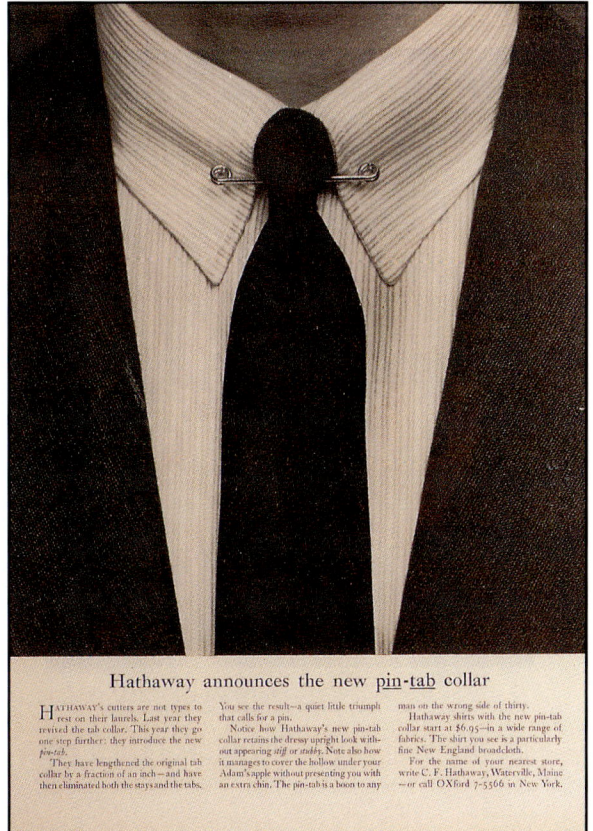

1958. The introductory advertisement for the Pin Tab collar.

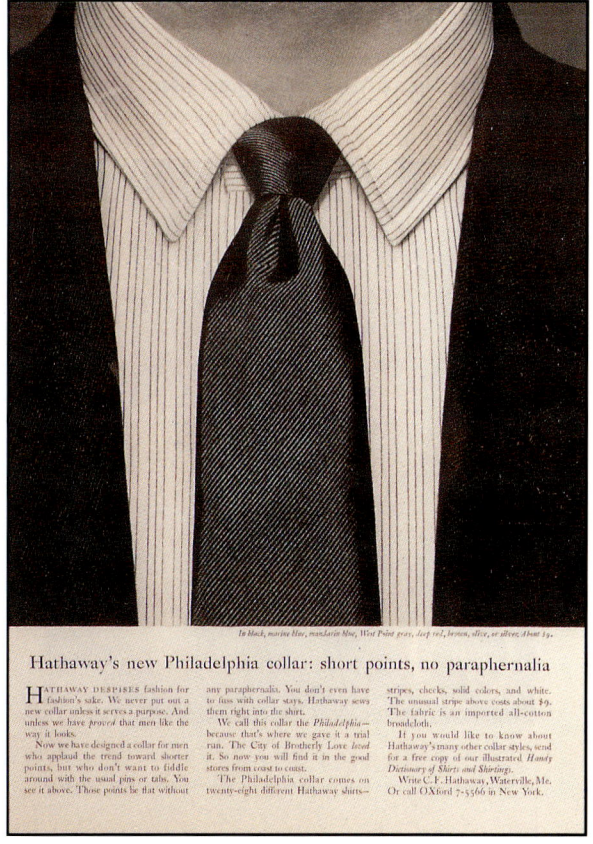

1958. Introducing the Philadelphia spread collar. $18–20.

45

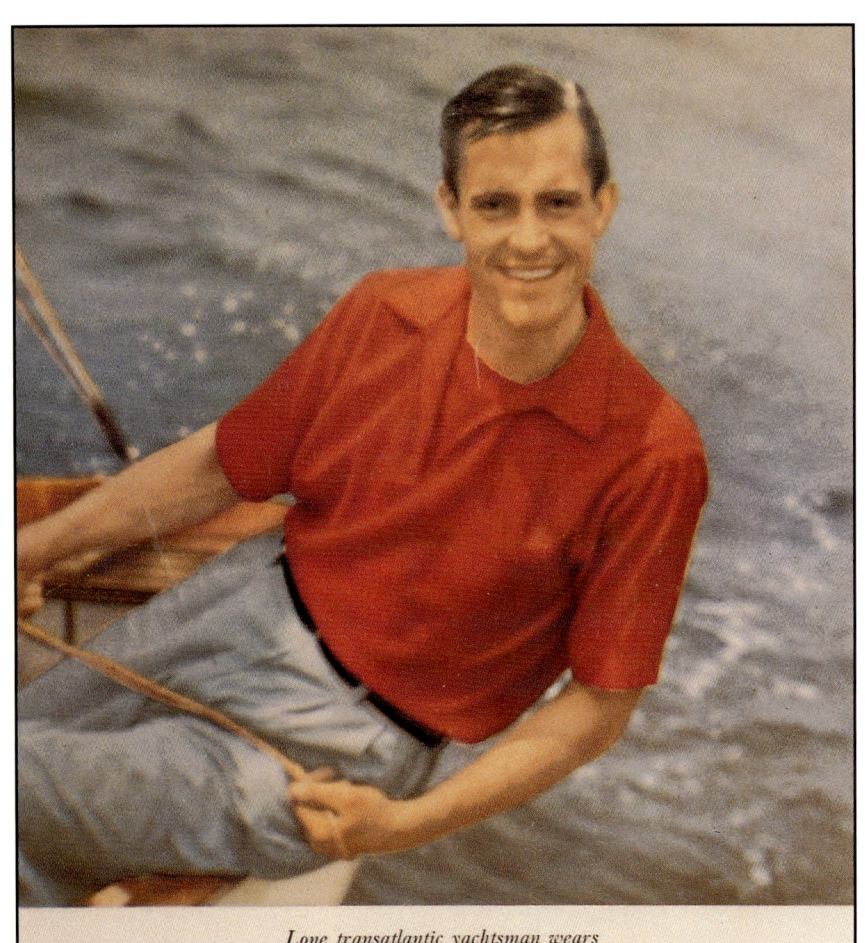

Left: 1958. The model here is yachtsman Colin Leslie Fox, who sailed his 24-foot cutter across the Atlantic single-handed and alternated two Viyella shirts for eighty-nine days. In 1963 Fox would return to Hathaway advertising as the new "Man in the Hathaway Shirt," sporting a moustache and a sophisticated air. Wrangell resigned in 1962. $20–22.

Lower left: 1959. Indian Madras in solids and plaids. $20–22.

Lower right: 1959. Introducing Bermuda Blue, a light fabric with a pin stripe. It recalls Hathaway's old dictum about never wearing white before sundown, and adds a new one: "White looks like a uniform in the morning, and like murder by midafternoon. $18–20.

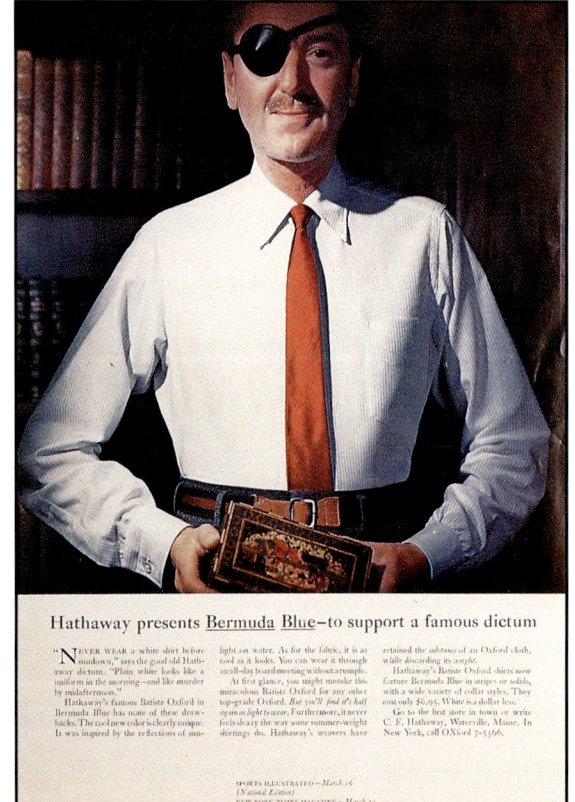

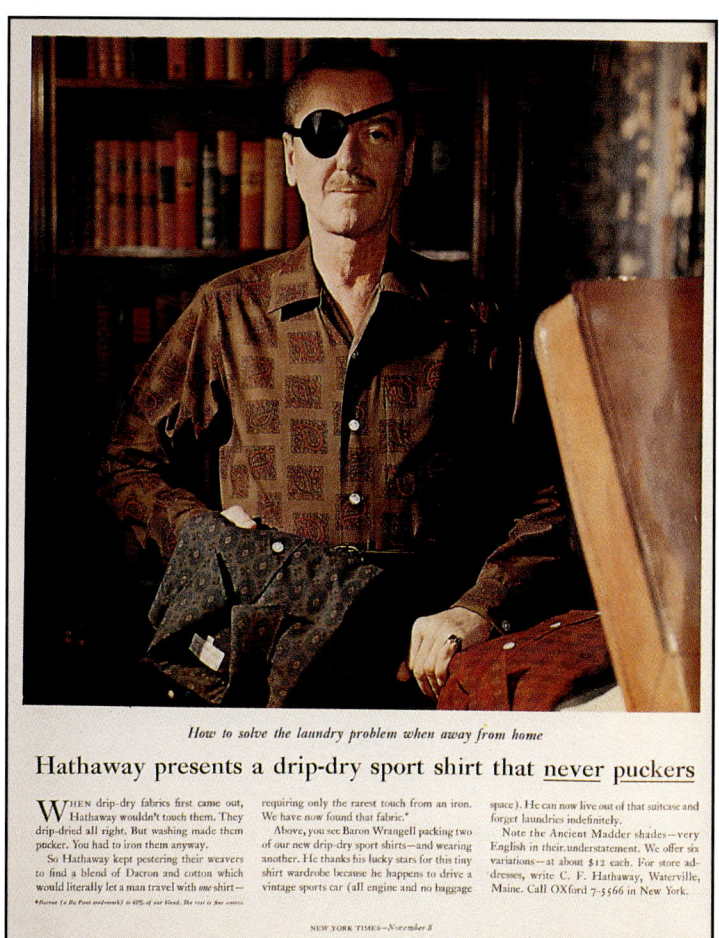

c. 1959. Introducing a new sports shirt in a drip dry Dacron polyester and cotton blend. $24–28.

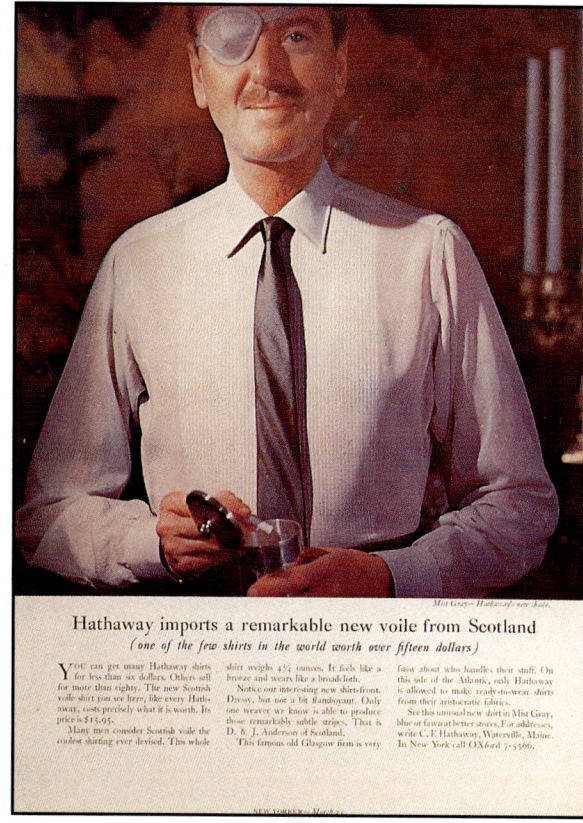

1959. A Scottish voile dress shirt with fabric by Anderson. $18–20.

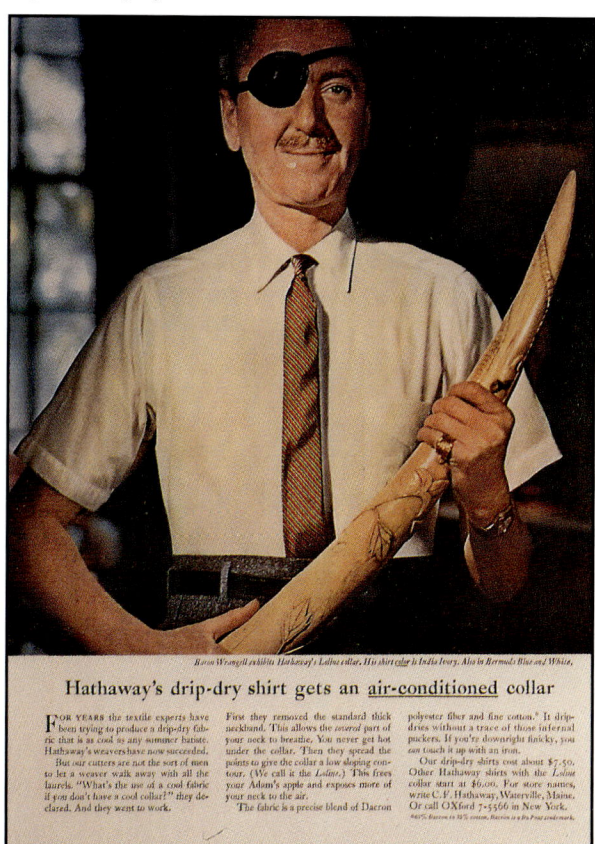

1959. A drip dry blended cotton shirt with a "loline" collar designed for coolness. $15–18.

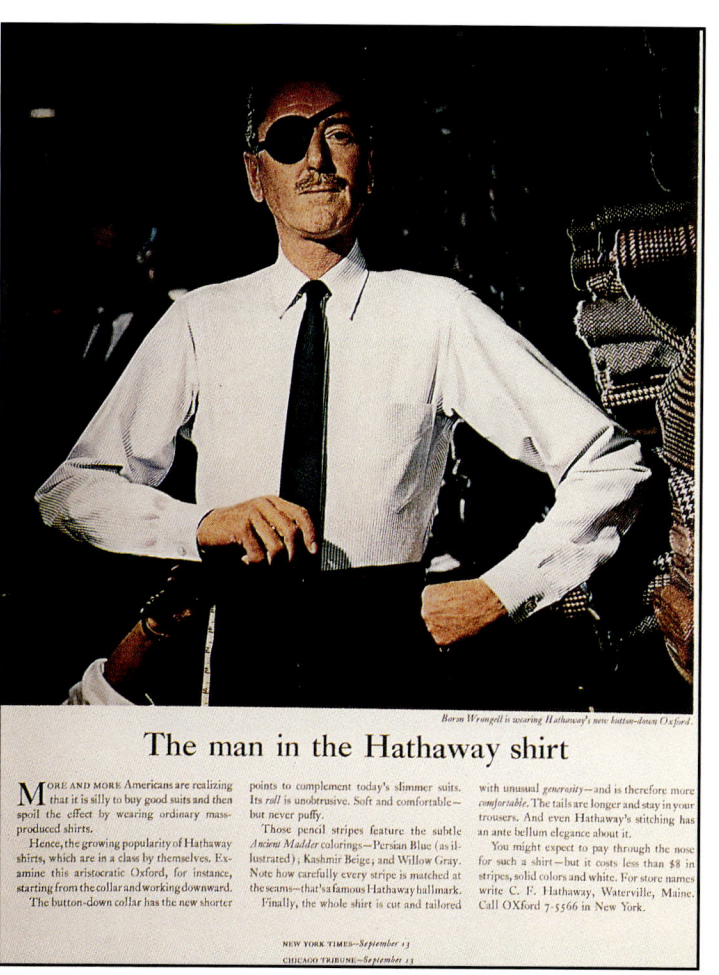

c. 1959. Revisiting the original Hathaway advertisement, this time in a button down pin stripe dress shirt.

47

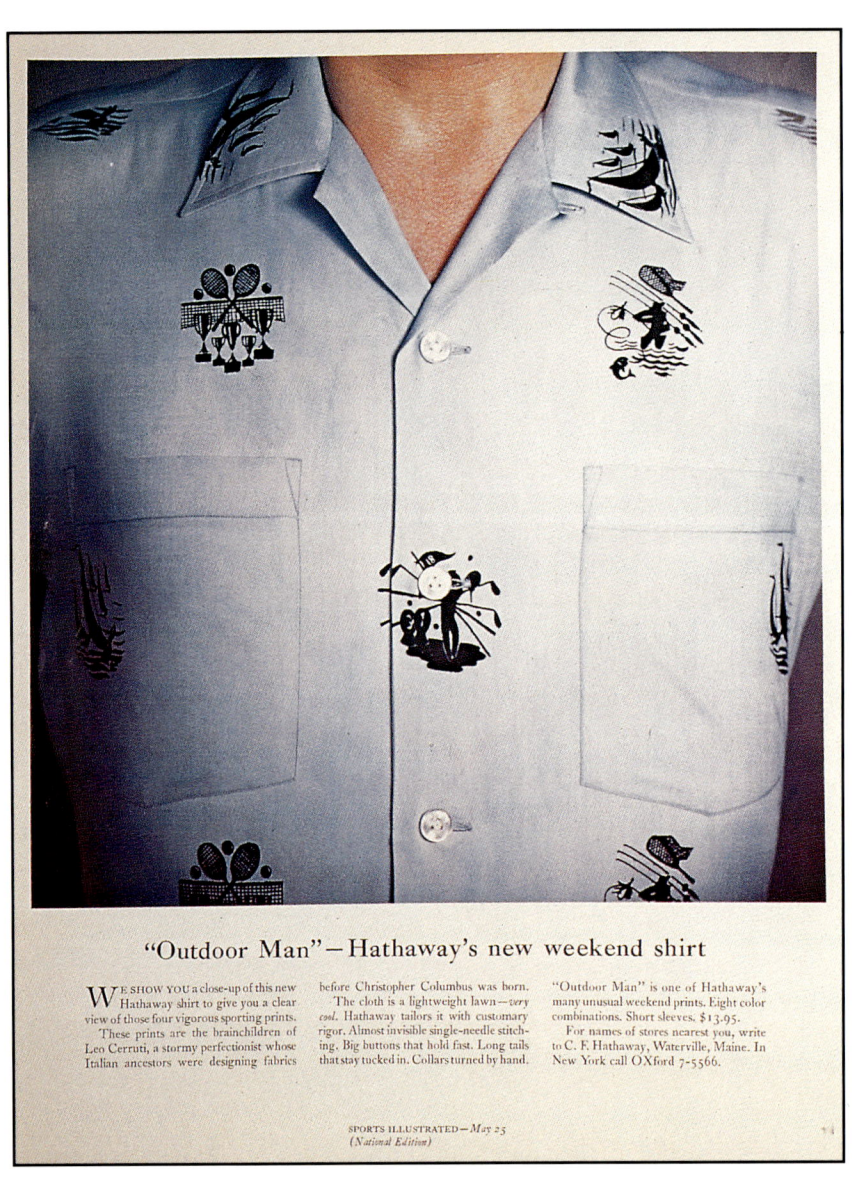

Left: 1959. "Outdoor Man," a light weight printed fabric designed by Leo Cerutti. $35–40.

Lower left: 1959. Viyella shirts in tartan and solids. $20–22.

Lower right: 1959. "How to choose a collar," a guide for the woman buying a shirt for a man.

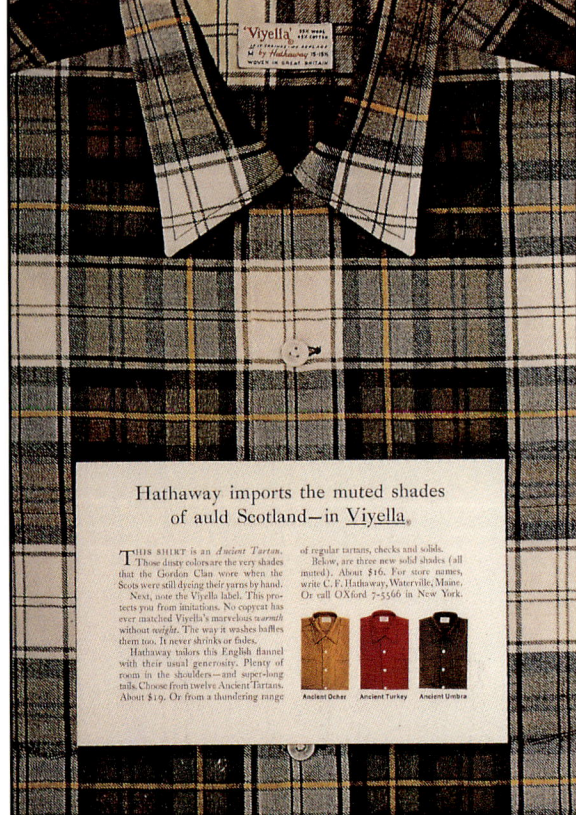

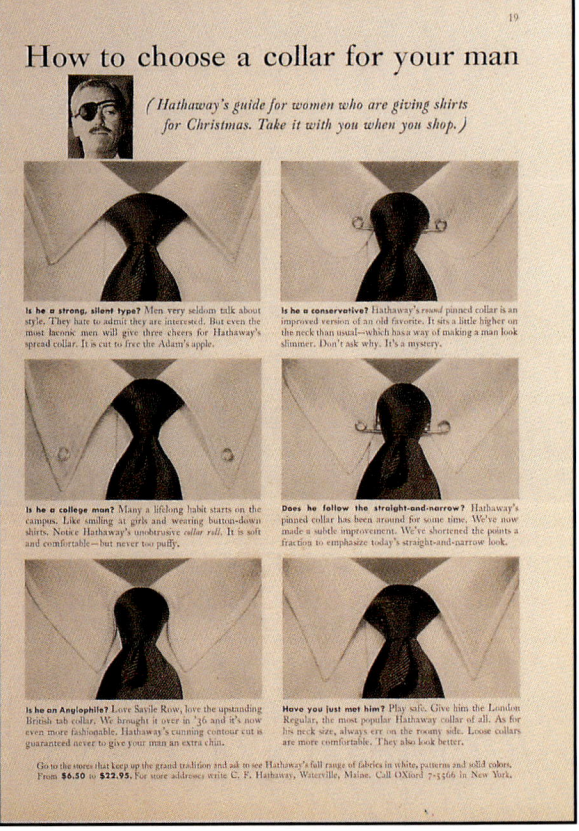

The Warner/Warnaco Years

Sometime in 1959 it became clear to Jette that the company needed to be part of a larger concern if its long term viability was to be insured. So, in June, 1960, it was sold to a Baltimore syndicate headed by Samuel J. Holtzman. Hathaway continued on unchanged in personnel or policies. It was a short-lived arrangement.

In August, 1960, it was announced that all of the assets of Hathaway were to be purchased by the Warner Brothers Company. Warner Brothers was another well established New England firm that had manufactured women's foundation garments since 1875. Writing in 1964, Pearce analyzes the relationship: "*Newsweek* magazine referred somewhat humorously to the marriage of the 'Merry Widow and the Man with the Eye-Patch,' but it has indeed been a happy marriage. It has united two family-built companies, each with a rich tradition of quality of product, of inventiveness in design and the use of fabrics, and each having demonstrated and imaginative approach to marketing and promotion."

In 1961, Leonard Saulter, who had spent his whole professional life at Hathaway, was named president. Under his leadership Hathaway continued to grow and the company moved into the growing sportswear field. In 1961 Hathaway held an exhibit of fabrics from India, including Indian Madras, tie-dyed cotton, India Hopsach, hand-woven silks and printed fabrics. Designed to celebrate the 25th anniversary of Hathaway's first importation of Madras into the United States, the exhibit also gave a new impetus to the use of the colorful fabric. Similarly Hathaway continued to promote Viyella a knitted fabric from the British Isles, used principally in sportswear. (LaPierre, pp. 110-111.)

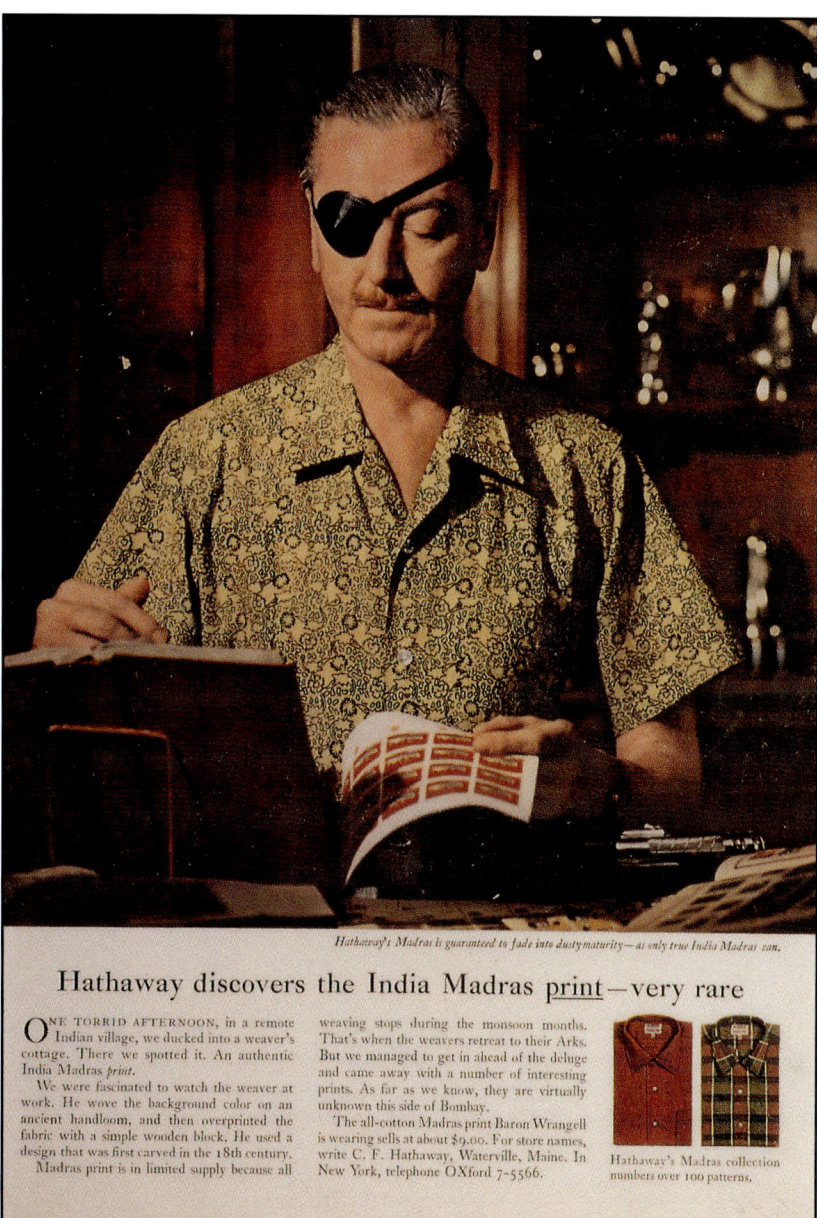

1960. Introducing the Madras print. The ad cites over 100 Madras patterns in the Hathaway line. $28–32.

Another revival of the 1960s was the "Trim Shirt," a fitted shirt made for a special account in the late 1930s. The name and the concept were reintroduced at the 1963 sales meeting, along with a new suede and leather line for Lady Hathaway.

Viyella was replaced in 1963 with a new fabric called Lochlana. Produced by the Moos Company of Switzerland, it was a cotton-wool blend which was light weight and perfect for winter sportshirts. It was offered in four tartan designs series, Classics, Olde, Dress, and Black. Each of these had several tartan choices. (LaPierre, pp. 120-121.)

In 1964 Hathaway introduced a stretch dress shirt, in a dacron polyester-cotton-lycra spandex blend. It came in blue or white with spread collar and French cuffs. It retailed for $12.95.

In spring 1965 the Club Line was introduced. Consisting of both dress and sports shirts, it was designed to appeal to the younger wearer. The collars were button down, and the designs were made for comfort and a trendy "sloppiness." The advertising featured entertainers and athletes. (LaPierre, pg. 129.)

Other significant Hathaway developments in the 1960s included:

The exclusive use in the U.S. of Donald Davies woolen shirtings, 1966
The introduction of the Elegant Dot Collection, packaging tie and shirt together, 1966
The increasing popularity of blended fabric, permanent press shirts, 1966
The addition of the Lanvin dress shirt line, 1966
The introduction of the Chelsea collar, slightly longer and fuller, with more linen showing above the jacket, 1967
After years of confusion with Warner Brothers, the movie company, the parent company changed its name to Warnaco in 1967.

In 1970 the advertising account was switch from Ogilvy & Mather to Green Domatch, Inc., ending a relationship of nearly 20 years. Paula Green, a principal in the new firm, commented on the Hathaway man: "It seems to me the Hathaway man always has been elegant, refined, delightful, witty, genteelly expensive and quietly chic, but by today's mores, he doesn't have the kind of bold masculine strength which I admire." (Quoted in LaPierre, p.150 ff.)

Reluctant to throw out the baby with the bath, Green Dolmatch's new campaign kept the patch while losing the man. They used the patch to replace the first "a" in Hathaway for the company logo. In their color advertisements, the face of the model was obscured by a white box with the drawing of an eyepatch in it.

Perhaps more significant were the ads featuring Jack Nicklaus in a Hathaway shirt. Nicklaus had been associated with Peerless, another part of the Warnaco family for a number of years before he became the model for the Hathaway Golf Classic knit shirt.

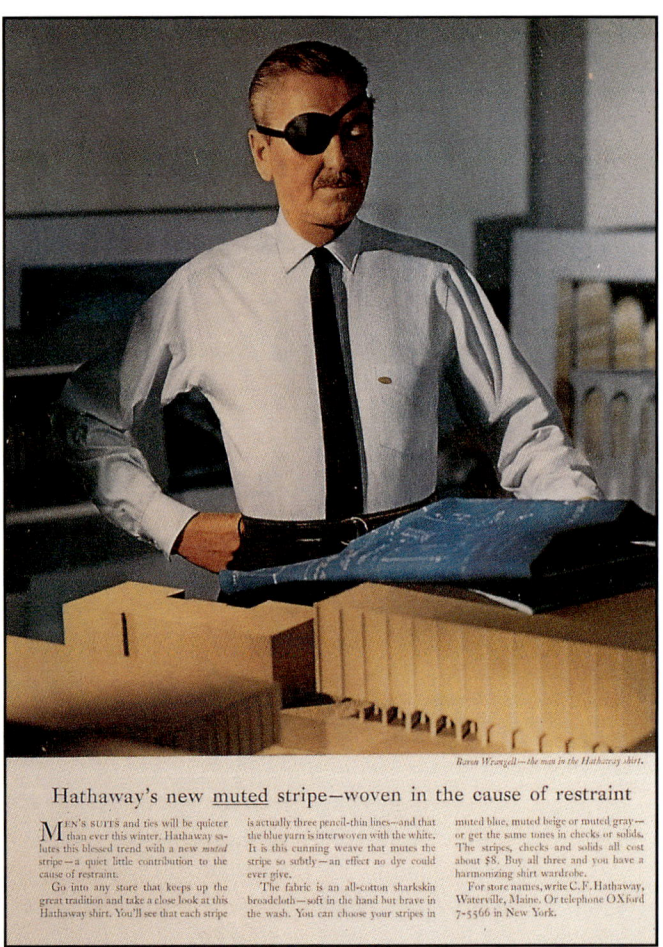

1960. Perfectly hand-matched pockets mark the quality of this drip dry print shirt. $28–30.

1960. $18–20.

Other highlights of the decade:

1971: Having established a separate operation for Lady Hathaway in 1962, Hathaway returned to the lady's shirt field with the Hathaway Patch line.

1974: The Concept line was introduced offering the younger man European tapered shirts with square bottoms, higher armholes, darted waists, tapered sleeves, and buttons placed higher on the band.

1974: Patch II was introduced in the fall as an extension of the Concepts line.

1974: The advertising account moved A.C. & R. Advertising of New York, a member of the Ted Bates Group.

1974: In August, Hathaway announced a licensing agreement to produce Christian Dior designer dress shirts.

In 1977 Hathaway returned its advertising account to Ogilvy & Mathers. Both companies had grown immensely over the years. Ogilvy & Mathers was now a $340 million company (compared to $9 million in 1951), and ranked 6th in the nation. Hathaway had had sales of $2,000,000 in 1951, and in 1977 the sales were in excess of $40,000,000.

In a Hathaway press release from February 1977, the president, Robert Matura is quoted as saying:

> For 140 years, Hathaway has been known for quality and fashion leadership in men's dress shirts. In the early 1950s, David Ogilvy created a distinctive and memorable brand image for our company, and the image persists. 26 years later, retailers and consumers recognize the famous Hathaway Eyepatch as a symbol of superb quality and workmanship.

In the same press release David Ogilvy said, "I am always happy when former clients come back to us—Hathaway most of all, because our campaign for them put Ogilvy & Mather on the map."

The account included Hathaway dress shirts, Jack Nicklaus Golf Classics, the Christian Dior line of dress shirts, and the Hathaway owned Stern-Merritt line of Christian Dior ties.

Ogilvy & Mather's first campaign brought the eyepatch back on the face of Ned Philips, in a print campaign that included *Newsweek, Time, The New Yorker, New York Magazine, The New York Times, New West, Vogue,* and *Harper's Bazaar.*

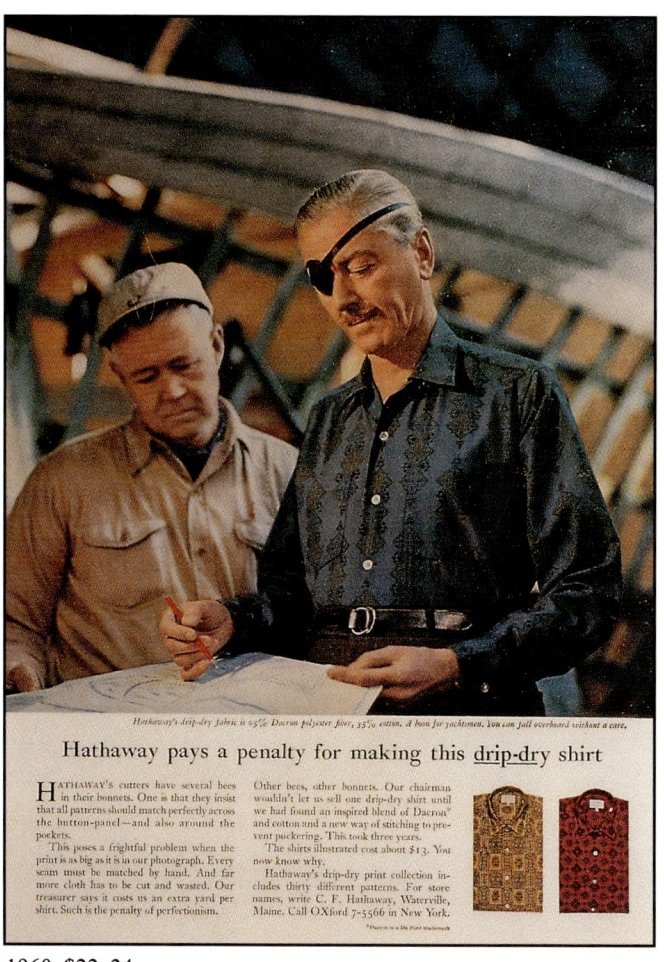

1960. $22–24.

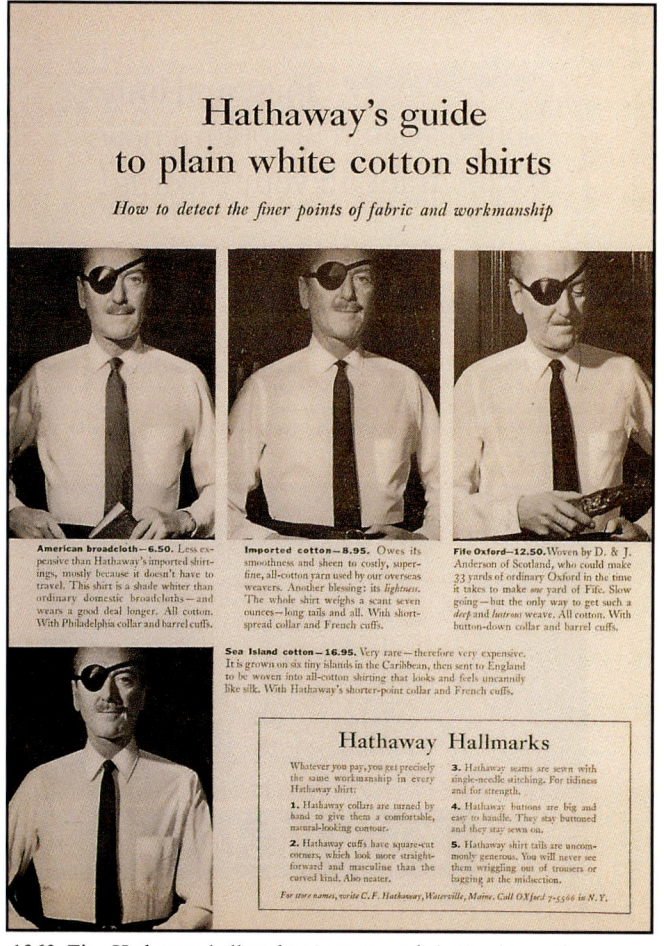

1960. Five Hathaway hallmarks are presented: 1. Hand-turned collars for comfort; 2. Square-cornered cuffs for appearance; 3. Single needle stitching for strength and tidiness; 4. Big buttons for ease of use; and 4. Generous shirt tails for comfort and fit. $15–18.

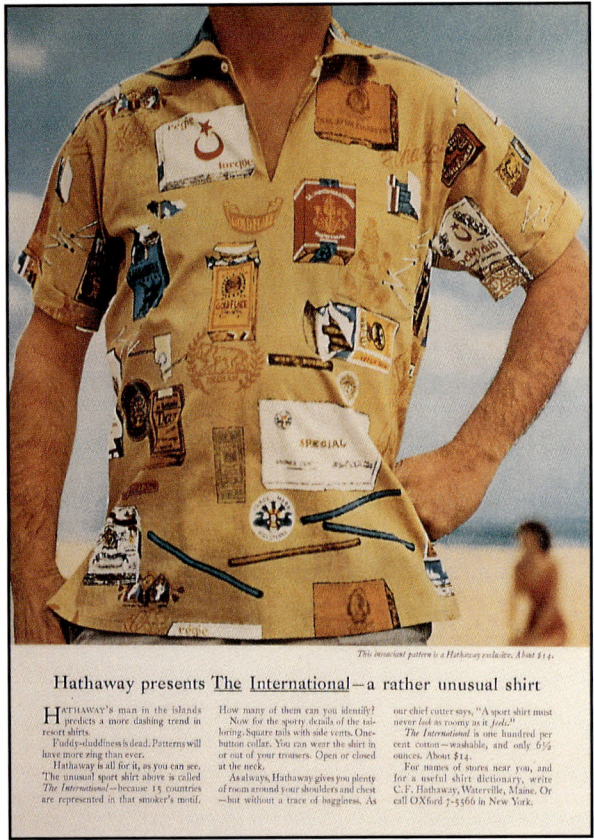

1960. Predicting a trend in "resort shirts," Hathaway introduces the International, with a tobacco motif representing 15 countries. Cotton. $35–40.

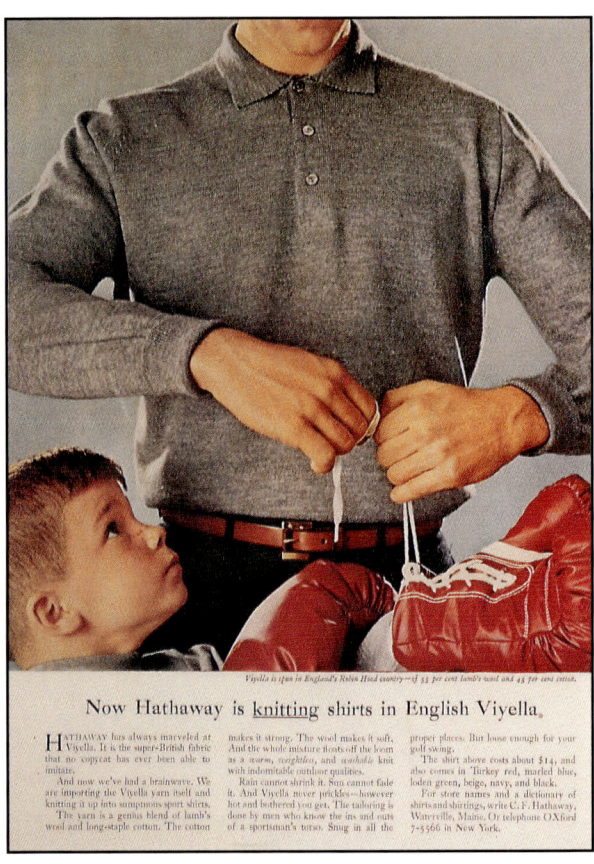

1960. A knit shirt of imported Viyella cotton yarn. $18–20.

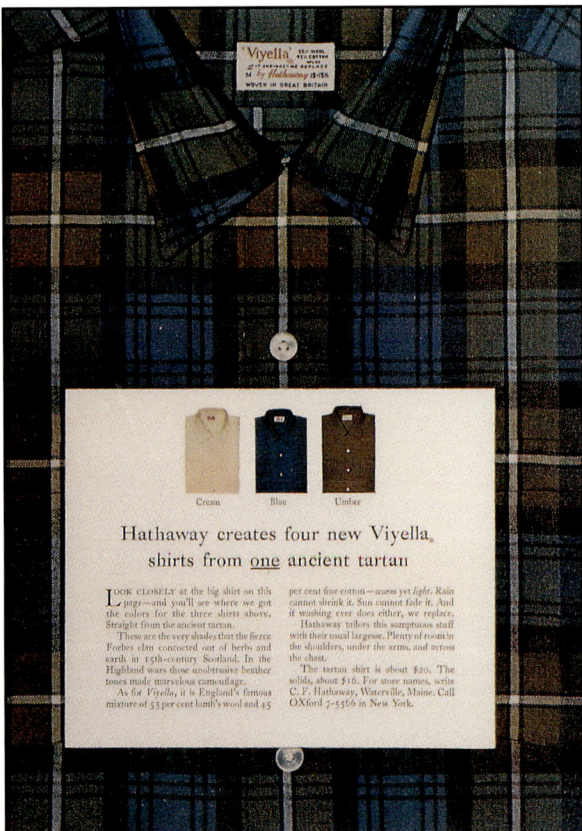

1960. Viyella tartan and coordinated solids. $20–22.

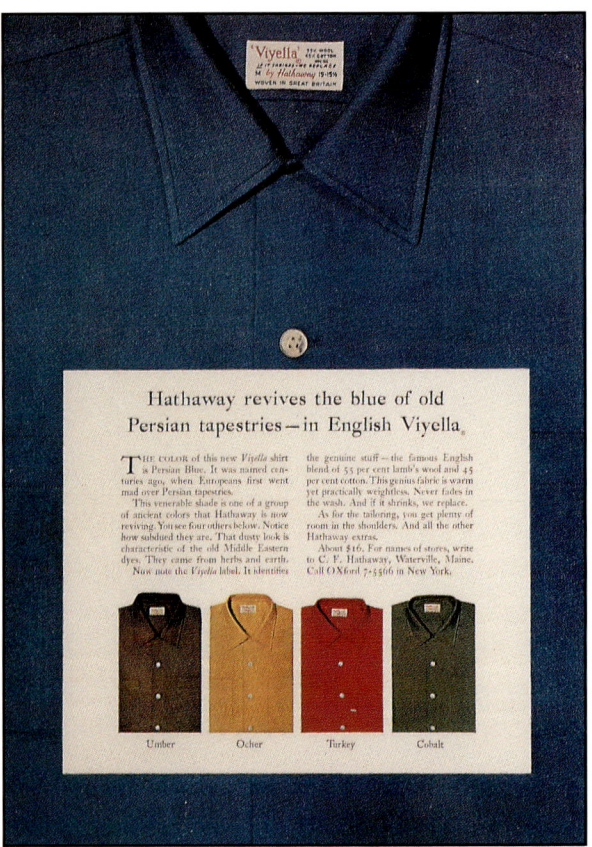

1960. Persian colors in Viyella. $18–22.

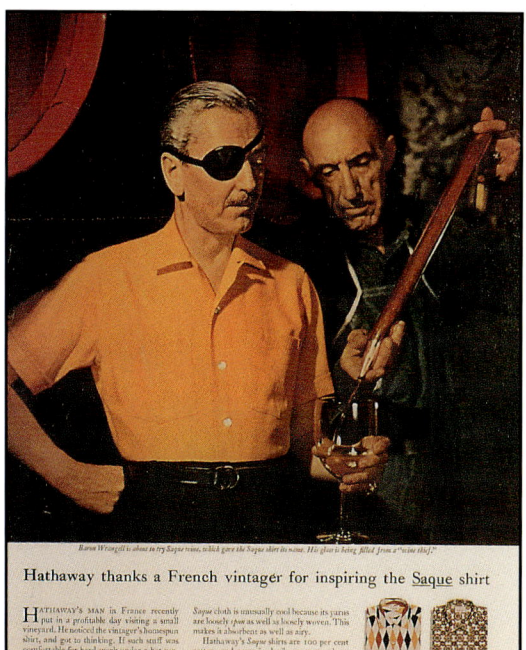
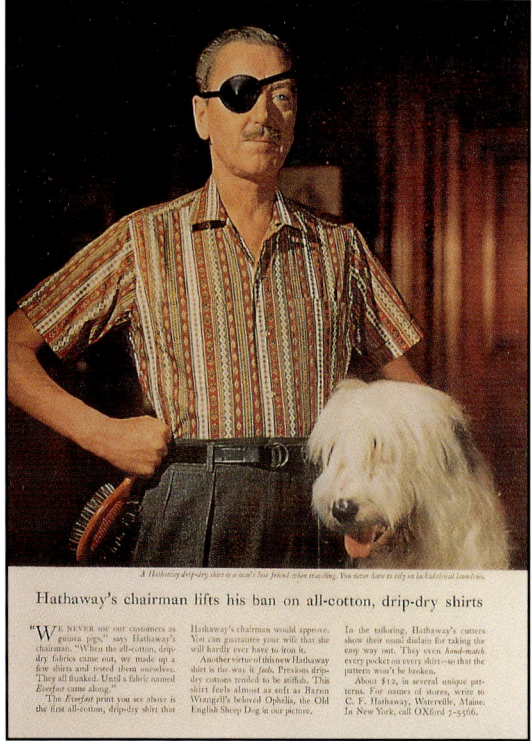
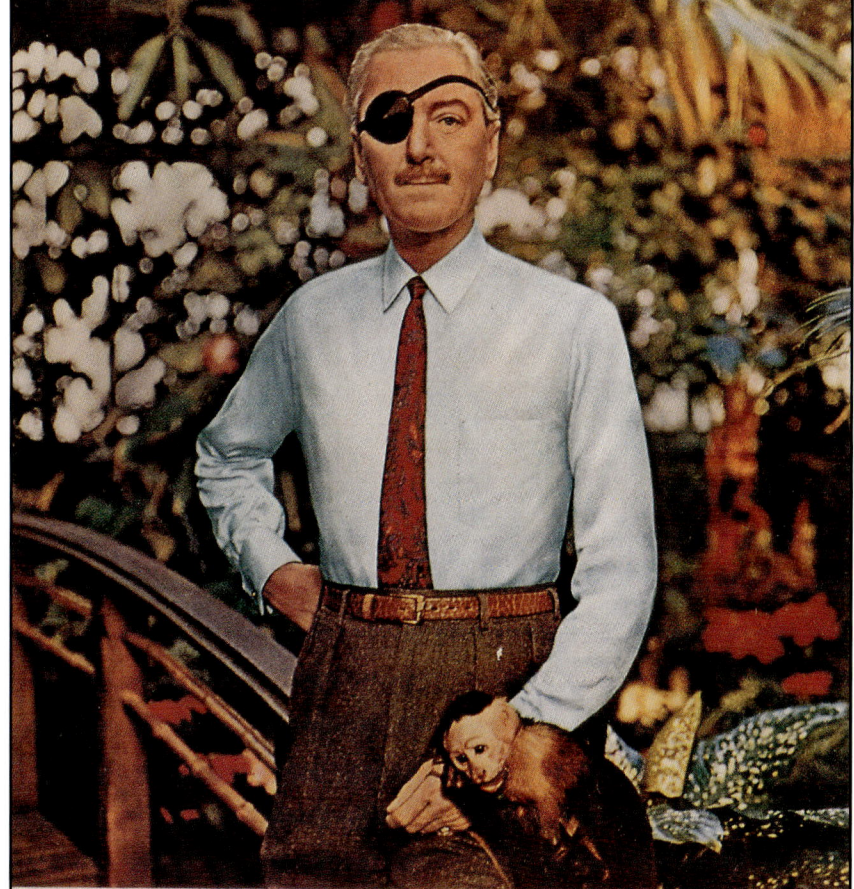

Above left: 1961. This shirt introduced the fabric called Everfast, the first all cotton, drip-dry shirt approved by Hathaway's chairman. $22–24.

Above right: 1961. A cotton fabric of loosely spun yarn that Hathaway called *Saque cloth*. $18–20.

Right: 1961. Lovat blue, discovered in Scotland by Ellerton Jette. $18–20.

53

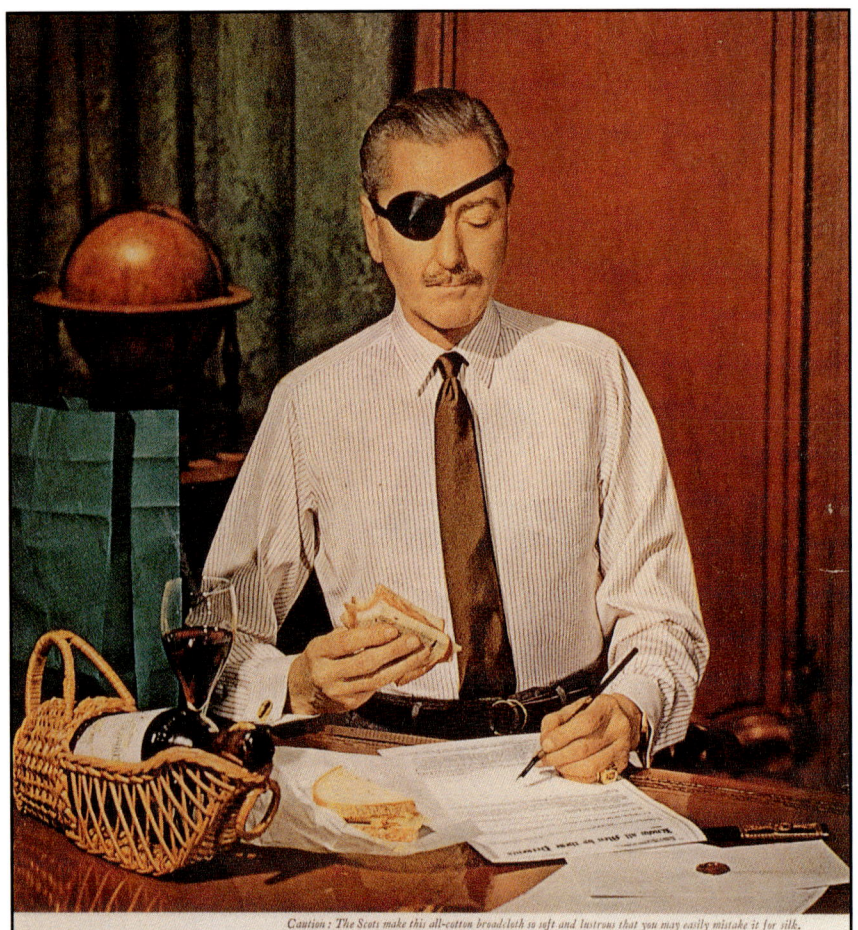

Left: 1961. A subtle stripe from D & J Anderson. $15–18.

Lower left: 1961. A cotton fabric woven on the silk looms of M. & W. Thomas, achieving a raw silk character. $22–24.

Lower right: 1961. $18–20.

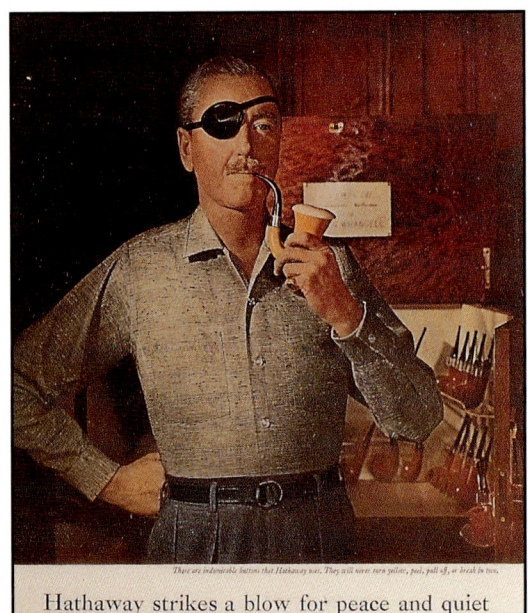

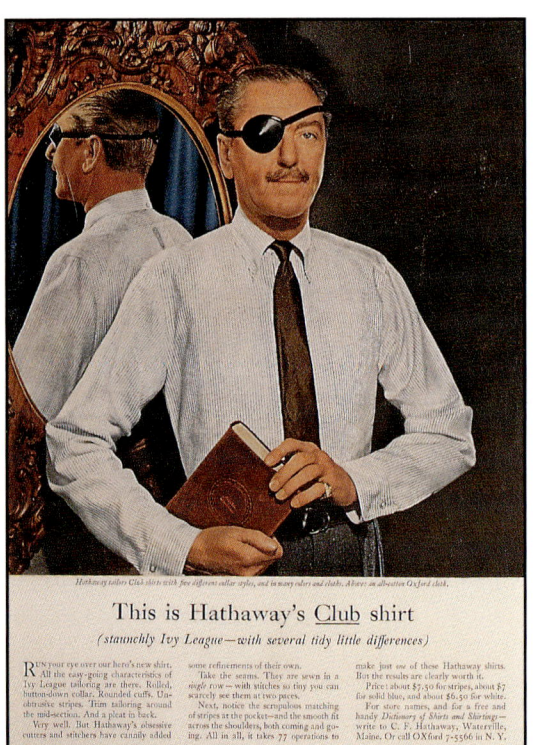

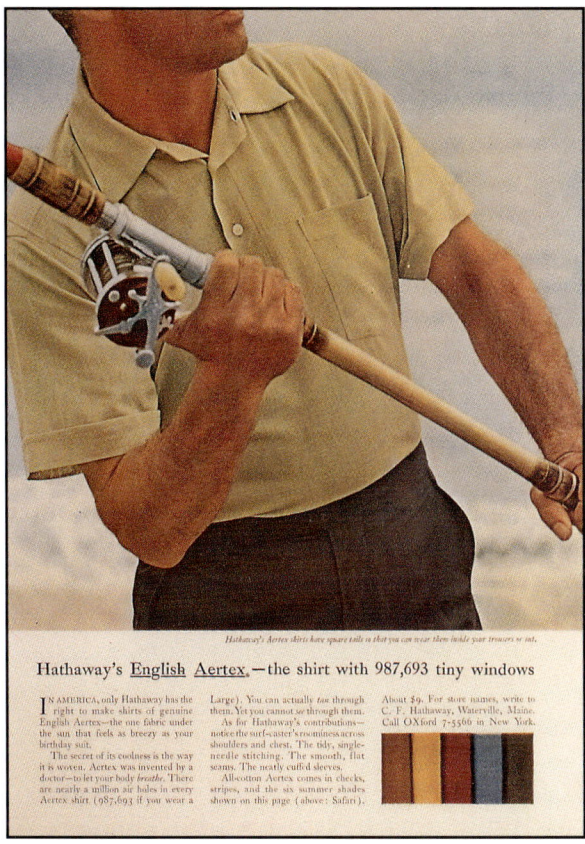

1961. An airy weave and loose fit made English Aertex great sportshirt. $22–24.

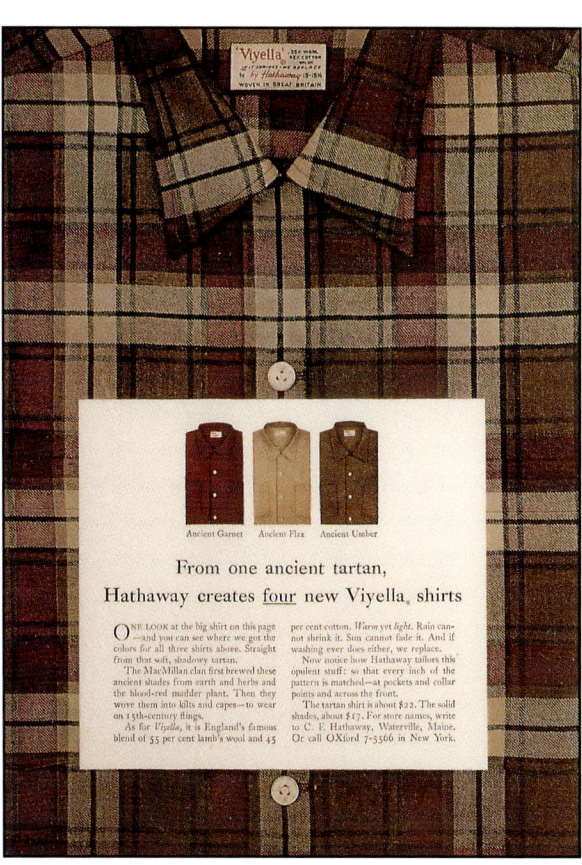

1961. Viyella in a clan Tartan and matching solids. $22–24.

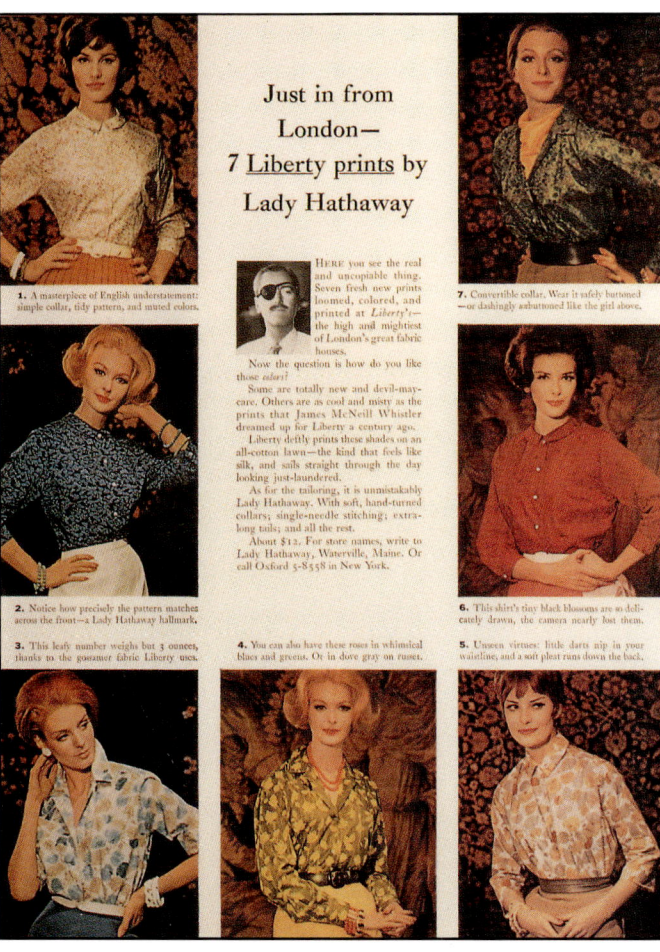

1961. Lady Hathaway Liberty prints. $24–28

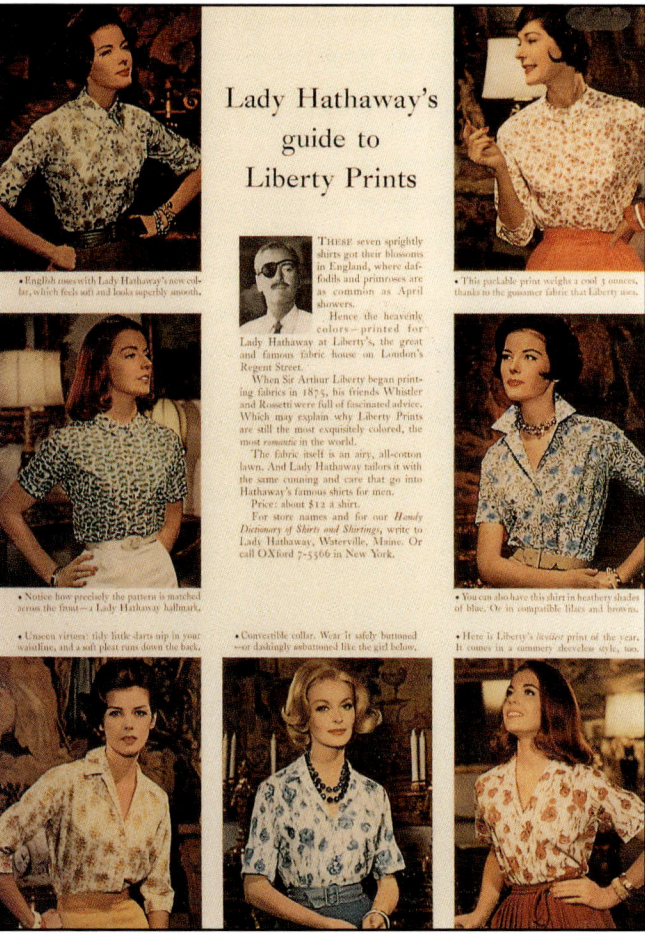

1961. Lady Hathaway's guide to Liberty prints. $24–68.

55

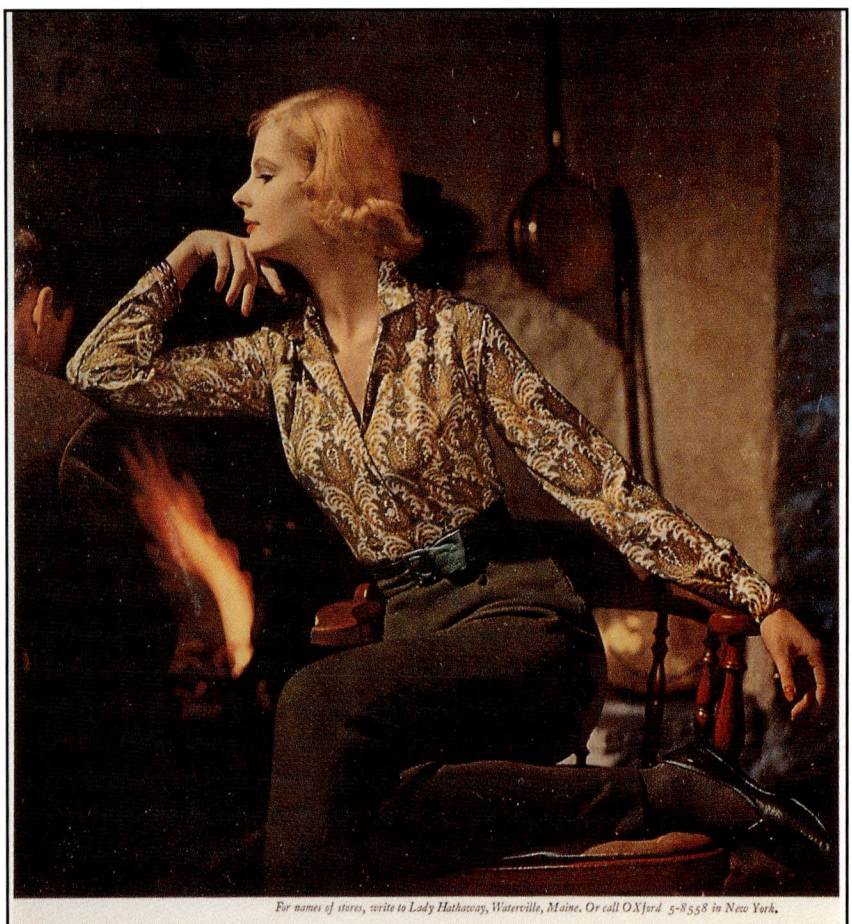

New from Lady Hathaway: Persian prints in soft and sumptuous Viyella.

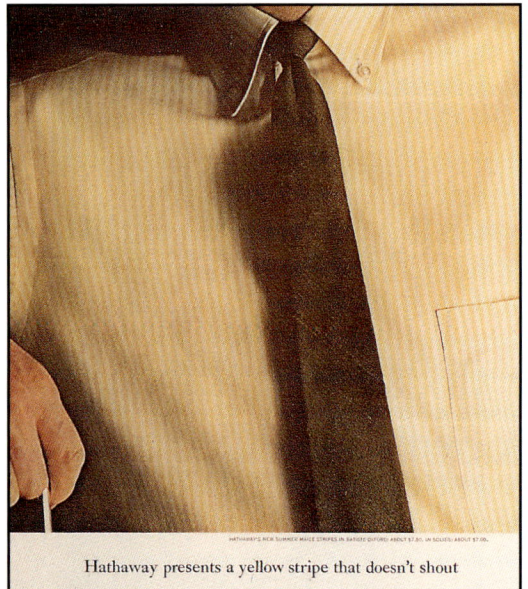

Hathaway presents a yellow stripe that doesn't shout

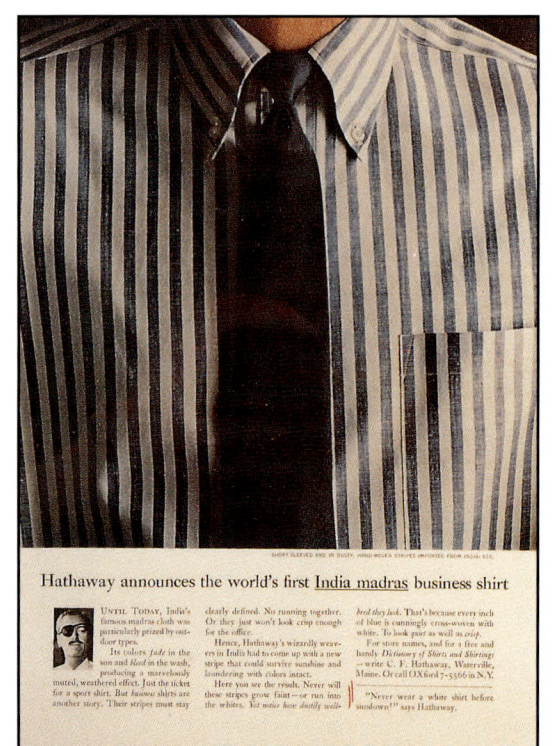

Hathaway announces the world's first India madras business shirt

Left: 1961. Persian prints on Viyella. $24–28.

Lower left: 1963. $18–20.

Lower right: 1963. Indian Madras striped business shirt. $18–20.

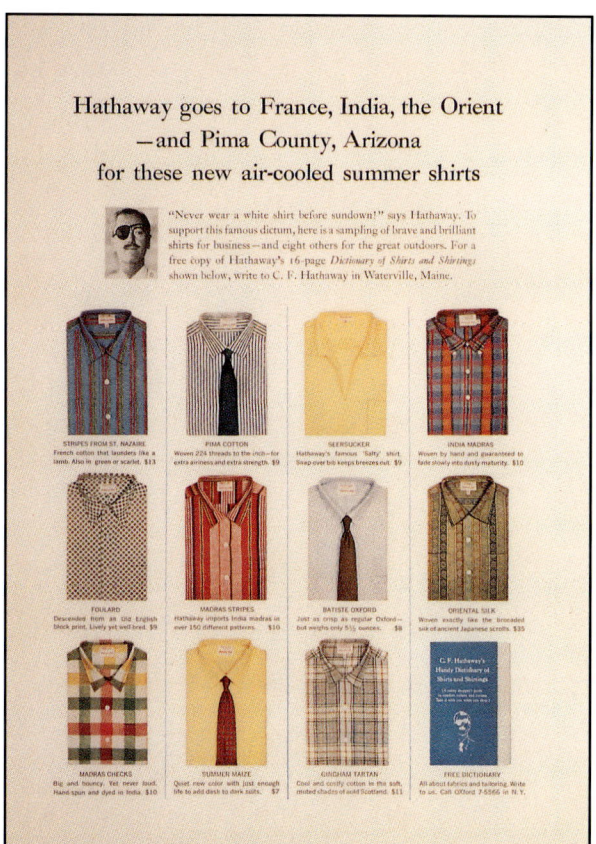

1963. This ad samples the variety of styles produced by Hathaway. $22–24.

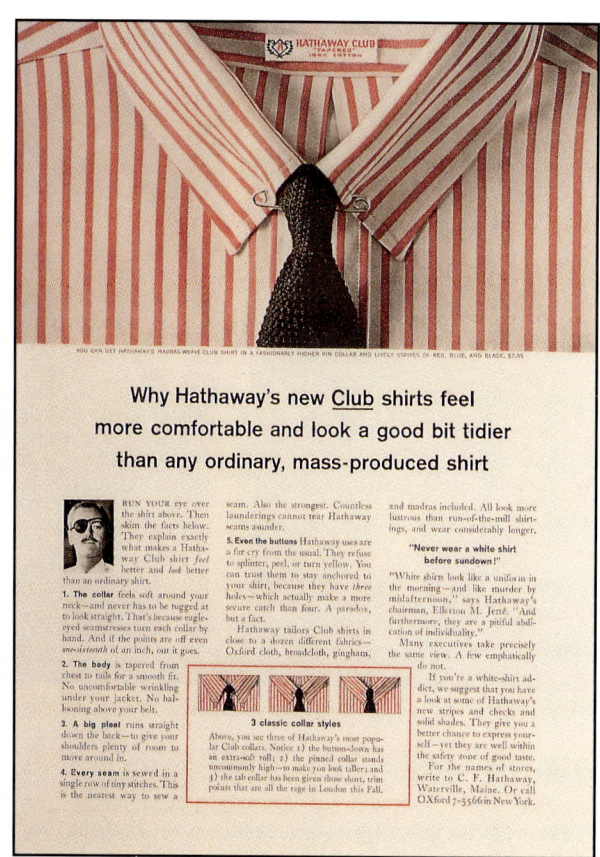

1963. $18–20.

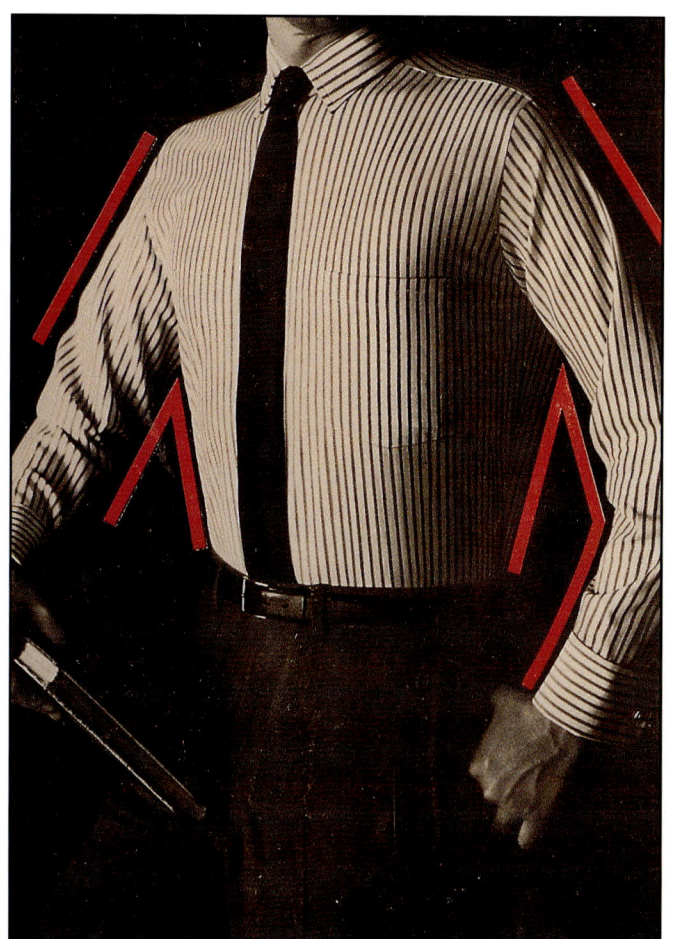

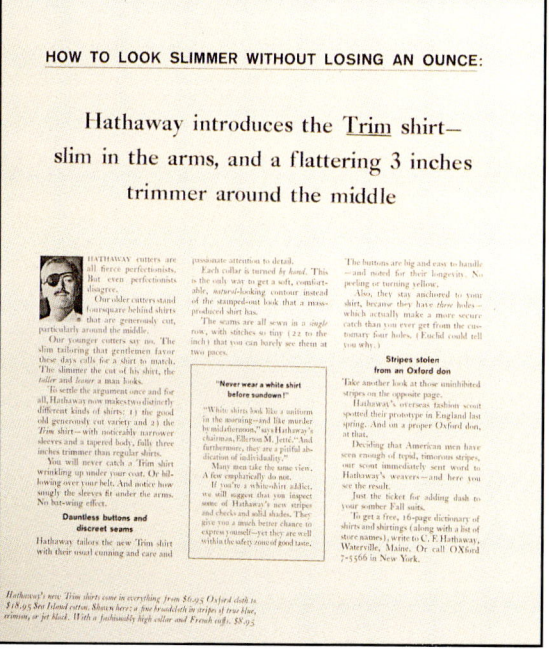

Left & above: 1963. The introduction of the "Trim Shirt," a fitted shirt. A shirt of a similar name and concept was introduced in the 1930s for one of Hathaway's bigger accounts.

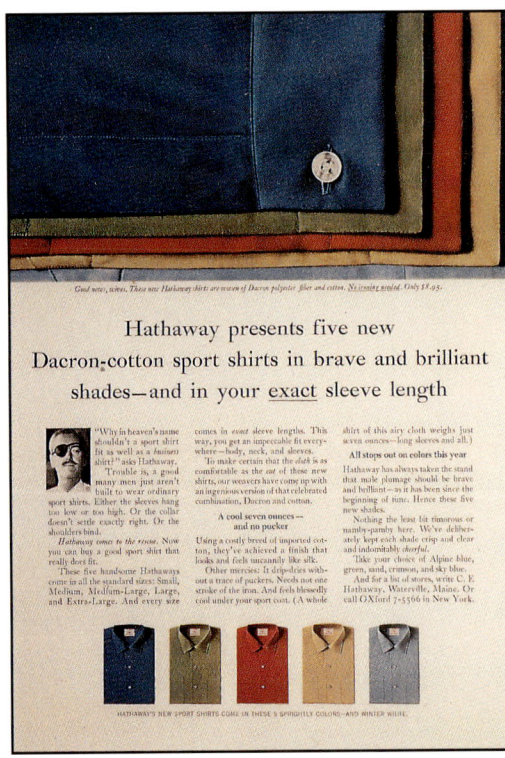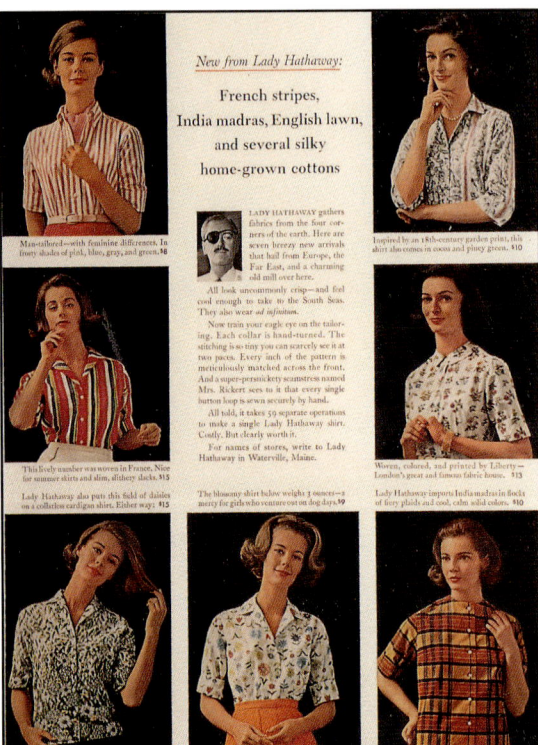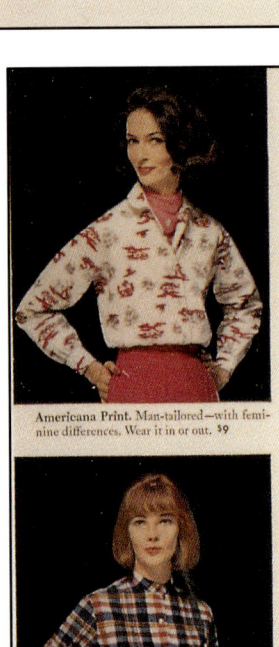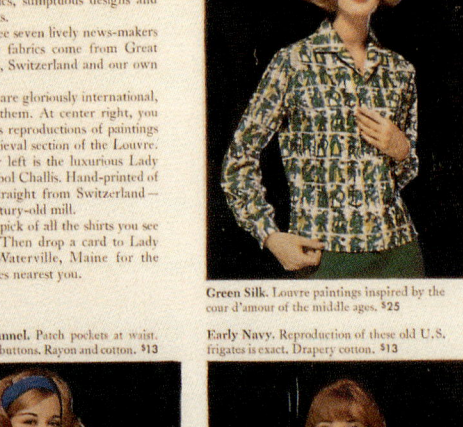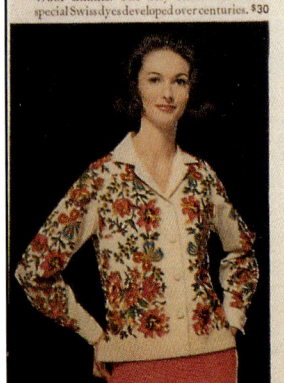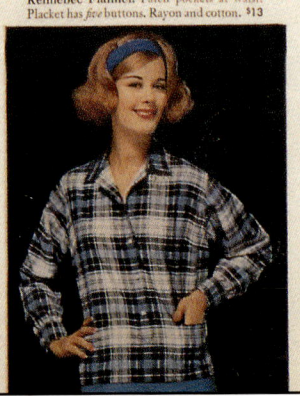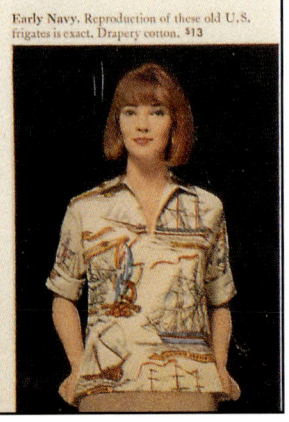

Above left: 1963. Dacron-cotton sportshirts with exact sleeve lengths for a better fit. $20–22.

Above right & right: 1963. Lady Hathaway styles. $22–24.

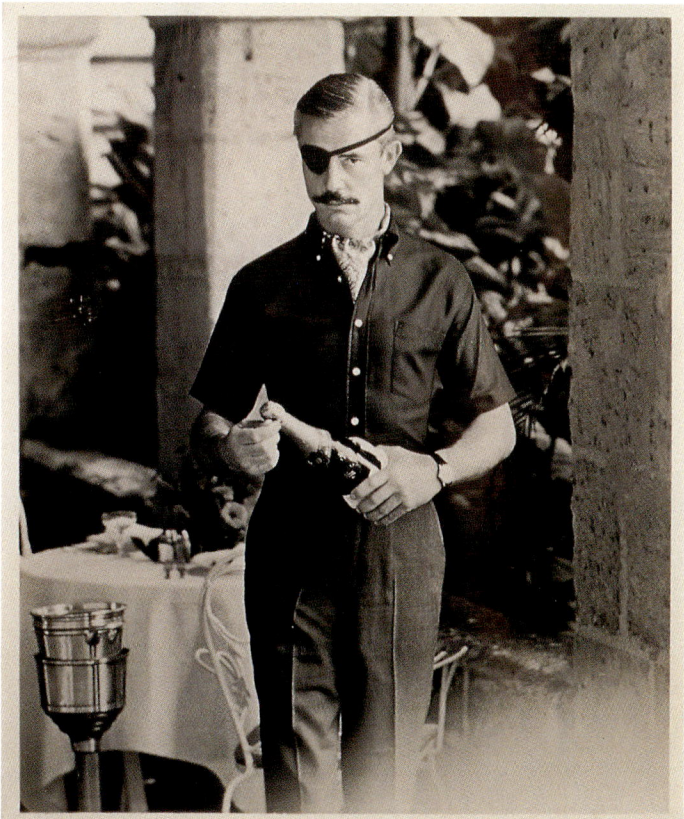

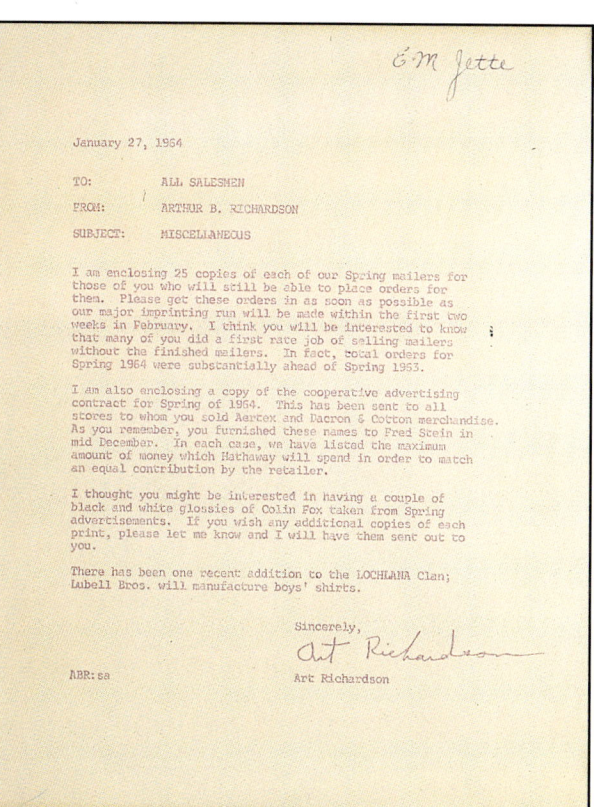

January 27, 1964

TO: ALL SALESMEN
FROM: ARTHUR B. RICHARDSON
SUBJECT: MISCELLANEOUS

I am enclosing 25 copies of each of our Spring mailers for those of you who will still be able to place orders for them. Please get these orders in as soon as possible as our major imprinting run will be made within the first two weeks in February. I think you will be interested to know that many of you did a first rate job of selling mailers without the finished mailers. In fact, total orders for Spring 1964 were substantially ahead of Spring 1963.

I am also enclosing a copy of the cooperative advertising contract for Spring of 1964. This has been sent to all stores to whom you sold Aertex and Dacron & Cotton merchandise. As you remember, you furnished these names to Fred Stein in mid December. In each case, we have listed the maximum amount of money which Hathaway will spend in order to match an equal contribution by the retailer.

I thought you might be interested in having a couple of black and white glossies of Colin Fox taken from Spring advertisements. If you wish any additional copies of each print, please let me know and I will have them sent out to you.

There has been one recent addition to the LOCHLANA Clan; Lubell Bros. will manufacture boys' shirts.

Sincerely,

Art Richardson

ABR:sa

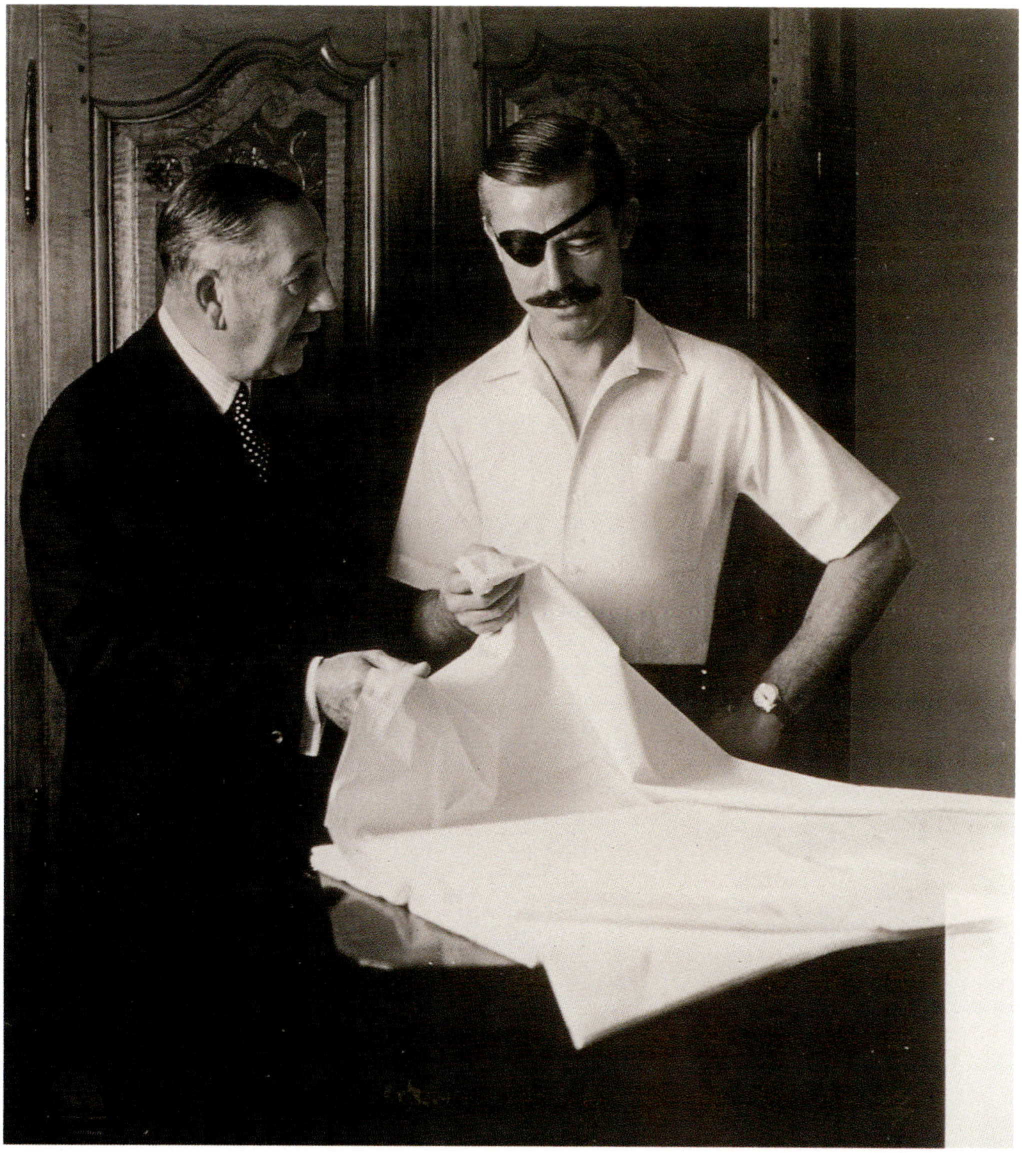

Above left & right: 1964. When Colin Leslie Fox became the new Hathaway man, this photo and accompanying memo from Art Richardson was sent to salesmen.

Left: Ellerton Jette and Collin Leslie Fox.

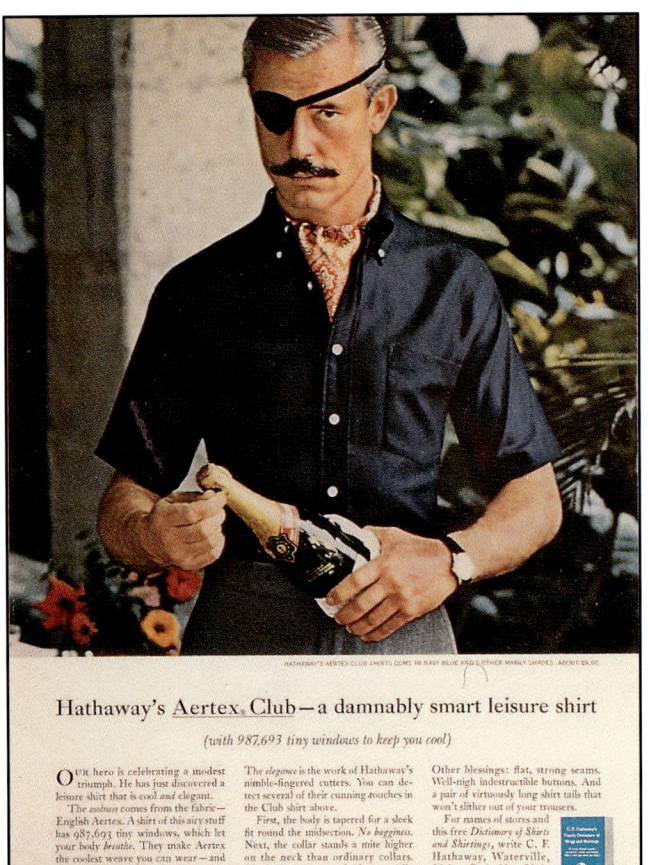

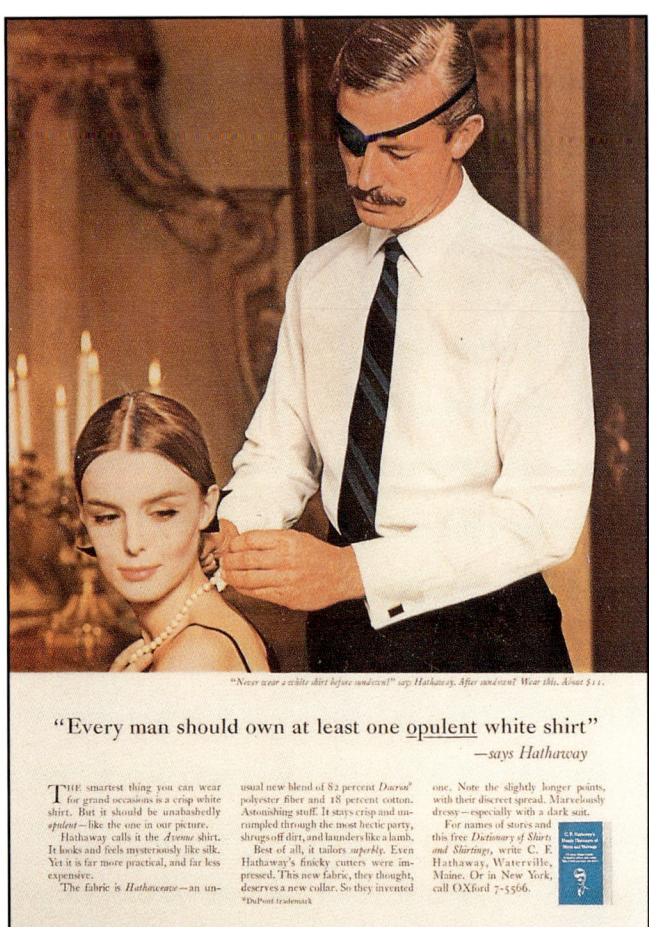

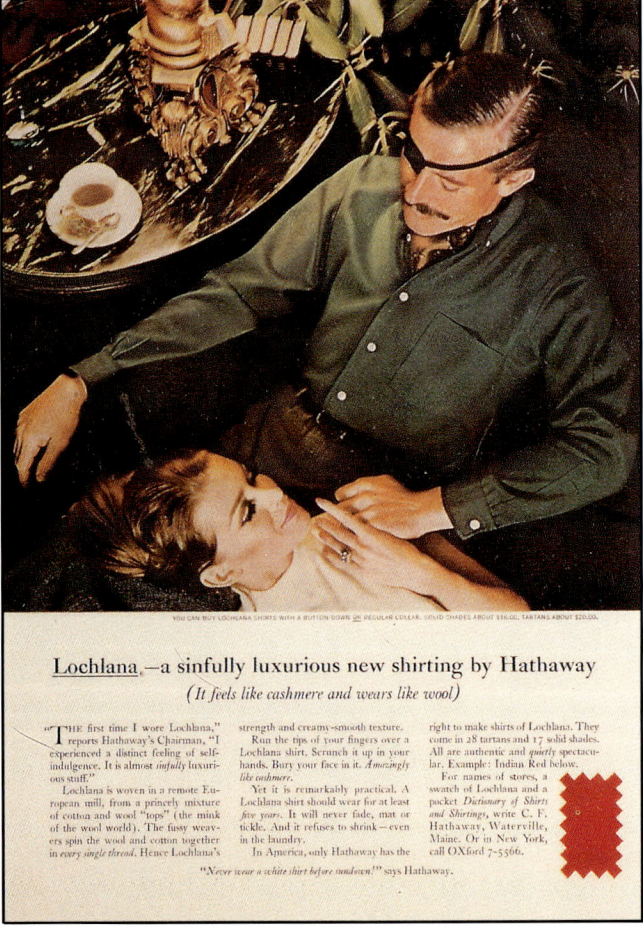

Above: 1964. It is clear that Fox was more than able to take up where Wrangell left off. $18–20.

Above right: 1964. The *Avenue* shirt, featuring a blend of 82% Dacron with 18% cotton. $18–20.

Right: 1964. Introduced in 1963, Lochlana took the place of Hathaway's longtime standard, Viyella. This new blend of wool and cotton was milled in Europe and, according to the ad, should wear for "at least five years." $22–24.

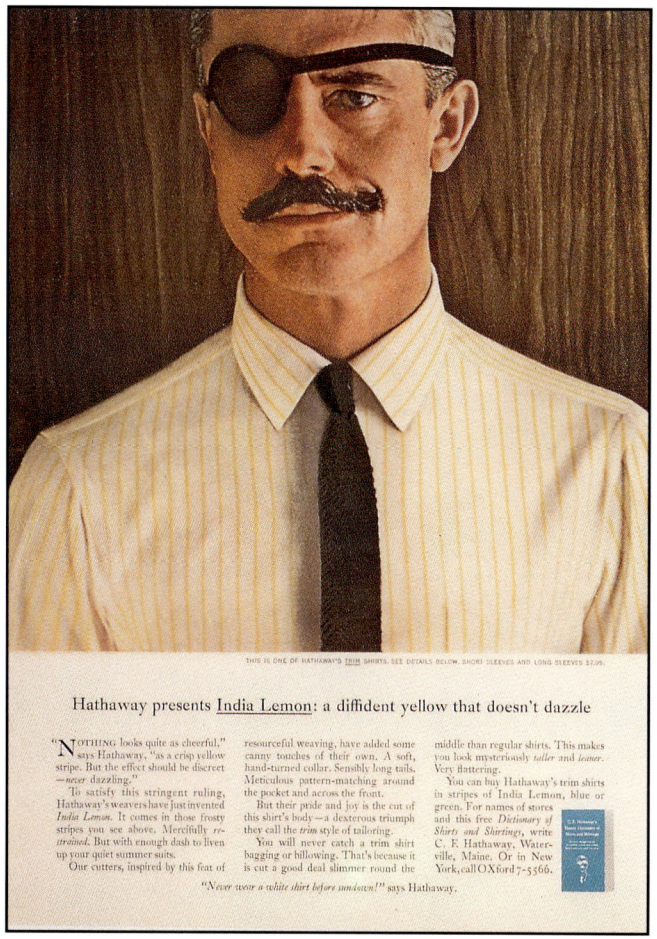

1964. $18–20.

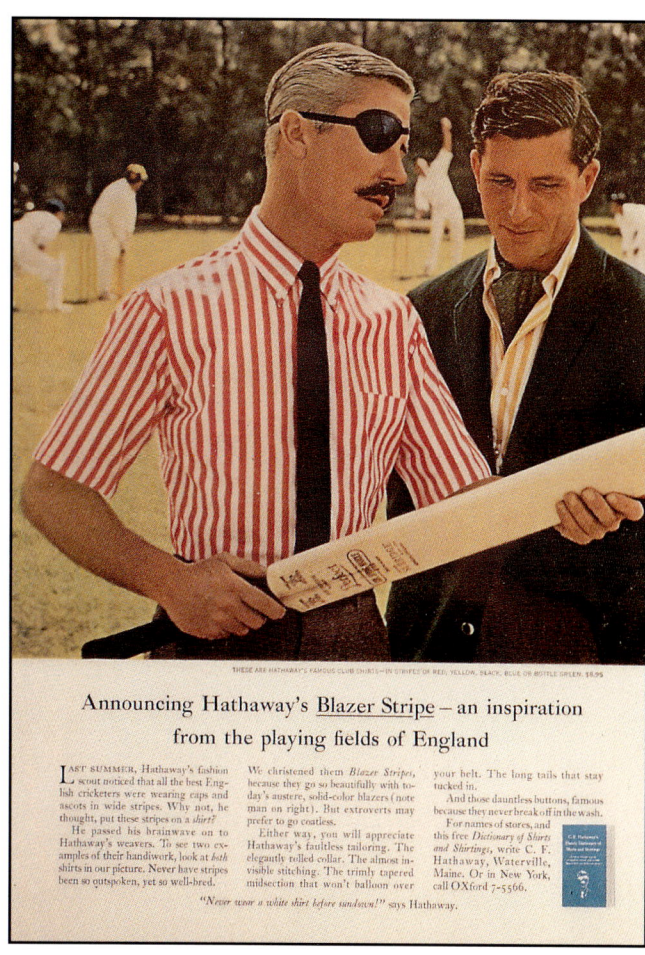

1964. The introduction of the wide Blazer Stripe. $18–20.

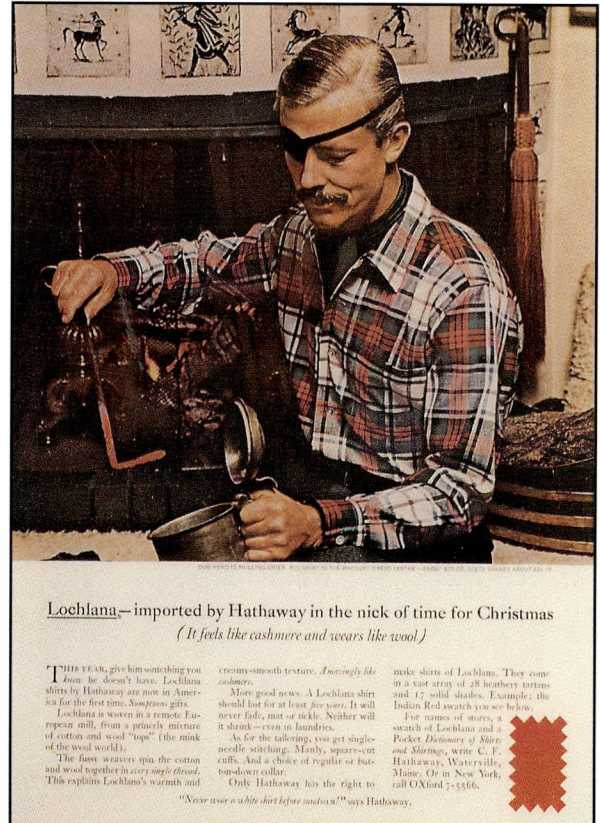

1964. Lochlana came in 28 tartans and 17 solid colors. $24–28.

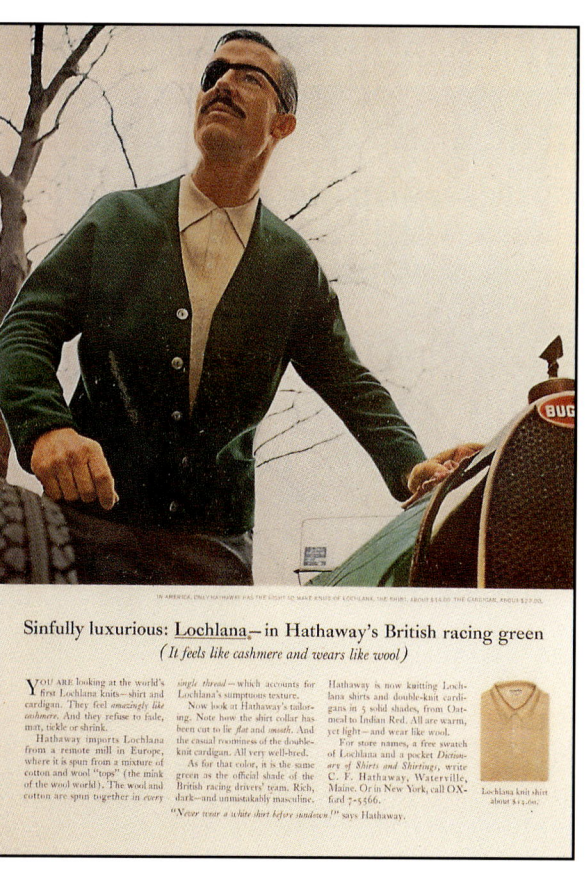

1964. Knit Lochlana shirt and cardigan sweater. $24–28.

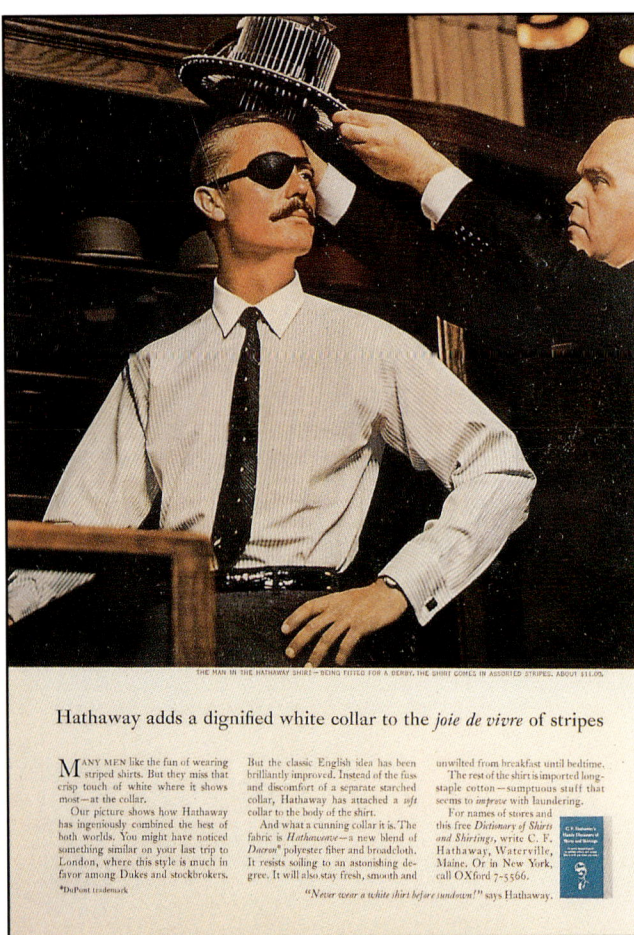

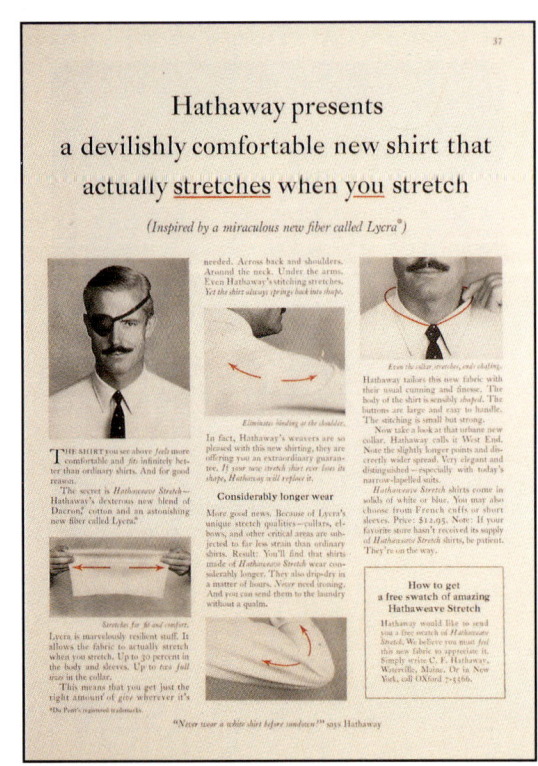

Left: 1964. An early example of the revival of the white collar on a colored shirt, a growing trend in the 1960s. $15–18.

Below: 1964. The introduction of the *Hathaweave Stretch* shirt, a blend of cotton and Lycra.

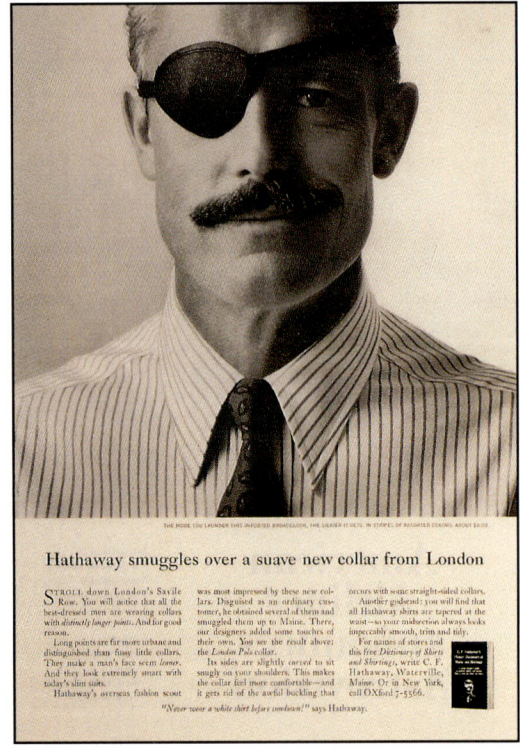

Above: 1964. A new collar "smuggled" from Saville Row, London. $18–20.

Right: 1964. Reminiscent of Fox's first appearance in a Hathaway ad, back in 1958, this is for an Aertex sport shirt. $22–24.

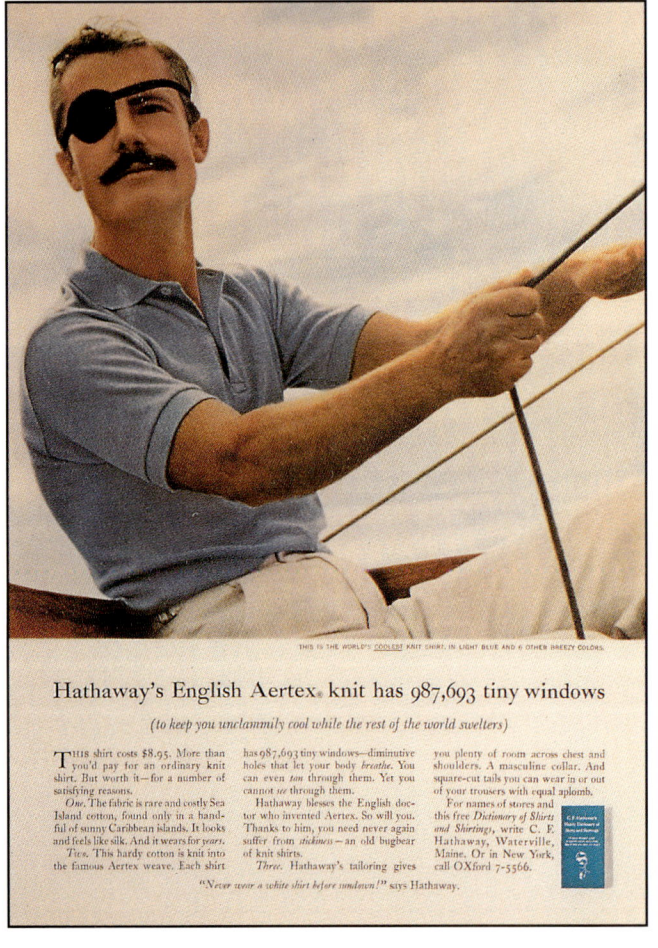

62

Right: 1964. Liberty strawberry pattern in a Lady Hathaway shirt. Wool challis. $28–30.

Below: 1964. Ellerton Jette appears with the Hathaway man to endorse this drip dry, *Hathaweave* fabric of 65% Dacron, 35% Batiste cotton. $20–22.

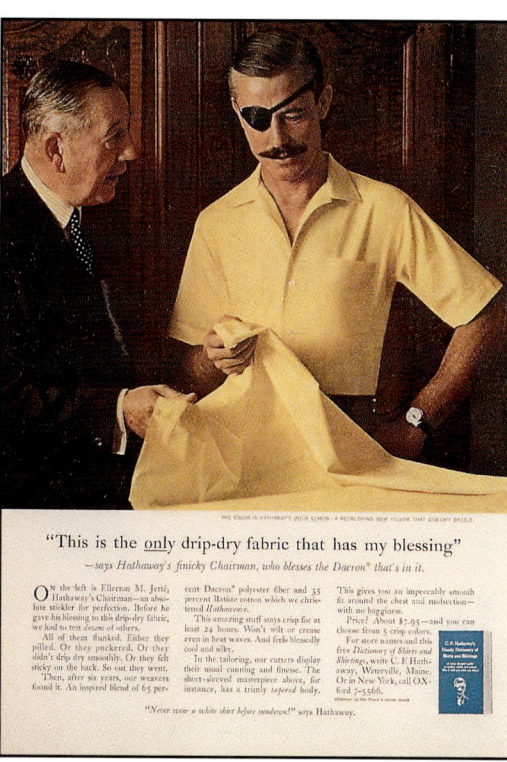

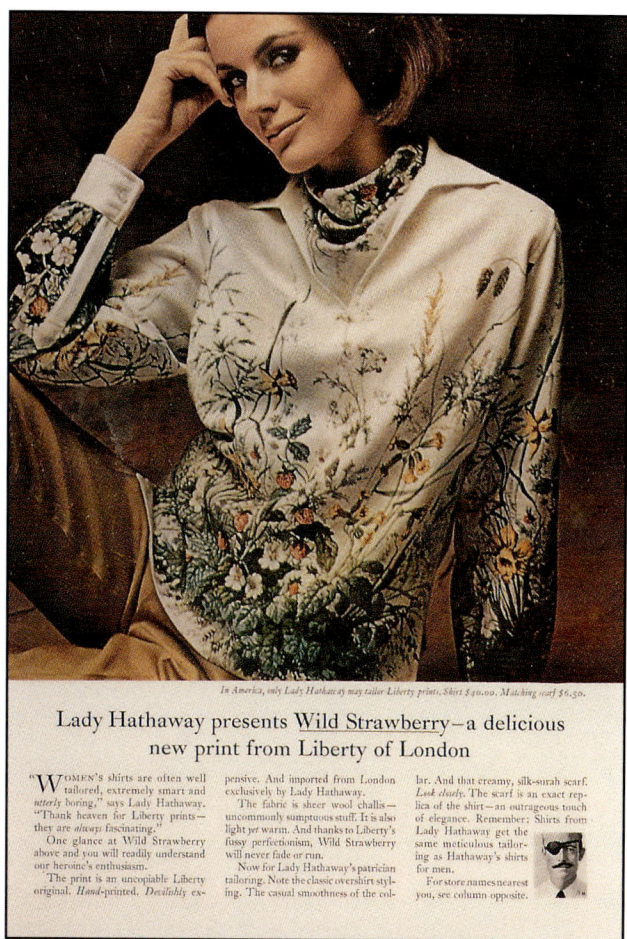

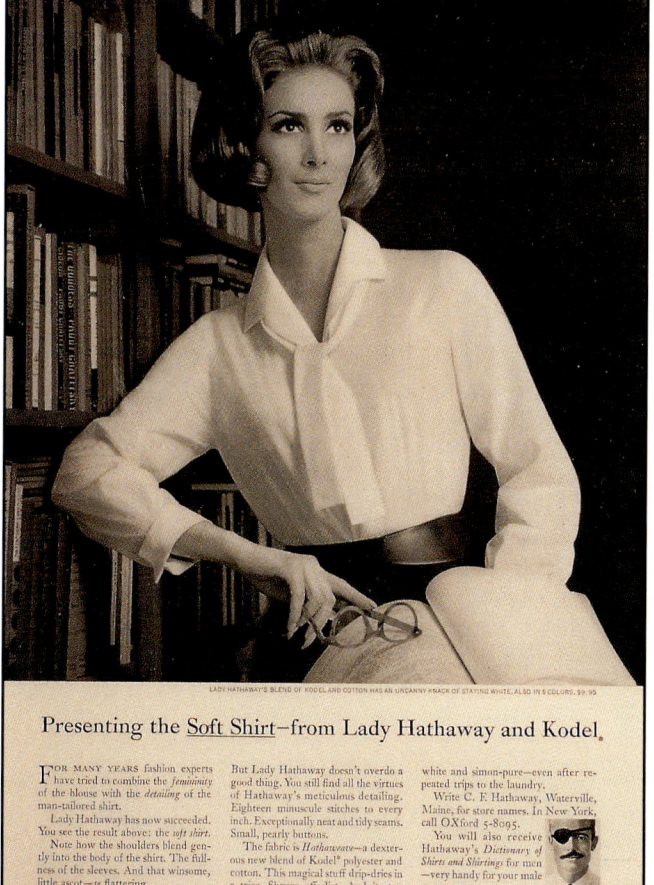

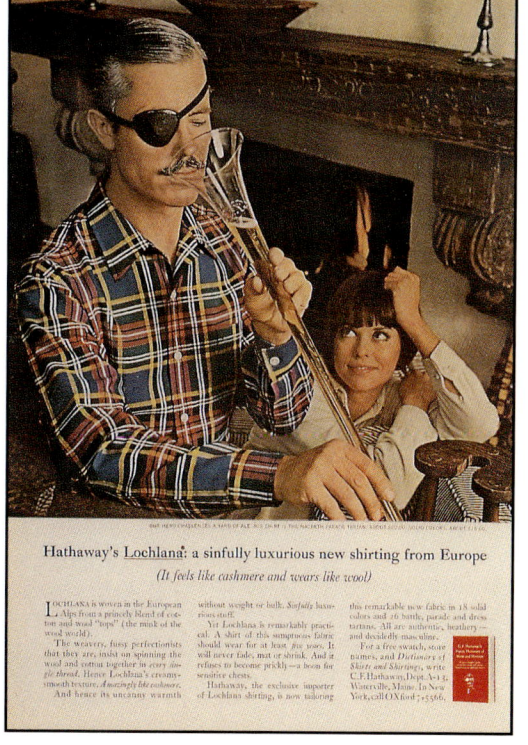

Above: 1965. Lochlana. $24–28.

Left: 1965. Another *Hathaweave*, this time of Kodel and cotton, give this shirt a new, feminine softness. $18–20.

63

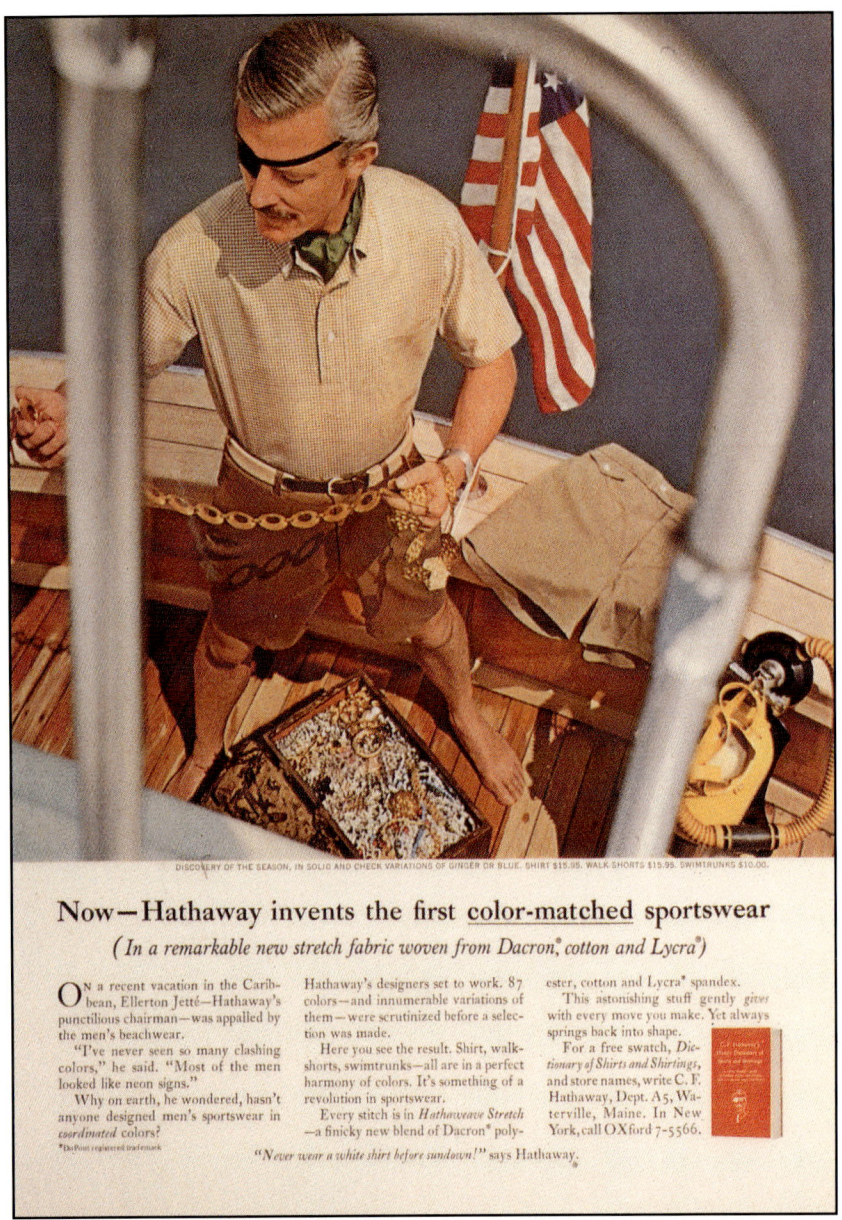

Left: 1965. Coordinated sportswear for men, including shirt, shorts, and bathing trunks. All are of a *Hathaweave* blend of Dacron, cotton, and Lycra. This is an early exploration of men's wear beyond shirts. $20–22.

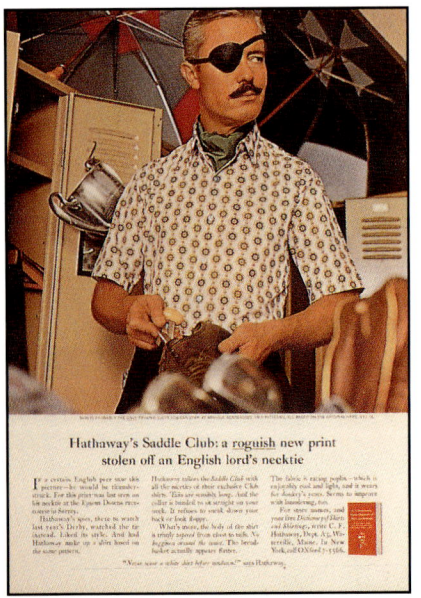

1965. $28–30.

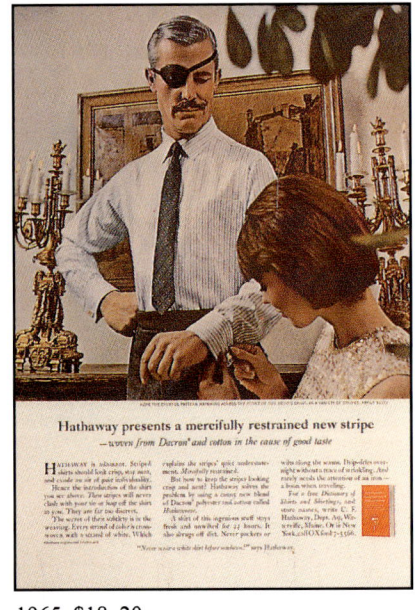

1965. $18–20.

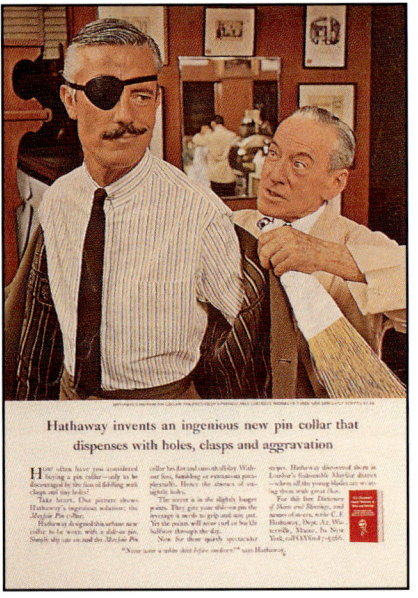

1965. $18–20.

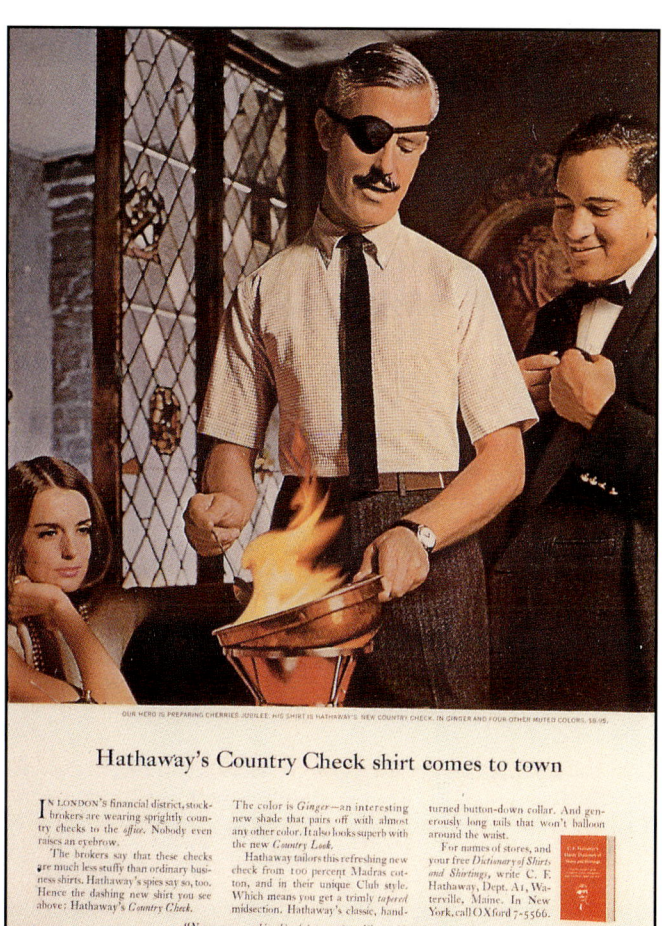

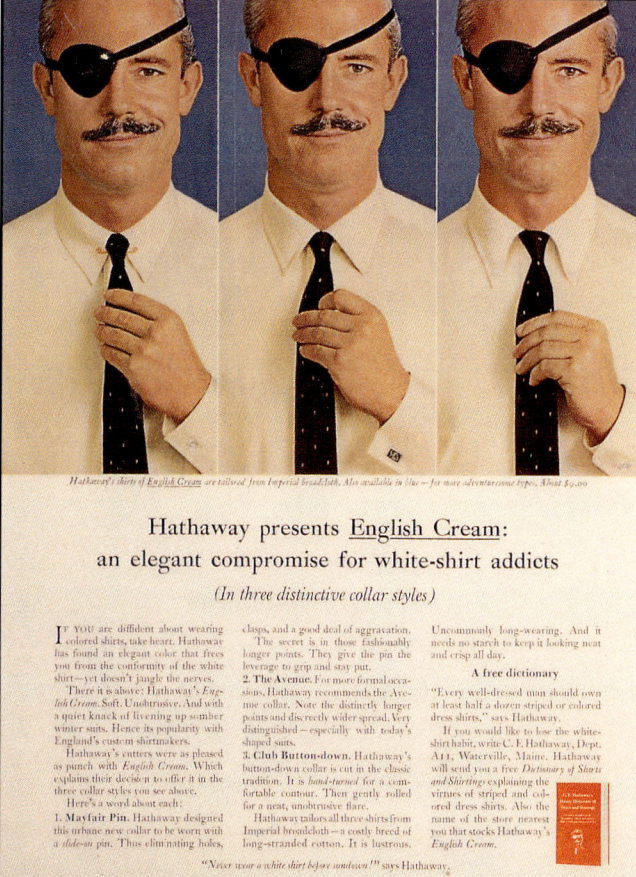

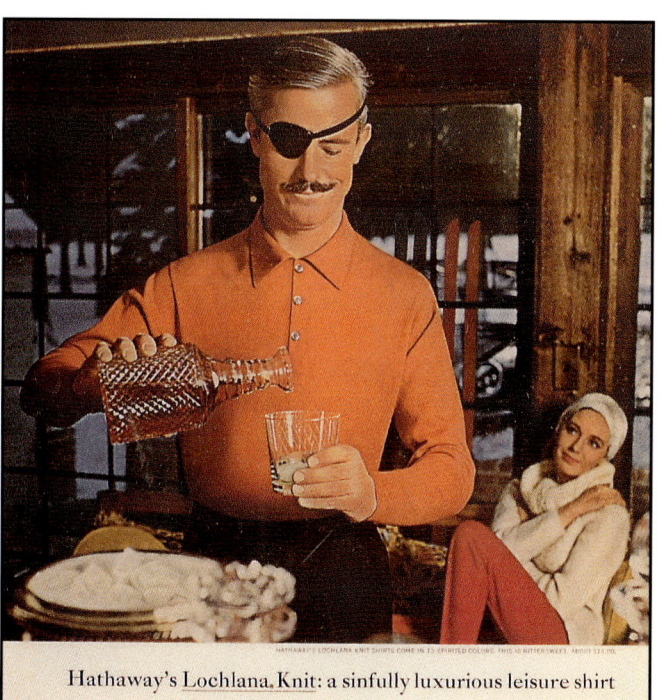

This page: 1965. Above left, $18–20. Below left, $20–22. Above, $20–22.

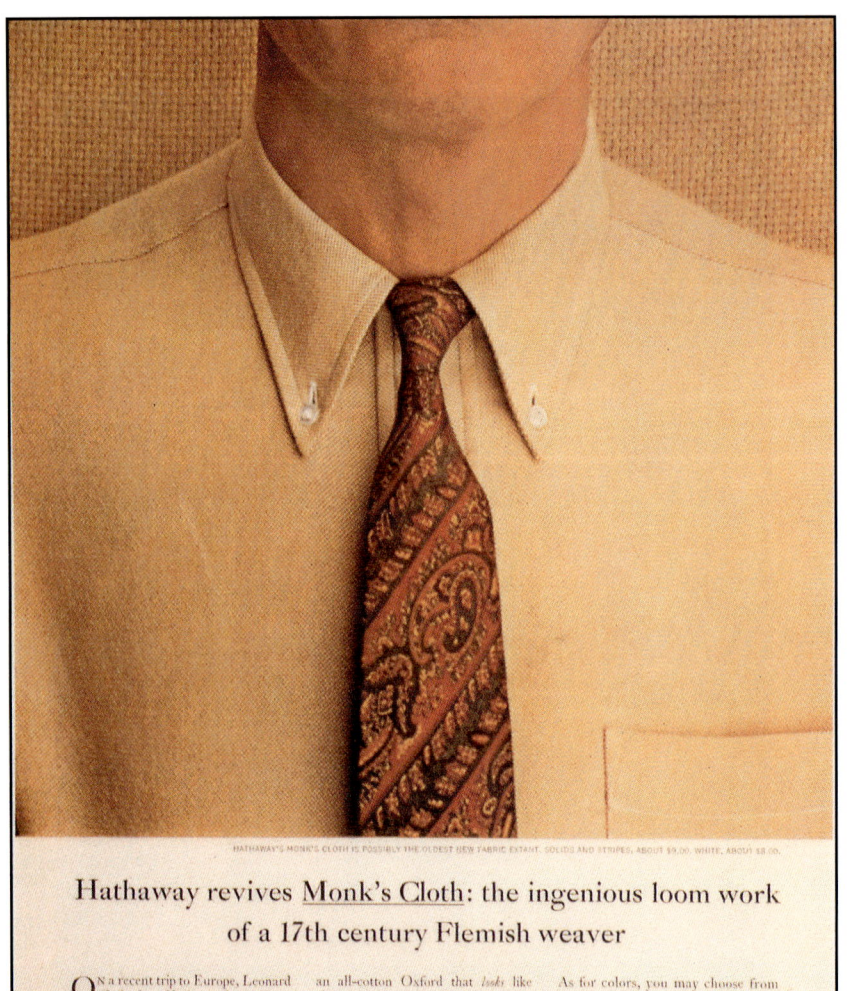

Left: 1965. Monk's Cloth, discovered in Europe by Hathaway's new president, Leonard Saulter, this 17th century Flemish weave was reproduced for a soft loose Oxford weave. $15–18.

Lower left: 1965. Lochlana. $24–28.

Lower right: 1965. Club Oxford. $15–18.

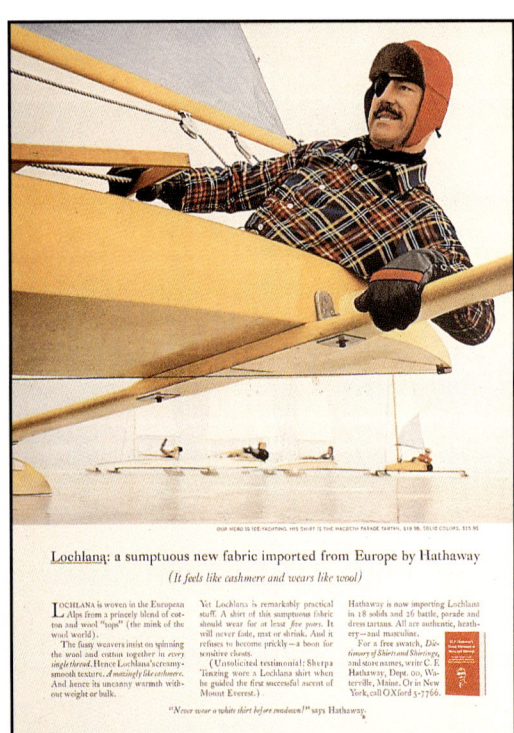

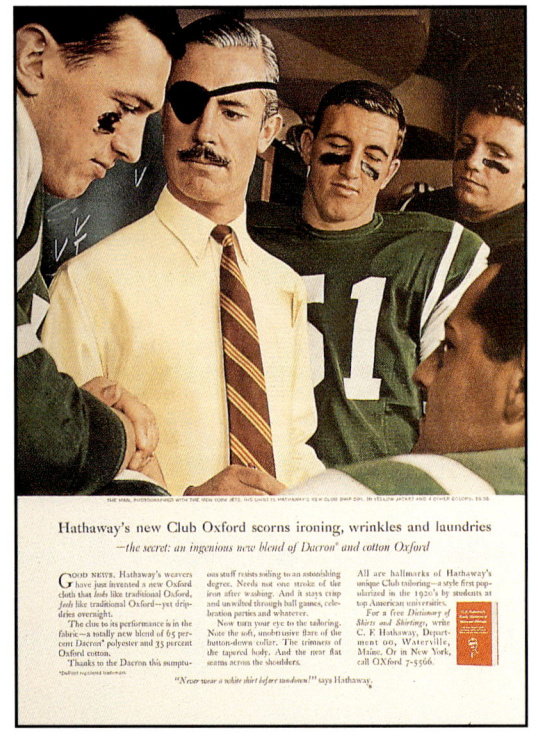

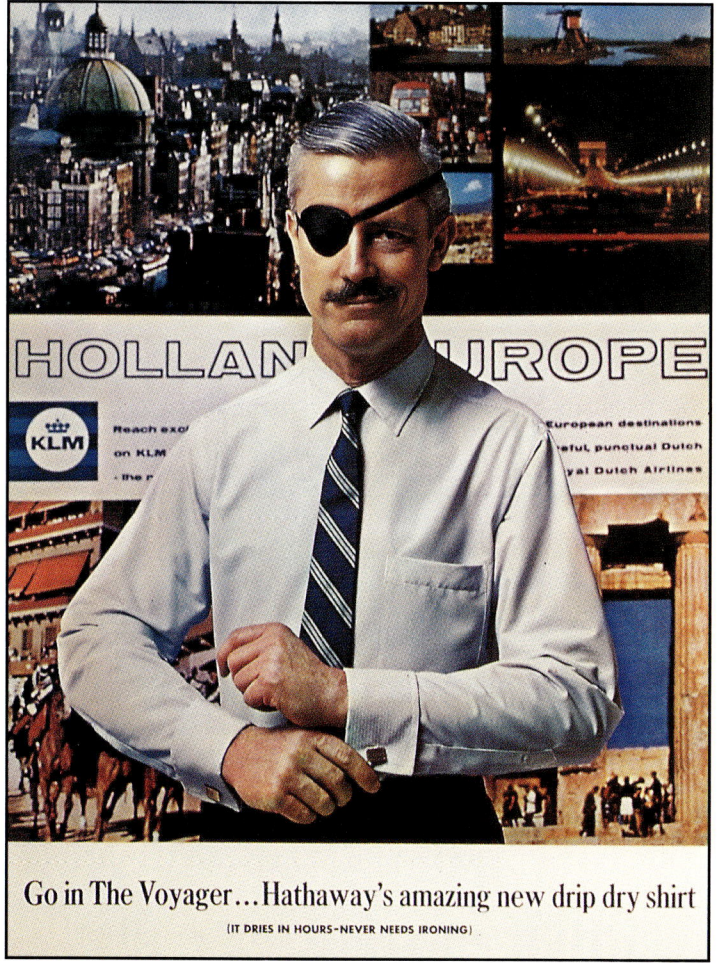

1965. $15–18.

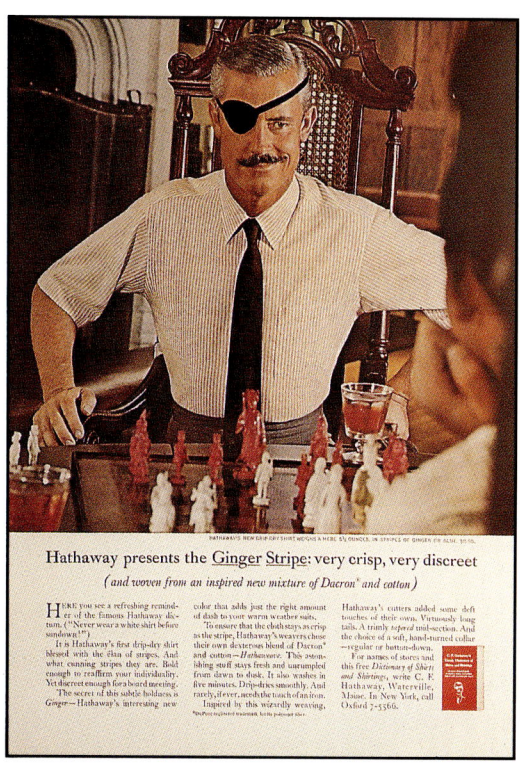

1965. Ginger Stripe. $15–18.

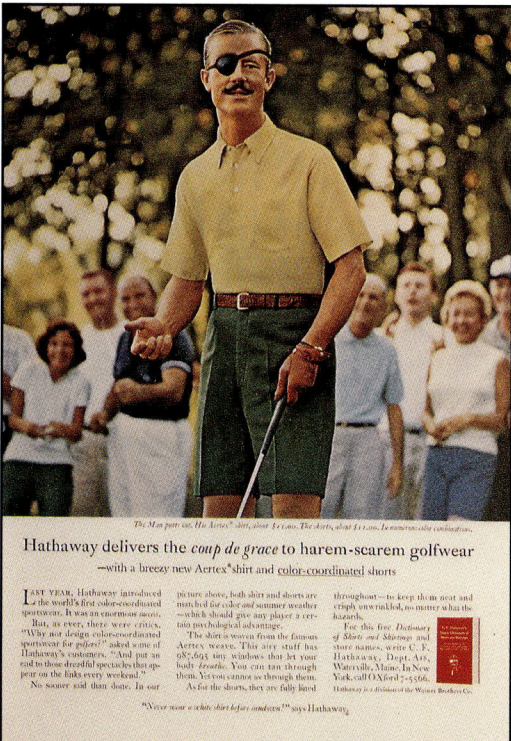

1966. Moving forward from coordinated sportswear, Hathaway introduces coordinated golf wear. $15–18.

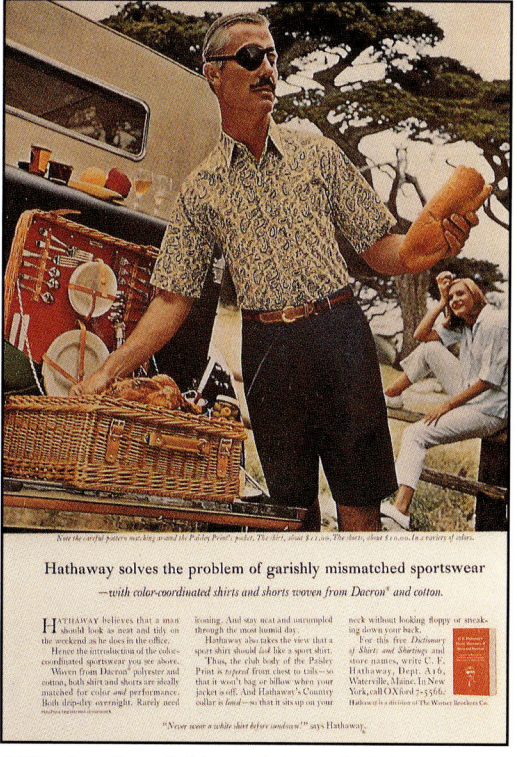

1966. Coordinated shirts and shorts. $20–22.

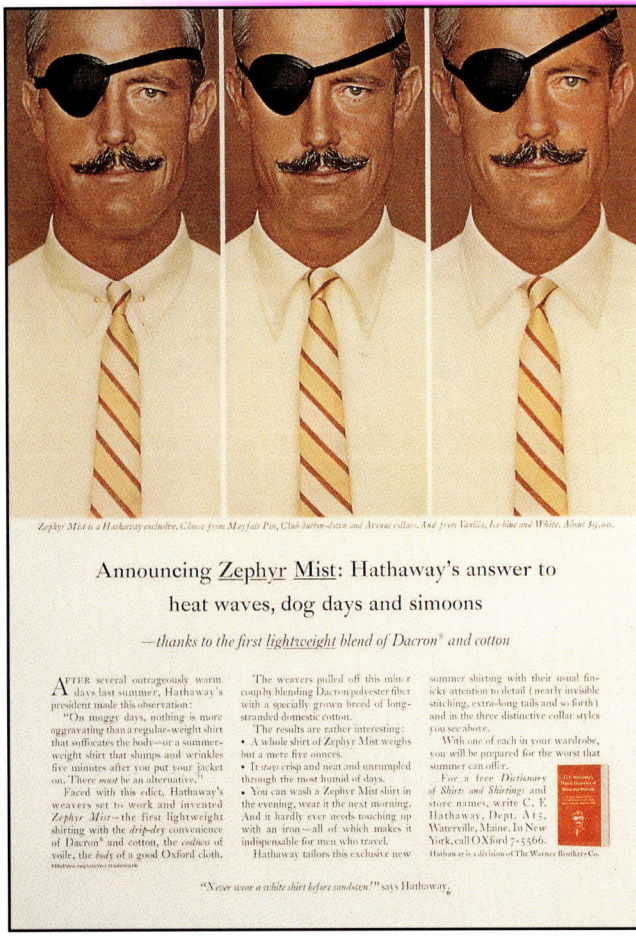

1966. Announcing Zephyr Mista lightweight shirting blend of Dacron and cotton. $15–18.

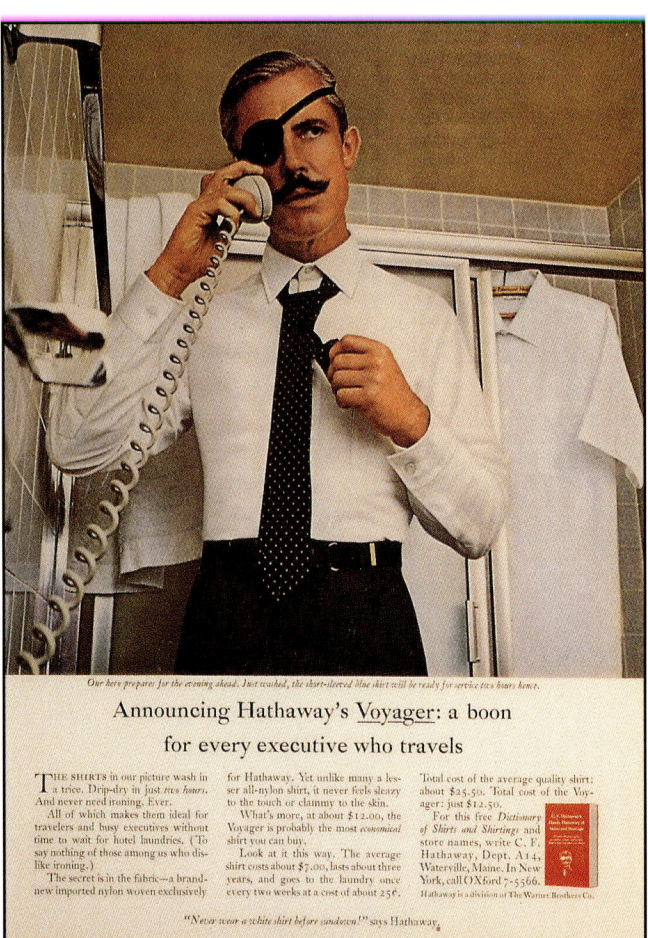

1966. Voyager was a comfortable nylon shirt designed for travelers. It would be washed and dried in 2 hours. $15–18.

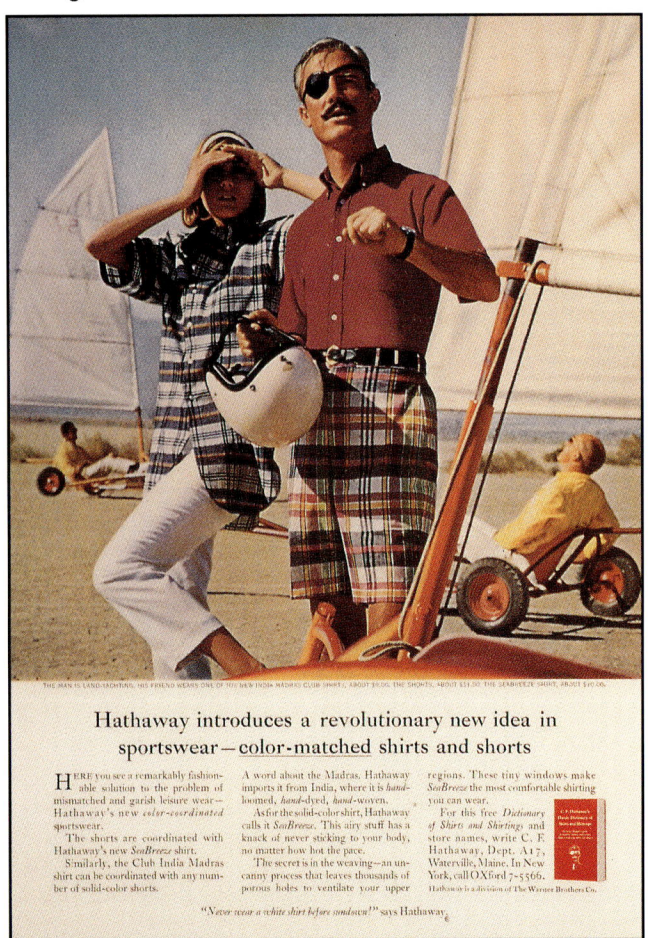

1966. Color matched shirts and shorts. $20–22.

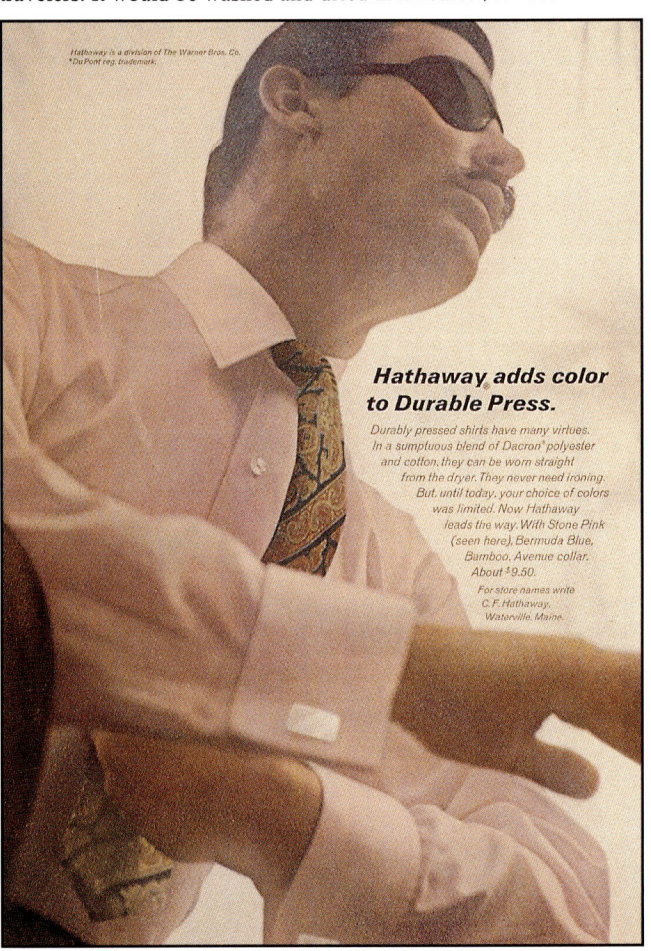

1966. The same Hathaway man but a new look in these late 1966 advertisements. $20–22.

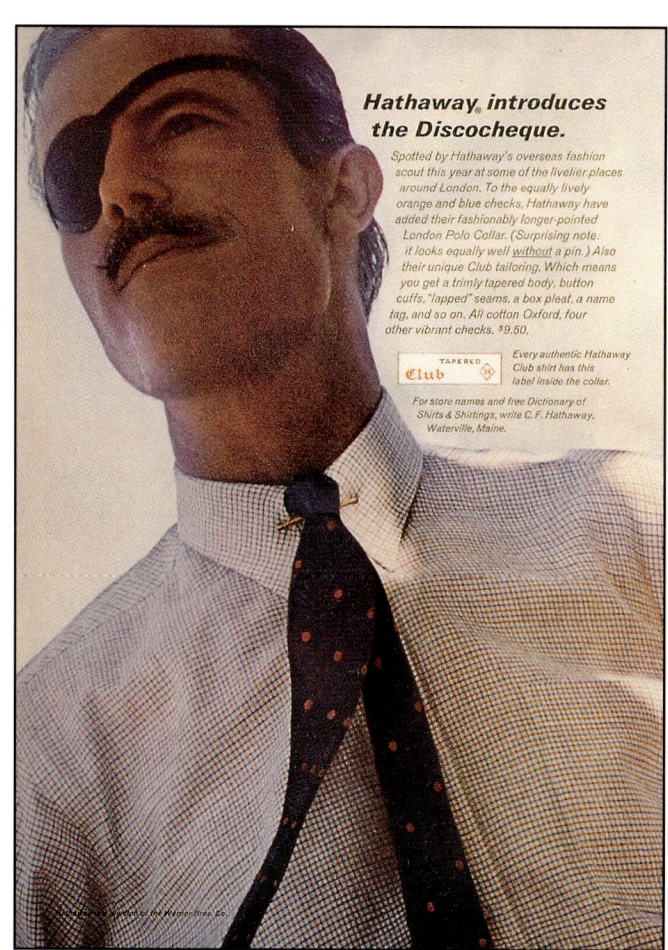

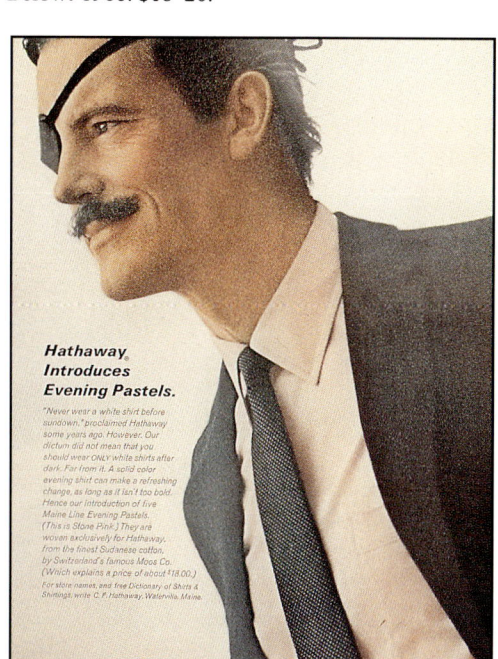

Left: 1966. $18–20.

Below: 1966. $18–20.

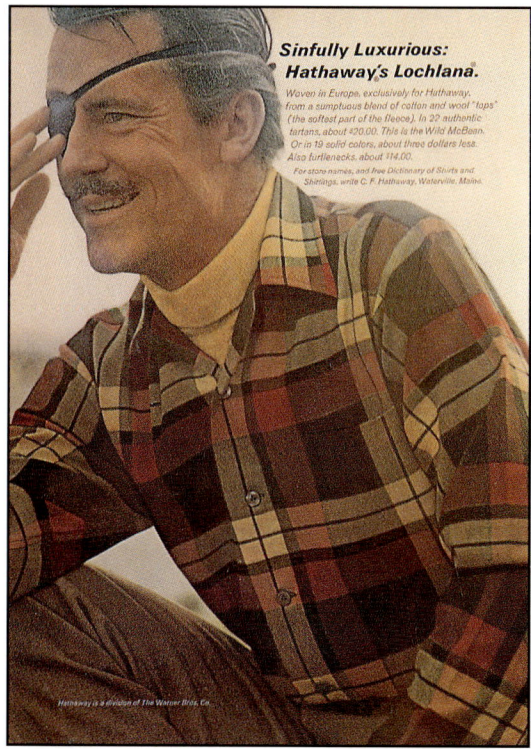

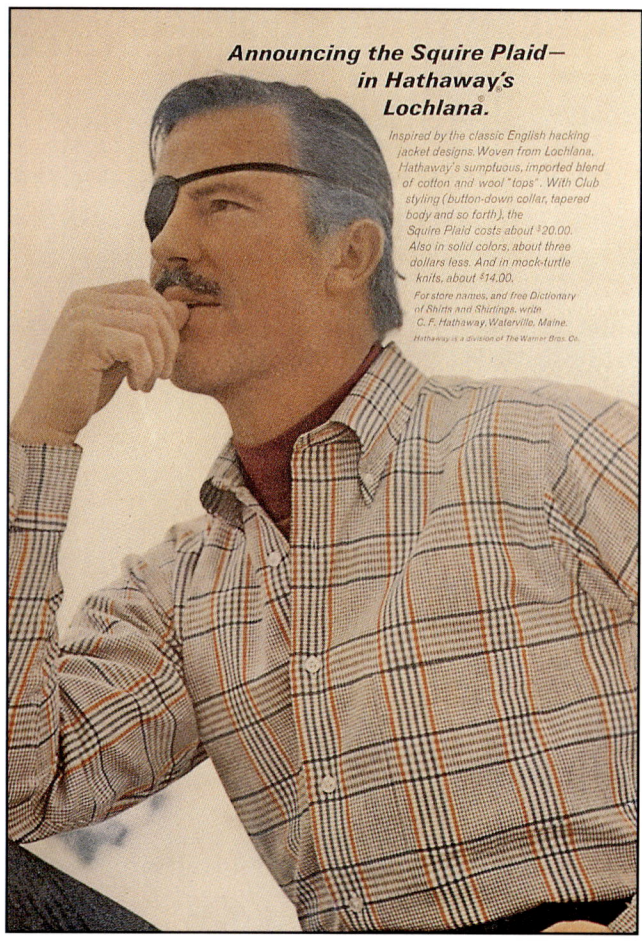

Above: 1966. $24–28.

Right: 1966. $22–24.

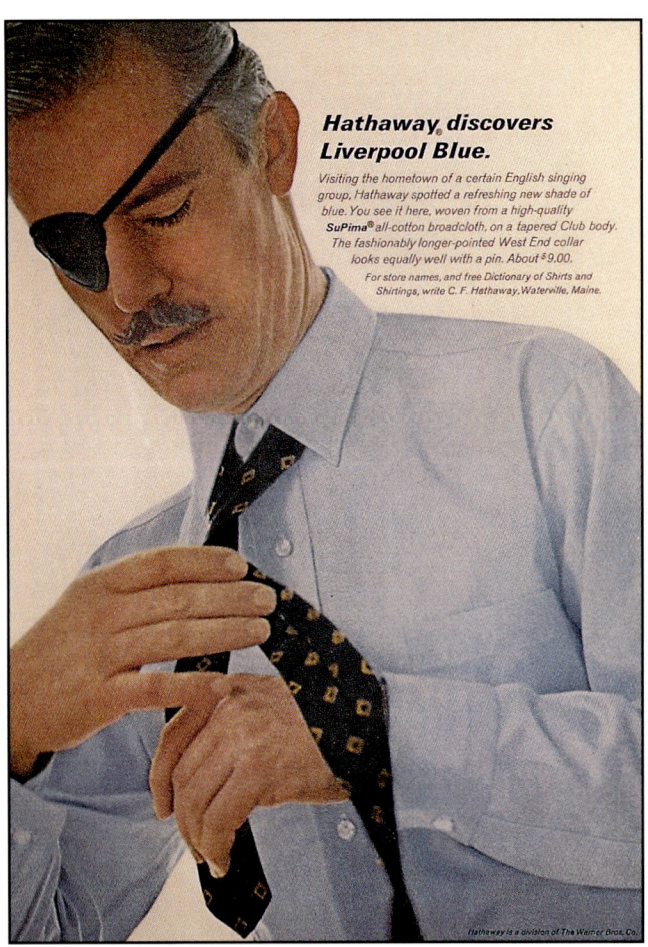

Left: 1966. $18–20.

Below: 1966. One of 11 designs for Hathaway from Britain's Donald Davies, hand loomed in Australian wool at his estate. $18–20.

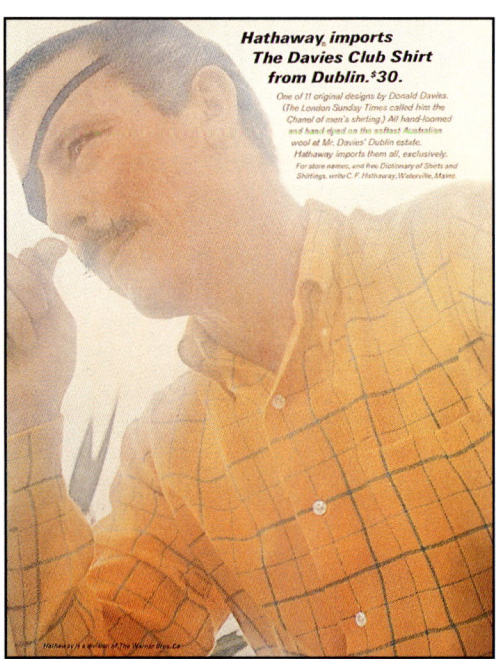

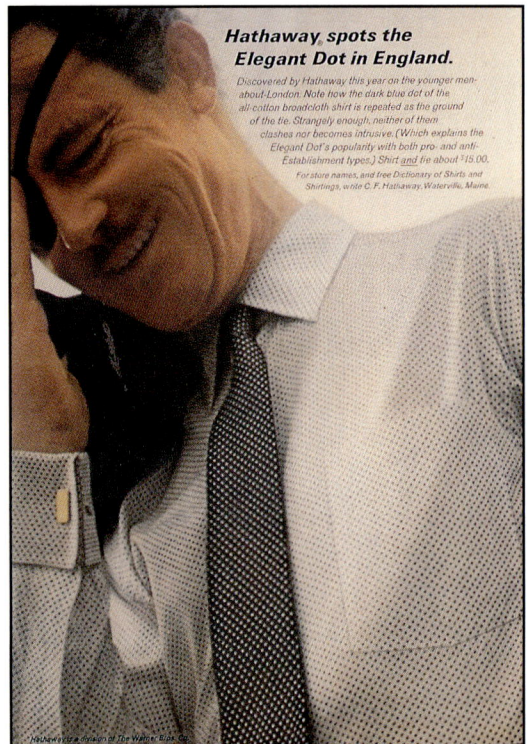

Above: 1966. $15–18.

Right: 1966. $22–24.

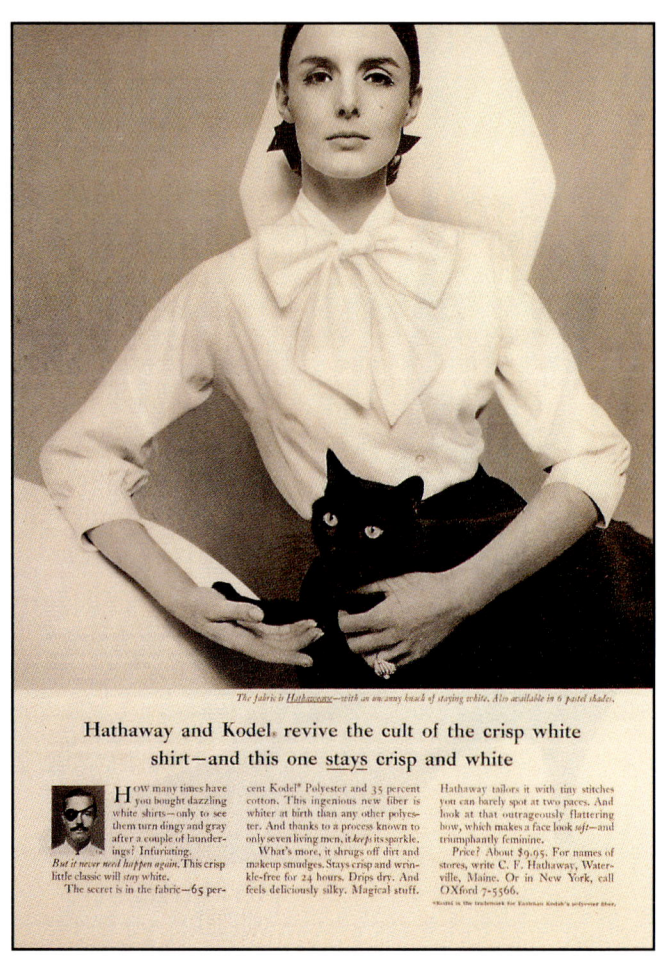

Right: 1967. Coordinated shirt and slacks, for more formal casual affairs. $18–20.

Lower left: 1967. A bit of the boldness in the late 60s shows in this lime green shirt with navy stripes. $18–20.

Lower right: 1967. A "more elegant" summer shirt. $18–20.

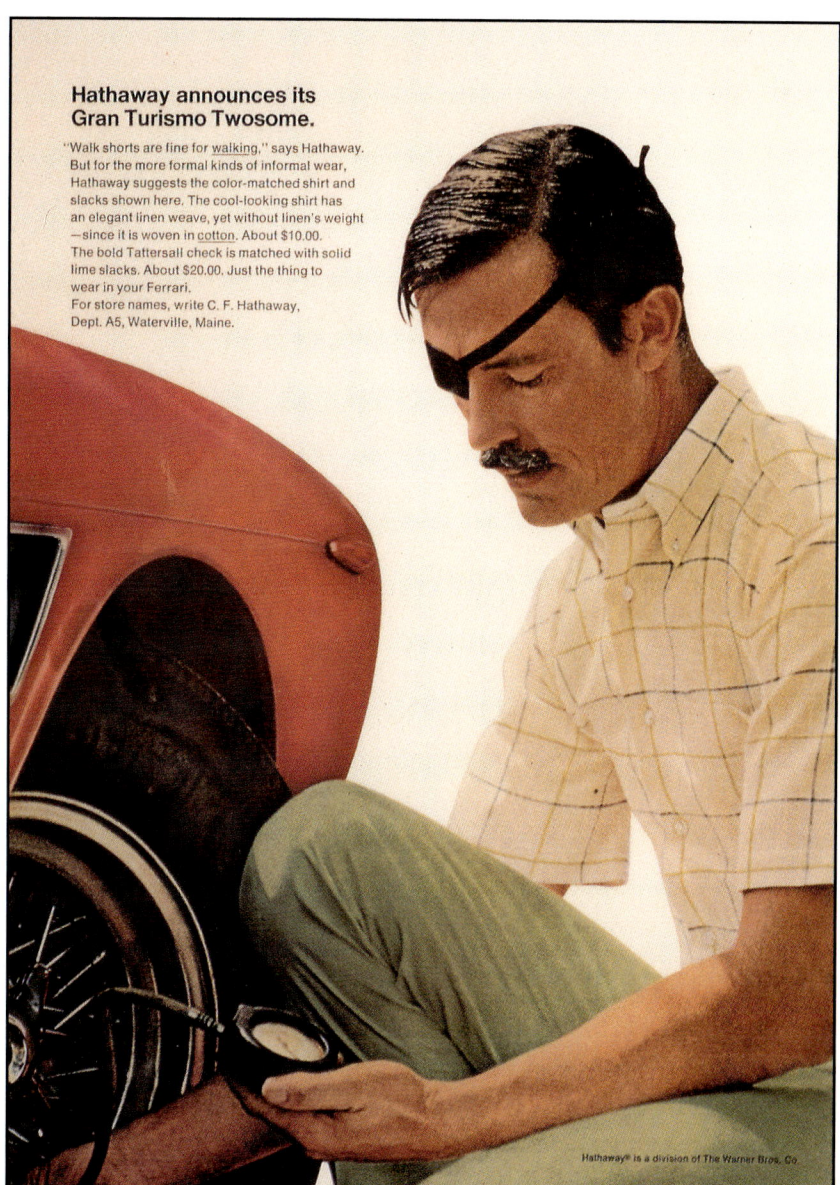

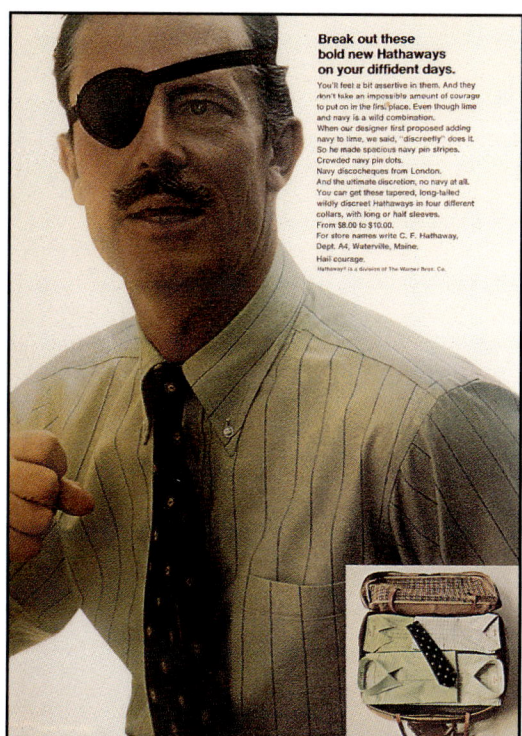

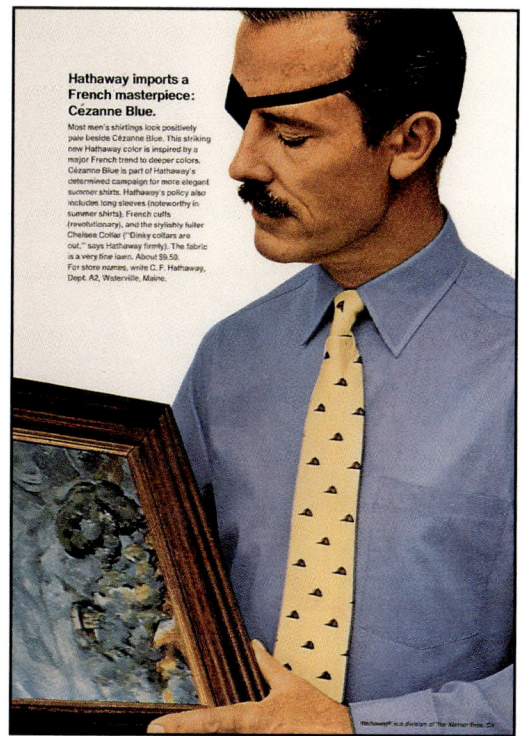

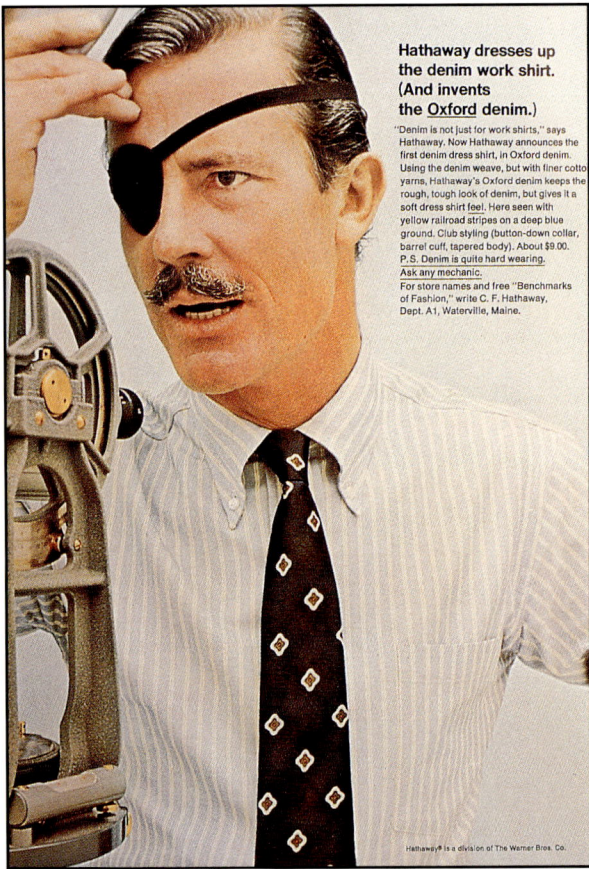

1967. A denim Oxford dress shirt. $18–20.

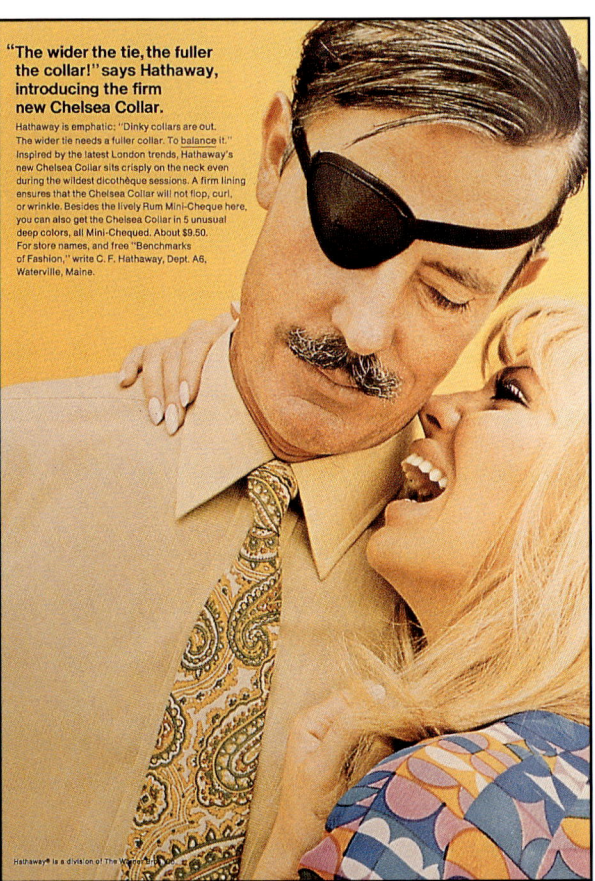

1967. The wider ties of the late 1960s required a wider collar, like this *Chelsea*. "Dinky collars are out." $15–18.

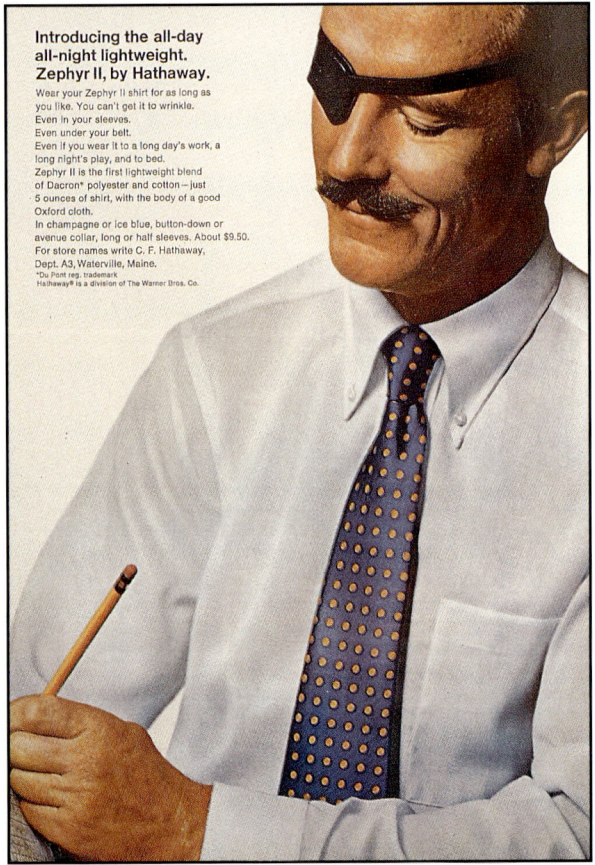

1967. Following the introduction of Zephyr Mist in 1966, Hathaway introduces Zephyr II. While there may have been some improvements, it is not clear from the ad copy what they were. $15–18.

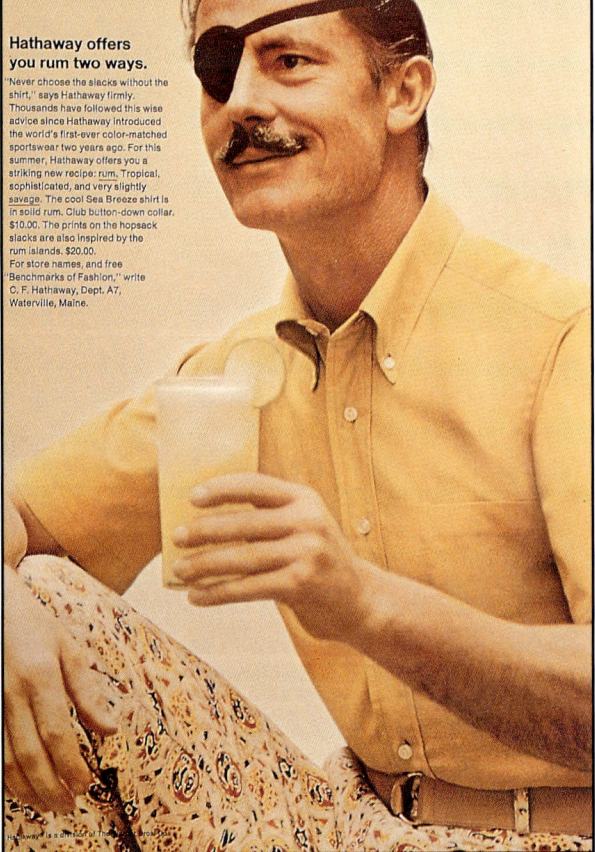

1967. Coordinated shirt and slacks in rum tones. $15–18.

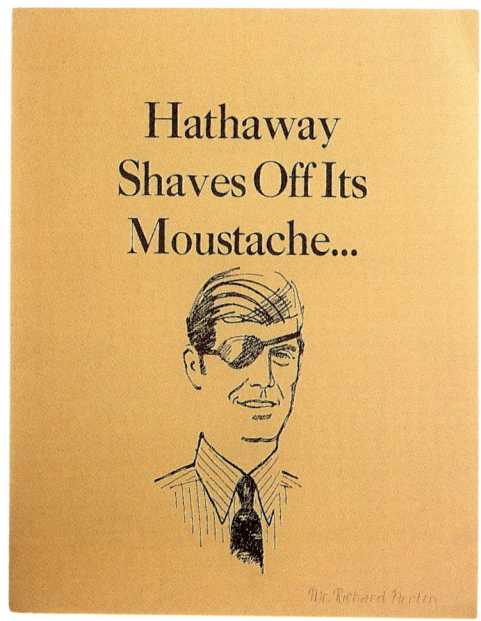

Left: 1967. Looking to appeal to a younger consumer, late 1967 brought the introduction of a new Hathaway man, younger and *sans moustache*. He was billed as elegant enough to hold on to older customers, yet with "the kind of vigor that will extend" as far as college campuses.

Below: 1967. Unlike his two predecessors, Wrangell and Fox, this third Hathaway man is a professional model. He is wearing an Oxford Tweed dress shirt. $18–20.

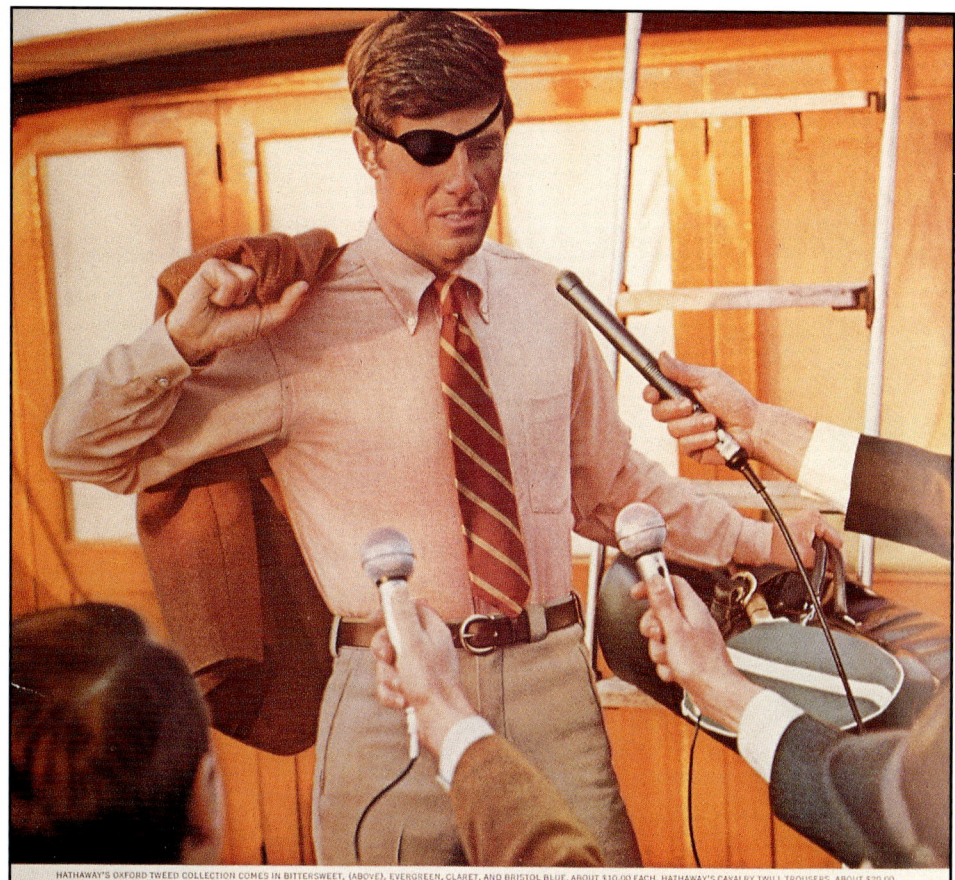

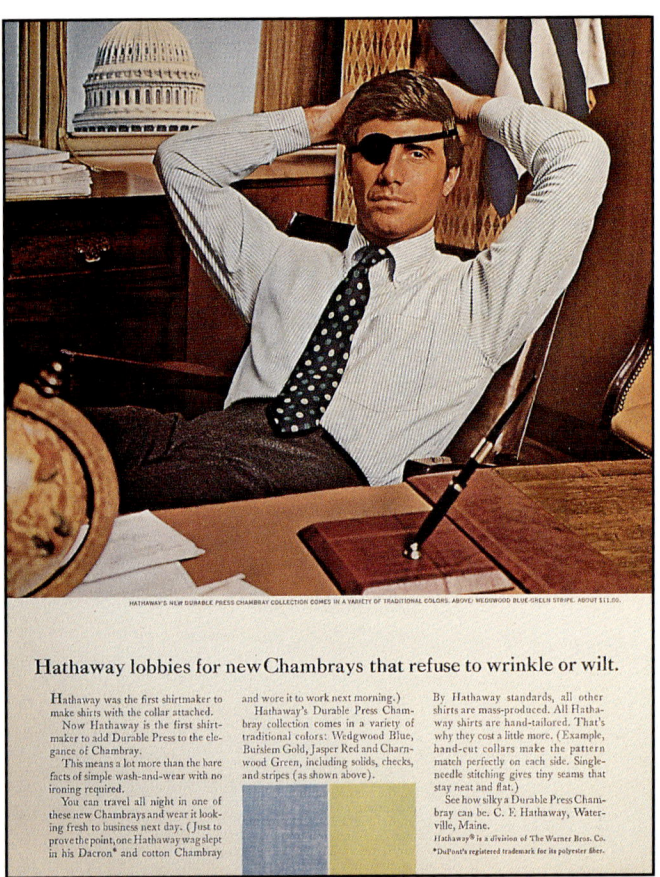

1967. A Dacron/cotton Chambray shirt. $18–20.

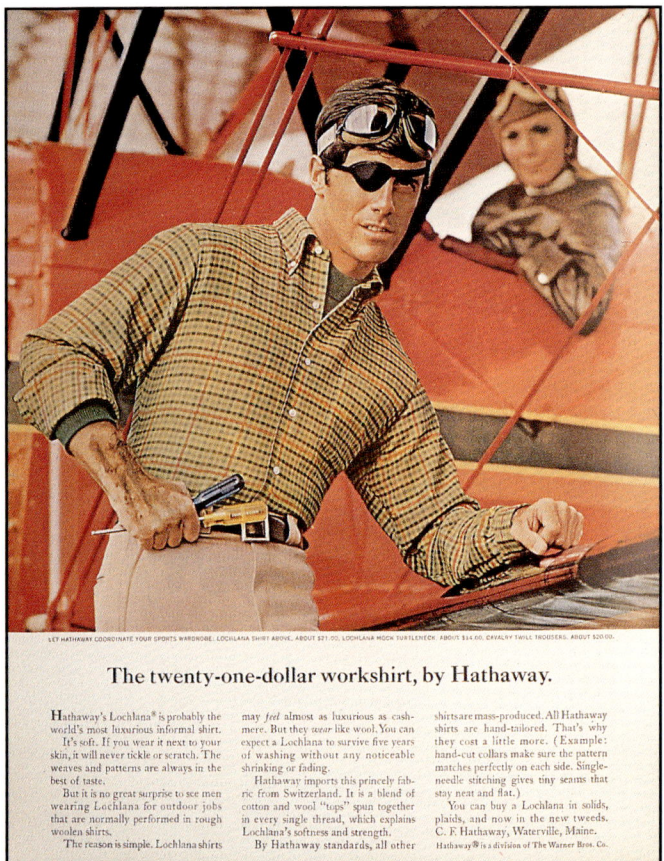

1967. Lochlana.

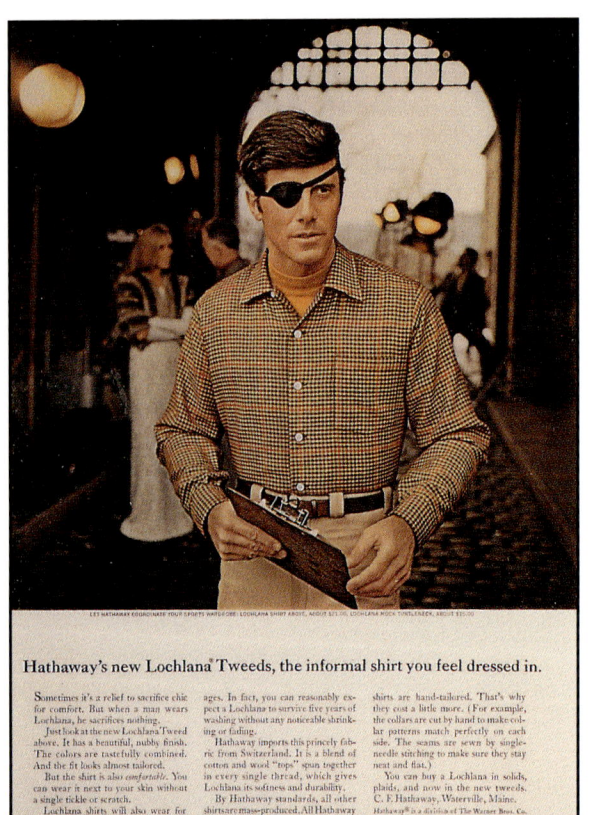

1967. New Lochlana tweeds. $24–28.

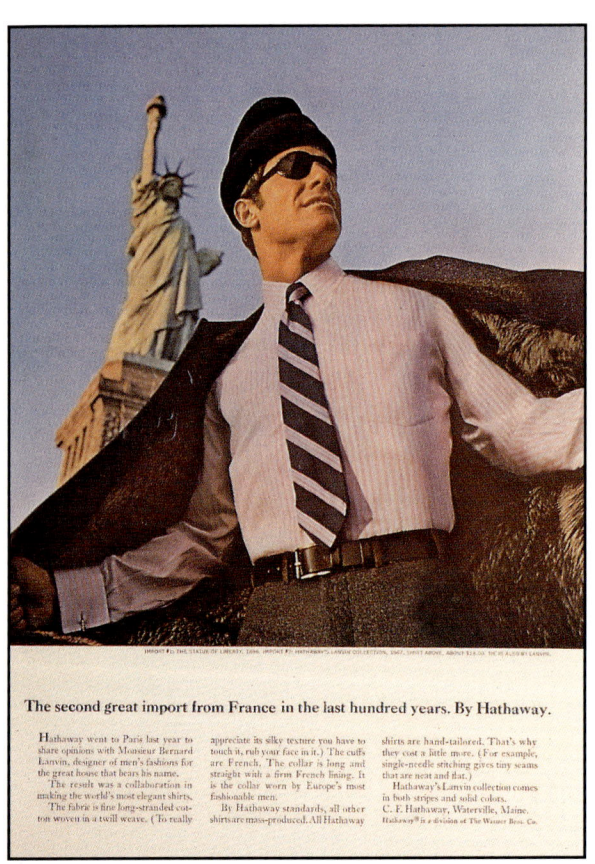

1967. Hathaway was licensed to make Lanvin shirts in 1966. Here is one of the first ads to celebrate that relationship. $20–22.

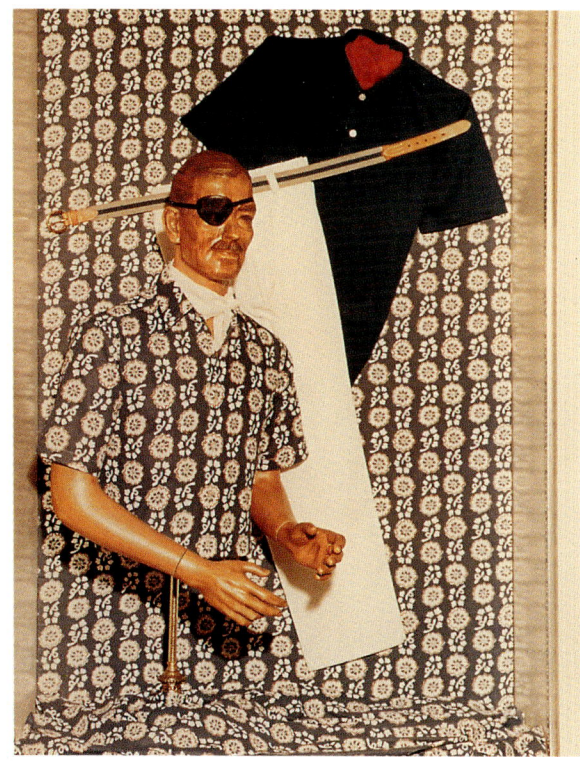
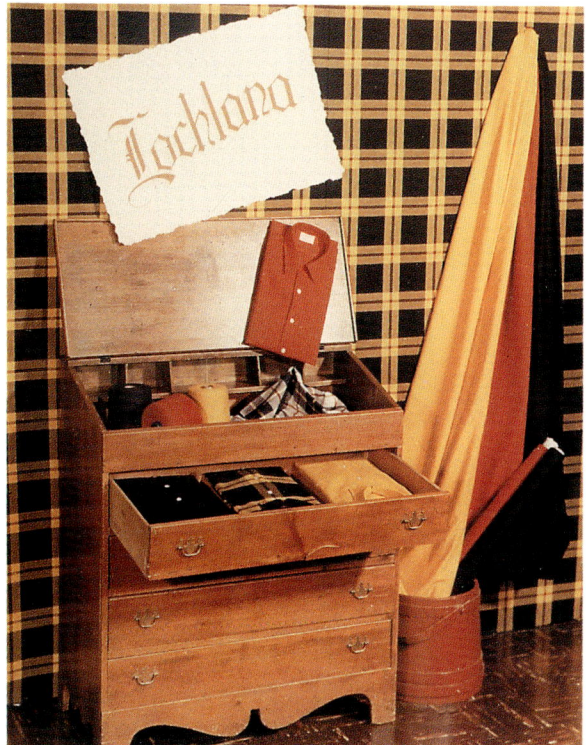

Above left: 1967. Store window display for coordinated Hathaway men's clothes. $28–30.

Above right: Late 1960s. Lochlana store display. $18–20.

Right: c. 1960s. This advertisement featuring a young Woody Allen was designed to appeal to younger consumers. Why did he wear Hathaway Club shirts in college? "I found they would hold more answers on the cuffs than any other kind."

Hathaway has a bizarre conversation with Woody Allen

Hathaway: Mr. Allen, when did you start wearing Hathaway Club shirts?

Allen: In college. I found they would hold more exam answers on the cuffs than any other kind.

Hathaway: You cheated in college?

Allen: Constantly. I wrote test answers on my sleeves. Sometimes, for a long test, on my entire shirt. Once, for three exams in a day, I had my parents buy me an all-white suit.

Hathaway: Well, to turn to other matters, did you know that every Hathaway Club shirt has a tapered midsection?

Allen: No.

Hathaway: Do you think it's important?

Allen: Viewed in the overall scale of things? Vital.

Hathaway: Mr. Allen, this interview has turned out to be something of a bomb.

Allen: Sorry.

Hathaway: Isn't there *anything* nice you can say about our product?

Allen: Well, Mr. Hathaway, let me put it this way— I think it's a pussycat.

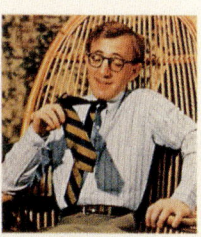

Hathaway Hallmarks
(Or what we hoped Woody Allen would mention)

1. *A tag for your name:* Sewn on the shirt tail of every Hathaway Club Shirt.
2. *Traditional button-down collar:* Hand-turned for a soft, comfortable roll and a casual flare.
3. *Tapered body:* Hathaway trimly tapers each and every Club shirt, so it won't bag, billow, and bulge over your waistband.
4. *Perfect pattern matching of* pockets, fronts and collars: Ordinarily found only on custom-made shirts. Reason: it costs more.
5. *The Red "H":* Found where the front tail meets the back— but only when the shirt passes 18 inspections.
6. *Three-hole buttons:* Used exclusively by Hathaway. It is much stronger than the four-hole kind. (Euclid knows why.)

Hear more of Woody Allen on Colpix's Woody Allen Volume 2. His shirt, incidentally, is one of Hathaway's new Club Ocean Stripes. $8.95.

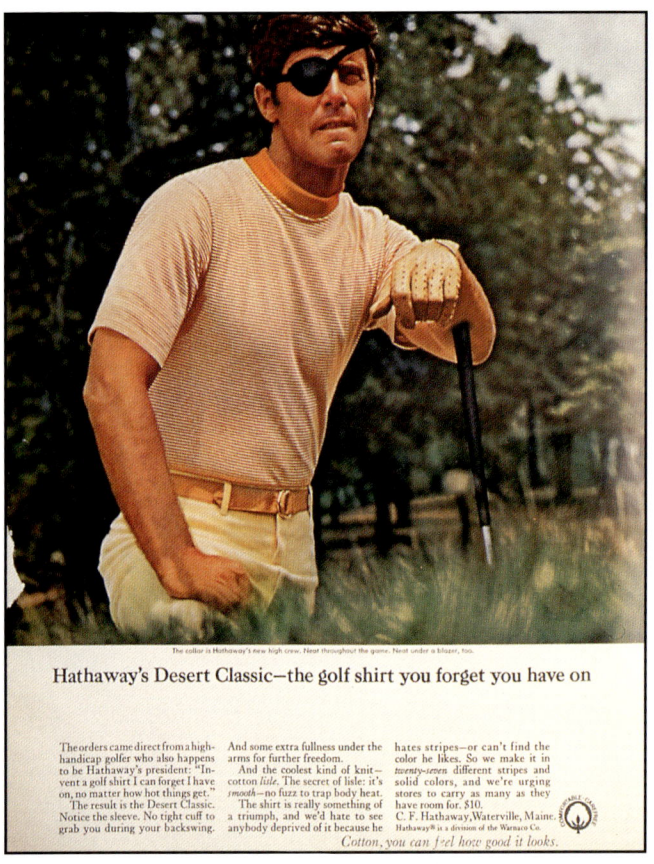

1968. Desert Classic golf shirt. $15–18.

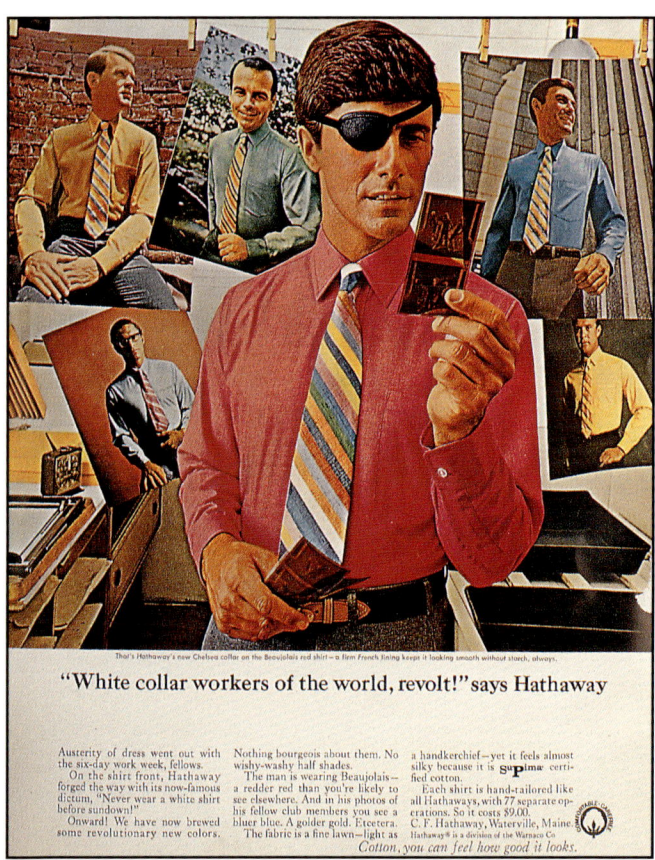

1968. Beaujolais red shirt with Chelsea collar. $18–20.

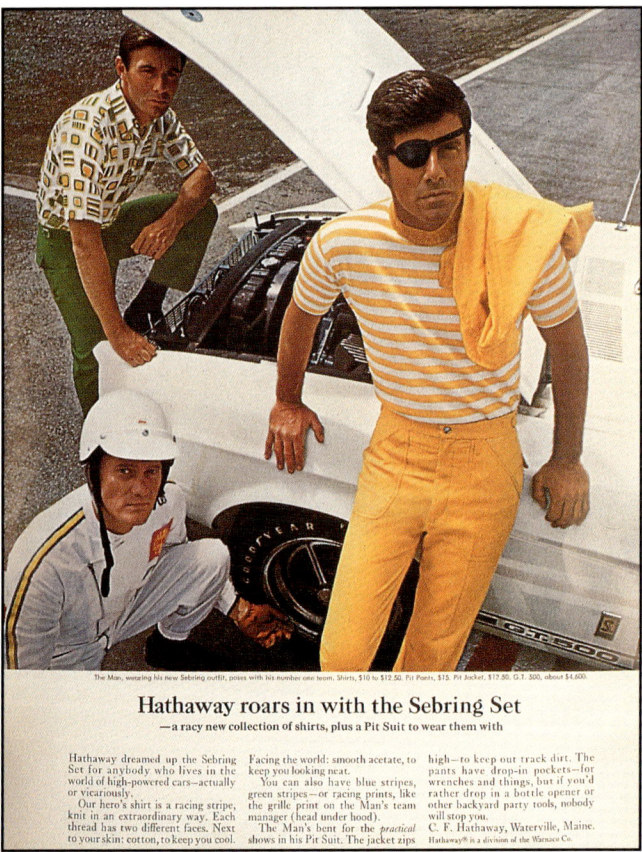

1968. A Sebring ensemble, featuring a shirt, pants, and a zipper jacket. $18–20.

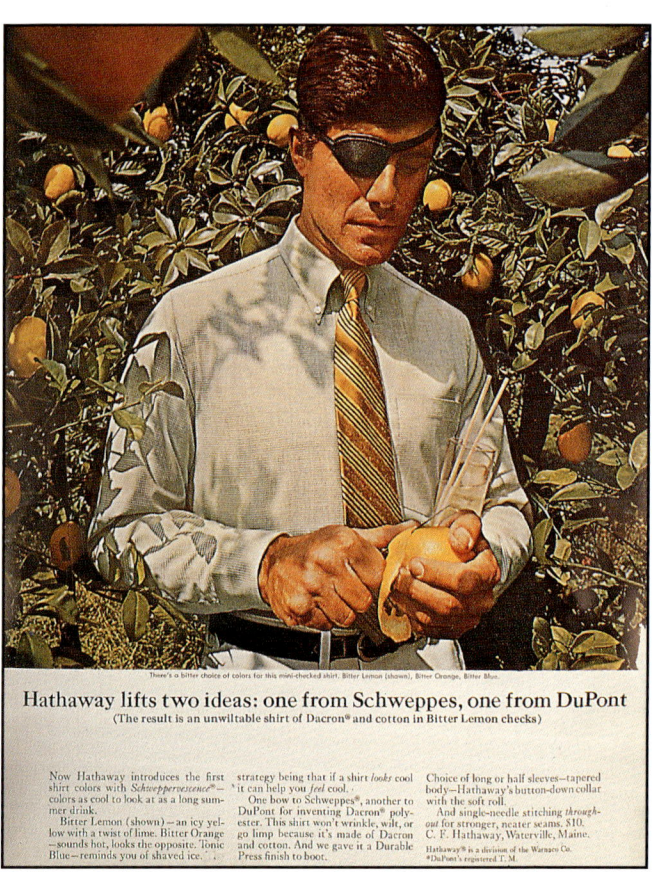

1968. Cooperative advertising for Hathaway and Schweppes. The colors offered are Bitter Lemon, Bitter Orange, and Tonic Blue. $15–18.

Right: 1968. A Jameson twill shirt advertised with John Jameson whisky. $18–20.

Lower left: 1968. Dacron-cotton dress shirts in mini-checks. $18–20.

Below right: 1968. Lochlana shirts with Lochlana turtlenecks, for a "layered look," the new fashion trend. $22–24.

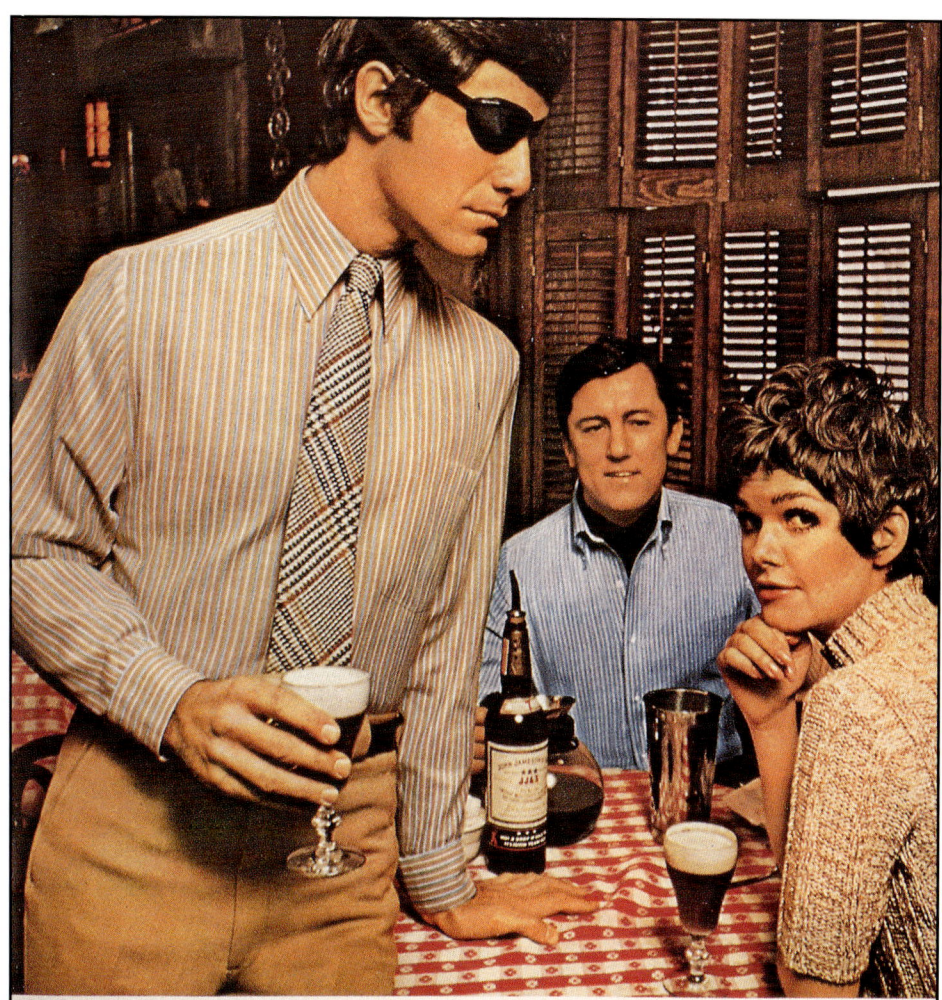

A remarkable fabric and a remarkable coincidence—from Hathaway

The first time Hathaway's scout saw this fabric, that unusually mellow shade of brown instantly reminded him of Irish coffee—the good drink made with John Jameson whisky. By an almost uncanny coincidence, the name of the fabric turned out to be Jameson twill.

It's a fine and closely woven cotton—very soft to the hand—but remarkably staunch stuff, as all twills are. We've had it made in stripes, tattersalls and miniature checks. Besides Irish coffee, colors include Kerry blue, Galway green, Cork gold.

Our hero's shirt has a London Polo collar. It stays neat all day because it has a firm inner lining to keep it smooth, without starch. The other fellow is wearing *two* Hathaways—a button-down over a knit—illustrating the popular "layered look."

About $10 each. For store names, write C. F. Hathaway in Waterville, Maine.

Hathaway

Cotton, you can feel how good it looks.

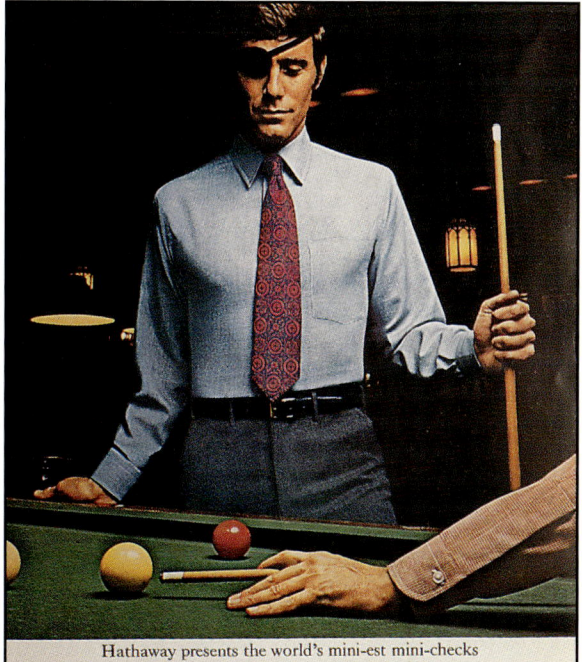

Hathaway presents the world's mini-est mini-checks
(Version H—made of Dacron® and cotton—with a Durable Press finish)

Hathaway introduced mini-checks for men two years ago. We seem to have started a rage. Here is our *fourth* version of the mini-check—and the smallest yet.

Above you see it close up in red. And in blue you see how it looks at a distance. Like a solid color but more interesting. It takes threads of four different colors to get this effect.

The wrinkle-resistant Dacron and cotton fabric means that your shirt ought to look morning-fresh all through the day and evening. The Durable Press finish means it positively *will*. The collar is Hathaway's Chelsea, just in from London.

This shirt, like every Hathaway shirt, is hand-tailored. So it costs about $11. For store names, write C. F. Hathaway, Waterville, Me.

Hathaway

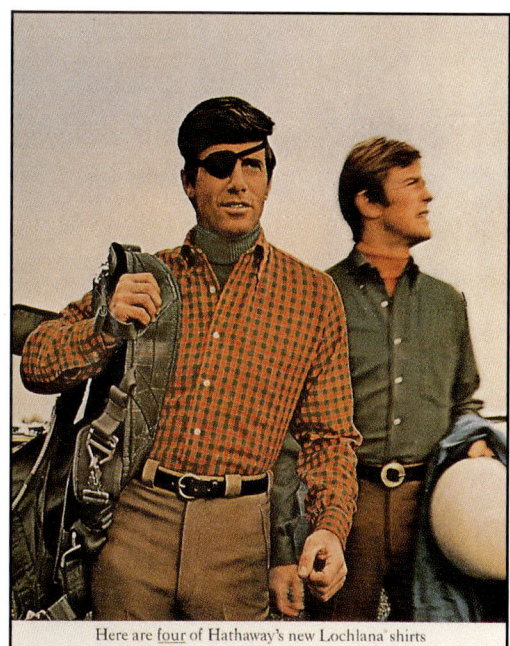

Here are *four* of Hathaway's new Lochlana shirts

The Man and his pilot are wearing four Lochlana shirts between them. This illustrates what young fashion-setters call "the layered look"—an idea that's growing more popular by the hour.

It also shows a few of the many styles in which Hathaway is now making its wonderfully soft Lochlana shirts. Heather-toned turtlenecks, button-downs in big bonnie checks and subtler solids. And of course we still make Lochlanas with the traditional sport shirt collar, and in many familiar plaids.

Lochlana is woven for Hathaway in Switzerland of 50% wool and 50% cotton, so it's warm without being bulky. And washable. Lochlana *mellows* with each washing.

Hathaway are still hand-tailors its shirts. These button-downs are $23 in checks, $18 in solid colors. The turtlenecks are $13. For stores, write C. F. Hathaway, Waterville, Maine.

Hathaway

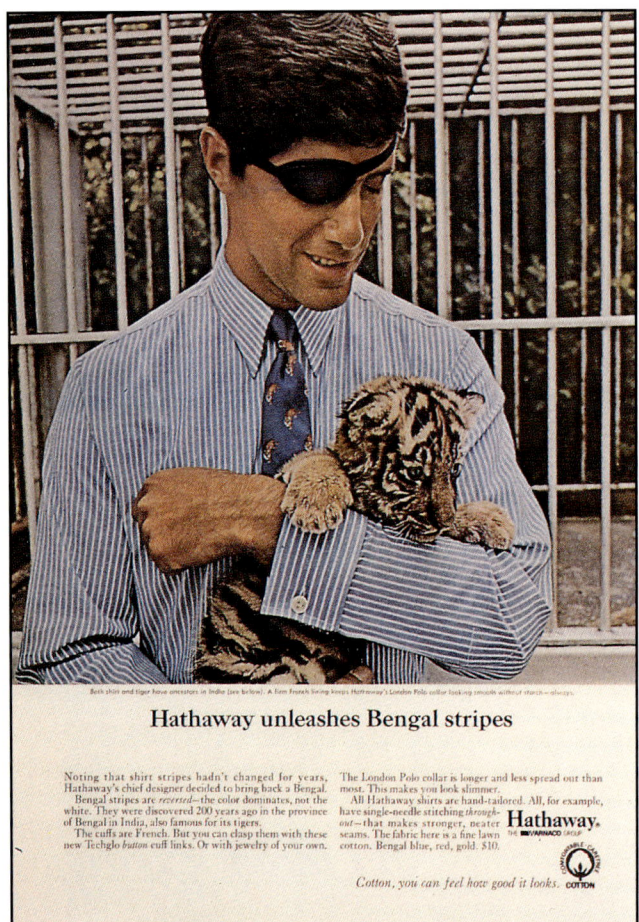

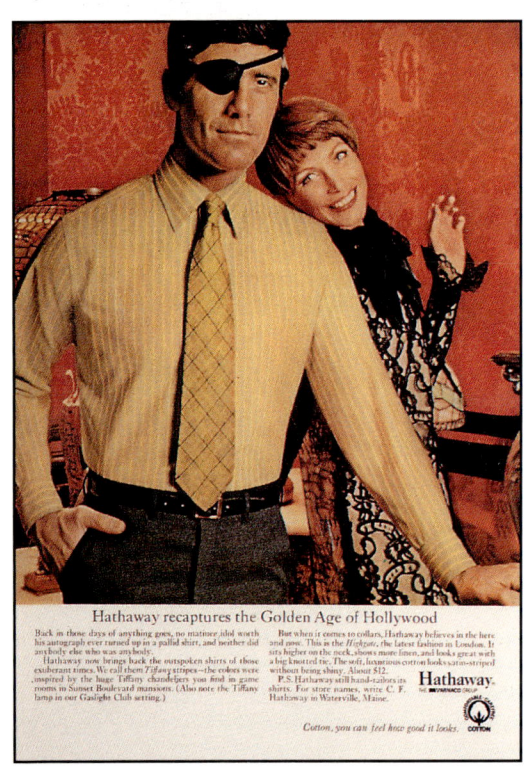

Left: 1968. $20–22.

Below: 1968. A Highgate collar and Tiffany stripes. $18–20.

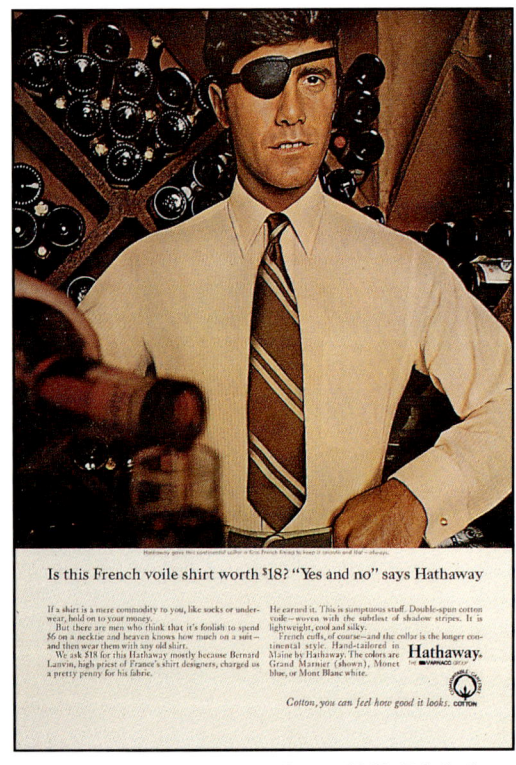

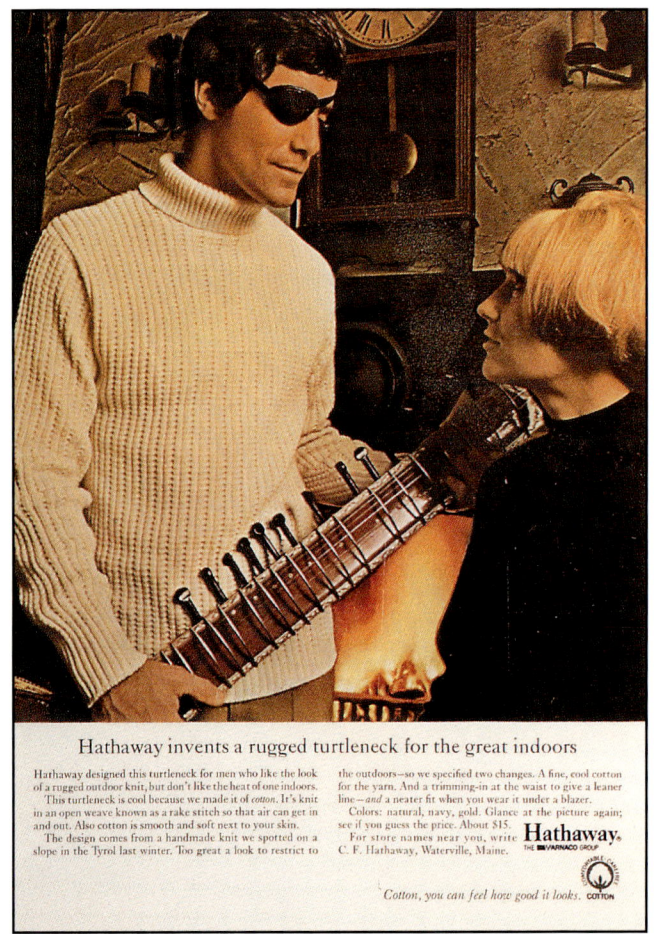

Above: 1968. Fabric from Bernhard Lanvin. $15–18.

Right: 1968. A cotton turtleneck sweater. $28–30.

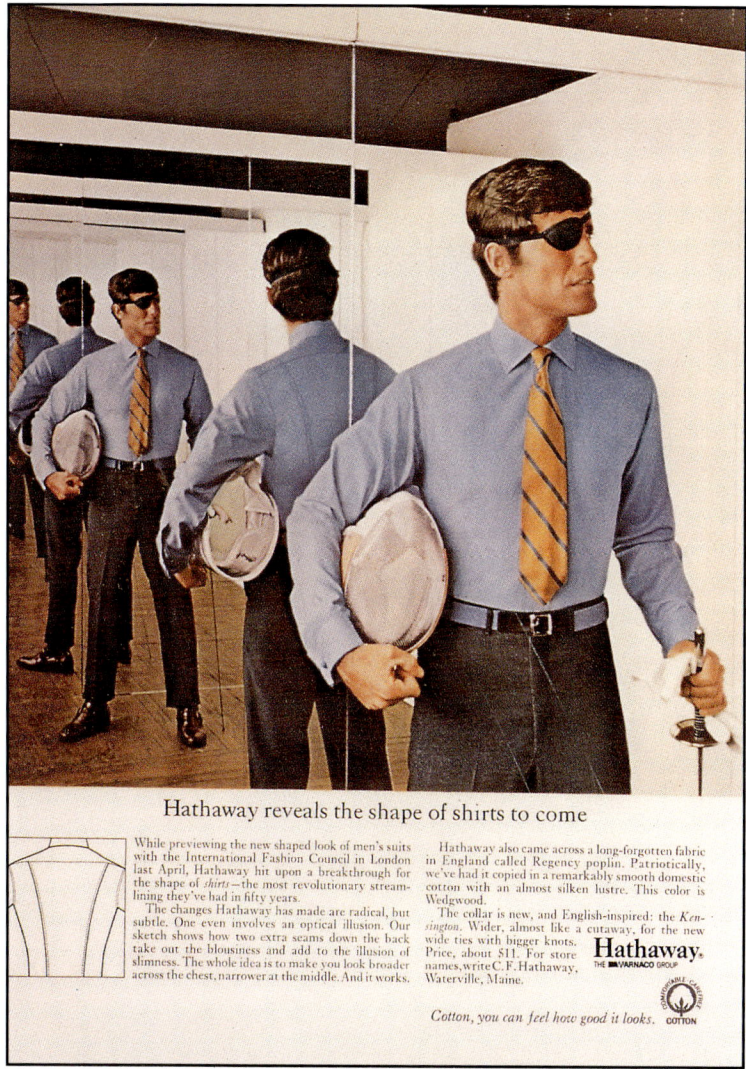

1968. A Kensington collar on a new fitted design, using two extra seams in the back to take out blousiness. $15–18.

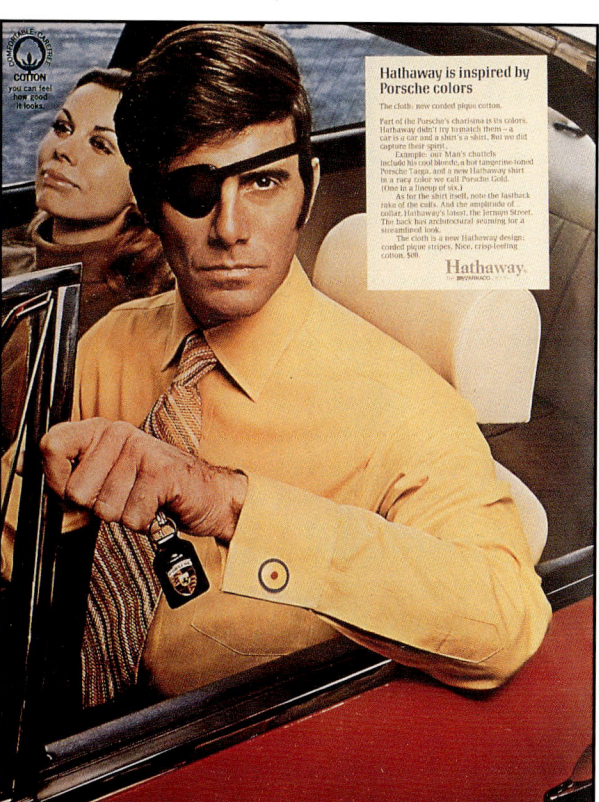

1969. Another tie-in with a recognized name is this Porsche connection. The color of the corded cotton shirt is Porsche gold, meant to complement the color of the car. $22–24.

Right: 1969. A cotton shirt with stripes in the color of Cherry Heering. $18–20.

Far right: 1969. $18–20.

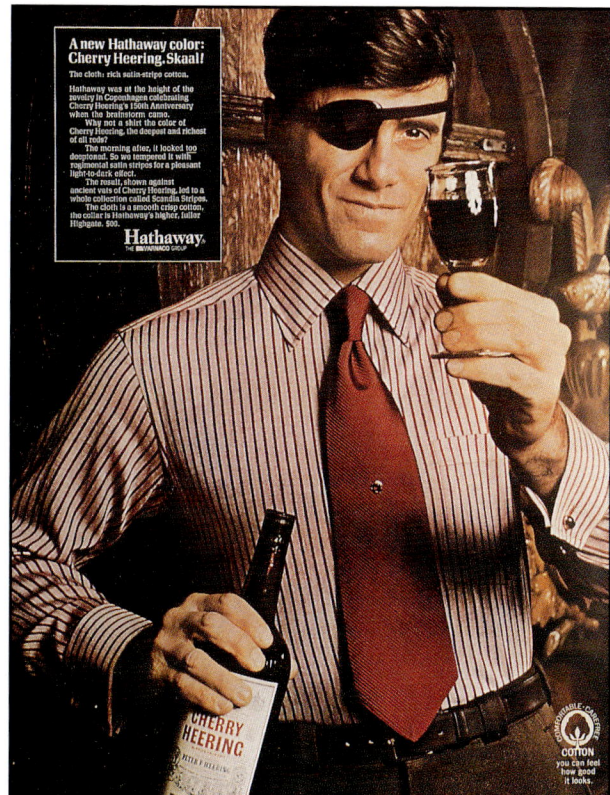

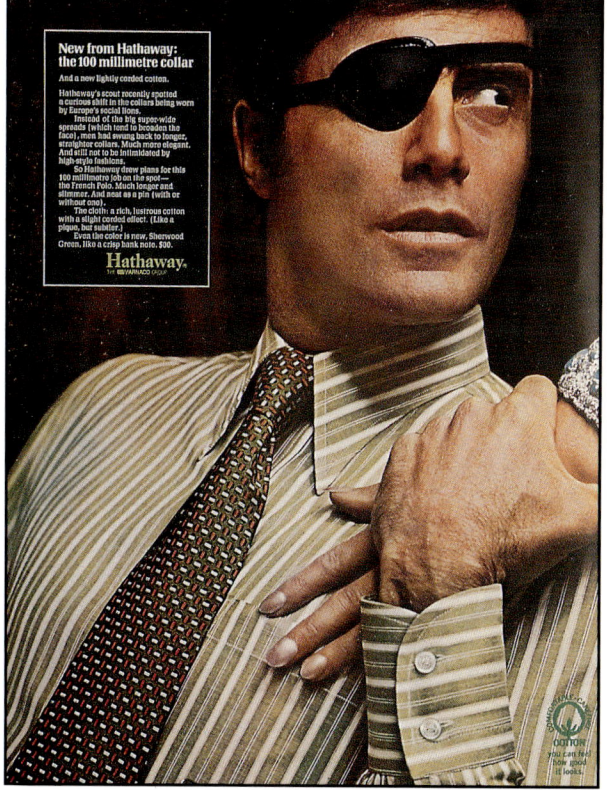

79

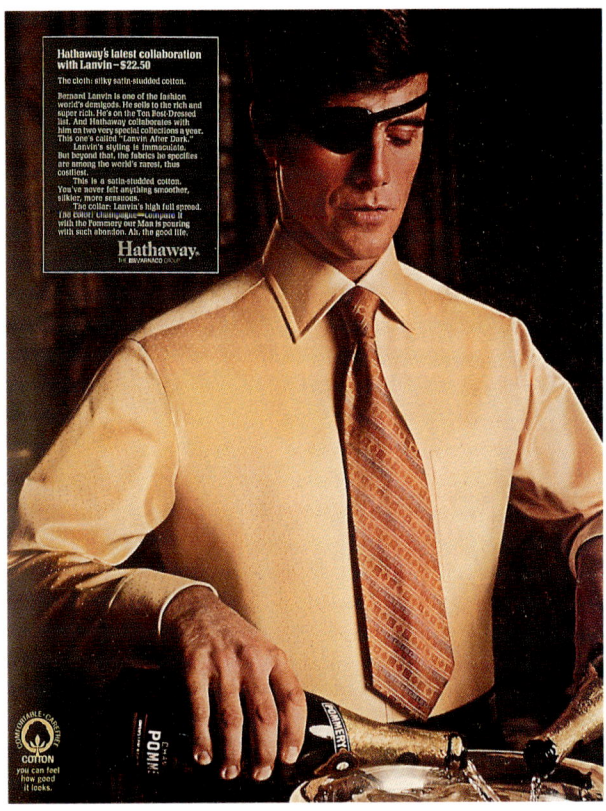

1969. One of the Lanvin After Dark shirts. $18–20.

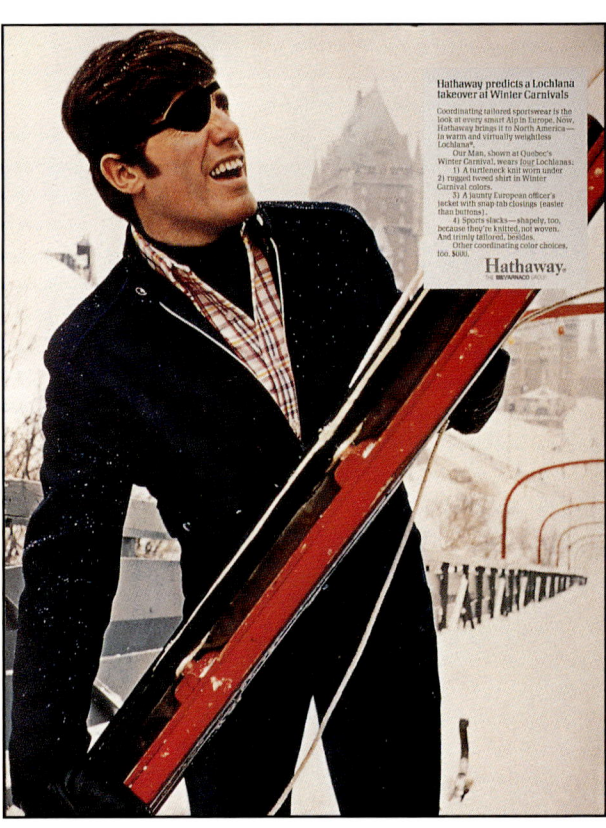

1969. Lochlana in four forms: turtleneck, shirt, jacket, and slacks. $20–22.

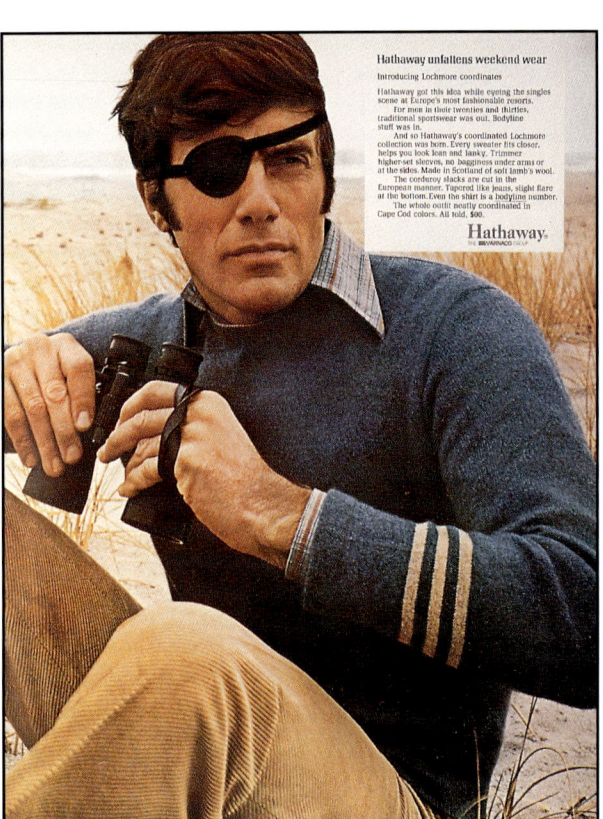

1969. Lochmore coordinates, Bodyline shirt, sweater, and corduroy slacks. $20–22.

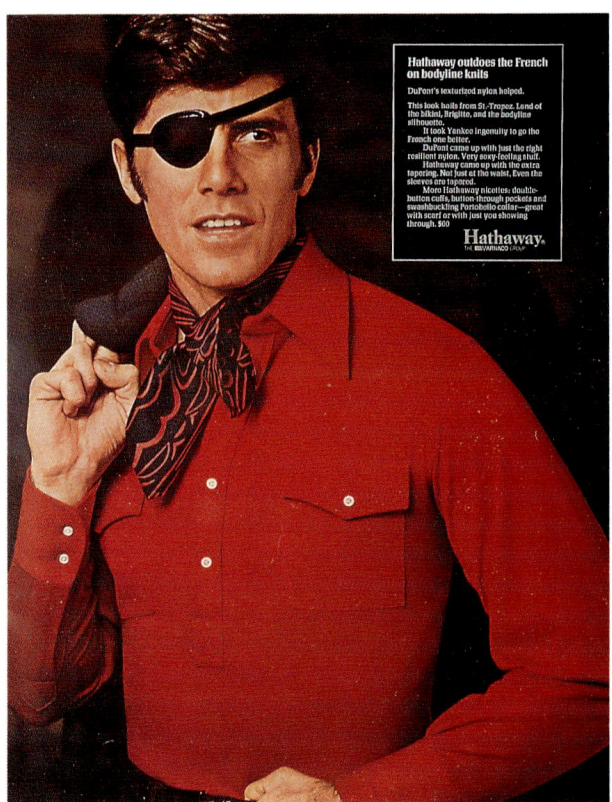

1969. Bodyline shirt of nylon. $20–22.

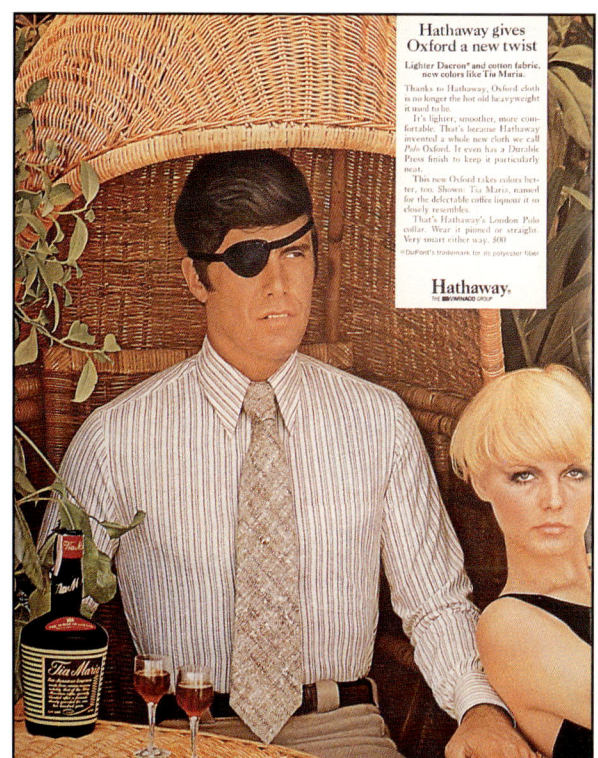
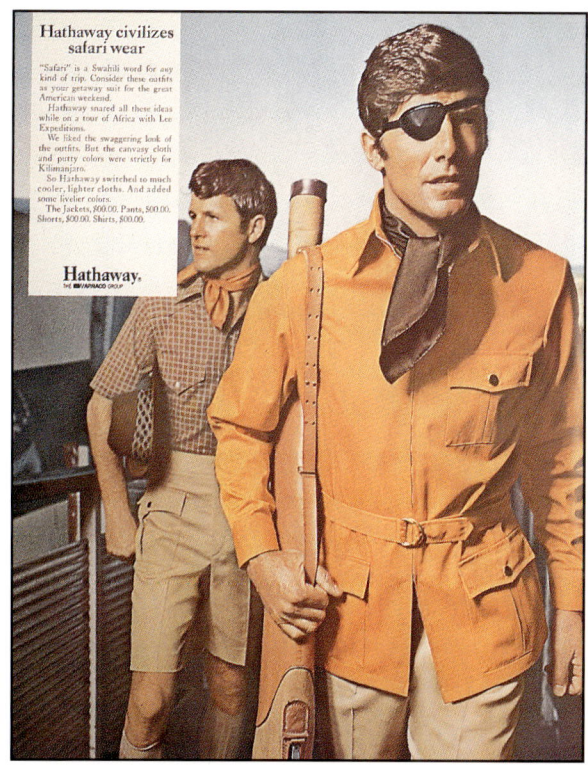

Above left: 1969. Another liquor tie-in, this time with Tia Maria. $18–20.

Above right: 1969. Safari wear. $30–35.

Right: 1969. Buy a dozen Hathaway shirts in different colors…just for starters. $20–22.

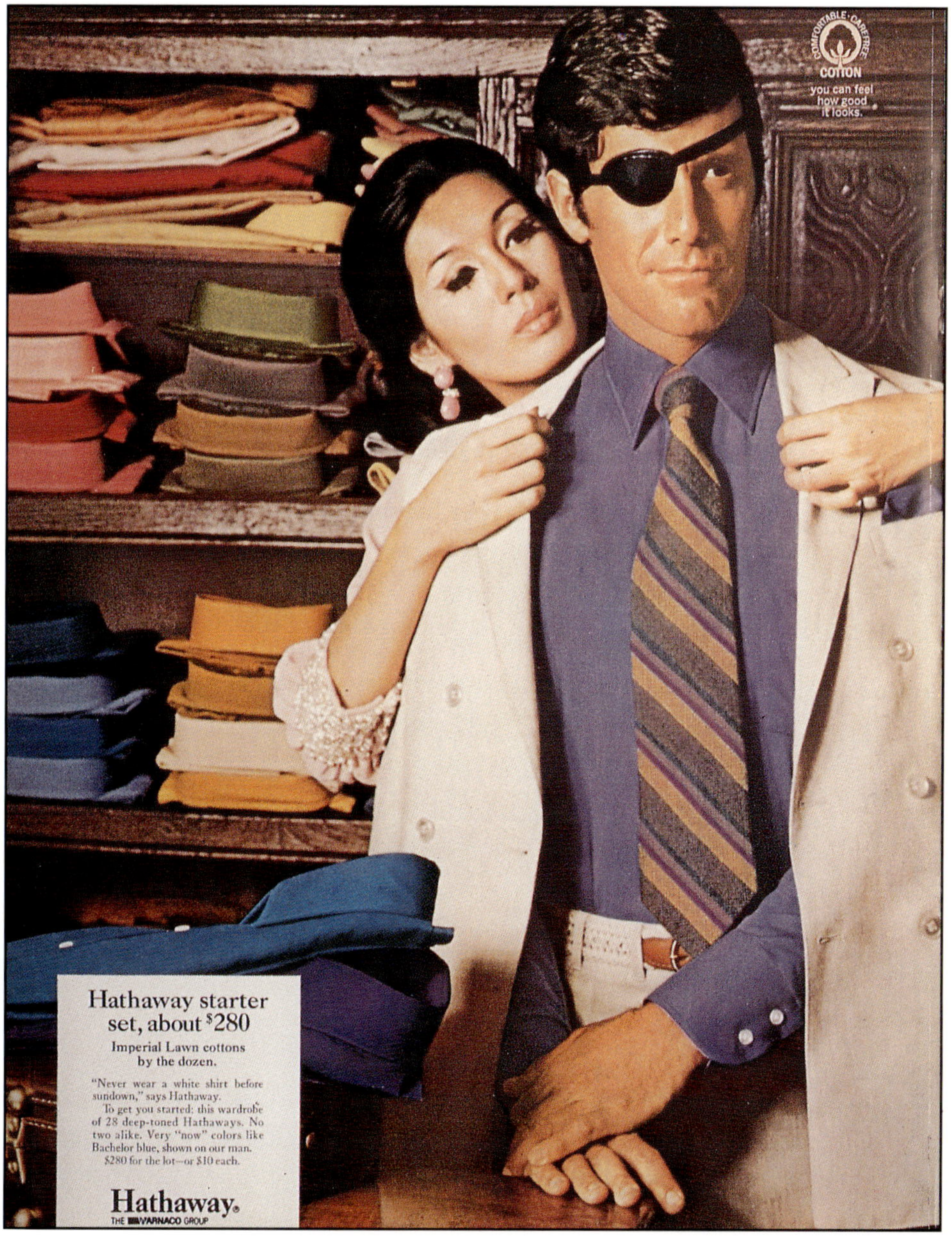

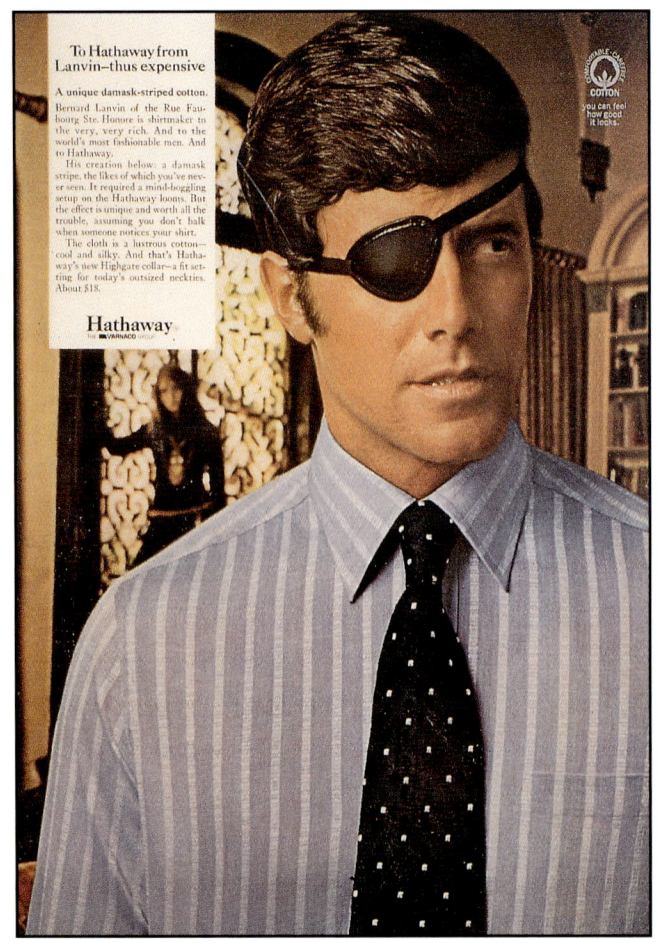

1969. Damask striped cotton in a Lanvin design. $18–20.

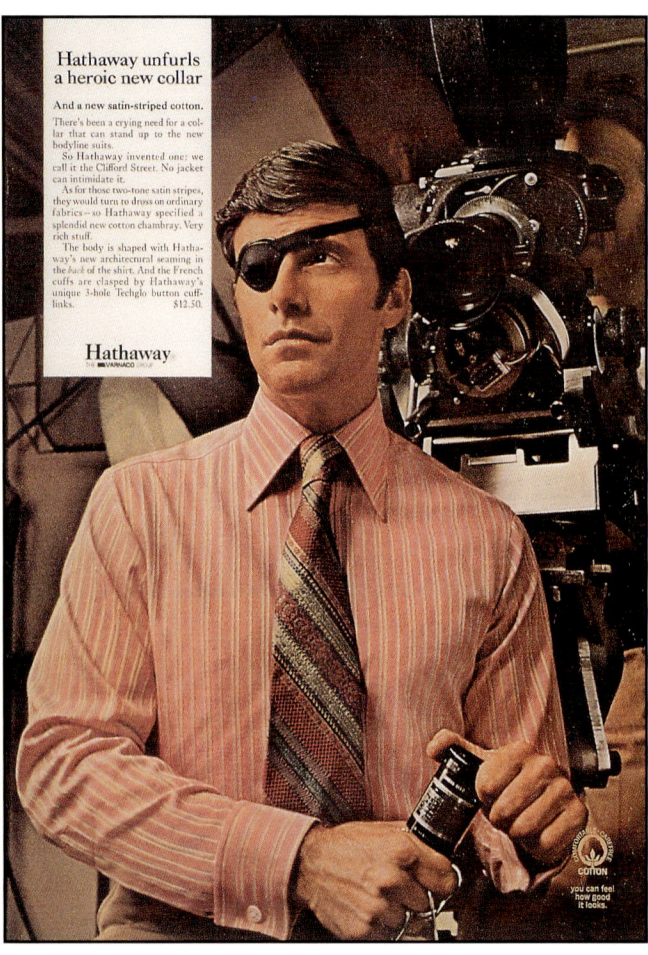

1969. The long Clifford Street collar. $18–20.

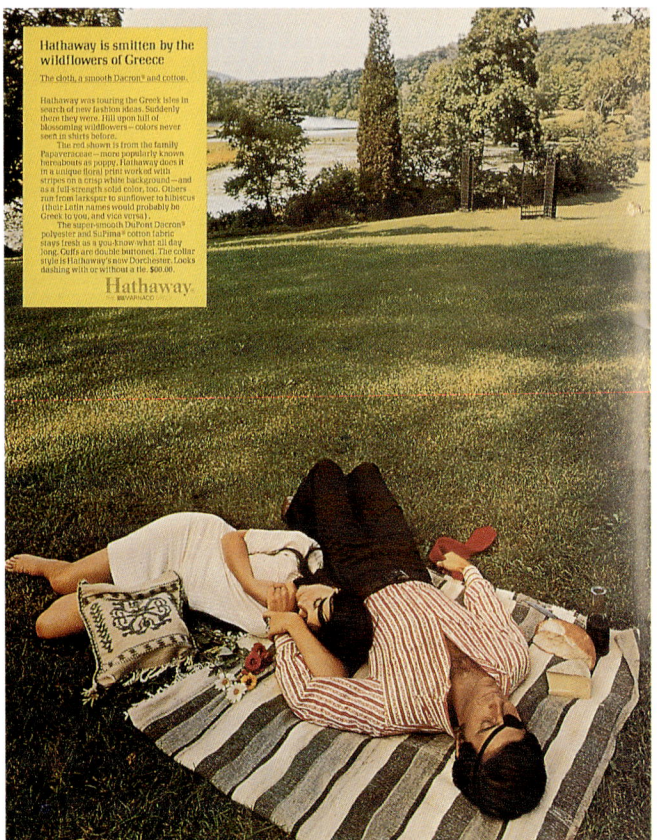

1970. $18–20.

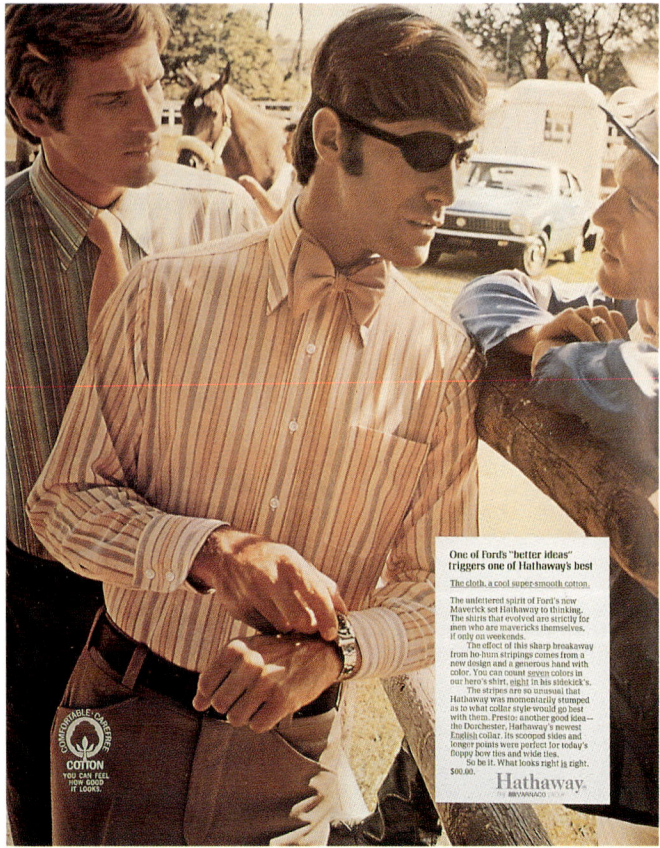

1970. A tie-in with the new Ford Maverick. $18–20.

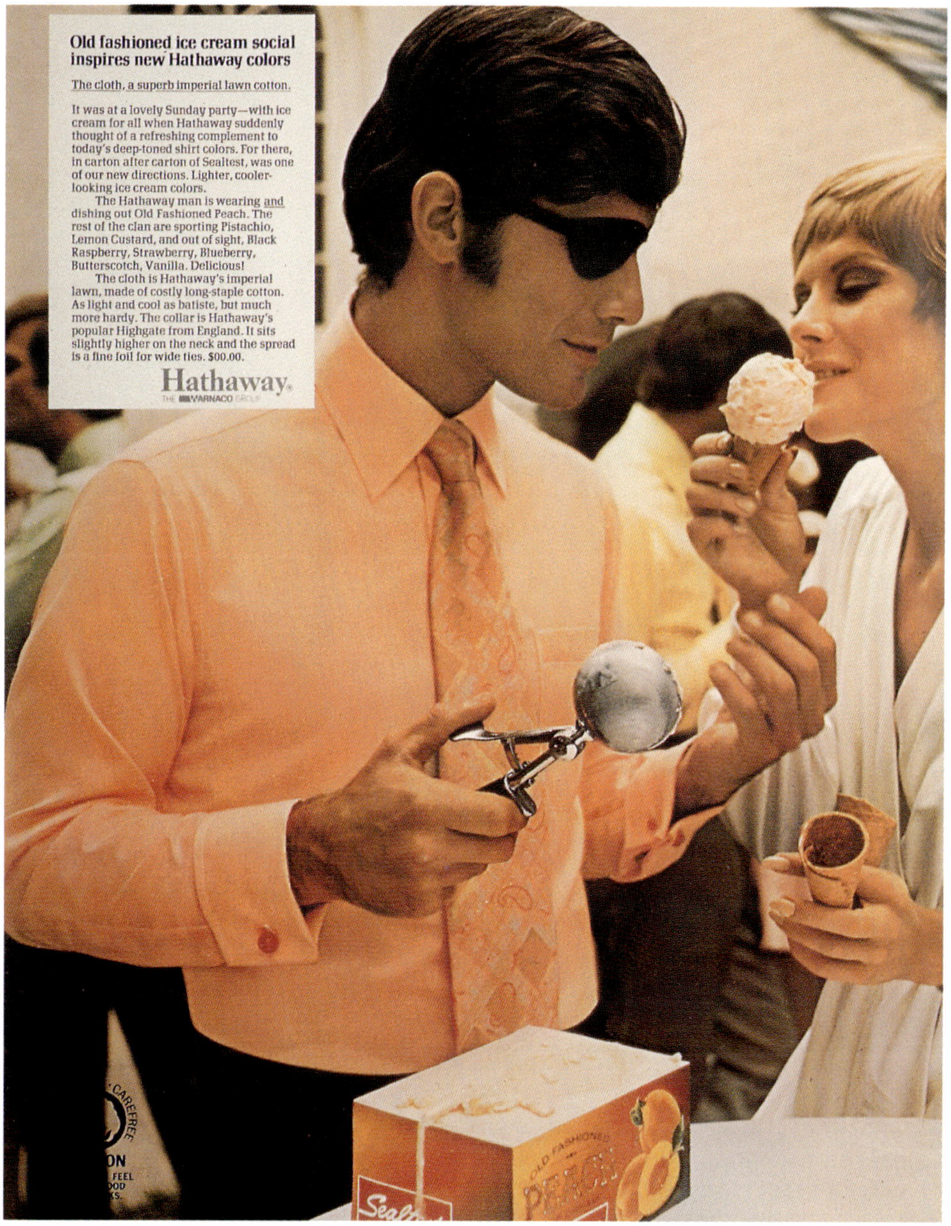

Right: 1970. $15–18.

Lower left: 1970. Hathaway's Lanvin shirt from the "armoire" series. $18–20.

Lower right: 1970. A cotton stripe with a Milano collar. $20–22.

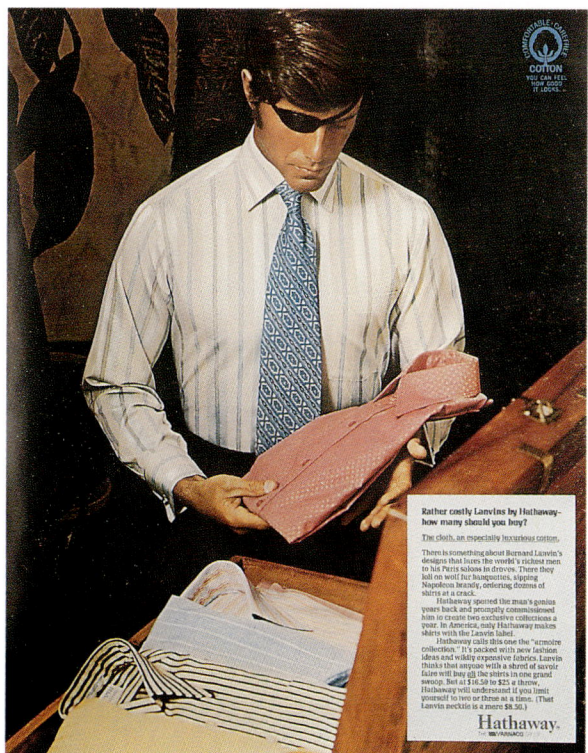

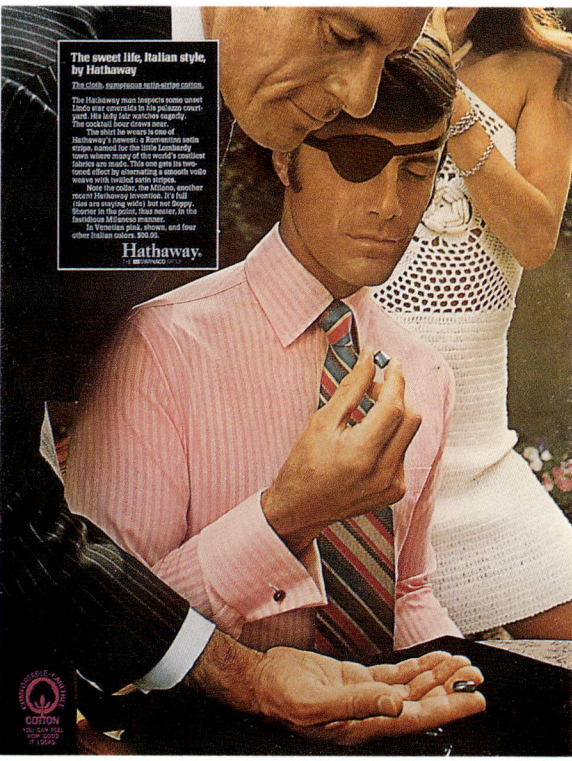

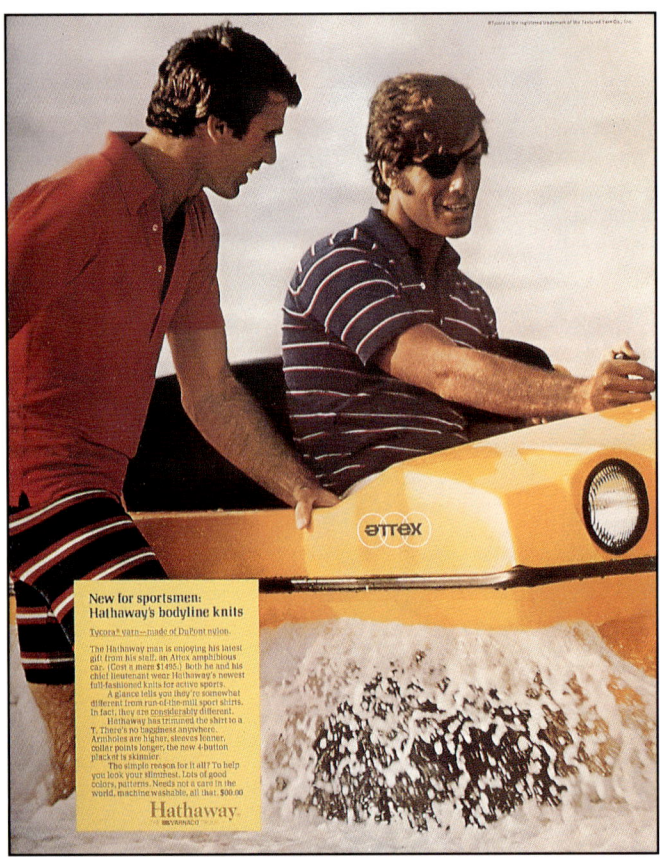

1970. Fitted knit sportshirt. $15–18.

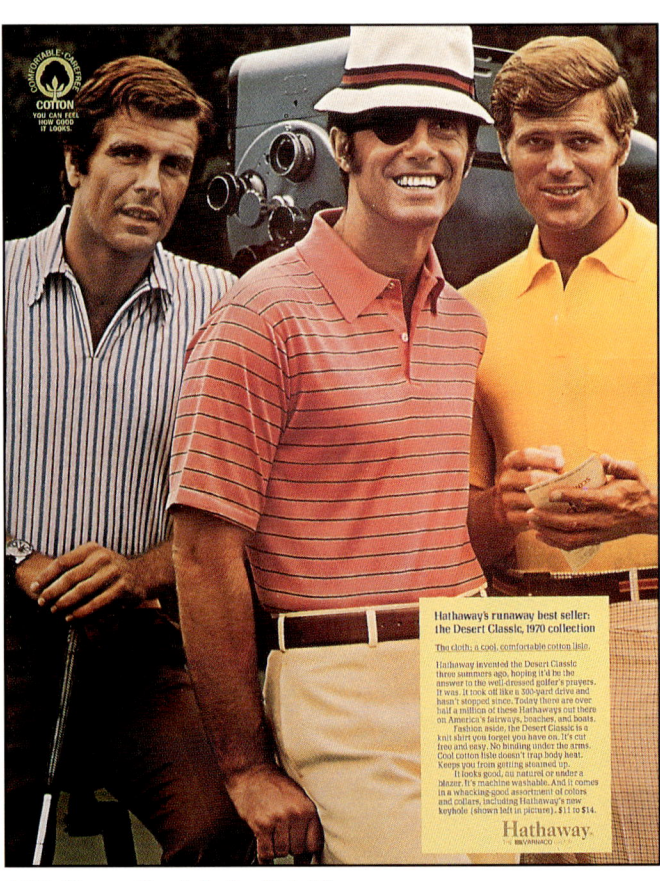

1970. Desert Classic knits. $15–18.

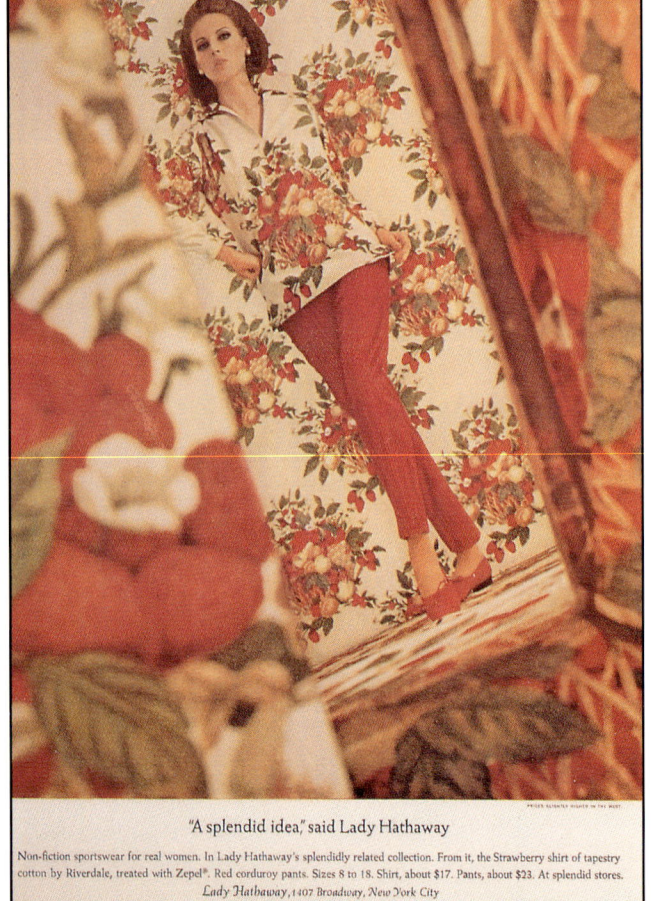

1970. Lady Hathaway continued to actively market the name, though in a separate operation from Hathaway shirts. $24–28.

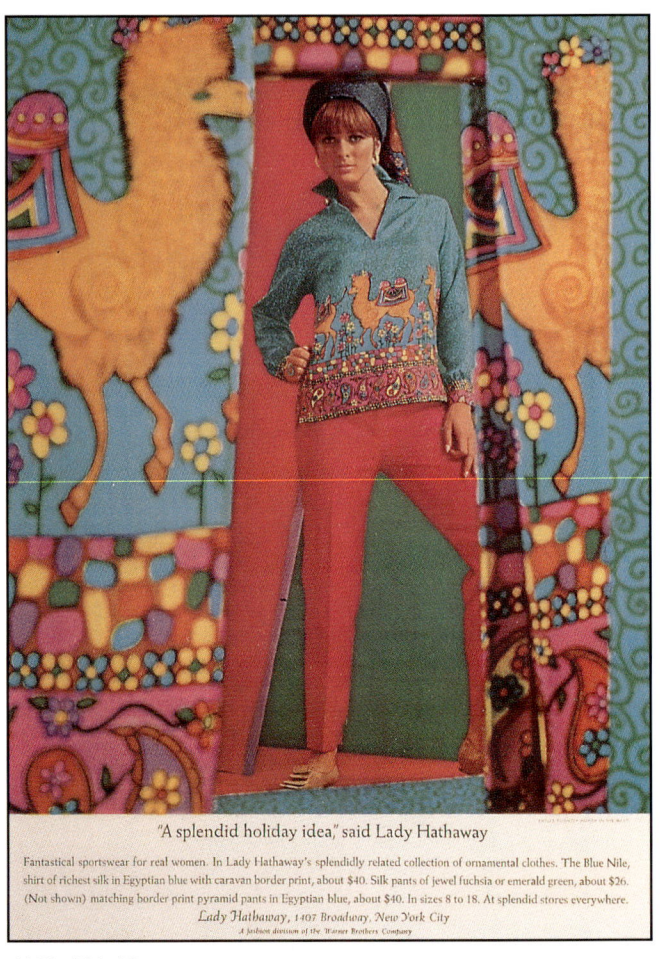

1970. $24–28.

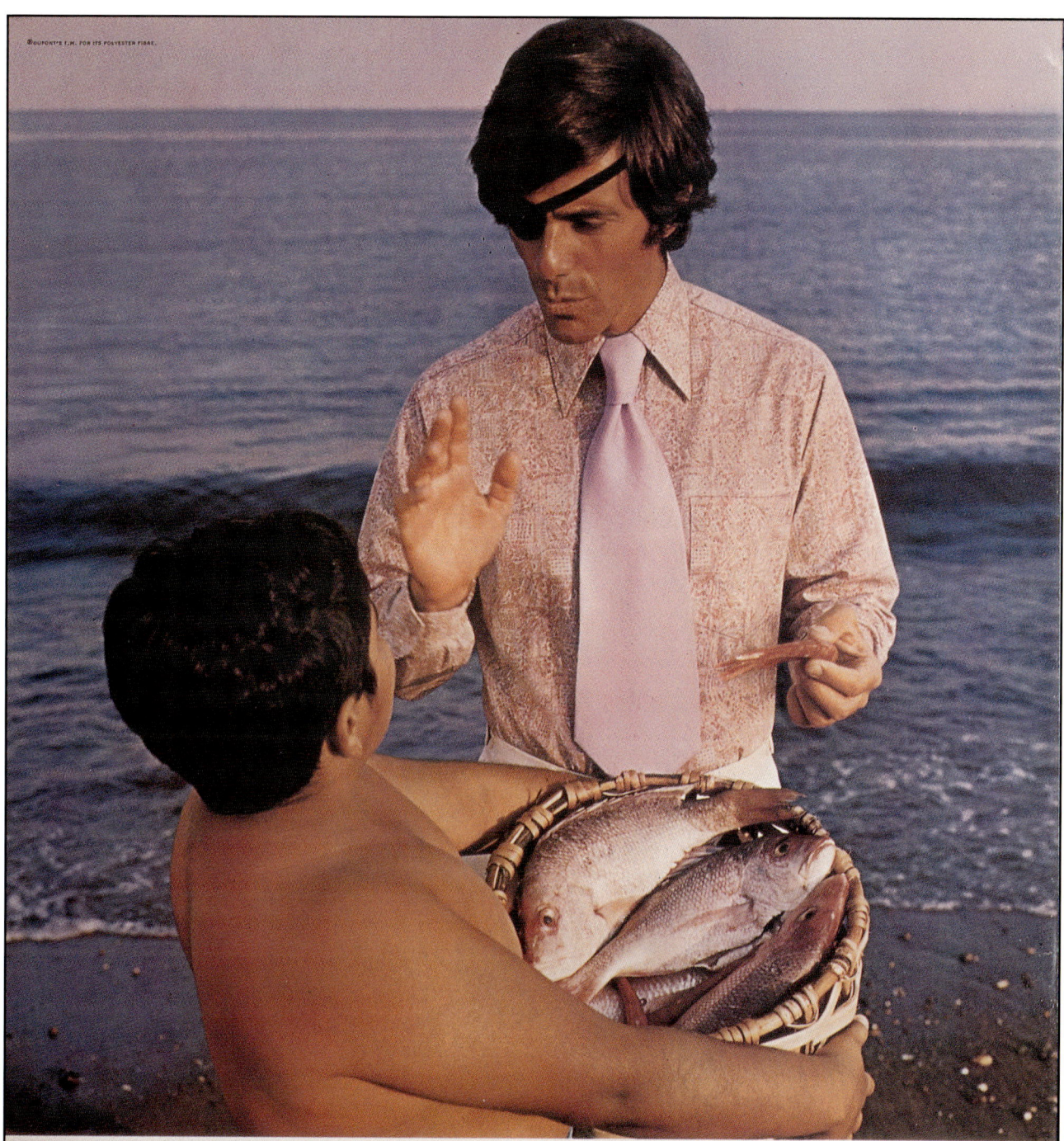

1971. In 1970 the advertising account moved from Ogilvy & Mathers to Green Domatch, Inc. Their earliest ads followed the tradition of their predecessors. The wide Warwick collar was designed to go with the fashionable wide ties. $22–24.

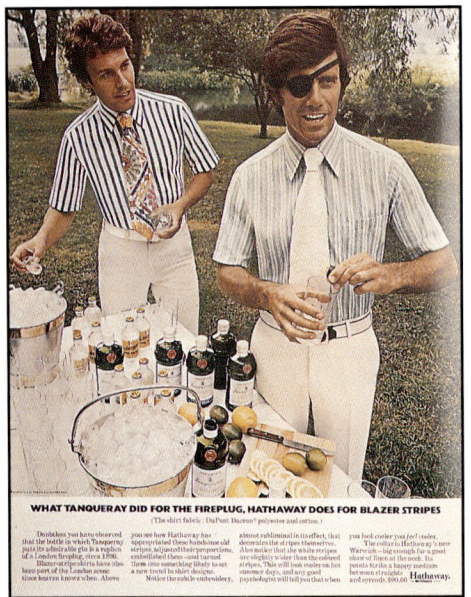

1971. Blazer stripes revisited for the 1970s. $20–22.

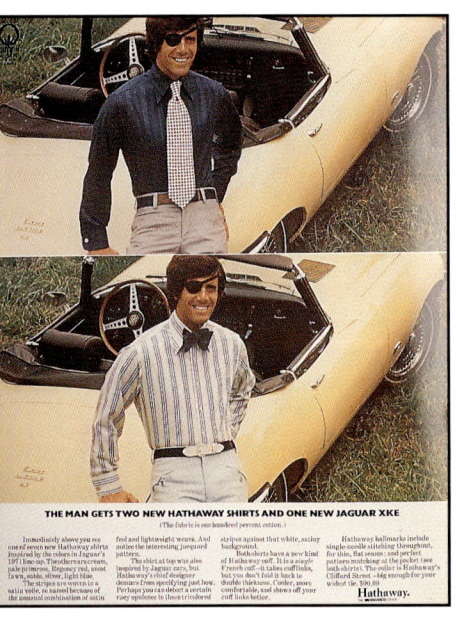

1971. This tie-in with Jaguar features the Clifford Street collar, "wide enough for your widest ties." $18–20.

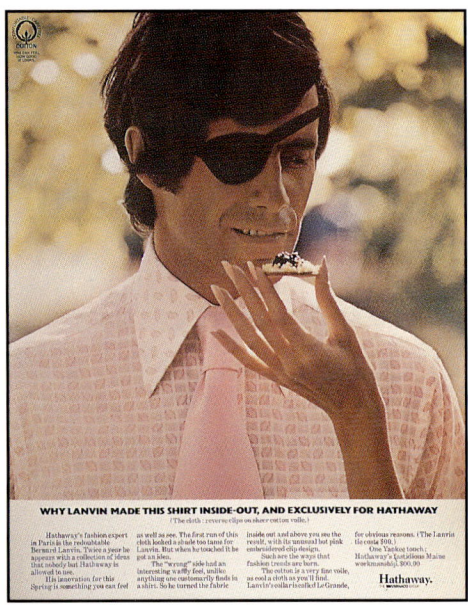

1971. A Lanvin design with LeGrand collar. $22–24.

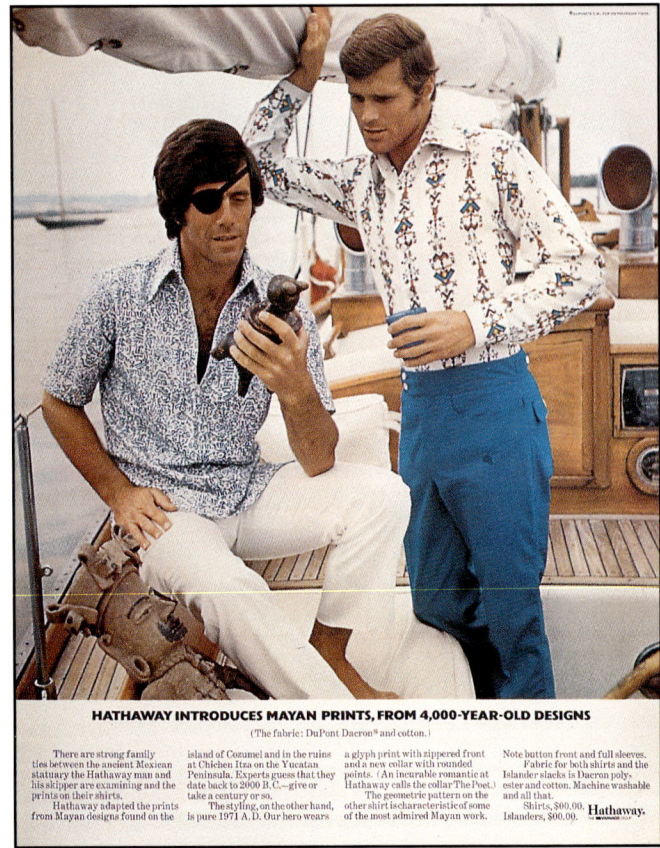

1971. Dacron-cotton blend Mayan print shirt with new rounded-point Poet collars. $28–32.

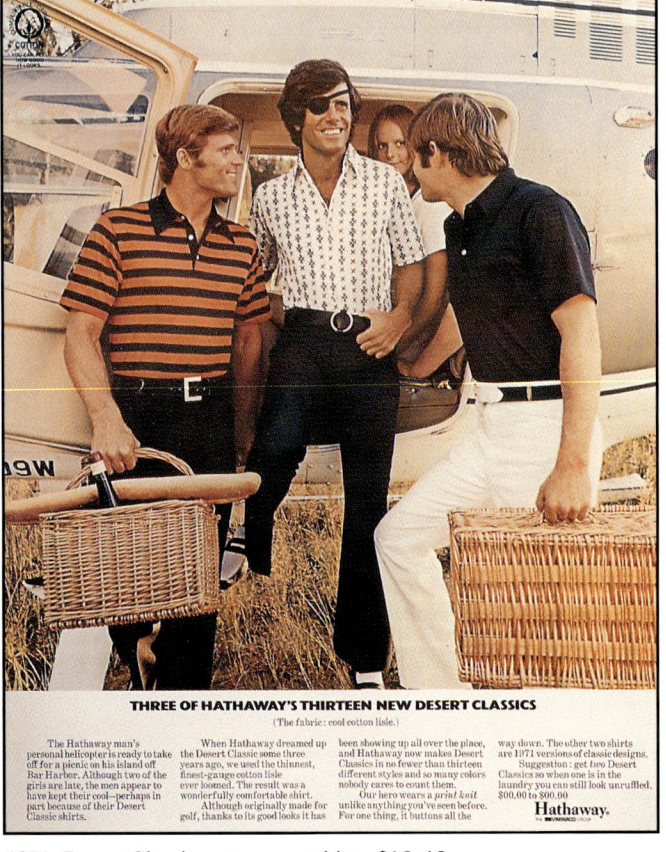

1971. Desert Classic cotton sportshirts. $15–18.

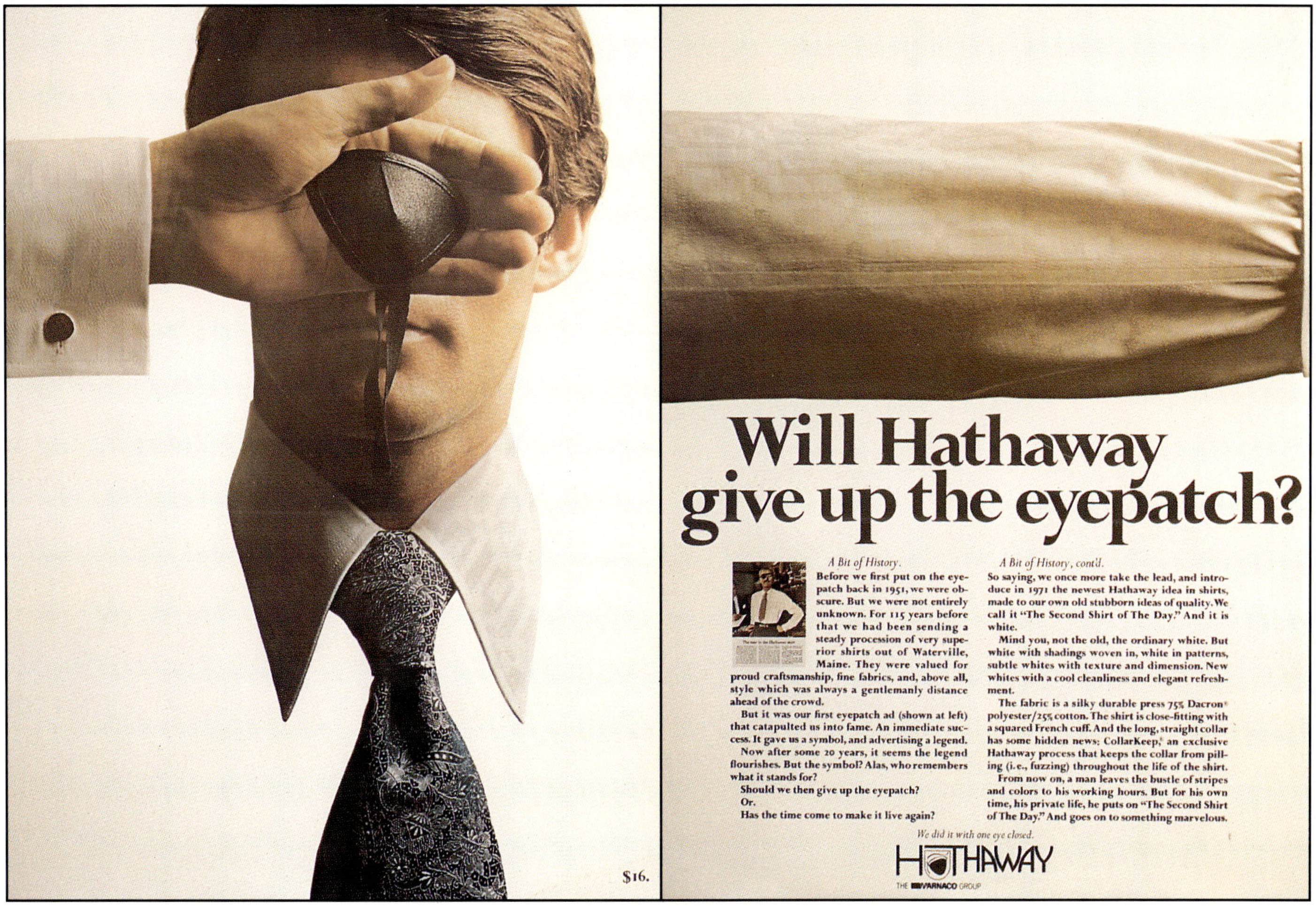

1971. With this teasing ad, Green Domatch introduced an original campaign. The patch becomes part of the logo, replacing the first "a" in Hathaway. It also reemphasizes white shirts as the "second shirt of the day," proposing that they be used for evening wear at home.

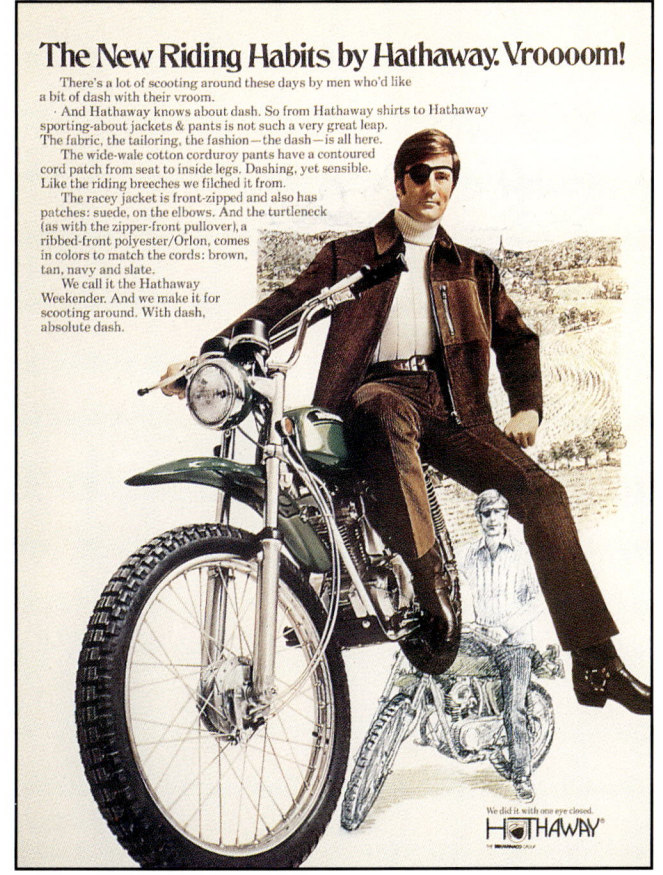

1972. A corduroy suit with Orlon turtleneck. $28–32.

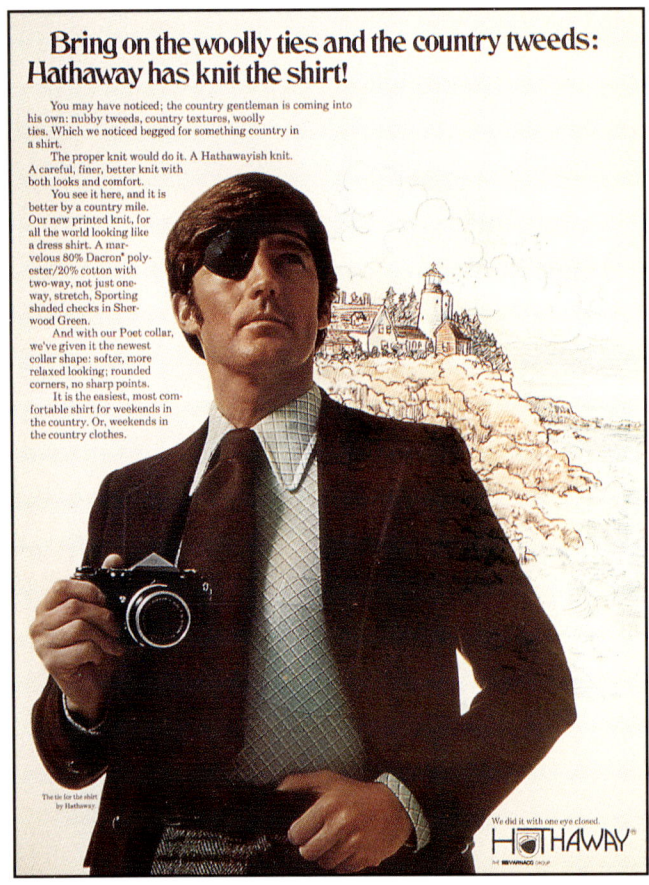

1972. Dacron-cotton knit dress shirt with Poet collar. $15–18.

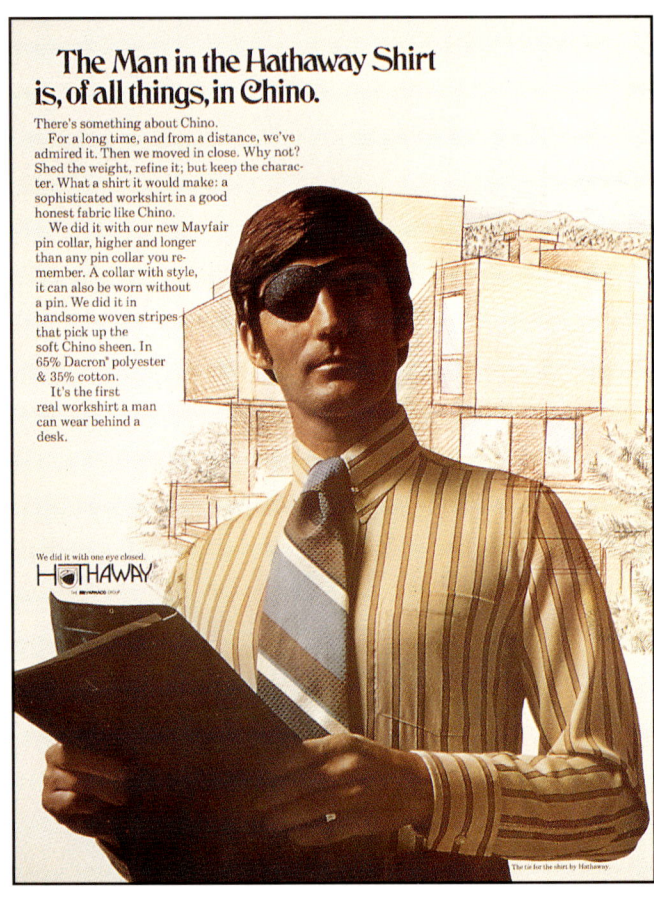

1972. A Chino work/dress shirt in Dacron-cotton with Mayfair pin collar. $18–20.

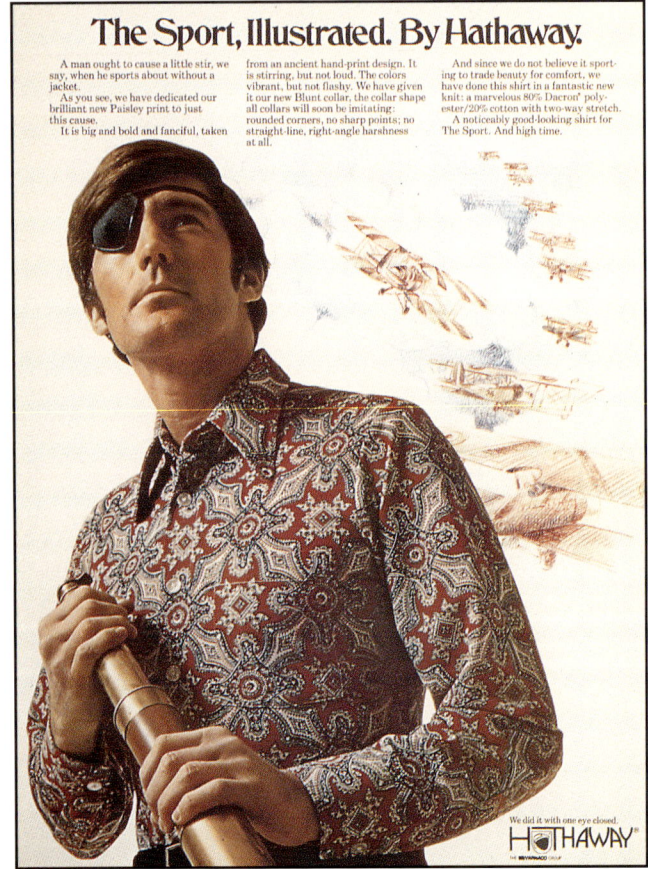

1972. Dacron-cotton with new Blunt collar. $28–30.

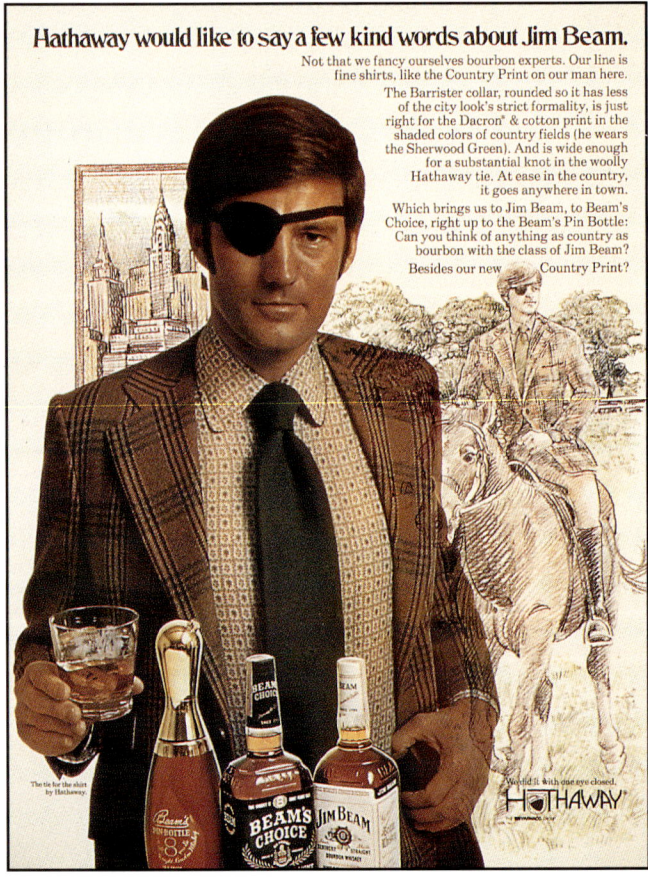

1972. Tie-in ad with Jim Beam bourbon. The shirt is Dacron-cotton with a Barrister collar. $22–26.

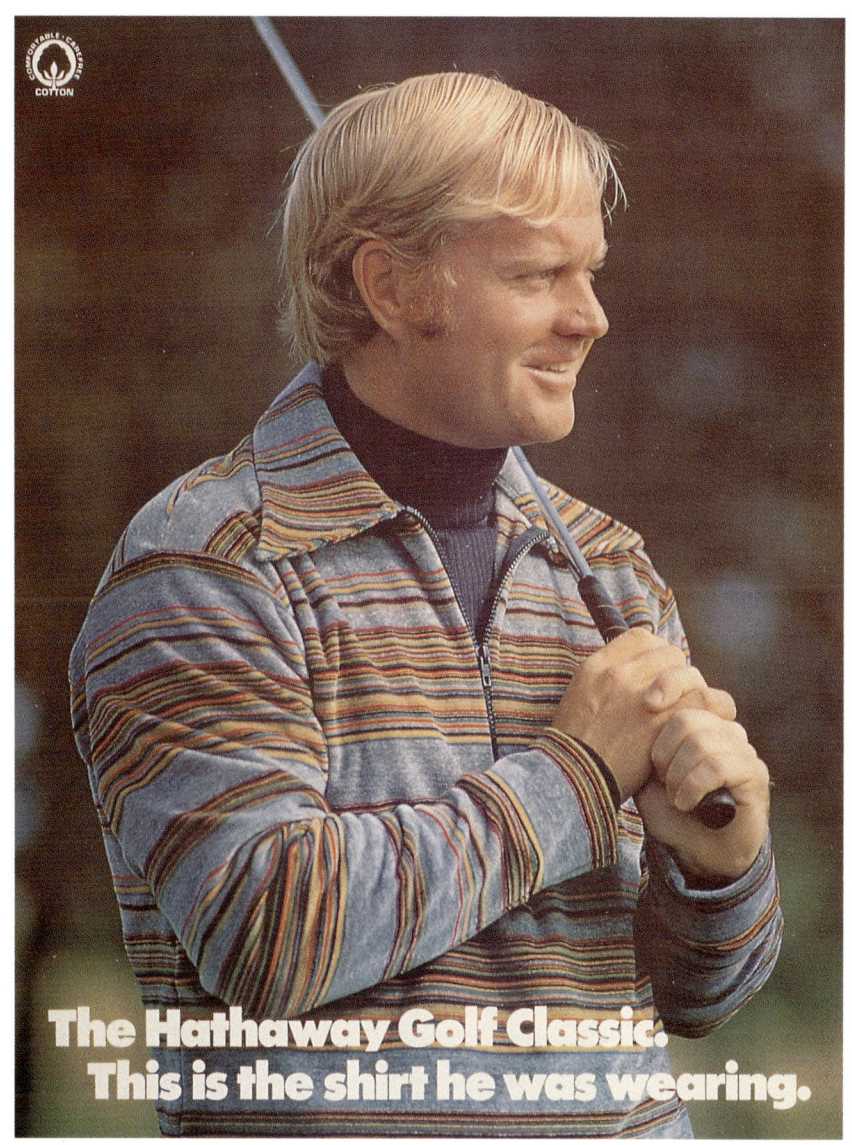

Right: 1972. The beginning of the Jack Nicklaus "This is the shirt he was wearing" advertising campaign. $20–22.

Lower two: 1972. $20–22.

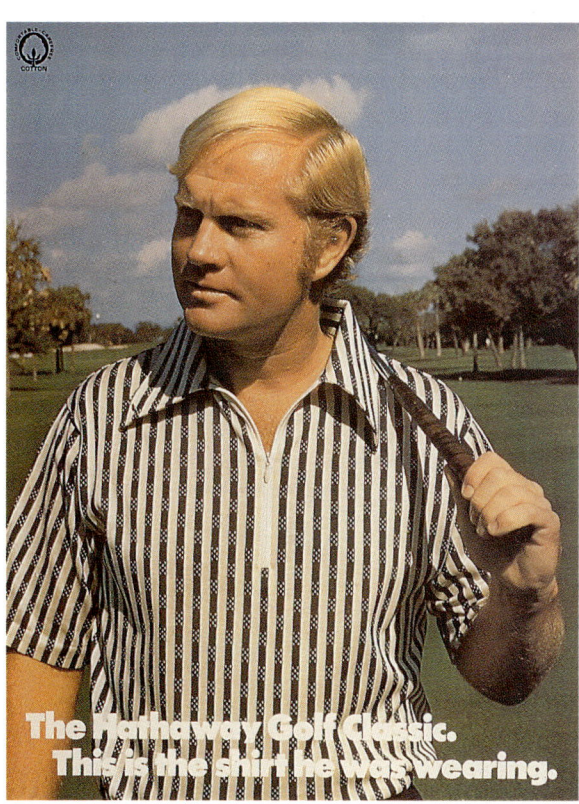

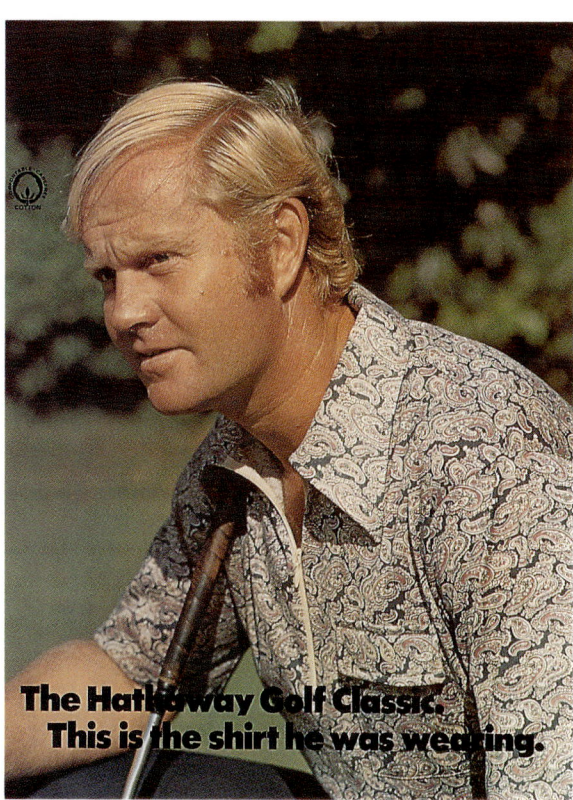

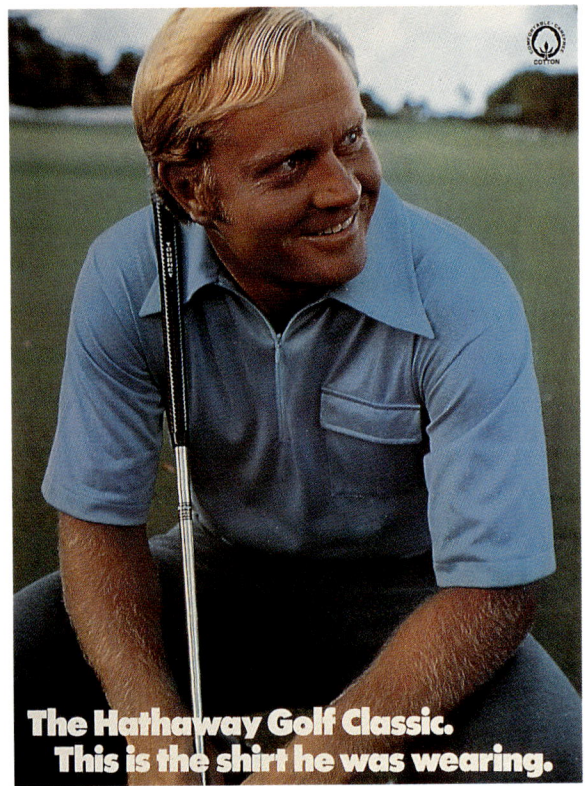

1972. $18–20.

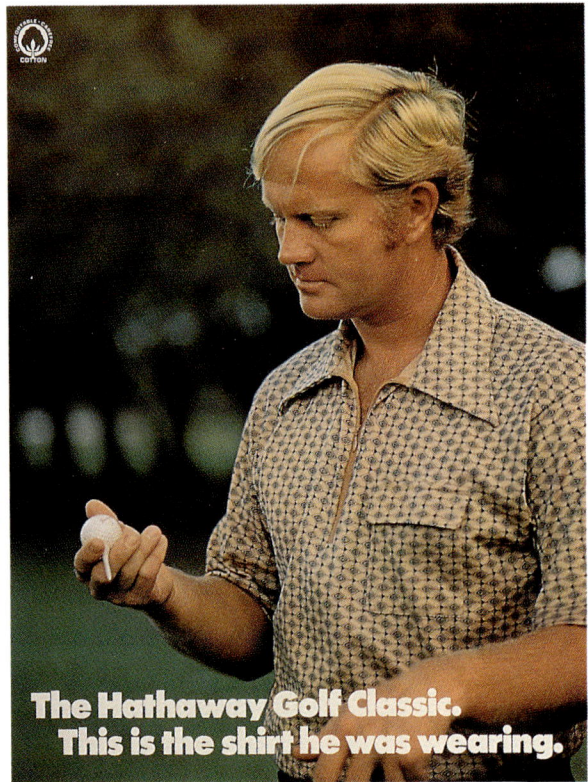

1972. $18–20.

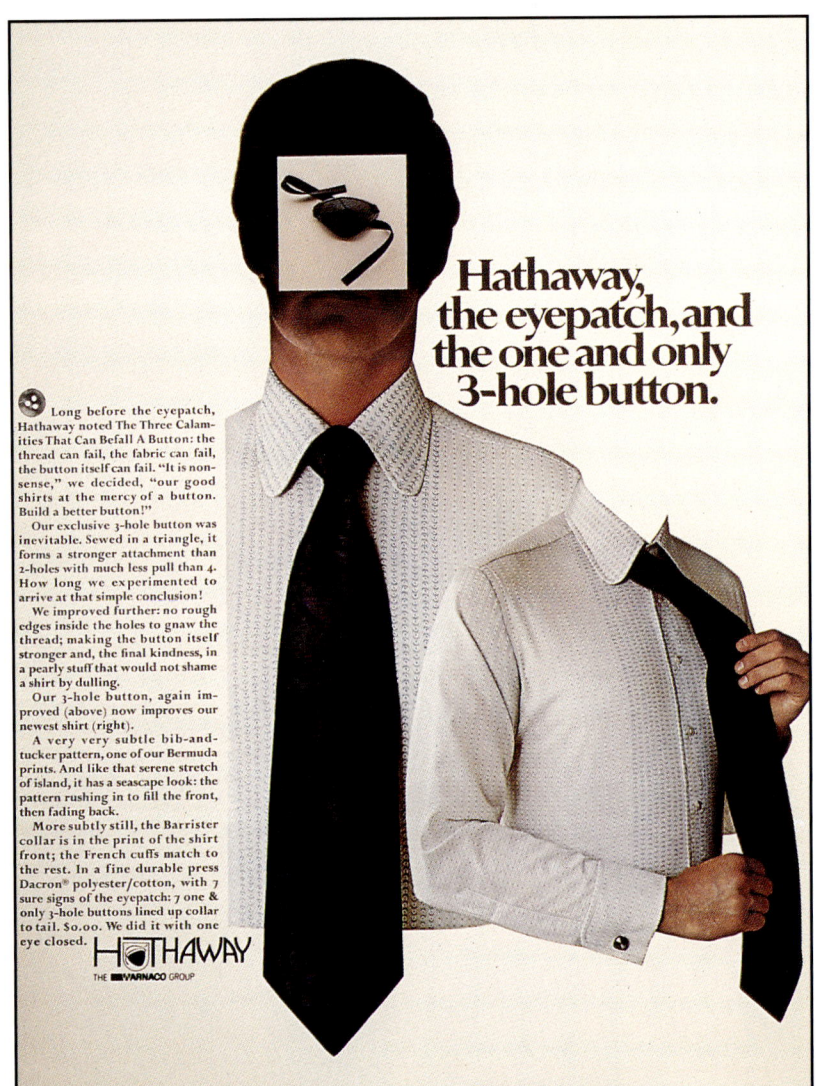

1972. Green Domatch became even more creative for this campaign. Though keeping the eyepatch, they put it in a white box, superimposed over the model's face. This dress shirt has the Barrister collar, and the copy highlights the three-hole button, introduced in the 1930s. $15–18.

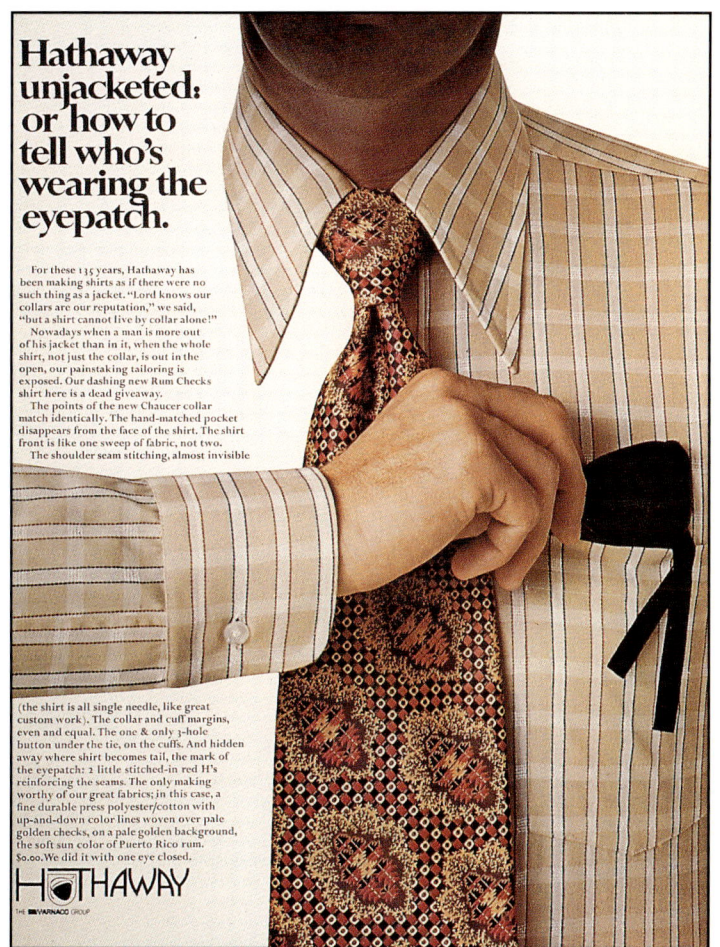

1972. Emphasizing the hand-matched pockets, this is a cotton-polyester blend with a Chaucer collar. $18–20

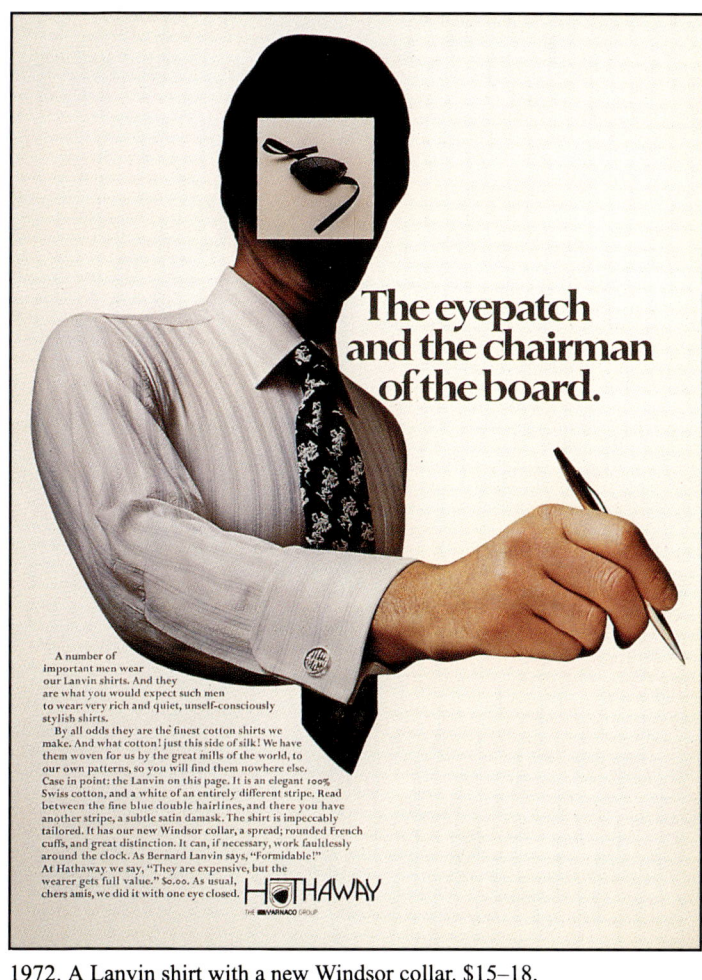

1972. A Lanvin shirt with a new Windsor collar. $15–18.

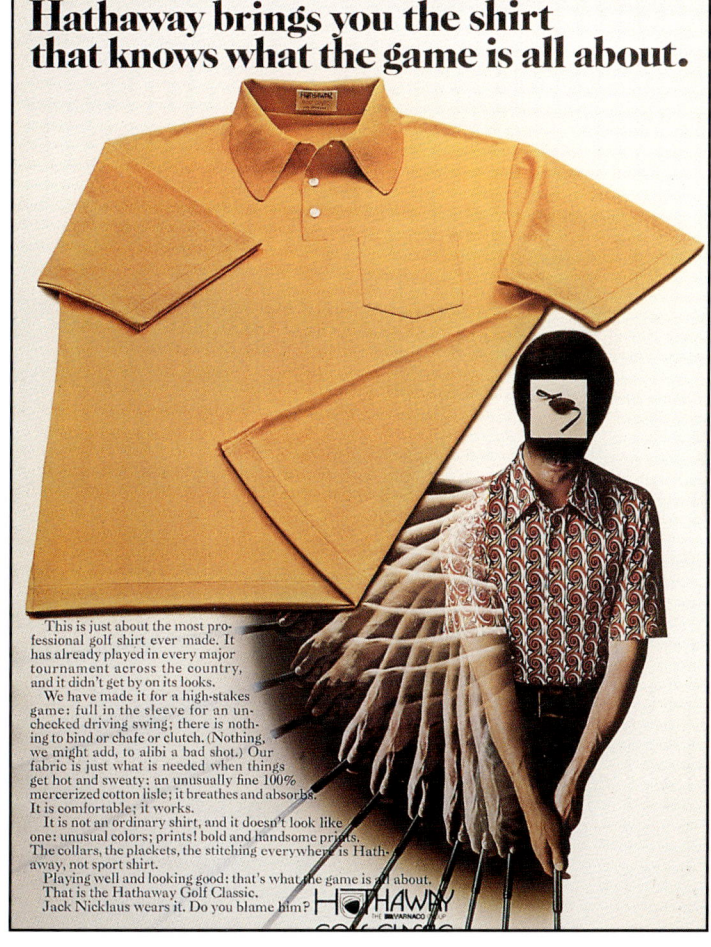

1972. The ad mentions Nicklaus, but does not show him. $15–18.

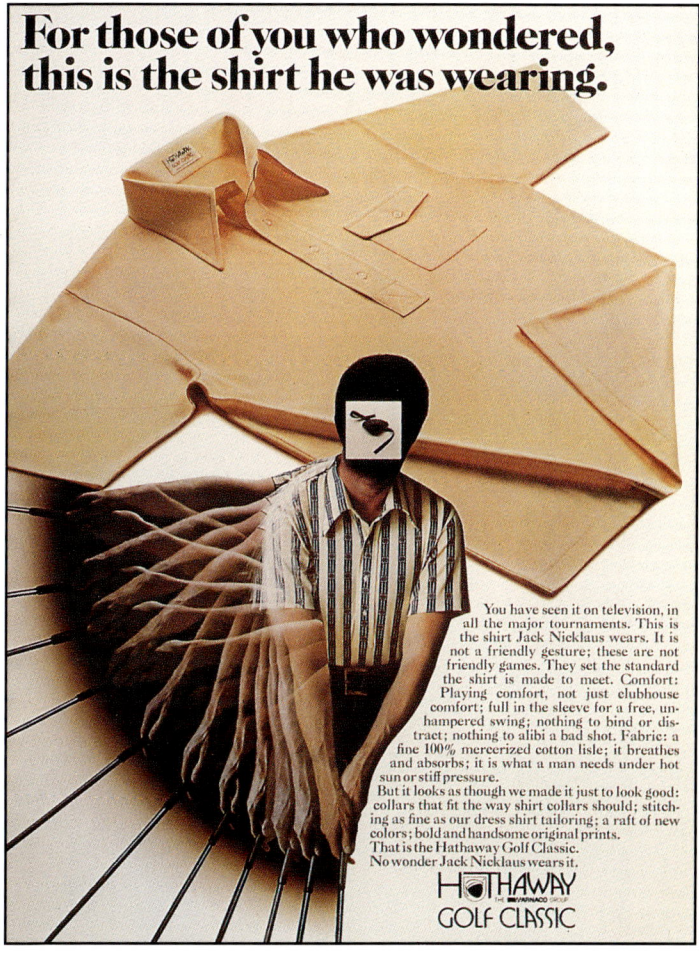

1972. The shirt that Jack wears. $15–18.

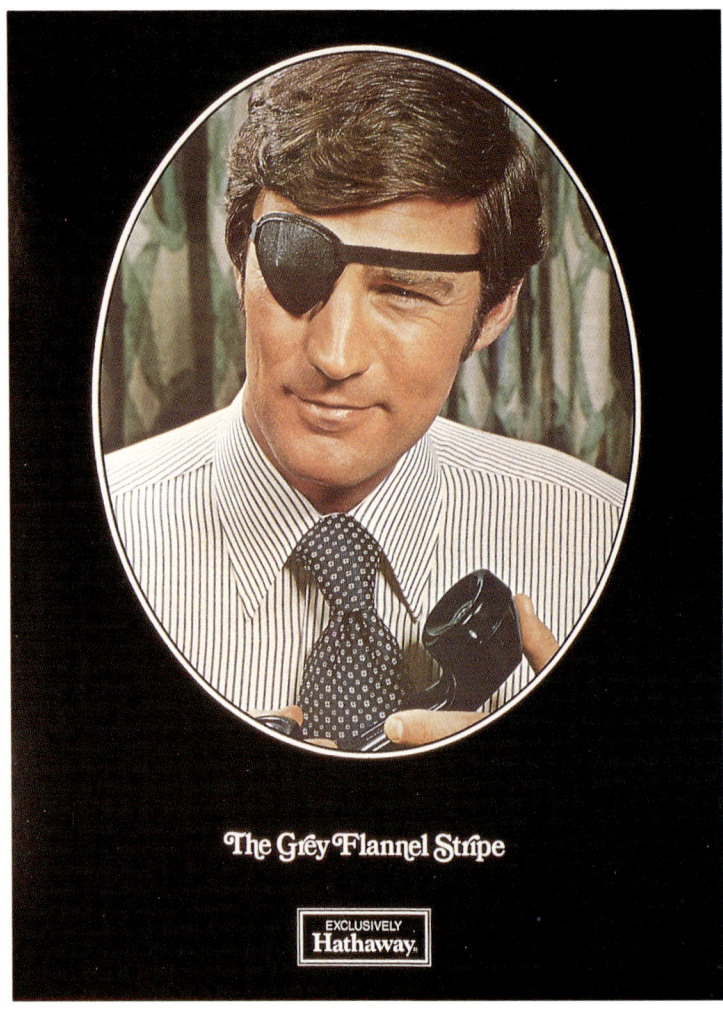

Left: 1973. The disembodied campaign quickly gave way to a more traditional approach. $18–20.

Lower left: 1973. $22–24.

Lower right: 1973. $20–22.

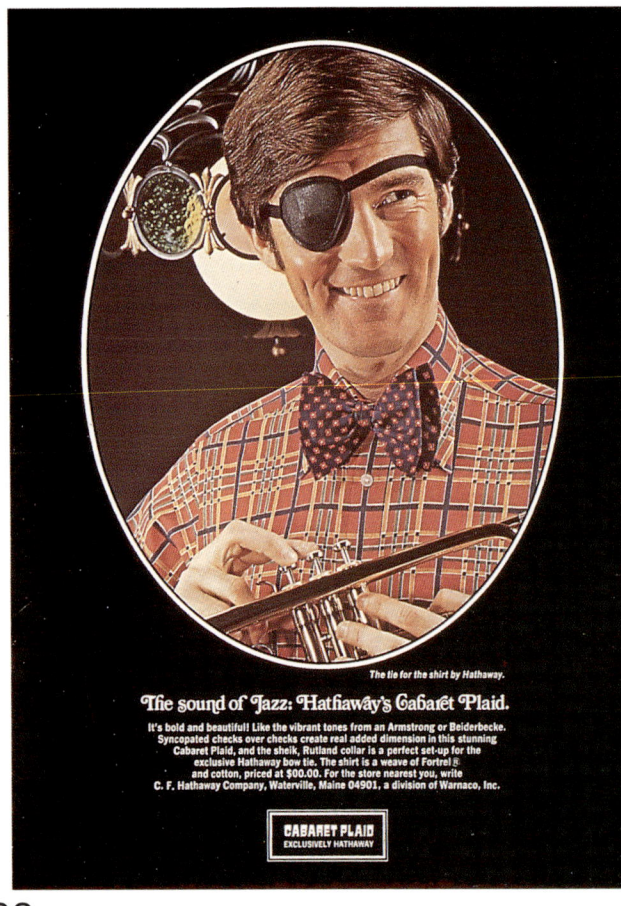

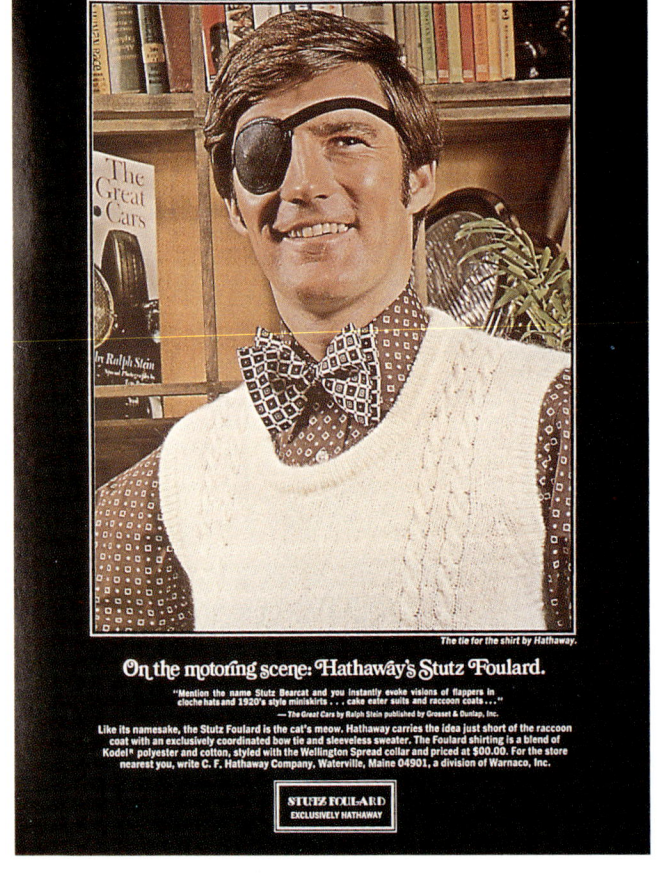

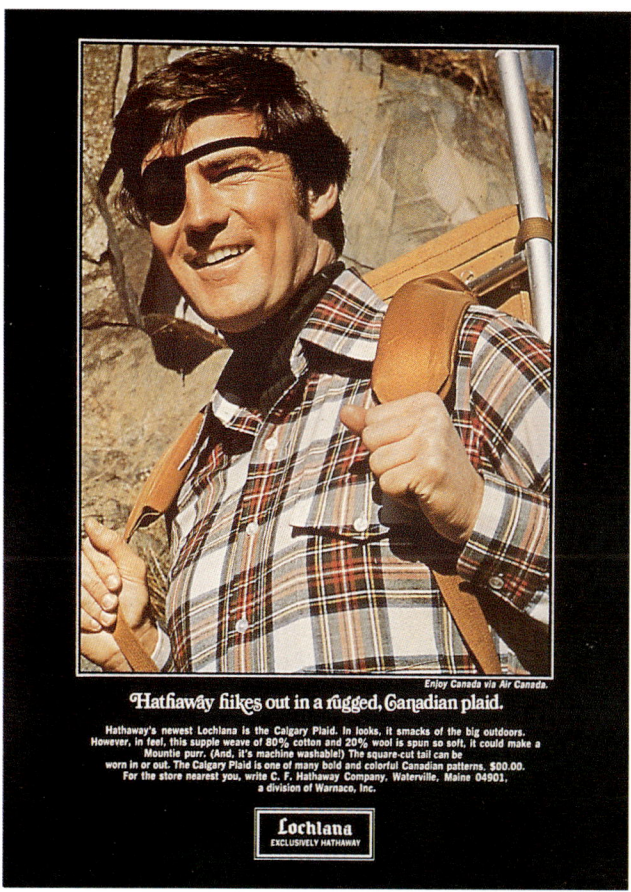
1973. A cotton-wool Lochlana blend for the sporting life. $22–24.

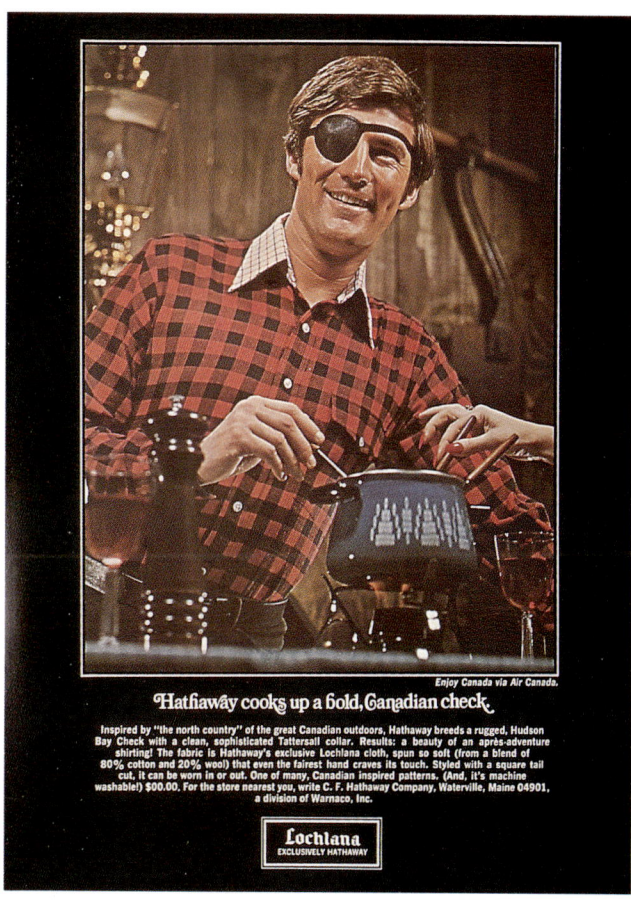
1973. Lochlana plaid. $24–28.

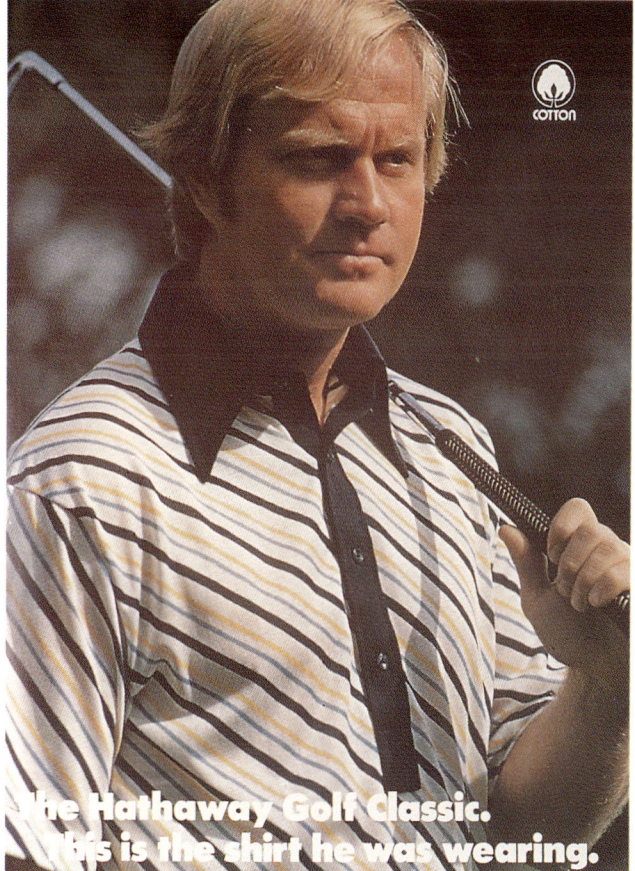
1973. The appeal of Nicklaus and the Hathaway Golf Classic continued. $24–28.

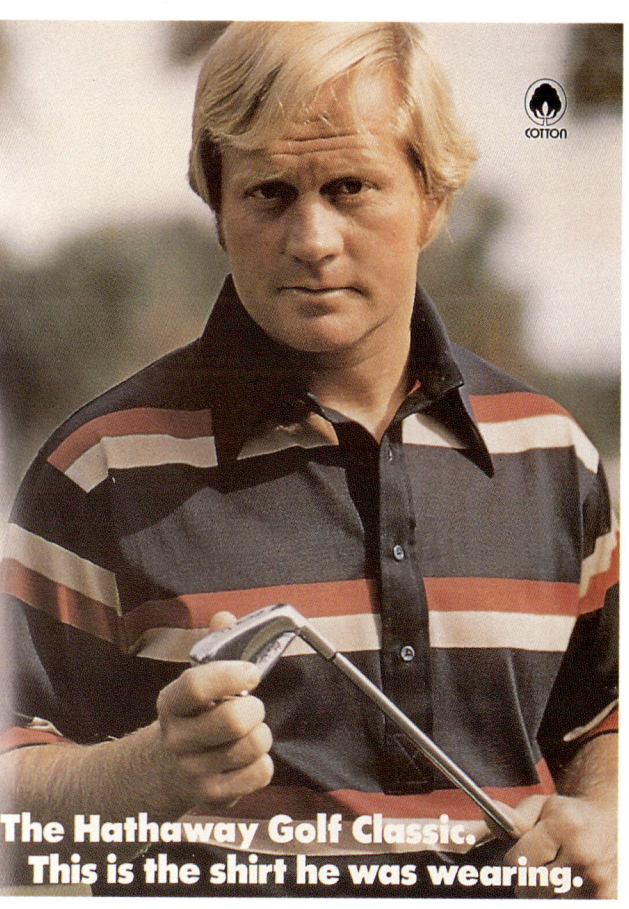
1973. $18–20.

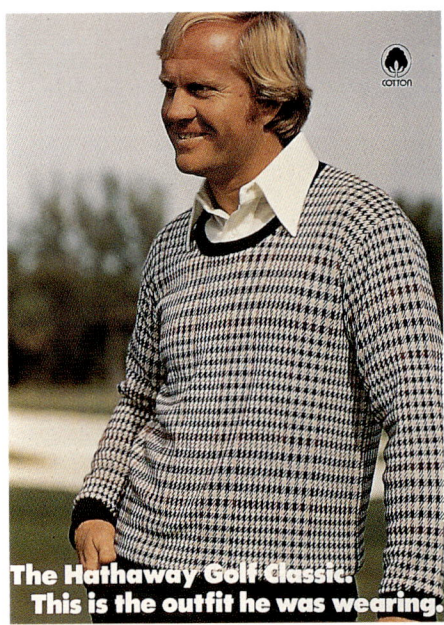
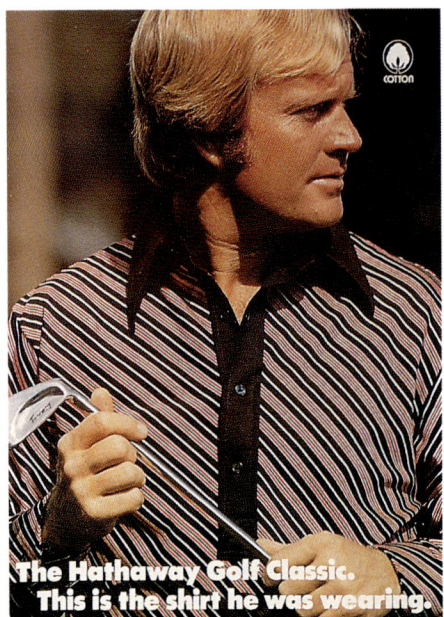
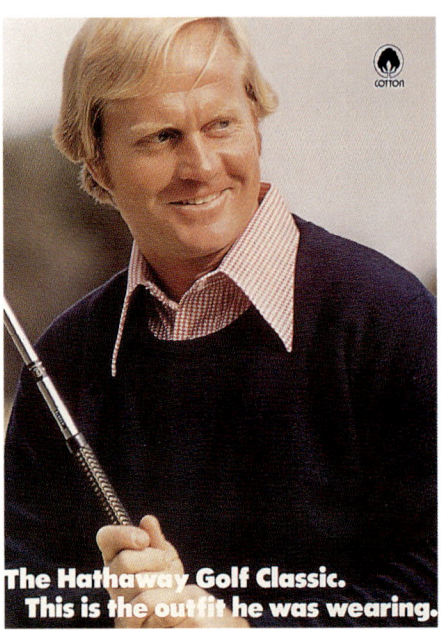
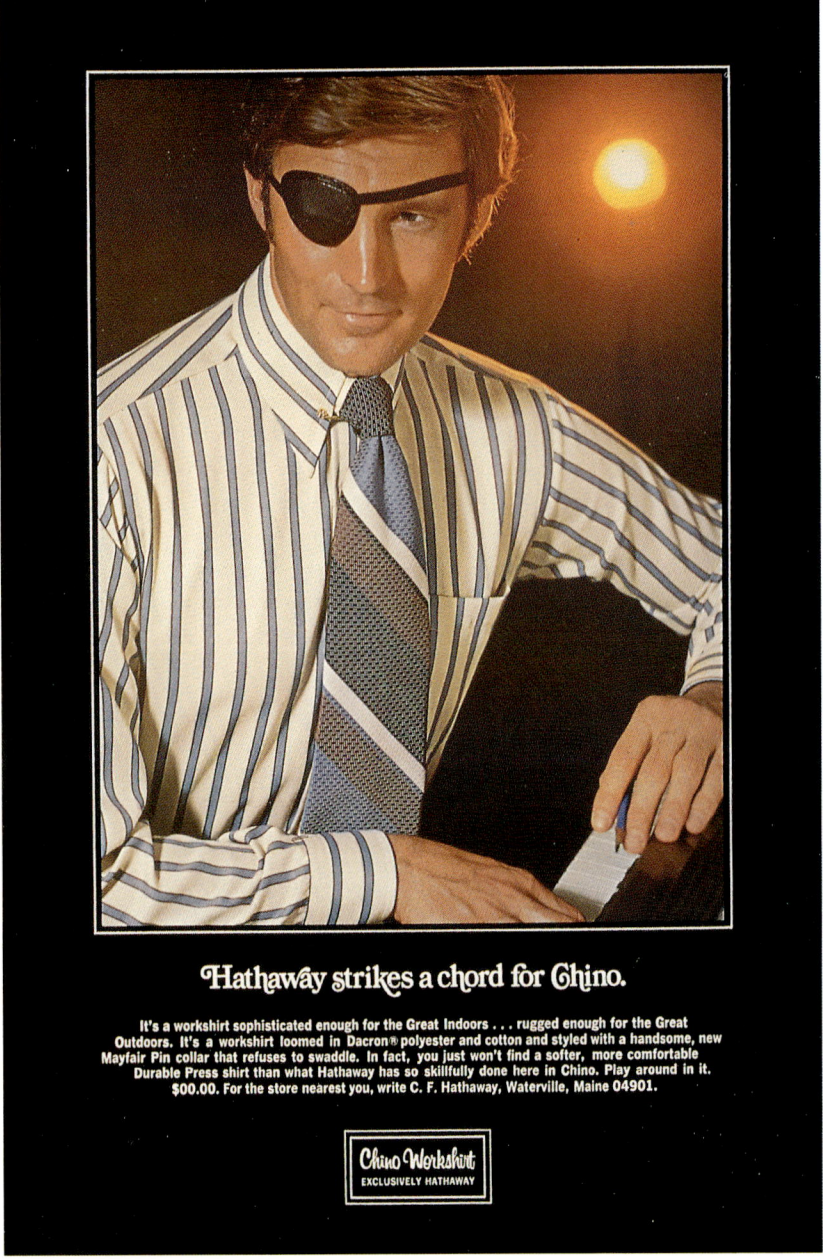

Top left: 1973. $28–30.

Top center: 1973. $20–22.

Top right: 1973. $20–22.

Left: 1973. Chino work shirt. $18–20.

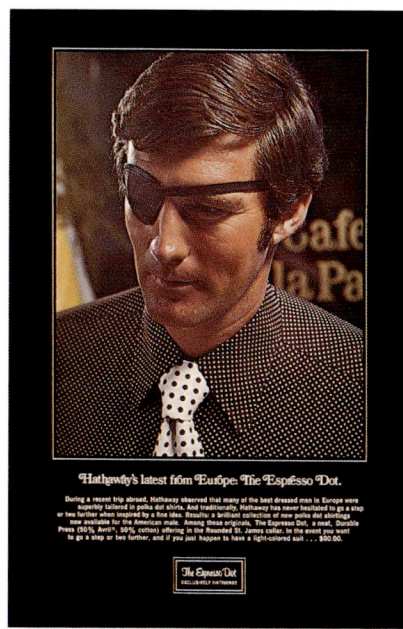

1973. Espresso Dot with a rounded St. James collar. $24–28.

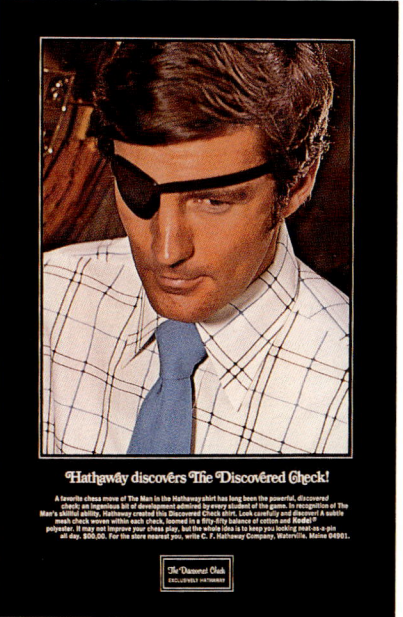

1973. $18–20.

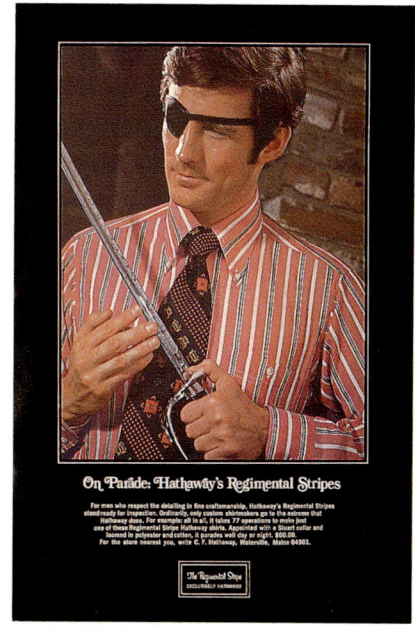

1973. Regimental stripes with a Stuart collar. $18–20.

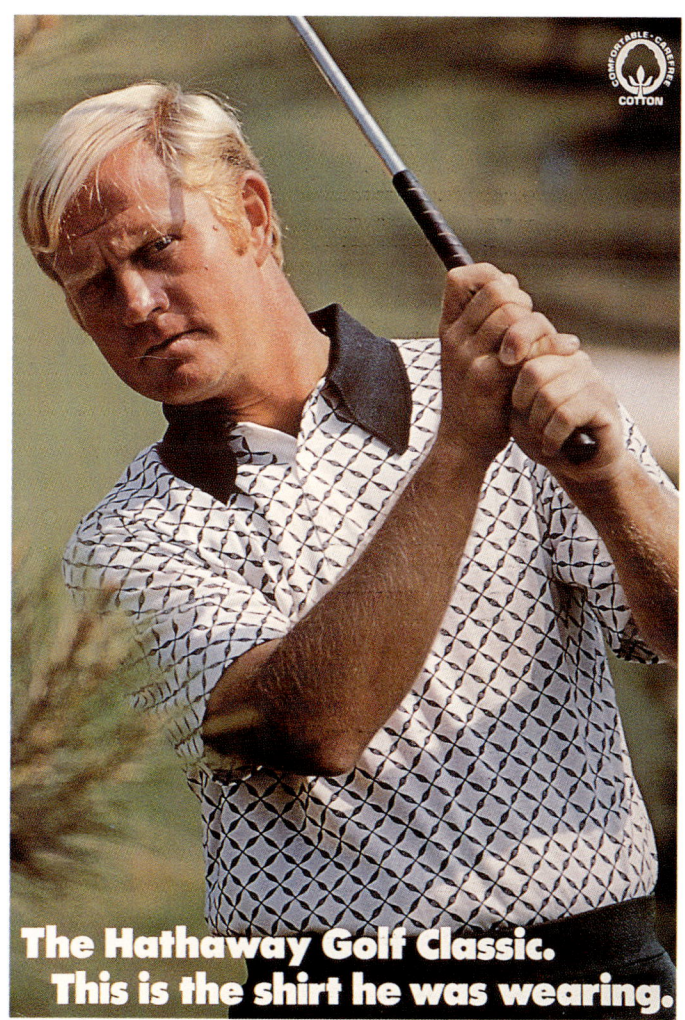

1973. $18–20.

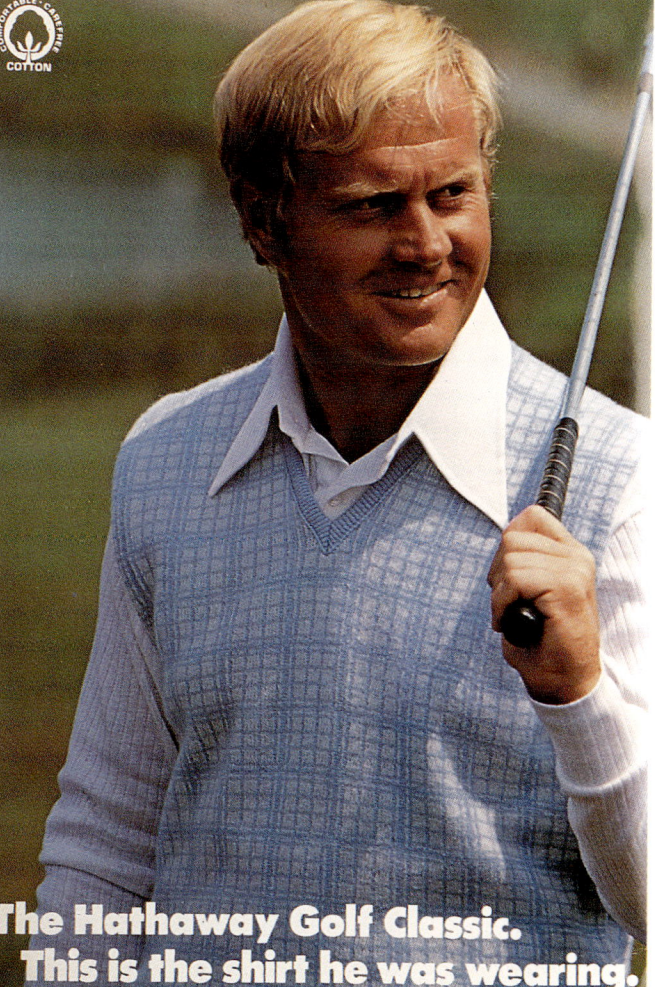

1973. $20–22.

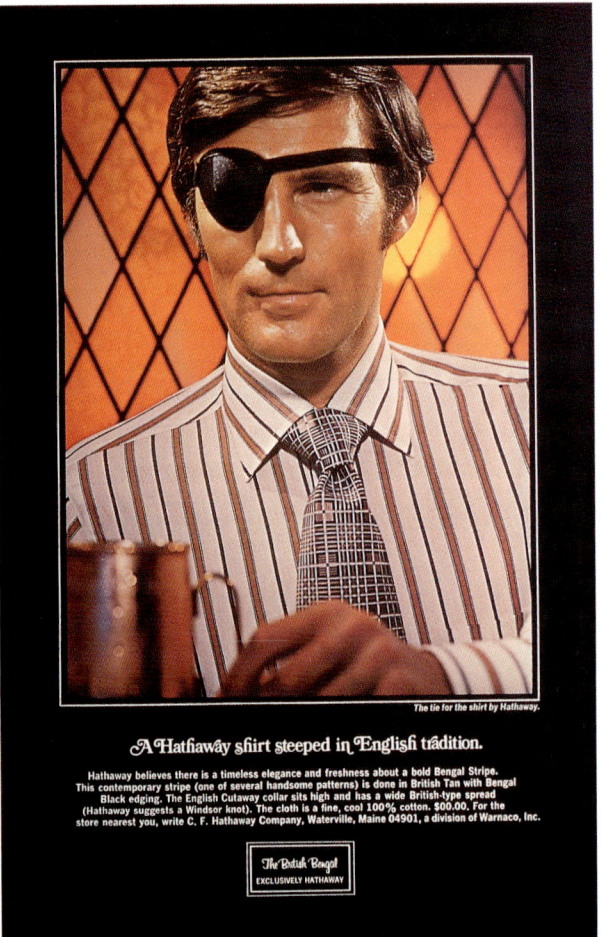

1973. English Cutaway collar, Hathaway also produced the ties in this period. $18–20.

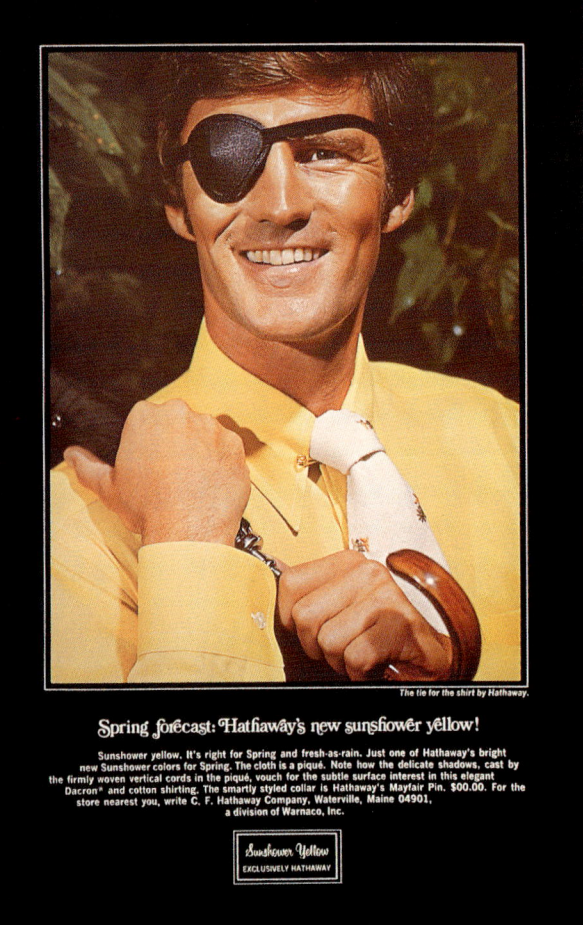

1973. $20–22.

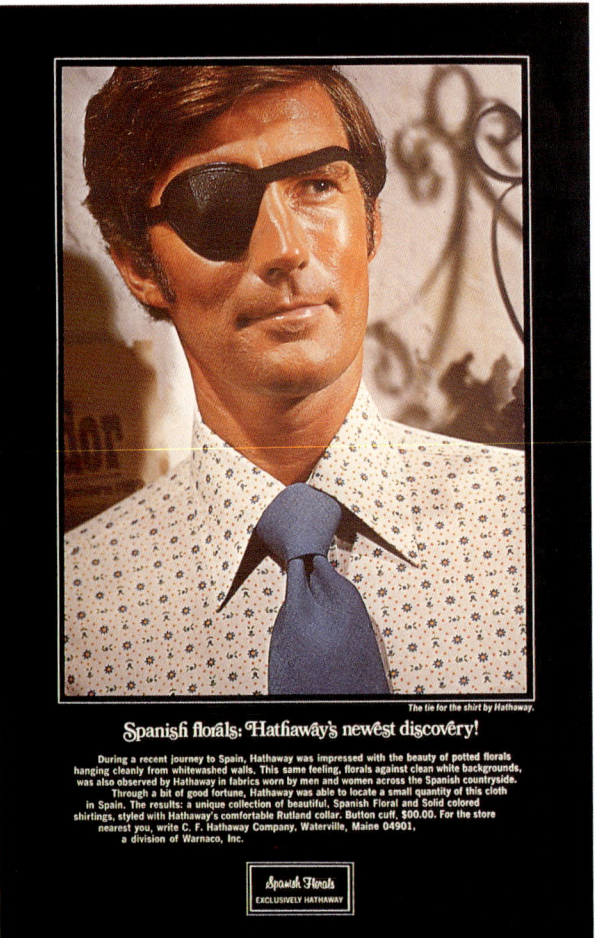

1973. Floral pattern with Rutland collar. $20–22.

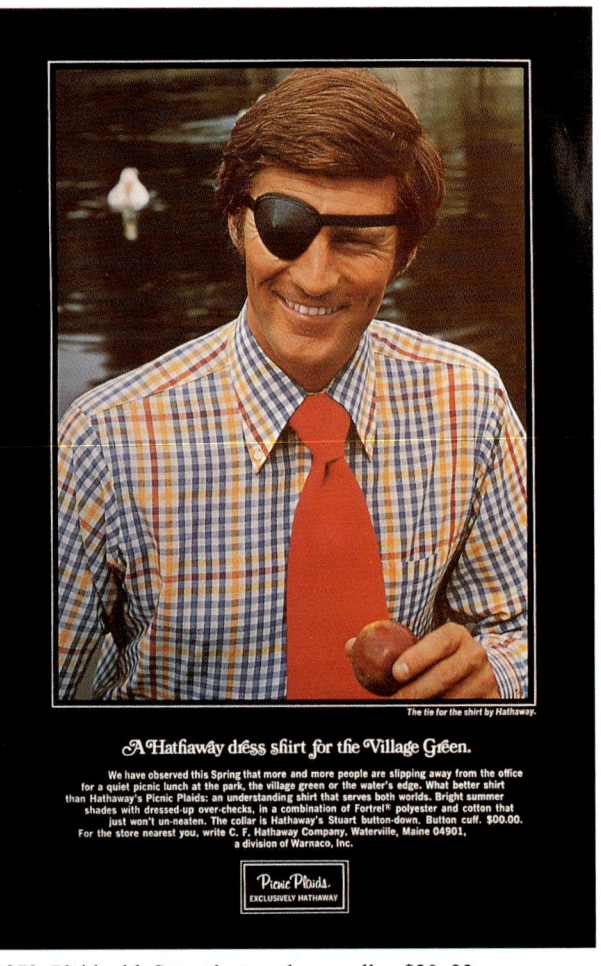

1973. Plaid with Stuart button-down collar. $20–22.

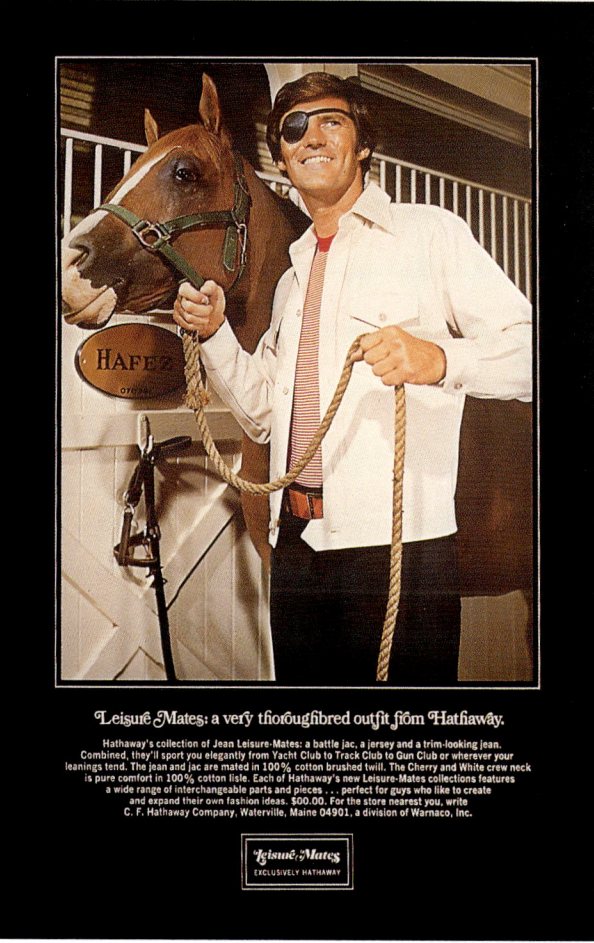

1973. An ensemble of jacket, jersey, and jean. $28–30.

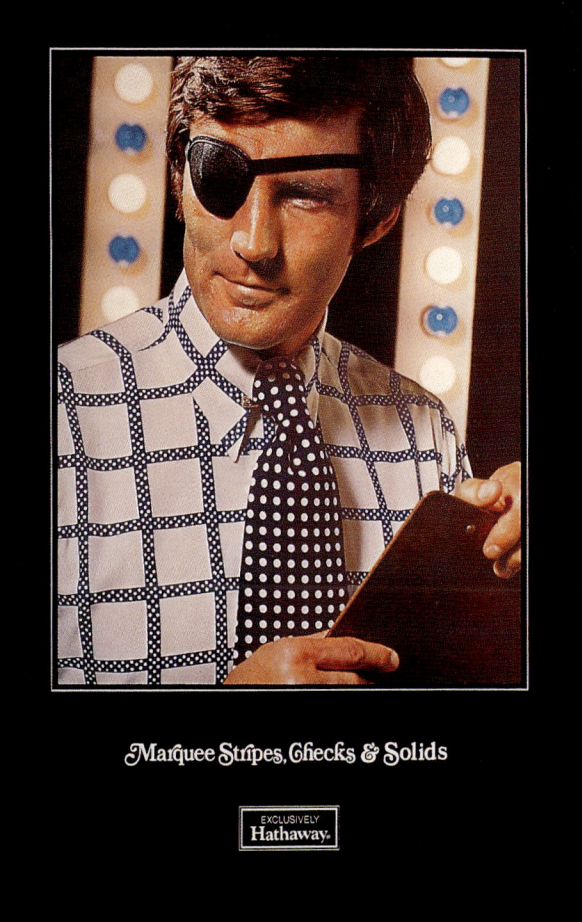

1973. $20–22.

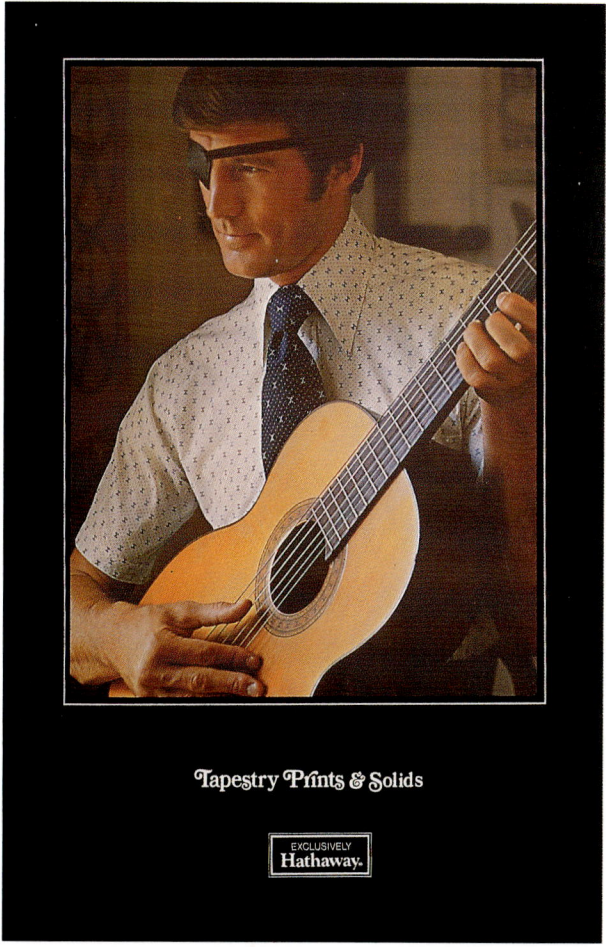

1973. $18–20.

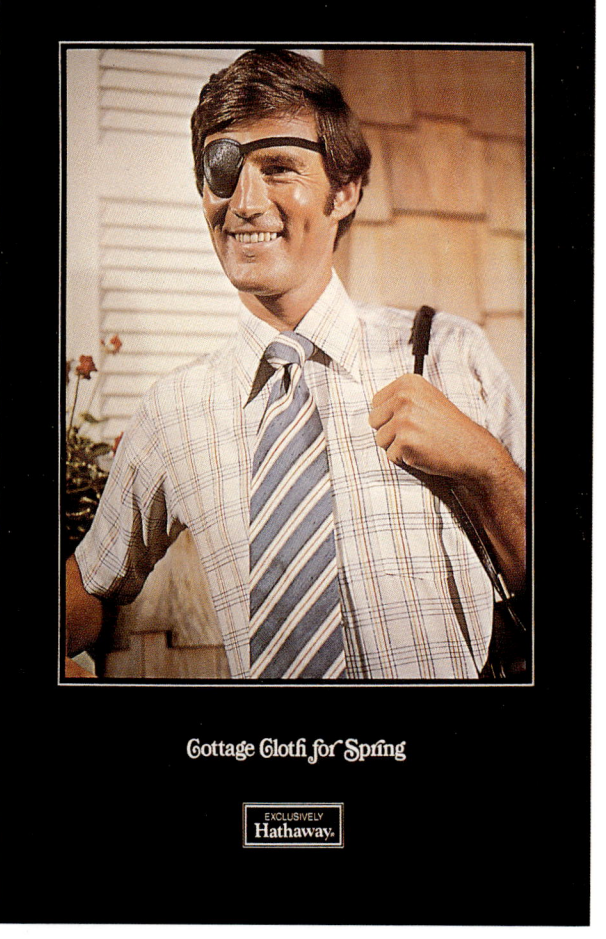

1973. $20–22.

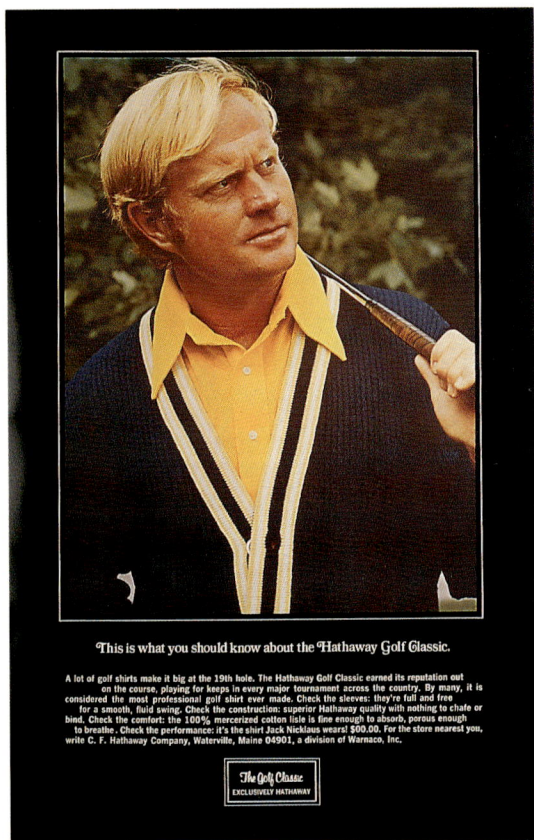
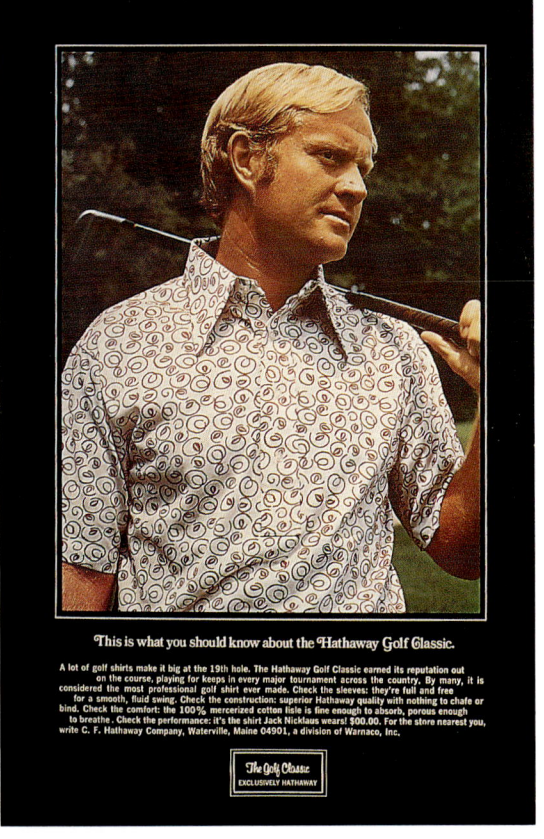

Above left: 1973. Hathaway Golf Classics. $24–28.

Above right: 1973. $24–28.

Left: 1973. $15–18.

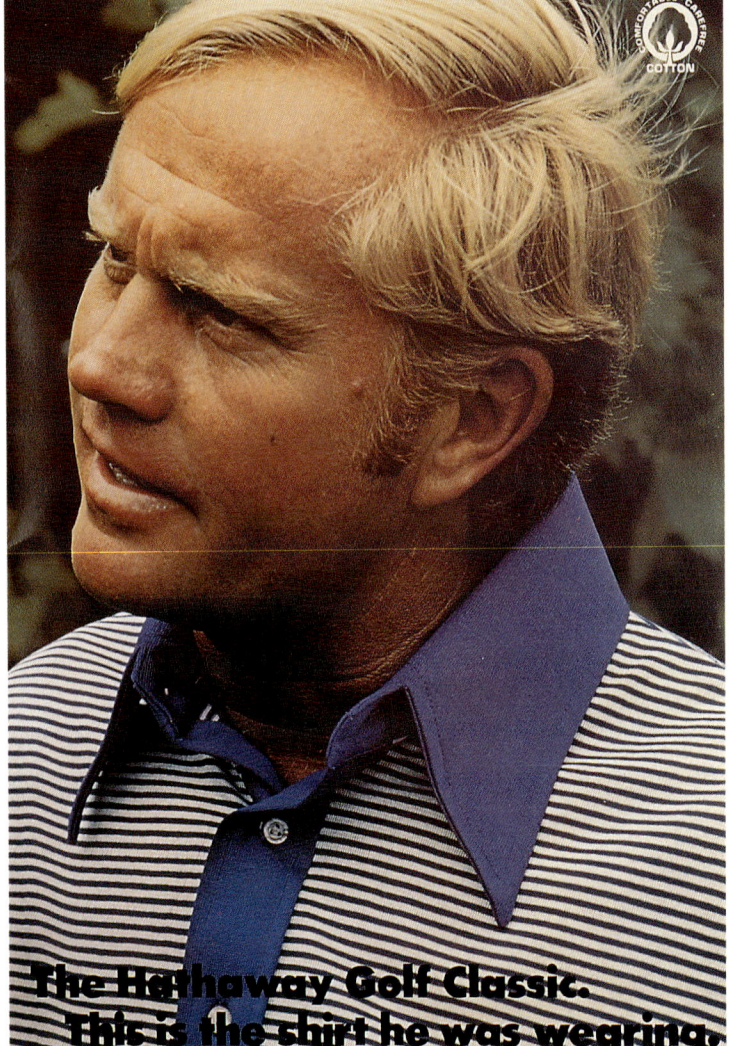

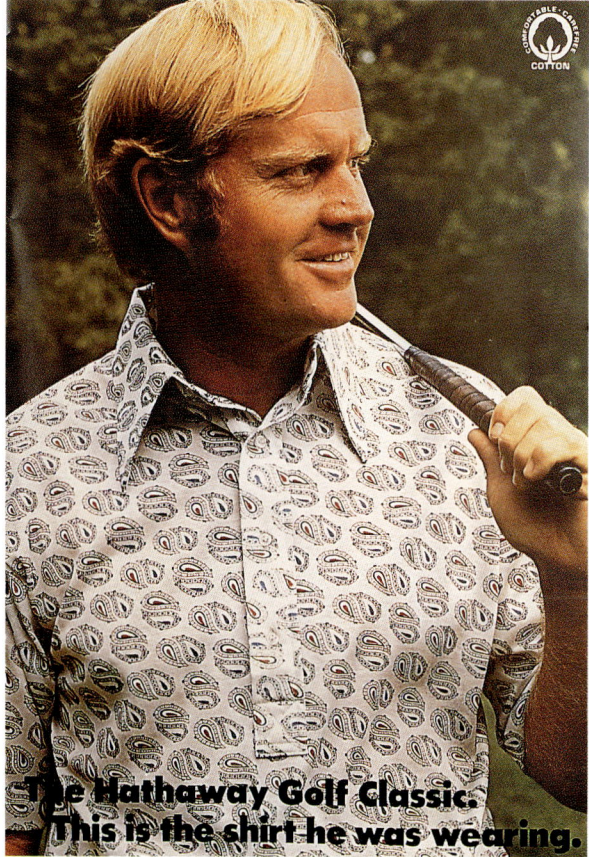

1973. $20–22.

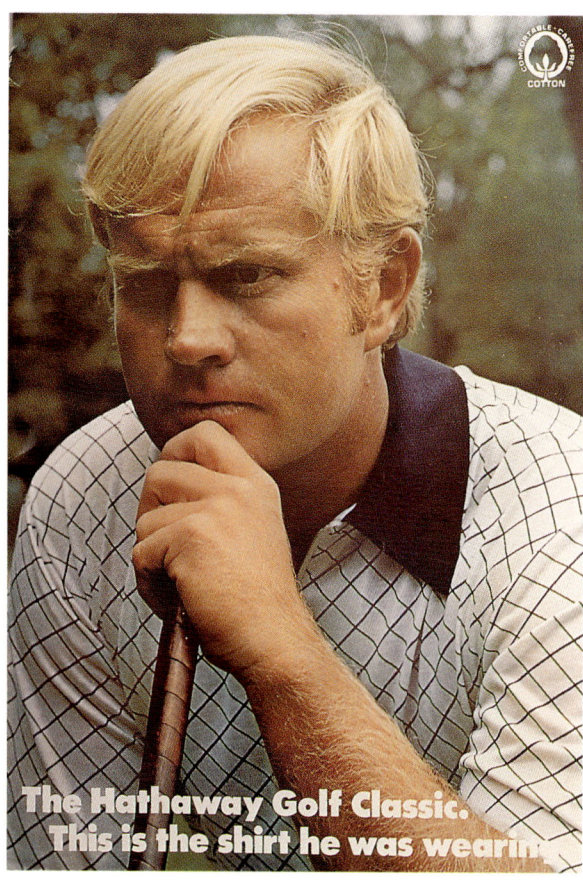

1973. $18–20.

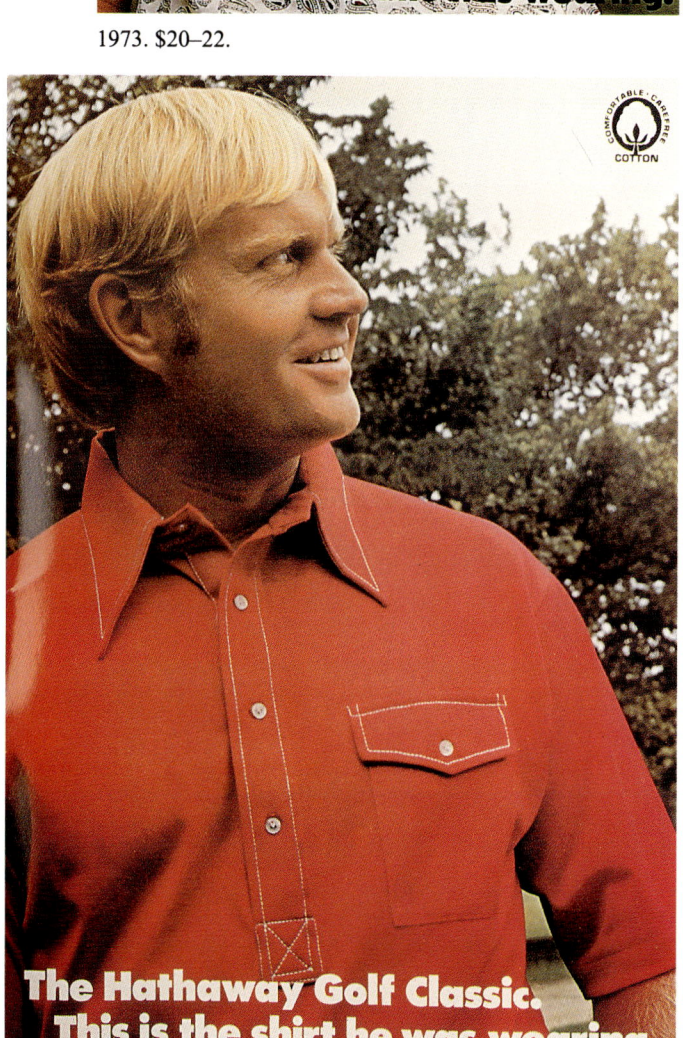

1973. $15–18.

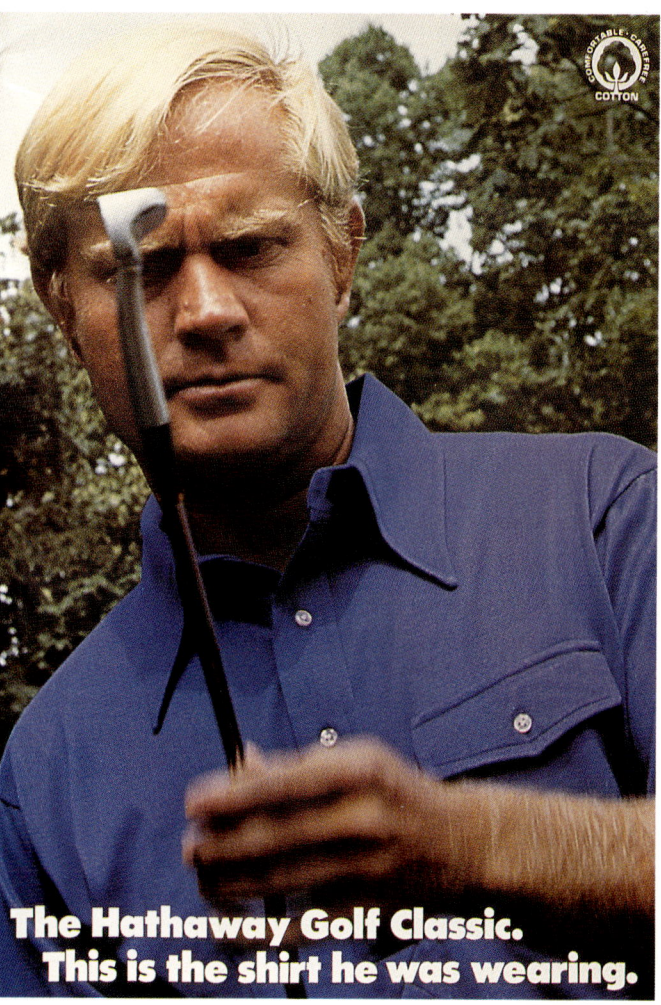

1973. $15–18.

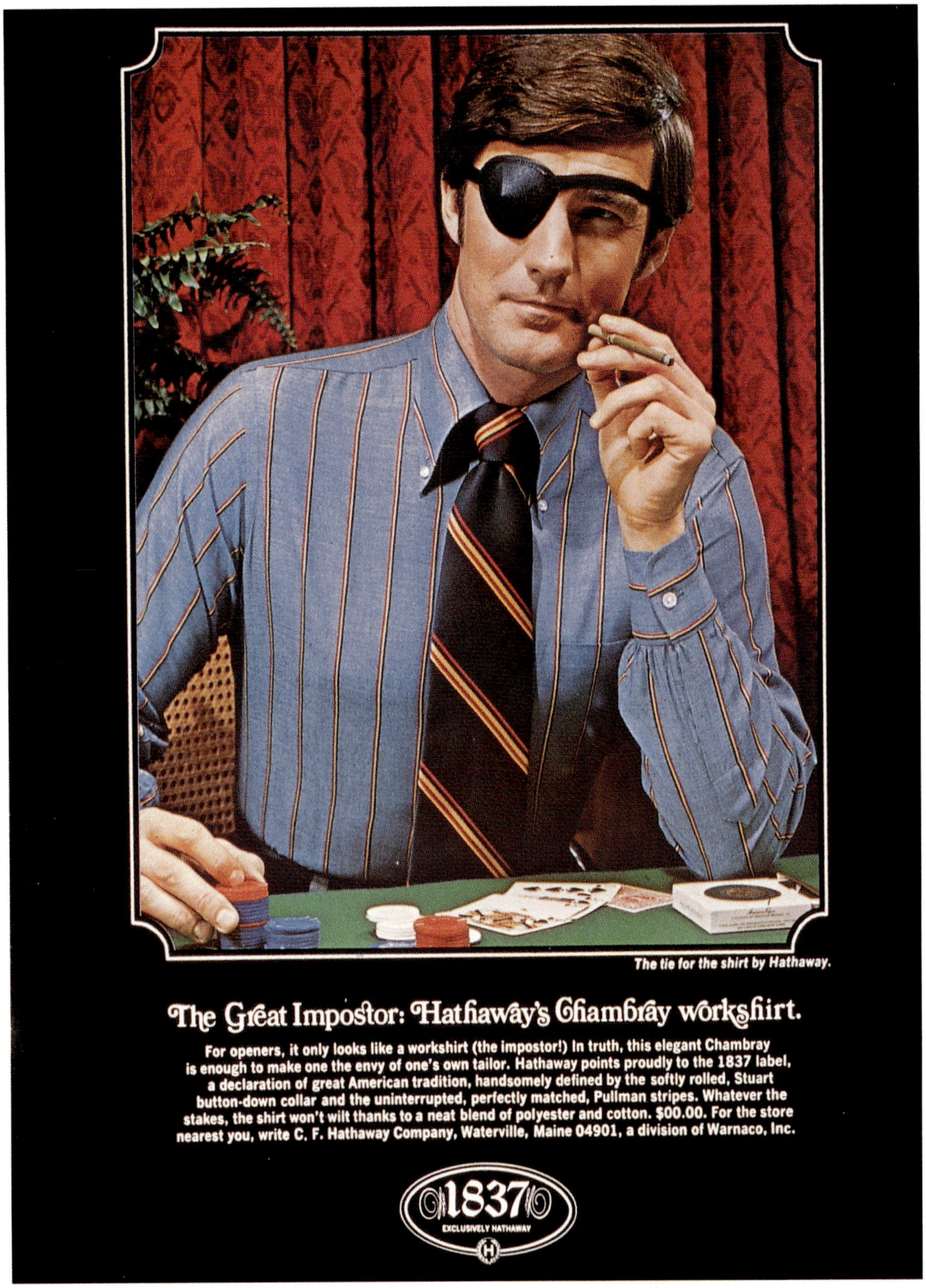

The Great Impostor: Hathaway's Chambray workshirt.

For openers, it only looks like a workshirt (the impostor!) In truth, this elegant Chambray is enough to make one the envy of one's own tailor. Hathaway points proudly to the 1837 label, a declaration of great American tradition, handsomely defined by the softly rolled, Stuart button-down collar and the uninterrupted, perfectly matched, Pullman stripes. Whatever the stakes, the shirt won't wilt thanks to a neat blend of polyester and cotton. $00.00. For the store nearest you, write C. F. Hathaway Company, Waterville, Maine 04901, a division of Warnaco, Inc.

The tie for the shirt by Hathaway.

1837 EXCLUSIVELY HATHAWAY

Above: 1973. Introduction of new "1837" label. $18–20.

Right two: 1973. $18–20.

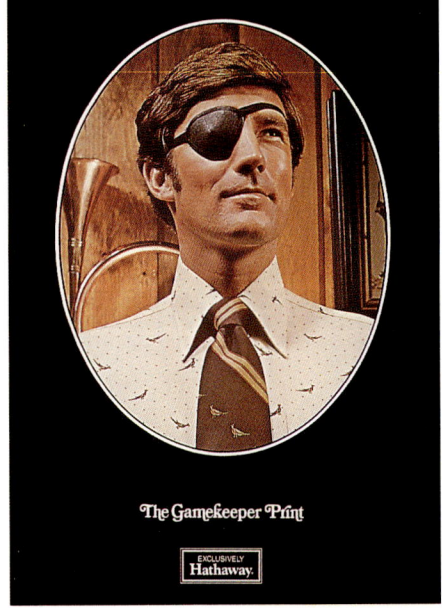

The Gamekeeper Print

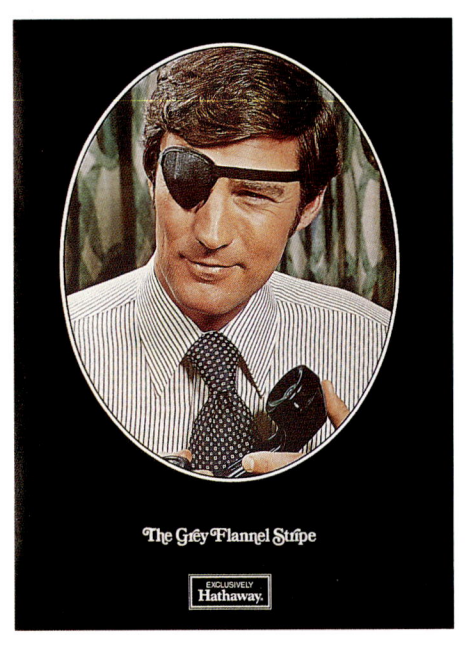

The Grey Flannel Stripe

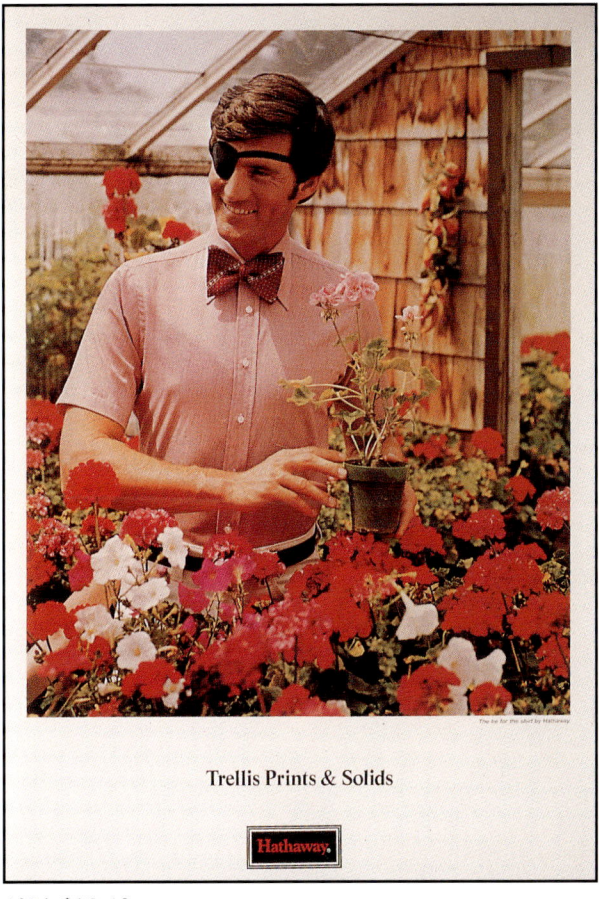

1974. $15–18.

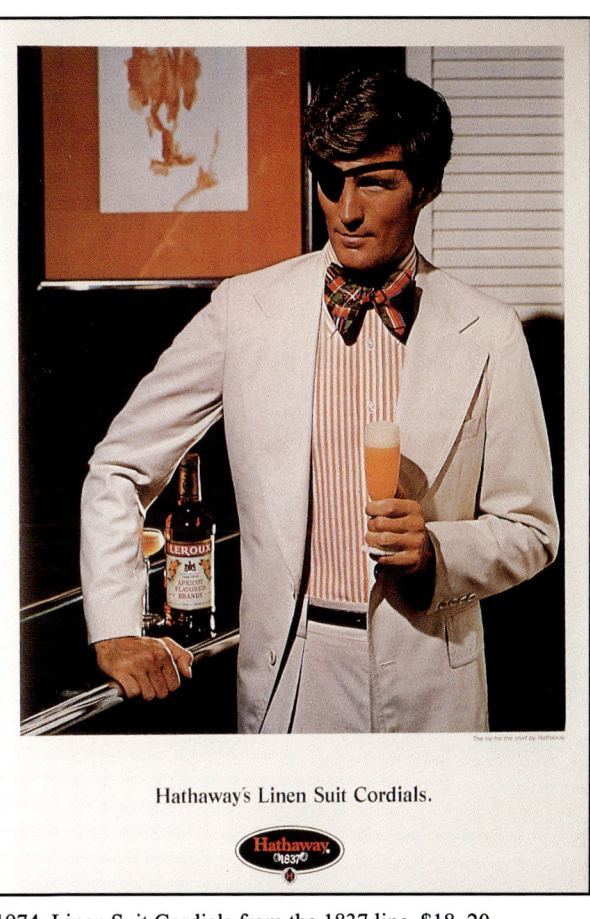

1974. Linen Suit Cordials from the 1837 line. $18–20.

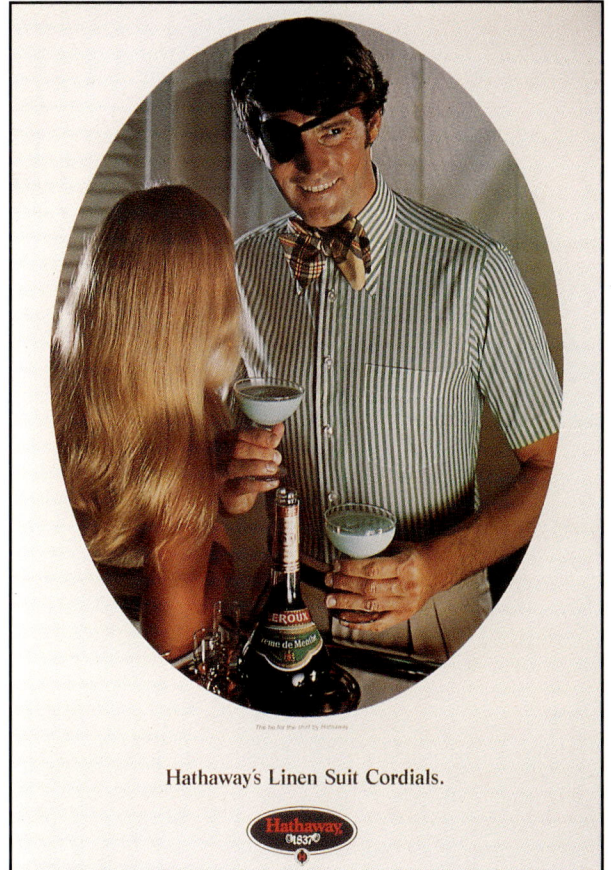

1974. The 1837 line. $18–20.

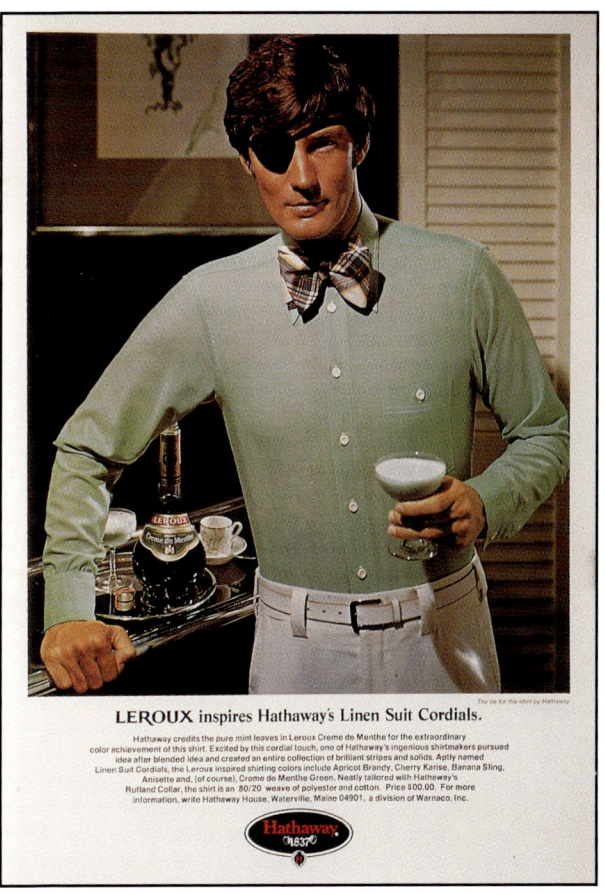

1974. The 1837 line. $20–22.

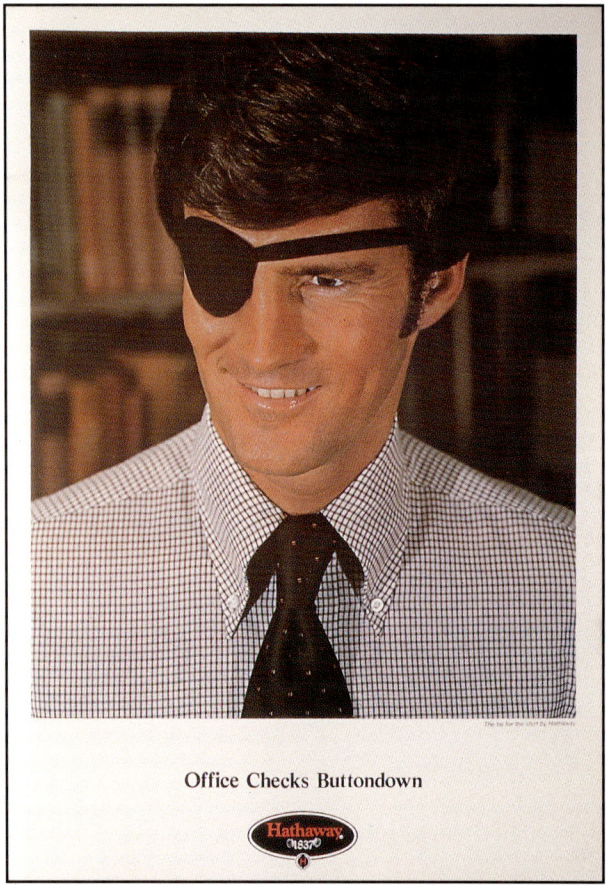

1974. The 1837 line. $18–20.

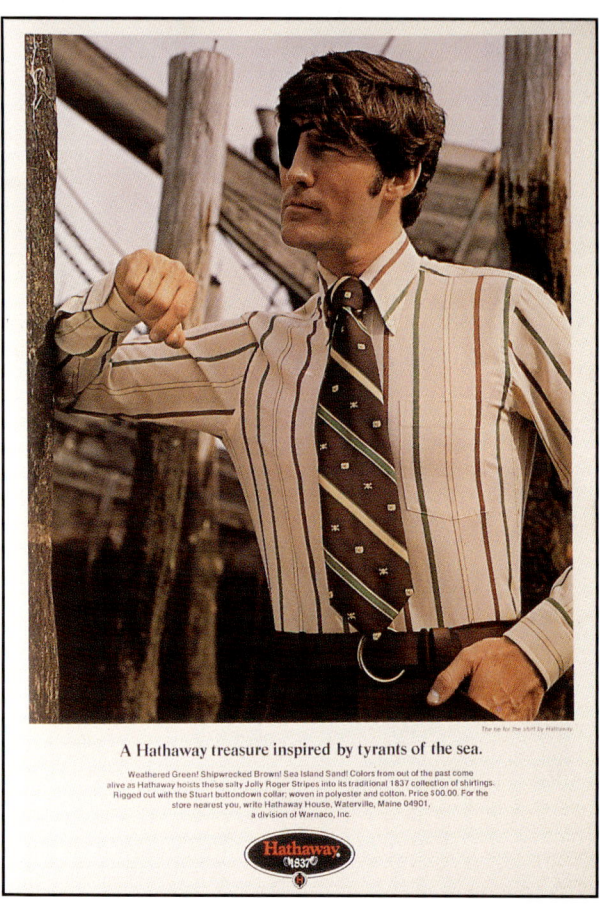

1974. The 1837 line. $18–20.

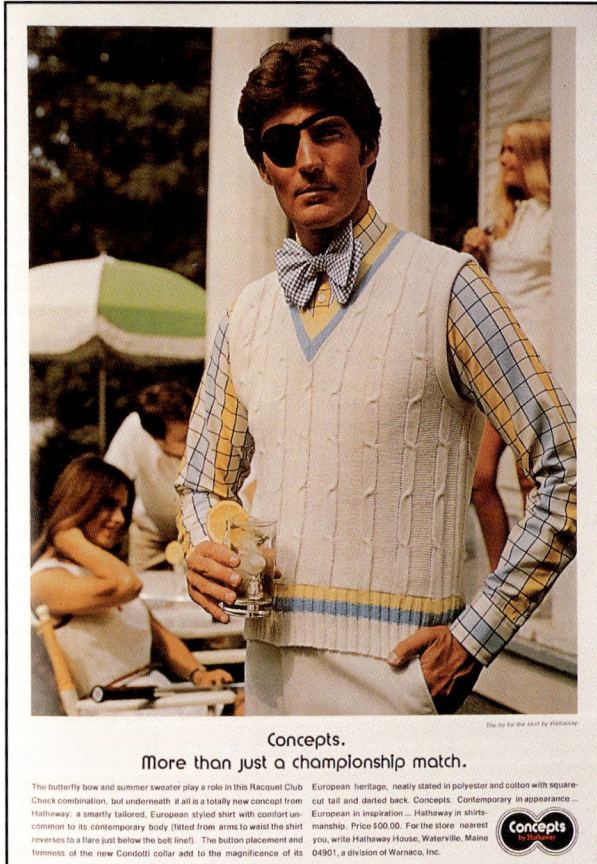

1974. Part of the Concepts line introduced in 1974 offering the younger man European tapered shirts with square bottoms, higher armholes, darted waists, tapered sleeves, and buttons placed higher on the band. $20–22.

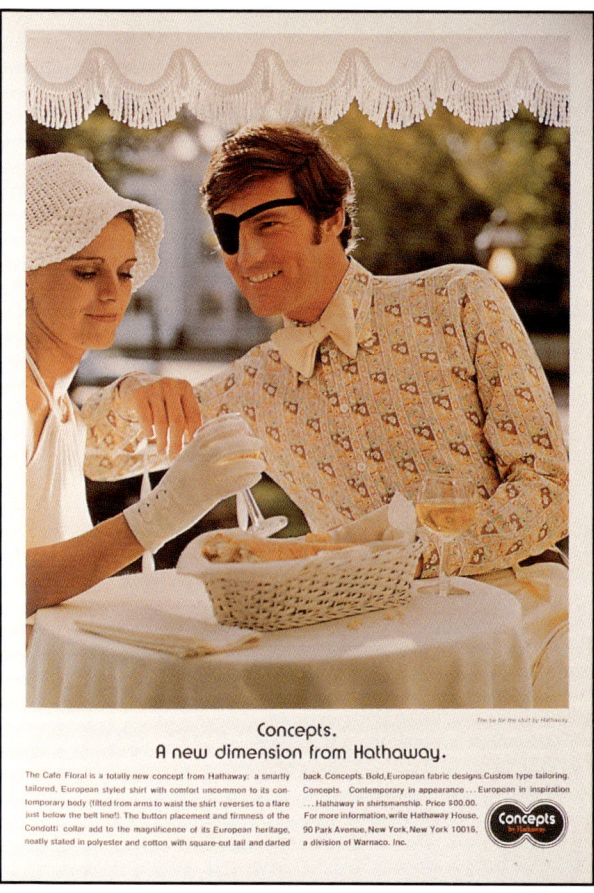

1974. Racquet Club Check with the new Condotti collar from the Concepts line. $22–24.

1974. $24–28

1974. $15–18.

1974. $18–20.

1974. $18–20.

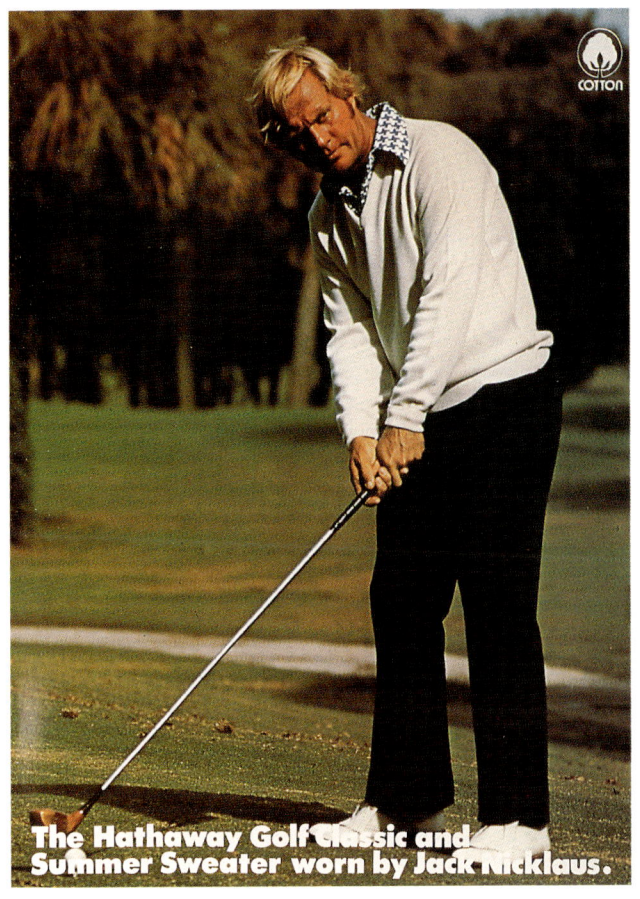
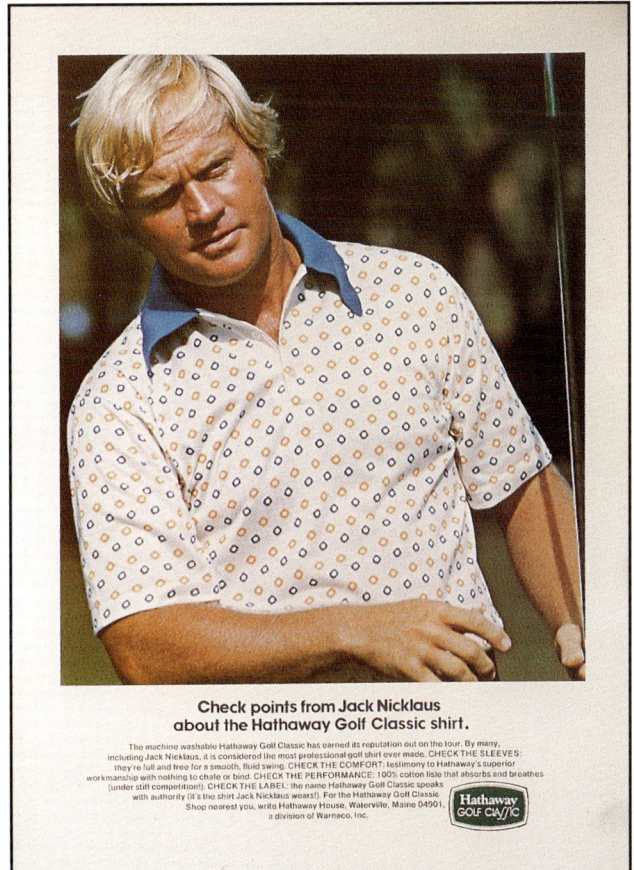
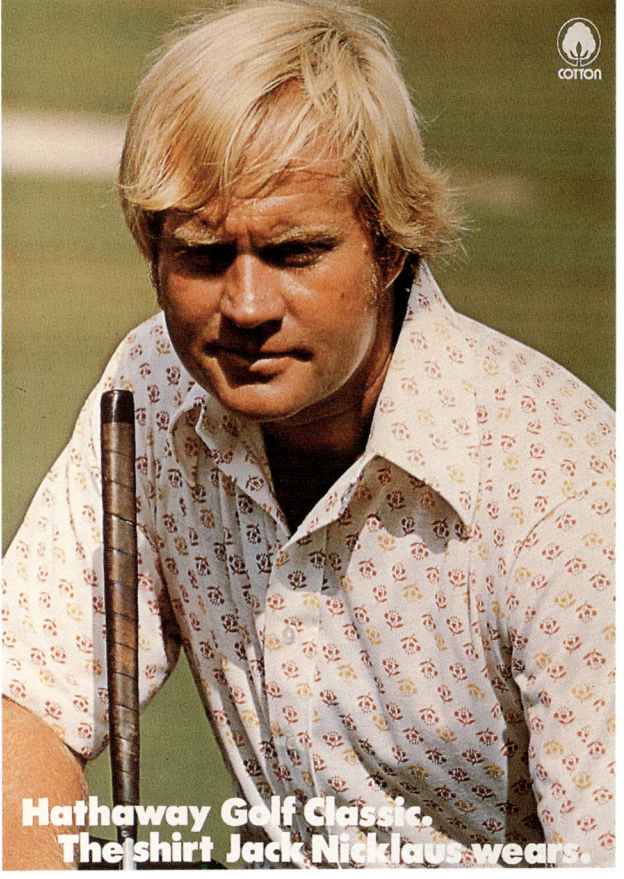

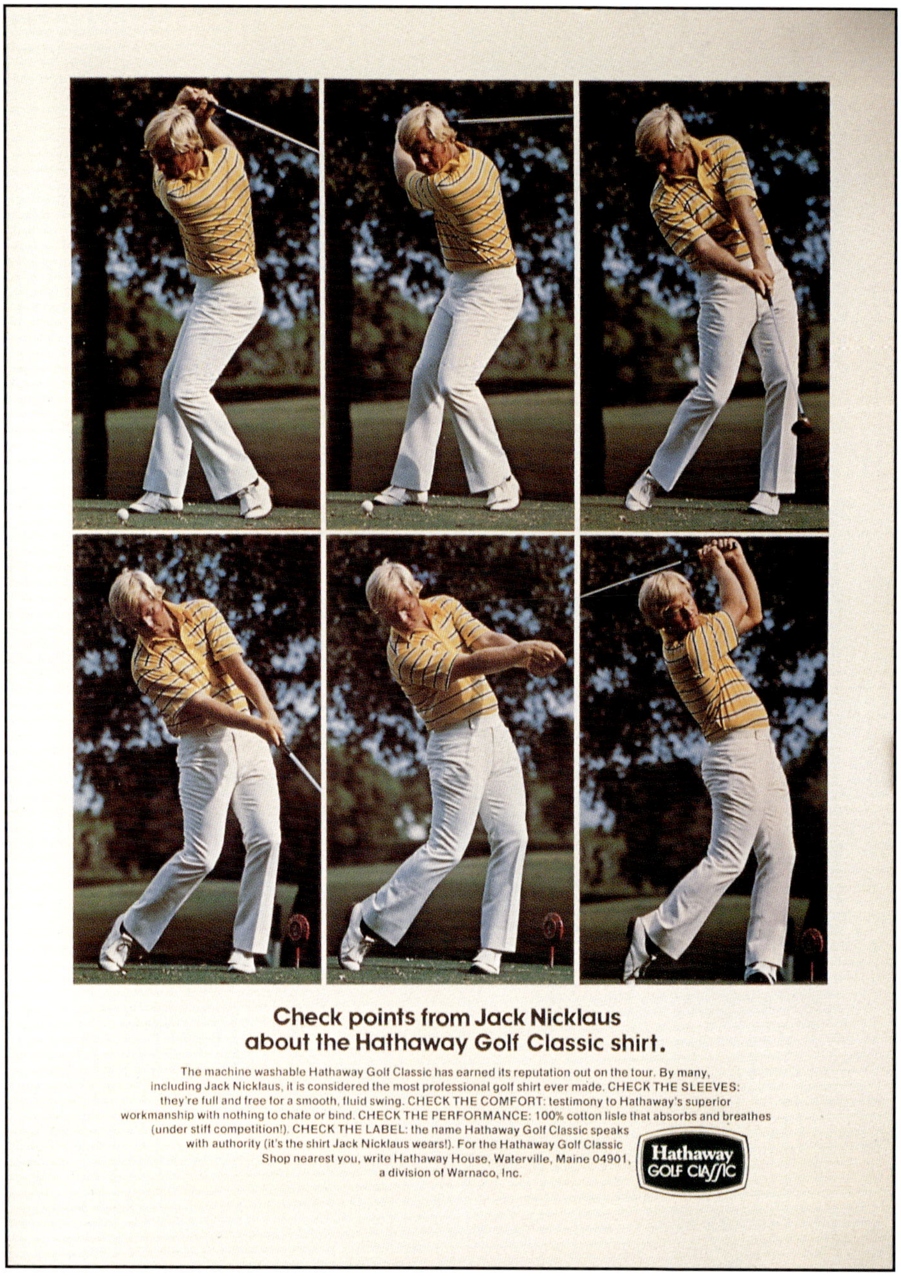

This page: 1974. $18–20.

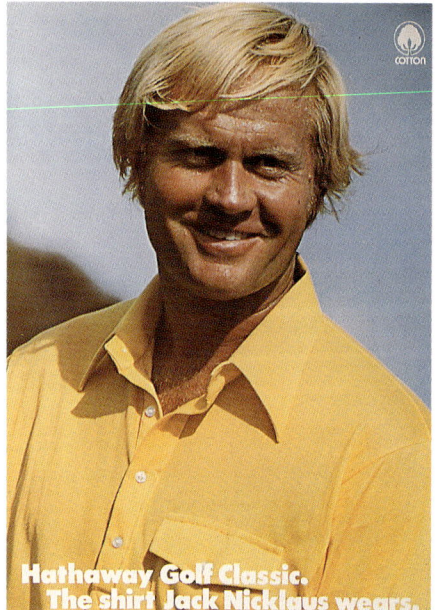

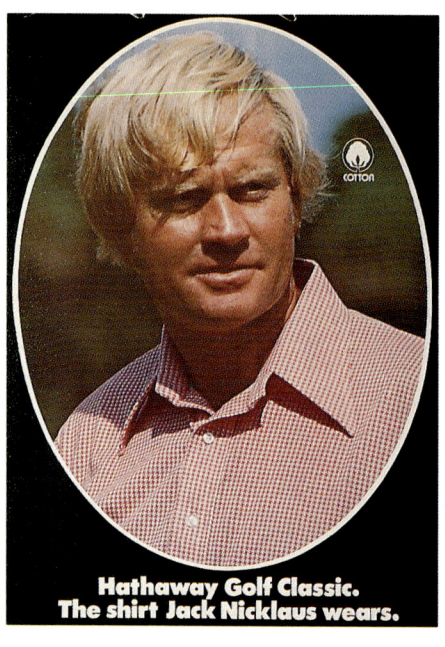

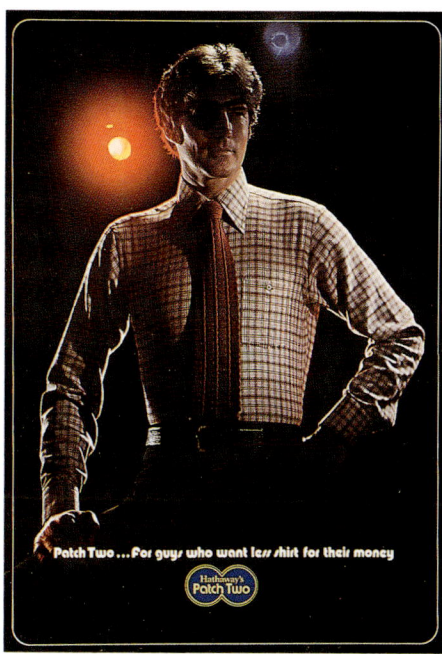

1974. The introduction of the Patch Two line in Fall, 1974 continued and expanded the Concepts line, introduced in the spring. $20–22.

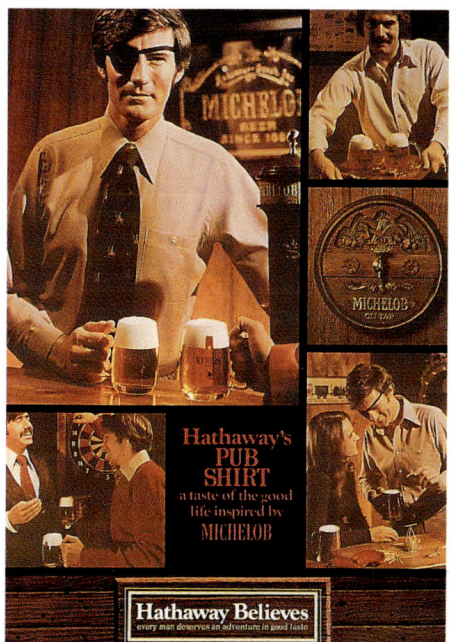

1974. The Pub Shirt, a tie-in with Michelob beer.

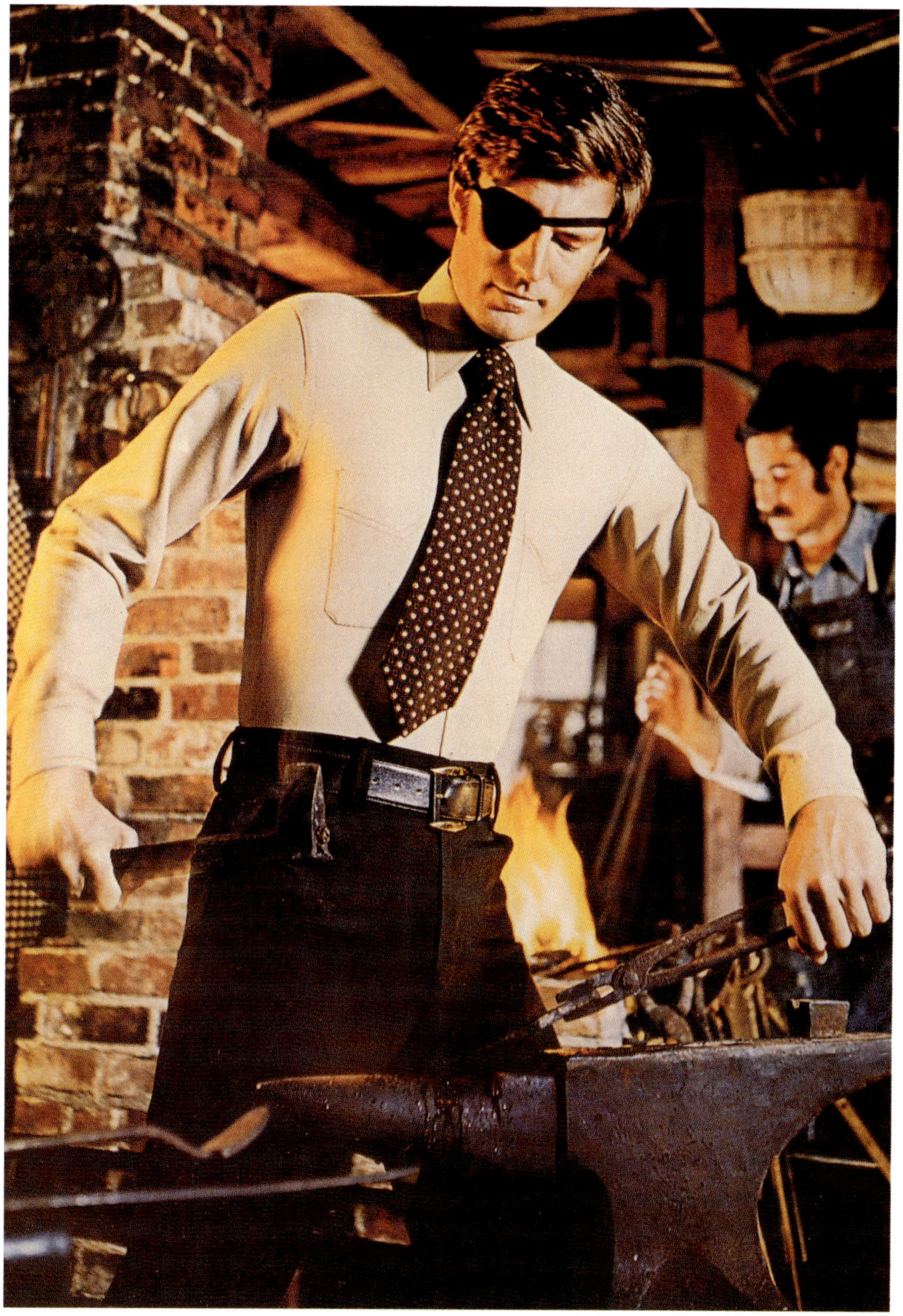

1974. $15–18.

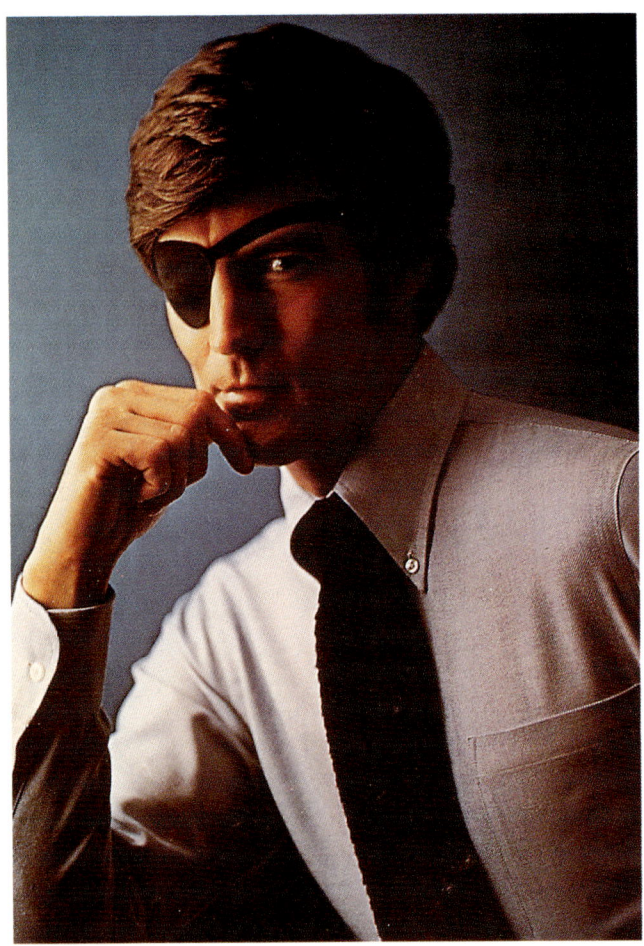

1974. $18–20.

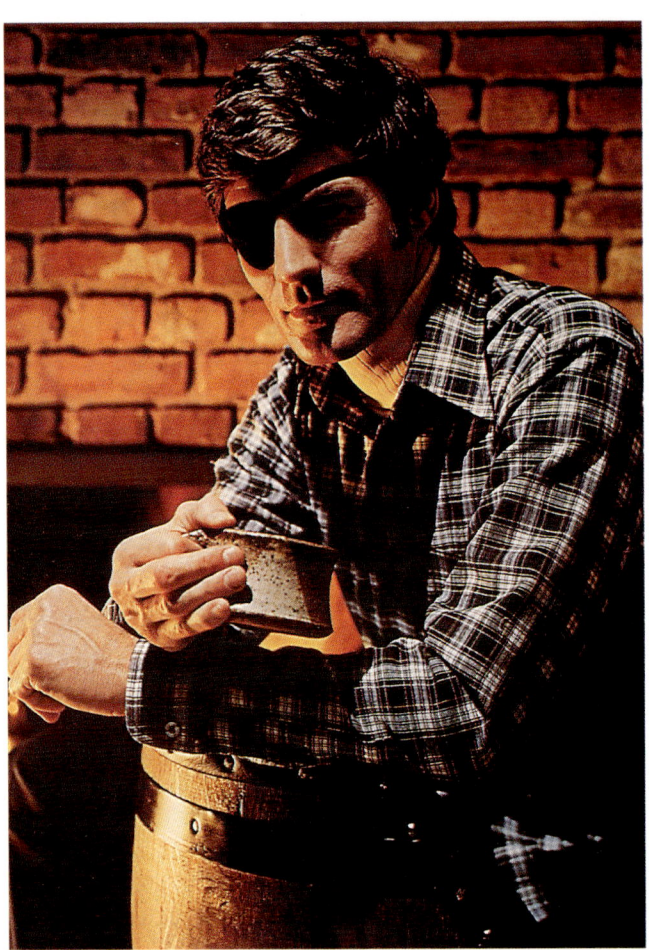

1974. $15–18.

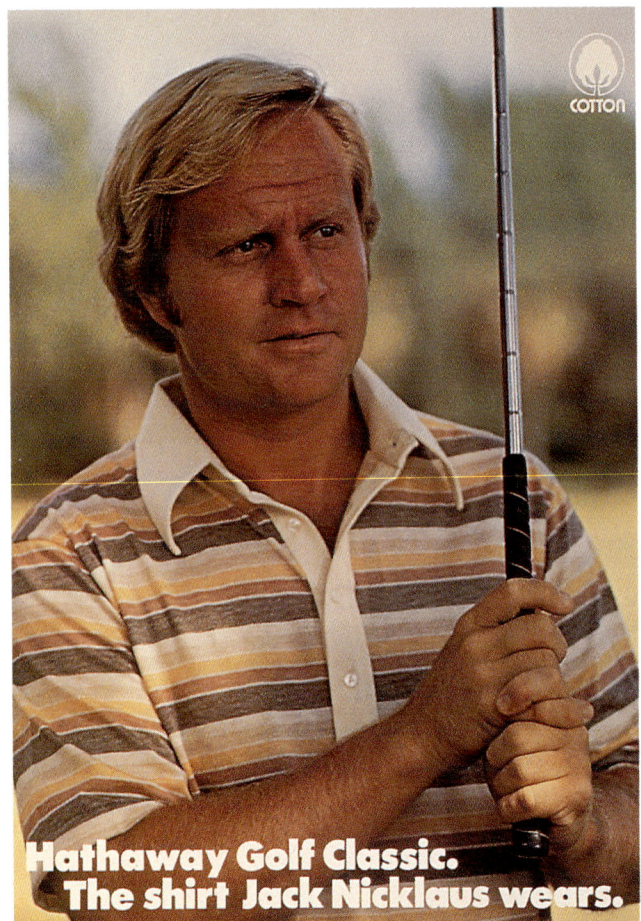

1974. Hathaway Golf Classic, "The shirt Jack Nicklaus wears." $18–20.

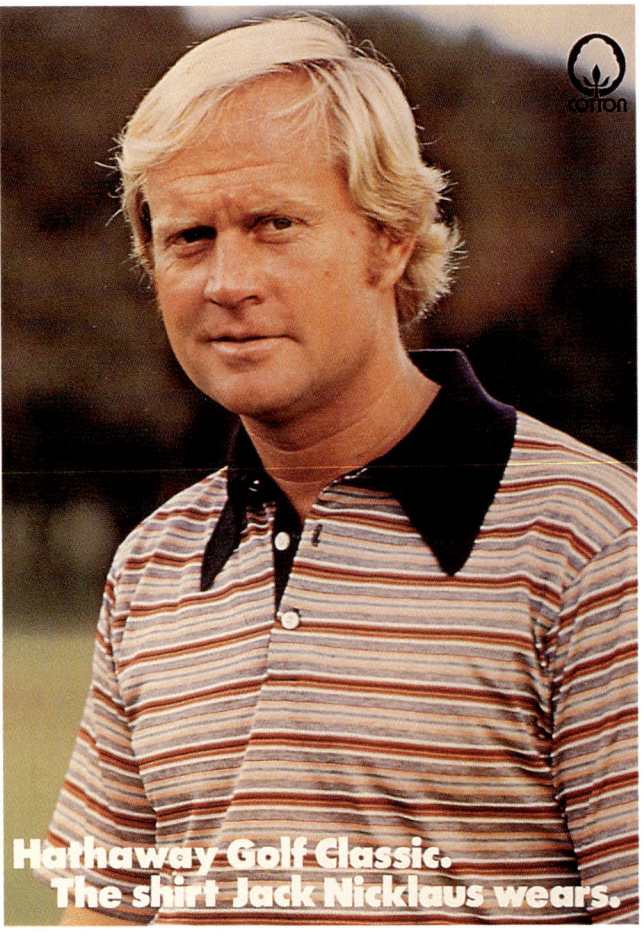

1974. $18–20.

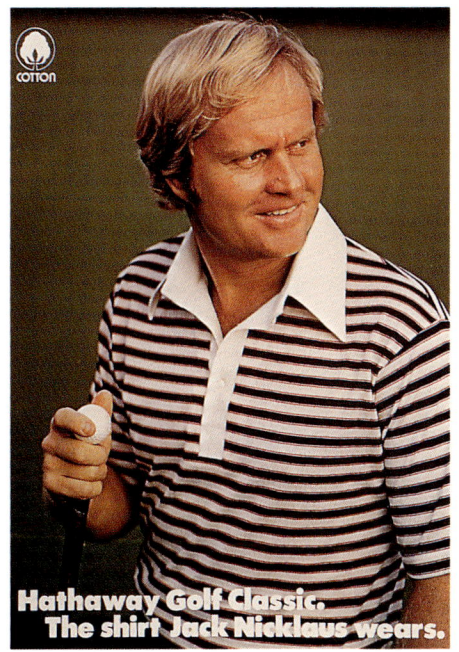
1974. $18–20.

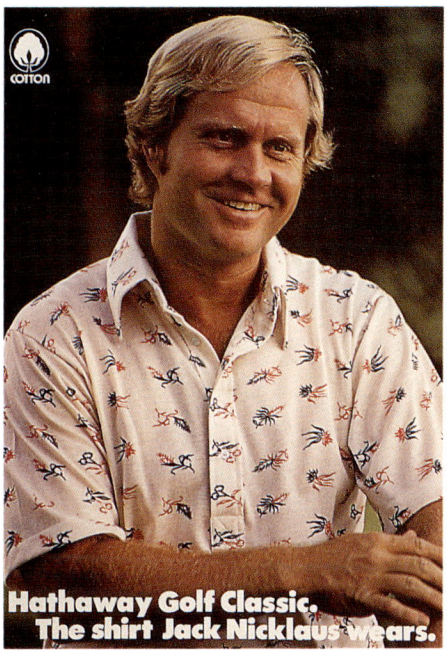
1974. $20–22.

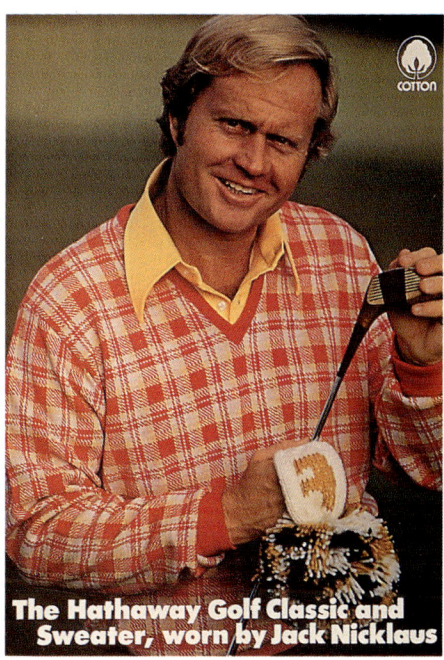
1974. $30–32.

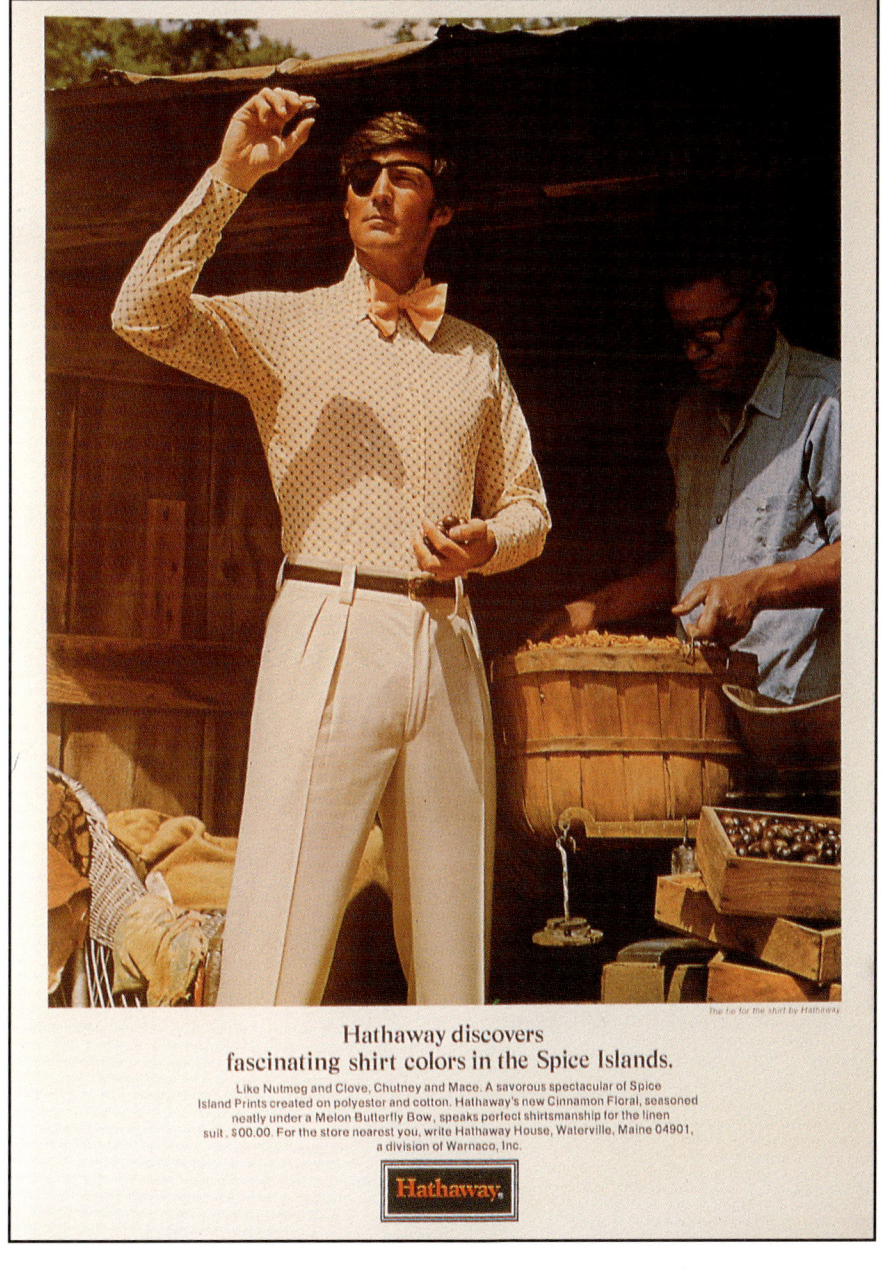
1974. $18–20.

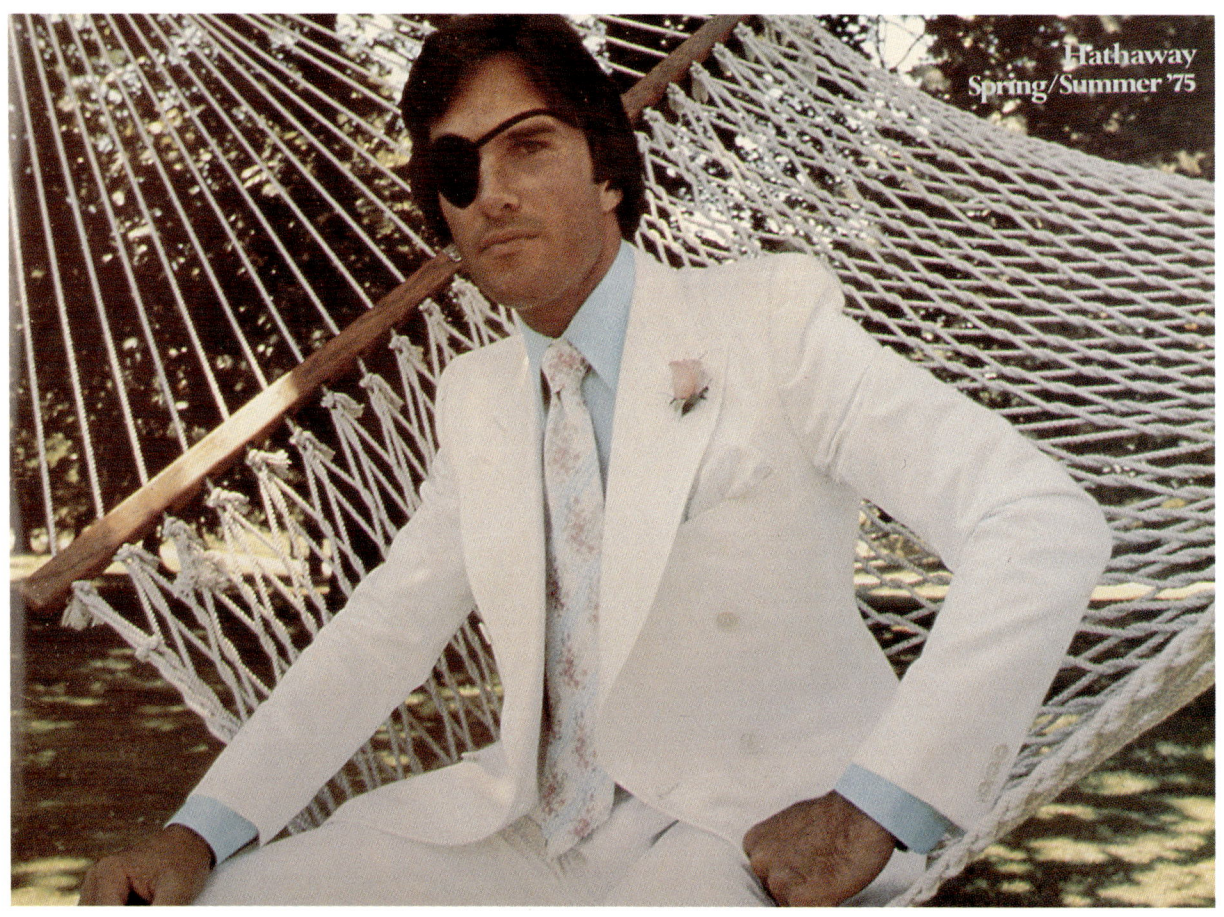

1975. Spring-Summer catalog.

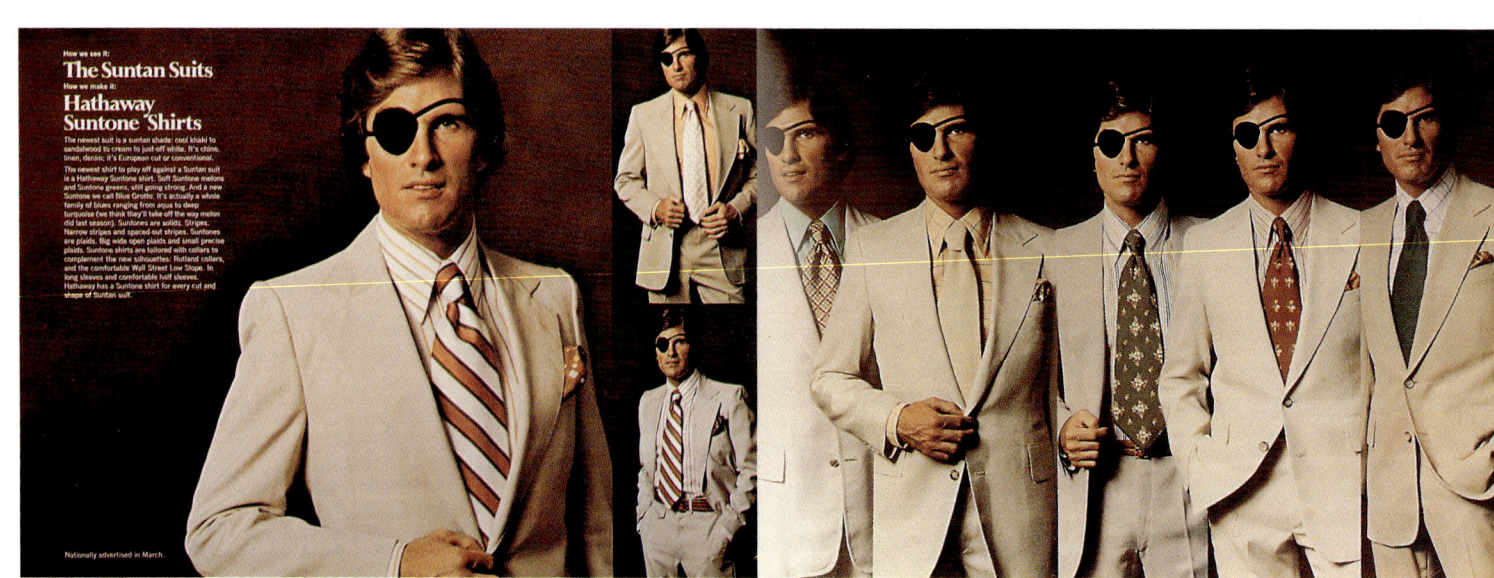

1975. Suntone shirts to go with the latest Suntan suits. Rutland collars. $15–18.

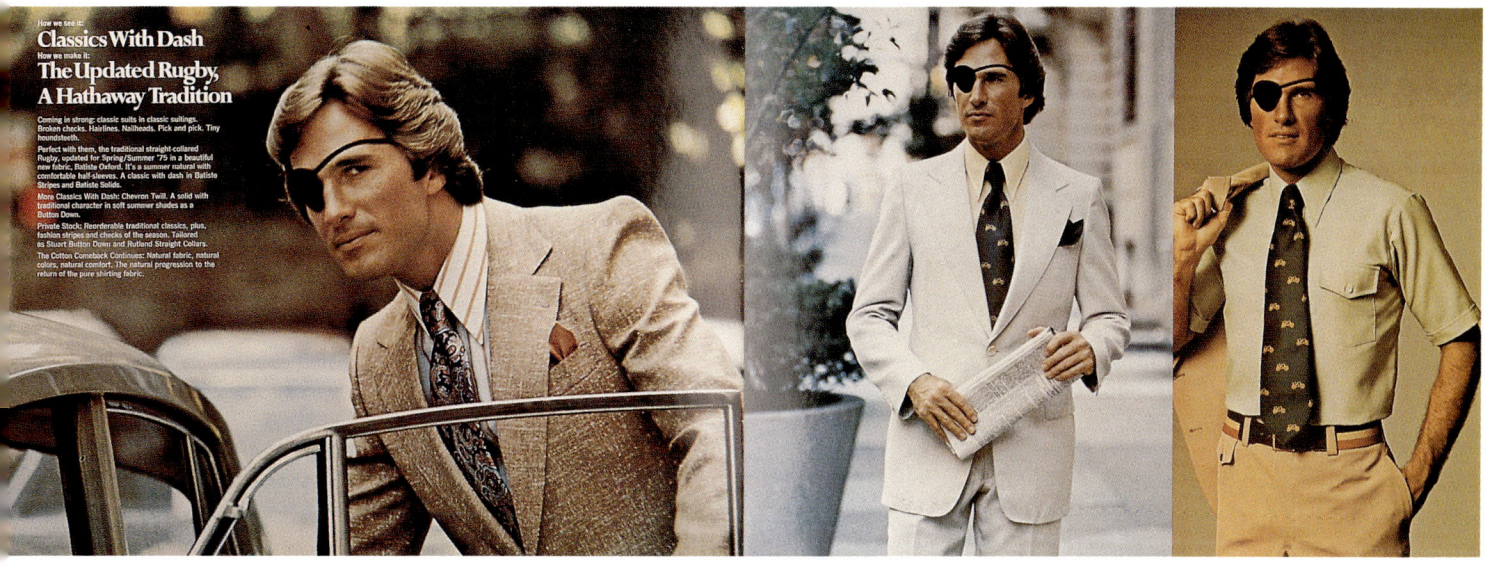

1975. Batiste Oxford Rugby shirts. Left, $18–20. Right, $15–18.

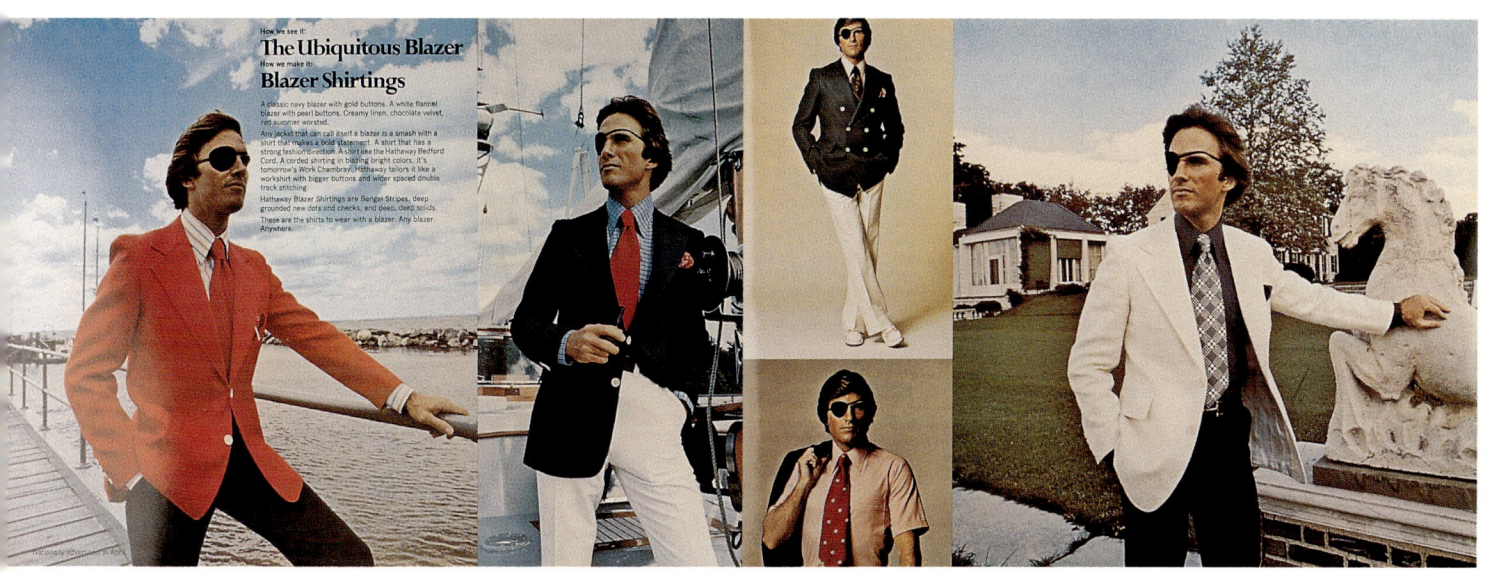

1975. Blazer Shirtings. $15–18.

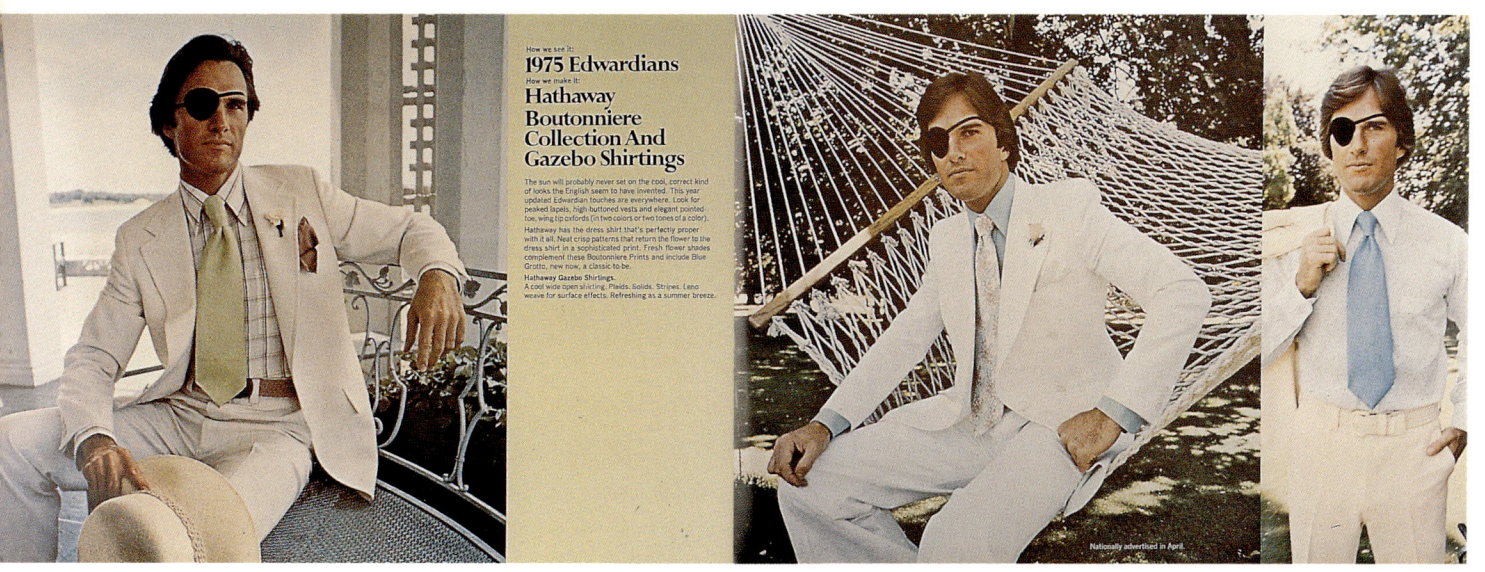

1975. Shirts to accompany the Edwardian renaissance of the mid-70s.
Left, $20–22. Right, $18–20.

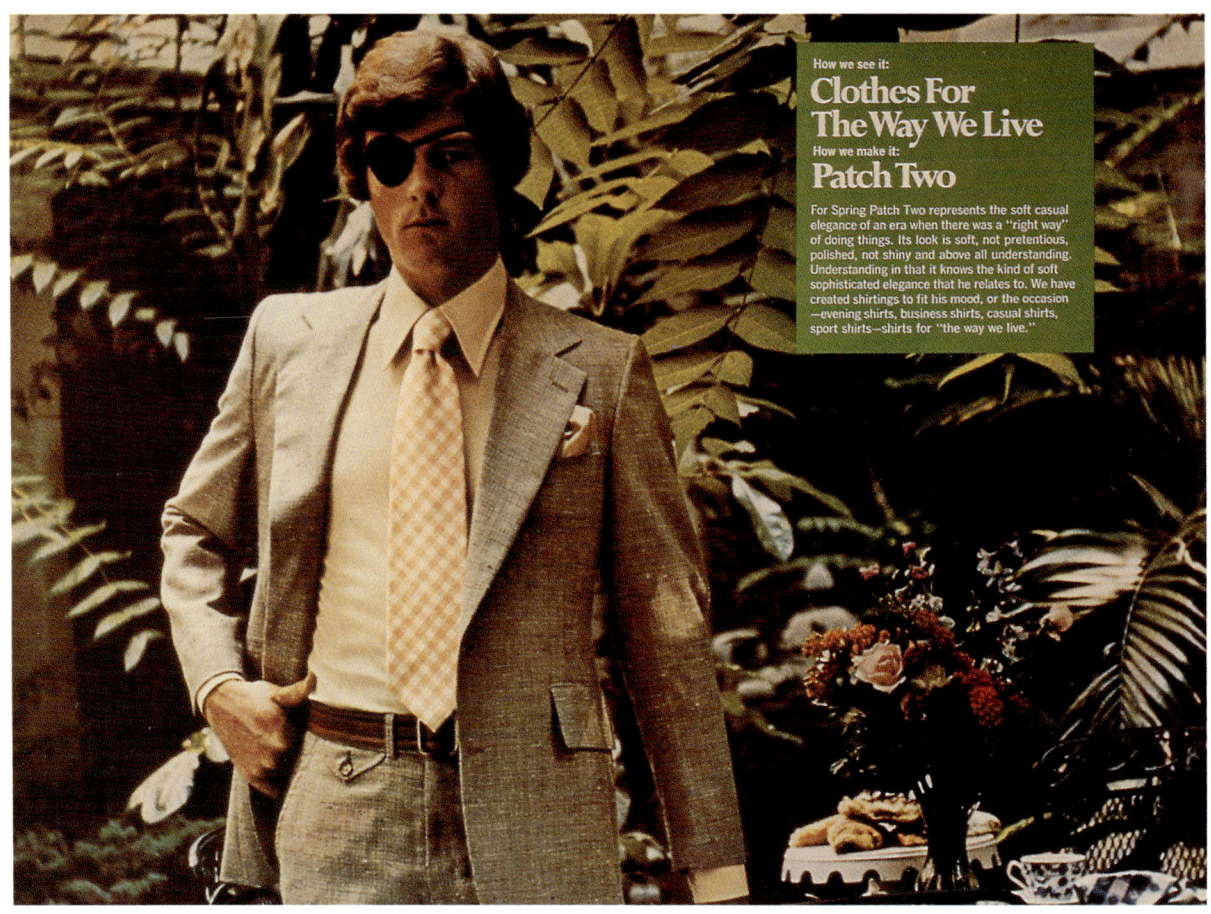

Above & below: 1975. Patch Two for spring. $15–18.

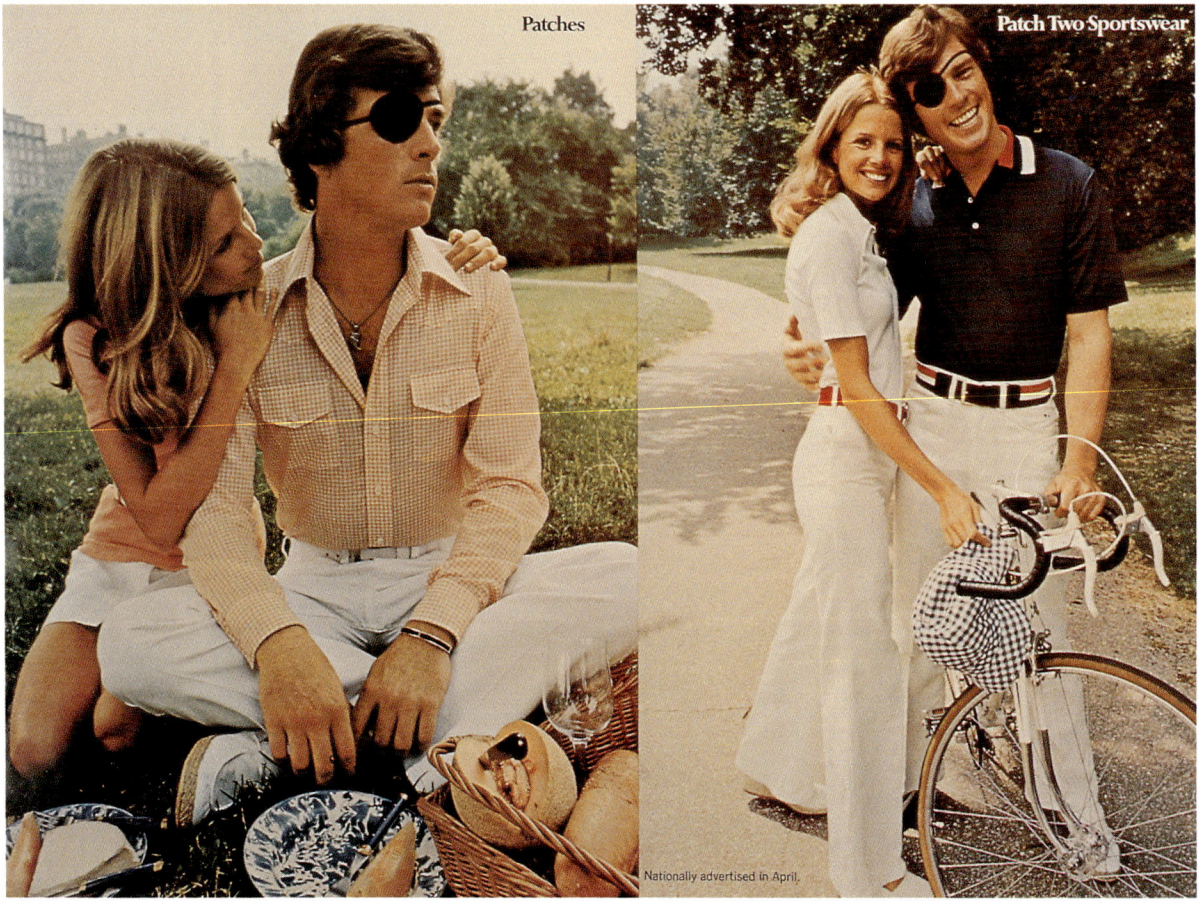

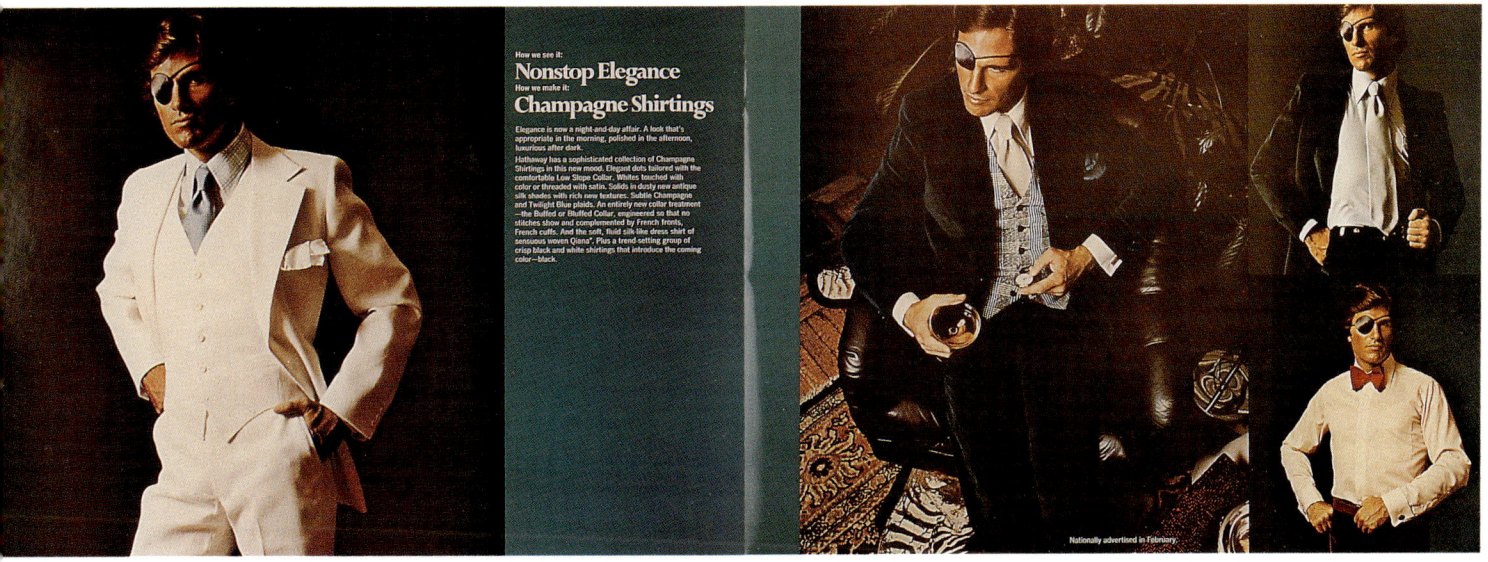

1975. Champagne Shirtings for day and evening wear in Qiana fabric.
Left, $20–22. Right, $18–20.

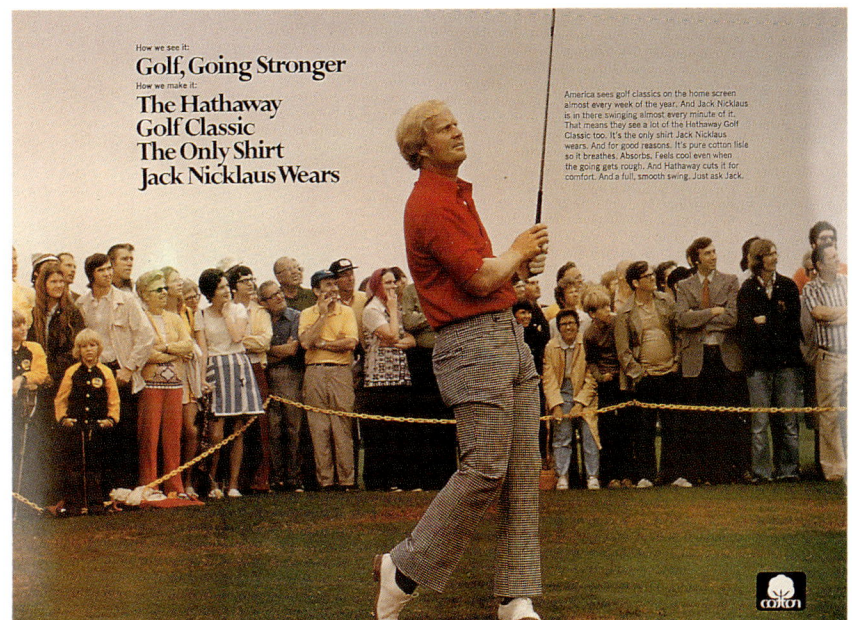

1975. The Golf Classic and Jack Nicklaus continue. $15–18.

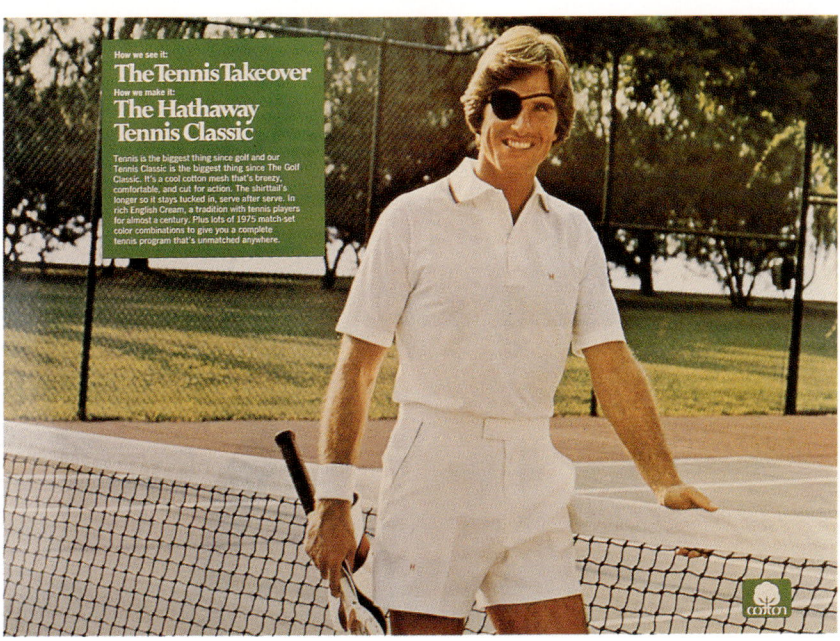

1975. A recognition of the growing presence of tennis as a recreational activity, brings the Tennis Classic shirts and shorts. $15–18.

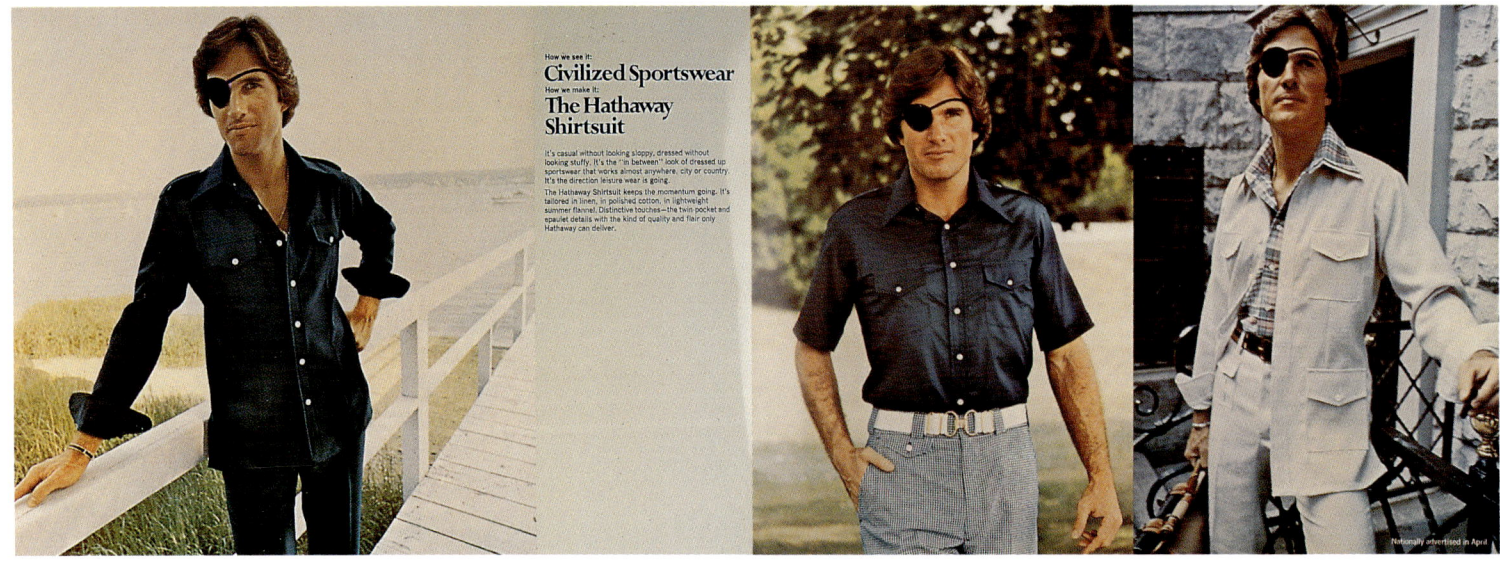

1975. The Shirtsuit was Hathaway's entry into the leisure suit arena. $18–20.

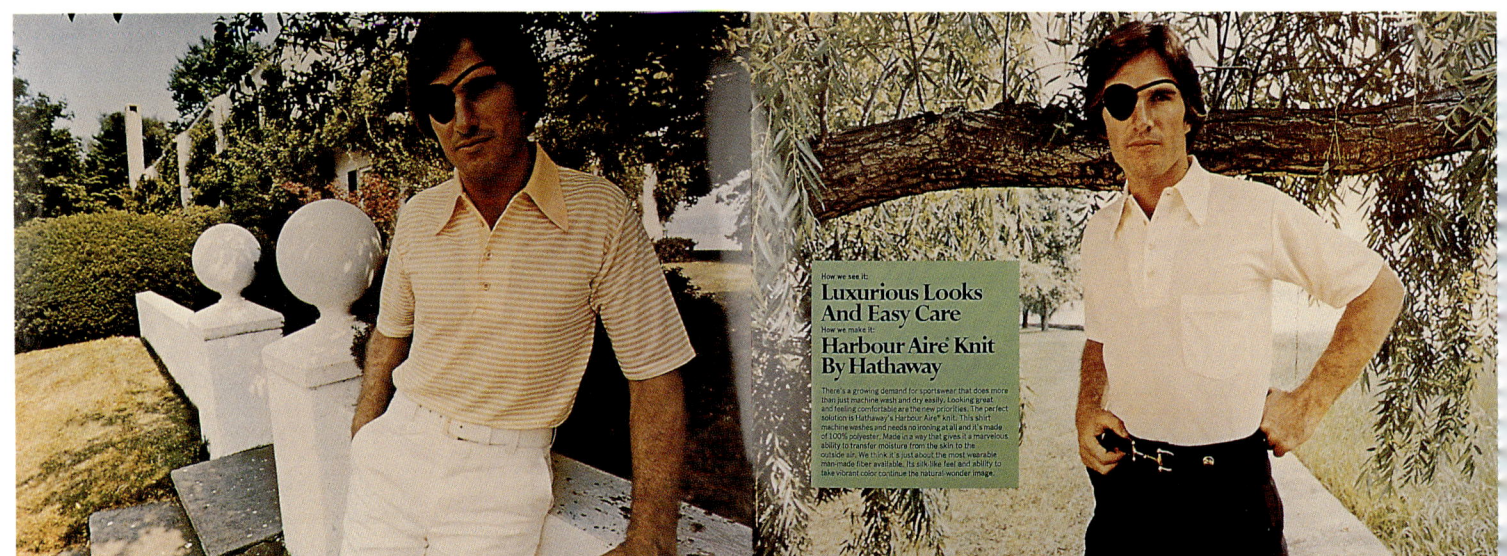

1975. Harbour Aire, polyester knit casual shirts. $15–18.

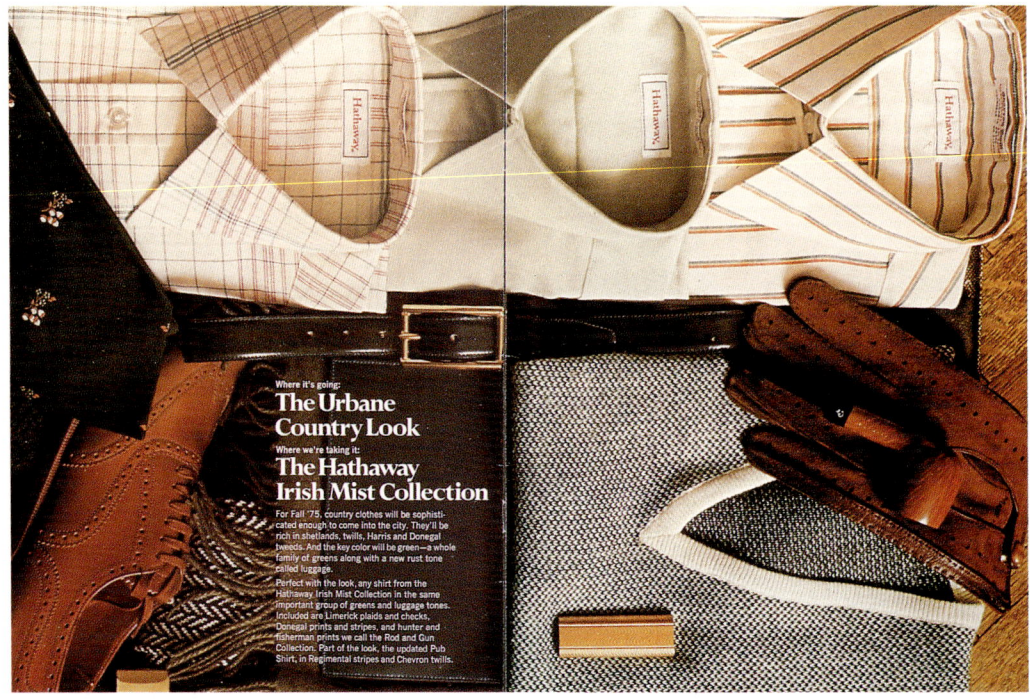

1975. Introducing the country look for Fall, 1975, with the Irish Mist Collection. $18–20.

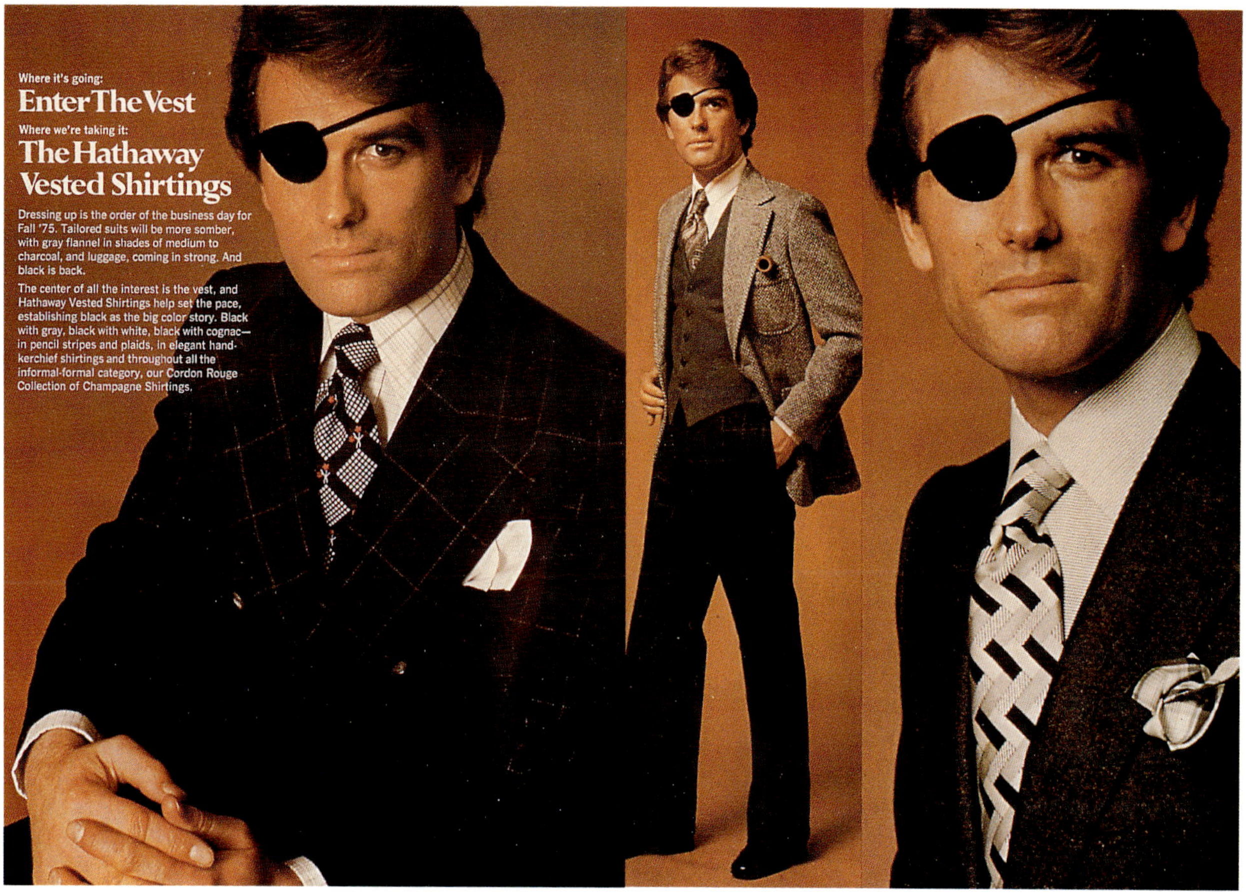

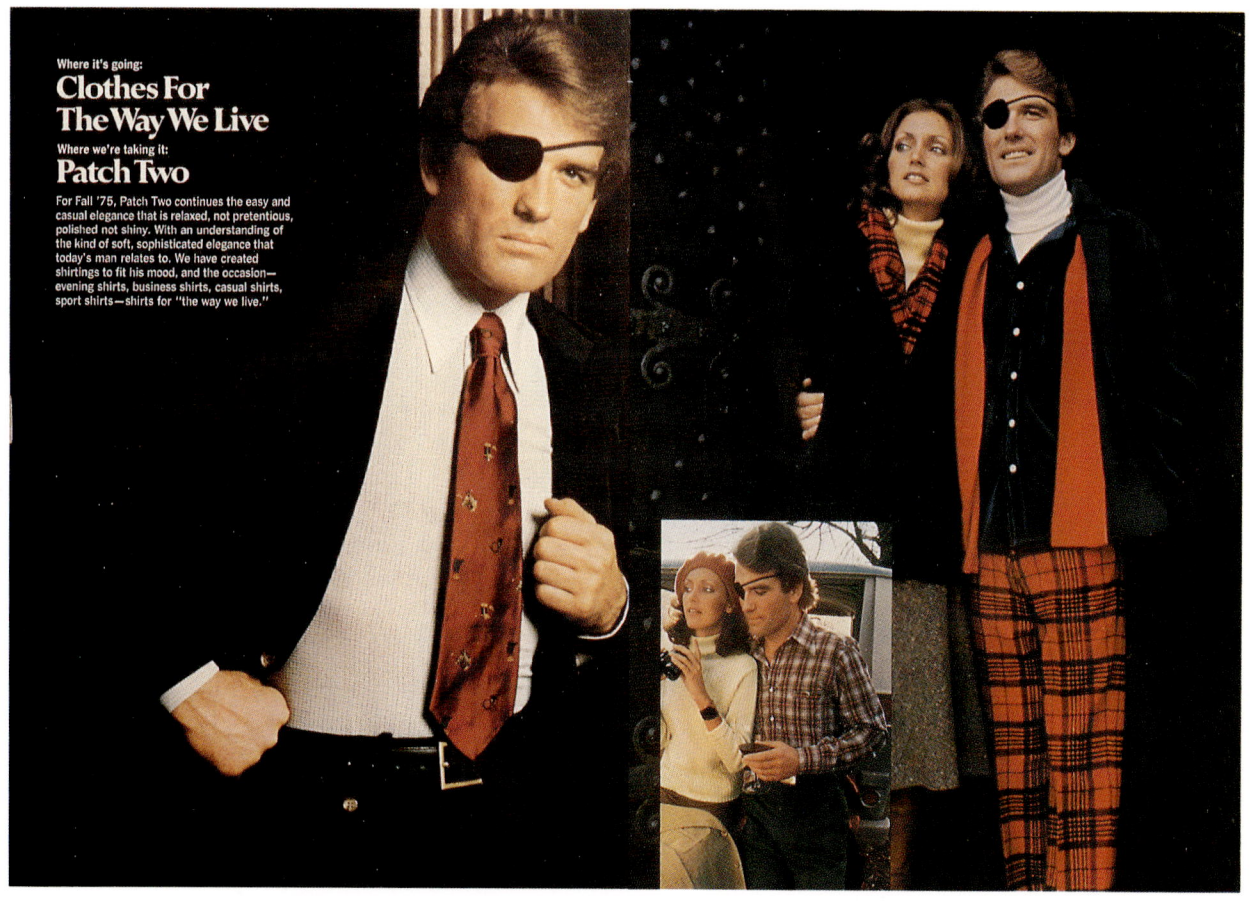

Where it's going:
Enter The Vest
Where we're taking it:
The Hathaway Vested Shirtings

Dressing up is the order of the business day for Fall '75. Tailored suits will be more somber, with gray flannel in shades of medium to charcoal, and luggage, coming in strong. And black is back.

The center of all the interest is the vest, and Hathaway Vested Shirtings help set the pace, establishing black as the big color story. Black with gray, black with white, black with cognac— in pencil stripes and plaids, in elegant handkerchief shirtings and throughout all the informal-formal category, our Cordon Rouge Collection of Champagne Shirtings.

1975. Vested Shirtings were designed in black, gray, and white tones to go with the somber suits of the Fall, 1975 season. $15–18.

Where it's going:
Clothes For The Way We Live
Where we're taking it:
Patch Two

For Fall '75, Patch Two continues the easy and casual elegance that is relaxed, not pretentious, polished not shiny. With an understanding of the kind of soft, sophisticated elegance that today's man relates to. We have created shirtings to fit his mood, and the occasion— evening shirts, business shirts, casual shirts, sport shirts—shirts for "the way we live."

1975. Patch Two continued into 1975, offering clothes with European design and an "easy and casual elegance." Left, $15–18. Right, $18–20.

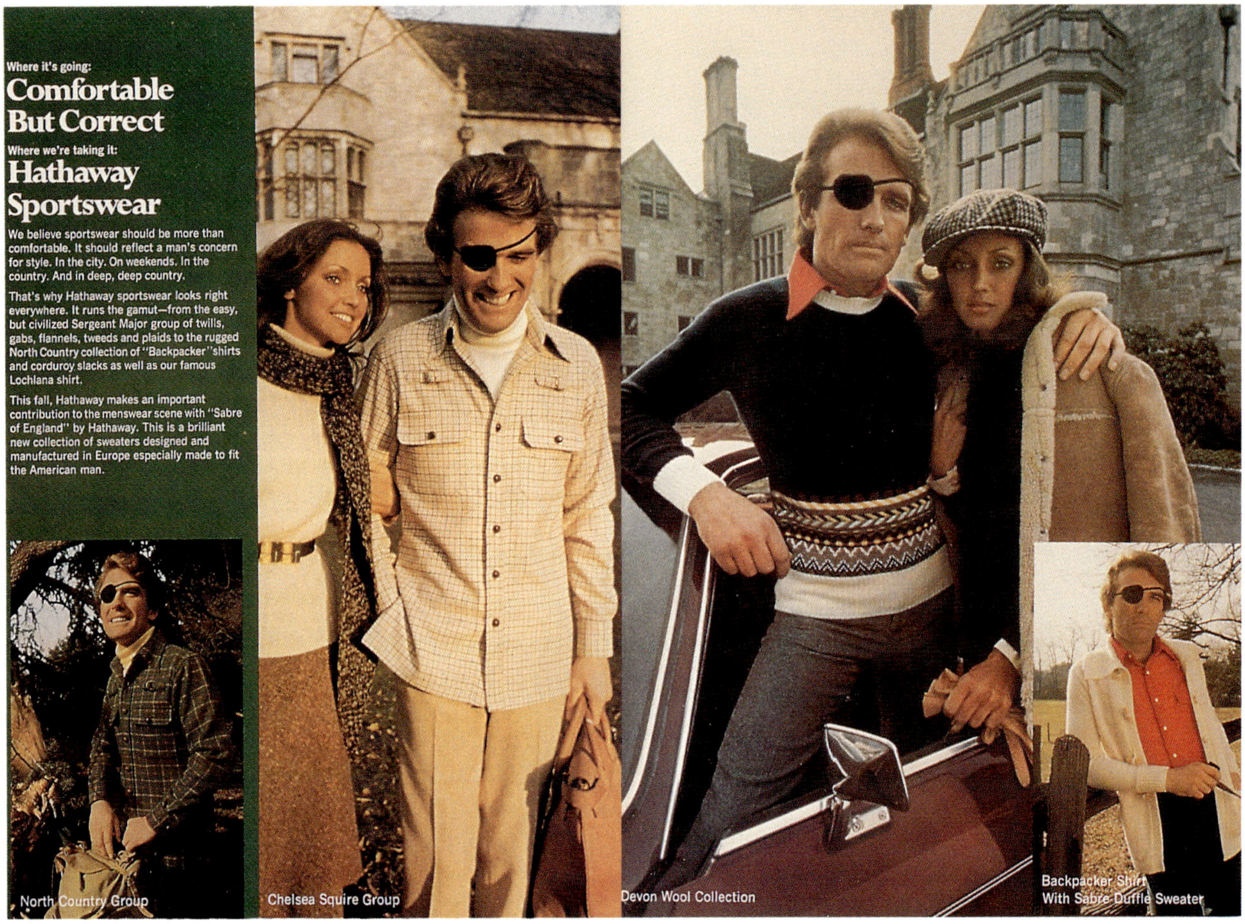

1975. Hathaway Sportswear included the North Country collection of shirts and corduroy pants, and "Sabre of England" sweaters. Left, $28–30. Right, $30–32.

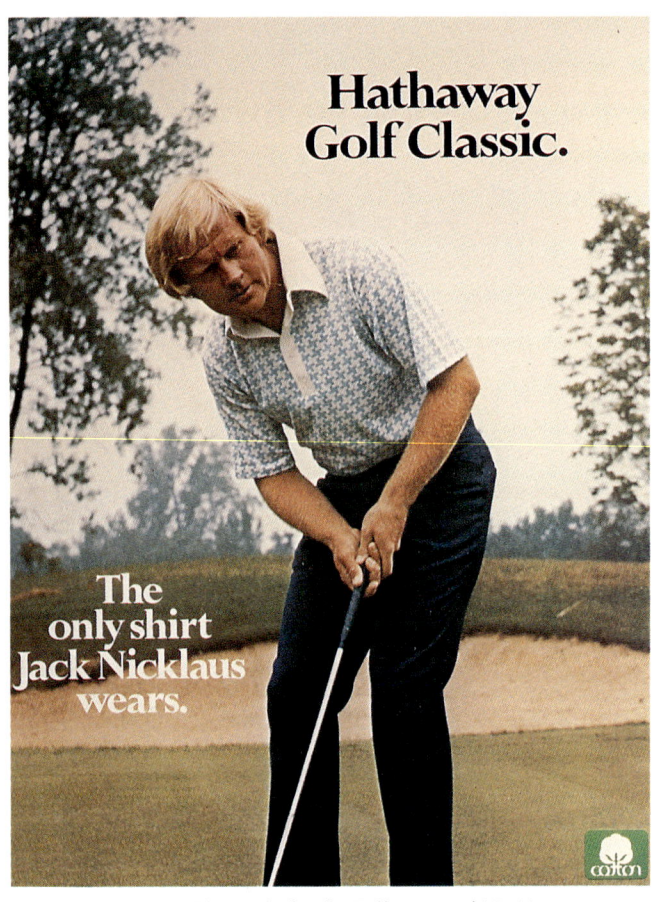

1975. Hathaway Golf Classic for the Fall season. $15–18.

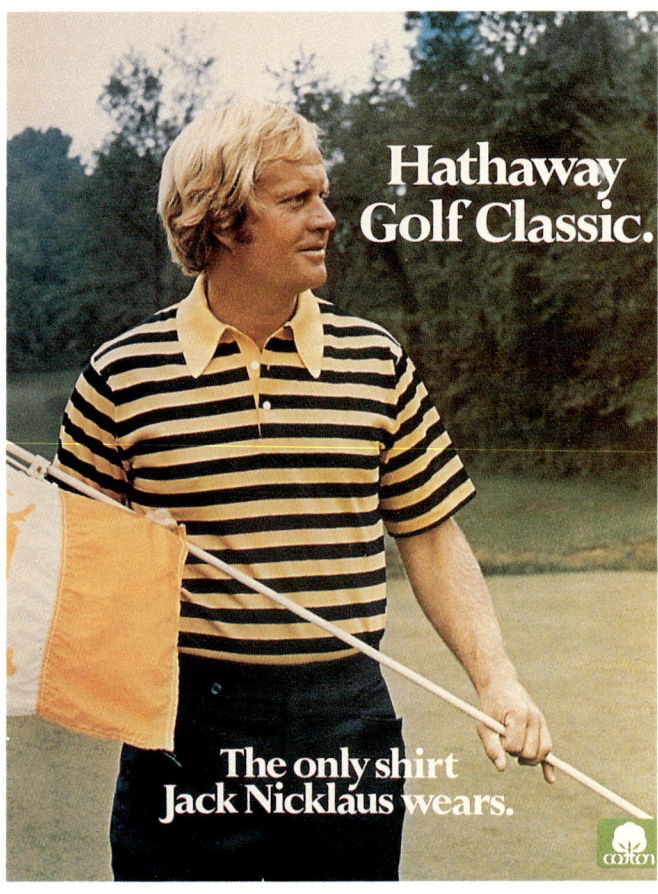

1975. Hathaway Golf Classic. $15–18.

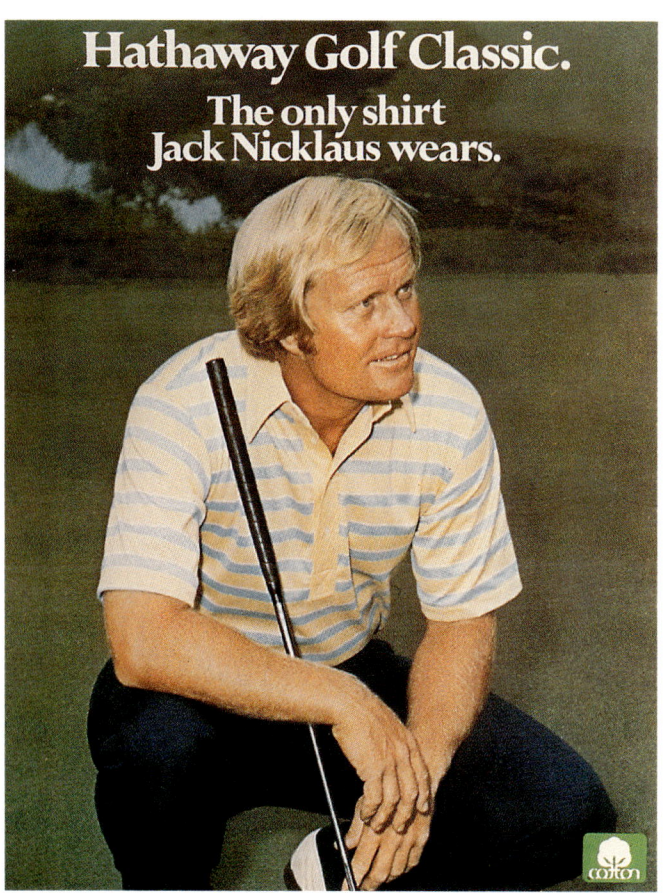
1975. Hathaway Golf Classic. $15–18.

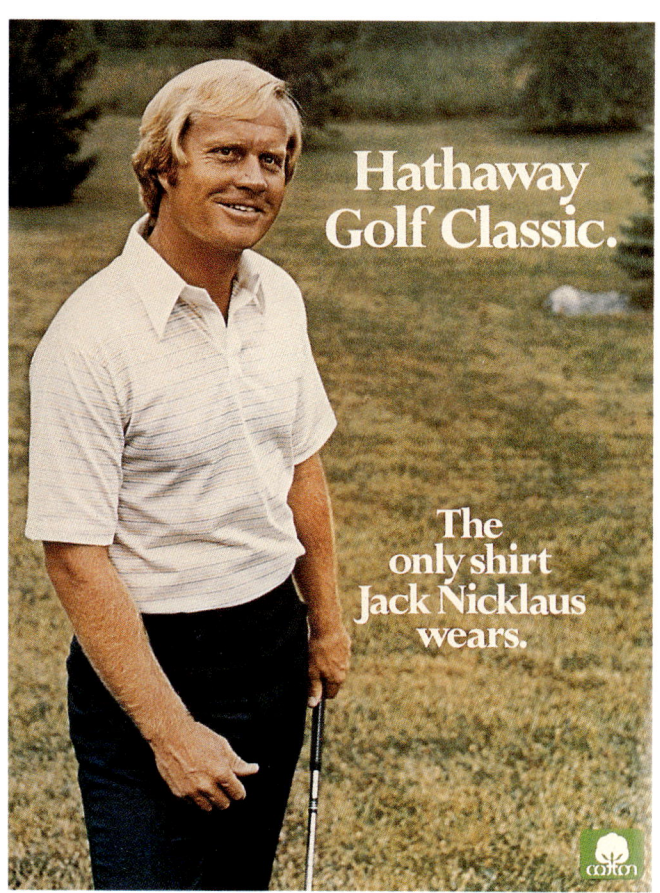
1975. Hathaway Golf Classic. $15–18.

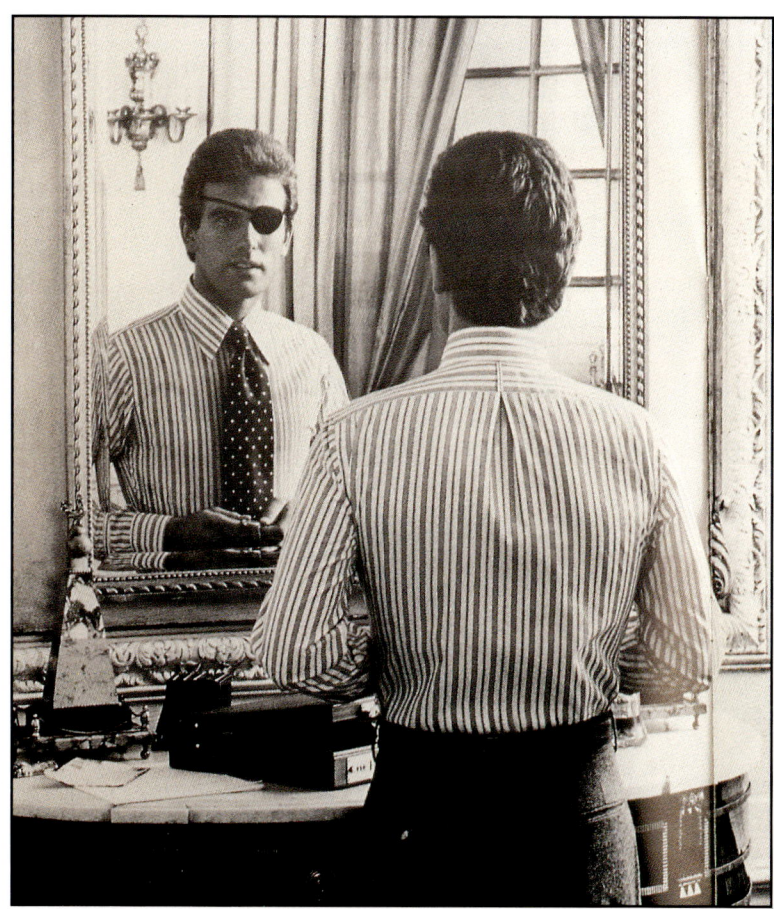
1976. The emphasis is decidedly dressy in this 1976 collection. $18–20.

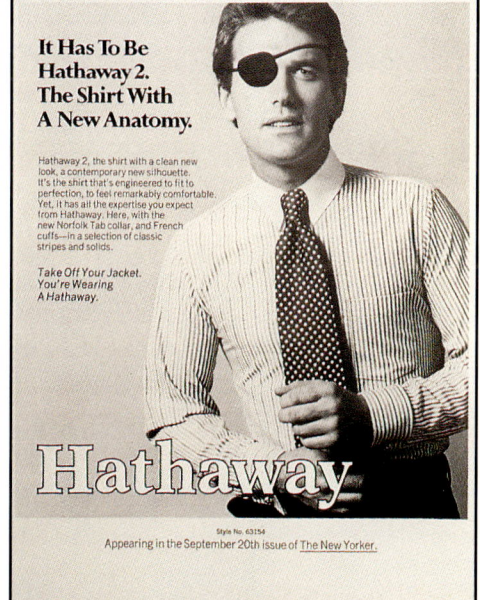
1976. Hathaway 2 shirt. Newly styled fitted shirt in solids and stripes. $15–20.

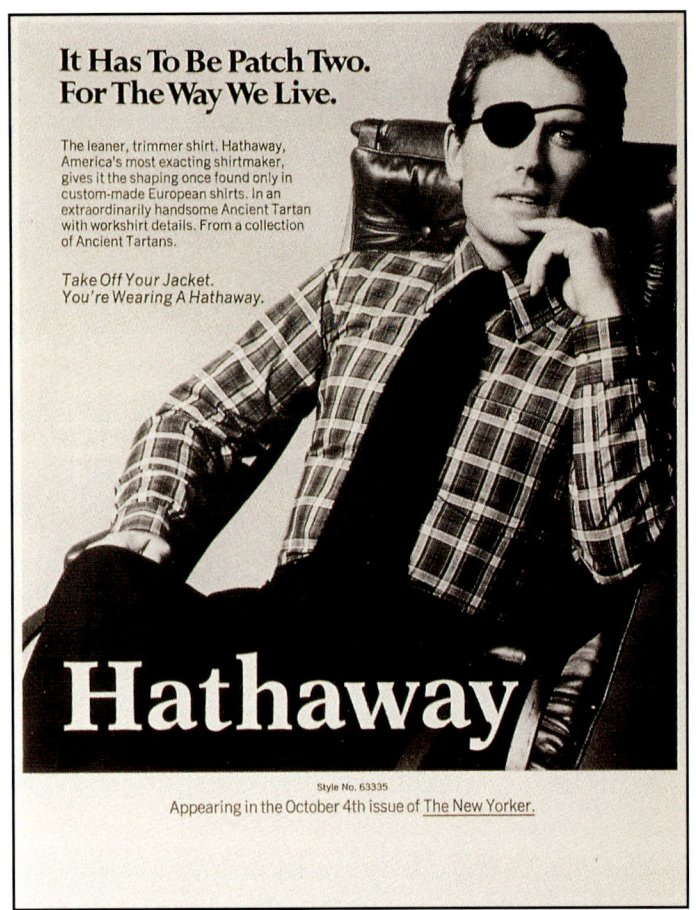

1976. The Patch Two was designed for a younger consumer, using a combination of European tailoring and trendy fabrics. $24–28.

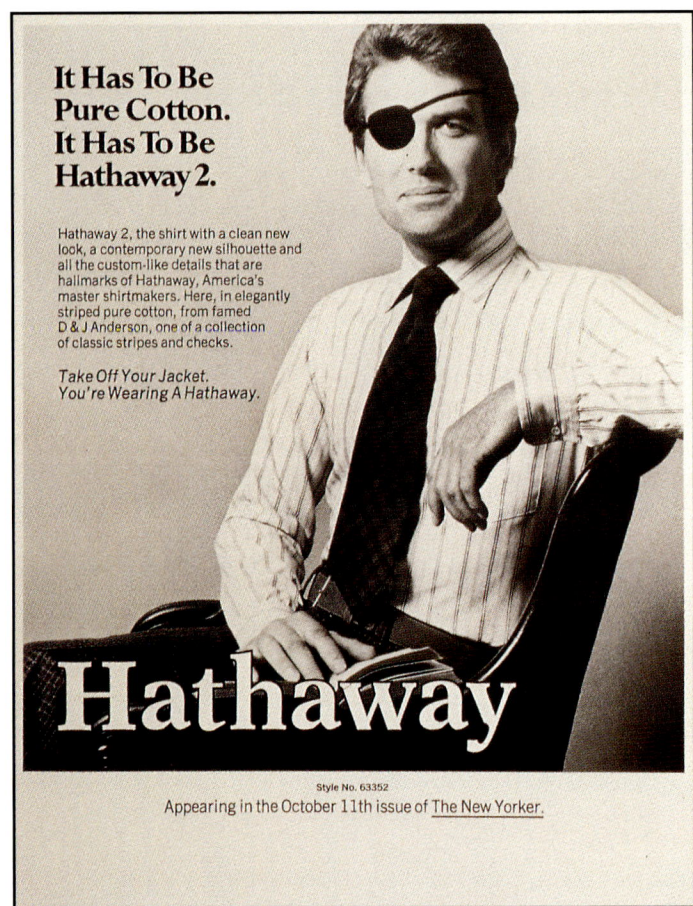

1976. Hathaway 2. The emphasis on pure cotton underscores the return, in the late 1970s, to natural products. $15–18.

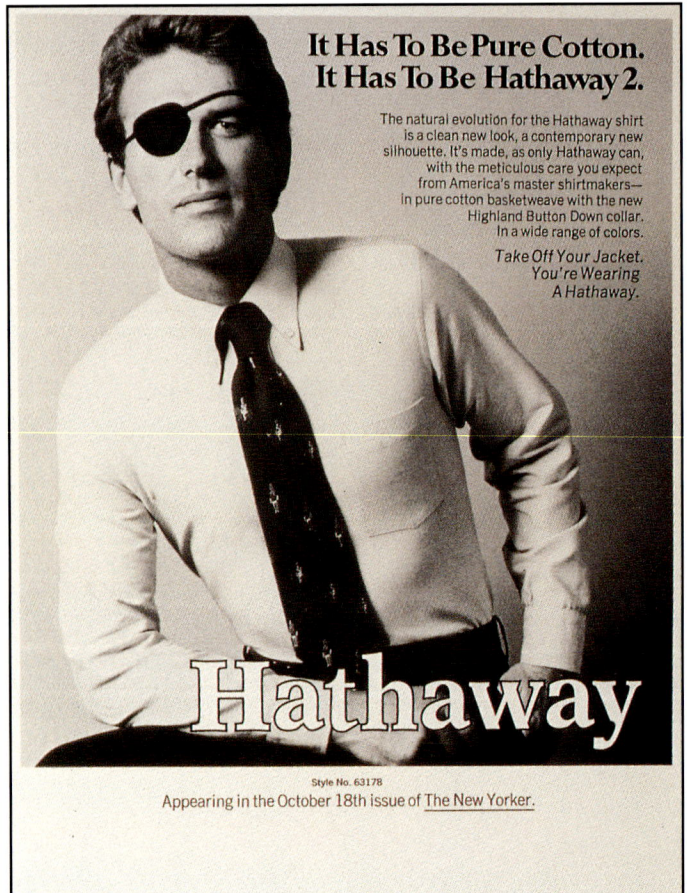

1976. $15–18.

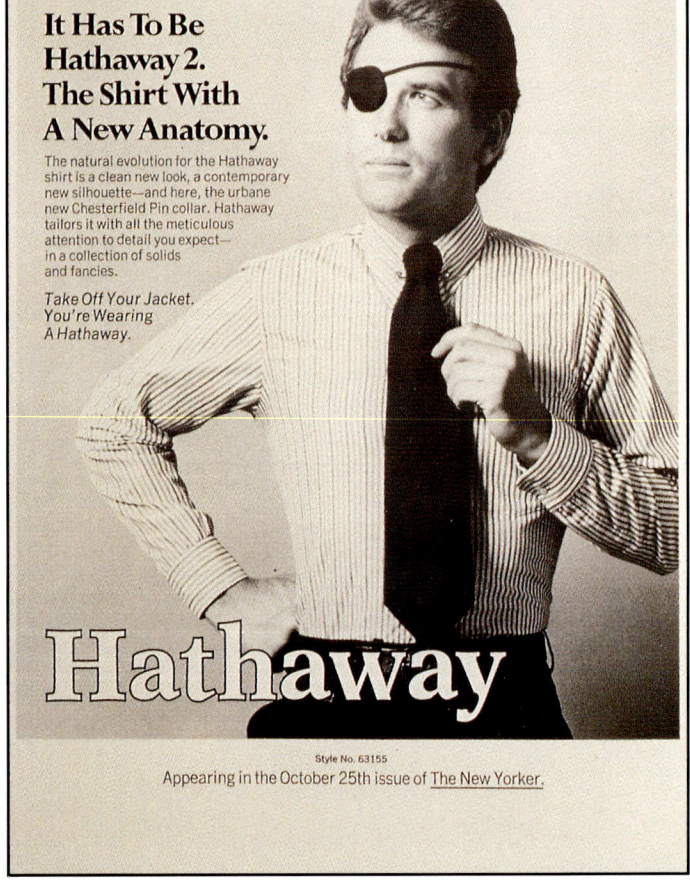

1976. $15–18.

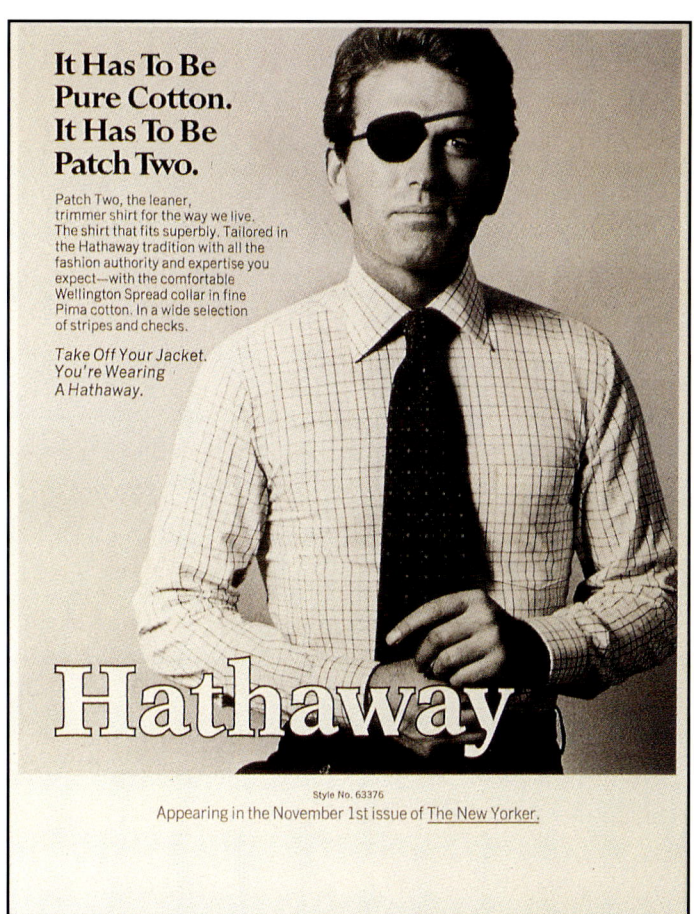

1976. $15–18.

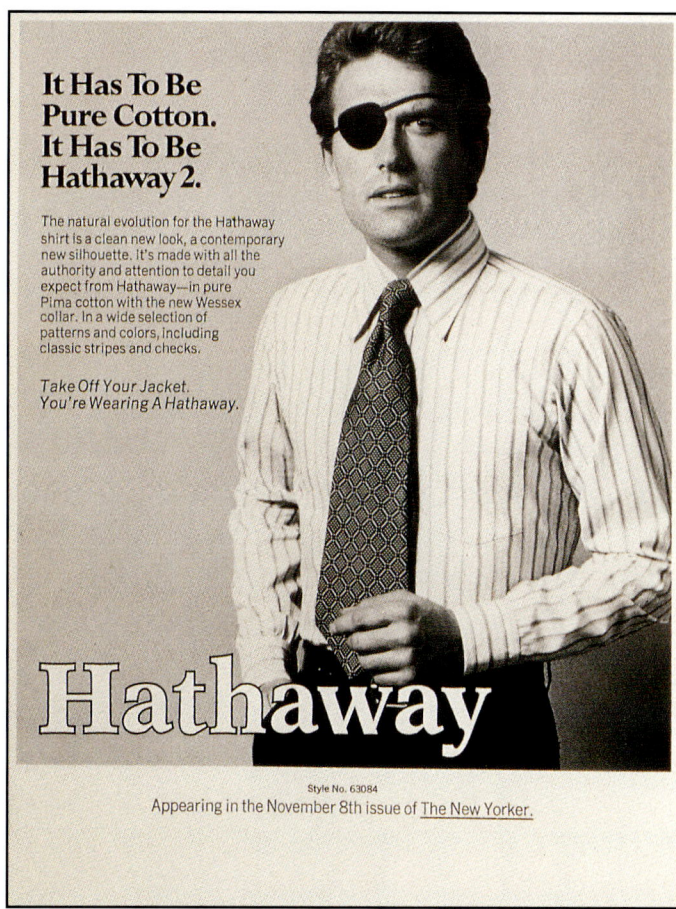

1976. $15–18.

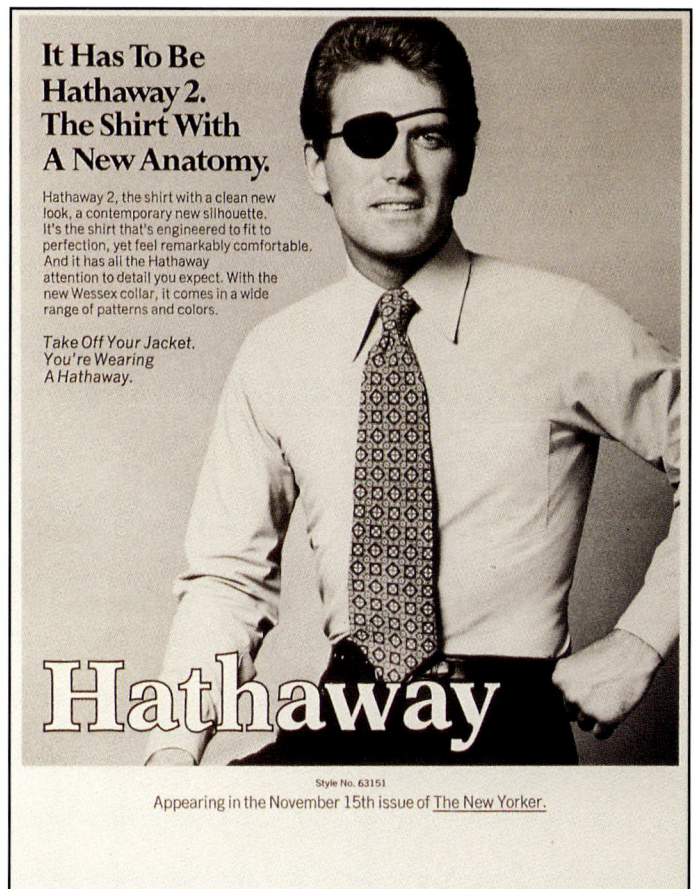

1976. $15–18.

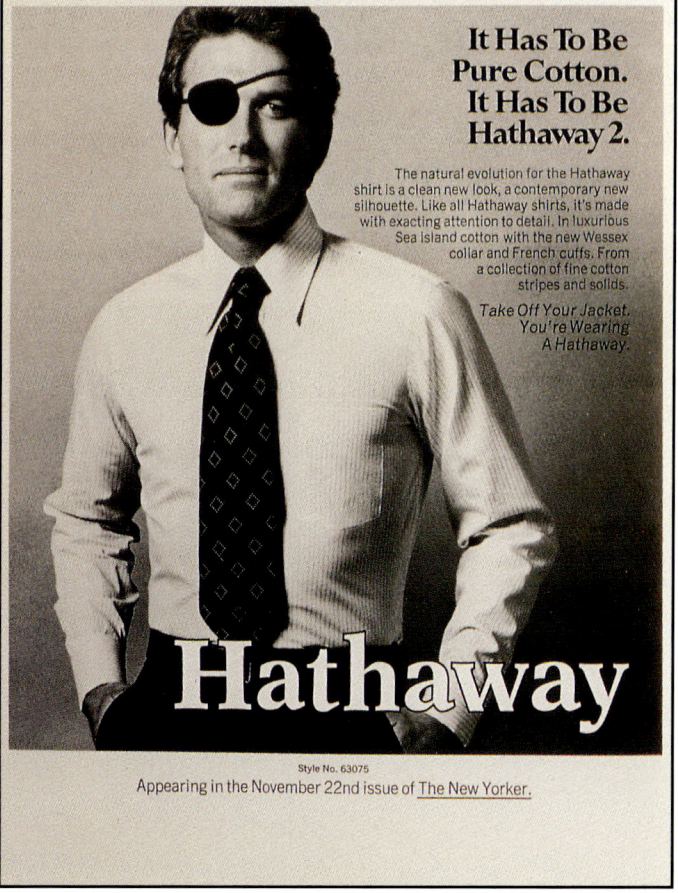

1976. $15–18.

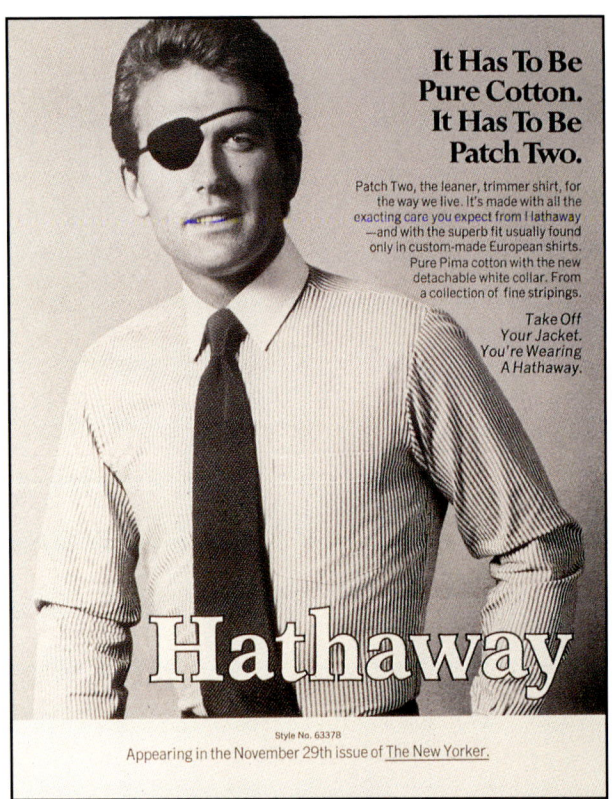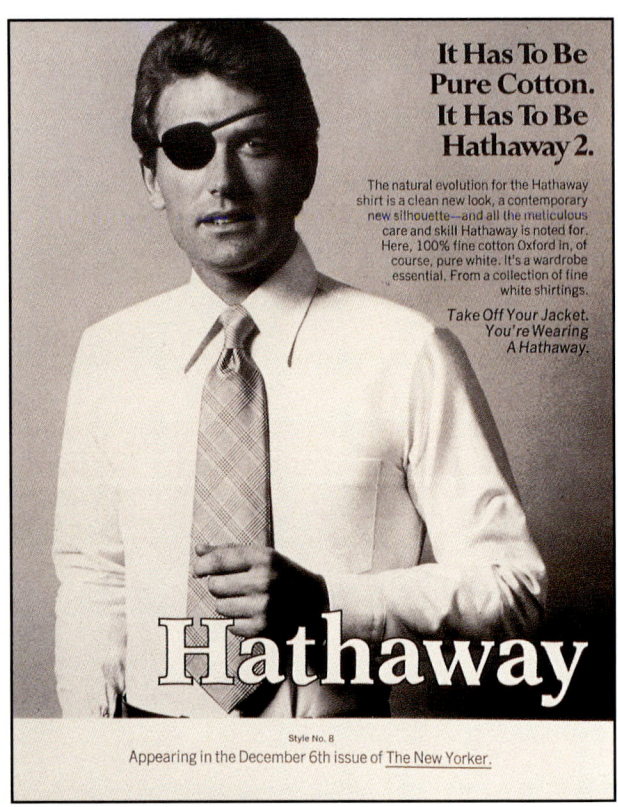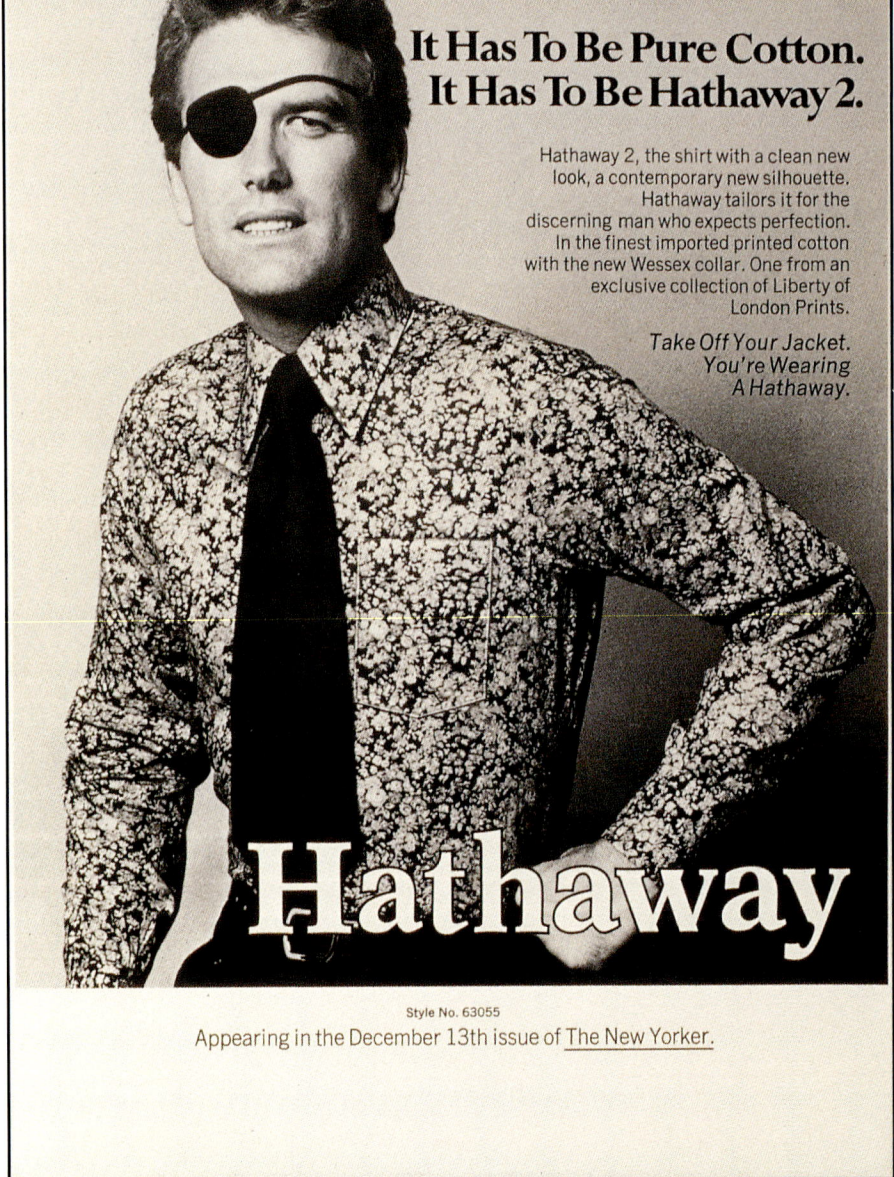

Above: 1976. $15–18.

Below: 1976. $28–30.

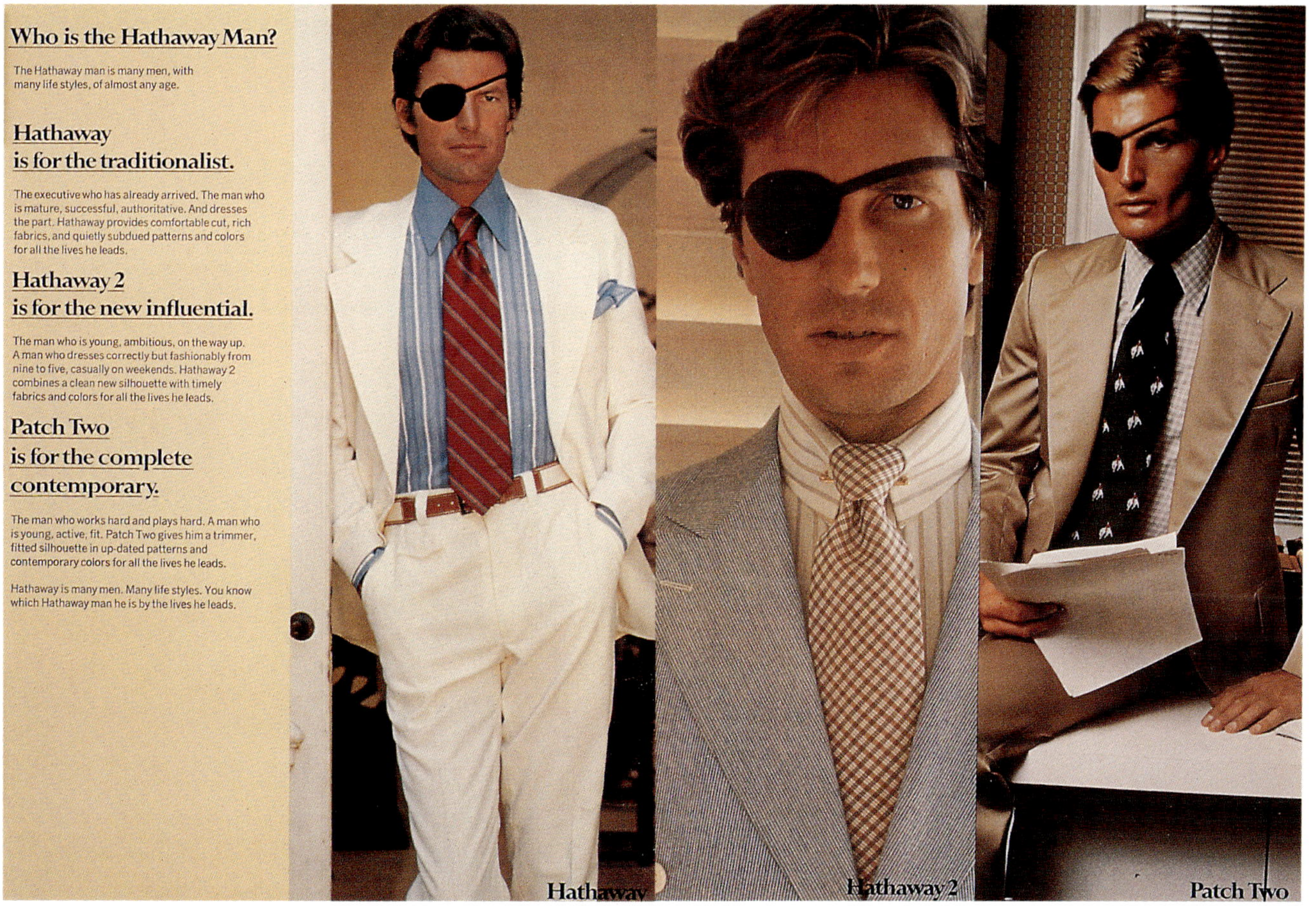

Who is the Hathaway Man?

The Hathaway man is many men, with many life styles, of almost any age.

Hathaway is for the traditionalist.

The executive who has already arrived. The man who is mature, successful, authoritative. And dresses the part. Hathaway provides comfortable cut, rich fabrics, and quietly subdued patterns and colors for all the lives he leads.

Hathaway 2 is for the new influential.

The man who is young, ambitious, on the way up. A man who dresses correctly but fashionably from nine to five, casually on weekends. Hathaway 2 combines a clean new silhouette with timely fabrics and colors for all the lives he leads.

Patch Two is for the complete contemporary.

The man who works hard and plays hard. A man who is young, active, fit. Patch Two gives him a trimmer, fitted silhouette in up-dated patterns and contemporary colors for all the lives he leads.

Hathaway is many men. Many life styles. You know which Hathaway man he is by the lives he leads.

1977. Who is the Hathaway Man? According to this he is really three men, the established executive (Hathaway), the up-and-coming young professional (Hathaway 2), and active contemporary man (Patch Two). $18–20.

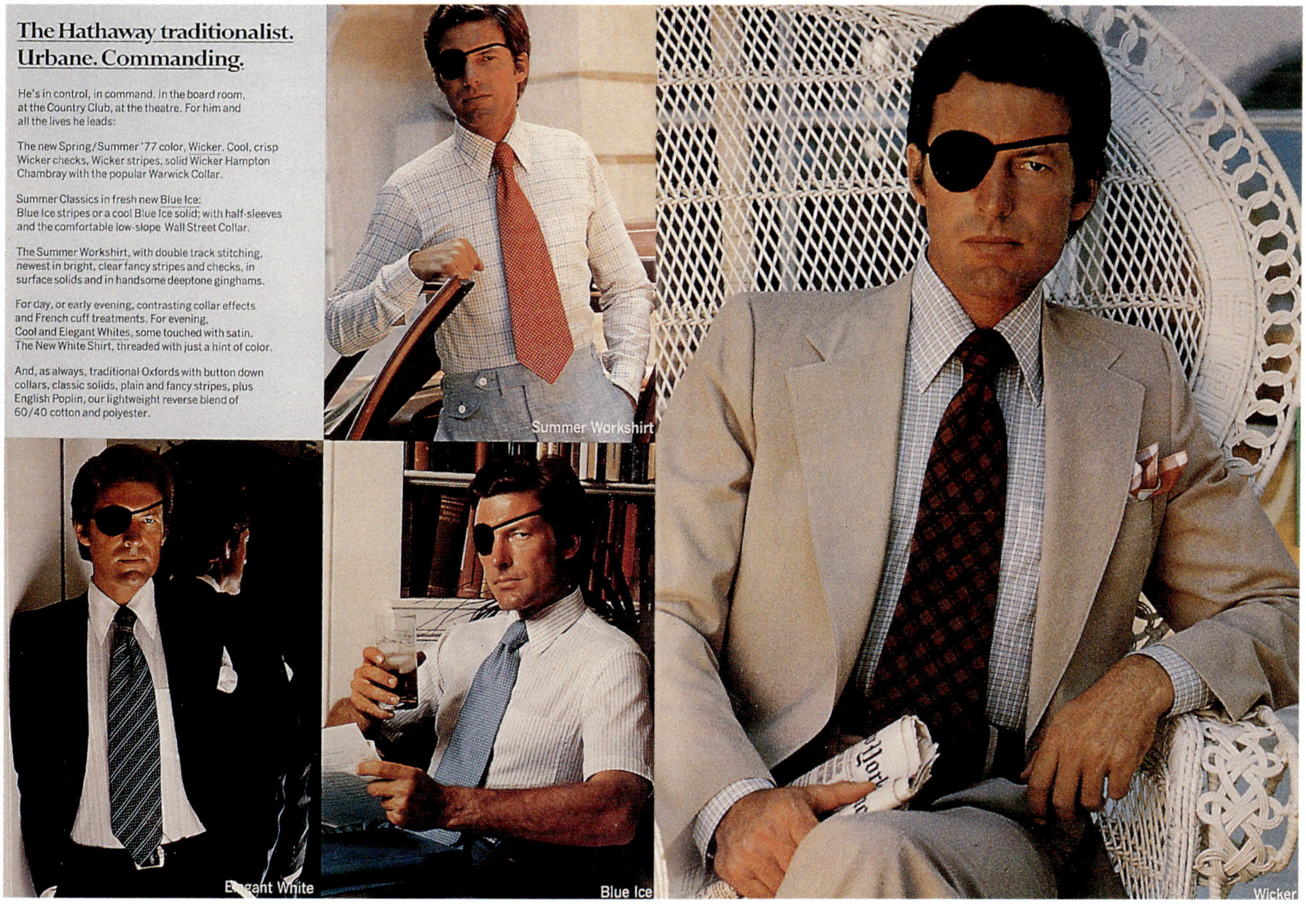

The Hathaway traditionalist. Urbane. Commanding.

He's in control, in command. In the board room, at the Country Club, at the theatre. For him and all the lives he leads:

The new Spring/Summer '77 color, Wicker. Cool, crisp Wicker checks, Wicker stripes, solid Wicker Hampton Chambray with the popular Warwick Collar.

Summer Classics in fresh new Blue Ice: Blue Ice stripes or a cool Blue Ice solid; with half-sleeves and the comfortable low-slope Wall Street Collar.

The Summer Workshirt, with double track stitching, newest in bright, clear fancy stripes and checks, in surface solids and in handsome deeptone ginghams.

For day, or early evening, contrasting collar effects and French cuff treatments. For evening, Cool and Elegant Whites, some touched with satin. The New White Shirt, threaded with just a hint of color.

And, as always, traditional Oxfords with button down collars, classic solids, plain and fancy stripes, plus English Poplin, our lightweight reverse blend of 60/40 cotton and polyester.

1977. New colors for Spring-Summer, 1977, included Wicker and Blue Ice. $18–20.

119

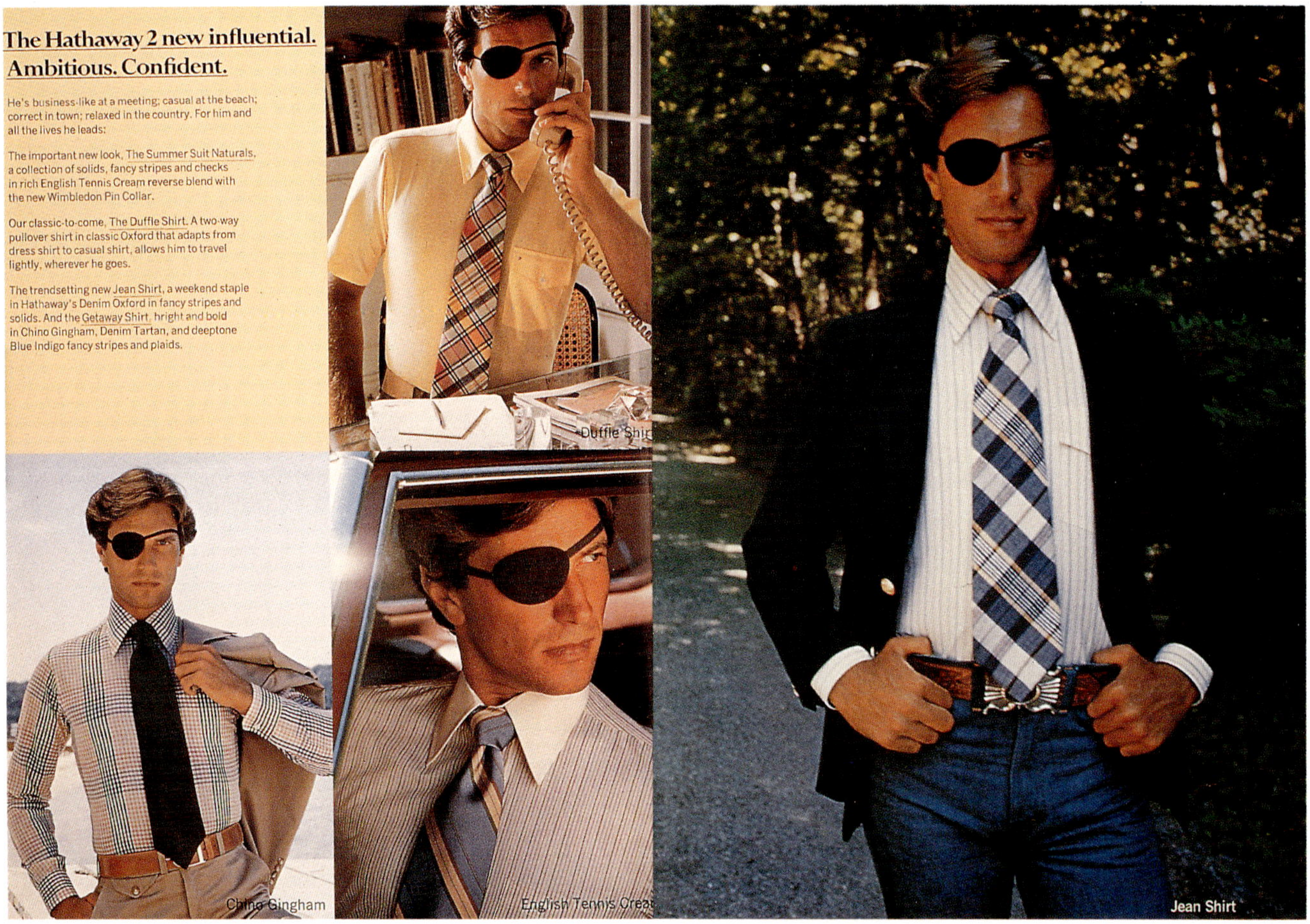

The Hathaway 2 new influential. Ambitious. Confident.

He's business-like at a meeting; casual at the beach; correct in town; relaxed in the country. For him and all the lives he leads:

The important new look, The Summer Suit Naturals, a collection of solids, fancy stripes and checks in rich English Tennis Cream reverse blend with the new Wimbledon Pin Collar.

Our classic-to-come, The Duffle Shirt. A two-way pullover shirt in classic Oxford that adapts from dress shirt to casual shirt, allows him to travel lightly, wherever he goes.

The trendsetting new Jean Shirt, a weekend staple in Hathaway's Denim Oxford in fancy stripes and solids. And the Getaway Shirt, bright and bold in Chino Gingham, Denim Tartan, and deeptone Blue Indigo fancy stripes and plaids.

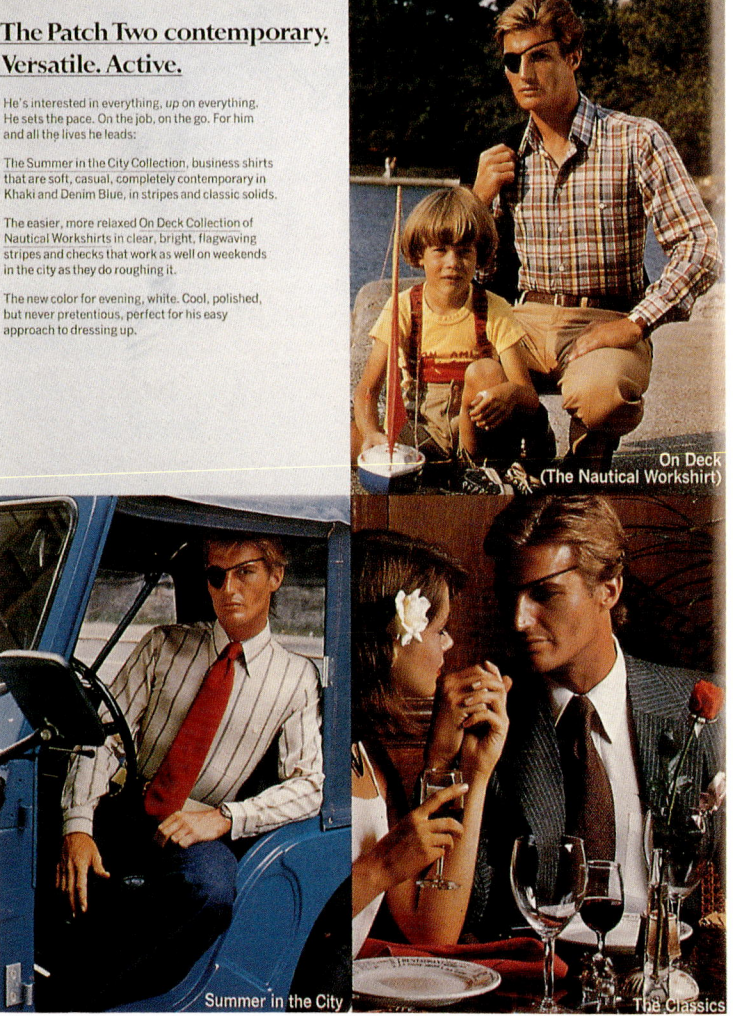

The Patch Two contemporary. Versatile. Active.

He's interested in everything, *up* on everything. He sets the pace. On the job, on the go. For him and all the lives he leads:

The Summer in the City Collection, business shirts that are soft, casual, completely contemporary in Khaki and Denim Blue, in stripes and classic solids.

The easier, more relaxed On Deck Collection of Nautical Workshirts in clear, bright, flagwaving stripes and checks that work as well on weekends in the city as they do roughing it.

The new color for evening, white. Cool, polished, but never pretentious, perfect for his easy approach to dressing up.

Above: 1977. Hathaway 2 designs. $18–20.

Left: 1977. Patch Two designs. $18–20.

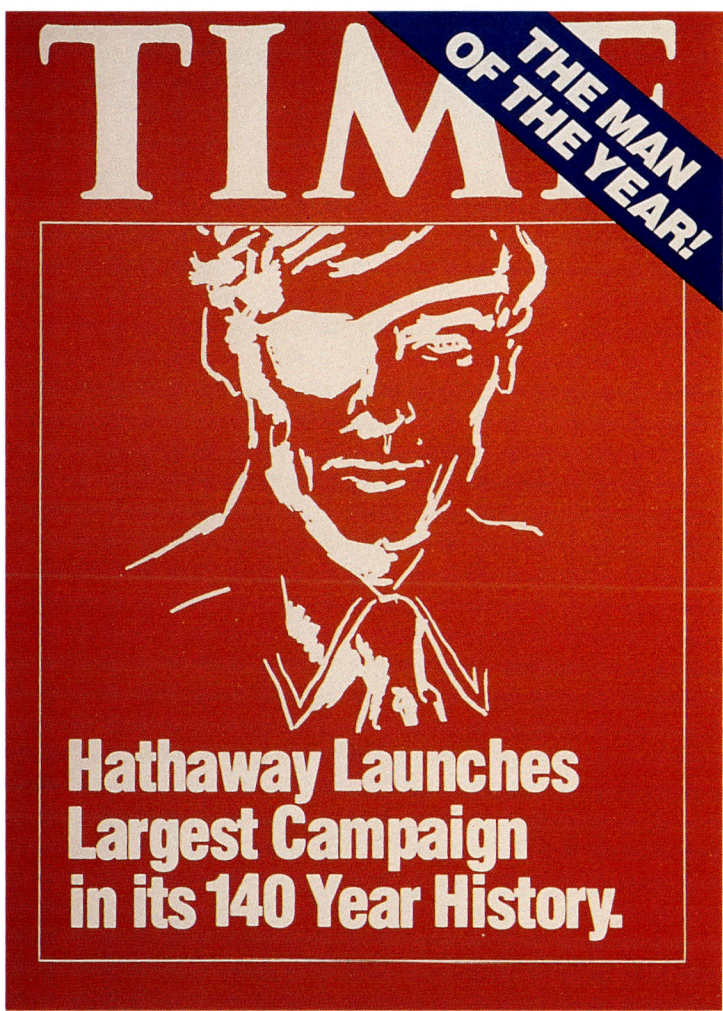

1977. In the fall of 1977 Ogilvy & Mathers again took on the Hathaway account, and announced a new campaign with this simulated *Time* magazine cover.

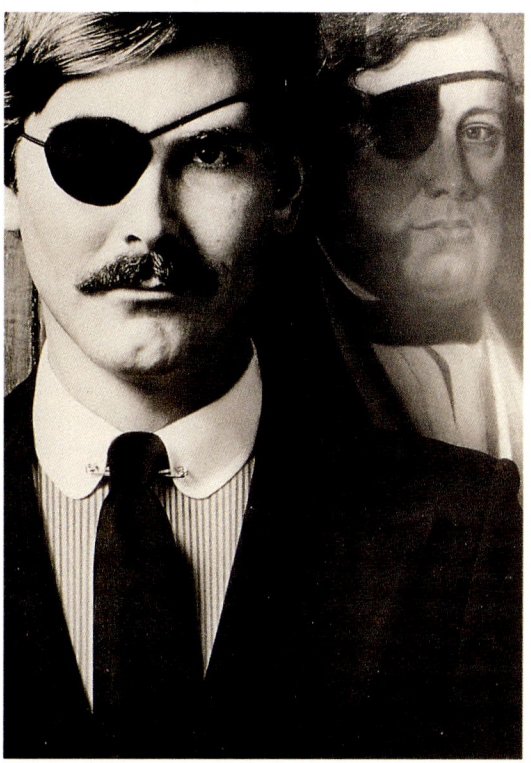

Ned Phillips, the new Man in the Hathaway Shirt.

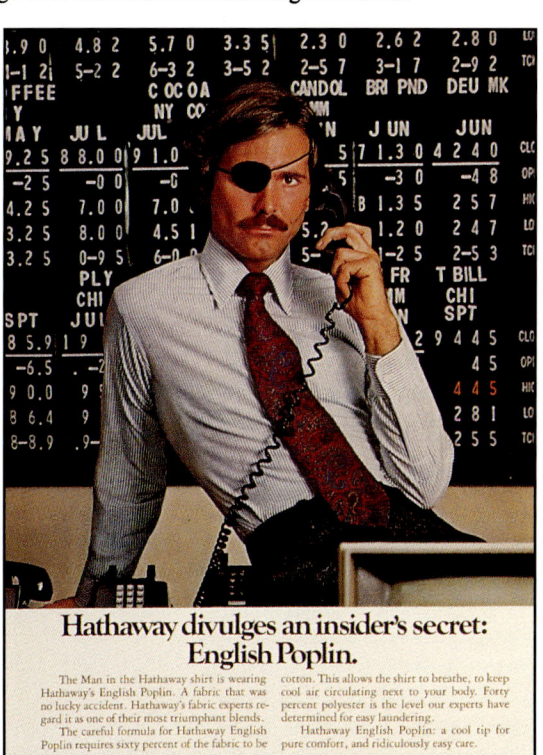

1978. The advertising echoed back to Ogilvy & Mathers original campaign, presenting an elegant, moustached man in an eyepatch in "manly" situations portrayed by Phillips. The Hathaway 2 line disappeared. $15–18.

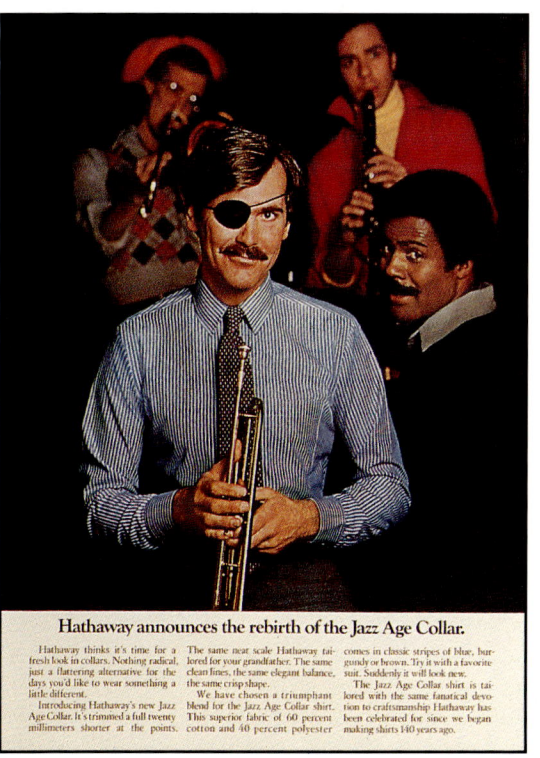

1978. The Jazz Age Collar is much shorter, reversing a trend from earlier in the decade. $15–18.

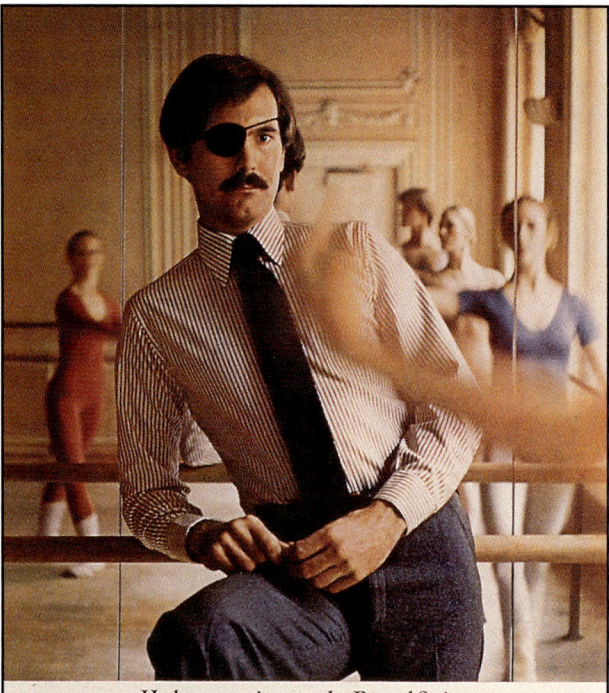

Hathaway re-invents the Bengal Stripe.

Hathaway created their original Bengal Stripe in the early 1920's. But we think the time has come for a tiny tampering with tradition.

Your first look at Hathaway's new Bengal Stripes will convince you that this is a splendid shirt, fit for men of incredibly high expectations.

Ah, but only your second attentive inspection reveals the secret behind the colorations. Each stripe is edged with two thin black lines. So the color seems more vivid, more completely separated from the white ground.

The shirt is available in stripes of Bengal blue, burgundy or brown.

The front placket and chest pocket are so carefully matched they practically dissolve into the pattern.

Hathaway has tailored the Bengal Stripe shirt from a most triumphant blend. It's 60% cotton to keep you unruffled and 40% polyester to keep you unwrinkled, as well.

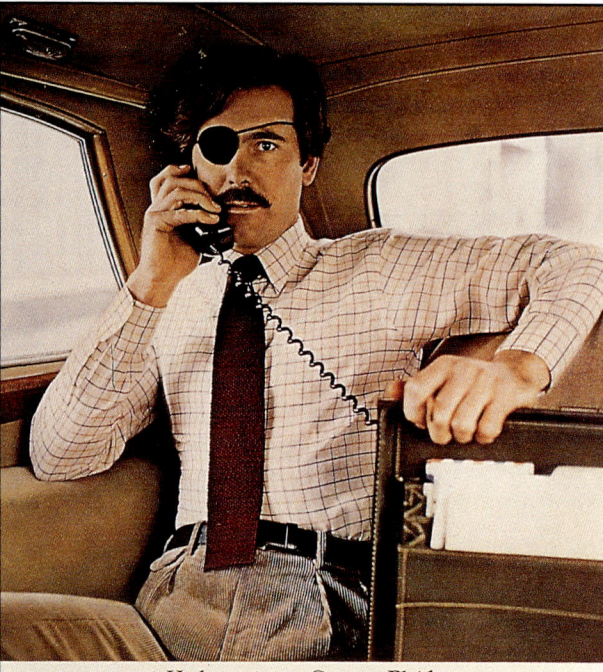

Hathaway's new Country Plaids.
If you're tempted to wear them to work, please do.

Hathaway created their new Country Plaids for weekends. But clever men refuse to give them up on Monday morning. And why should they? The plaids thrive in the city. The colorations are designed to complement the new corduroy suits, favorite blazers, soft tweeds.

Hathaway's new Country Plaids are meticulously tailored in a soft, brushed twill fabric. The front placket, the chest pocket, the collar and cuffs are hand-matched. And the seams! Single needle stitches take extra time and trouble. In a world of compromise, Hathaway doesn't.

Hathaway's new Country Plaids. When temptation strikes, give in.

True, Hathaway's Country Plaids might not be everyone's choice in the boardroom. But at meetings, business luncheons or cocktails, they add a dash of insouciance. They move you miles ahead of the crowd.

Above left: 1978. Resurrecting the Bengal Stripe. $15–18.

Above right: 1978. $15–18.

Left: c. 1978. $18–20.

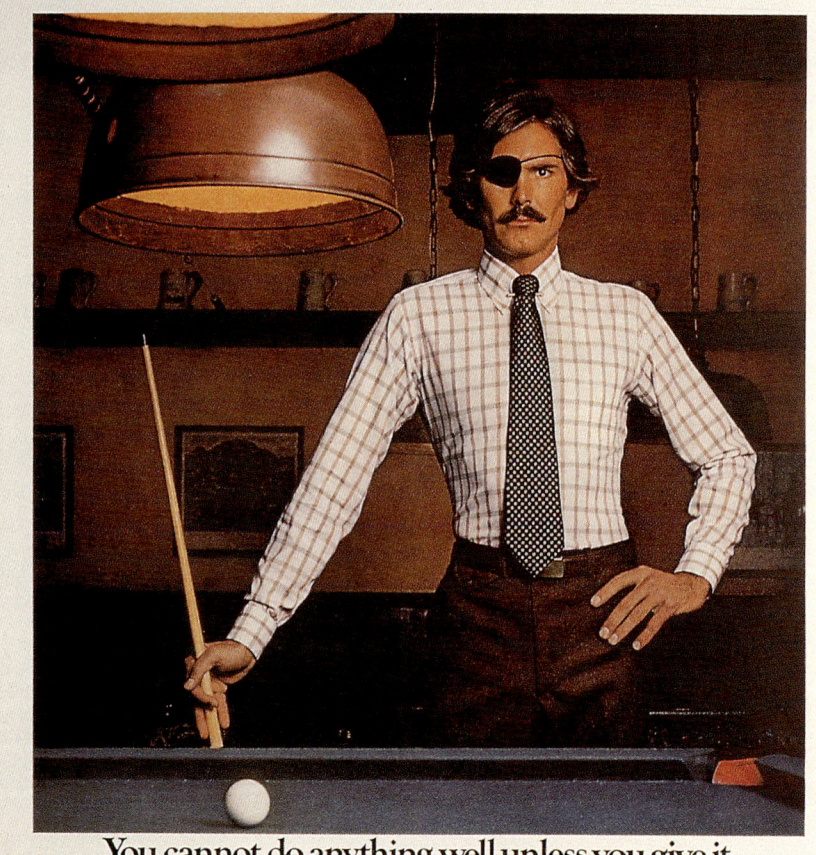

You cannot do anything well unless you give it your full attention, says Hathaway.

Hathaway doesn't trust the tricky business of matching plaids to a machine. We give it our full attention. Every line of plaid is carefully matched by hand. So each side of the collar is a mirror image of the other. The cuffs are identical. The front pocket is perfectly aligned to the shirt. It practically dissolves into the pattern.

It takes seventy-five separate tailoring processes to craft a Hathaway shirt. The hand-turned collar, alone, requires twelve precise operations.

But all this meticulous attention to detail is not enough for Hathaway. We have 14 sharp-eyed inspectors who won't pass a shirt unless they can say "This Hathaway is perfect."

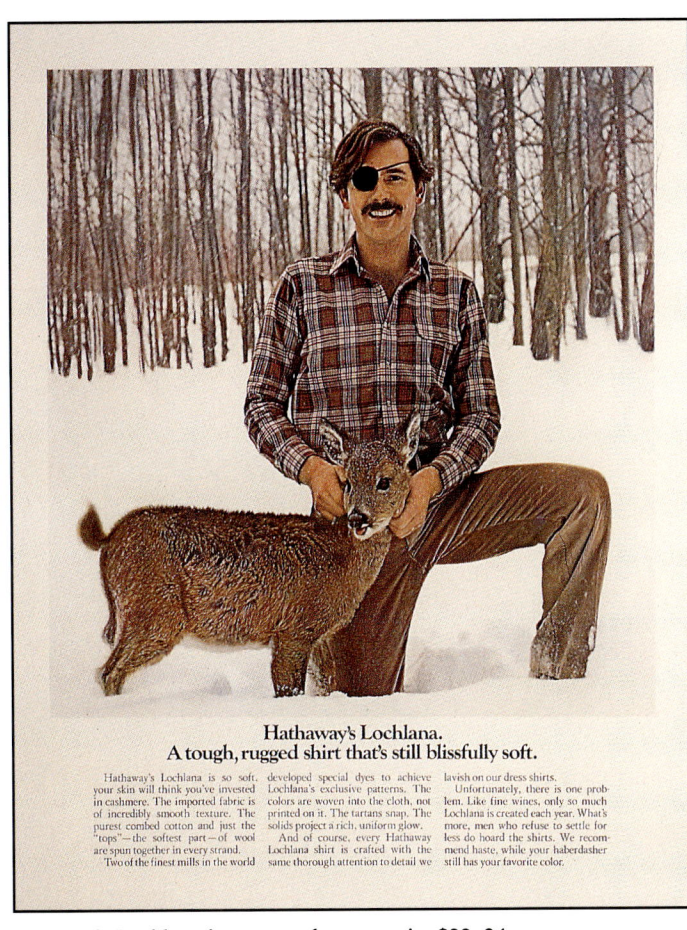

c. 1978. Lochlana is promoted once again. $22–24.

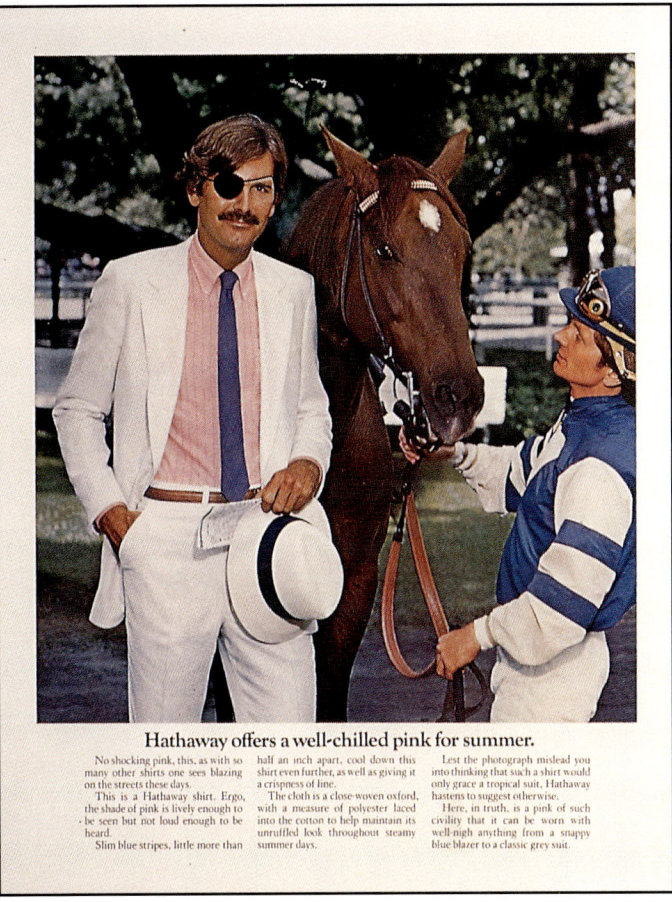

c. 1978. $18–20.

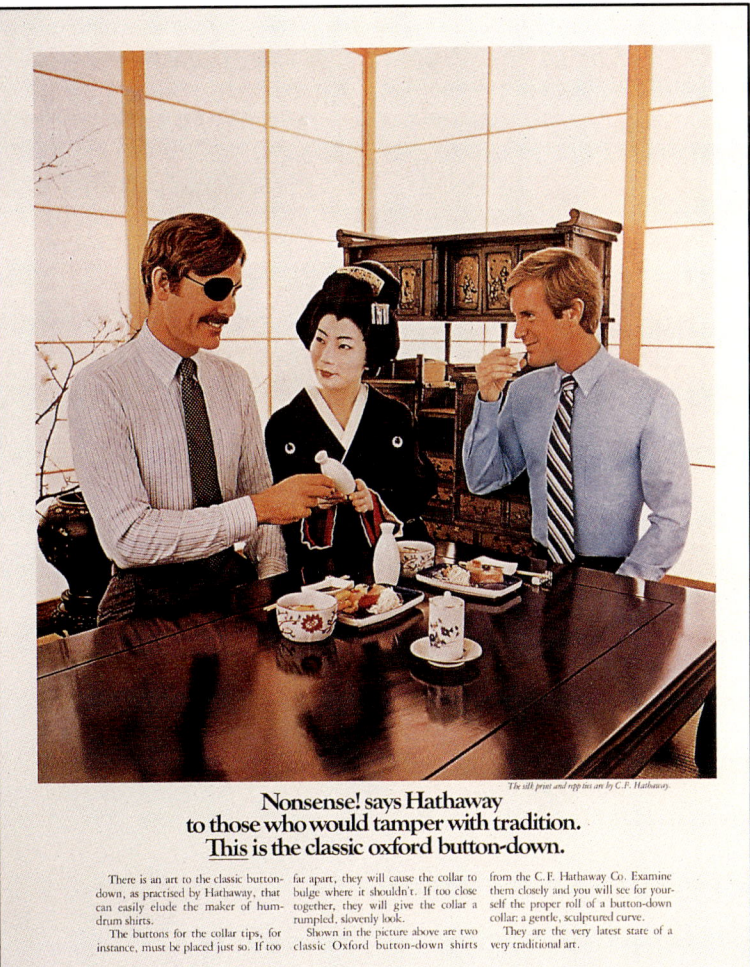

c. 1978. $15–18.

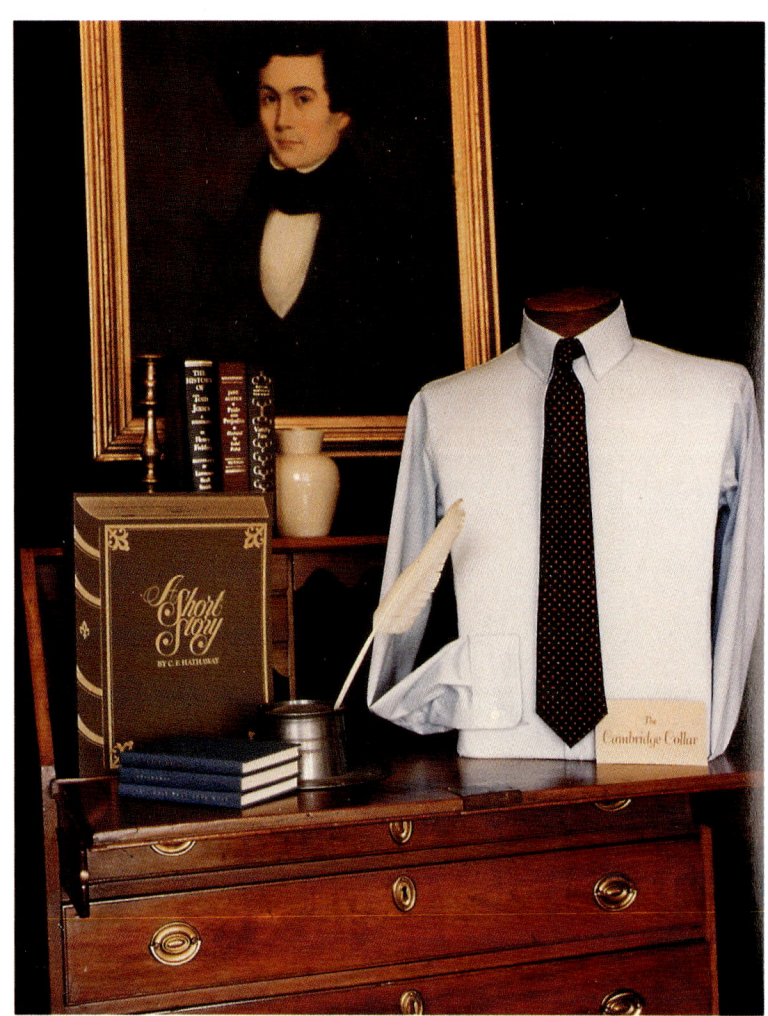

c. 1978. To introduce the shorter collar designs, Hathaway developed "A Short Story" campaign, providing stores with possible window designs for the promotion.

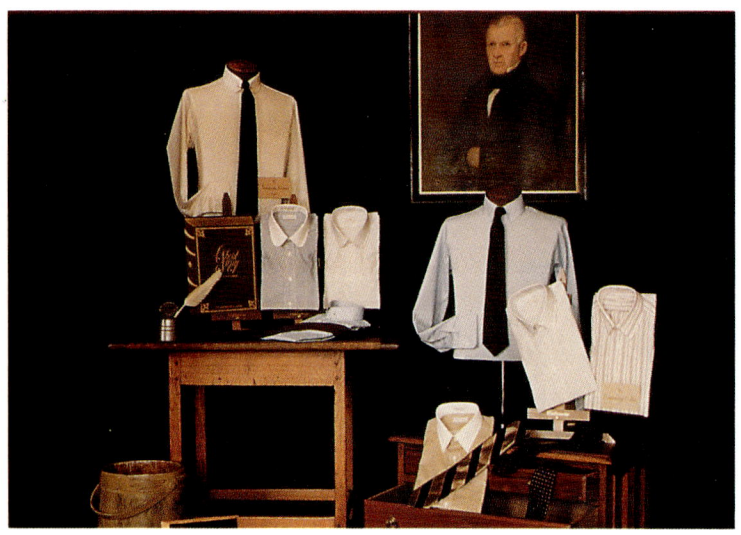

c. 1978. $15–18.

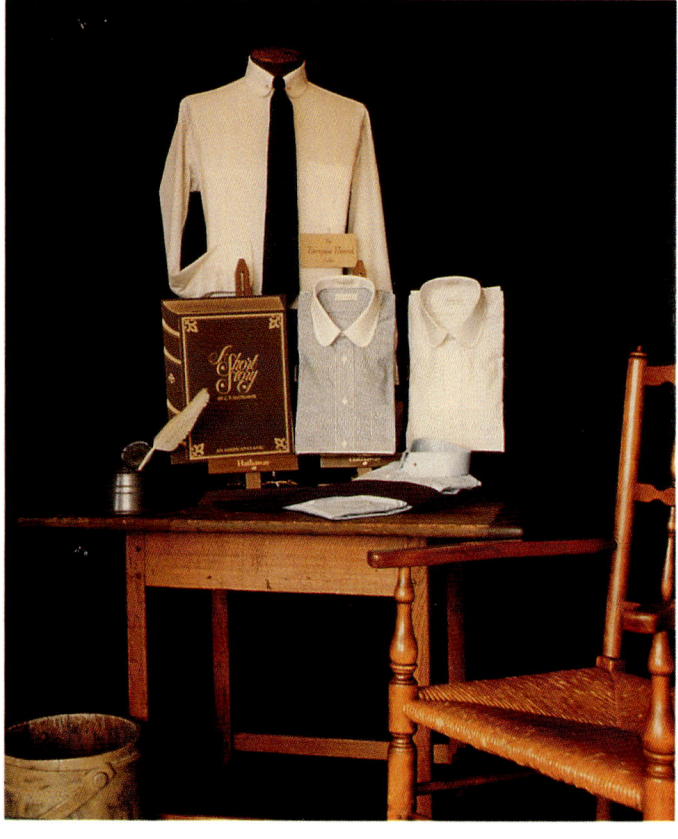

c. 1978. $15–18.

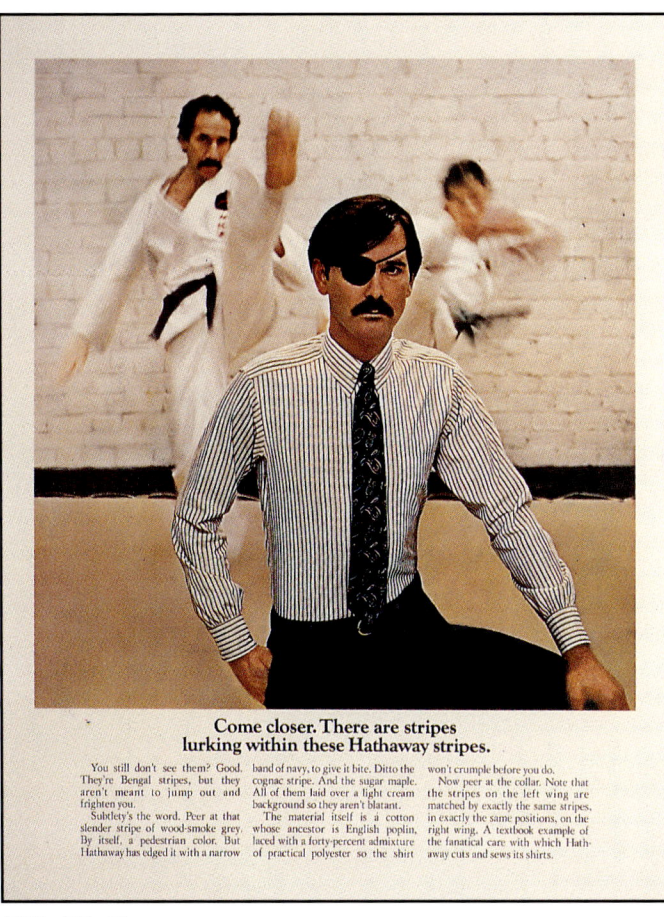

1979. $18–20.

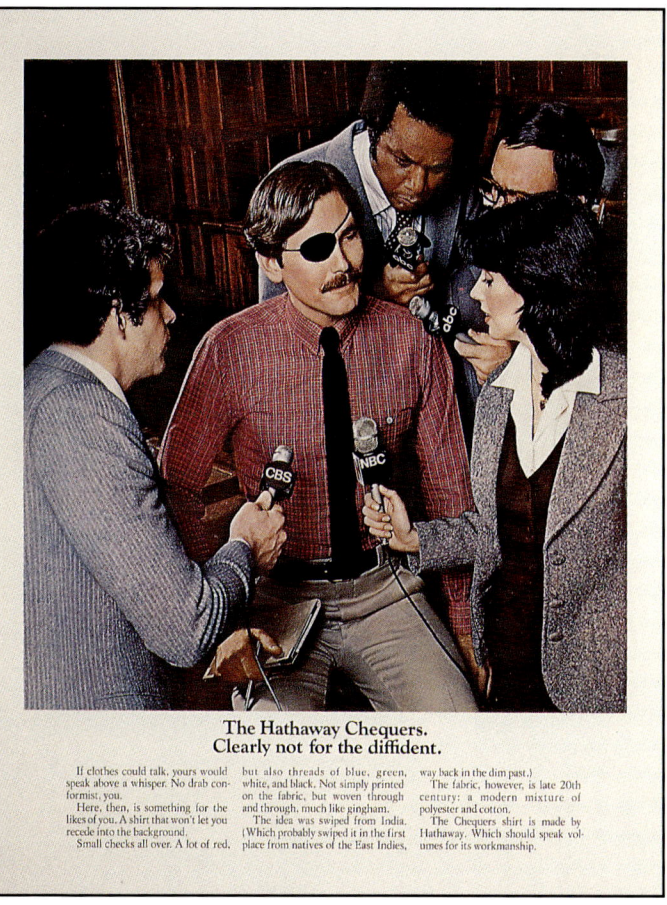

1979. Hathaway Chequers. $18–20.

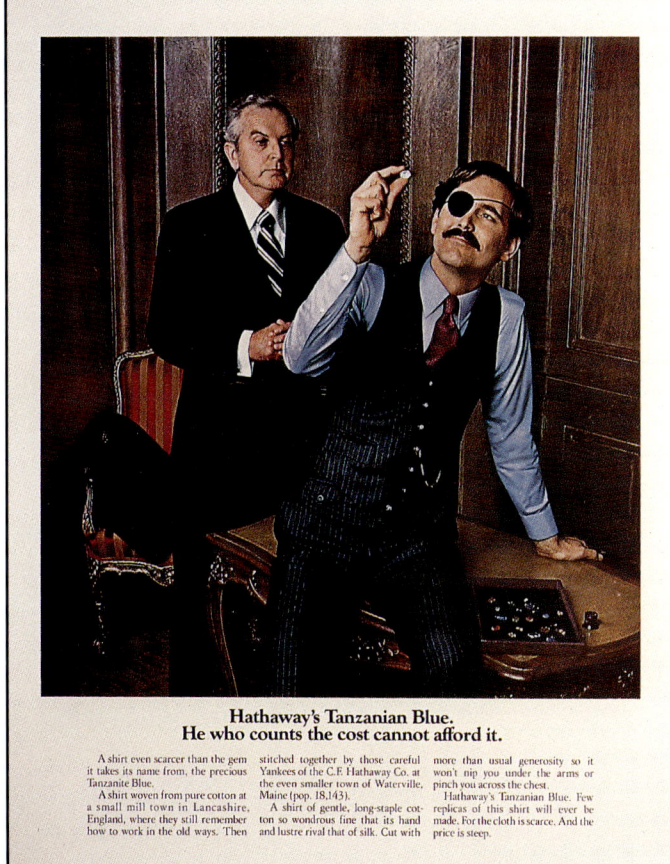

1979. $15–18.

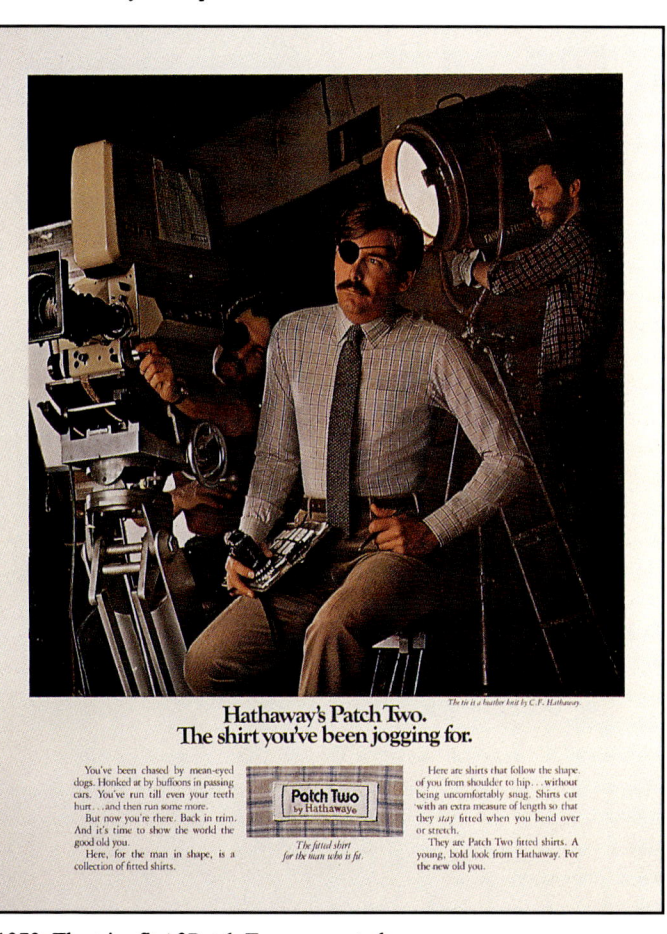

1979. The trim fit of Patch Two connected to the growing interest in jogging. $18–20.

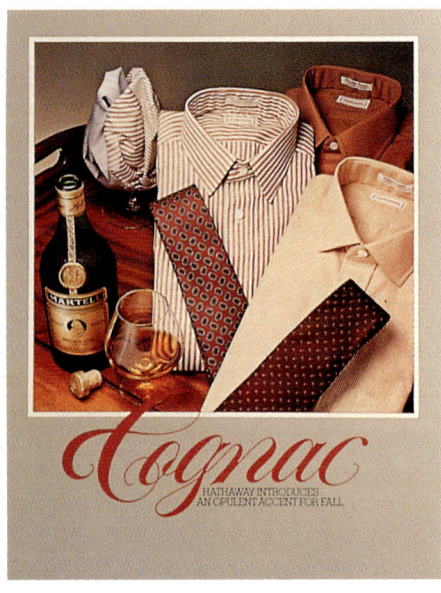 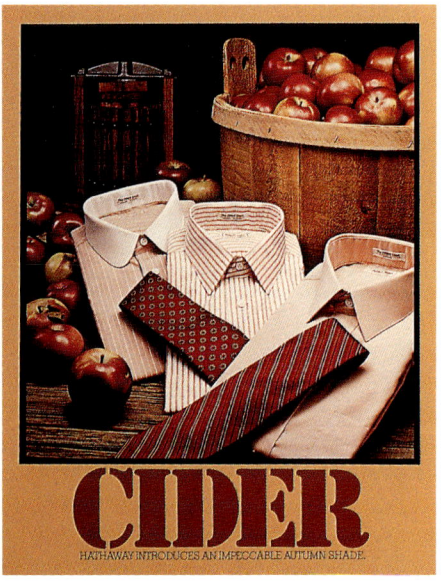 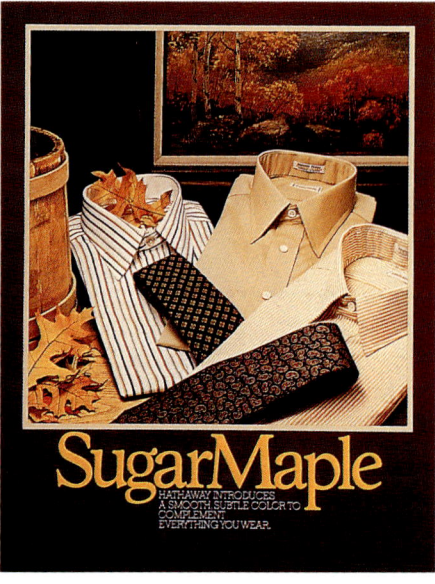

1979. Cognac, a new color for fall. $15–18. 1979. Cider, the epitome of autumn. $15–18. 1979. Sugar Maple. $15–18.

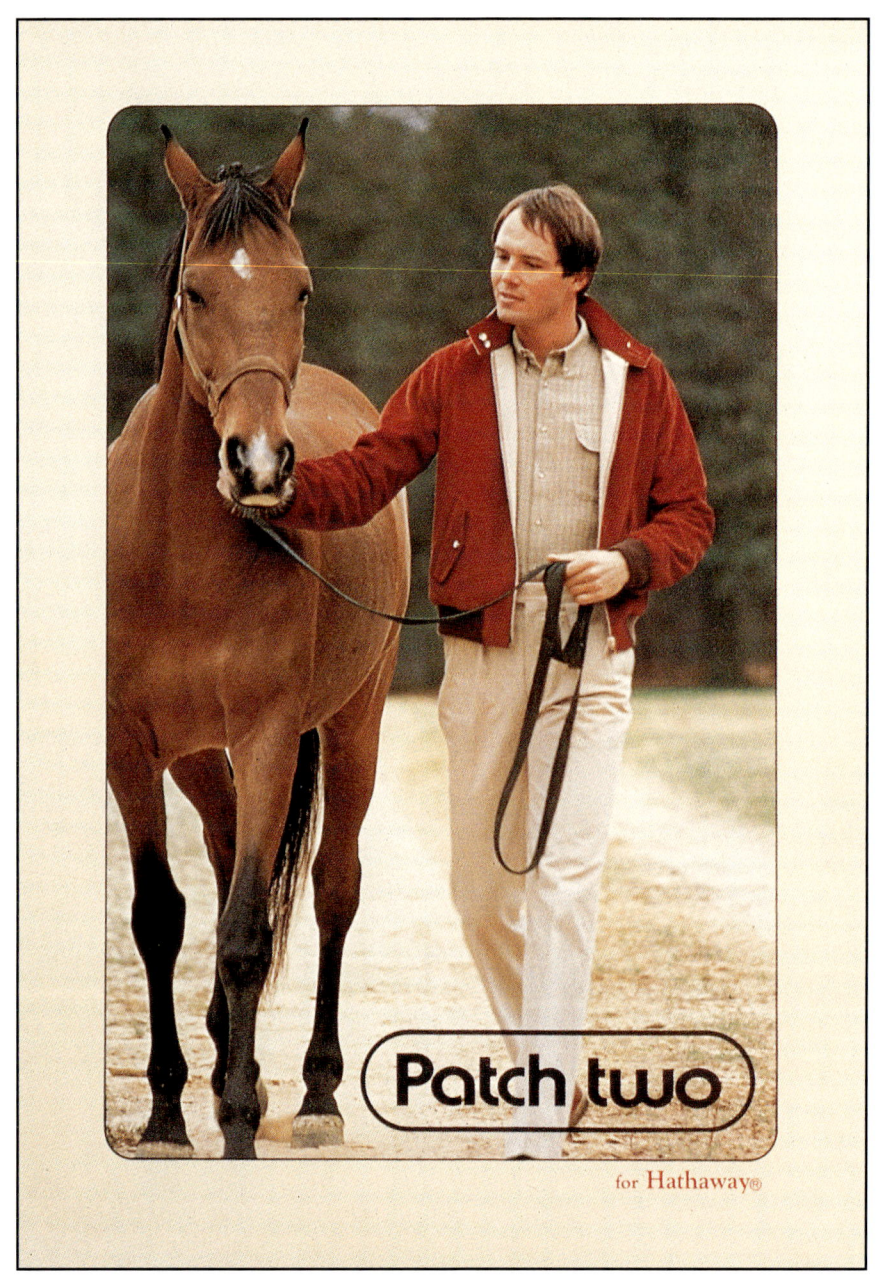

Left & following two pages: 1979. The Patch Two collection featuring a young, unpatched model, consistent with the target consumer. Left: $24–28.

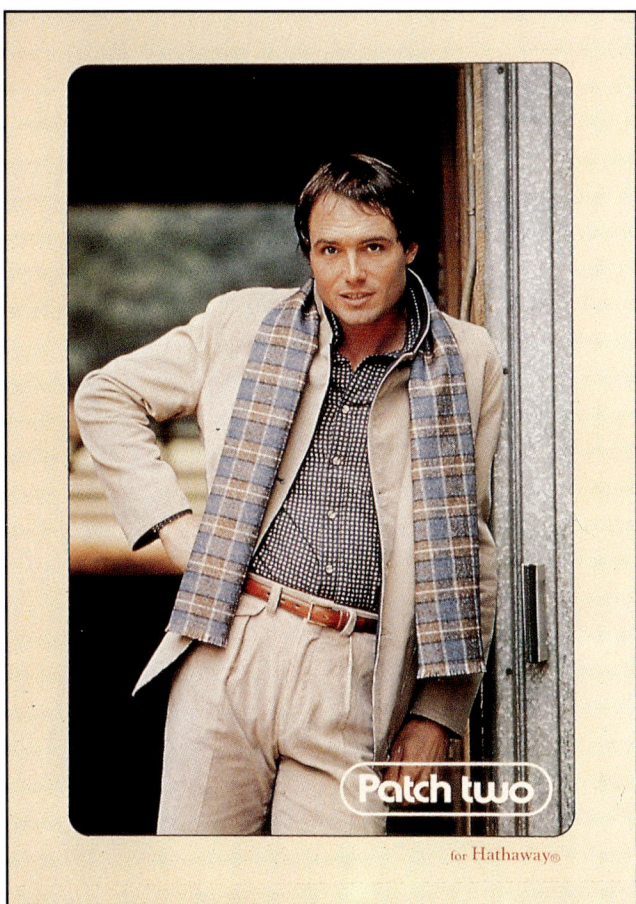

$18–20.

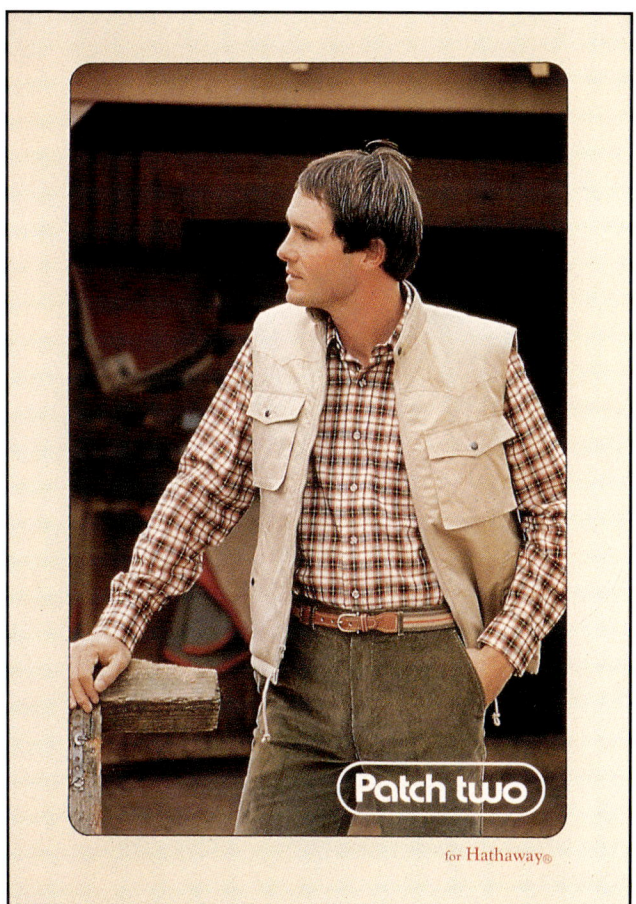

$24–28.

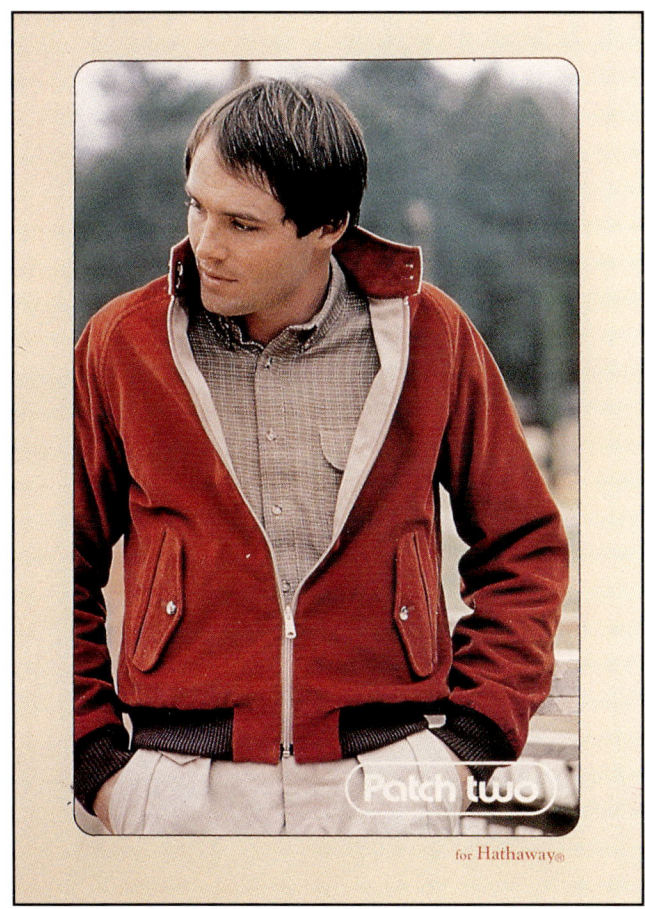

$30–32.

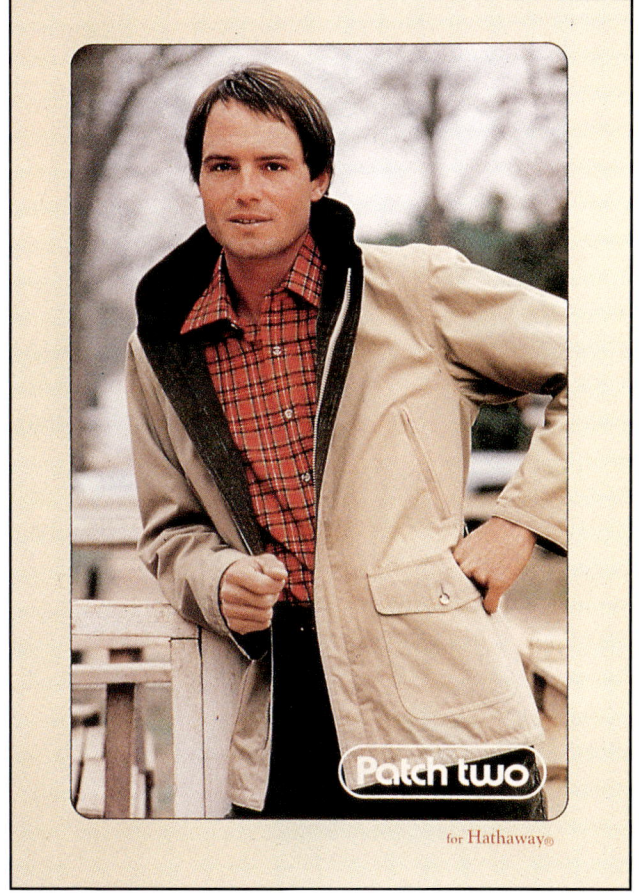

$30–32.

127

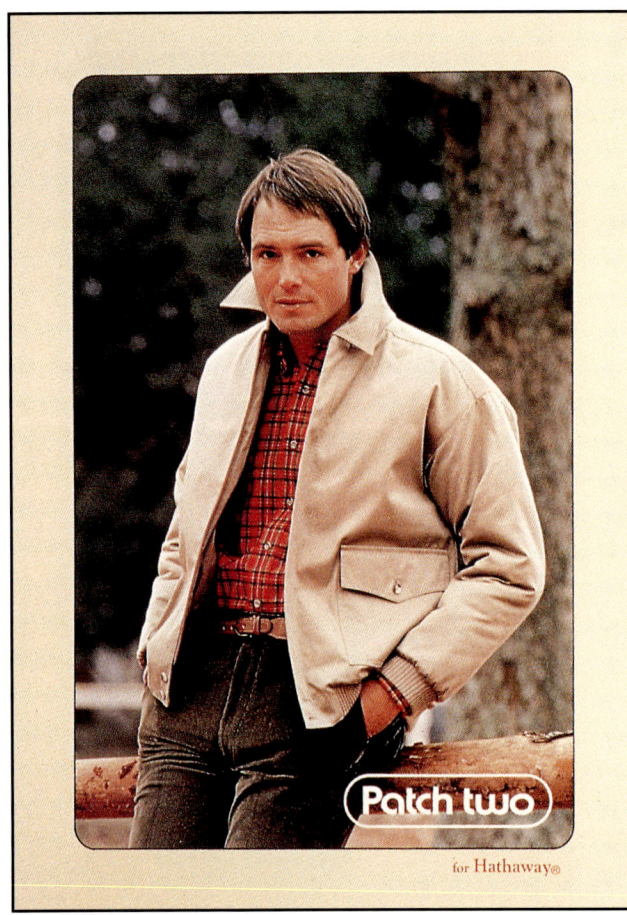

$30–32.

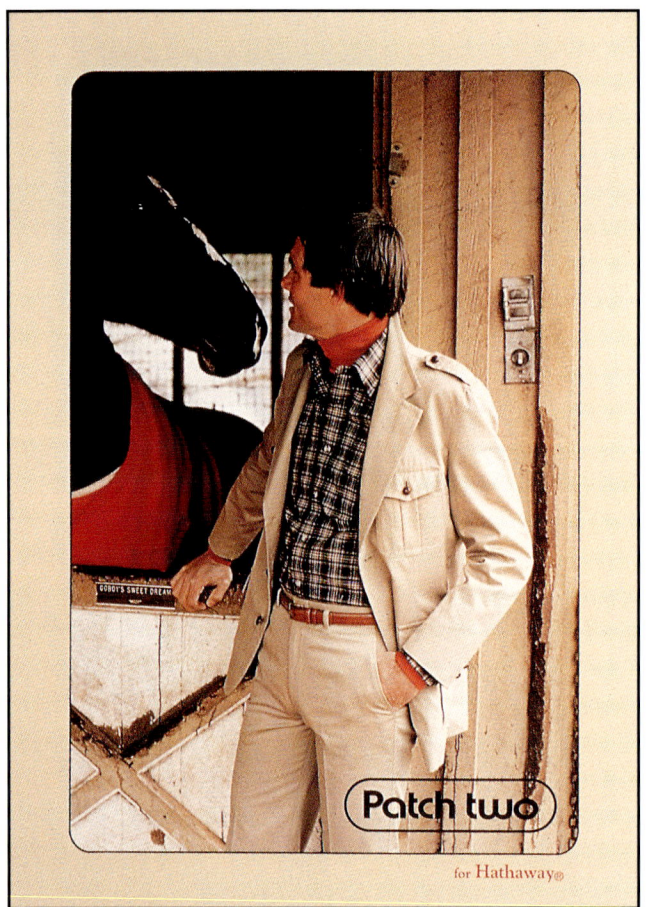

$30–32.

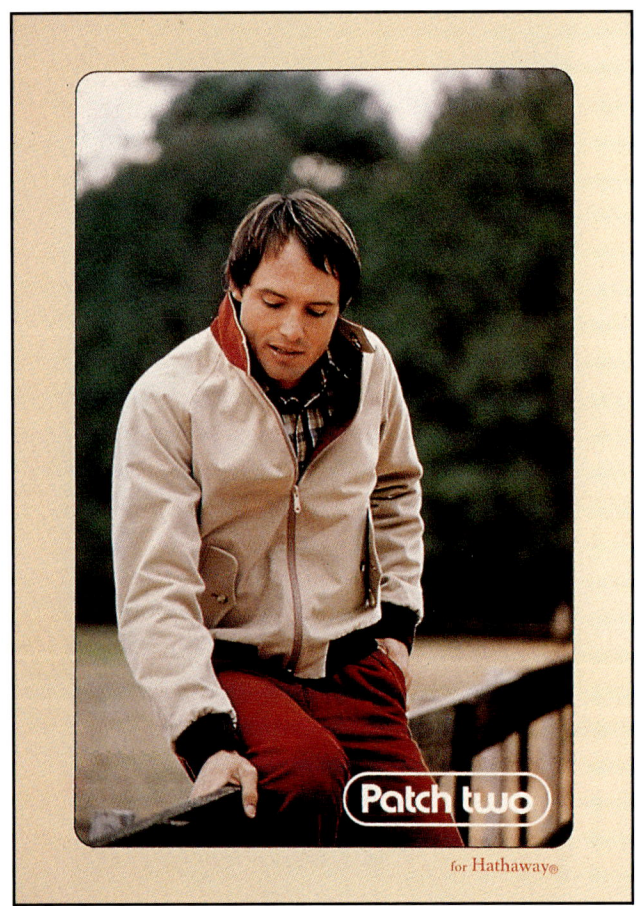

$30–32.

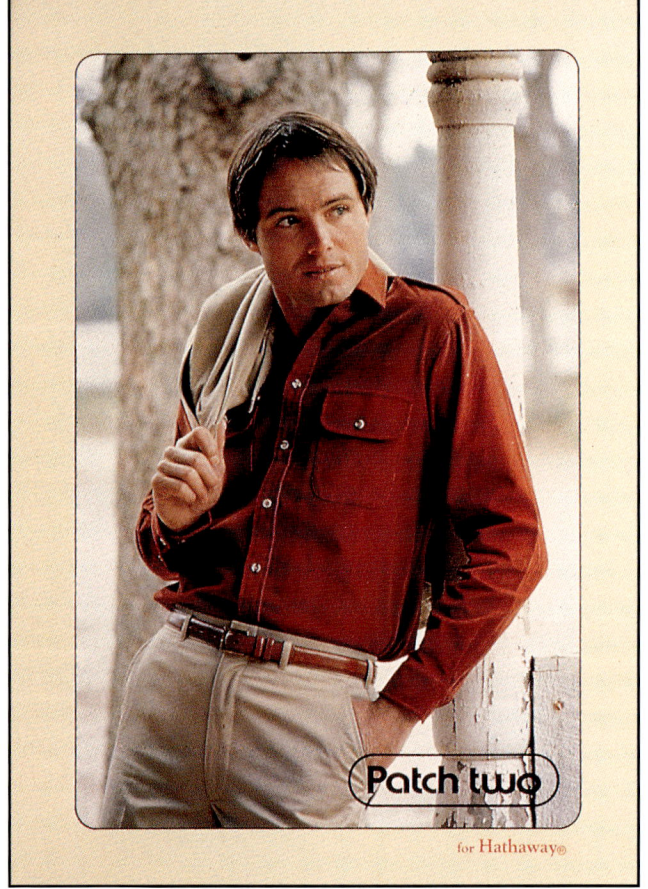

$30–32.

Entering the 1980s

In 1981 Hathaway and Ogilvy & Mather initiated "Operation Eyepatch," the search for the new Hathaway man. In the press release announcing the search, Danal Epstein, the Hathaway president, said that his firm was searching for: "the one American male who best epitomizes the well-dressed, well-groomed Hathaway man of the '80's." The search was open to any man in the United States, models and non-models alike. The requirements? "We have very few," said Epstein, "Quite simply, we are looking for a gentleman between the ages of 25 and 49 who helps to reinforce the high quality and traditional fashion excellence image so long associated with Hathaway."

The winner of the search was Clark Halstead, a real estate executive. The advertisement introducing him read in part:

> We've looked from Maine to California for six months. We've pulled men off the street. We've pored over 1200 photos from 1200 applicants. We've had phone calls and secret letters from wives and girlfriends.
>
> Now the search is over. We've found our man.

He's not an actor. Or a model. He's the Sr. Vice President of one of the world's most prestigious real estate firms. He holds degrees in architecture and business. He has a wonderful wife and a beautiful six year-old daughter. He stands 6'4" in his socks. And he looks fantastic in our Hathaway shirts."

Not exactly your average Joe, but a handsome choice. His run as the Hathaway man went through 1982.

In 1983, advertising was turned over to the Silverman Mower agency of Syracuse, New York. When asked why Hathaway left Ogilvy & Mather, Albert DiMarco, senior vice president at Hathaway, told an interviewer "They were probably way past their ability to service a small account. When you're spending only a million, you get lost in the shuffle. We were there because of sentimental reasons on our management side and on their management side. So we decided to go to a smaller shop which we could abuse." (*The New York Times*, September 9, 1983.)

They did not become totally unsentimental, however. They recognized the public's identification of the patch with Hathaway, so rather than give up a time-tested symbol, they changed the person behind the patch. They used celebrities, "real life Hathaway men," as DiMarco called them.

The consumers they sought for their high end shirts were men over 35 years old and earning over $35,000. The celebrities that spoke to this group were business celebrities. The series kicked off with Ted Turner, followed by *Megatrends* author, John Naisbitt, J.W. Marriott. In time the list would include other business men like Jacuzzi, Roy Jacuzzi and Michael Mondavi, sports figures Don and David Shula, Bob Costas, and Pete Dawkins, John Connally the politician, and Robert Jarvik, scientist and inventor.

The advertising budget for this campaign exceeded $1 million for the first time in Hathaway's history, jumping to $2 million. To justify this expenditure DiMarco said "the only way we'll increase our market share is to take it away from the competition." Philip Dougherty, *The New York Times* columnist writing the story, correctly identified just who the competition was: "[It] is not in lesser priced dress shirts, which make up 80 percent of the sales volume, but in house labels of Brooks Brothers, Paul Stuart, Saks Fifth Avenue and Bloomingdale's, as well as Gant, Polo, and Eagle." (*The New York Times*, September 9, 1983) The celebrity series ran until 1986 with good results.

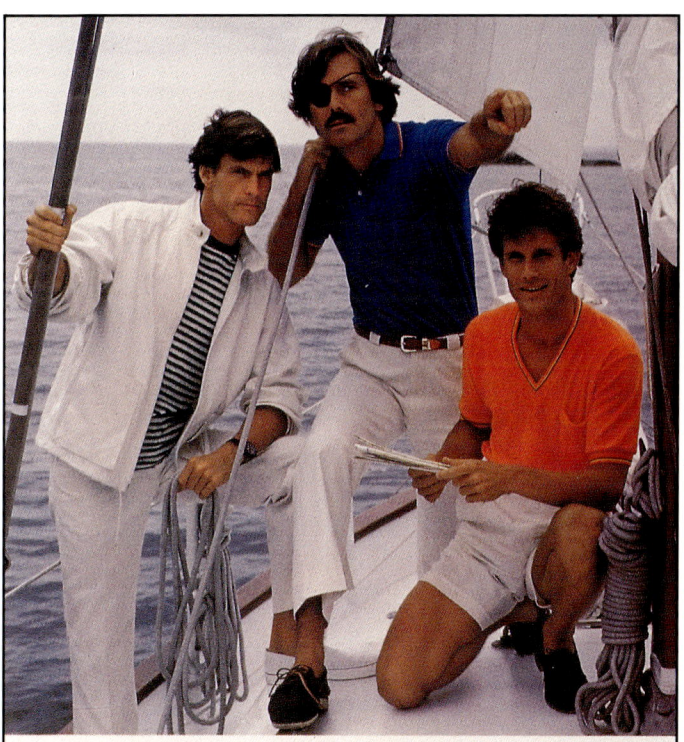

1980. $18–20.

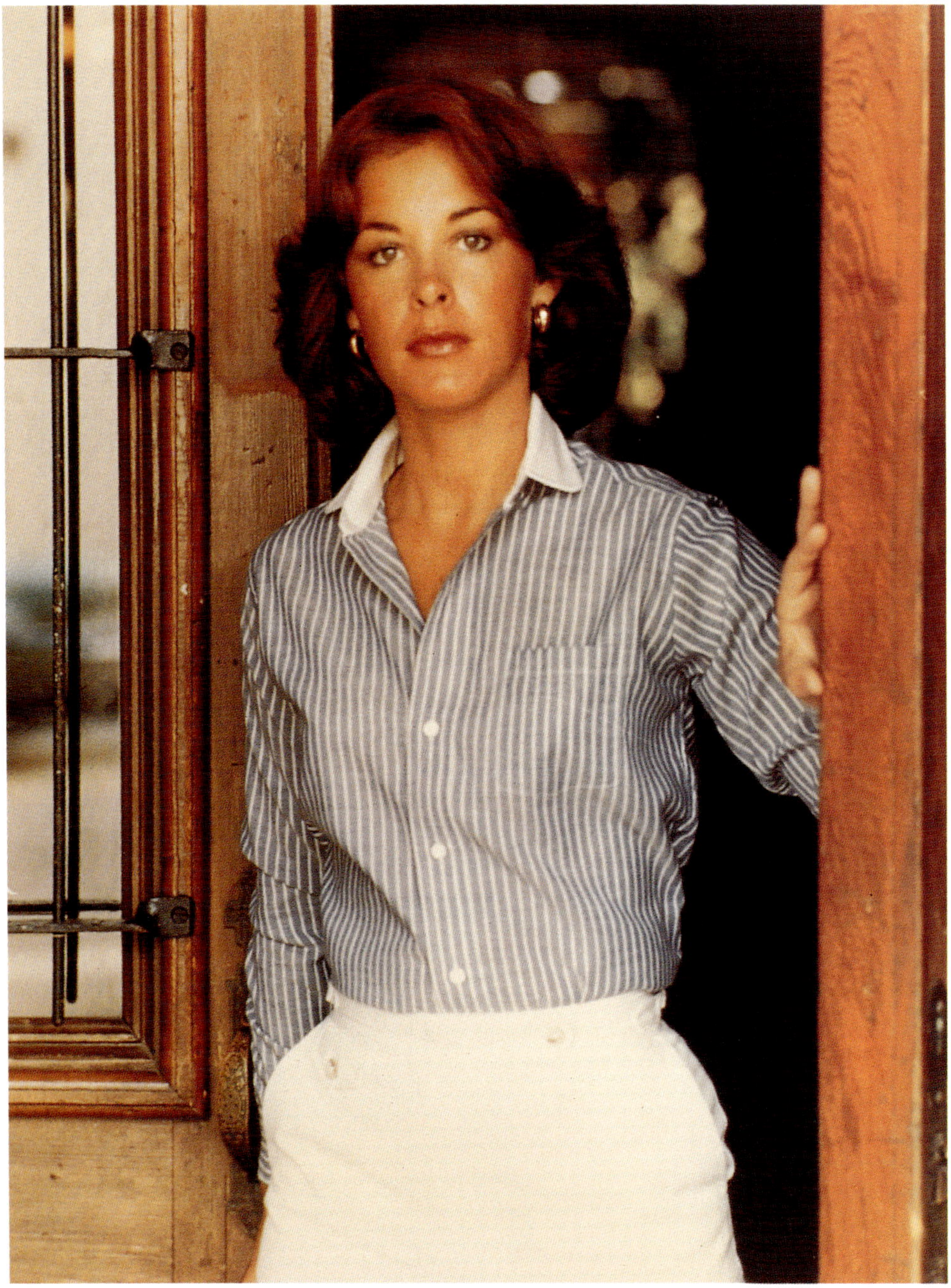

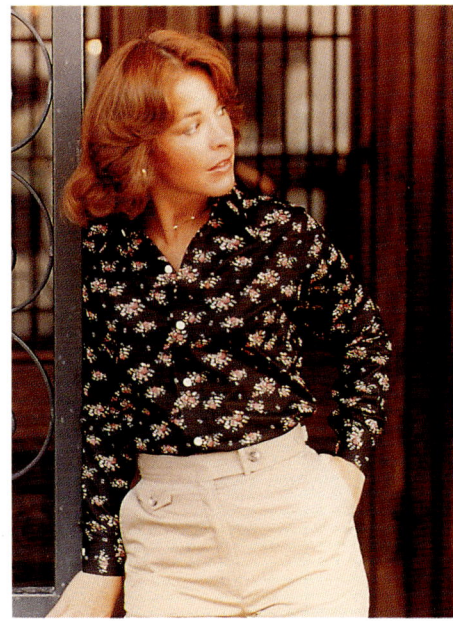

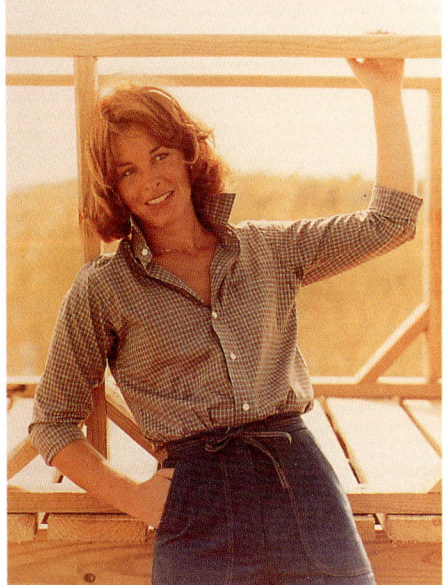

This & following three pages: c. 1980. Lady Hathaway had been established as a separate division by Warnaco in 1964. Hathaway reintroduced women's shirts in 1971. These are offerings from the late seventies and early 1980s under the Hathaway name and as "Hathaway for Her." $15–20.

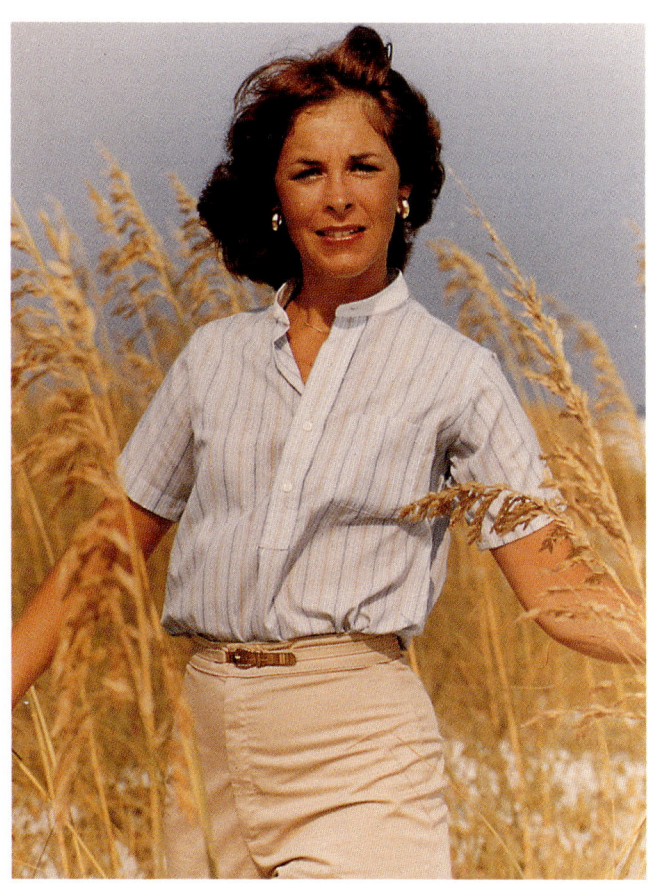
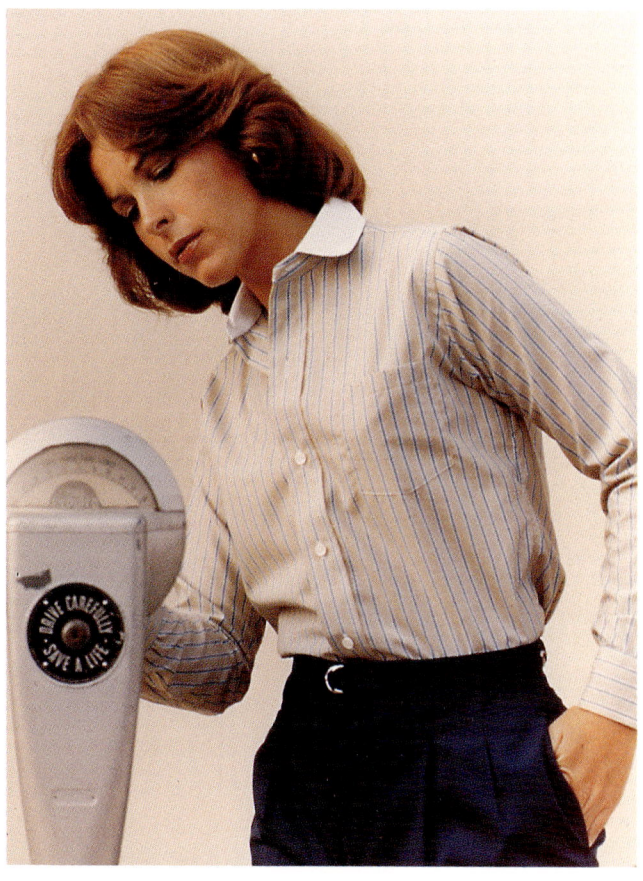
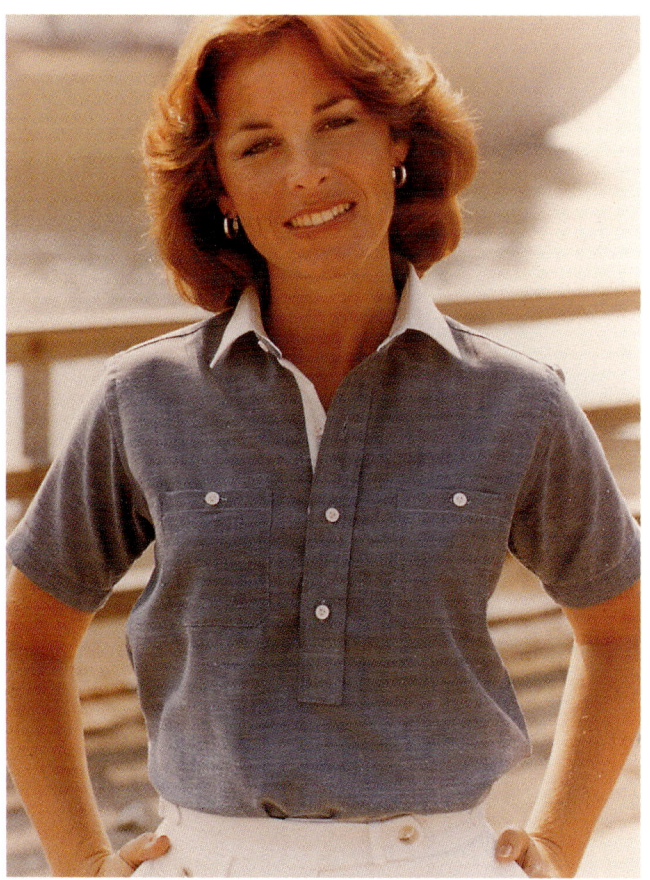
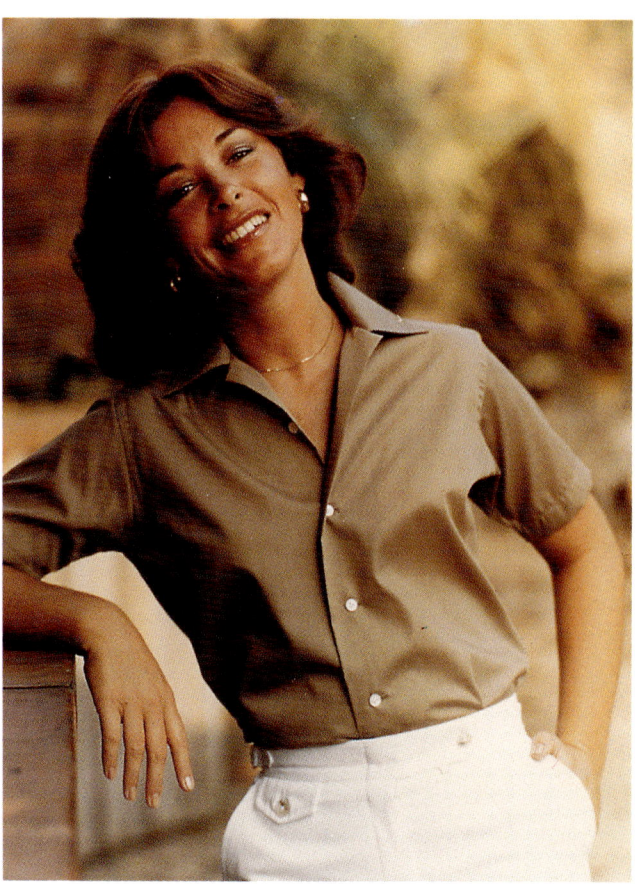

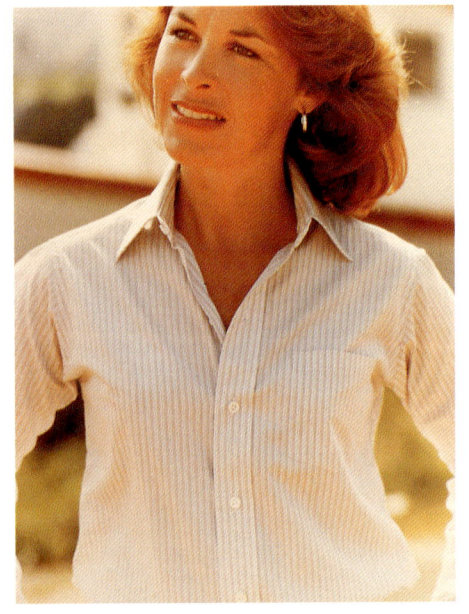
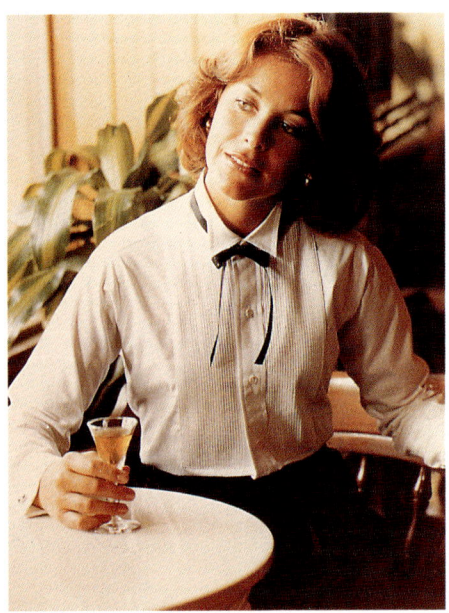
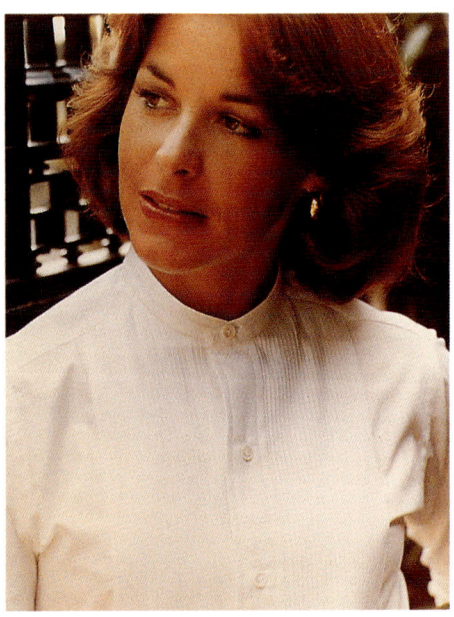

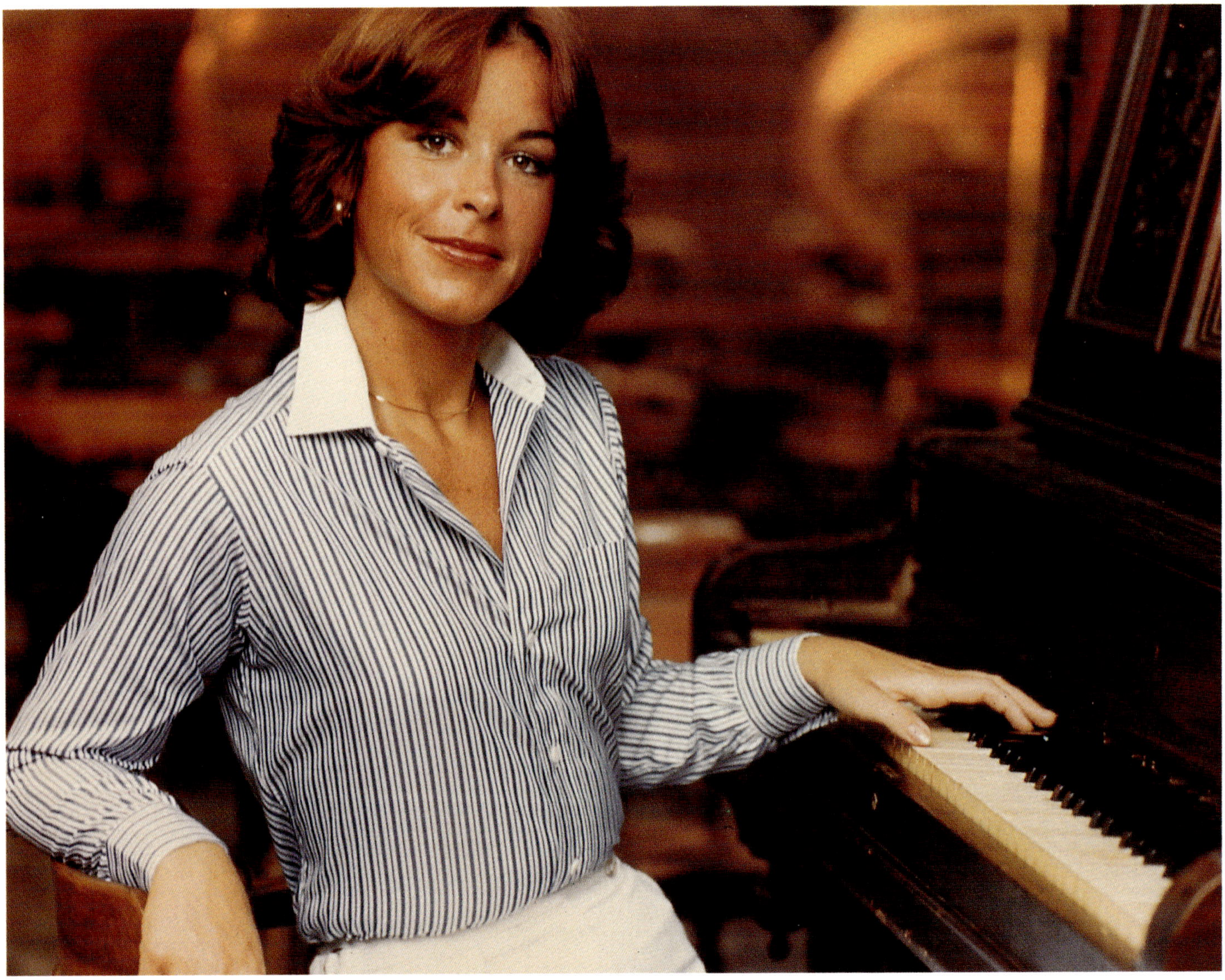

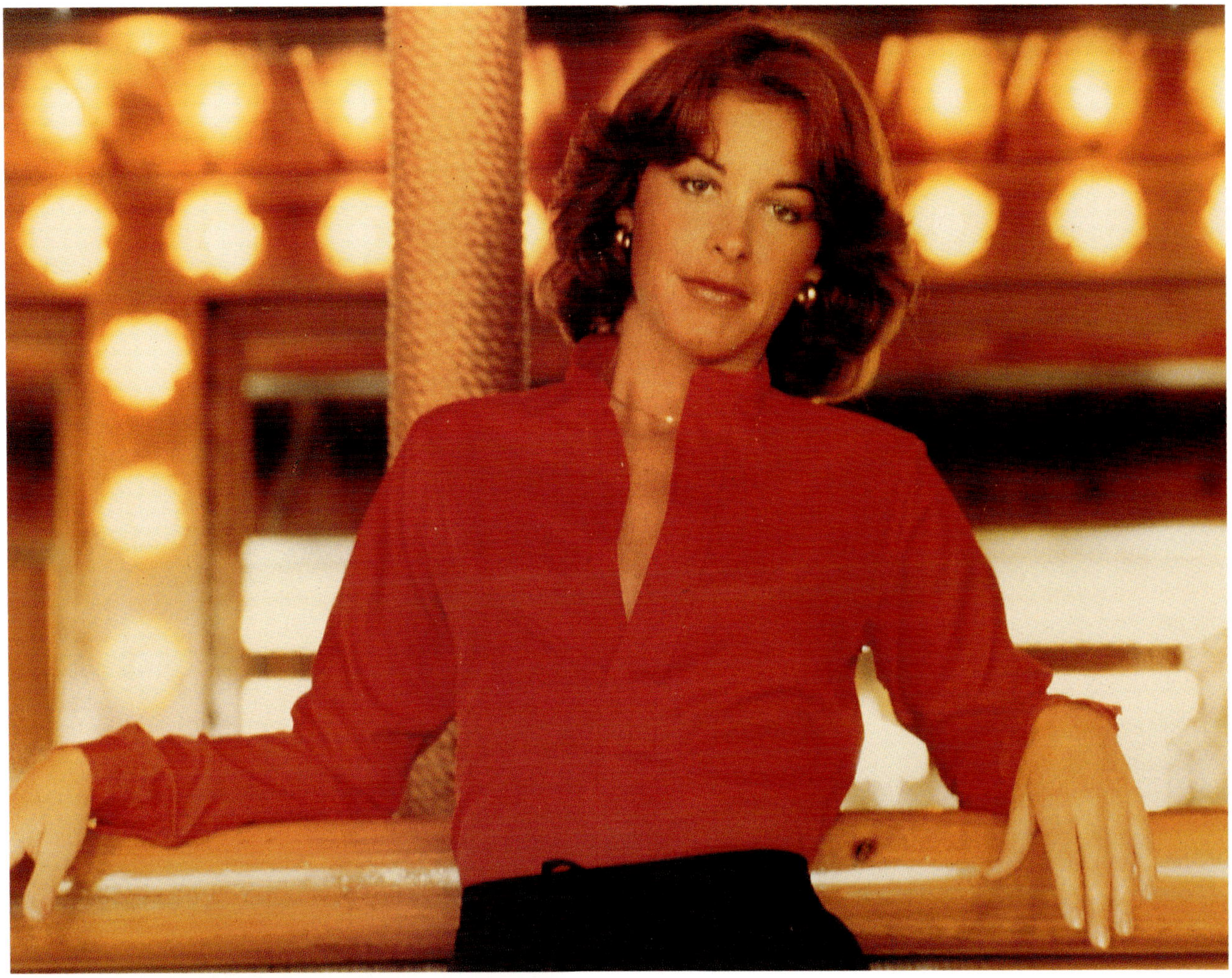

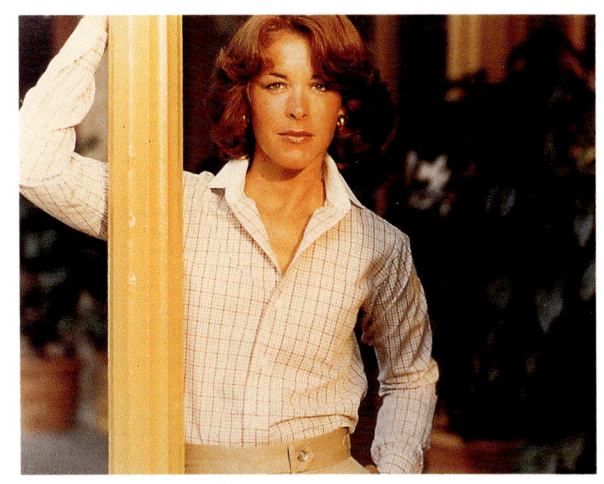
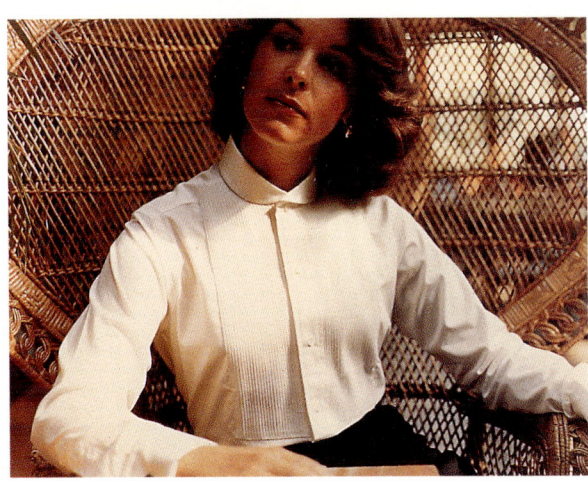

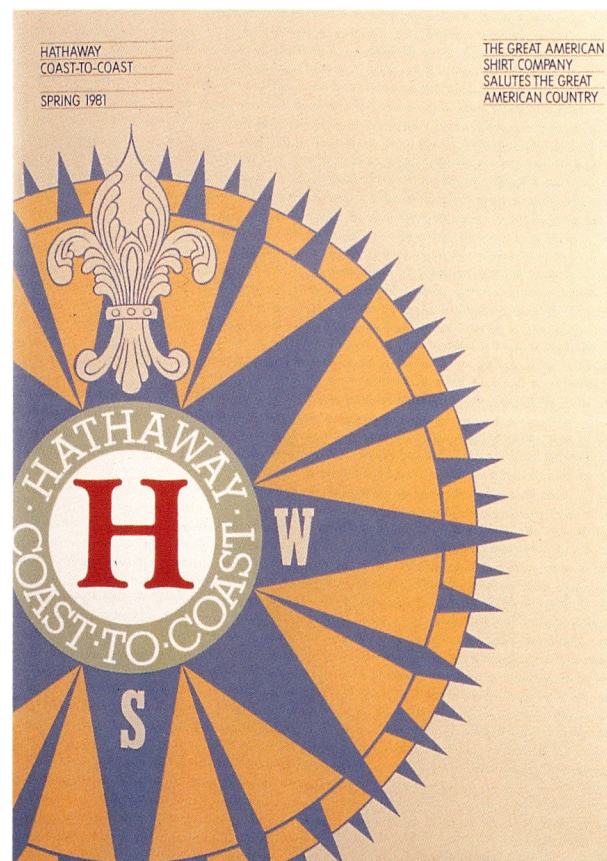

1981. "Hathaway Coast-to-Coast" catalog of Spring-Summer, 1981. Advertising materials included suggested events and displays for five promotions based on "The Great American Shirt Company Salutes the Great American Country."

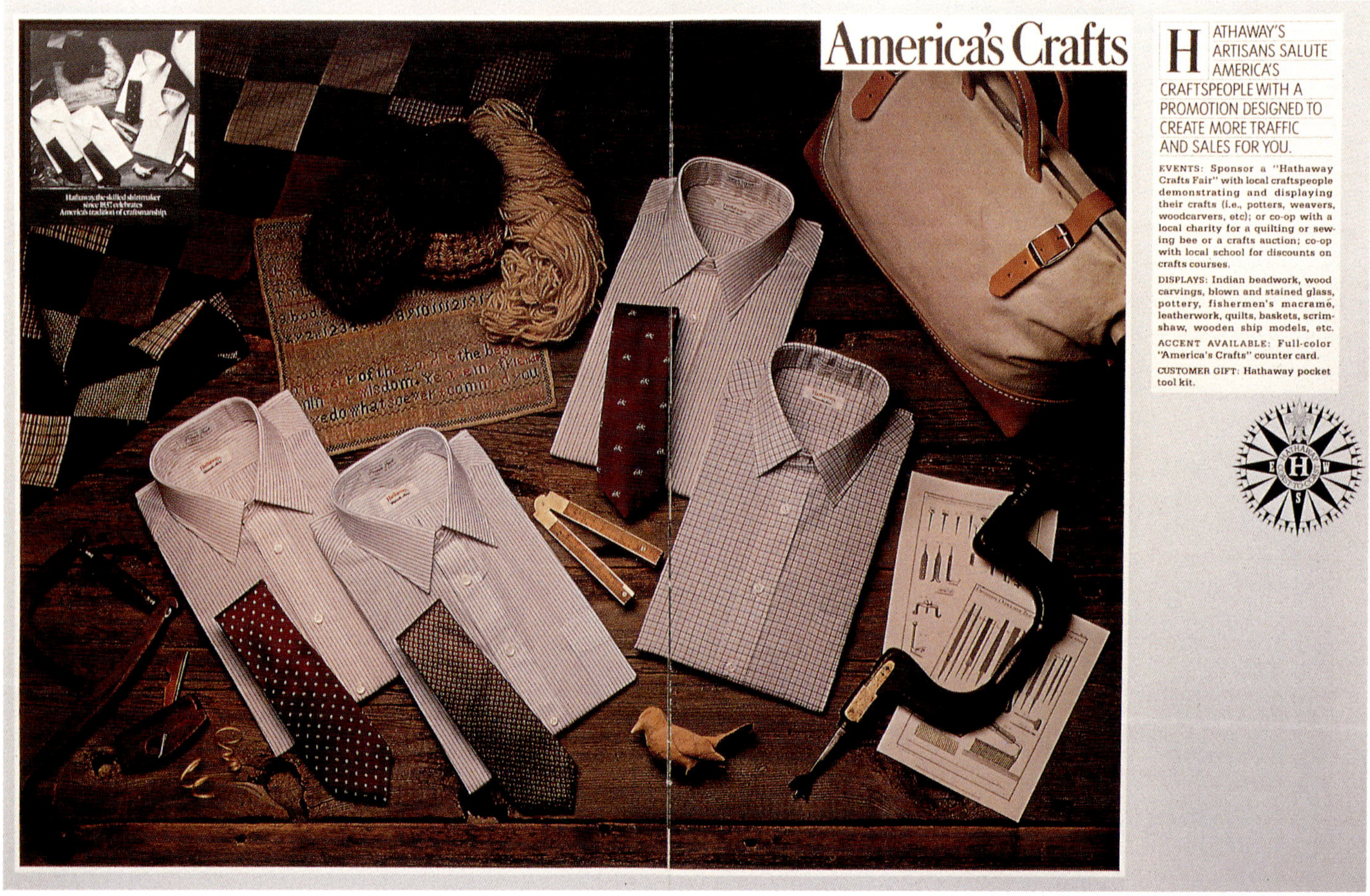

1981. America's Crafts. $18–20.

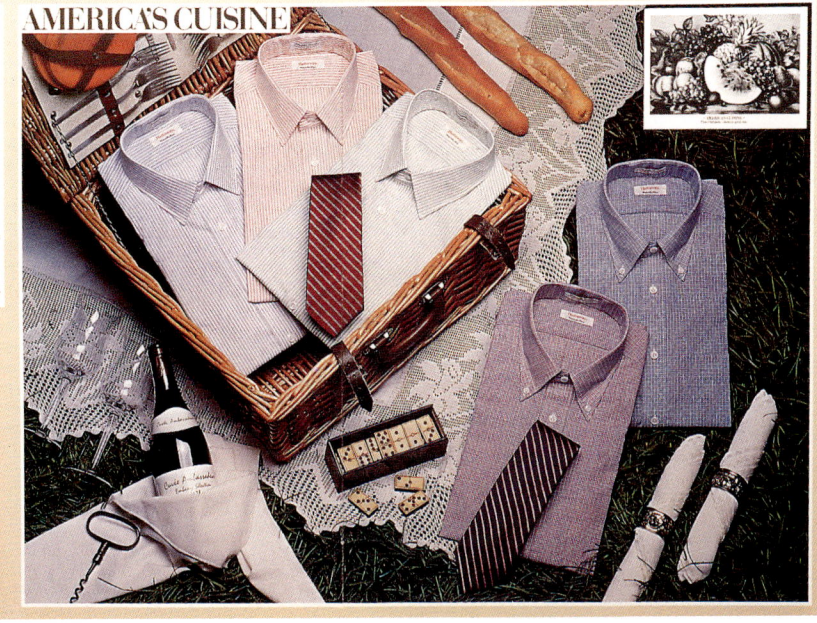

HATHAWAY HELPS YOU COOK UP GREAT SALES WITH THIS MOUTH-WATERING PROMOTION

EVENTS: Sponsor local bake-off tasting with gift certificates as prizes; tie in with charity or sponsor self-liquidating local style food event; i.e., Texas barbecue, Wisconsin cheese tasting, New England clambake, California wine-tasting, etc. Co-op with local gourmet restaurant for discount or "dinner-for-two" contest.

DISPLAYS: Menus from local restaurants, antique cooking/baking utensils, recipe boxes, cookbooks, trays, napkins, silver, crystal (tie in with other stores or departmental). Theme displays on local cuisine; i.e., clambake's lobster pots, buoys, etc.; barbecue's checked napkins, aprons, etc; cheese boards and knives; wine corkscrews, ice buckets, etc.

ACCENT AVAILABLE: Full-color Currier & Ives counter card.

CUSTOMER GIFT: C.F. Hathaway's cookbook: "A Taste of Early American Cooking."

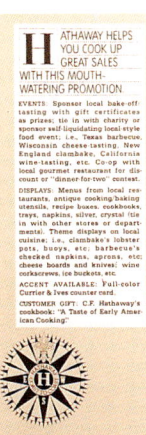

1981. America's Cuisine. $18–20.

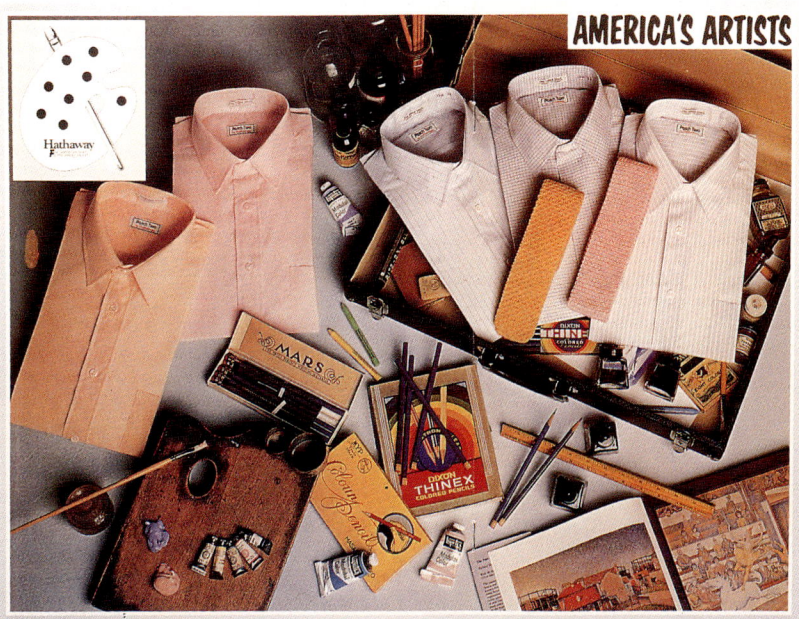

FINE HATHAWAY SHIRTS AND FINE AMERICAN ART— A CLASSIC COMBINATION IN A PROMOTION WHICH WILL REFINE YOUR MERCHANDISING ARTS.

EVENTS: Co-op with local gallery or museum for free admission or discounts with purchase; stage American art exhibit with cooperation of local artists or gallery; invite local artist to paint or sculpt at store; offer free-with-purchase portraits with cooperation of local pastel portrait artist.

DISPLAYS: Real or reproduction local or "name" American art, possibly focused on local interest or area (i.e., Winslow Homer for the sea, Frederick Remington for the West, Jasper Johns for cities, etc.); artists' materials: easels, palettes, brushes, rags, palette knives, smocks, berets; use shirts and art together to highlight color themes.

ACCENT AVAILABLE: Colorful Hathaway palette counter card with fabric swatches.

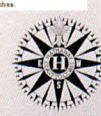

1981. America's Artists. $18–20.

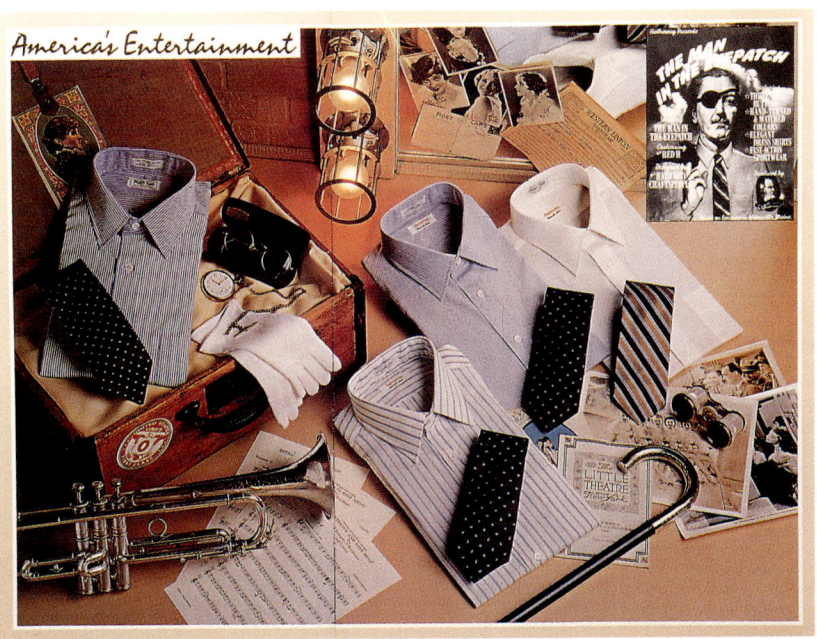

FROM HOLLYWOOD TO SUMMER STOCK, YOUR CUSTOMERS WILL ENJOY IT MORE IN A HATHAWAY

EVENTS: Feature "Hathaway Saturday Matinee" with popcorn, soda and old silent movies on a Fairchild recorder; co-op for local theatre or movie tickets with purchase; feature mime or "mechanical model" for entertainment; co-op with local travel agent for "night-on-the-town" contest.

IN-STORE SALES CONTEST: Run a one- or two-week "Academy Award" sales contest just before the awards in April: Reward your shirt department's best salesclerk with an "Academy Award night on the town for two" (movie tickets and dinner).

DISPLAYS: Lighted stage mirror and makeup, tap and ballet shoes, masks, sheet music from American musicals, tuxedo accessories, opera, ballet and theatre tickets, posters and programs, circus memorabilia, old movie posters, photos of Academy Award-winning stars and films.

ACCENT AVAILABLE: Full-color counter card of "Hathaway presents 'The Man in the Eyepatch'" movie poster.

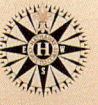

1981. America's Entertainment. $18–20.

135

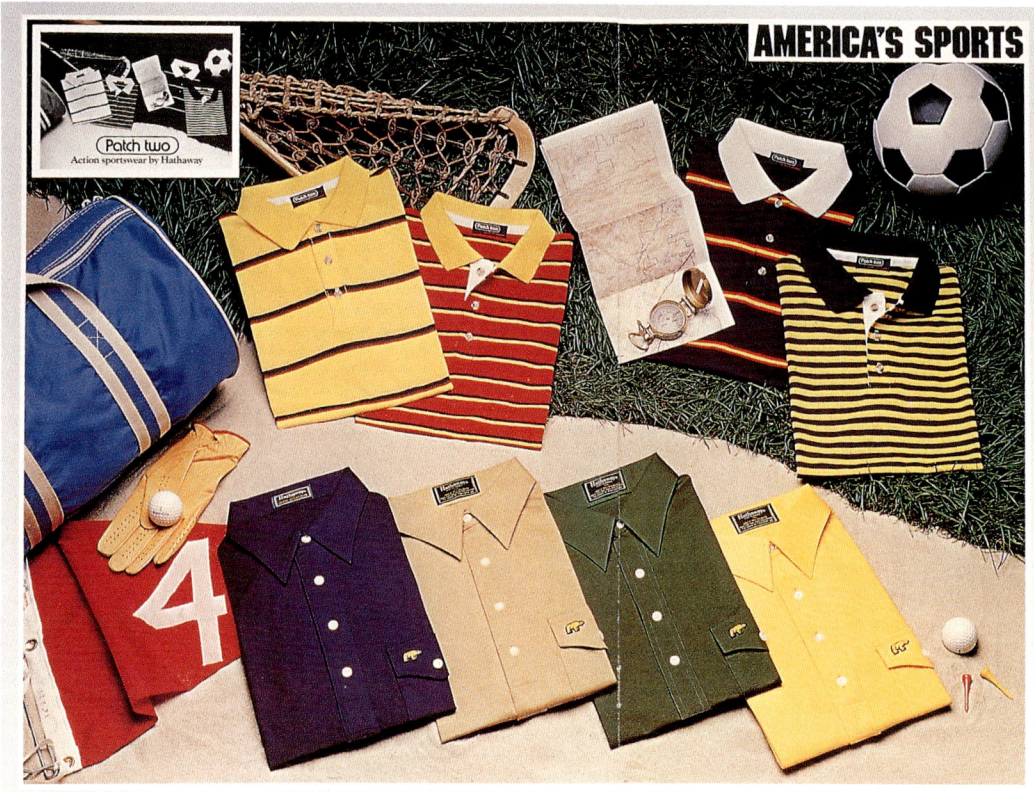

1981. America's Sports. $18–20.

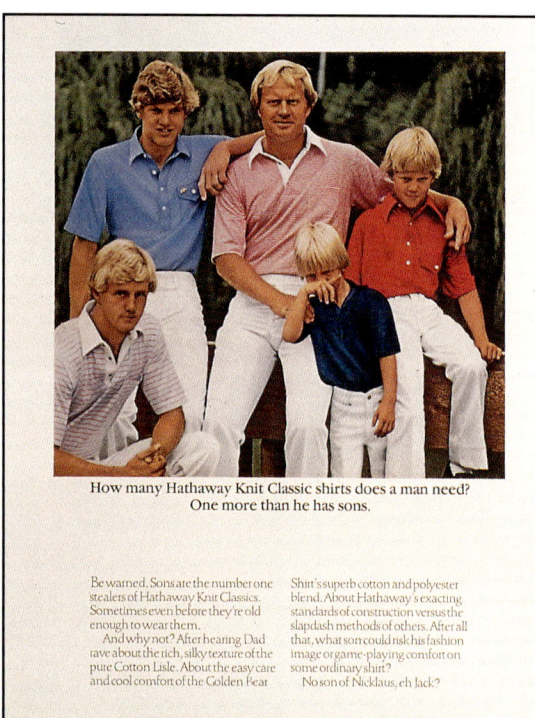

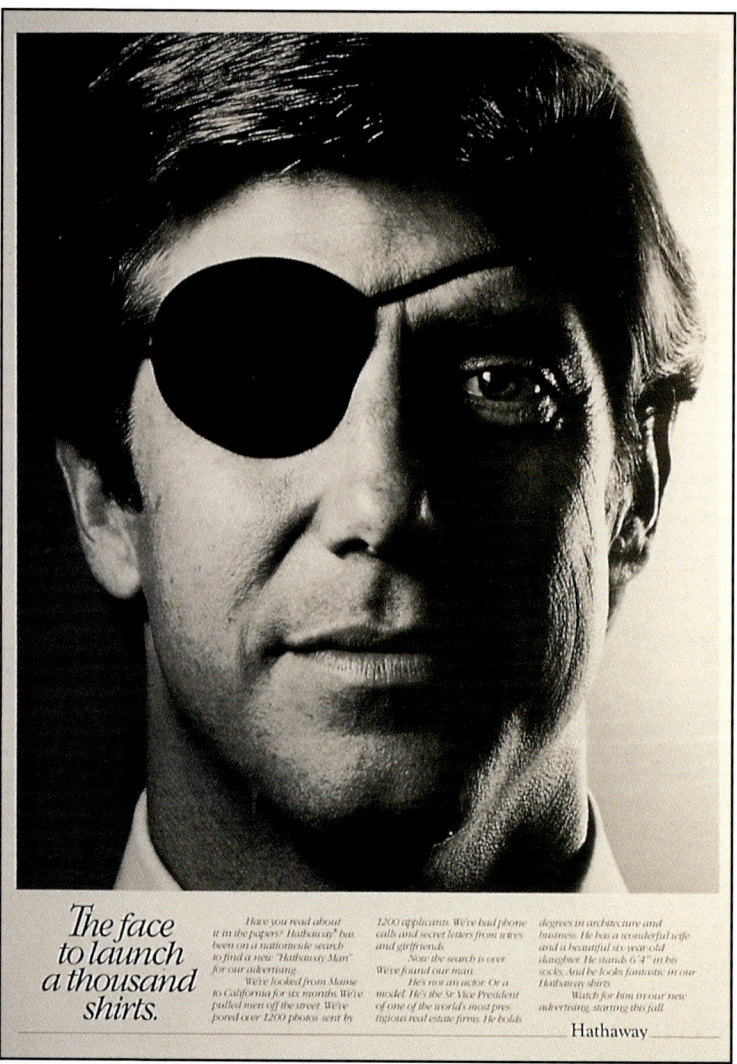

Above: 1981. The Nicklaus connection continues, this time with the next generation. $18–20.

Right: 1981-82. The winner of the nationwide search to find a new "Hathaway Man" was Clark Halstead, a real estate executive. This ad introduced him.

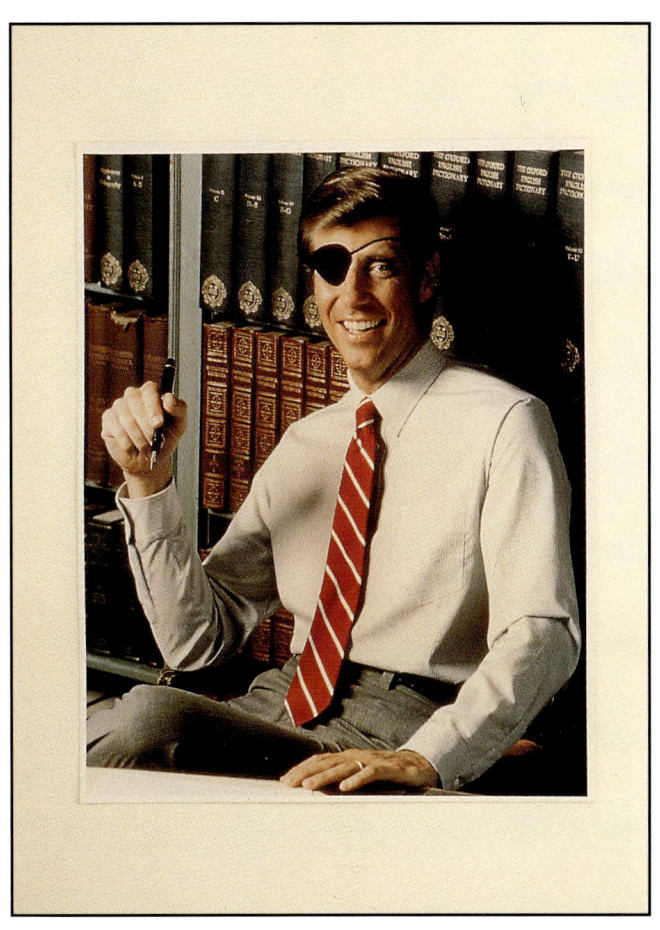

1982. Halstead in color. $15–18.

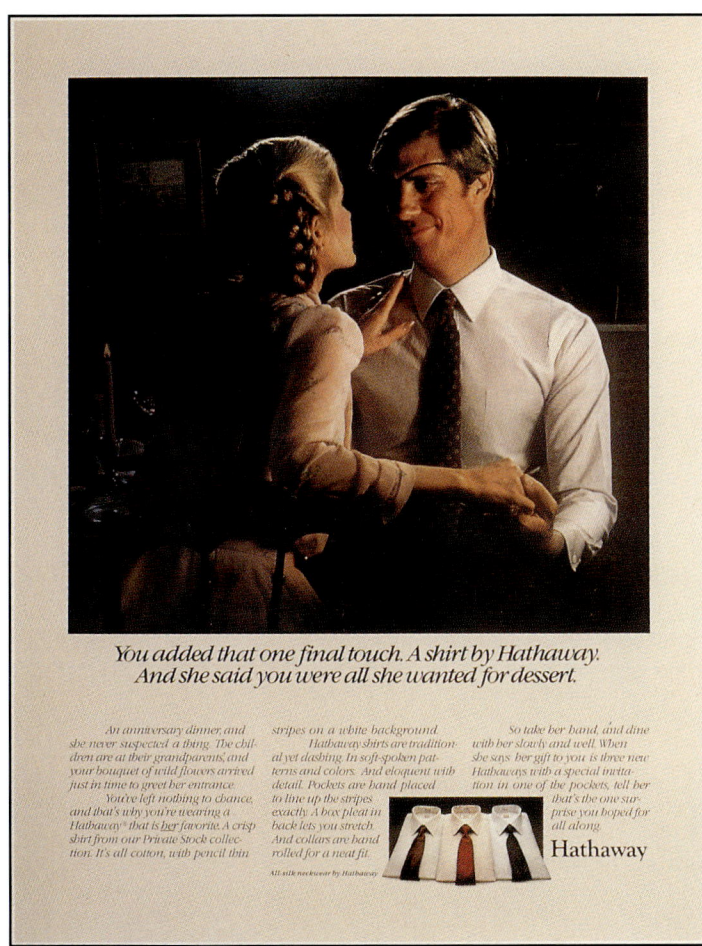

1982. The Private Stock Collection. $15–18.

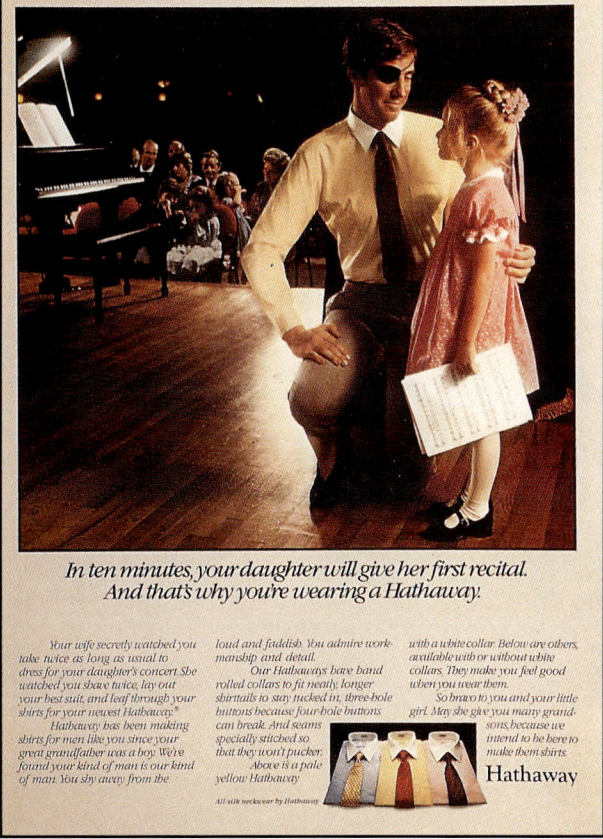

1986. In ten minutes, your daughter $18–20.

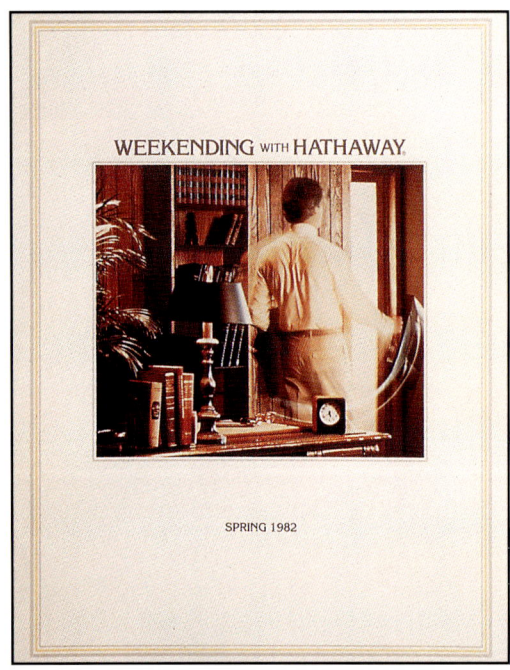

1982. "Weekending with Hathaway, the spring catalog. Clark Halstead appears throughout this publication wearing the eyepatch. $15–18.

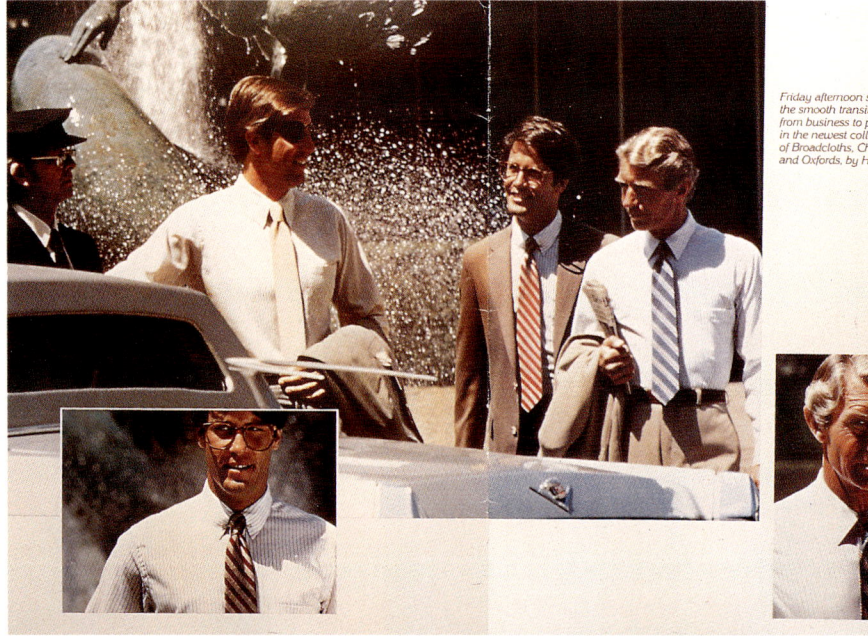

1982. Friday afternoon, business shirts of broadcloth, chambray, and Oxford. $15–18.

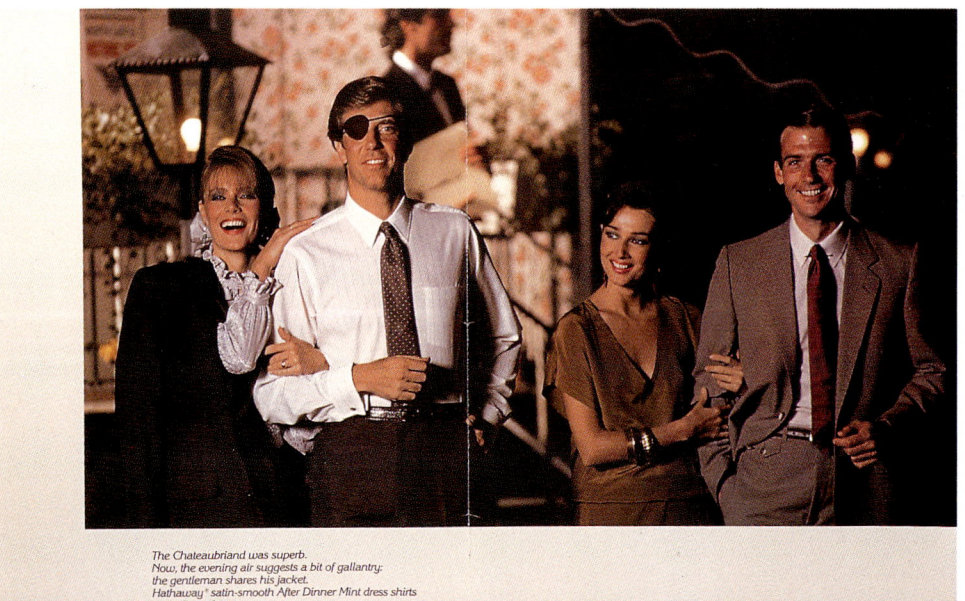

1982. Friday evening in After Dinner Mint dress shirts and Hathaway silk ties. $15–18.

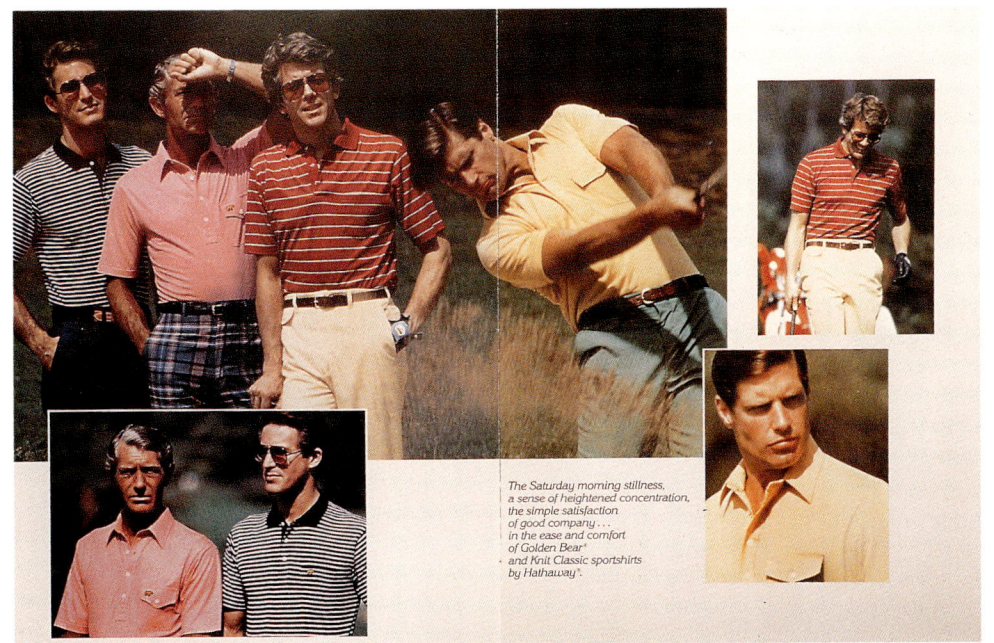

The Saturday morning stillness, a sense of heightened concentration, the simple satisfaction of good company... in the ease and comfort of Golden Bear® and Knit Classic sportshirts by Hathaway®.

1982. Saturday morning golf wear. Golden Bear, Nicklaus's nick name has replaced Golf Classics as a brand name, along with Knit Classic. $15–18.

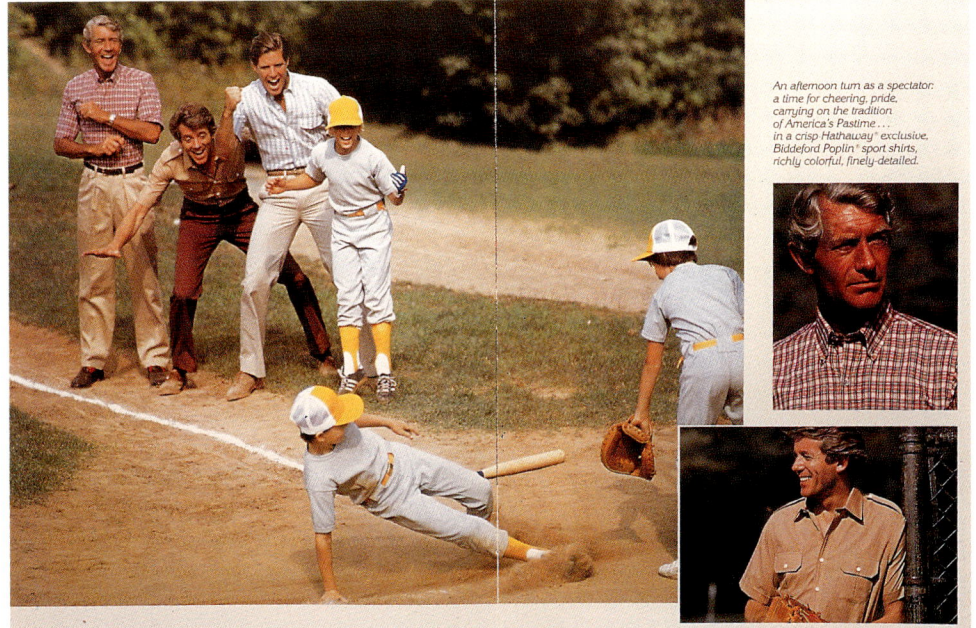

An afternoon turn as a spectator: a time for cheering, pride, carrying on the tradition of America's Pastime... in a crisp Hathaway® exclusive, Biddeford Poplin® sport shirts, richly colorful, finely-detailed.

1982. Saturday afternoon calls for Biddeford poplin sportshirts. $18–20.

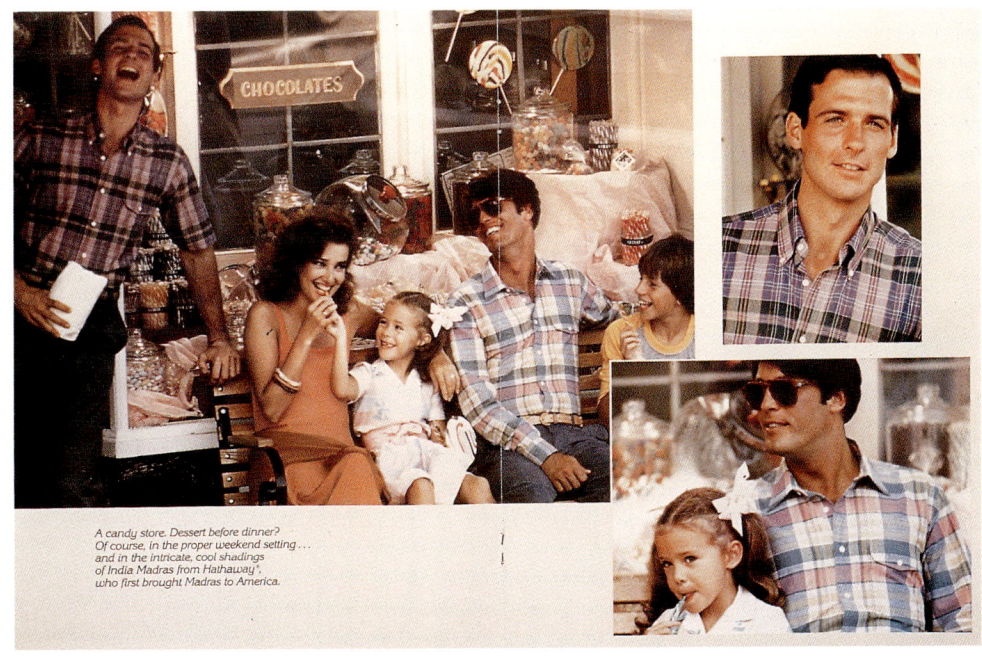

A candy store. Dessert before dinner? Of course, in the proper weekend setting... and in the intricate, cool shadings of India Madras from Hathaway®, who first brought Madras to America.

1982. Later he wears Madras. $18–20.

139

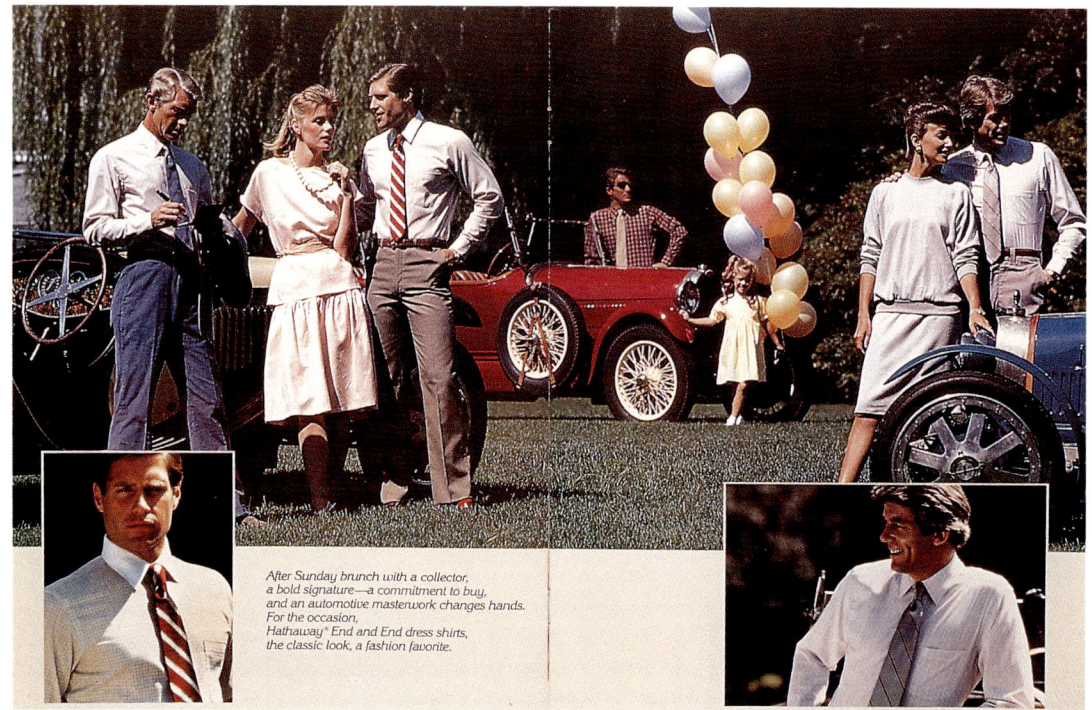

1982. Sunday brunch dress wear. $18–20.

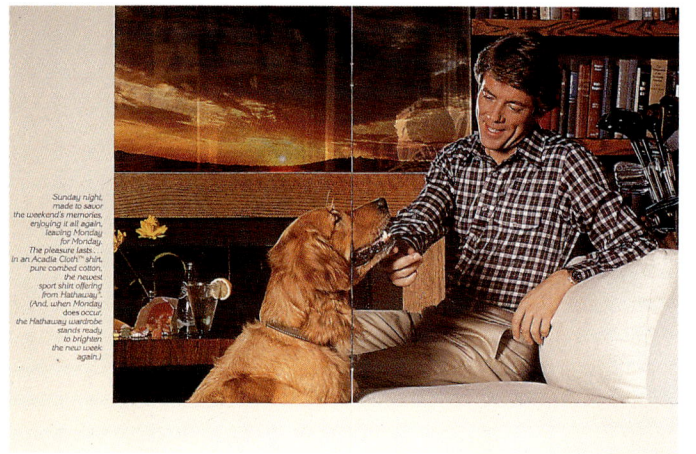

1982. Private Stock sportswear in cotton and cotton/silk blends. $20–22.

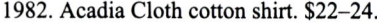

1982. Acadia Cloth cotton shirt. $22–24.

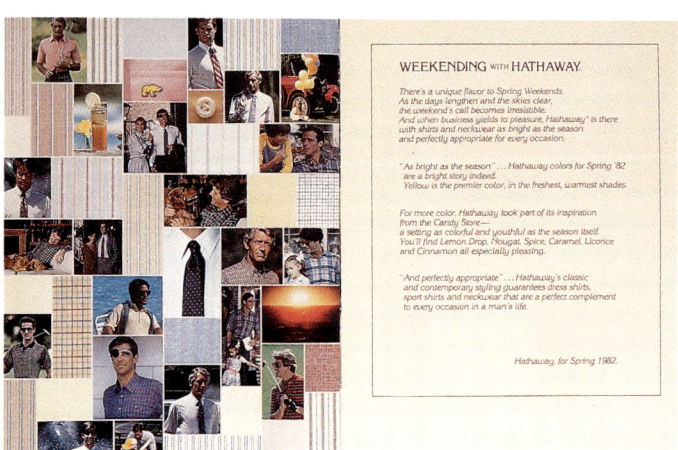

1982. The closing page of the Spring, 1982 catalog.

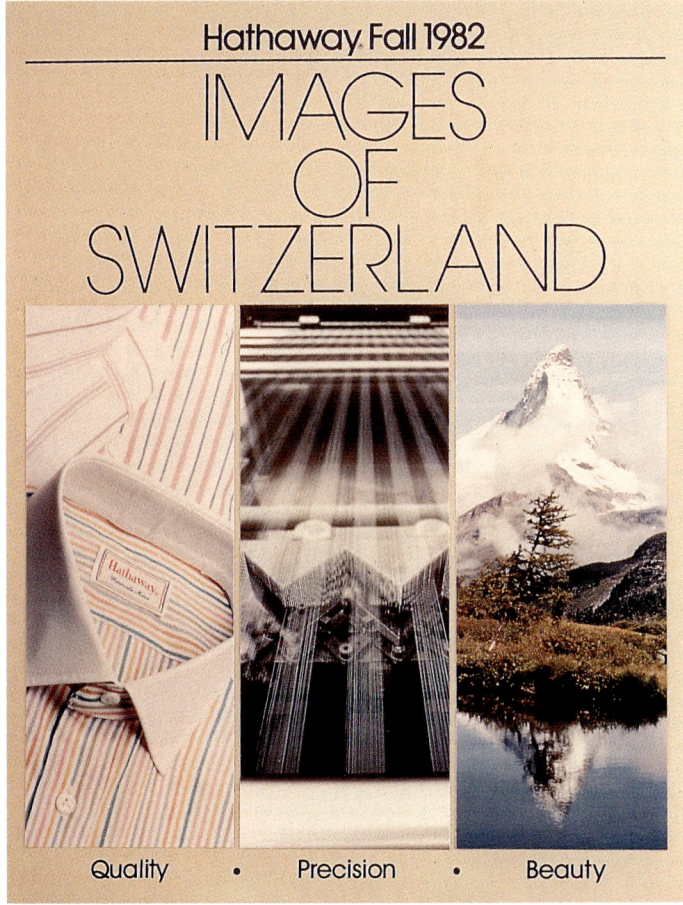

1982. "Images of Switzerland," the Fall 1982 catalog. The images featured only the shirts. No sign of the Hathaway Man. $18–20.

1982. Dress shirts. $18–20.

1982. Wovens. $18–20.

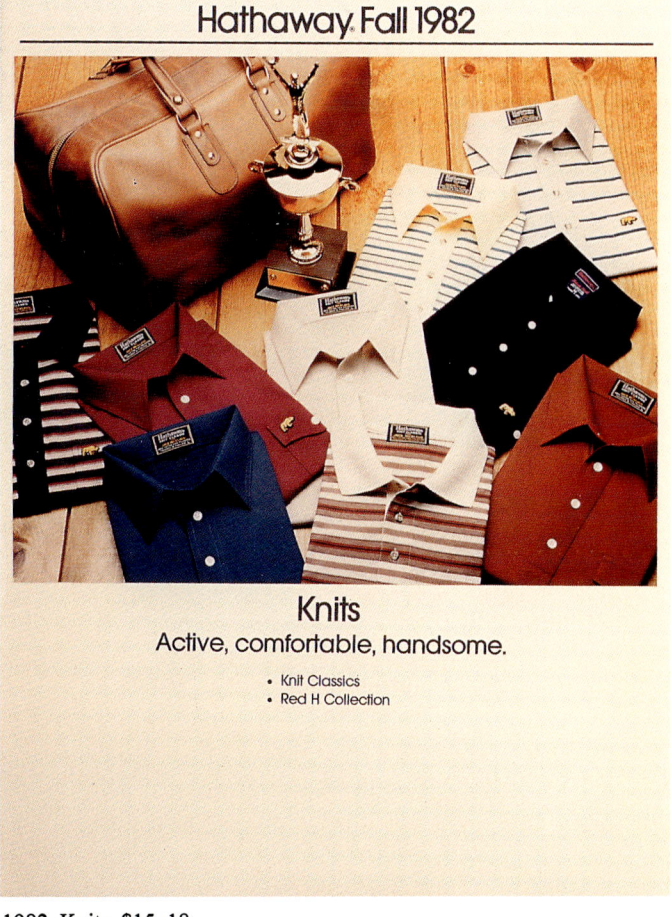

1982. Knits. $15–18.

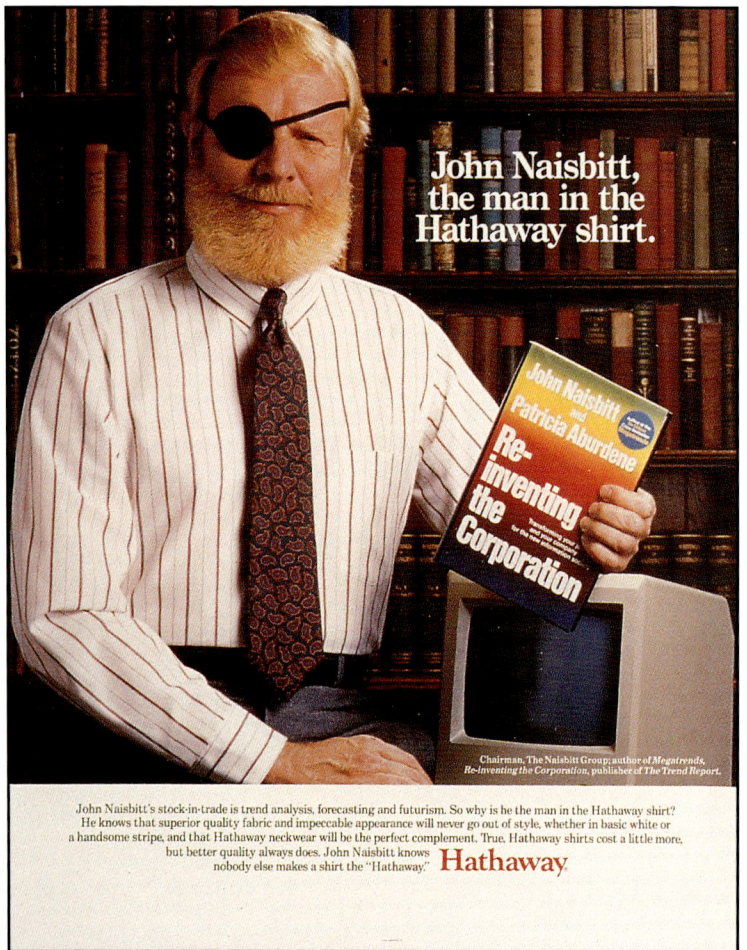

c. 1986. Silverman Mower agency of Syracuse, New York took over the advertising account from Ogilvy & Mathers in 1983. In 1985-86 they produced this series using celebrities from business, entertainment, politics, and sports as the new Hathaway Men. John Naisbitt, the *Megatrends* and *Reinventing the Corporation*, led off the series. Shirts ranging $18–20.

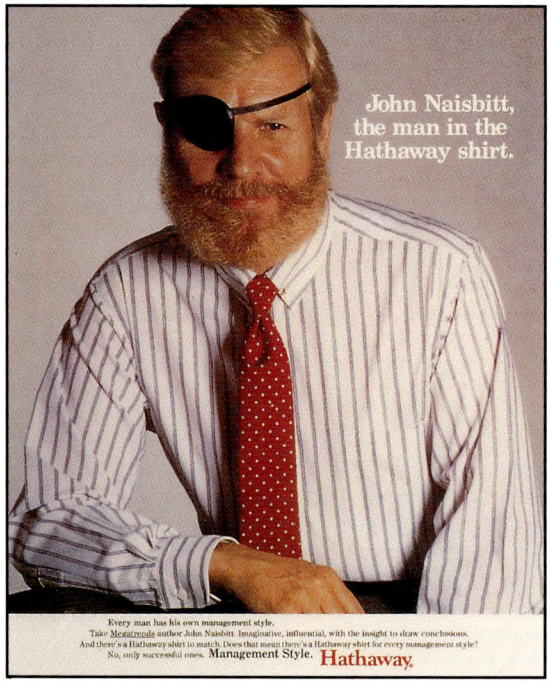

1986. John Naisbitt.

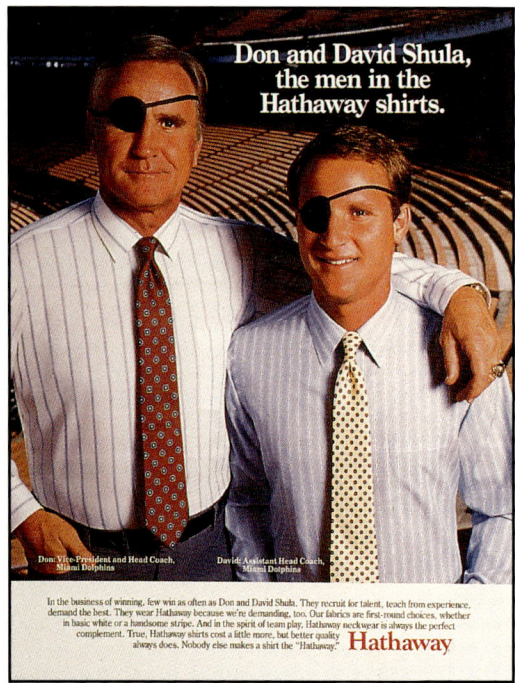

1986. Don and David Shula.

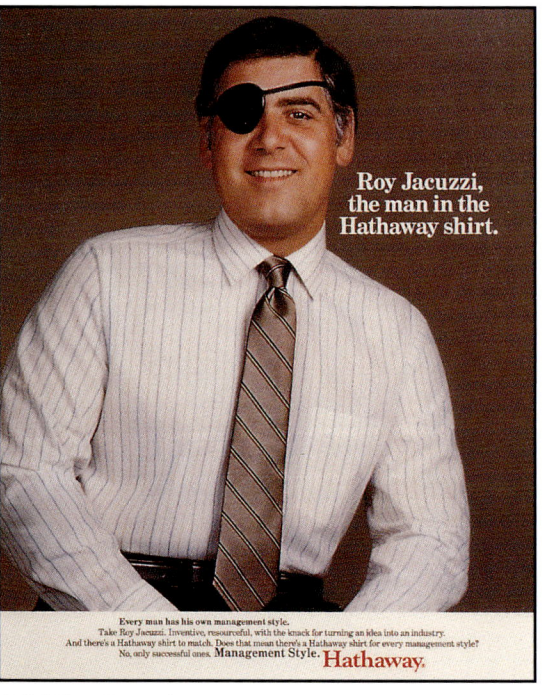

1986. Roy Jacuzzi.

142

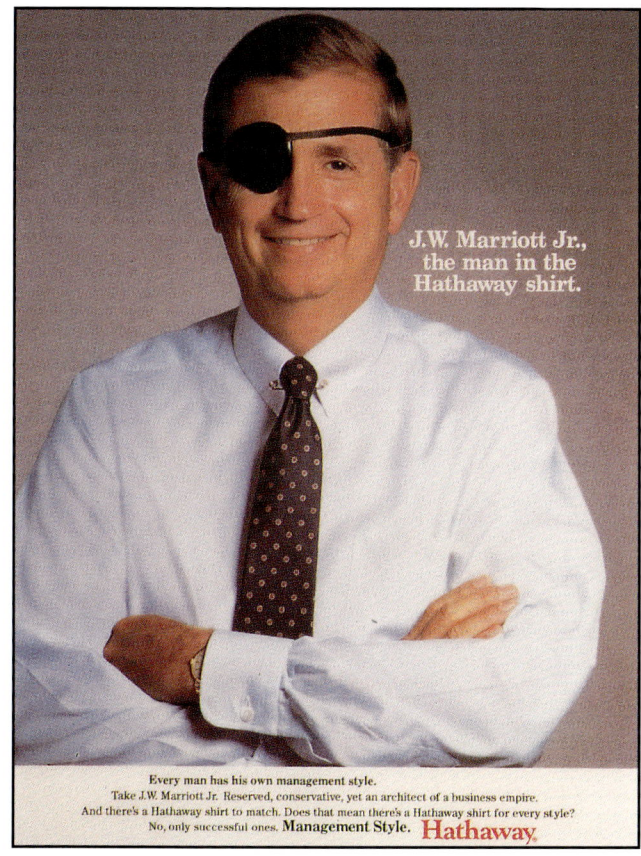

1986. J.W. Marriott.

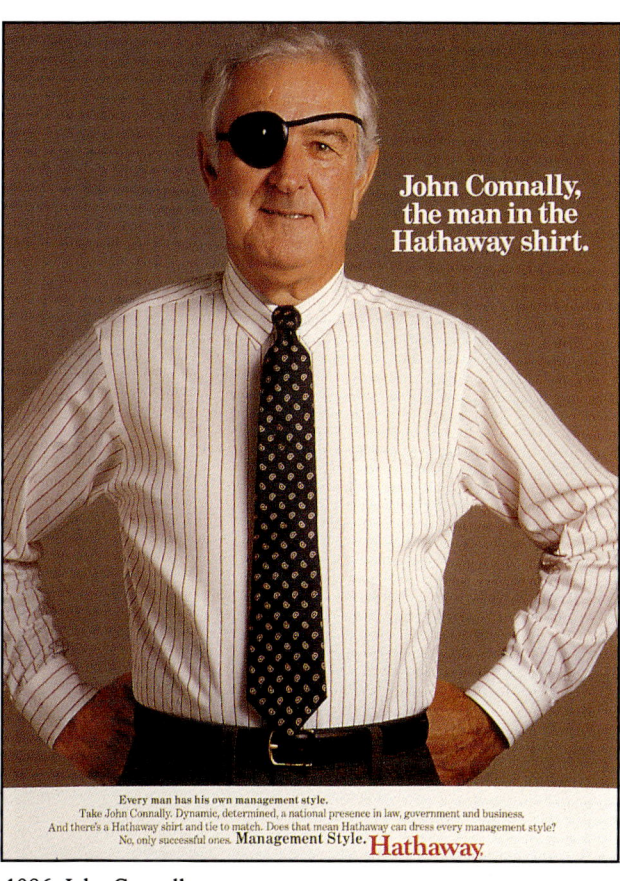

1986. John Connally.

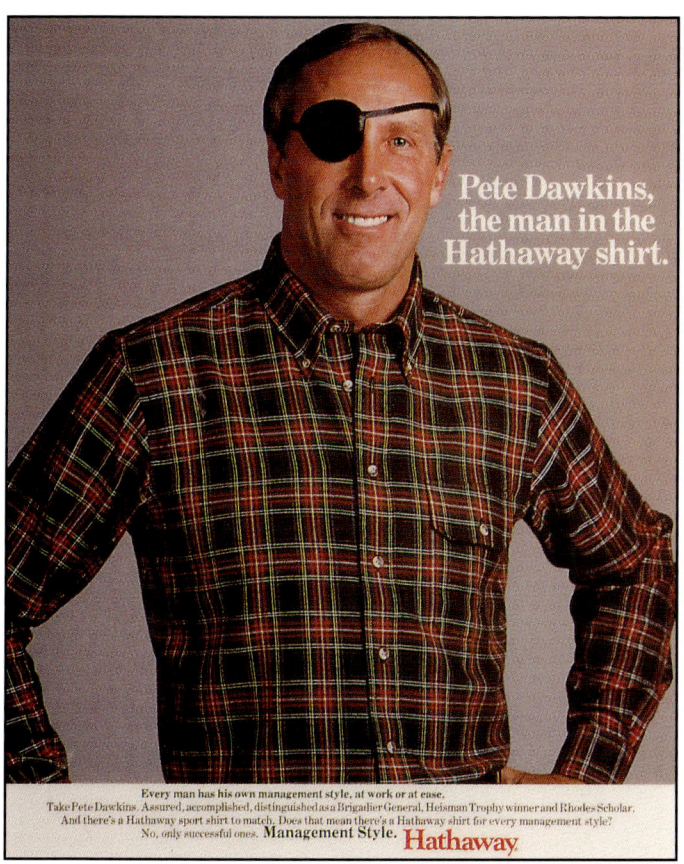

1986. Pete Dawkins.

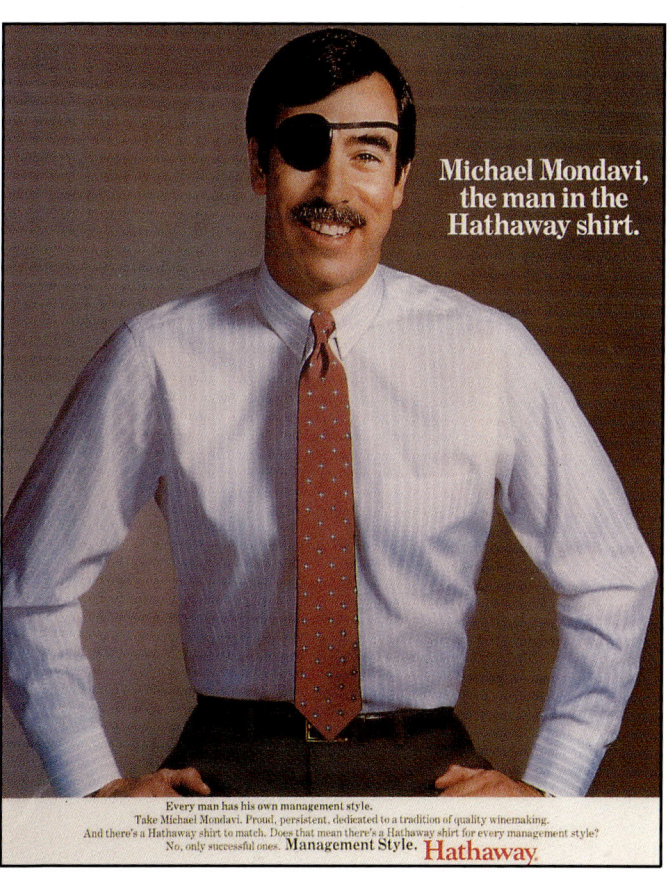

1986. Michael Mondavi.

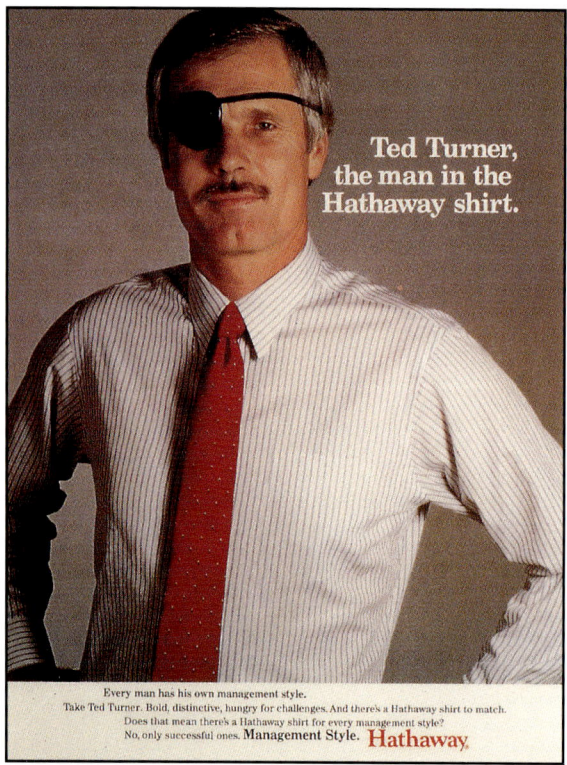
1986. Ted Turner.

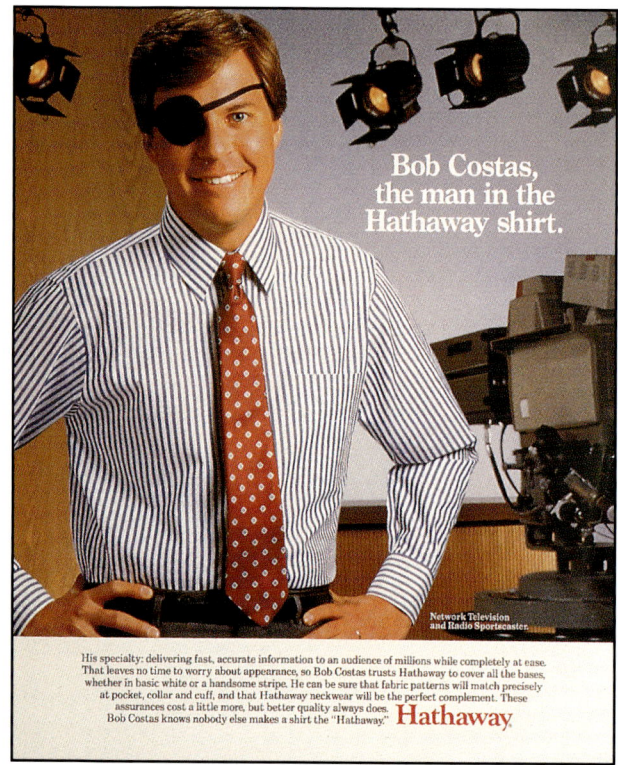
1986. Bob Costas.

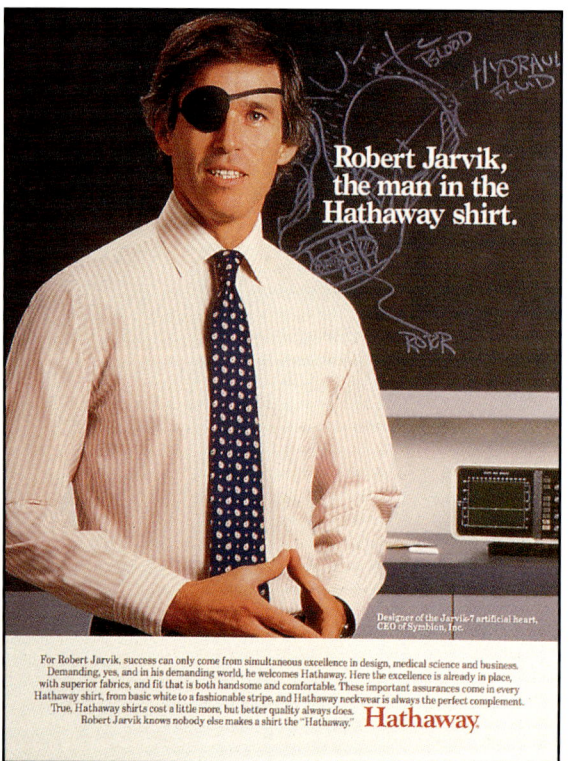
1986. Robert Jarvik.

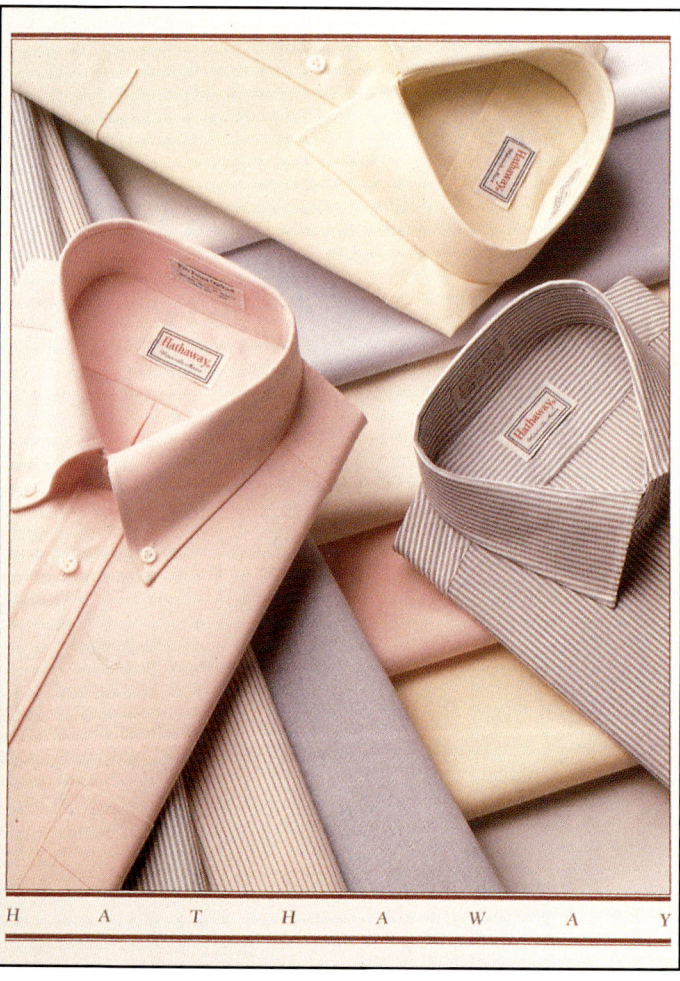
1986. Cover of the product list.

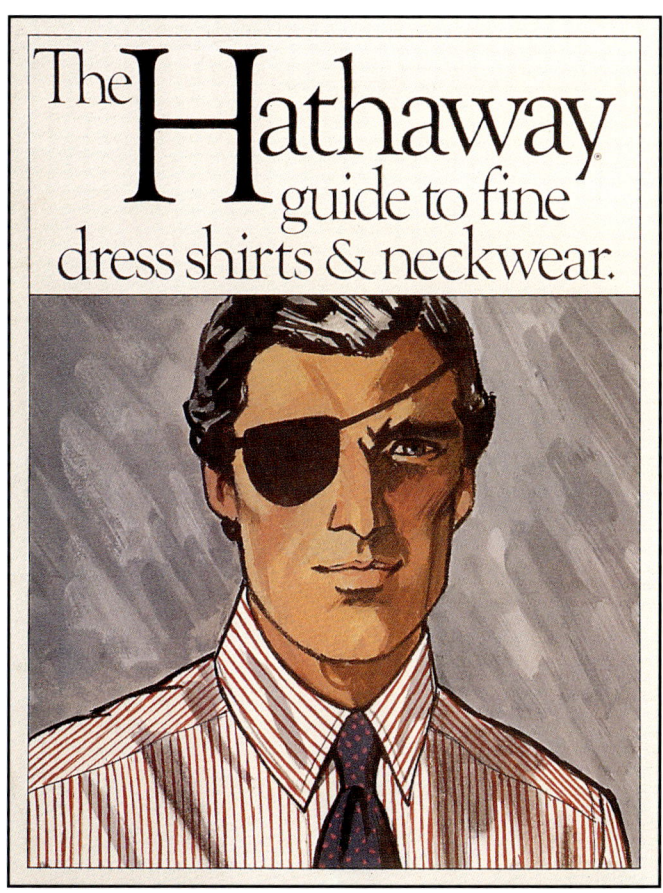
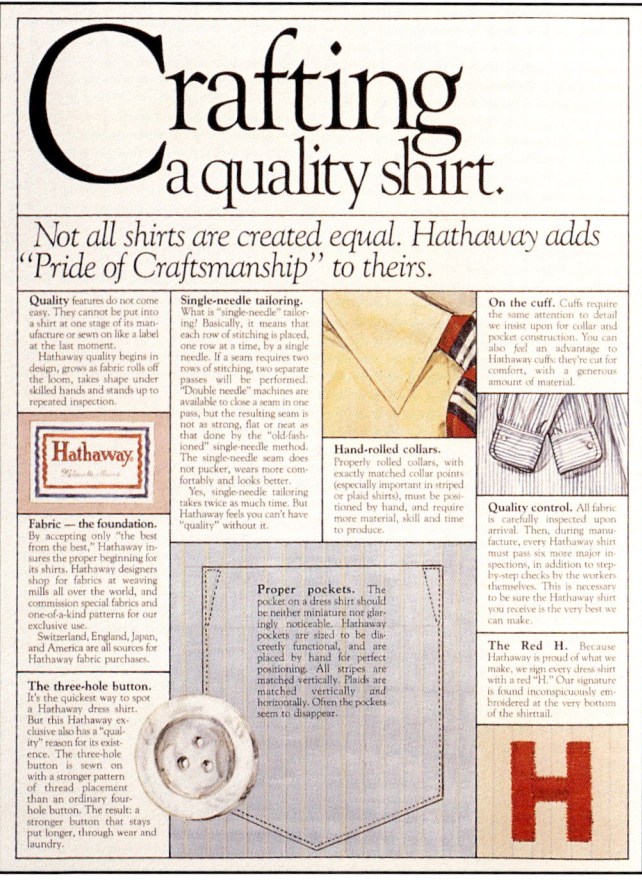
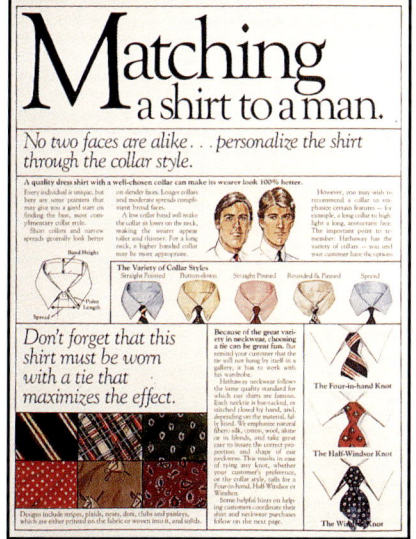
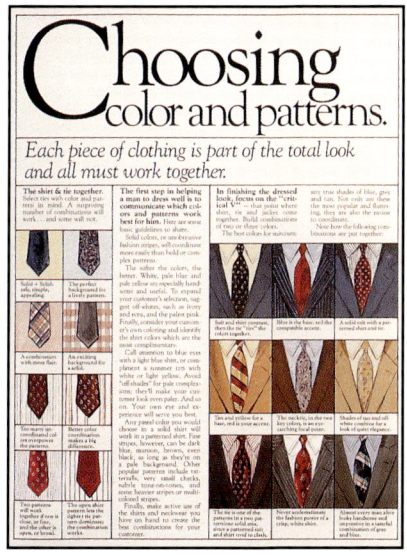
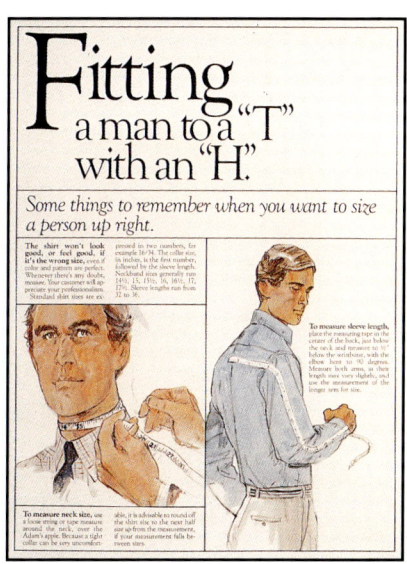

c. 1987. The Hathaway Guide to Fine Dress Shirts & Neckwear.
All you ever needed to know about color, style, fit, and fabric

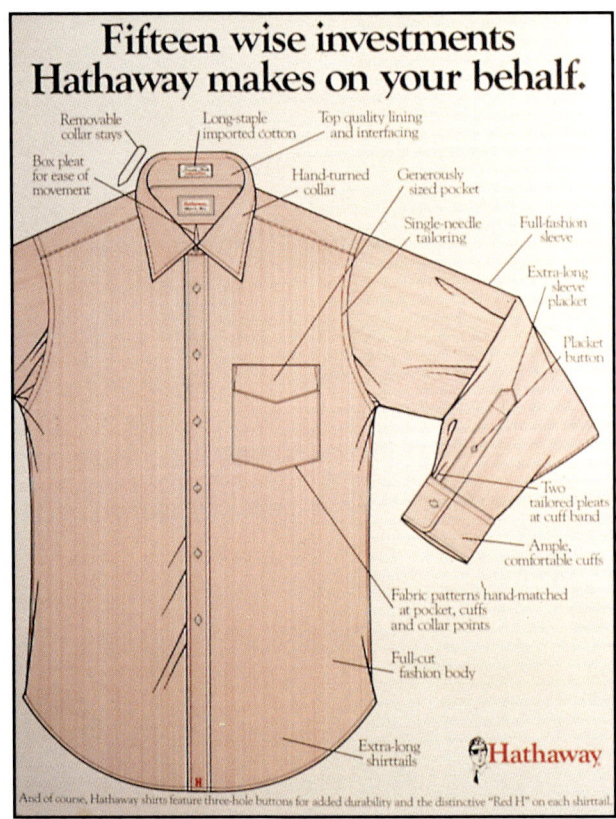

c. 1987. "Fifteen wise investments Hathaway makes on your behalf."

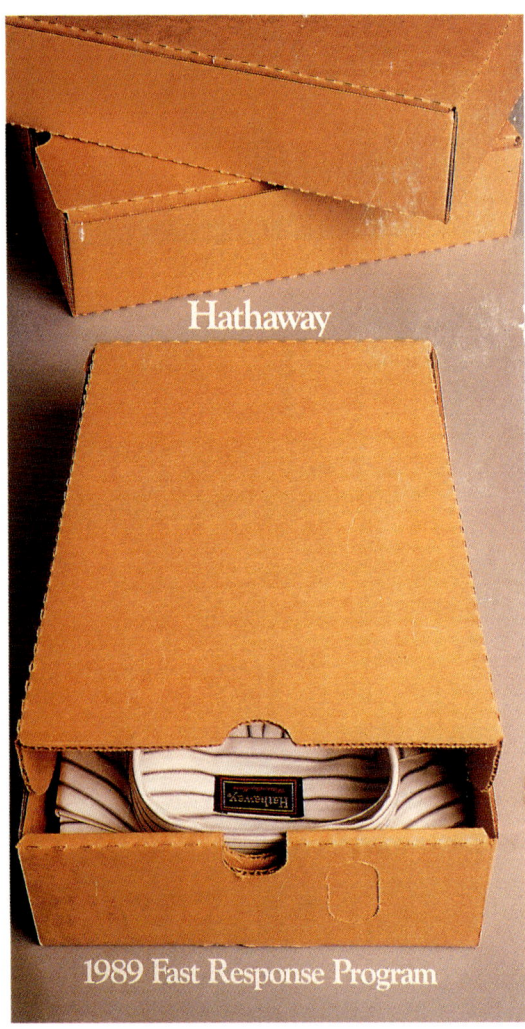

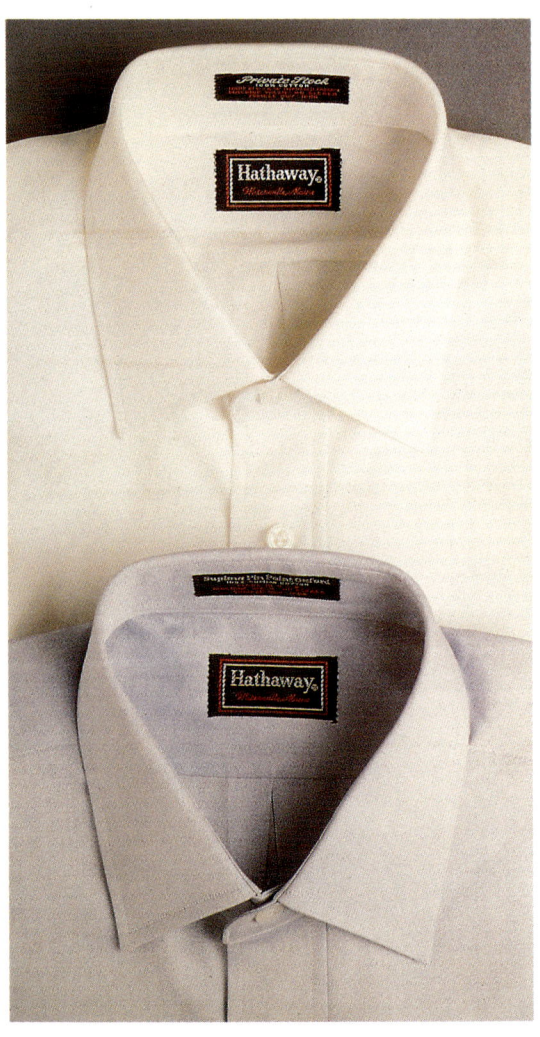

Above, right, & opposite: 1989. Illustrations from the 1989 product list. It is interesting to note that the product illustrated in exclusively dress wear, at a time when the national trend was toward more casual clothing. Shirts ranging $15–20.

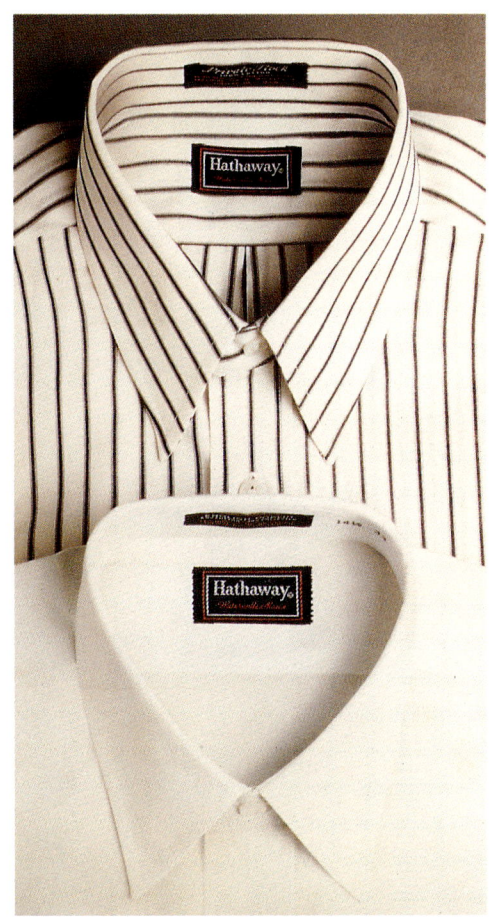
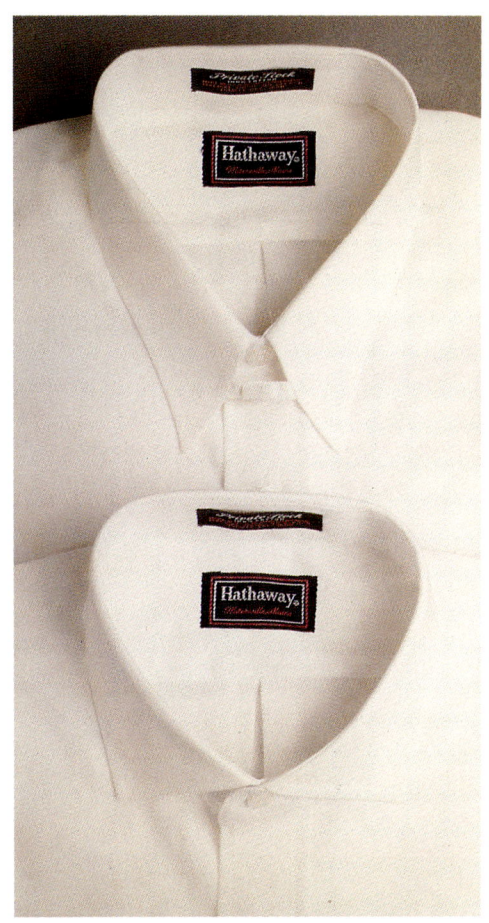
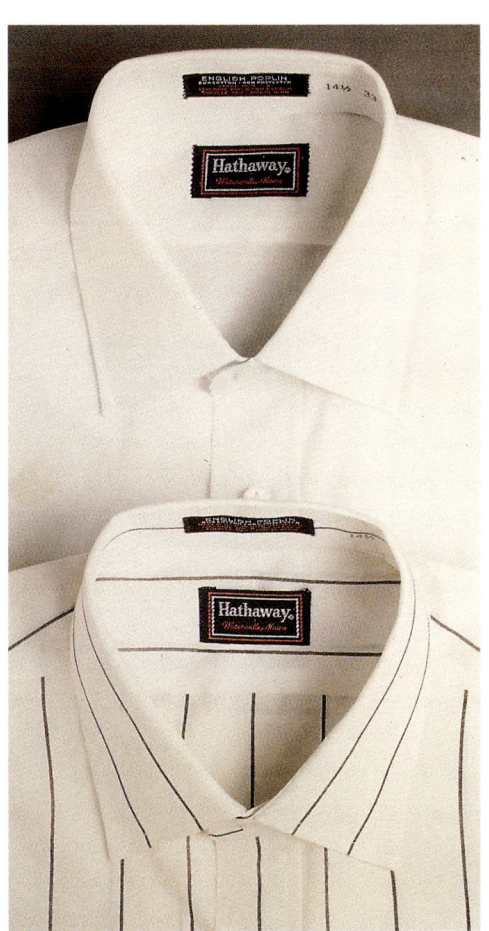
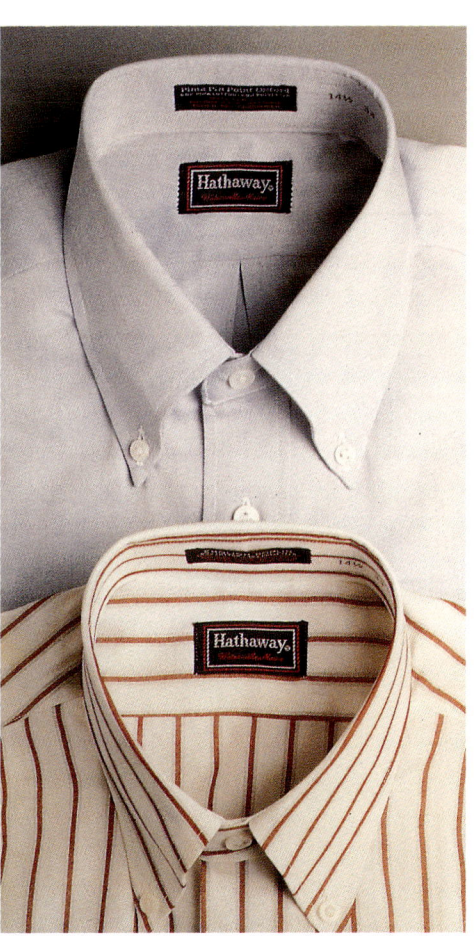

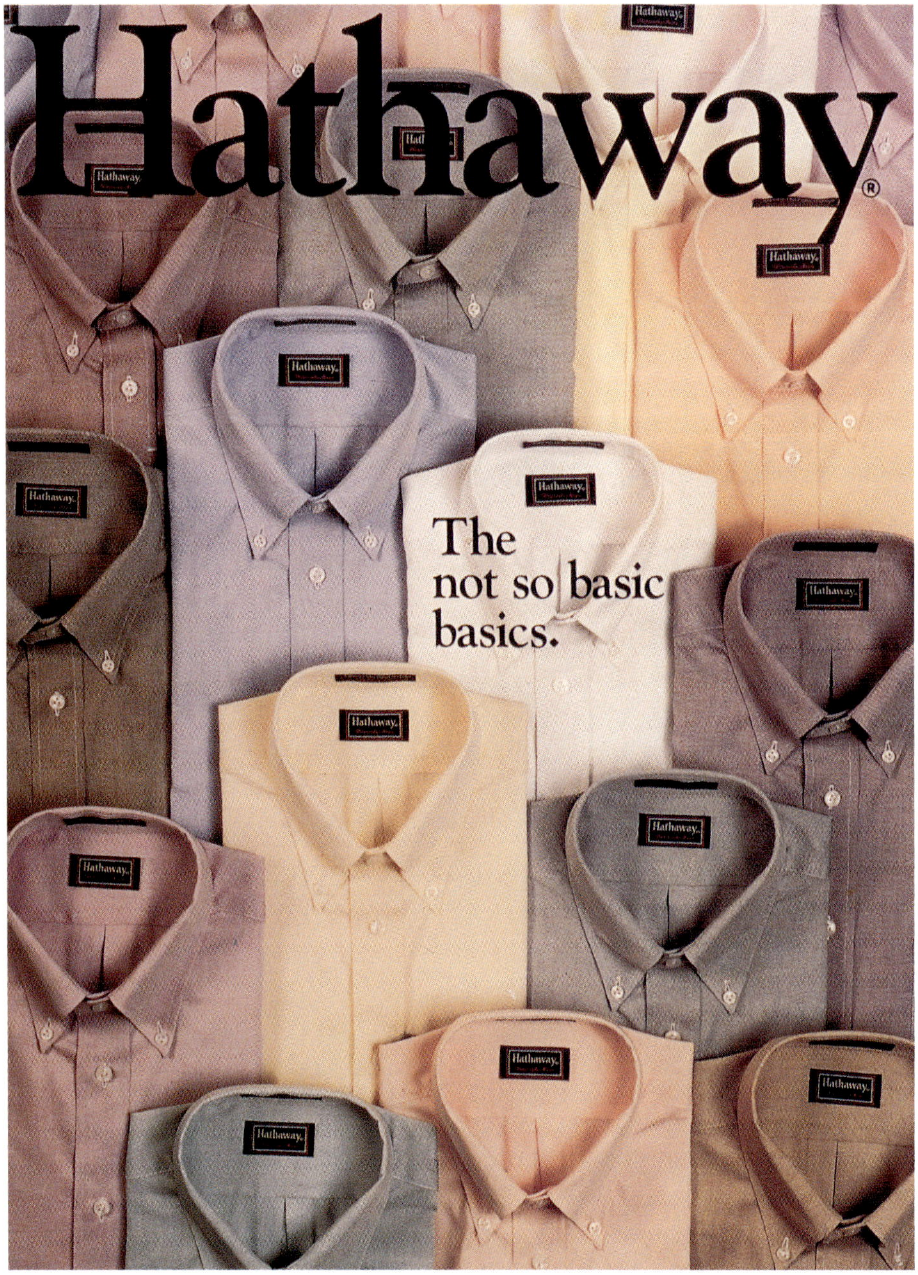

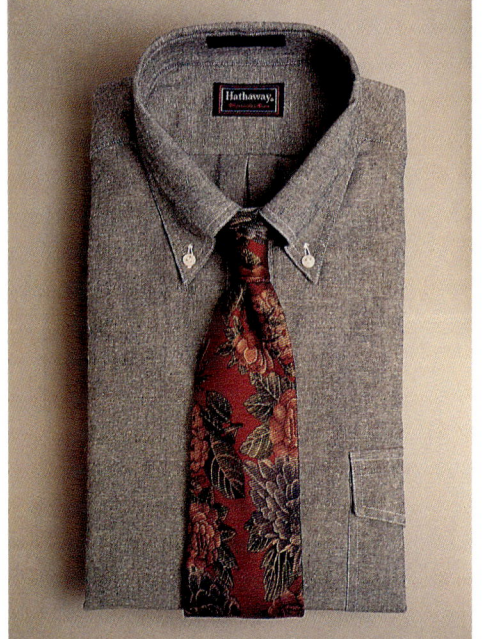
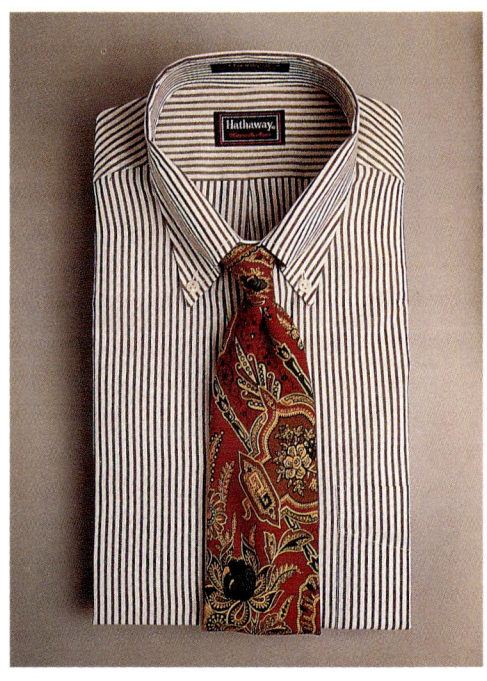

This & following three pages: 1991. Illustrations from the product list. Shirts ranging $15–20.

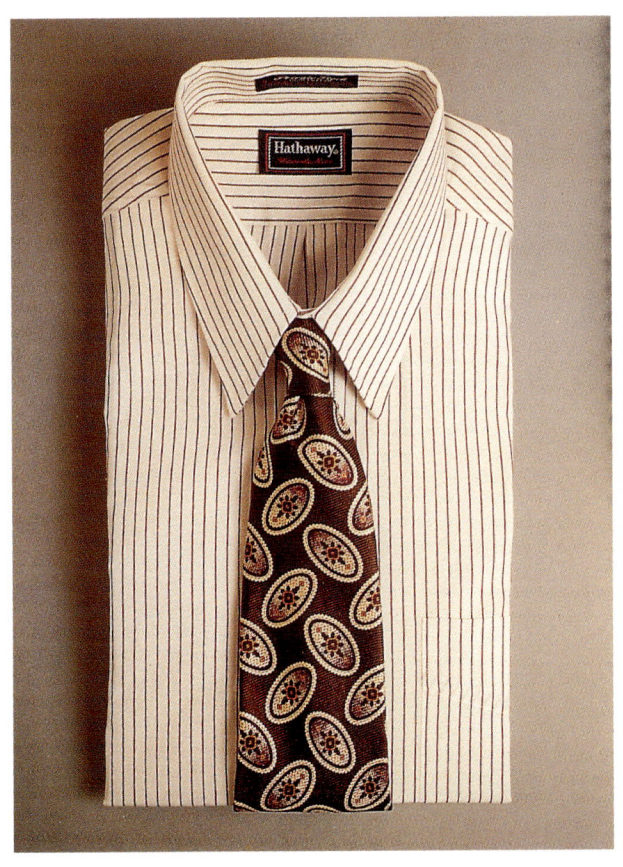
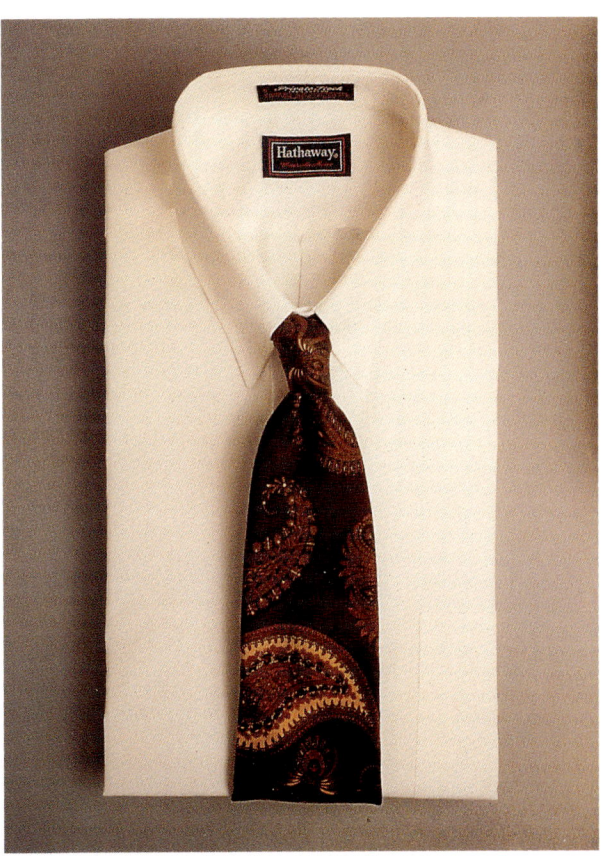
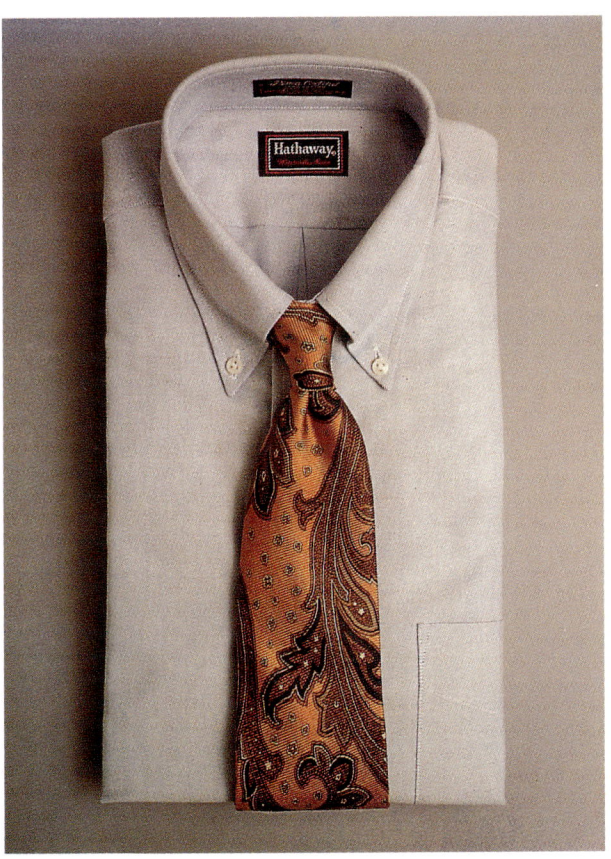
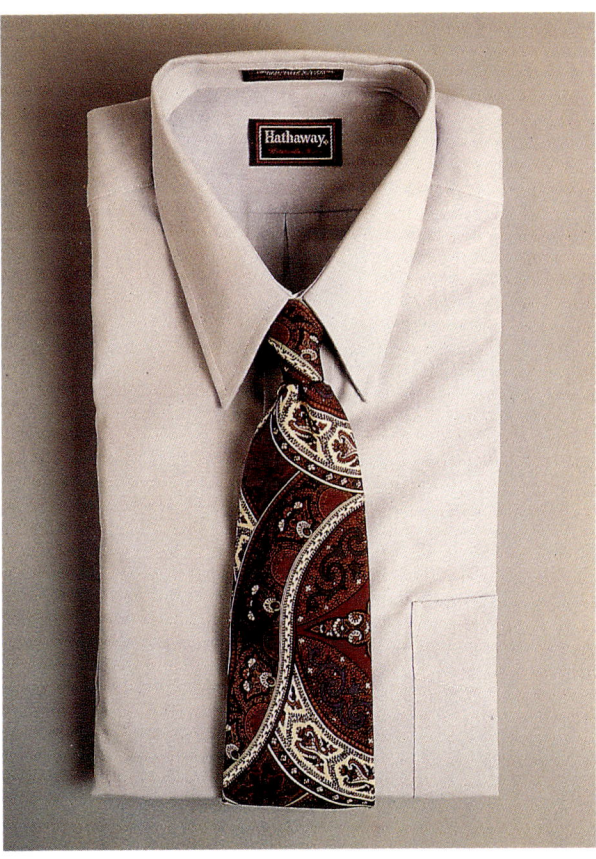

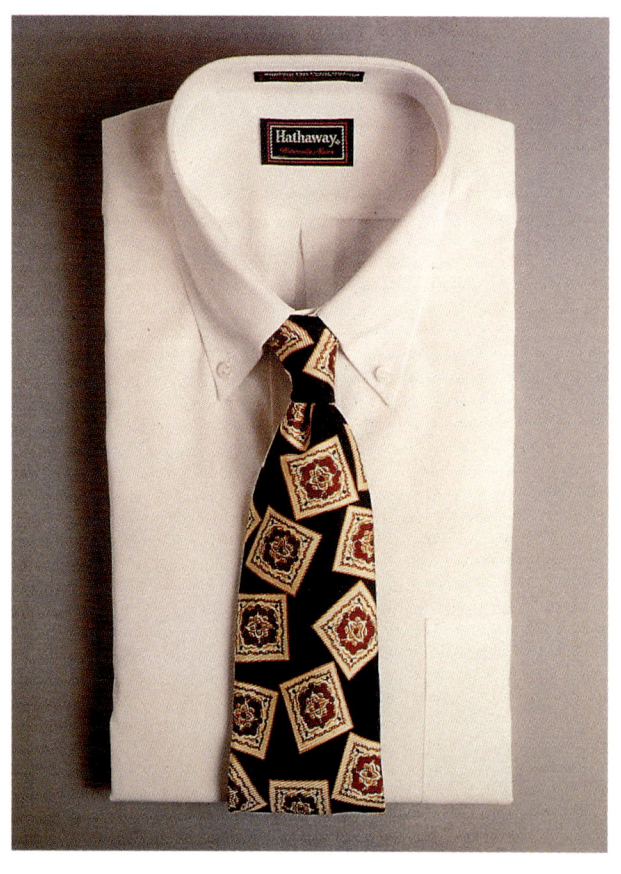
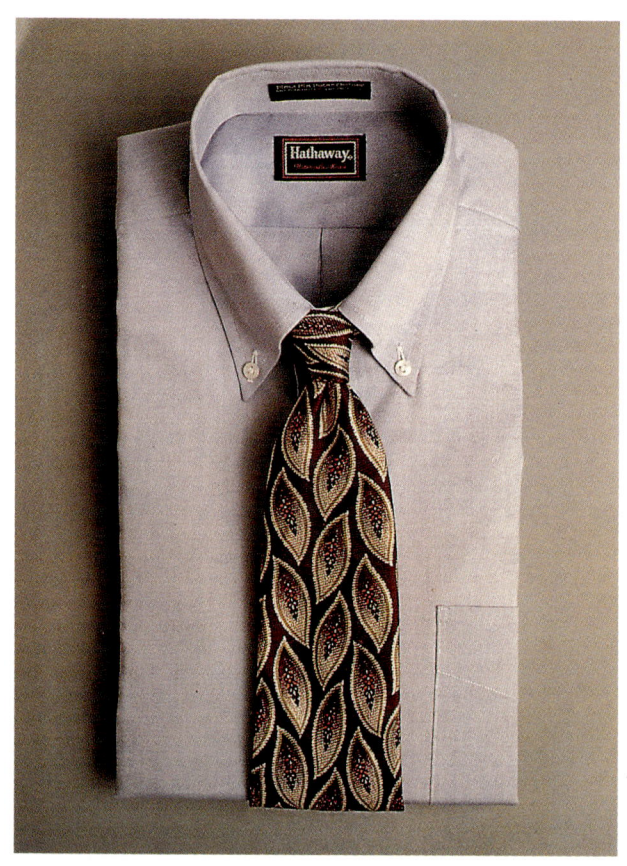
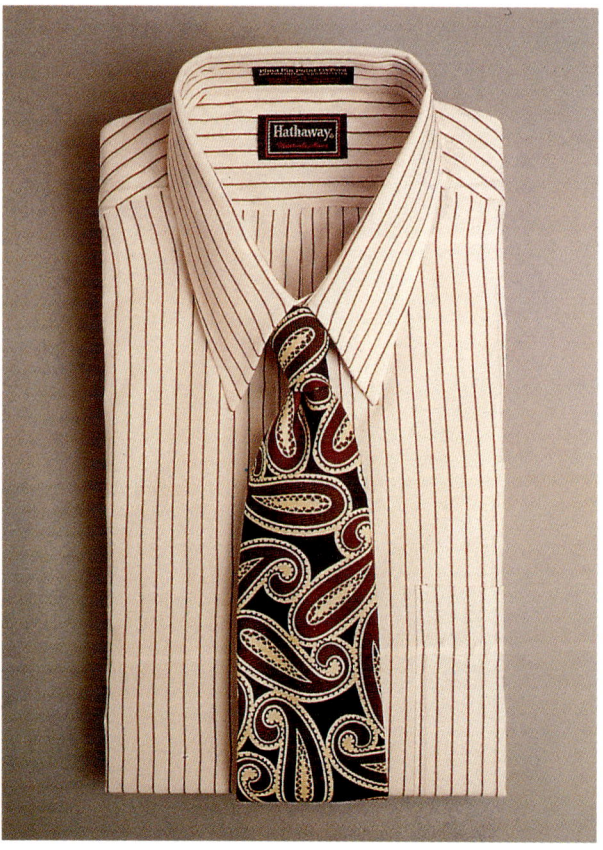
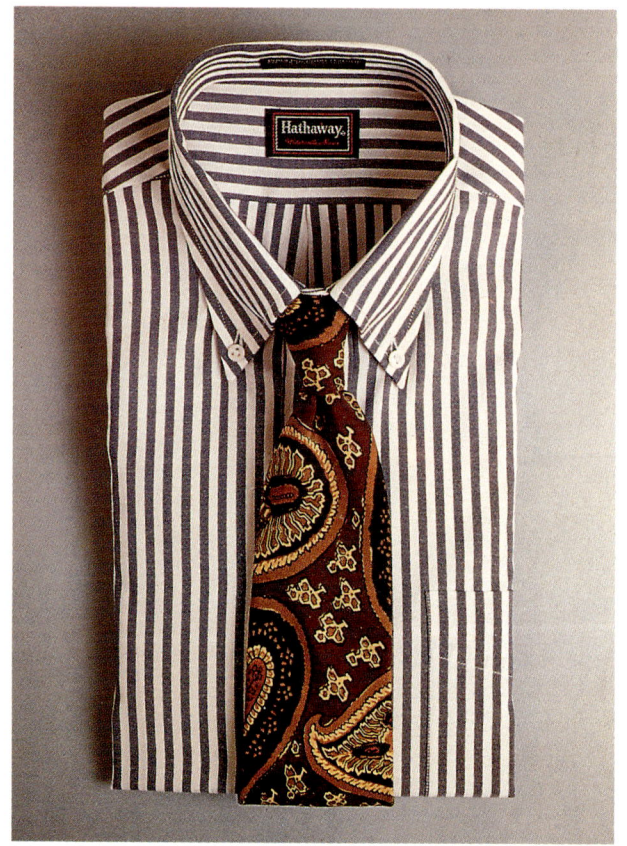

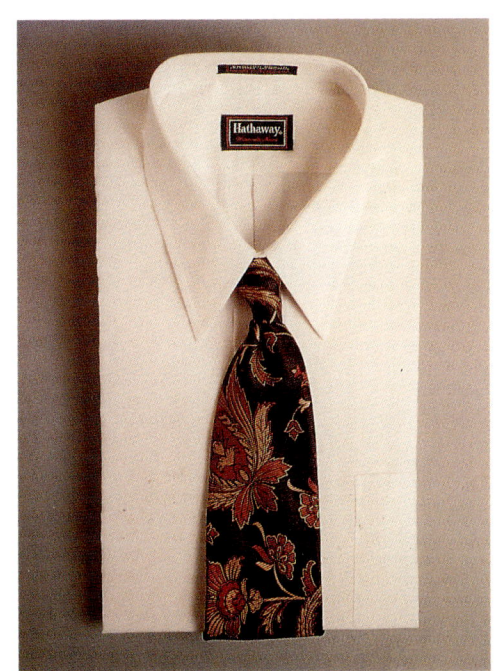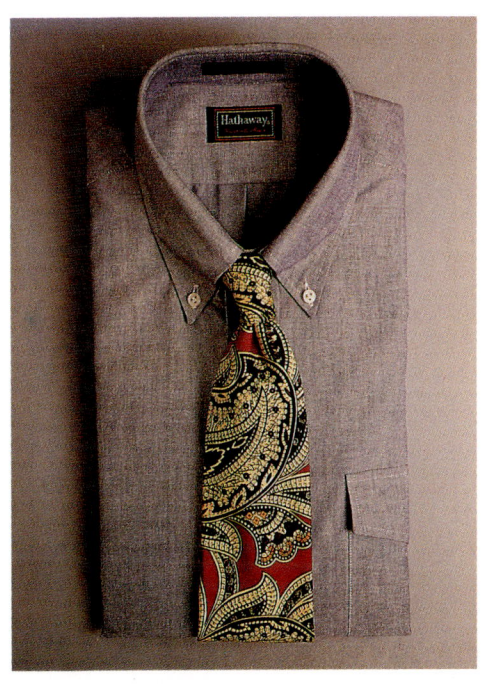

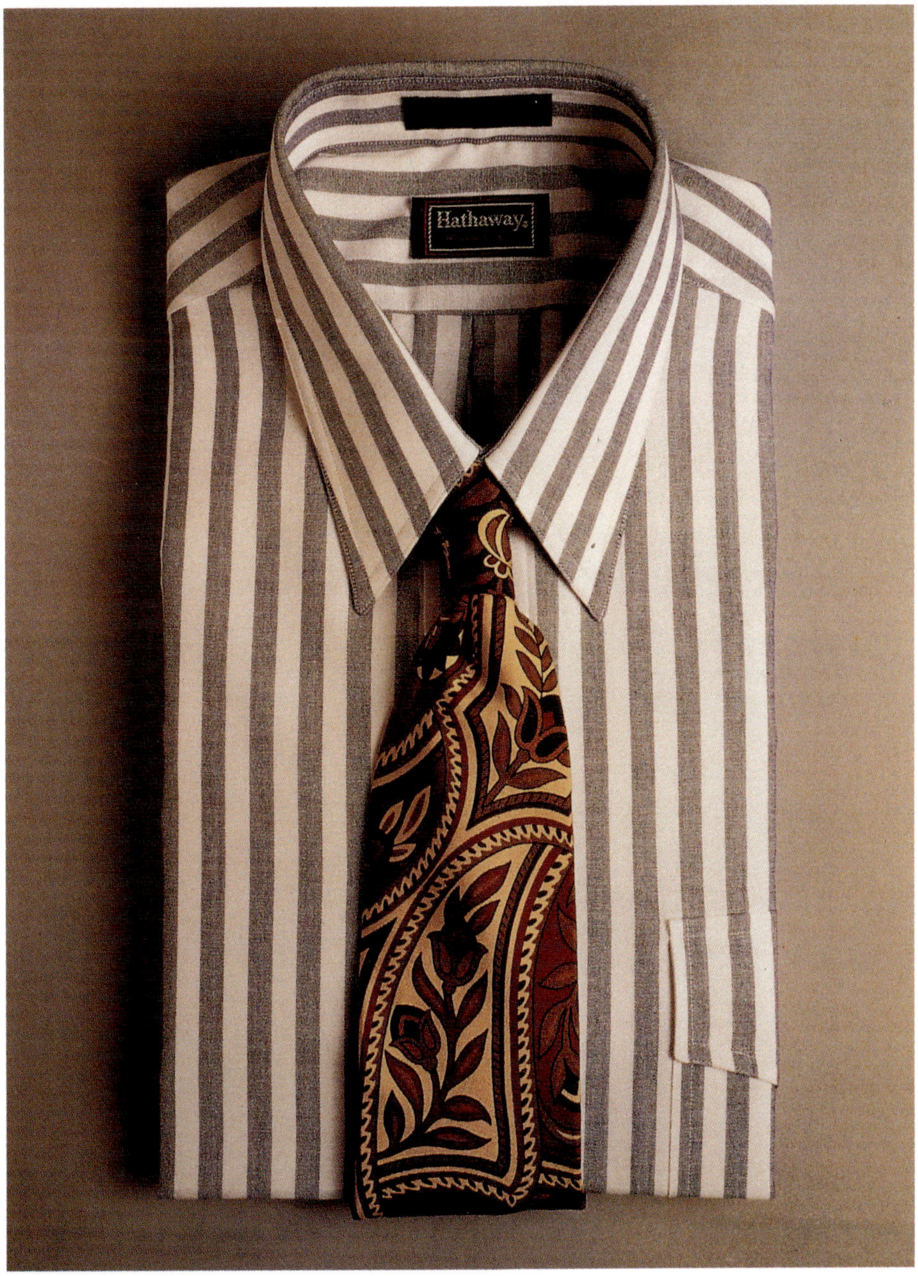

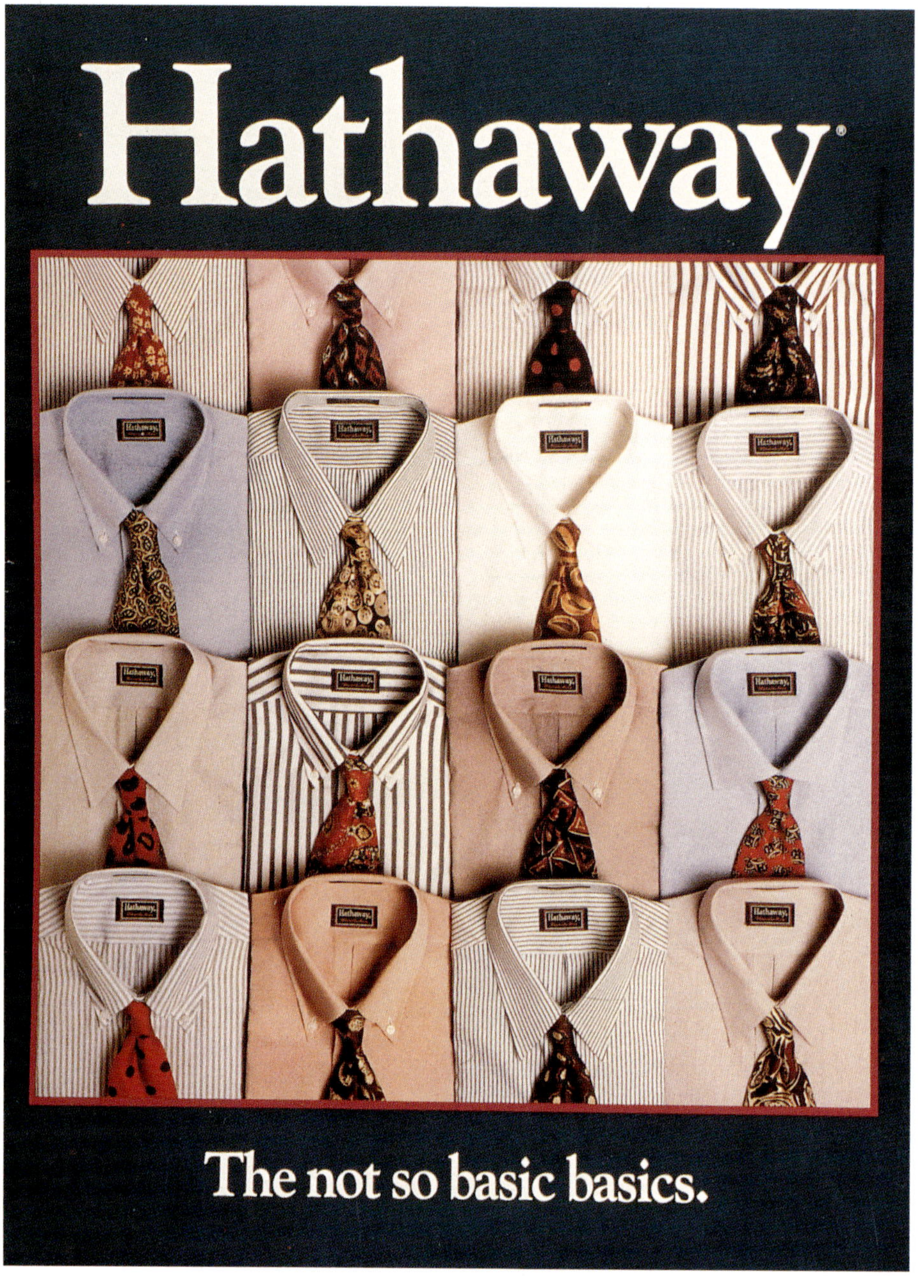

Hathaway

The not so basic basics.

This & following three pages: 1992. Illustrations from the product list. Shirts ranging $15–20.

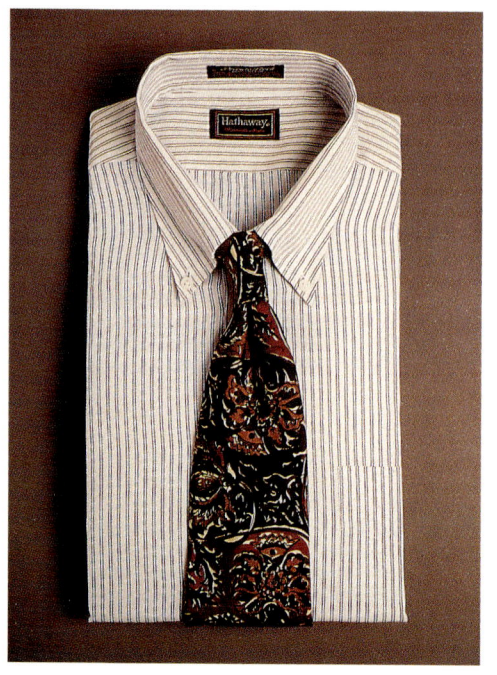

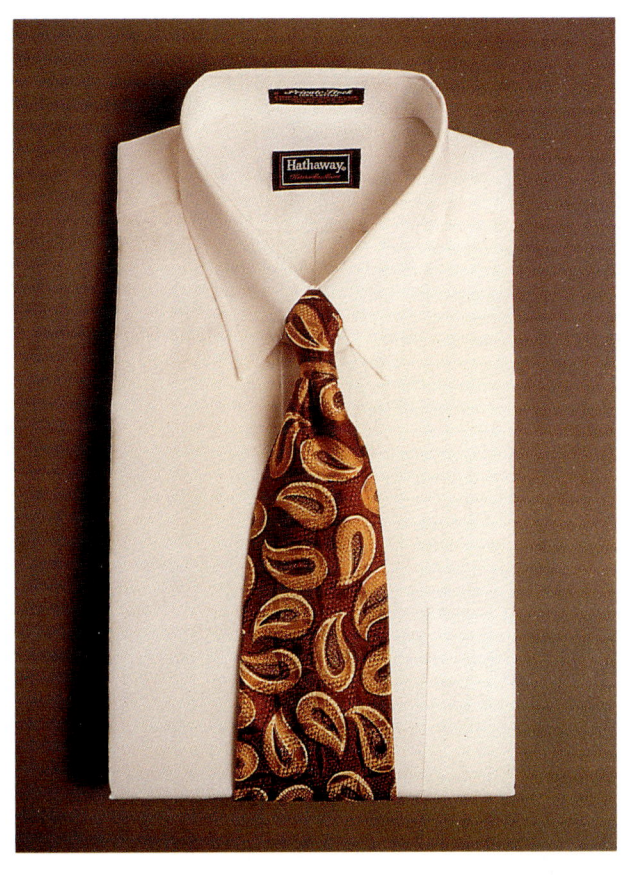
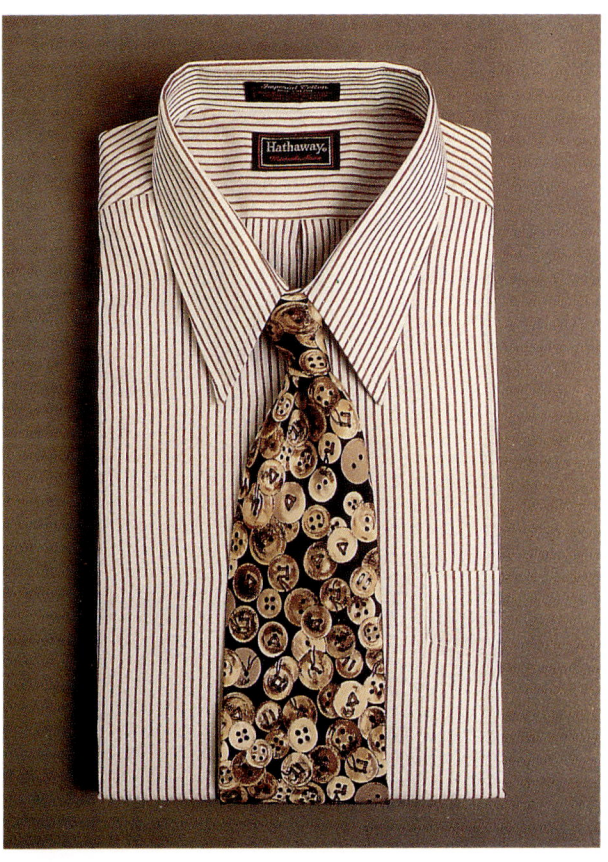
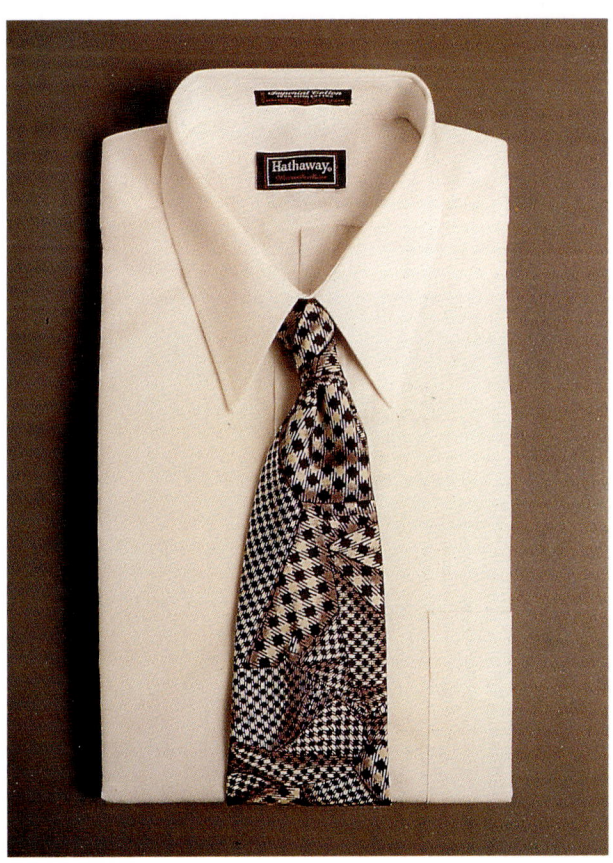
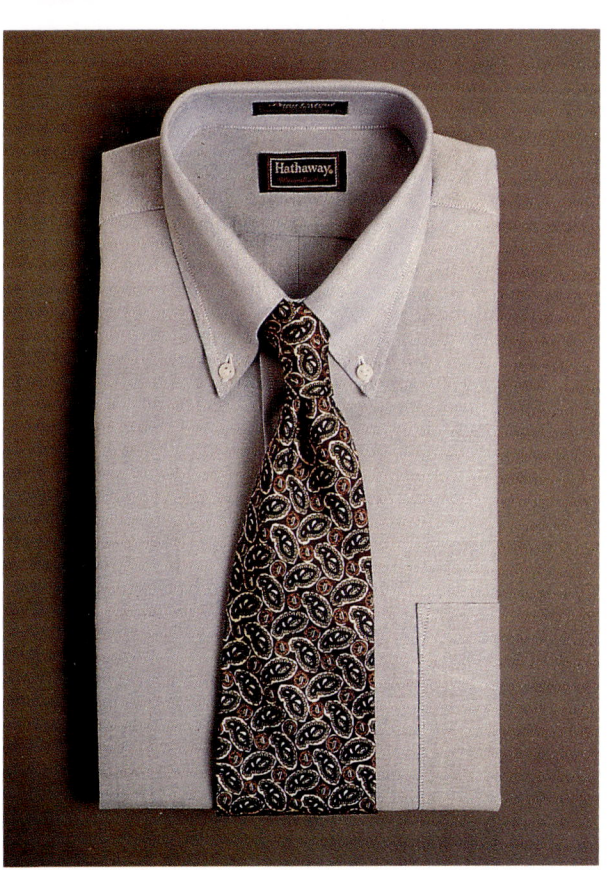

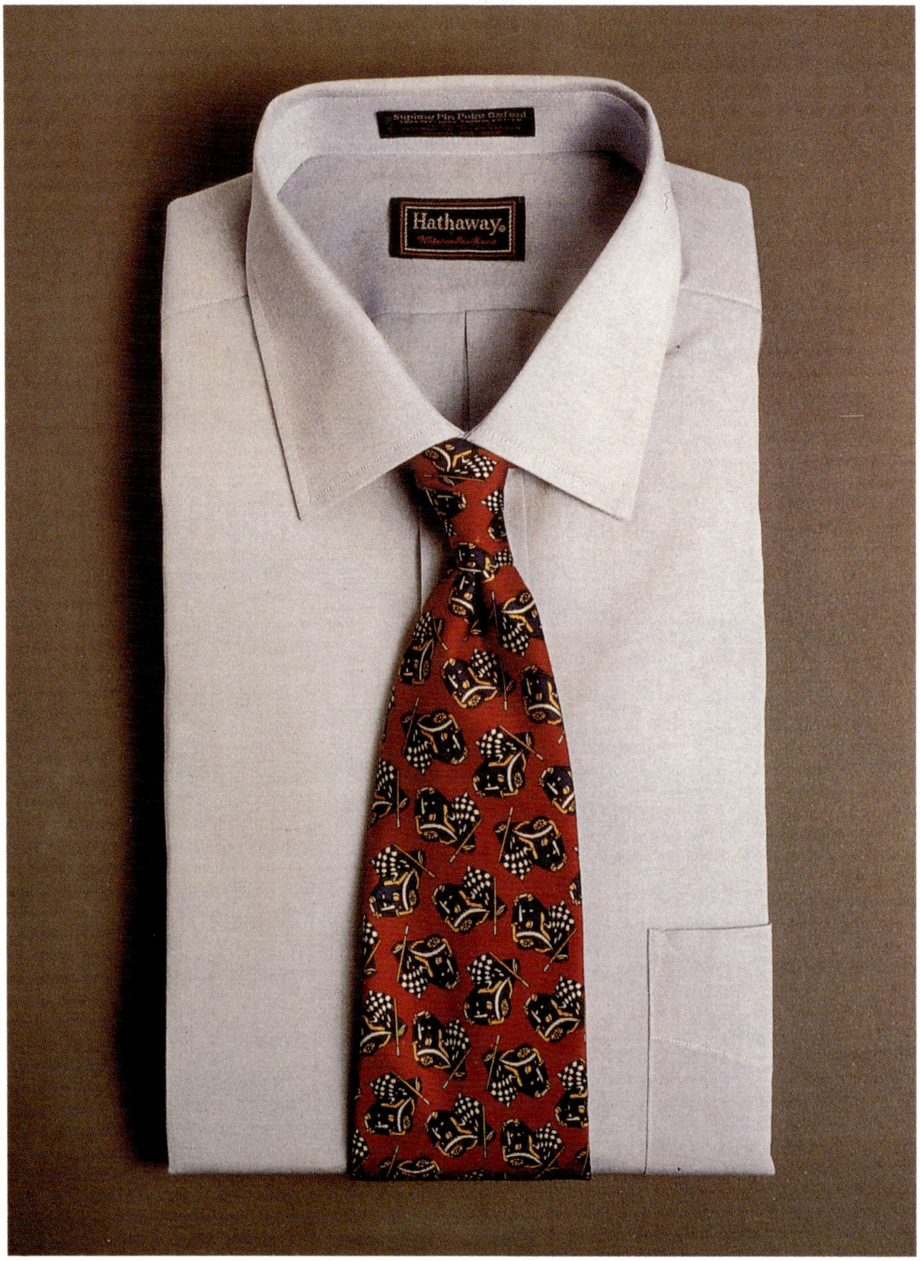

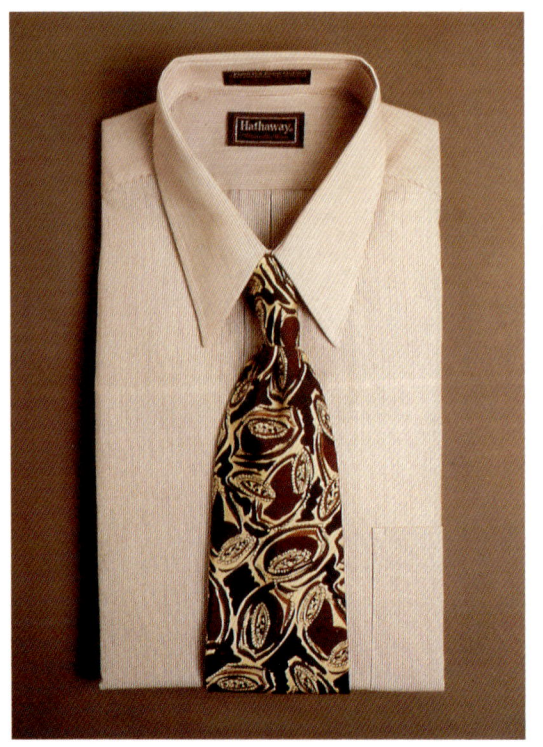
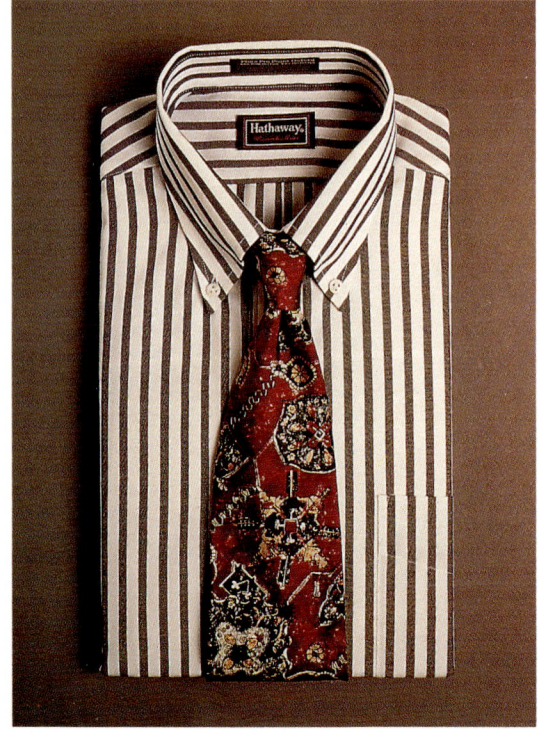

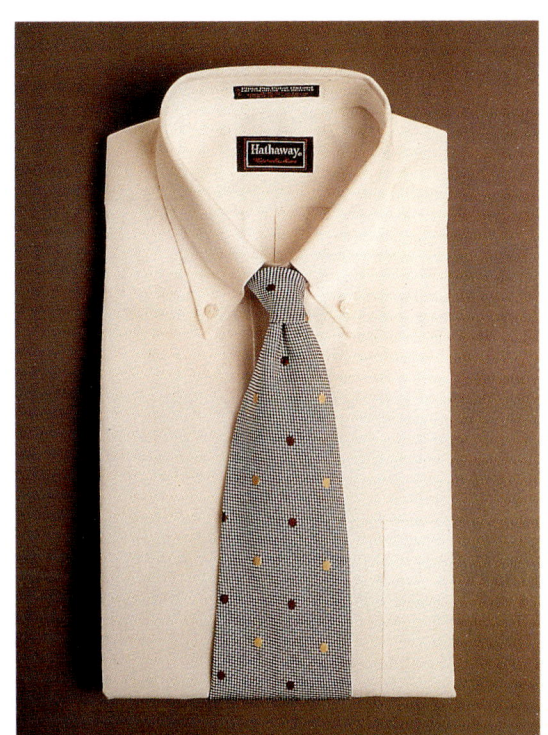
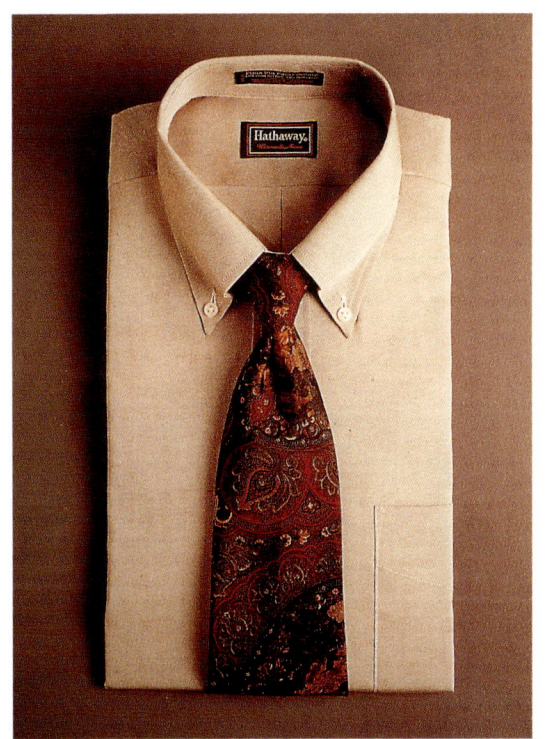

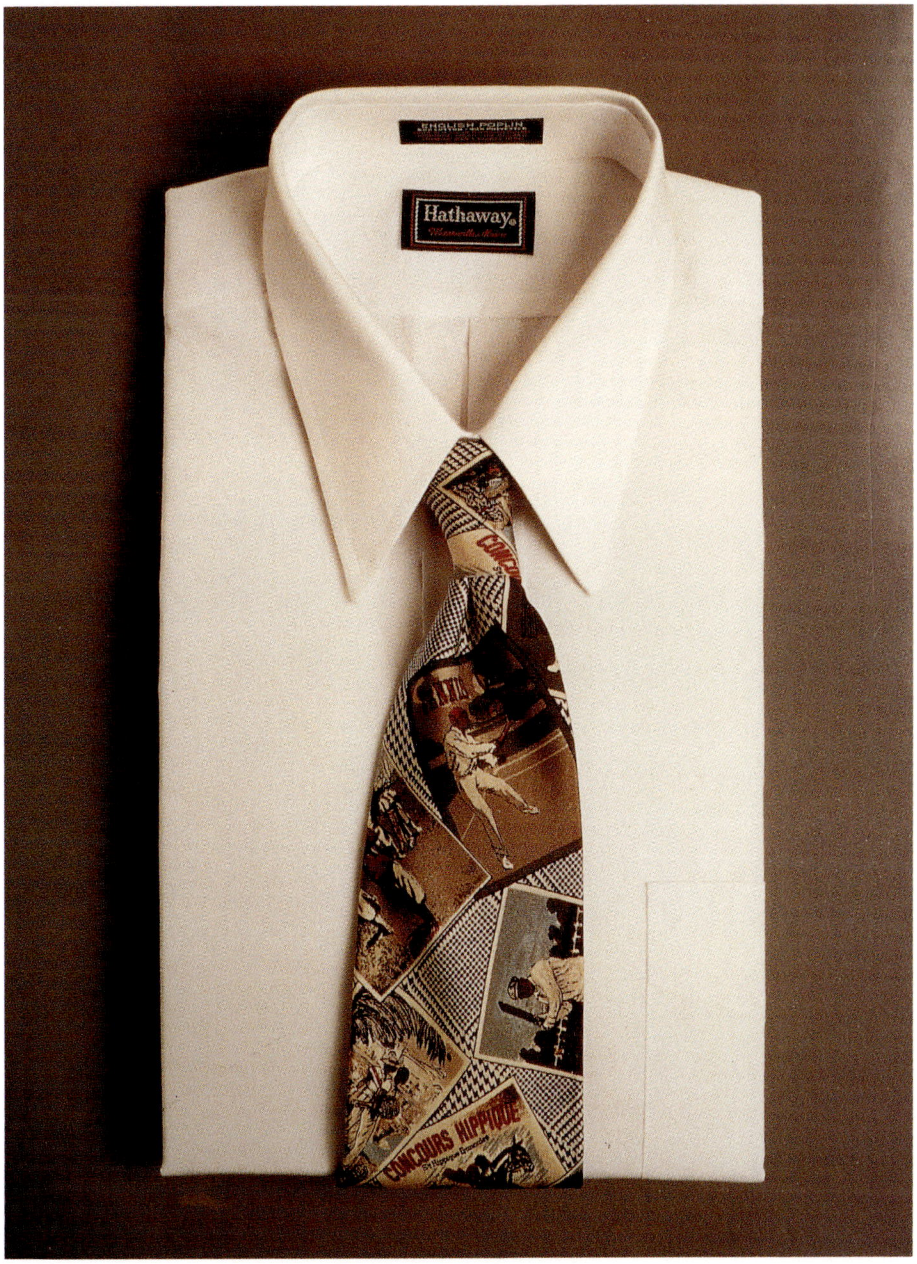

Saving a Great Shirt Company

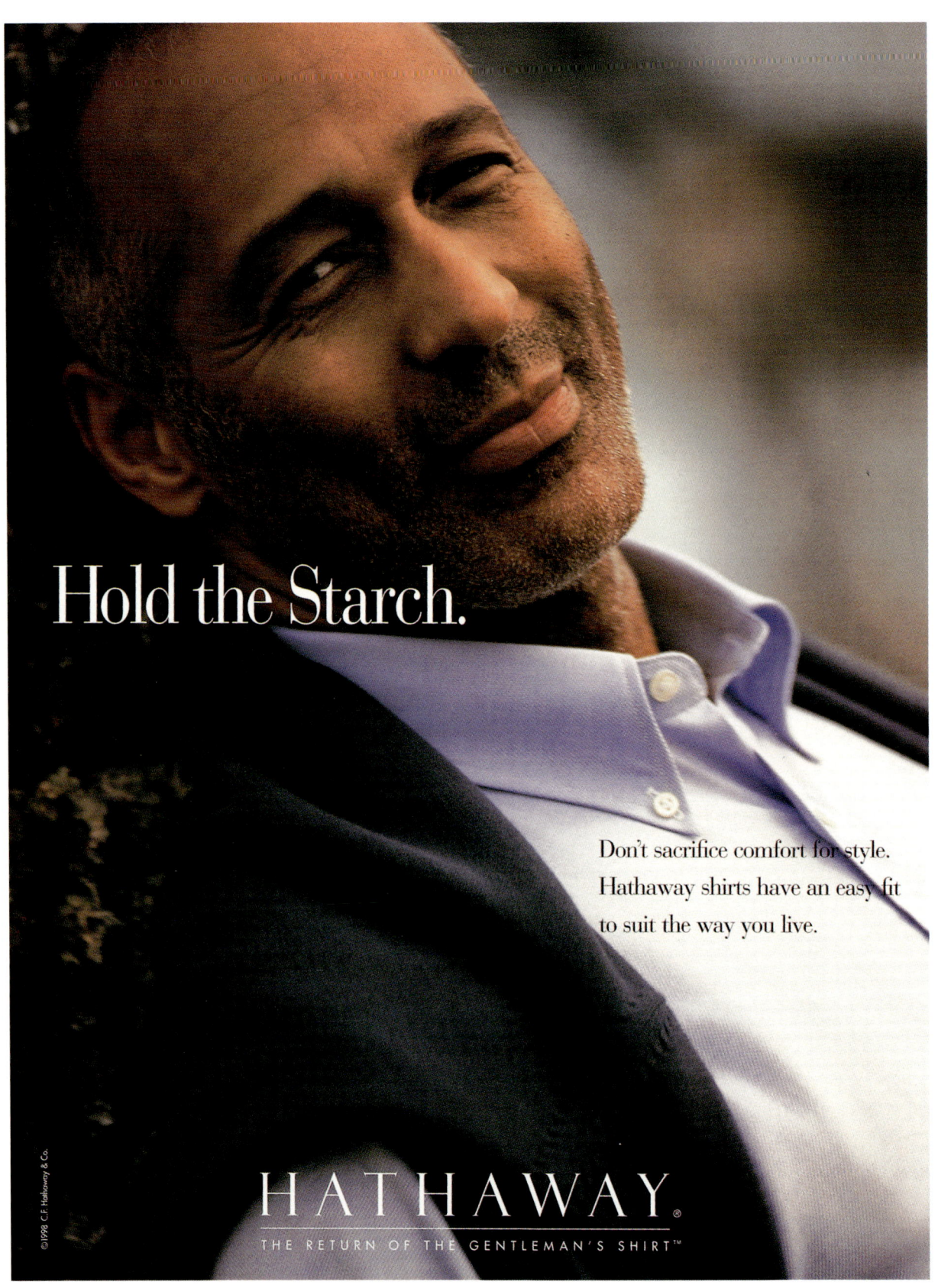

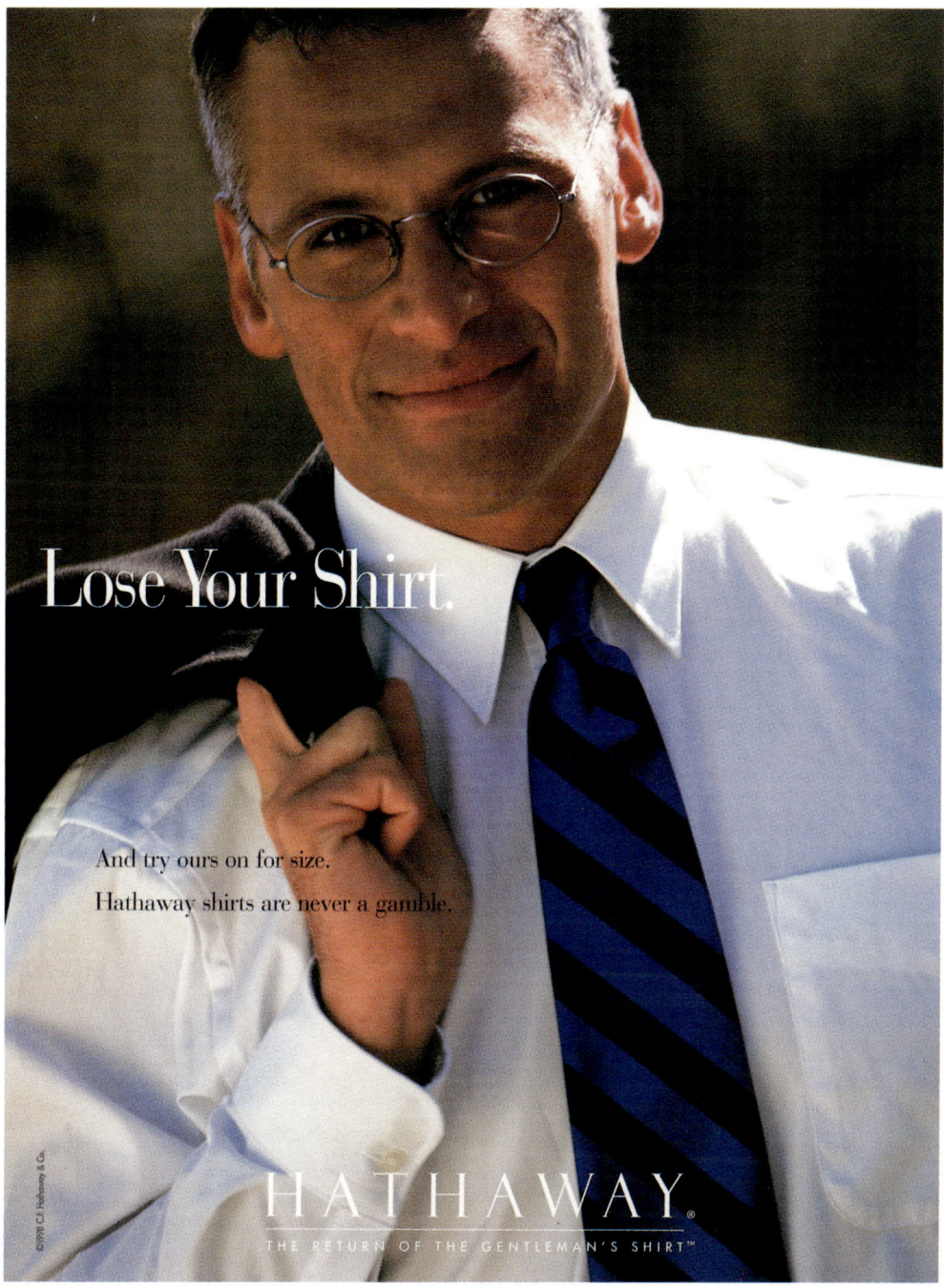

In 1986 Warnaco was acquired by W Acquisition Group, in a hostile takeover led by Linda Wachner. As Don Sappington evaluated the years from 1986 to 1996 in an article for *Apparel Industry Magazine (November, 1997)*, the new group "did a good job of keeping the factory updated, but it didn't market the brand." As the American market for dress shirts gave way to a more casual style, national advertising shrank, competition from foreign factories grew and Hathaway struggled to be profitable. In 1994 the UNITE, the Union of Needletrades, Industrial, and Textile Employees, which represent Hathaway workers, facing an uncertain future, agreed to a contract that provided for a joint labor-management effort "to increase and secure employment." The employees at Hathaway gave up increases in pay and doubled their productivity. According to Michael Cavanaugh, a UNITE official, "The amount of production went from an average of 2,000 dozen a week to 3,000 dozen a week and the cost of that production went down almost in half." (Quoted in Barlett & Steele, the *Philadelphia Inquirer*, 1996.)

Despite these efforts Warnaco surprised everyone by announcing, on May 6, 1996, that they were closing Hathaway for good. The 159-year-old company would be only a memory by September of that year.

The personal and political repercussions were immediate. Workers felt betrayed. State politicians felt the blow of one more "traditional" industry falling prey to international pressure. Governor Angus King was in Waterville on May 7, promising workers to keep the

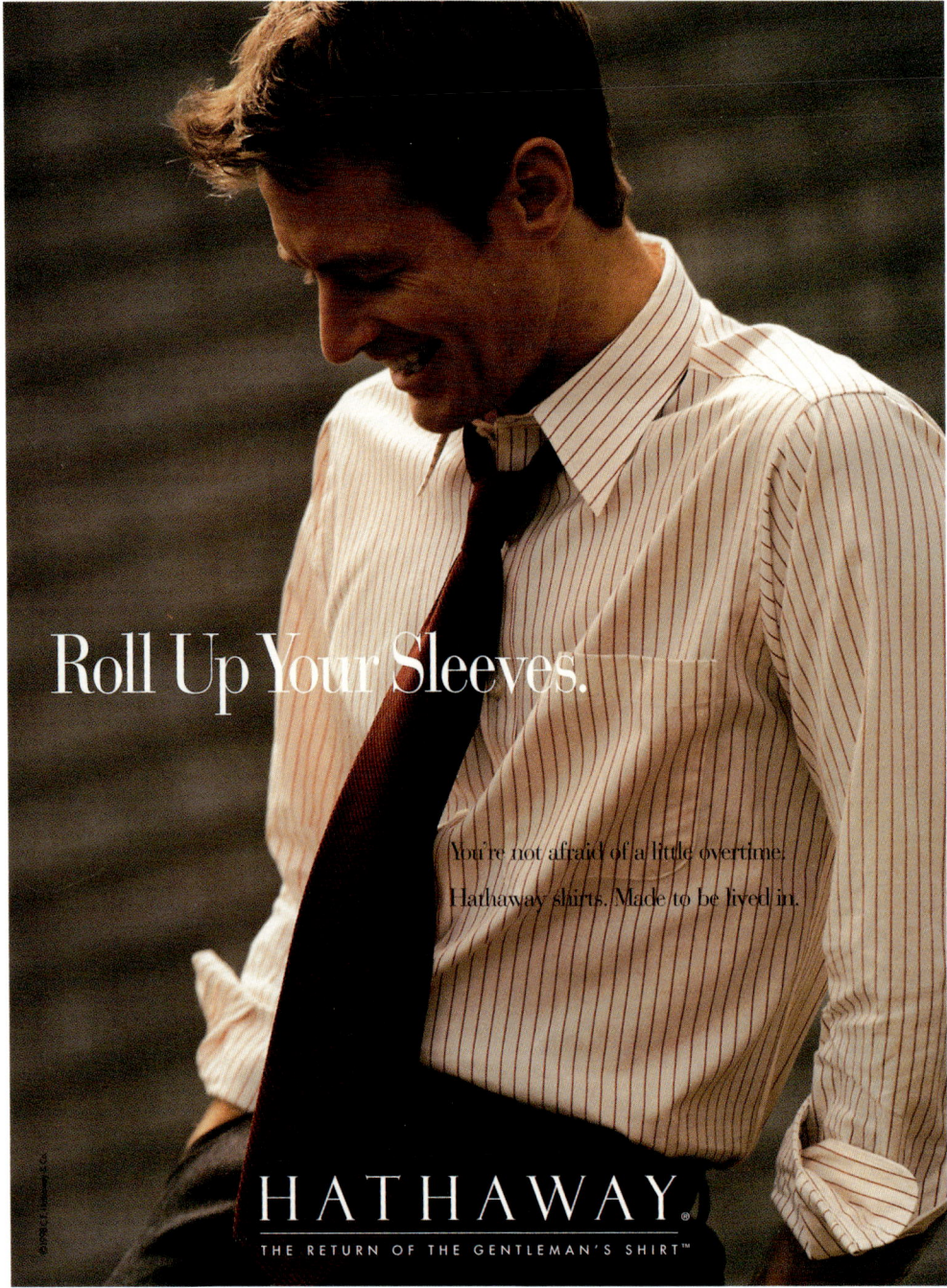

plant open until a new buyer could be found. On May 14, he put together a task force to conduct the search. Hillary Rodham Clinton championed the cause at the State Democratic Convention meeting in Portland on May 17 through 19. UNITE hired American Capital Strategies, a Maryland company specializing in buyout deals, to look for investors.

Enter John R. McKernan, the Republican governor of Maine from 1987 to 1994, and viewed by many in the union as being anti-labor. With the assistance of his wife, U.S. Senator Olympia Snowe, he was able to convince Wachner, on May 22, to agree that he had the exclusive right to develop a purchase proposal over a period of 90 days. He enlisted Michael Liberty and Kevin Mahaney, both prominent Maine business, and the three of them announced on May 26 that they would keep the factory alive by purchasing it from Warnaco. By August 1, 1996, the deal was announced. An investor group headed by McKernan bought the company for an undisclosed amount. In a statement from Linda Wachner it was said: "It has been our objective to reach an agreement that would preserve the jobs of Hathaway employees and the Hathaway trade name, while enabling Warnaco to exit a business that is not in line with its long-term objectives." The deal enjoyed the support of the Maine legislature, the federal government and the city, to put together a deal that provided $1.6 in aide, plus much more from private investors, providing enough to buy the factory and make improvements. Final signing of the deal took place on November 13, 1996.

Don Sappington, an industry veteran, was brought in to oversee the operation. He turned his attention first to the product, "We asked, 'Is this what the customer wants?' and the answer was no. We spent several months redesigning the entire shirt, down to where the buttons are positioned. We are establishing it as a better quality, better price-point shirt." In other words, Hathaway was returning to its roots.

But that does not mean it was going backwards. The changes relied on the latest pattern designing computers and marking and cutting technology. The results are shirts that have an updated collar, larger pocket, two extra inches in the chest, waist and hips for comfort. According to Sappington "We spent several months redesigning the entire shirt, down to where the buttons are positioned."

To launch the new Hathaway, an extensive advertising program was developed, first in retail trade publications and then to the general public. Since the brand had not been advertised in years, it was important for Hathaway to create a unique and up-to-date image for the brand. Elaine Scott, the Director of Marketing describes their motivations:

We wanted to define "who the Hathaway man is for the late 1990s and beyond" and we wanted to do it in a way that people could relate to. By doing this you create an emotional connection and can break the tie in the purchase decision making process between competing brands.

We also wanted to communicate comfort, quality and style. The line "The Return of hte Gentleman's Shirt" is a nice way of saying we are back adn refers to Hathaway's heritage.

With its name once again equated with quality and style, the hope is that the company will double in size by the end of the century. And with the commitment and energy exhibited by the people of Hathaway they are well on their way.

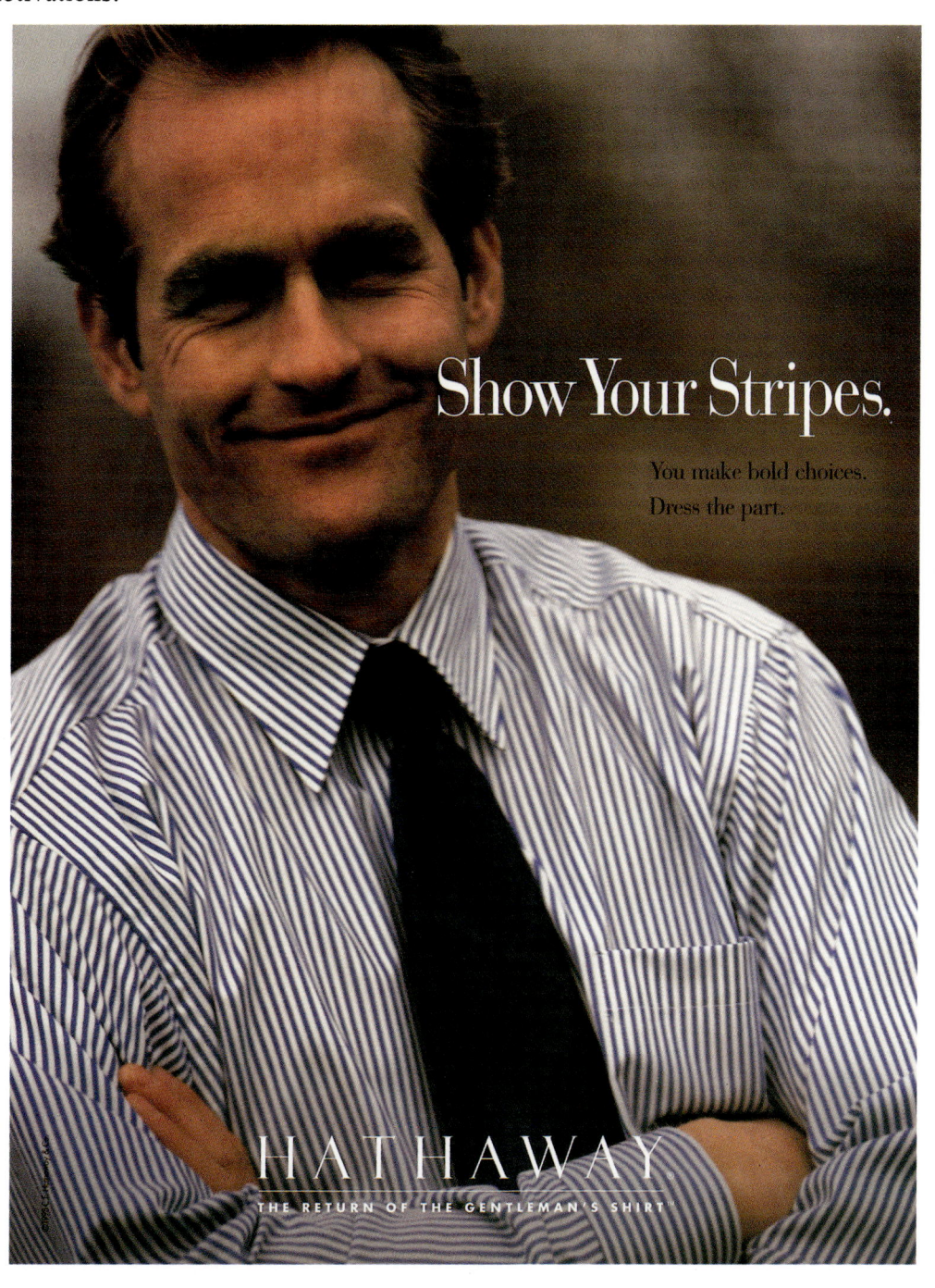

Bibliography

Barlett, Donald L. and James B. Steele. "America: Who Stole the Dream? The Burden of the Working Woman." *The Philadelphia Inquirer*, September 8, 1996.

Dougherty, Philip H. "Eye Patch Lives on at Hathaway." *The New York Times. New York:* September 9, 1983.

"The Hathaway Story." An uncredited history of the company, probably given as a speech in 1950.

Jette, Ellerton. "History of Hathaway," A speech given on August 25, 1953, at the Third Annual Sales Meeting.

LaPierre, Louis Leonard. "C.F. Hathaway Company: The First One Hundred and Twenty-Five Years." A masters thesis at the Thomas College Graduate School of Management. 1978

-----. "C.F. Hathaway Co.: The First One Hundred and Twenty-Five Years." Thomas Business Review, Vol. 8, No. 1, Fall 1981. Waterville, Maine: 1981.

"Maine Is Losing Traditional Factory Jobs." Staff report, *Portland Press Herald.* Portland, Maine: March 16, 1997.

Nemitz, Bill. "Boy Wonder Grows Up, Reaches Out." *Portland Press Herald*. Portland, Maine: May 26, 1996.

"The One Hundred Fiftieth Anniversary of the C.F. Hathaway Company." Hathaway publication, 1987.

Pearce, Arthur W. "The Future Out of the Past." Hartford: The Warner Brothers Company, 1964.

Perry, Nancy. "B&W Confirms Commonwealth Deal." *Portland Press Herald.* Portland, Maine: June 2, 1996.

Smith, Jeff. "Hathaway Tax-Break Plan Gaining." *Portland Press Herald*. Portland, Maine: September 4, 1996.

"U.S. Apparel Manufacturing Returns to Its Roots." Apparel Industry Magazine, Conrad, Andrée, editor. Shore-Varrone, Inc.: November, 1997.